International Federation of Library Associations and Institutions
Fédération Internationale des Associations de Bibliothécaires et des Bibliothèques
Internationaler Verband der bibliothekarischen Vereine und Institutionen
Международная Федерация Библиотечных Ассоциаций и Учреждений
Federación Internacional de Asociaciones de Bibliotecarios y Bibliotecas
国际图书馆协会与机构联合会
الاتحاد الدولي لجمعيات ومؤسسات المكتبات

About IFLA   www.ifla.org

IFLA (The International Federation of Library Associations and Institutions) is the leading international body representing the interests of library and information services and their users. It is the global voice of the library and information profession.

IFLA provides information specialists throughout the world with a forum for exchanging ideas and promoting international cooperation, research, and development in all fields of library activity and information service. IFLA is one of the means through which libraries, information centres, and information professionals worldwide can formulate their goals, exert their influence as a group, protect their interests, and find solutions to global problems.

IFLA's aims, objectives, and professional programme can only be fulfilled with the cooperation and active involvement of its members and affiliates. Currently, approximately 1,600 associations, institutions and individuals, from widely divergent cultural back-grounds, are working together to further the goals of the Federation and to promote librarianship on a global level. Through its formal membership, IFLA directly or indirectly represents some 500,000 library and information professionals worldwide.

IFLA pursues its aims through a variety of channels, including the publication of a major journal, as well as guidelines, reports and monographs on a wide range of topics. IFLA organizes workshops and seminars around the world to enhance professional practice and increase awareness of the growing importance of libraries in the digital age. All this is done in collaboration with a number of other non-governmental organizations, funding bodies and international agencies such as UNESCO and WIPO. IFLANET, the Federation's website, is a prime source of information about IFLA, its policies and activities: www.ifla.org

Library and information professionals gather annually at the IFLA World Library and Information Congress, held in August each year in cities around the world.

IFLA was founded in Edinburgh, Scotland, in 1927 at an international conference of national library directors. IFLA was registered in the Netherlands in 1971. The Koninklijke Bibliotheek (Royal Library), the national library of the Netherlands, in The Hague, generously provides the facilities for our headquarters. Regional offices are located in Rio de Janeiro, Brazil; Pretoria, South Africa; and Singapore.

IFLA Publications 142–143

World Guide to Library, Archive, and Information Science Associations

3rd, completely revised edition

Edited by
Alexandra Meinhold

De Gruyter Saur

IFLA Publications
edited by Sjoerd Koopman

Library of Congress Cataloging-in-Publication Data

> World Guide to Library, Archive, and Information Science Associations. -- 3rd, completely rev. ed. / edited by Alexandra Meinhold.
>   p. cm. -- (IFLA publications, ISSN 0344-6891 ; 142-143)
>   Includes indexes.
>   ISBN 978-3-11-022637-9
>   1. Library science--Societies, etc.--Directories. 2. Information science--Societies, etc.--Directories. 3. Archives--Societies, etc.--Directories. I. Meinhold, Alexandra. II. International Federation of Library Associations and Institutions.
>   Z673.A1W67 2010
>   020.6'2025--dc22
>   2010020074

ISBN 978-3-11-022637-9
e-ISBN 978-3-11-022638-6
ISSN 0344-6891

Bibliographic information published by the Deutsche Nationalbibliothek
The Deutsche Nationalbibliothek lists this publication in the Deutsche Nationalbibliografie; detailed bibliographic data are available in the Internet at http://dnb.d-nb.de.

Walter de Gruyter GmbH & Co. KG, Berlin/New York
Data conversion and typesetting by Dr. Rainer Ostermann, München
Printing and binding by Strauss GmbH, Mörlenbach

© 2010 by International Federation and Library Associations and Institutions, The Hague, The Netherlands

∞ Printed on permanent paper
The paper used in this publication meets the minimum requirements of American National Standard – Permanence of Paper for Productions and Documents in Libraries and Archives
ANSI/NISO Z39.48-1992 (R1997)

Printed in Germany

www.degruyter.com

Contents

Contents 5
Preface 7
Introduction 9
Guide to Use 11
Part I: International Associations **15**
Part II: National Associations **91**
Index of Associations 395
List of Acronyms 417
Index of Official Journals 429
Index of Officers 443
Subject Index 479
Countries with International Associations 483
Countries with National Associations 485

Preface

This is the new edition of a well-established IFLA reference source. Previous editions of The *World Guide to Library, Archive, and Information Science Associations* were published in 1990 and 2005. These have made important contributions to the professional community worldwide and have been well received by the profession.

De Gruyter Saur Verlag undertook the challenging task of updating and revising this book and their staff used extensive resources and expertise to produce this new edition.

During the last two decades the Library, Archive and Information Science profession has grown and has developed more specializations. Within the same period countries changed their names, while others were dissolved or – on the contrary – created!

The number of national and international associations increased from 587 in 1990 to 633 in 2005, but the number included in the present edition went slightly down to 603.
Although there are 57 new entries, quite a few entries could not be confirmed and do not seem to exist any longer.

The overall structure and arrangement of entries, which makes for easy use, has been preserved, and information on the associations was revised and expanded. Contact details, e-mail addresses and websites enable easy communication with each association for further information.

We are grateful to the De Gruyter Saur editors for producing this revised and enhanced reference tool, which will be an indispensable source for the networking of our profession. IFLA is very happy to sponsor this latest edition, of which we can be proud.

Sjoerd Koopman
IFLA Professional Programmes Director

Introduction

The associations included in this reference work are non-profit associations in the fields of librarianship, documentation, information science, and archives, including associations formed by institutions, staff (both professional and non-professional), and associations for professional education. Associations depending on commercial support are omitted. The term "library association" is used throughout the book for the sake of simplification and also because it seems to be accepted in many countries. However, the meaning should be understood in the broadest context of including all types of associations in the information fields.

The associations selected belong to two categories:
1. International Associations: Those organisations whose membership includes two or more countries (e.g., Scandinavia, Africa, Europe, Southeast Asia). They may be general in nature (e.g., the International Federation of Library Associations and Institutions), or specialised (e.g., the International Association of Law Libraries).
2. National Associations: Those organisations operating on a national level, either general in nature or specialised by subject, type of library, staff, etc., but open to all qualified members of a country. Associations covering only certain districts, provinces, or regions within a country are generally not within the scope of this World Guide.

The format of the book is designed to facilitate use and allow for easy identification and comparison of different aspects concerning the associations. Thus, the outline for each association follows the same pattern under established uniform headings. Whatever pertinent information could be obtained is listed, and if a negative answer was ascertained, it is so stated (e.g., Staff: None). When no definite information was available, or could be verified, headings are usually omitted.

The associations are grouped according to the two above-mentioned categories: First, the international associations in alphabetical order (totalling 95 associations); second, the national associations listed by countries of the world (508 associations). The countries are in alphabetical order, and the associations are listed alphabetically under each country. Countries without evidence of existing associations are not listed. All efforts were made to be as inclusive as possible of newly established independent nations.

The present third edition contains a total of 603 entries, all updated using thorough internet research and first-hand information from questionnaires. With 57 new entries, the latest trends and developments in the field are well documented.

The editorial staff is greatly indebted to the many people who assisted us, foremost the officers of the associations who took the time and effort to fill out questionnaires and provide us with information. We are very grateful for the many responses from all over the world. The comments and advice from this international community were essential and important in making this book a useful information source and an aid in making professional contacts throughout the world.

Guide to Use

The information for each association is given as follows:

Name. Each association is entered under its official name as listed by the association, followed by the acronym, if one is used, and in parenthesis the English translation of the official name. In the case of languages using a non-Roman alphabet, some associations may list the English version first. In the case of associations using more than one official language for their name, the first title is in the language officially used by the association itself, separated by a slash from the titles in other languages (e.g., the International Council on Archives is listed under the French name, Conseil International des Archives; EID under Federation Internationale d'Information et de Documentation; IFLA under International Federation of Library Associations and Institutions). Each association is assigned an Arabic number for identification purposes. This number is referred to in the various indexes.

Address. The current address (mailing and visiting address) is given, followed by telephone and fax numbers, e-mail address and web site.

Languages. The official language(s) used by the association in its publications and activities.

Established. Date, place, and occasion of founding. A brief summary of any changes in the name of the association, the constitution or bylaws, with corresponding dates.

Officers. The main executive officers, whether they are elected or appointed, and their term of office are listed. The total number of members on the Executive Board/Committee is given.

Staff. Whether there is any staff at Headquarters, and if so, number of staff and whether paid or voluntary.

General Assembly. How often the general membership meets; date and place of recent and future meetings whenever available.

Membership. Total number of members, both individual and institutional members. Number of chapters, divisions, sections, or any other subgroups (with brief listings). Types of membership available. Requirements for joining the association for each type of membership. Amount of dues for each category of membership, usually in the currency of the country.

Structure. How the association is governed and name of the governing body. Affiliations with other organisations, e.g. IFLA, and whether the association is part of a parent organisation.

Sources of Support. How the association is financed, whether through membership dues, sale of publications, and any other means, especially whether any forms of government subsidies are received.

Major Fields of Interest. The broad areas of concern of the association.

Major Goals and Objectives. The mission statement and objectives of the association as specified in the statutes.

Activities. Major accomplishments in recent years. Current major activities and projected activities in the immediate future. Library legislation with which the association has been involved. Specific information on any continuing education programs, and sponsorship of Book Week, Exhibits, and other activities.

Publications. Official journal and any newsletters of the association with all available bibliographical information: Title (also in English translation, if needed), date of founding, frequency, price, name of editor, address (if different from that of the association), telephone number, language(s), circulation, and where indexed and/or abstracted. Other major publication programs. Types of material published (including annual reports, proceedings of conferences, bibliographies). Some recent publications representative of the association's publishing activities. Whether publications are for sale, whether price lists are available, whether publications are listed in the journal. Any publications exchange programs in existence.

Bibliography. Useful references with emphasis on the most recent years, or highlights of the association's past, are appended whenever possible, providing additional information on policies, activities, and the history of the organisation.

Comment. Further details and information. It is also noted here if there is no further information or proof of current activity.

Note regarding the use of the asterisk *. Every effort has been made to update all information in this Guide. All entries listed in this Guide have been updated either via extensive internet research and with the help of the IFLA network or by the associations themselves. Entries of associations having submitted first-hand details are marked with *.

Indexes

Index of Associations. An alphabetical listing of all associations, both international and national, usually by the official name, but occasionally by the English version, if the official name was not available. This index is useful for locating an association known only by name and not by country of origin. The country of origin (or "International") is listed in parenthesis, followed by the entry number of the association.

List of Acronyms. An alphabetical index of acronyms used by the associations, with the full name of the association listed in parenthesis, followed by the entry number to facilitate quick identification and reference. This feature is useful due to the extensive use of acronyms in current publications.

Official Journals. The official journals and selected newsletters published by the associations are grouped together in one alphabetical listing. Each entry is followed by the name of the association in parenthesis and the entry number for easy reference.

Index of Officers. An alphabetical index of the presidents, chairpersons and other important functionaries of the association. Each entry is followed by the name of the association in parenthesis and the entry number for easy reference. This is a world wide guide to prominent professionals active in associations in the information fields.

Subject Index. This index of broad areas of concern to associations in the information fields gives an indication of the extent of specialisation and identifies current issues. Subject entries are followed by the entry number for each association. This index is useful for identifying similar interest groups in other parts of the world.

Countries with International Associations. This alphabetical list identifies countries in which international associations in the information fields are currently located. The entry number for each association is provided. This index is useful for identifying countries that are internationally active.

Countries with National Associations. An alphabetical index by the English names of the countries with national associations, for which information has been given in the book.

Part I
International Associations

001 American Indian Library Association (AILA)*
Address c/o Kelly Webster, 12 Highfield Rd. No. 2, Roslindale, MA 02131 Tel.: + 1 617-552-0164, ailawebsite@gmail.com; www.ailanet.org
Languages English
Established 1979
Officers Pres: Liana Juliano; VP/Pres-elect: Jody Gray; Secr: Heather Devine; Interim Treas: Carlene Engstom
Staff All volunteers
General Assembly Membership meetings held twice a year in conjunction with the American Library Association annual conferences and midwinter meetings. Annual Conference 2010: Washington, DC
Membership Approximately 300 members. Requirements: Interest in aims of Association. Dues (US Dollar) 20, individuals; 40 libraries; 15 students
Structure Governed by executive officers. Affiliations: ALA
Sources of Support Membership dues
Major Fields of Interest Library services to American Indians
Major Goals and Objectives Address the library-related needs of American Indians and Alaska Natives; to improve Indian library, cultural, and informational services in school, public, and research libraries on reservations. AILA is also committed to disseminating information about Indian cultures, languages, values, and information needs to the library community
Activities Carried out in accordance with goals and objectives
Publications Official journal: American Indian Libraries Newsletter. 2/yr. Free to members. Editor: Mary Johnson. email: MJohnson@thenicc.edu
Bibliography Blumer, T.J., "Library Service for American Indian People and American Indian Library Association," Library of Congress Information Bulletin 42 (Sept. 10, 1984):296–298; Mathews, VH., "American Indians," in ALA Yearbook 1989. pp. 25–26. Chicago: American Library Association, 1989

002 Arab Club for Information (Arabcin)*
Address PO Box 33092, Damskus Tel.: +963 11-5921740, arabcin@net.sy; www.arabcin.net
Established 25th of October 1998
Officers Head: Dr. Abdel Majid Al Rifai Syria
Major Fields of Interest Networking, Coordinating and Information
Publications Areen (monthly). Arabia 3000 (quarterly)

003 Arab Federation for Libraries and Information (AFLI)
Address BP 1603, Tunis 1055 alsereihy@yahoo.com; www.afli.info(onlyarabic)
Established Dec. 1986, during Fourth Arab Conference organized by the Institut Supérieur de Documentation in Hammamet, Tunisia
Major Fields of Interest Cooperation between library associations and institutions in the Arab world
Major Goals and Objectives To re-enforce cooperation between library associations and institutions in the Arab world; to conserve the Arab heritage everywhere in its written or audiovisual form and to make it known; to promote the profession; to prepare and

encourage scientific research and studies in the field of librarianship and to organize special conferences and seminars; and to try to improve the quality of curricula dispersed in schools and institutes which educate and train librarians and information specialists
Activities   Establish mutual help relationships with national, Arab, and international organizations and institutions which share the same concerns; publish a magazine and year-book on libraries and information in the Arab world; hold conferences on the Arab level which deal with technical subjects in the field of information; form working commissions such as: Intellectual production, Bibliographical, Education and training, and standards and professional lexicon

004   Arab Regional Branch of the International Council on Archives (ARBICA)
Address   c/o M. Abdelmadjid Chikhi, President, B.P. 61, Alger Gare   Tel.: +213 21 542160, Fax +213 21 449624; www.arbica.org
Languages   Arabic, English, French
Established   1972, Rome, by leading archivists from 9 Arab countries: M. Touili (Algeria), E. M. ElSheneti (Egypt), M. Abdulhamid (Iraq), S. Mousa (Jordan), C. Muemne (Lebanon), W. Wakili (Morocco), M. J. Abdusalim (Sudan), A. Rifai (Syria), and O. Salah Ahmed (People's Republic of Yemen)
Officers   Pres: M. Abdelmadjid Chikhi; 1st VP: Riffat Hilal; 2nd VP: Qasem Abu Harb; GenSecr: Hedi Jallab; Treas: Baho Al Ibrahim
General Assembly   General assembly meets once a year
Membership   Total members: 46. Type of membership: National documentation centers, Associations, research and information centers, universities or any other side related to documents, Specialized and other people working in the field of documentation, Honorary members, who had prominent roles in the fields of National or Arabic or International documentation; 4 committees (Media and Publications, Scientific Committee, Research and Translation, Training and Preparation)
Structure   Governed by Executive Board. Affiliation: ICA
Major Fields of Interest   Regional cooperation among national archival institutions of Arab States
Major Goals and Objectives   Spread documentary awareness in the Arab Countries, fulfill integration in practical and learning activities in documentary aspects among the Arab National Centers, and promote cooperation and coordination between them and the International Council of Archives, acquaint or identify the centers of Arab National documentation and the documents they own, achieve cooperation and coordination among the Arab National centers in order to procure the historical documents relevant to the Arab Countries from countries and international organizations, unite the regulations, rules, plans programs, procedures, terminology, criteria and examples in the Arab National documentation Centers, promote the educational standard and practical skills for all those involved in the field of documentation and preservation of records in the Arab countries, maintain the use of Arabic language among the other languages used in the ICA, allow Arab experts and specialized personnel to participate in the fields of documentation and preservation of records in the ICA and activate their role in its activities, find an Arab instructional legalized regulation to unite the organizations of the Arab Documents, make access to reading the documents, use or enter the latest applications in the field of Information Technology in the process of work in the Arab Documentation organizations

Activities Holds scientific seminars and training sessions, issues scientific periodicals and instructional guides and news bulletin
Publications Official journal: The Arab Archives (al-Watha'ig al Arabiyah)

005 Arkib Negara Malaysia
(National Archives of Malaysia)

Address Jl. Duta, 50568 Kuala Lumpur Tel.: +60 3 6510688, Fax +60 3 6515679; http://arkib.gov.my
Languages English
General Assembly Executive Board meets once a year. General conference every 2 years. 2004: Hanoi
Membership Total members: 8 (institutional). 8 countries represented. Requirements: Open to archival institutions in countries of Southeast Asia only
Structure Governed by constitution. Affiliations: Regional Branch of ICA
Sources of Support Membership dues, sale of publications, government subsidies, international organizations (including ICA)
Major Fields of Interest Administration of archives
Major Goals and Objectives To establish, maintain and strengthen relations between archivists of all countries in the region and between all institutions, professional bodies and organizations which are concerned with the custody, organization or administration of archives; to promote all measures for the preservation, protection and defense against all manner of hazards of the archival heritage of the region, and to further the progress of all aspects of the administration and preservation of these archives; to facilitate the use of archives of the region by making them more widely known and by encouraging greater ease of access; to promote, organize and coordinate activities in the field of archives in the region; to sponsor professional training of archivists in the region; to cooperate with other organizations or institutions concerned with the documentation of human experience and the use of that documentation for the benefit of mankind; to generally carry out the aims and objectives of the International Council on Archives
Activities Past achievements: (1) Projects completed under contract with the Regional Office of Unesco for Asia and Pacific: Inventory of cartographic records in the Arsip Nasional, 1612–1816 (Indonesia); Guide to the Royal Archives of Perak (1945–69), Johore (1874–1984) and Perlis (1984–1985) (Malaysia); Purchase of aerial photographs of Thailand preserved in the Williams Hunt Collection, United Kingdom (Thailand); (2) Testing of Records and Archives Management Programme (RAMP) Guidelines Projects: Appraisal of moving images (Indonesia); Sampling techniques; legislation and regulations; and preservation and restoration of paper records (Malaysia); Surveying archival records management systems; and preservation and restoration of photographic materials (Thailand); (3) Training courses in archival handling of audiovisual materials in Malaysia and Singapore; (4) Colloquium on Access and Use of Archives in Jakarta, in conjunction with the 7th General Conference of SARBICA, 1987. Current: Project on Guide to the Sources of Asian History; publications. Future: (1) Preparation of a model kit for the training of users of archives; (2) guidelines for simplified access procedures. Association sponsors exhibits and continuing education lectures, seminars, workshops
Publications Official journal: SARBICA Journal. 1968-. 1/yr. US$ 6.00 for non-members. Address same as the Association. Circ: 500. English. Other publications:

Southeast Asian Microfilms Newsletter (SARBICA/CONSAL publication). Senior ASEAN Statemen – A Catalogue of Oral History Interviews. Published by the Oral History Centre, National Archives of Singapore, in 1998 to commemorate 25th year of ASEAN. Directory of Experts in Records Management and Archives Adminstration in SARBICA countries. Published by the SARBICA Secretariat c/o National Archives of Malaysia, in 1997. This directory provides information on experts in records and archives fields available in SARBICA countries. Publications available for sale. Price list issued
Bibliography Tan, L., "SARBICA," Singapore Libraries 12 (1982):21–23

006 ARLIS/Norden
(Art Libraries Society Norden)

Address c/o University of Art and Design Helsinki UIAH, Hämeentie 135 A, 00560 Helsinki Tel.: +358 975 630243, Fax +358 975 630246, eila.ramo@uiah.fi; www.arlisnorden.org
Languages Swedish, Norwegian, Danish
Established 1986
General Assembly Annual meeting and conference, which normally takes place during 2–3 days, is arranged on a rotating basis in the Nordic countries
Membership Consists of both institutional and individual members in the five Nordic countries
Structure Affiliations: IFLA
Major Fields of Interest Art librarianship
Major Goals and Objectives Aims to further every aspect of art librarianship in the Nordic countries
Publications ARLIS/Norden Info

007 Art Libraries Society of North America (ARLIS/NA)*

Address 7044 S. 13th St., Oak Creek, WI 53154 Tel.: +1 414 768-8000, Fax +1 414 768-8001, arlisna@arlisna.org; www.arlisna.org
Languages English, French, Spanish
Established 1972, Chicago, Illinois
Officers Pres: Marilyn Russell; VP/Pres-elect: Jon Evans; Past Pres: Amy Lucker; Secr: V. Heidi Hass; Treas: Tom Riedel
General Assembly Entire membership meets once a year.
Membership Total members: nearly 1100 (individual and institutional from the United States, Canada, Mexico, and overseas). Requirements: An interest in and support for the fields of art librarianship and visual resources curatorship, e. g. professional librarians, students, library assistants, art book publishers, art book dealers, art historians, archivists, architects, slide and photograph curators, or retired associates in these fields
Structure Governed by Executive Board. Affiliations: American Library Association, Arbeitsgemeinschaft der Kunst und Museumsbibliotheken, ARLIS/Australia & New Zealand, ARLIS/Netherlands, ARLIS/Norden / in English, ARLIS/United Kingdom & Ireland, Association of Architecture School Librarians, College Art Association, International Federation of Library Associations and Institutions, Japan Art Documentation Society, Tokyo, Museum Computer Network, Society of American

Archivists, Society of Architectural Historians, Sous-section des Bibliothèques d'art, Association des bibliothécaires français, Visual Resources Association
Sources of Support Membership dues, sale of publications, conference fees, donations
Major Fields of Interest Art librarianship and visual resources curatorship
Major Goals and Objectives To provide leadership in the development and use of art libraries and visual resource collections, particularly by acting as a forum for the interchange of information and materials on the visual arts
Activities Sponsors exhibits, conferences, seminars and workshops. Active in promoting library-related legislation and standards in art cataloging. Presents awards for publications and research in the visual arts, and scholarships to library students
Publications Official journal: Art Documentation, 1982-, published twice annually, circulation 1400, ISSN 0730-7187. Editor Judy Dyki, email jdyki@cranbrook.edu. Other publications: Occasional Papers Series, ISSN 0730-7160. Example: Occasional Paper No. 16, Art Museum Libraries and Librarianship, edited by Joan M. Benedetti, co-published with the Scarecrow Press. 336 p., 90 illustrations. Cloth: $75.00. Paper: $45.00. Also: online publications, book reviews, conference proceedings: see website www.arlisna.org
Bibliography Ciccone, A. N. Judith A. Hoffberg: The Early Years of ARLIS/NA. Art Documentation v. 27 no. 1 (Spring 2008) p. 41–51; Chapin, M. L. The 27th Annual George Wittenborn Memorial Book Awards: Interviews With Some of the Winning Authors and Editors. Art Documentation v. 26 no. 1 (Spring 2007) p. 59–6; Jacoby, T., et. al., Reminiscing, Looking Ahead: An Interview with Joan Benedetti. Art Documentation v. 23 no. 1 (Spring 2004) p. 26–32; Parry, P. J. The way we were: reflections on my years (1980–1993) as ARLIS/NA's executive director. Art Documentation v. 21 no. 1 (Spring 2002) p. 4–6 By-Laws, Policy manual and other administrative documents at www.arlis.org

008 Arts Libraries Society of Australia and New Zealand (ARLIS-ANZ)*

Address c/o Cheryl Stevens, 226 Grey Street, South Bank Queensland, PO Box 3370, 4101 South Bank Queensland Tel.: +61 7 373 53131, Fax +61 7 373 53133, secretary@arlis.org.au; www.arlis.org.au
Languages English
Established 1975 as Art Libraries Society, Name change 1980 following a national seminar on arts information in Australia organized by the Sydney-based Museums, Arts and Humanities Group. The adoption of the name Arts Libraries Society instead of Art Libraries society, reflected its broadly based origins, the absence of bodies representing some other arts sectors, and a desire to be an integral part of the ARLIS international network
Officers Chair: Volker Joye; Secr: Cheryl Stevens; Treas: Vicki Marsh
General Assembly Entire membership meets biennially in conference
Membership Total members: 130 (71 individual, 59 institutional). Types of membership: Individual, institutional. Requirements: Interest in the aims of the Association
Structure Governed by Executive Committee, meeting querterly. Affiliation: IFLA
Sources of Support Membership dues
Major Fields of Interest Art librarianship
Major Goals and Objectives To develop and promote arts and museum librarianship and information practices. To strengthen the operation of the Society to ensure the

continued vitality and progress of ARLIS/ANZ. To co-operate with other national and international organisations in the fields of the arts, museology and librarianship
Activities   Holds biennial conferences. Maintains an electronic discussion list for members and those interested in Arts Librarianship. Developed projects to fill directory and database gaps in the visual arts. Sponsors lectures open to the public, seminars, workshps, and other continuing education activities
Publications   Official journal: ARLIS-ANZ Journal (ISSN 0157–4043) will move from a print to an online journal in 2010+. See website: http://www.arlis.org.au for updated information on the society's journal
Bibliography   Richards, V., "ARLIS/ANZ and Art Libraries in the Antipodes," Art Libraries Journal 11 (1986):12–16. The View From "Down under" : ARLIS/ANZ and the World of Art Librarianship (2000): http://www.fh-potsdam.de/ IFLA/INSPEL/00–1shma.pdf

009   Asociación de Estados Iberoamericanos para el Desarrollo de la Bibliotecas de Iberoamérica (ABINIA)

Address   Final Av. Panteón. Sede Administrativa de la Biblioteca Nacional de Venezuela, Caracas 1010   Fax +58 212 5643189, sea@abinia.org; http://abinia.ucol.mx
Languages   Spanish, Portugese
Established   1989

010   Asociación Hispana de Documentalistas en Internet (AHDI) (Documentation Sciences Foundation)

Address   C/ Dulzaina 3, 2º – A, 28033 Madrid, Postcode 545, 10600 Plasencia   Tel.: +34 327 41 66 06, Fax +34 91 5735858; www.documentalistas.com
Languages   Spanish
Established   2002
Membership   Requirements: Spanish speaking professionals in documentation
Major Fields of Interest   Internet in the work of documentalists
Major Goals and Objectives   Collaboration between professionals, to inform on new technologies concerning the work with the internet
Activities   Organizes conventions, conferences, further education opportunities, seminars, round tables
Publications   Official publication: Boletín Online

011   Asociación Interamericana de Bibliotecarios, Documentalistas y Especialistas en Información Agrícola (AIBDA) (Inter-American Association of Agricultural Librarians, Documentalists and Information Specialists)

Address   elizabeth.ascencio@aibdaperu.org
Languages   Spanish, Portuguese or English for articles in the AIBDA Journal
Established   1953, at the First Inter-American Meeting of Agricultural Librarians and Documentalists. Reactivated 1965 at the Third World Congress of the International Association of Agricultural Librarians and Documentalists (IAALD), in Washington, DC
General Assembly   General membership meets every 3 years

Membership Individual and Institutional members. Requirements: Individuals working in agricultural library or documentation centers, librarians working in other fields, library school professors, individuals in other fields interested in the aims of the Association. Institutions with an agricultural interest. Dues including AIBDA Journal (US Dollar): 40, individual; 108, institution
Structure Governed by executive officers and council meeting annually. Affiliations: IFLA, IAALD
Sources of Support Membership dues, sale of publications, annual economic support of the Inter-American Institute of Cooperation for Agriculture. Donations for special projects from other donor organizations
Major Fields of Interest Agricultural librarianship and information; training of agricultural librarians; continuing education
Major Goals and Objectives To promote librarianship and documentation in the field of agriculture in Latin America and the Caribbean; to establish cooperation among librarians and information science specialists; to promote professional education
Activities Association sponsors exhibits, continuing education, short courses. Members participate in congresses, seminars and meetings
Publications Official journal: Revista AIBDA
Bibliography Moretti, D.M.B., "A evoluçao de AIBDA," Revista AIBDA 4 (1983):53–54 (in Spanish); Chavez, M., "Las Filiales de AIBDA," Revista AIBDA 4 (1983):55–58 (in Spanish); "AIBDA ha cumplido viente años," Boletín de Informativa de AIBDA 21 (1986):1–2 (in Spanish); Paz de Erickson, A.M., "Recursos humanos: un recurso renovable?" (Human Resources: A Renewable Resource? Revista AIBDA 7 (1986):85–94 (AIBDA's program for continuing education); Márquez, O., "La Asociación Interamericana de bibliotecarios y Documentalistas Agrícolas (AIBDA) y sus organismos componentes – Cronología y análisis de actividades," (The Interamerican Association of Agricultural Librarians and Documentalists (AIBDA) and its consistituent bodies – chronology and analysis of activities) Revista AIBDA 7 (1986):63–83 (survey and evaluation of activities 1966–83); "AIBDA in Guatemala: Looking to the Future," (80th Conference, 1987); Quarterly Bulletin of IAALD 32 (1987):229–230; "Inter-American Association of Agricultural Librarians and Documentalists," in The Bowker Annual: Library and Book Trade Almanac. 34th Edition 1989–90. p. 728. New York: R. R. Bowker, 1989
Comment No adress available

012 Asociación Latinoamericana de Archivos (ALA)
(Latin American Association of Archives)
Address Carrea 6a No 6–91, Bogota Tel.: +57 1 3373111, Fax +57 1 3372019, ancost@ice.co.cr; www.ala.or.cr
Languages Spanish
Established April 6, 1973 in Lima, Peru
Membership 15 archives, associations, historical and regional administration archives, centers for archival education and individual archivists
Structure A regional branch of ICA
Major Goals and Objectives To further the aims of ICA and to strengthen co-operation within the Spanish and Portuguese speaking countries of Latin America, and Spain and

Portugal. ALA is responsible for carrying out the policy and programmes of ICA in this region, where these are relevant to ALA members
Activities Sponsors regional and international seminars and meetings
Publications Official journal: Boletín Interamericano de Archivos. 1/yr. Address: Centro Interamericano de Formación de Archiveros, Cordoba, Argentina; Revista ALA
Bibliography Revista ALA Nos. 1 al 25

013   Asociación Mexicana de Bibliotecarios, A.C. (AMBAC) (Mexican Association of Librarians)*

Address Angel Urraza 817-A, Col. Del Valle, México Tel.: +52 55 55753396, Fax +52 55 55751135, correo@ambac.org.mx; www.ambac.org.mx
Languages Spanish
Established Founded 1924 in Mexico City
Officers Pres: Jesus Lau; VP: Oscar Saavedra; Secr: Victor Cid; Treas: Anibal Ramirez; Pro-Secr: Julio Zetter; Pro-Treas: Raul Ramirez
Staff Paid: 1 Full-Time voluntary o; Partial-Time voluntary 20
General Assembly Annual Congress Congress, 2009: Acapulco, Guerrero, Sept 9–11. 2010: Zacatecas, Zacatecas, May 3–5
Membership 340 members, 10 divisions. Personal and institutional memebership. Personal membership $35, institucional memebership $175. There are no special requirements for joining.
Structure Officers: President, Vicepresident, Secretary, Treasurer, Pro-Secretretary, Pro-treasurer. Technical Council, 4 members. Affiliate to IFLA, ALA
Sources of Support The association is financed through memebership dues, advertising sales and congress fees.
Major Fields of Interest Librarianship and information science
Major Goals and Objectives Our goal is professional advancement of our parteners and promote and encourage library, the library service and librarianship
Activities Organize an annual meeting with the purpose of analyze and discuss the problems of the library and information services. Calles to 4 meetings to the year to infor, parteners on the activies of the board. Organizes courses and workshops training with relevant subjects.
Publications Quarterly Newsletter "Noticero de AMBAC" (AMBAC Newsletter) since 1966 in spanish. Publish their memories of the annuaö meetings and other monographs about librarianship. Publications available for sale. Most recent publications: XXXV Jornadas Mexicanas de Biblioteconomía (CD) : 11 al 14 de mayo de 2004, Cancún, Quintana Roo. Quintana Roo, México: Asociación Mexicana de Bibliotecarios (CD): BiblioNep (2005). XXXIII Jornadas Mexicanas de Biblioteconomía : memoria 5, 6 y 7 de junio de 2002 Monterrey, Nuevo León. México, D.F.: Asociación Mexicana de Bibliotecarios (2003) 331 p.
Bibliography Fernández Esquivel, Rosa María: La Asociación Mexicana de Bibliotecarios : notas para su historia (The Mexican Library Association, Notes for its History) México: Asociación Mexicana de Bibliotecarios (1995), 151 p.; Asociación Mexicana de Bibliotecarios. Reglamento (Regulation) México: Asociación Mexicana de Bibliotecarios (2002), 27 p.; Asociación Mexicana de Bibliotecarios. Testimonio del acta

constitutiva (Testimony of charter) México: Asociación Mexicana de Bibliotecarios (1965), 8 p.

014 Associação Portuguesa de Bibliotecários, Arquivistas e Documentalistas (BAD)
(Portuguese Association of Librarians, Archivists and Documentalists)*
Address R. Morais Soares n°43-C, 1° Drt, 1900–341 Lisbon Tel.: +351 21 8161980, Fax +351 21 8154508, apdad@apdad.pt; www.apbad.pt
Languages Portuguese
Established 1974, Portugal
Officers Pres: António José de Pina Falãdo; VP: Cristina Maria Realinho Ribeiro; Secr: Maria José Vitarino Gonçalves; Lis Training: Rosa Maria Barreto Pereira Silva; Editorial: João Carlos Salvador da Silva de Oliveira; Finance: Leonarda de Jesus Rodrigues Galhanas
Staff 5 paid – secretariat
General Assembly Last general assemblies: 7th April 2010, 22nd May 2010
Membership 1500 members
Structure Affiliations: IFLA, EBLIDA, ICA, IASL
Sources of Support Membership dues, sale of publications, continuing education
Major Fields of Interest Librarianship, archives, documentation
Major Goals and Objectives To promote the development of libraries, archives, and documentation centers in Portugal; to represent the members and promote their status and professional development
Activities Extensive training programs and continuing education offerings; establishing an information network for a national information system
Publications Official journal: Cadernos BAD. 1963. Semestral 15 EUR. Portugese, Spanish, French, English

015 Association for Health Information and Libraries in Africa (AHILA)
Address c/o Cheick Oumar Diawara, BP 1805, Bamako Tel.: +223 225277, secretary@ahila.org; www.ahila.org
Languages English
Established 1984, as African Medical Library Association (AMLA); new name adopted 1988
Officers Pres: Vimbai Hungwe; 1st VP: Cristina Horta; 2nd VP: Marcel Singirankabo; Secr Gen: Flatiel Vilanculos; Treas: Grace Ajuwon
Membership 46 country members and many partners and collaborators worldwide
Structure Affiliations: IFLA
Sources of Support Subscription as well as donations and grants
Major Fields of Interest Medical librarianship and health information services
Major Goals and Objectives Purpose: 1. To promote closer association among health information professionals in Africa: 2. To promote a high standard of library practice for health information services, education and research in Africa; 3. To work in close collaboration with the World Health Organization Regional Office for Africa and cooperate with national and international health organizations and learned societies in full mutual respect of their objectives; 4. To participate in international activities in the field of

health sciences information; 5. To carry out other activities on which the General Assembly agrees
Activities Electronic discussion group moderated by the World Health Organization Regional Office for Africa (AFRO), headquartered in Brazzaville, Congo (email: ahila@afro.who.int). Congresses (Bamako/Mali 2002)

016 Association for Information Management Professionals (ARMA International)
Address 11880 College Blvd., Suite 450, Overland Park, KS 66210 Tel.: +1 913 341 3808, Fax +1 913 341 3742; www.arma.org
Languages English
Established 1955
Officers Exec Dir: Marilyn Bier
Staff 24
General Assembly Annual Conference and Expo, 49th Long Beach, CA Okt. 3–6, 04
Membership ARMA International members include records and information managers, MIS and ADP professionals, imaging specialists, archivists, hospital administrators, legal administrators, librarians, and educators
Sources of Support Membership dues, sale of publications, annual conference, advertising
Major Fields of Interest Information retrieval, files and forms management, historical documentation, micrographics, retention schedules, vital records protection, computer-assisted information management programs, correspondence and reports management
Major Goals and Objectives To provide education, research, and networking opportunities to information professionals, to enable them to use their skills and experience to leverage the value of records, information, and knowledge as corporate assets and as contributors to organizational success
Publications The Information Management Journal
Bibliography "ARMA International," in The Bowker Annual: Library and Book Trade Almanac. 34th Edition 1989–90. pp. 665–666. New York: R. R. Bowker, 1989

017 Association for Information Systems (AIS)
Address P.O.Box 2712, Atlanta, GA 30301 Tel.: +1 404 4137441, pete@aisnet.org; www.aisnet.org
Languages English
Established 1994
Officers Exec Dir: Pete Timsley
Staff 3, paid
Membership 30 institutional and 4110 personal members
Structure Governed by Executive Board. Chapters: 14; Special Interest Groups: 24
Major Fields of Interest Information Systems
Major Goals and Objectives To create and maintain a professional identity for IS educators, researchers and professionals, researchers, and educators; promote communications and interaction among members; provide a focal point for contact and relations with bodies in government, the private sector, and in education that influence and/or control the nature of information systems; improve curricula, pedagogy, and other

aspects of IS education; create a vision for the future of the IS field and profession; create and implement a modern, technologically sophisticated professional society; establish standards of practice, ethics, and education where appropriate; include professionals worldwide

Activities Sponsors conferences, chapters, special interest groups, events, awards; offers Information System Electronic Library (AISeL), CAIS, SAIS, AMUS, ICIS

Publications Official journals: Journal of the Association of Information Systems (JAIS). Editor: Kalle Lyttinen, Case Western Reserve Univ., kjll3@po.cwru.edu, phone +1 216 3685353, fax +1 216 3684776; Communications of the Association for Information Systems (CAIS). Editor: Paul Gray, Claremont Graduate University, e-mail: cais@cgu.edu

018   Association for Population/Family Planning Libraries and Information Centers – International (APLIC-I)

Address   c/o Family Health International Library, P.O. Box 13950, Research Triangle Park, NC 27709   info@aplici.org; www.aplici.org
Languages   English
Established   1968, at the Carolina Population Center, Chapel Hill, North Carolina
Staff   None
General Assembly   Entire membership meets annually in April
Membership   Type of membership: Individual, institutional. Requirements: Payment of fee for both categories: individual (developed countries) $25.00; individual (developing countries) $15.00; student $15; sustaining (up to 5 individuals) $75.00
Structure   Governed by executive officers. Affiliations: AICIP, ASIS, MLA, IFLA
Sources of Support   Membership dues, private gifts
Major Fields of Interest   Population and family planning information centers
Major Goals and Objectives   Provide Opportunities for: Capacity and community building among population/reproductive health communication, information, and resource professionals. Worldwide professional networking for the exchange of ideas, information, and resources. Professional development and continuing education. Innovating effective documentation and information systems and services in the field of population and reproductive health
Activities   International technical assistance in development of population/family planning librarianship. Training seminars for Africa and Latin America. Special publications, international family planning population networking. Active in promoting library-related legislation in the field of training seminars and development of teaching materials. Sponsors exhibits, seminars, workshops, continuing education, Duplicate Materials Exchange Program
Publications   Official journal: AppliCommunicator. 3 times annually. Free to members. Editor varies. Address same as Association. APLIC-I Union List of Serials (1995); POPIN-APLIC Electronic Resource Guides (Adobe Acrobat PDF files)

019   Association Francophone d'Informatique en Agriculture (AFIA)

Address   c/o I.S.A.R.A, 31 place Bellecour, 69288 Lyon, cedex 02   Fax +33 4 72773235; www.acta-informatique.fr
Languages   French

Officers Pres: Guy Walksman; VP: Jerôme Steffe; Secr: Francis Sevila; Treas: Jean-Marc Ferrero

020 Association Internationale des Archives Francophones (AIAF)

Address c/o Secrétaire-trésorière, Pavillon Louis-Jacques-Casault, Case Postale 10450, Sainte-Foy, Québec G1V 4N1 Tel.: +1 418 644-4800, Fax +1 418 644-0868, carol.couture@banq.qc.ca; www.aiaf.org
Languages French
Established 1989
General Assembly Membership meets every 4 years
Membership Institutional membership. Dues: 100 euro/yr
Structure Governed by executive council. Affiliation: CIA
Major Fields of Interest Archives in French speaking countries
Major Goals and Objectives Information exchange, dissemination of technical literature, organization and modernization of archival services
Activities Préparation d'un Portail international archivistique francophone (PIAF)

021 Association Internationale des Bibliothèques, Archives et Centres de Documentation Musicaux/Internationale Vereinigung der Musikbibliotheken, Musikarchive und Musikdokumentationszentren (IAML; AIBM; IVMB) (International Association of Music Libraries, Archives and Documentation Centres)*

Address c/o Roger Flury, Secretary General, POB 1467, Wellington Tel.: +64 4 474 3039, Fax +64 4 474 3035, roger.flury@natlib.govt.nz; www.iaml.info
Languages English, French, German
Established 1951, Paris
Officers Pres: Martie Severt; Secr Gen: Roger Flury; Treas: Kathy Adamson; Past Pres: Massimo Gentili-Tedeschi; VP: Jon Bagûés; Jim Cassaro; Jutta Lambrecht
Staff None
General Assembly General membership meets once a year. Conferences: 2008 Naples; 2009 Amsterdam; 2010 Moscow (27 June – 2 July), 2011 Dublin (24–29 July); 2012 Montreal (22–27 July); 2013 Århus; 2014 Vienna; 2015 New York
Membership Total members:about 1,900 individual and institutional members in some 57 countries throughout the world. National Branches: 25. Professional Branches: 5 (Archives and Music Documentation Centres, Broadcasting and Orchestra Libraries, Libraries in Music Teaching Institutions, Public Libraries, Research Libraries). Commissions: 5 (Bibliography, Cataloguing, Audio-Visual, Service and Training). Committees: 6 (Constitution, Copyright, IT, Outreach, Programme, Publications). Requirements: Any person or institution wishing to further the goals of the Association. Dues: 36,00 EUR (individual); 60,00 EUR (institutional)
Structure Governed by a Council, made up of national branch and professional branch representatives, a Board, made up of elected and appointed officers, and the General Assembly. Affiliations: IFLA, International Music Council, International Musicological Society (IMS)

Sources of Support Membership dues

Major Fields of Interest Source inventories in the field of music, music librarianship including cataloging

Major Goals and Objectives To encourage and promote the activities of music libraries, archives and documentation centers and to strengthen the cooperation among institutions and individuals in these fields of interest

Activities Through a series of joint Committees with other international organizations, IAML sponsors the preparation and publication of significant works in music and bibliographic scholarship: (1) Répertoire International des Sources Musicales (RISM)/International Inventory of Music Sources (RISM). 1952-, concerned with bibliographies of all sources in music until 1800; The Directory of Music Research Libraries (RISM Series C); (2) Repertoire International de Littérature Musicale (RILM)/International Inventory of Music Literature. 1966-, deals with current literature; sponsors RILM Abstracts. 1967-, also available online through Dialog database; (3) Répertoire International d'Iconographie Musicale (RIdIM)/The International Repertory of Musical Iconography. 1971-, concerned with visual materials relating to music; the Research Center for Musical Iconography at the City University of New York (founded 1972) serves as the international RIdIM center; (4) The International Repertory of the Musical Press (RIPM). Other IAML-assisted publications include Documenta Musicologica. Catalogus Musicus. Terminorum Musicae Index Septum Linguis Redactus, The Guide for Dating Early Published Music. The Association has been involved in a Unesco-sponsored plan to assist Third World countries in developing music libraries and documentation centers

Publications Official journal: Fontes artis musicae. 1954-, 4/yr. Free to members. Editor: Maureen Buja, PhD, Hong Kong Gold Coast, Block 22, Flat 1-A,1 Castle Peak Road, Tuen Mun, NT, Hong Kong. Phone: +852–2146–8047. Email: mbuja@earthlink.net. English, French, German. Circ: Membership. Indexed in RILM abstracts (Dialog). IAML Electronic Newsletter. (1999-). Editor: Brian McMillan, email: brian.mcmillan@mcgill.ca. Other publications: Documenta musicologica. Kassel : Bärenreiter (in progress). Reihe 1: Druckschriften-Faksimiles. 1951-. 38 vols. to 1990. Reihe 2: Handschriften-Faksimiles. 1955-. 27 vols. to 1990. Catalogus musicus Kassel : Bärenreiter, 1963- (in progress). 15 vols. to 1995. Code international de catalogage de la musique. Frankfurt : Peters, 1957–1983. 5 vols. (complete). Guide for dating early published music. Hackensack, NJ : Boonin; Kassel: Bärenreiter, 1974. Terminorum musicae index septem linguis redactus. Budapest : Akád. Kiadó; Kassel: Bärenreiter, 1978

Bibliography "IAML Annual Conference, 1984 in Como, Italy," Fontis Artis Musicae 32 (Jan. 1985):1–86 (special issue); "1985 IAML/IASA Conference, Berlin, GDR, 7–14 September," Fontis Artis Musicae 33 (1986):1–91, 246–247; Brook, B. S. and Ratliff, N., "International Association of Music Libraries, Archives and Documentation Centres (IAML)," in ALA World Encyclopedia of Library and Information Services. 2nd ed., pp. 369–370. Chicago: American Library Association, 1986; Crudge, R., "The Constitution of IAML: A United Kingdom View," Brio 23 (1986):8–11; Lonn, A., "The IAML Constitution Revisited-A Progress Report," Fontes Artis Musicae 35 (1988):3–6; "International Association of Music Libraries, Archives and Documentation Centres (IAML)," in The Bowker Annual: Library and Book Trade Almanac. 34th Edition 1989–90. pp. 730–731. New York: R. R. Bowker, 1989. 50th anniversary celebrated at

Conference in Périgueux, 2001. Heckmann, Harold. "Half a century", in www.iaml.info/organization/what_is_iaml/history

022 Association Internationale des Écoles des Sciences de l'Information (AIESI) (International Association of Schools of Information Science)

Address c/o Doina Banciu, 8–10 Averescu Avenue, 71316 Bucarest 1 Tel.: +40 1 2245262, Fax +40 1 2241030, Doina.Banciu@ici.ro; www.aiesi.refer.org
Languages French
Established 1997, Geneva, Switzerland
Staff None
General Assembly General membership meets every 2 years
Membership Total members: 38 (5 individual, 33 institutional). 10 countries represented (Belgium, Benin, Ivory Coast, France, Libanon, Marocco, Romania, Senegal, Suisse, Tunisia). Requirements: Affiliation with school of information science or educational program of university level of an organization that uses French
Structure Governed by an Executive Board and a Secretariat meeting twice yearly. Affiliations: IFLA, AUPELF (Association des Universités Partiellement ou Entièrement de Langue Française)
Sources of Support Membership dues. Receives financial aid from FICU (Fonds International de Coopération Interuniversitaire)
Major Fields of Interest All fields related to the training of specialists in information science
Major Goals and Objectives To encourage the development of the education of librarians, information scientists and other information professionals and to encourage a higher quality of such personnel; to stimulate original French-language research in this area; to establish and maintain a liaison between French-language schools, and promote instructional material in the French language
Activities Major accomplishments in the last 5 years: sponsored workshops on "Teaching Methods and the Information Sciences" (Rabat, Morocco, 1984); "Continuing Education and Information Science" (University of Bordeaux, France, 1986). Current: Cooperation between schools of information sciences. Future: Further cooperation between schools, publication of teaching materials in French
Publications No official journal. Other publications: Répertoire des Écoles francophones en sciences de l'Information (Directory of French-language Schools of Information Science)
Bibliography Lajeunesse, M., "Les relations internationales à l'École de Bibliothéconomie et des Sciences de l'Information," (The International Relations of the School of Library and Information Science [University of Montreal], Argus 16 (1987):31–33

023 Association of Caribbean University, Research and Institutional Libraries (ACURIL)

Address POB 23317, UPR Station, San Juan 00931–3317 Tel.: +1 787 7640000, Fax +1 787 7642311; http://acuril.rrp.upr.edu/que.htm
Languages Spanish, French, Dutch, English
Established June, 1969 in San Juan during the East Caribbean Conference. Originally

founded as the Association of Caribbean University and Research Institute Libraries (hence the acronym ACURIL), but changed to present name in order to broaden the membership to include public libraries, which in many areas serve as research sources
Officers   Pres: Bea Bazile; Exec Secr: Luisa Vigo-Cepeda
Staff   2 (volunteer, partial pay)
General Assembly   General membership meets annually in May. The Executive Council usually meets in November and during the annual meetings
Membership   Three categories of membership open to libraries, archives, organizations, and individuals living within the area of the Caribbean archipelago, the mainland countries (including the Guianas), and the states of the United States of America which border on the Caribbean Sea or Gulf of Mexico: Institutional : open to libraries, archives and schools conducting programmes of library or archival education. Organizational : available to national library associations, and regional and other special organizations and associations. Personal : open to librarians and archivists, other employees of libraries or archives, and other interested in library, archival, or related services and activities
Structure   Governed by Executive Council. Affiliations: IFLA, UNICA (Association of Caribbean Universities and Research Institutions)
Sources of Support   Membership dues
Major Fields of Interest   Libraries, archives, information services and library associations and workers in these areas in the Caribbean
Major Goals and Objectives   To facilitate the development and use of libraries, archives, and information services, and the identification, collection and preservation of information resources in support of the whole range of intellectual and educational endeavors throughout the Caribbean area; to strengthen the archival, library and information professions in the region; to unite workers in them; and to promote cooperative activities in pursuit of these objectives
Activities   Organization of regional projects aimed at improving access to information produced or published in the region. Examples are the provision of opportunities for special interest groups to meet, review and plan for the progress of library development and growth in the region. Common problems are identified, solutions are discussed, and ideas are shared on general trends, and the publication of most the Proceedings of its annual conferences. Services Provided: a forum for professional discussion and meetings, continuing education programmes in the form of pre, during and post conference workshops, seminars, symposia, etc., promotion of cooperative activities including the sharing of resources in the region, promotion of the dissemination and exchange of information in the region, providing an environment for scholarly interaction and stimulating research and publication activities, information on the Association's activities, as well as of its members by a regular publication programme
Publications   Official journal: ACURIL Newsletter/Carta Informativa. Free to members. Address same as Association. Other publications: Proceedings of meetings; reports of seminars, workshops; CARINDEX: Social Sciences and Humanities. 1977-; bibliography. Publications available for sale. No publications exchange program
Bibliography   Jordan, A., "ACURIL – Treasure of My Dreams," COMLA Newsletter 35 (Mar. 1982):3–4; de la Garza, P.J., "Report on the 16th Annual Meeting of ACURIL," Library of Congress Information Bulletin 44 (Aug. 12, 1985):225–228; "ACURIL XVII Stresses Continuing Education," Quarterly Bulletin of IAALD 31 (1986):175; Douglas, D.,

"Association of Caribbean University, Research and Institutional Libraries," in ALA World Encyclopedia of Library and Information Services. 2nd ed., pp. 81–82. Chicago: American Library Association, 1986; de la Garza, P.J., "Report on the 17th Annual Meeting of the Association of Caribbean University, Research and Institutional Libraries," Library of Congress Informaton Bulletin 45 (Sept. 8, 1986):312–315; "SALALM and ACURIL Consider Strategies for Coping with Shrinking Budgets," Library of Congress Information Bulletin 46 (Nov. 16, 1987):483–491; Jordan, A., "The Association of Caribbean University, Research and Institutional Libraries (ACURIL)," IFLA Journal 15 (1989):233–236; ALA (American Library Association): Report of visit to ACURIL XXXI and its host country, Cuba, May 23 – May 30, 2001 (www.ala.org/ala/iro/iroactivities/alacubanlibrariesreport.htm)

Comment   formerly Association of Caribbean University and Research Libraries

024   Association of Commonwealth Archivists and Records Managers (ACARM)

Address   c/o IRMT, Rm 14–15, 88/90 Hatton Garden, London EC1N 8PN newsletter@acarm.org; www.acarm.org

Languages   English

Established   Sept., 1984, at 10th International Congress on Archives

Officers   Chair: Charles Farrugia; Vice-Chair: Joel das Neves Tembe

Staff   Volunteers (officers)

General Assembly   General membership meets every 4 years

Structure   Governed by an elected Executive Committee consisting of a Chairman, Secretary, Treasurer and 6 other members. Affiliations: ICA

Sources of Support   Membership dues, quasi-government subsidies from the Commonwealth Foundation

Major Fields of Interest   Archives and records management

Major Goals and Objectives   Promote the development of professional archival standards in the Commonwealth; reinforce the importance which archives and records have in national heritage and development programmes; promote the development of professional archival and records management education and training throughout the Commonwealth; permit archivists and records managers who share a common heritage to compare, exchange, share and develop their common experience; encourage the dissemination of information; promote an increased awareness of the Commonwealth through the exploitation of archives and records in teaching; encourage the formation and continued development of professional archival and records management associations in individual countries of the Commonwealth

Activities   Networking organisation, seeks to lay the foundations for the electronic exchange of professional information, sponsors continuing education lectures, seminars, and workshops, preparation of guidelines on records and archives legislation

Publications   Official journal: ACARM Newsletter. Other publications: Venter, L., "Guide to the Internet and World Wide Web For Archivists and Records Managers (2005); Rhys-Lewis, J., "Conservation and Preservation Activities in Archives and Libraries in Developing Countries (2000); Parer, D., "Archival Legislation for Commonwealth Countries; Annual Report 2007

025   Association of Parliamentary Libraries of Australasia (APLA)

Address   c/o Judy Ballantyne, Harvest Tce, Perth, WA 6000   secretaryapla@apla.org.au; www.apla.org.au
Languages   English
Established   1984
General Assembly   Entire membership meets once a year
Major Fields of Interest   Parliamentary Librarianship
Major Goals and Objectives   To encourage understanding of, and co-operation between, research and information services attached to National and State Legislatures; to consider any matters affecting the common interests or operations of Parliamentary Libraries; to initiate, develop, establish and support ideas, methods and techniques likely to result in the better functioning of Parliamentary Libraries generally, and in particular their effective provision of information relevant to the needs of the Parliamentarians they serve; to foster a clearer understanding of the respective needs and roles of Members of Parliament and their Parliamentary Libraries by establishing a forum for better communication between the two; to provide a body which can speak and act on behalf of its several constituents on matters coming within the ambit of its authority; to advance the cause of Parliamentary Librarianship generally

026   Australian and New Zealand Theological Library Association Ltd (ANZTLA)

Address   c/o Wendy Davis   Tel.: +61 8 8416 8416, secretary@anztla.org; www.anztla.org
Languages   English
Staff   Volunteer members
Membership   Members: individual and institutional
Structure   Elected Board with chapters for each Australian state and for New Zealand
Sources of Support   Membership fees and income from publications
Major Fields of Interest   Theological libraries and librarianship
Major Goals and Objectives   To foster the study of theology and religion by enhancing the development of theological and religious libraries and librarianship
Activities   To provide a framework whereby librarians and other people and groups interested in theological and religious libraries and librarianship can interact, learn and work towards the development and improvement of theological and religious libraries and the role and function of such libraries in theological education; to educate persons on acceptable standards of librarianship among theological and religious libraries, and to support the implementation and development of such standards; to promote information services in support of teaching, learning and research in theology, religion and related disciplines, and to create such tools and aids as may be helpful in accomplishing this; to foster, as part of an education program, inter-library cooperation at both regional and national levels; to publish and disseminate literature and information in respect of theological and religious librarianship
Publications   Official journal: ANZTLA Newsletter. 1987-. 3/y. Other publications: ARI – Australasian Religion Index. 1989-. 2/y. Australasian Union List of Serials In Theological Collections. New Zealand Bibliography of Religion and Theology

027 Beta Phi Mu (International Library Science Honor Society) (BPM)*
Address c/o John Paul Walters, Program Director, 101 Louis Shores Building, 142 Collegiate Loop, P.O. Box 3062100, Tallahassee, FL 32306–2100 Tel.: +1 850 6443907, Fax +1 850 6449763, betaphimuinfo@admin.fsu.edu; www.beta-phi-mu.org
Languages English
Established Aug. 1948, at the University of Illinois
Officers Program Dir: John Paul Walters; Exec Dir: Christie Koontz, Ph.D.
Staff 1 (paid)
General Assembly General membership meets during ALA annual conference. Executive Board also meets during ALA Mid-Winter Conference
Membership Total members: 35,000. Chapters: 44. Requirements: Graduates of ALA-accredited schools who complete course requirements leading to a fifth year or other advanced degree in librarianship with a scholastic average of 3.75 on a 4.0 scale and recommended by the dean of their school and by invitation only from the faculty
Structure Beta Phi Mu is guided and governed by an Executive Board of Directors. Beta Phi Mu is a member in good standing with the American Library Association and the Association of College Honor Societies
Sources of Support Membership dues, sale of products, and publication royalties
Major Fields of Interest Librarianship and Information Studies
Major Goals and Objectives The society was proposed by a group of leading librarians and library educators who were aware of the notable achievements of honorary societies in other professions and who believed that such a society might have much to offer in the service of librarianship and library education. Its objectives are to recognize high scholarship in the study of librarianship and to sponsor appropriate professional and scholarly projects. The motto, Aliis inserviendo consumor, meaning "Consumed in the service of others," was selected by the founders based on the concept of dedication of librarians and other information professionals to the service of others
Activities Annual scholarship program includes: Sarah Rebecca Reed Scholarship for Beginning Professional Education ($2,250), Harold Lancour Scholarship for Foreign Study ($1,750), Frank B. Sessa Scholarship for Continuing Education of a Beta Phi Mu Member ($1,500), Blanche E. Woolls Scholarship for School Media ($2,250) and up to six Eugene Garfield Doctoral Dissertation Fellowships ($3,000 each). Also, the American Library Association offers annually the Beta Phi Mu Award ($1,000 and a 24k gold-framed Citation of Achievement) to a library school faculty member or to an individual for distinguisehd service to education for librarianship
Publications Newsletter: THE PIPELINE Beta Phi Mu Online Newsletter (www.beta-phi-mu.org). Monograph Series (1989-present), published by Greenwood Press for Beta Phi Mu. Proceeds from the sale of titles in this series are used to support the Beta Phi Mu Scholarship Program. As of 2000, titles in the series include: An Active Instrument for Propaganda – The American Public Library During World War I; Wayne A. Wiegand (4/26/1989); American Libraries before 1876, Haynes McMullen (8/30/2000); Carnegie Denied – Communities Rejecting Carnegie Library Construction Grants 1898–1925 Robert Sidney Martin (2/28/1993); Daring to Find Our Names – The Search for Lesbigay Library History, James V. Carmichael Jr. (8/30/1998); Defining Print Culture for Youth – The Cultural Work of Children's Literature, Anne Lundin, Wayne A. Wiegand (5/30/2003); Libraries and Scholarly Communication in the United States – The Historical

Dimension, Phyllis Dain, John Y. Cole (3/26/1990); Publishing and Readership in Revolutionary France and America – A Symposium at the Library of Congress, Sponsored by the Center for the Book and the European Division, Carol Armbruster (6/30/1993); Self-Examination – The Present and Future of Librarianship, Budd, John M. (11/30/2007); The Social Transcript: Uncovering Library Philosophy, Charles Osburn (12/30/2008); Renewing Professional Librarianship: A Fundamental Rethinking, Bill Crowley (3/30/2008); Leading from the Middle: A Selection of My Writings about Library Leadership, John Lubans, Jr. (Forthcoming)
Bibliography Holley, E. G., "Beta Phi Mu," in ALA Yearbook 1989. pp. 62–63. Chicago: American Library Association, 1989; "Beta Phi Mu," in The Bowker Annual: Library and Book Trade Almanac. 34th Edition 1989–90. pp. 677–679. New York: R. R. Bowker, 1989

028 Bibliographical Society of Australia and New Zealand (BSANZ)
Address c/o Rachel Salmond, POB 1463, Wagga Wagga, NSW 2650 Fax +61 2 69318669, rsalmond@pobox.com; www.csu.edu.au/community/BSANZ
Languages English
Established Feb. 1969 in Melbourne
Staff 6 (volunteers)
General Assembly General membership meets once a year. 1998: Melbourne, 1999: Brisbane, 2000: Melbourne, 2003: Canberra; 2004: Melbourne; 2005: Wellington: 2006 Adelaide
Membership Individual and institutional Membership 10 countries represented. Requirements: None. Dues: A$50.00 for personal members wherever located, A$30.00 for full-time students only, A$60.00 for institutional members in Australia and New Zealand, A$70.00 for institutional members outside Australia and New Zealand
Structure Governed by Council
Sources of Support Membership dues, sale of publications
Major Fields of Interest Bibliography of all types
Major Goals and Objectives To encourage and promote research in all aspects of physical bibliography in Australia and New Zealand: history of printing, publishing, bookselling, typefounding, papermaking, bookbinding; palaeography and codicology; and textual bibliography. Also has an interest in the general field of reference bibliography, involved in efforts to document the holdings in Australia of pre-1800 books through the recently completed Australian Book Heritage Project
Activities Annual conference, local meetings, participation in planning of EIP, Annual Essay Prize
Publications Official journal: BSANZ Bulletin, published quarterly (ISSN 0084–7852) (March 1970-); BSANZ newsletter, the Broadsheet, which is now delivered on-line; aktive publishing program. All pubs. available from: Ian Morrison Curator (Australia) Archives and Special Collections, Baillieu Library, University of Melbourne, Melbourne, Vic. 3010, Australia. Tel.: (61) 0383445366, Fax: 93478627, email: morrison@unimelb.edu.au

029 Bibliothèques Européenne de Théologie (BETH) (European Theological Libraries)
Address c/o Etienne D'hondt, Vicepresident prjhall@aol.com

Established Oct. 18, 1961 under the name "Comité International de Coordination des Associations de Bibliothèques de Théologie Catholique (CIC);" adopted new name under statutes, 1972, as registered association with seat in Nijmegen: International Council of Associations of Theological Libraries. 1999, in order to recognise the distinctive European nature of the organisation, the general assembly voted to change the name of the council to BETH
General Assembly 33rd General Assembly of BETH: 4.–8. 9. 2004, Lyon (France); 32nd : 13.–18. 9. 2003, Brixen (Bressanone); 31st: 21.–26. 9. 2002, Salamanca; 30th: 4.–9. 9. 2001, Erfurt; 29th: August 30 – September 2, University College of Ripon and York St. John
Membership Total members: 23 (12 ordinary, 11 extraordinary member associations). Requirements: None, but membership comprises mainly theological associations
Structure Governed by executive officers meeting several times a year. Affiliations: IFLA
Sources of Support Membership dues
Major Fields of Interest Theological library associations
Major Goals and Objectives To promote co-operation among the theological and ecclesiastical libraries in Europe. To stimulate the development of theological libraries through shared knowledge and experience and through training theological librarians. To serve the interests of European theological libraries in the scientific/academic sphere and on an international level. To preserve the rich cultural patrimony found in the theological and ecclesiastical libraries of Europe
Activities Furthering the aims of the association and carrying out an extensive publications program
Publications No official journal, but maintains an extensive publications program
Bibliography Cervelló-Margalef, J.A., ed., Le Conseil International des Associations de Bibliothèques de Théologie. 1961–1981. Cologne: Secrétariat du Conseil, 1982; Cervelló-Margalef, J.A., "Der Internationale Rat der Vereinigung Theologischer Bibliotheken," Zeitschrift für Bibliothekswesen und Bibliographie 30 (1983):257–262. Conseil International des Associations de Bibliothèques de Théologie. Leuven: Bibliotheek van de Faculteit Godgeleerdheid, 199
Comment Formerly: International Council of Associations of Theological Libraries

030 Caribbean Archives Association – Regional Branch of the International Council on Archives (CARBICA)

Address 19 av. Saint-John Perse, 97200 Fort-de-France Tel.: +869 46525211208, Fax +869 4651001, csylvester@sgu.edu; www.carbica.com
Languages English, French
Established 1965, Mona Kingston, Jamaica
Staff None
Membership Types of membership: Individual, institutional (17 national archives), honorary. Requirements: Individual: Archivists, historians, librarians, or persons approved by the Association for membership. Institutional: National or other institutions concerned with the custody and preservation of archives
Structure Governed by an Executive Committee, meeting once or twice a year. Affiliations: ICA, OAS (Organization of American States), Unesco

Sources of Support Membership dues, sale of publications
Major Fields of Interest Archival science
Major Goals and Objectives To establish, maintain and strengthen relations between archivists of the Caribbean; to study problems concerned with the conservation of archives in tropical countries; to contribute to a better mutual understanding among peoples of the Caribbean
Activities Holding Caribbean Archives Conferences; publication of journal. Establishing a training program for Caribbean archivists. The Association has succeeded in bringing together archivists of the English- and French-speaking Caribbean. The Spanish-speaking archivists have their own association (Asociación Latinoamericana de Archivos/Latin American Association of Archives)
Publications Official journal: Caribbean Archives. 1975-. 2/yr. Free to members. Address same as Association. English and French. Circ: 40. Issues proceedings of meetings. Publications issued for sale, price lists available. Publications exchanged with other associations

031 Comité français IFLA

Address c/o Bibliothèque Nationale de France, Direction des collections, Quai François Mauriac, 75706 Paris Cédex cfi.ifla@free.fr
Officers Pres: Pascal Sanz

032 Commonwealth Library Association (COMLA)

Address POB 144, Mona, Kingston 7 Tel.: +1 876 927 0083, Fax +1 876 9271926, nkpodo@uwimona.edu.jm; www.commonwealthfoundation.com/about/CA/CDP/Commonwealth\%20Library\%20Association\%20\%28COMLA\%29/index.cfm
Languages English
Established 1972, Lagos, Nigeria, at an inaugural conference. Sponsored by the Commonwealth Foundation, Mr. John Chadwick, Director. Constitution amended 1979 to restructure on a regional basis
Staff 2 (paid)
General Assembly General membership, Executive Committee, and COMLA Council meet every 3–4 years
Membership 50 countries represented. Types of membership: Full: National associations; affiliates: Libraries, documentation centers, etc. Requirements: Open to all associations, libraries, information centers, etc. in and out of the Commonwealth
Structure Governed by 6 Regional Councils, which send delegates to General Council meetings every 3 to 4 years. Regional Vice Presidents sit on the Chief Executive Committee, which meets every 12 to 18 months. Affiliations: ACURIL, FID, IFLA
Sources of Support Membership dues, grants from the Commonwealth Foundation
Major Fields of Interest Development of all types of libraries and library services in the Commonwealth
Major Goals and Objectives (1) To improve libraries in the Commonwealth; (2) to forge, maintain and strengthen professional links between librarians; (3) to support and encourage library associations; (4) to promote the status and education of librarians and the reciprocal recognition of qualifications; (5) to initiate research projects

Activities Past accomplishments: Greater emphasis on development of COMLA member organizations within their own regions through the activities of the Regional Councils (Europe, West Africa, Asia, East, Central and Southern Africa, Americas and Caribbean). Current and future: Promotion of rural libraries and resource centers; furthering of library and information work in developing countries; promotion of library skills amongst young readers. Proposed amendments to the Constitution to clarify certain articles. Active in promoting library-related legislation by providing background information and promotional activities. Sponsors conferences, seminars, workshops, and other continuing education programs

Publications Official journal: COMLA Newsletter. 1973-. 4/yr. Free to members. Circ: 600. English. Issues proceedings of seminars, workshops sponsored by the Organization. Has other occasional publications: Mungo, K. M. and Robertson, A., comps., Policy Guidelines for School Library Development (1987); Xuereb, P., ed., The Impact of Automation on the Functions. Administration and Staffing of Libraries: A COMLA Seminar. Singapore. Nov. 1–2, 1985 (Malta, 1988); etc. Publications issued for sale, price lists available, listed in official Journal, exchanged with other international associations and Commonwealth professional associations. Some publications sent free on request

Bibliography "COMLA: A Decade of Growth," COMLA Newsletter 37 (Sept. 1982):1–5, 12–13; Swaby, J.E., "Commonwealth Library Association," in ALA World Encyclopedia of Library and Information Services. 2nd ed., pp. 215–216. Chicago: American Library Association, 1986; "COMLA and the Library Profession," COMLA Newsletter 53 (Sept. 1986): 1; Ferguson, S., "Organising Library Associations in Small Countries," COMLA Newsletter 54 (Dec. 1986):8–9; "The Sydney Workshop on Rural Libraries," COMLA Newsletter 63 (Mar. 1989): 1–4 (COMLA organized a Workshop on Rural Libraries and Community Resource Centres in Sydney, Australia, 5–7 Sept. 1988); "Location of COMLA Secretariat," COMLA Newsletter 63 (Mar. 1989):6; "The COMLA Connection: An Interview between Michael Wooliscroft (Regional Councillor, COMLA South Pacific Region) and John Stringleman (former COMLA President)," New Zealand Libraries 46 (Mar. 1989):12–16; Swaby, J.E., "COMLINKS: News and Views from the COMLA Secretariat," COMLA Newsletter 64 (June 1989): 1–2, 12; Benoit, M., "COMLA Workshop, Malta, 2–5 April 1990," COMLA Newsletter 65 (Sept. 1989): 1,2; Swaby, J., "Regional Cooperation: The Role of COMLA in International Librarianship," IFLA Journal 15 (1989):243–245

033 Conference of Directors of Directors of National Libraries of Asia and Oceania (CDNLAO)

Address c/o Libraries of Asia Pacific Directory, Canberra, ACT 2600 Tel.: +61 2 62621481, Fax +61 2 62732545, lap@nla.gov.au; www.nla.gov.au/lap/aboutcd.html
Languages English
Established 1979
General Assembly Meets annually
Membership 26 national libraries in Asia and Oceania
Major Fields of Interest Resource and information sharing within the Asia Pacific region
Major Goals and Objectives To exchange information and promote cooperation for the development of libraries in Asia and Oceania; to assist libraries in lesser developed

countries through cooperation; to understand the state of the art of library development among libraries in Asia and Oceania
Publications Official journal: CDNLAO Newsletter. 3/yr. Web site: www.ndl.go.jp/en/publicationcdnlao. Address: Planning and Cooperation Division, Administrative Department, National Diet Library, 1–10–1 Nagata-cho, Chiyoda-ku, Tokyo 100–8924, JAPAN fax: +81–3-3508–2934, E-mail: newsl@ndl.go.jp

034 Conference of Directors of National Libraries (CDNL)

Address c/o Jasmine Cameron, Secretary, Canberra ACT 2600 Tel.: +61 2 62621262, Fax +61 2 62731133, jfullerton@nla.gov.au;jcameron@nla.gov.au; www.nla.gov.au/initiatives/meetings/cdnl/
Languages English
Established 1974
Staff None
General Assembly Meets annually, usually on the Wednesday of the IFLA conference at the National Library of the IFLA host country
Membership Requirements: Open to directors of national libraries
Structure Affiliations: IFLA
Sources of Support Not applicable
Major Fields of Interest Those aspects of librarianship that are pertinent among directors of national libraries
Major Goals and Objectives To provide a forum for communication among directors of national libraries
Activities CDNL List used to distribute information and communicate with members of the Conference of Directors of National Libraries (cdnl-l@infoserv.inist.fr); Establishes committes to take action on issues of importance to its members: The Committee on Digital Issues; Committee to review the IFLA Core programmes
Publications No official journal
Bibliography Strebl, M., "La préservation des resources documentaires dans les bibliothèques. Rapport de la conférence internationale de Vienne, 7–10 avril 1986," (The Preservation of Documentation Resources in Libraries. Report of the Vienna International Conference, 7–10 April 1986) Bulletin d'Information de l'Association des Bibliothécaires Français 137 (1987):19–22; Carroll, F.L., and Schwartz, P.J., Biographical Directory of National Librarians (London: Mansell, 1989). Scott, M.,Conference of Directors of National Libraries: forum for discussion and action, Alexandria; 7 (1) 1995, p.37–46; Rugaas, B., Past, present and future relations between the IFLA Section of National Libraries and the Conference of Directors of National Libraries, IFLA Journal; 20 (2) 1994, p.141–44

035 Conference of European National Librarians (CENL)*

Address c/o Dr. Britta Woldering, Secretary, Adickesallee 1, 60322 Frankfurt am Main Tel.: +49 69 1525-1541, Fax +49 69 1525-1010, cenl@d-nb.de; www.cenl.org
Languages English
Established 1987
Officers Chair: Dr. Elisabeth Niggemann; Secr: Dr. Britta Woldering
Staff 0,5 (voluntary)

General Assembly All members meet once a year. 2009: Madrid, 2010: London, 2011: Copenhagen
Membership National Librarians of all member states of the Council of Europe (49 members from 46 European countries)
Structure CENL Board: all members, CENL Executive Committee: 4 elected members
Sources of Support Association is financed through annual membership fees
Major Fields of Interest National libraries in Europe, digitisation,(traditional and digital) preservation of cultural heritage
Major Goals and Objectives To increase and reinforce the role of national libraries in Europe, in particular in respect of their responsibilities for maintaining the national cultural heritage and ensuring the accessibility of knowledge in that field
Activities Annual membership meetings as well as initiatives and support of research and development activities, joint projects, common web service: The European Library (www.theeuropeanlibrary.org), major player in the European digital library initiative Europeana (www.europeana.eu)
Publications Annual reports, available via CENL website

036   Congress of South-East Asian Libraries (CONSAL)

Address c/o Nguyen Huy Chuong, Secretary, 144 Xuan Thuy Street, Cau Giay District, Hanoi   Tel.: +64 4 37546558, Fax +84 4 3768-7900; www.consal.org
Established 1970, Singapore, as First Conference of Southeast Asian Librarians by the Library Associations of Malaya and Singapore. Current name assumed and constitution revised in 1975
Officers Pres: Nellie Dato Pakuda Haji Sunny; VP: Haji Abdullah Haji Tahir
Staff None
General Assembly CONSAL members meet at least once every 3 years with one member country acting as host for the conference
Membership Open to all national library associations of the Southeast Asian region (Brunei, Burma, Cambodia, Indonesia, Laos, Malaysia, the Philippines, Singapore, Thailand and Vietnam). National membership: National library associations; the national library and all libraries and related organizations within the member countries. Associate membership: Libraries and related organizations of non-member countries; and individuals interested in the objectives of CONSAL
Structure Governed by the CONSAL Committee, which includes the Executive Board and 3 delegates from each participating country
Sources of Support Financial support from int. organizations, governments and firms within the region as well as organizations outside the region, incl. UNESCO, IFLA, the Commonwealth Found. and the Nat. Libr. of Australia, also carries out various fund-raising activities
Major Fields of Interest Libraries and librarianship in the Southeast Asian region
Major Goals and Objectives 1) Establish, maintain, and strengthen networks, partnerships, and linkages with librarians, libraries, library schools and library associations and related institutions in the region; 2) Promote cooperation and provide assistance in the development of librarianship, library and information sciences, documentation, information and related services in the region; 3) Cooperate with regional and international organizations, and other institutions in the support of common undertakings and interests

of CONSAL; 4) Provide the fora for sharing and exchange of information and experiences on issues in the field of librarianship, library and information sciences, documentation, information and related services in the region; 5) Any other objectives that maybe approved by the Executive Board

Activities Provides opportunities for Southeast Asian librarians to come together to discuss matters of common professional interest. CONSAL has held an international conference every two to three years. Promotes the continuing education of librarians in the region. Contributes to the literature of librarianship

Publications No official journal. Publishes newsletter, proceedings, and other publications. Masterlist of Southeast Asia Microfilms, ed. by Winarti Partaningrat, 1978. Directory of Librarians in Southeast Asia, ed. by Marina G. Dayrit and Namnama P.Hidalgo, 1980. Southeast Asian Microfilms Newsletter, 1972–93, edited by Institute of Southeast Asian Studies

Bibliography Soosai, J.S., "Fifth Congress of the South-East Asian Librarians (CONSAL V)," IFLA Journal 7 (1981):416–418; Horton, A.R., "CONSAL VI," Australian Academic and Research Libraries 14 (1983):249–251; Mansor, N., "CONSAL VI: A Report and Personal Impressions," Singapore Libraries 13 (1983):28–30; Lim Pui Huen, P., "Congress of Southeast Asian Librarians (CONSAL)," in ALA World Encyclopedia of Library and Information Services. 2nd ed., pp. 218–219. Chicago: American Library Association, 1986; Khurshid, A., "Library Associations in Asia," Herald of Library Science 28 (1989):3–10; Anuar, H., "The Why and How of CONSAL as a Regional Library Association," IFLA Journal 15 (1989):237–242

037   Council of Australian University Librarians (CAUL)*

Address PO Box 8169, Canberra ACT 0200 Tel.: +61 2 61252990, Fax +61 2 62488571, caul@caul.edu.au; www.caul.edu.au
Languages English
Established 22 August, 1965 in Canberra, Australia
Officers Pres: Cathrine Harboe-Ree; Dep Pres: Ainslie Dewe; Exec Committee Members: Heather Gordon; Imogen Garner; Jogn Shipp
Staff 2,7
General Assembly Two council meetings per year. 2009/2 in Sydney, 2010/1 in Canberra, 2010/2 in Brisbane
Membership 40 CAUL members – annual fees AUD 3,600.00. 70 CEIRC members (CAUL Electronic Information Resources Committee – cooperative purchasing program) – annual fees AUD 2,450.00 / 3,675.00 (internal/external)
Structure Members are the library directors or university librarians or equivalent of institutions eligible for membership of Universities Australia
Sources of Support Membership fees
Major Fields of Interest Research resources, research training, research support, e-research, institutional repositories, open scholarship, copyright
Major Goals and Objectives To provide leadership in relevant higher education developments and information policy, and communicate activities to key stakeholders; to facilitate the members' role in supporting and maximising learning and teaching outcomes and contributing positively to the student experience; to facilitate the members' role in supporting and maximising research outcomes; to maximise access to information

resources and facilitate libraries' wider scholarly communication and information management roles; and to promote continuous improvement and best practice in pursuit of internationally recognised high quality library services and operations
Activities   COSI – CAUL Open Scholarship Initiative; CAIRSS – CAUL Australian Institutional Repository Support Service & ADT – Australasian Digital Theses Program; CEIRC – CAUL Electronic Information Resources Committee – cooperative purchasing program; ULA – University Library Australia – national borrowing program
Publications   The CAUL website is almost entirely open access, restricted only for those commercial documents relating to the CEIRC program
Bibliography   The CAUL Memoir: the Council of Australian University Librarians 1928–1998, with contributions by Alex Byrne, Ken McKinnon, Neil A Radford [and] Colin Steele. Canberra, University College & Research Libraries Section of the Australian Library and Information Association, 1998. ISBN 0 85889 723 7. See also www.caul.edu.au/caul-doc/publications.html

038   Council on Botanical and Horticultural Libraries, Inc. (CBHL)

Address   c/o Gayle Bradbeer, Secretary, 1100 Lawrence Street, Denver, CO 80204–2095 Tel.: +1 303-556-2791, Fax +1 303-556-3528, Gayle.Bradbeer@auraria.edu; www.cbhl.net
Languages   English
Established   1969, at Hunt Institute, Pittsburgh, PA, after a feasibility meeting in 1969 at the Massachusetts Horticultural Society, Boston, MA
Officers   Pres: Sheila Connor; 1st VP: Stanley Johnston; 2nd VP: Robin Everly; Past Pres: Leora Siegel; Treas: Brian R. Thompson; Secr: Gayle Bradbeer
Staff   None
General Assembly   Entire membership meets once a year, usually in the spring
Membership   Total members: 250+. 11 countries represented. Types of membership: Individual, institutional, commercial. Requirements: Individuals interest in the field and botanical and horticultural libraries of any size, worldwide
Structure   Governed by Board of Directors
Sources of Support   Membership dues, sale of publications
Major Fields of Interest   Botanical and horticultural libraries, literature, publications, information
Major Goals and Objectives   To initiate and improve communication and coordinate activities and programs of mutual interest and benefit to its membership
Activities   Computer Consortium, a botanical and horticultural resource sharing group, Online Distribution List, Annual Literature Award, various committees, annual meeting
Publications   Official journal: CBHL Newsletter. 1972-. 3–4/yr. Free to members. English. Other publications: Membership list, Seed catalog directories and the Plant Bibliography Series. Publications exchange program in effect of duplicate books and journals. Publications available for sale

039   Council on Library/Media Technicians (COLT)

Address   c/o Margaret Barron, Executive Director, 28262 Chardon Road, PMB 168, Wickcliffe, OH 44092–2793 Tel.: +1 202 231-3836, Fax +1 202 231-3838, jmhite0@dia.mil; http://colt.ucr.edu
Languages   English

Established 1967, as Council on Library Technical Assistants. 1976 became the Council on Library/Media Technical-Assistants, with new Constitution and Bylaws
Officers Pres: Jackie Hite; VP/Pres Elect: Chris Egan; Secr: Robin Martindill; Treas: Stan Cieplinski; Immediate Past Pres: Jackie Lakatos
Staff None
General Assembly Entire membership meets once a year. 2004: Orlando/FL
Membership Individual and institutional membership. Requirements: Open to anyone interested in the aims of the Association. Dues: Personal Membership in United States $45.00, Personal Membership outside of United States $70.00, Student Membership $35.00 Institution Membership in United States/Institution Representative $70.00, Institution Membership outside of United States/Institution Representative $95.00
Structure Governed by Board of Officers plus Regional Directors and Standing Committee Chairpersons. Affiliations: ALA, Ohio Association of Library Technicians
Sources of Support Membership dues, sale of publications
Major Fields of Interest Support staff in all types of libraries and information centers
Major Goals and Objectives To function as a clearinghouse for information relating to library support staff personnel. To advance the status of library support staff personnel. To initiate, promote and support activities leading toward the appropriate placement, employment and certification of library support staff personnel. To promote effective communication between and among library staff at all levels. To promote research projects. To study and develop curricula for the education of library support staff and develop appropriate standards for that education. To cooperate usefully with other organizations whose purposes and objectives are similar to and consistent with, those of COLT
Activities Sponsors exhibits, conferences, seminars, workshops, and other continuing education programs; sponsors awards
Publications No official journal. Other publications: U. S. Library Technician Programs (continually updated online directory of Library Technician education programs); Directory of Programs for the Training of Library/Media Technical Assistants (1997, print only); One Stop Guide to Workshop Planning (print only). Contact: Patricia McQuitty. email: pmcquitt@coin.org
Bibliography Halsted, D. D. and Neeley, D.M., "The Importance of the Library Technician," Library Journal 115 (1990):62–63

040   European Association for Health Information and Libraries (EAHIL)
Address Postbus 1393, 6300 BJ Utrecht Tel.: +31 302 619663, Fax +31 302 311830, EAHIL-secr@nic.surfnet.nl; www.eahil.org
Established 1987
Structure Affiliations: IFLA
Sources of Support Sponsors
Major Fields of Interest Health sciences and medical librarianship
Major Goals and Objectives To promote information and libraries in the health sciences in Europe
Activities Diskussion list EAHIL–L for all members. Workshops and conferences: 9th EUROPEAN CONFERENCE OF MEDICAL AND HEALTH LIBRARIES Santander, Spain, 20–25 September 2004; EAHIL Workshop 2005: "Overall quality – quality for all". Palermo, Italy, June 23–25, 2005; 9th ICML–International Congress on Medical

Librarianship, 19–23 September, 2005, Salvador, Bahia, Brazil http://www.icml.org/; 10th EUROPEAN CONFERENCE OF MEDICAL AND HEALTH LIBRARIES Cluj-Napoca, Romania,11th-16th of September 2006; EAHIL workshop 2007. Cracow, Poland. September 11–14, 2007. (Preliminary date)

041 European Association for Library and Information Education and Research (EUCLID)

Address c/o Prof. Ragnar Audunson, Chair, Pilestredet 52, 0617 Oslo Tel.: +47 22 452600, Fax +47 22 452605; www.jbi.hio.no/bibin/euclid/index.html
Membership Requirements: Departments or institutions providing education at the tertiary level and undertaking research in the field of library- and information science or information management in countries that are eligible for membership of the Council of Europe. Affiliate membership is open to research institutions in the field and teaching institusions at the secondary level; Corresponding membership is open to any other institutions or organisation involved in education and research in the field
Structure Governed by executive board
Major Fields of Interest Cooperation within library and information education and research
Major Goals and Objectives Facilitate exchange of students among the members; facilitate exchange of staff among members; encourage mutual recognition of curricula or parts of curricula; develop co-operation on research projects; develop co-operation with other international organisations; exchange mutual information about development in curricula and research; arrange meetings about the topics of organisation; encourage support from stronger to weaker members; represent the membership in relation to European and international bodies

042 European Association of Aquatic Sciences Libraries and Information Centres (EURASLIC)

Address c/o Snejina Bacheva, Exec Secretary, 40, Parvi mai Str., Asparuhovo living quarter, 9000 Varna, P.O. Box 152, 9000 Varna Tel.: +359 52 370484, Fax +359 52 370483, library@io-bas.bg; www.euraslic.org
Languages English
Established Officially registered in April 1990 as a Europe-wide association, with its own bank account and various categories of membership. Euraslic is a legal entity and as such can enter into contracts and agreements with other legally constituted organizations within the bounds of the Euraslic bylaws
Staff 12 (11 volunteers, 1 paid)
General Assembly EURASLIC has already held ten meetings, in Plymouth, Paris, Lelystad, Bremerhaven, Gdynia, Valletta, Athina, Aberdeen, Brest and Kiel. 2005: Split, Croatia
Membership 110 members
Structure Affiliation: a regional group of the International Association of Aquatic and Marine Science Libraries and Information Centres (IAMSLIC)
Major Fields of Interest Aquatic sciences libraries and information centers
Major Goals and Objectives To provide an organisation for the exchange of ideas and views on issues of mutual concern; collect and present views and proposals on behalf of

the members to other organisations; to encourage cooperation within Europe and to build links with other national, regional and international aquatic science libraries and information networks; to undertake joint projects, to improve the flow, exchange and dissemination of aquatic information
Activities Organizes conferences; Projects: Union List of serials available at the EURASLIC ECET Group aquatic libraries; BLICOP Black Sea Regional Library Co-Operation Project; Directory project
Publications Official journal: EURASLIC Newsletter. 2/yr. Editor: Snejina Bacheva. Address same as association. Other publications: Proceedings of the biennial conferences; Directory of European Aquatic Sciences Libraries and Information Centres; Press releases: No1, May 2003: Black Sea Scientific Information and Knowledge Base; No 2, May 2003: Tenth Euraslic Conference – Short Report; November 2002: Aquatic Sciences Libraries Benefit from Equipment Grants; October 2001: Important Scientific Collections either Underutilized or in Danger of Being Lost
Bibliography Baron, J., & Varley, A.:Euraslic: the first ten years. The origins and history of the European Association of Aquatic Sciences Libraries and Information Centres, 1988–1997. In: E. Charou, J. Baron & D. Kazepis (Eds.): People and technology. Sharing knowledge and shaping the future of aquatic information in Europe. Athens 1998, pp. 5–12; Baron, J.: Aquatic Library and Information Networks. In: F. L. Carroll & J. F. Harvey (Eds.): International Librarianship: Cooperation and Collaboration. Lanham, Maryland 2001, pp. 59–72; Moulder, D.: A Summary of the Proposals for the future of Euraslic. In: Euraslic 2: Proceedings of the Meeting, Paris, Institut océanographique, 26–27 April 1990. Oceanis Vol. 16 (1990), pp. 45–52

043   European Association of Information Services (EUSIDIC)
Address WG Plein 475, 1054 SH Amsterdam Tel.: +31 20 5893232, Fax +31 20 5893230; www.eusidic.org
Languages English
Established 1970
Staff 1 (paid)
General Assembly Entire membership meets annually
Membership Nearly 100 organizations, 16 countries represented. Requirements: Any organization involved in the electronic transfer of information. European members: Full membership with voting rights; outside Europe: Associate membership. Membership fee per year is EUR 990. For smaller organisations reductions are available upon request
Structure Governed by Executive Board and Council, elected annually from full membership. Affiliations: INTUG (International Telecommunications User Group)
Sources of Support Membership dues, subsidies
Major Fields of Interest Electronic transfer of information
Major Goals and Objectives To promote the unimpeded and efficient flow of information in machine-readable form both within Europe and between Europe and the rest of the world. Seeks to be a multi-faceted body bringing together information professionals and their organisations to share their knowledge and widen their perspective, to benefit from the experience and ideas of other members and to place their specialisation and expertise in the broader context of the industry as a whole
Activities Association has become an international forum for information producers,

hosts, users, and all groups interested in the handling, production, and dissemination of information in electronic form. Activities cover online services (both bibliographic and nonbibliographic), telecommunications, economics of information processing, microcomputing, office systems, transborder data flow, etc. Organizes yearly monitoring week of public data networks (PDNs) in Europe to determine the failure rate via the public data networks of members. Sponsors workshops, usually at end of annual conference. Maintains close contacts with relevant organizations
Publications Official journal: Newsidic (newsletter). 6/yr., circulated to members only. Other publications: EUSIDIC Members Directory (1/yr.); EUSIDIC Database Guide: various reports, Guidelines, and Codes of Practice, etc. on topics of interest to members
Bibliography Henderson, H., "European Association of Information Services (EUSIDIC)," in ALA World Encyclopedia of Library and Information Services. 2nd ed., p. 272. Chicago: American Library Association, 1986; "EUSIDIC Survey of Public Data Network," Herald of Library Science 28 (1989):289; "EUSIDIC 1989 Monitoring Week: The Results," Program: Automated Library and Information Systems 24 (1990):94

044   European Association of Libraries and Information Services on Alcohol and Other Drugs (ELISAD)*

Address c/o Brian Galvin, Secretary, Holbrook House, Holles Street, Dublin, 2 cgoodair@sgul.ac.uk; www.elisad.eu
Languages English
Established 1988
Officers Chair: Christine Goodair; Past Chair: Jorunn Moen; Treas: Brian Galvin; Secr: Daniela Zardo
General Assembly Meetings at least once a year, 2009 meeting held in Budapest
Membership Requirements: open to all those with an interest in the collection, the dissemination and the use of factual information on alcohol and other drugs in Europe. Dues: Full membership (120 Euro/year); Associate membership (80 Euro/year)
Structure Governed by an executive board. Affiliations: SALIS
Sources of Support Membership fees and any income derived from grants for underatking work
Major Fields of Interest Libraries and information services on addictions
Major Goals and Objectives To provide a forum for collaboration and exchange of information between European libraries, institutions, information services and centres as well as individuals in the field of addictions; to promote the role of documentation centres and libraries and the efficient flow of information in the field of addictions
Activities The activities of the association are: 1. To organise a conference – at least once a year in various cities in Europe – dealing with information, research and documentation matters in the field of addictions; 2. To be a European forum for the exchange of experience, development of ideas for the addictions information sector and the wider health information community; 3. To produce information resources, services and/or publications for the addictions sector; 4. To encourage the interaction of information specialists with scientists and others who require information on addictions
Publications Elisad journal. Only available for members
Bibliography Christine Goodair, Jorunn Moen, Susanna Prepeliczay & Thomas Rouault: Collaboration across Europe: Experience from Practice, in LIBRI, vol. 55, number 4,

December 2005 (http://librijournal.org/2005–4toc.html). The Elisad Gateway provides multilingual descriptions of and links to over 1000 evaluated European websites and other Internet resources on the use and misuse of drugs including those of Central and Eastern European countries

045 European Bureau of Library, Information and Documentation Associations (EBLIDA)*

Address POB 16359, 2500 BJ The Hague Tel.: +31 70 3090551, Fax +31 70 3090558, Eblida@eblida.org; www.eblida.org
Languages English
Established 1992
Officers Pres: Gerald Leitner; VP: Jill Martin; Dir: Yoanne Yeomans
Structure Governed by Executive Committee
Major Fields of Interest Umbrella association of national library, information, documentation and archive associations and organisations in Europe
Major Goals and Objectives Increase cohesion and influence of library, archive & information sectors & professionals in Europe; identify relevant European policy issues and lobby for favourable outcome; raise awareness & disseminate information; extend membership (new 10 EU members & applicant countries)
Activities Promotion of interests of its members, active involvement of members in European information policies, consultation and advice, information on European developments; sponsors workshops, meetings, events
Publications Official journal: EBLIDA Hot News. 12/yr

046 European Information Association (EIA)

Address c/o Eric Weber, coordinator, PO Box 28, CH7 6FE Mold, Flintshire Tel.: +44 1352 700051, eric@eia.org.uk; www.eia.org.uk
Languages English
Officers Chair: Paul Clarke; Secr: Angela Stogia; Treas: Ian Mayfield
General Assembly Membership meets once a year
Membership Membership includes public, academic and government libraries; information units of professional and voluntary groups; European Documentation Centres; Euro Info Centres; law firms; local authorities; publishers; companies
Structure Administered by a committee
Major Fields of Interest EU information
Major Goals and Objectives Objectives: To promote economic and social progress; to assert its identity on the international scene; to strengthen the protection of the rights and interests of the nationals of its Member States; to maintain and develop the Union as an area of freedom, security and justice; to maintain in full the acquis communautaire.
Activities Plays a major role in improving the quality of EU information through lobbying, and through the EIA Awards
Publications Official newletter: Focus. 12/yr. Editor: Eric Davies, European Information Services, Mold, UK, e-mail: euro.info@btinternet.com

047 Fédération Internationale des Archives du Film (FIAF) (International Federation of Film Archives)*

Address Rue Defacqz 1, 1000 Brussels Tel.: +322 538 3065, Fax +322 534 4774, info@fiafnet.org; www.fiafnet.org

Languages English, French; Spanish also used as a working language (Federación International de Archivos Filmicos)

Established 1938, Paris

Officers Secr Gen: Meg Labrum; Treas: Patrick Loughney; VP: Vladimir Opela; èric LeRoy; Luca Giuliani

Staff 4 (paid)

General Assembly Affiliates meet once a year in different countries. The Congress combines a General Assembly at which the formal business of the Federation is transacted with a programme of symposia and workshops on technical or legal aspects of film archive work and on aspects of film history and culture

Membership Total number of affliates: 151 institutions in over 70 countries. Types of membership: Institutional. Requirements: Autonomous, non-profit film and audiovisual archives, working on a national, regional or specialized level, accessible to the public, devoted to the history and aesthetics of cinema and all moving immage tecnologies

Structure Governed by general assembly and executive committee. Affiliations: Unesco

Sources of Support Membership dues. Budget (US Dollar): Approx. 150,000

Major Fields of Interest Association of the world's leading film archives The preservation of film as art and historical document, including all forms of the moving image

Major Goals and Objectives To promote the preservation of films; encourage the formation and development of film archives in all countries; facilitate the collection and the international exchange of films and documents relating to the cinema; develop cooperation among its members

Activities Publication of the half-yearly specialized Journal of Film Preservation. Publication of the International Film Archives Database and the FIAF Databases Online. Publication of several manuals on film preservation, film cataloging, and bibliographical tools. Publication of the Advanced Manual of Film Projections. The Association's practical work is also carried out by individual archives and by 3 Commissions (Technical commission, Cataloguing and Documentation Commission, Programming and Access to Collections Commission). Educational projects in Africa, Asia, Latin America, through the FIAF Summer School and the FIAF School on Wheels. Cooperative preservation projects through the Reel Emergency Project. Contribution to film and media studies through the FIAF Oral History Project.

Publications Main main periodical publication: Journal of Film Preservation. 2/yr.; FIAF International FilmArchive Database (Contains the International Index to Film/TV Periodicals offering in-depth coverage of the world's foremost film journals. Full citations, abstracts and subject headings for nearly 300.000 records from over 300 titles. Also includes Treasures from the Film Archives. info: pip@fiafnet.org; Treasures from the Film Archives annually updated; International Index to Film Periodicals (1972-; Standing order: 160.00 EUR; Single order: 2009, (latest published volume): 180.00 EUR; Back volumes: 1982, 1983, 1986–2009 (each volume): 150.00 E; Annual Bibliography of FIAF Members' Publications (1979- : 12 EUR (each volume); FIAF Directory (Brochure including the complete list of FIAF affiliates and Subscribers 1/yr: 5.00 EUR)

Bibliography   King, B.E., "International Federation of Film Archives," Archives and Manuscripts 9 (1981):87–91; "Fourth Round Table Meeting on Audiovisual Archives," IFLA Journal 10 (1984):421–422 (repr. from Unisist Newsletter): "International Federation of Film Archives," in The Bowker Annual: Library and Book Trade Almanac. 34th Edition 1989–90. pp. 735–736. New York: R. R. Bowker, 1989; Smither, R.B.N., "Formats and Standards: A Film Archive Perspective on Exchanging Computerized Data (paper given at 42nd Annual Congress of FIAF)," American Archivist 50 (1987): 324–339; "News in the Field of Audio-visual Archives," Unisist Newsletter 17 (1989):66–67

048   Forum of Asian Theological Libraries (For ATL)

Address   c/o Karmito, Librarian, Jl. Dr. Wahidin S. 5–19, Yogyakarta 55224 bethpulanco@gmail.com
Membership   Requirements: represents librarians from India, Korea, Indonesia, the Philippines, Malaysia and Taiwan, the colleagues from Australia and New Zealand are also invited; includes Protestant libraries only
Publications   No official journal. Other publications: Directory Asian Theological Libraries 1992–1993

049   Friends of African Village Libraries (FAVL)*

Address   POB 90533, San Jose, CA 95109–3533   Tel.: +408 5546888, mkevane@scu.edu; www.favl.org
Languages   French, English, local languages
Established   2001 in San Jose, California
Officers   Pres: Michael Kevane; VP: Leslie Gray; Dir: Sue Frey; Deborah Garvey; Lori Zink
Staff   All nine board members are volunteers; One paid intern. In Burkina Faso FAVL employs five librarians and three coordinators, including a representative in Ouagadougou
General Assembly   Regular board meetings normally hosted in San Jose, CA (various locations)
Membership   n/a
Structure   Nine-member board and led by two co-Directors.
Sources of Support   Occasional grants and donations from individuals
Major Fields of Interest   Long-term management of and support for small community libraries in rural Africa; increasing access to reading material and other information in rural villages in sub-Saharan Africa
Major Goals and Objectives   To assist the rural poor of Africa with the creation of village libraries. This is accomplished by working closely with the communities in which the libraries are established
Activities   FAVL has established and continues to manage and improve upon13 village libraries, eight in Burkina Faso, three in Ghana, one in Tanzania, and one in Uganda. FAVL also founded and supports the Uganda Community Library Association(UgCLA) with over 50 library members. FAVL employs or has a liaison with staff persons in each country of operation and librarians receive regular training to maximize leadership capacity. FAVL coordinates numerous volunteers (undergraduate students, graduate students in library sciences, professors of library science and photography) who spend from one week to three months in the community libraries. FAVL also has a small book

production unit that creates and publishes appropriate children's reading material. We currently have 30 children's books undergoing the publishing process.
Publications Friends of African Village Libraries Newsletter, mailed biannually, English
Bibliography see website

050   Indian Association of Teachers of Library and Information Science (IATLIS)*

Address Patiala (Punjab) 147002 Tel.: +91 175 6046179, Fax +91 175 2283073, iatlis.patiala@mail.com; www.sites.google.com/site/iatlishome
Languages English
Established 1969, Nagpur (Maharashtra
Officers Pres: Dr. Jagtar Singh; VP: Dr. Inder Vir Malhan; Dr. B.D. Kumber; Gen Secr: Dr. Trishanit Kaur; Joint Secr: Dr. H.P.S. Kalra
Staff Voluntary
General Assembly Executive meeting once in two months. General Assembly once a year, but a special general assembly meeting can also be held on demand or in case of an emergency situation
Membership Total members: 516. Type of membership: Life. Requirements: Library and Information Science Teachers, Library Professionals, Research Scholars, etc. Life Membership Fee: INR. 1,000
Structure Governed by Executive Committee of the office bearers
Sources of Support Sale of Publications, Membership fee and endowments
Major Fields of Interest Library and information science education research and training
Major Goals and Objectives To promote exchange of ideas on education in library science; to promot research in education in Library science; to promote publication of books and periodicals on education in library science; to hold conferences, seminars and colooquia for the development and propagation of ideas on education in Lubrary science; to give consultaion service on education in library science; to promote welfare of teachers of library science in India
Activities Organizing training workshops for Library and Information Professionels
Publications Official journal: IATLIS Communication (Newsletter). IATLIS plans to start a peer-reviewed Journal. The name of the journal should be IATLIS Journal of Information and Konowöedge Management

051   International Association for Social Sciences Information Services and Technology (IASSIST)

Address c/o Karsten Boye Rasmussen, SDU-OU, Campusvej 55, 5230 Odense M laine@chass.utoronto.ca; www.iassistdata.org
Languages English, some French
Staff None
General Assembly Entire membership meets annually in May. 2004: Madison/Wisconsin, USA; 2003: Ottawa/Canada; Storrs/Connecticut, USA
Membership 200 members from a variety of workplaces, incl. data archives, statistical agencies, research centers, libraries, academic departments, government departments, and non-profit organizations. Dues: regular 50$, Student 25$, Institutions 75 $
Major Fields of Interest Social Sciences information services

Major Goals and Objectives   To foster and promote a network of excellence for data service delivery; to advance infrastructure in the social sciences; to provide opportunities for collegial exchange of sound professional practices
Activities   Training, workshops, seminars,actions groups
Publications   IASSIST Quarterly (IQ) 4/yr. Editor: Karsten Boye Rasmussen, Department of Organization and Management, SDU-OU, Campusvej 55, DK-5230 Odense M, Denmark, Tel: +45 6550 2115, email: kbr@sam.sdu.dk. IASST-L@columbia.edu (email discussion list for IASSIST members)
Bibliography   Geraci, D., "The International Association for Social Science Information Services and Technology (IASSIST) [1988 Annual Meeting]," College & Research Libraries News 8 (1988):530–532

052   International Association of Agricultural Infornation Specialities (IAALD)
Address   c/o Margot Bellamy, Secretary/Treasurer, 14 Queen Street, Dorchester-on-Thames Wallingford OX10 7HR   Tel.: +44 1865 340054, info@iaald.org; www.iaald.org
Languages   English
Established   1955, Ghent, Belgium
Officers   Pres: Peter Ballantyne; VP: Stephen Rudgard; Secr/Treas: Toni Greider; Edi: Debbie Currie
Staff   1 (volunteer)
General Assembly   General membership meets every five years in a World Congress. Regional conferences held in between. XI. World Congress: May 15–21, 2005, Lexington/USA
Membership   Total members: over 300 in 80 countries. No membership requirements. Dues (US Dollar): 45/1 yr, 80/2yrs, individual; 95/1 yr, 180/2yrs, institutional
Structure   Governed by executive officers meeting annually. Affiliations: AFITA, INFITA
Sources of Support   Membership dues
Major Fields of Interest   Agricultural information management on an international scale
Major Goals and Objectives   To enable our members to create, capture, access and disseminate information to achieve a more productive and sustainable use of the world's land, water, and renewable natural resources
Activities   To connect agricultural information specialists worldwide, providing platforms and spaces for information dissemination, exchange and knowledge sharing; to convene agricultural information specialists worldwide, organising meetings and catalyzing dialogue among all agricultural information stakeholders; to communicate and advocate the value of knowledge and information to its members and others, improving the status and practice of agricultural information management and dissemination; to collaborate with members and other partner organisations, facilitating and catalyzing educational and other opportunities across agricultural information communities
Publications   Official journal: Quarterly Bulletin of IAALD. 1956-. 4/yr.Free to members. Other publications: Agricultural Information Resource Centers A World Directory 2000 by Jane S. Johnson, Rita C. Fisher, Carol Boast. IAALD News
Bibliography   Butler, R.W., "International Association of Agricultural Librarians and Documentalists," in ALA World Encyclopedia of Library and Information Services. 2nd

ed., p. 367. Chicago: American Library Association, 1986; Paz de Erickson, AM., "Recursos humanos: un recurso renovable?" (Human Resources: A Renewable Resource?) Revista AIBDA 7 (1986):85–94 (reviews role of AIBDA in continuing education); "IAALD Members," Quarterly Bulletin of IAALD 33 (1988):13–45; "International Association of Agricultural Librarians and Documentalists," in The Bowker Annual: Library and Book Trade Almanac. 34th Edition 1989–90. pp. 728–729. New York: R. R. Bowker, 1989

053   International Association of Aquatic and Marine Science Libraries and Information Centers (IAMSLIC)

Address   c/o Janet Webster, Librarian, 2030 S. Marine Science Drive, Newport, OR 97365   Tel.: +1 772 4652400 ext. 201, Fax +1 772 4652446, janet.webster@oregonstate.edu; www.iamslic.org
Languages   English
Established   1975, Woods Hole, Massachusetts, USA
Officers   Pres: Ruth Gustafson; Secr: Kathleen Heil; Treas: Sandra Abbott-Stout; Pres-Elect: Marcia Croy-Vanwely; Amy Butros; Past-Pres: Elizabeth Winiarz
Staff   None
General Assembly   Entire membership meets annually. 2004: Hobart/Tasmania, Australia. 2005: Rome. 2006: Portland/Oregon, USA
Membership   Types of membership: Individual, institutional. Requirements: Interest in marine science librarianship/information/documentation. Members include all types and sizes of libraries and information centers, including marine research and policy institutions, government agencies, colleges, universities, non-profit and profit-making institutions. Dues (US Dollar): 35
Structure   Governed by Executive Board
Sources of Support   Membership dues, sale of publications
Major Fields of Interest   Libraries and information centers in aquatic and marine science
Major Goals and Objectives   To promote the cooperation and sharing of resources among libraries and information centers which specialize in any aspect of marine science. To provide a forum for exchange and exploration of ideas and issues of mutual concern
Activities   Provides continuing education workshops for members. Annual Conference, Document Transmission, GLODIR & IDALIC Directories, Grants
Publications   No official journal. IAMSLIC Newsletter. 1977-. 4/yr.Circ: Membership only. English. Available in the members' area of the web site. Publishes proceedings of meetings

054   International Association of Law Librarians (IALL)*

Address   17 Russell Square, London WC1B 5DR   Tel.: +44 20 7862 5884, Fax +44 20 7862 5850, jules.winterton@sas.ac.uk; www.iall.org
Languages   English
Officers   Pres: Jules Winterton
Staff   None
General Assembly   Annual, December 2008 San Juan Puerto Rico, December 2009 Istanbul, September 2010 The Hague

Membership 750, US$60 personal, US$95 institutional, see website for details and application form http://iall.org/membership.html

Structure Non-profit corporation registered in Washington DC, elected Board

Sources of Support Membership dues

Major Fields of Interest Law librarianship

Major Goals and Objectives Promotes the work of individuals, libraries, and other organizations concerned with the dissemination of legal information; Advances the education of law librarians and other legal information professionals by providing substantive educational programs on foreign and international legal systems in venues all around the world; Supports educational and professional opportunities for newer legal information professionals, especially those from developing nations, by providing financial support in the form of bursaries and scholarships for annual course attendance and internships; shares legal knowledge and scholarship and increases access to legal information on a worldwide basis through the International Journal of Legal Information and other publications, and its website; fosters networking and mentoring among legal information professionals on a worldwide basis by creating and maintaining ongoing relationships between IALL and other international, national and regional law library and legal information organizations; and supports and encourages the development of national and international legal information policies and promotes free access to legal information on a worldwide basis through policy statements and scholarship

Activities Major annual conference and course in international law librarianship, journal International Journal of Legal Information, three conference grants p.a., major grant for individual research project /overseas placement, IALL International Handbook on Legal Information Management in progress, sponsored the establishment of the IFLA section of Law Libraries

Publications Andrews, Joseph L. et al. The Law in the United States of America: A Selective Bibliographical Guide. (New York): New York University Press, 1965; Australian and South Pacific Law: Structure and Legal Materials: Papers and Proceedings of the 8th IALL Course on Law Librarianship, May 10–15, 1981; Igor I. Kavass, ed. Buffalo, N.Y.: William S. Hein, 1983; Catalonia, Spain, Europe, and Latin America: Regional Legal Systems and Their Literature: Papers Presented at the 12th International Association of Law Libraries Course on International Law Librarianship, August 17–21, 1993 at Universitat Pompeu Fabra, Barcelona, Catalonia, Spain. Jürgen Christoph Gödan & Bernard D. Reams, Jr., comps. Buffalo, N.Y.: William S. Hein, 1995; Courts, Law Libraries and Legal Information in a Changing Society: 25. IALL Anniversary. Freiburg i.Br., July 15–20, 1984. International Association of Law Libraries, 1984; European Law Libraries Guide/Guide européen des bibliothPques de droit. Prepared by the International Association of Law Libraries under the auspices of the Council of Europe/Préparé par l'Association internationale des BibliothPques de droit sous les auspices du Conseil de l'Europe. London: Morgan-Grampian, 1971; The IALL Messenger. No. 1 (1986); IALL Newsletter. No. 1 (Mar. 1975) – no. 25 (Dec. 1979); International Association of Law Libraries Bulletin. No. 1–29/30 (Sept. 1960 – Dec. 1972); International Association of Law Libraries. Directory – International Association of Law Libraries. Buffalo, N.Y.: Published for the International Association of Law Libraries with the compliments of William S. Hein & Co., Inc., 1977, 1980, 1988.1; International Association of Law Libraries: Proceedings of the Meeting at the Harvard Law School Cambridge,

Massachusetts, June 24–25, 1961. Kurt Schwerin, ed. 1962; International Journal of Legal Information. Vol. 10- (1982-); International Journal of Law Libraries. Vol. 1–9 (1973–1981); Law in Multicultural Societies: Proceedings of the IALL Meeting, Jerusalem, July 21–26, 1985. E. I. Cuomo, ed. Jerusalem : International Association of Law Libraries; B. G. Segal Law Library Center, The Hebrew University of Jerusalem, 1989; Sloan, Irving J. Chronology of American Constitutional History and Law. Dobbs Ferry, NY: Oceana, 1987; Supranational and Constitutional Courts in Europe: Functions and Sources: Papers Presented at the 30th Anniversary Meeting of the International Association of Law Libraries, Bibliotheque Cujas,Paris, August 1989. Igor I. Kavass, ed. Buffalo, N.Y.: William S. Hein, 1992; The Unification of Private Law and Law and Legal Literature in Italy: 4th Course in Rome, September 4–8, 1972. Marburg, Germany: International Association of Law Libraries, 1974

Bibliography Dahlmanns, Gerhard, J. "The International Association of Law Libraries." The Law Librarian 4(3) (Dec. 1973/Mar. 1974): 40–41; Dahlmanns, Gerhard J. "The International Association of Law Libraries: An Interim Account." IALL Bulletin No. 28 (June 1972): 7–12; Dahlmanns, Gerhard. "Serving Legal Information: Twenty-Five Years of IALL." In Courts, Law Libraries, and Legal Information in a Changing Society: 25th IALL Anniversary Meeting 4–23 (Freiburg, Germany: International Association of Law Libraries, 1984); Landheer, Bart. "Ten Years International Association of Law Libraries." International Association of Law Libraries Bulletin XXIII (June 1969):5–6; Schwerin, Kurt. "The International Association of Law Libraries: Its Beginnings." International Journal of Legal Information 12 (1&2) (Feb./April 1984): 1–6; Sprudzs, Adolf. "The International Association of Law Libraries and its Twenty-Five Years of Activities." The Law Librarian 15(3) (Dec. 1984): 50–53; Sprudzs, Adolf. "Thirty-Five Years of International Cooperation: The Case of the IALL." The Law Librarian 26(2) (June 1995): 321–326. Wenger, Larry B. "IALL at 40." International Journal of Legal Information 27(1) (Spring 1999): 1–2; Winterton, Jules. "IALL: Law Libraries in an Era of Globalisation." Novaya Justitsiya No.2 (2009): 114–117

055   International Association of Law Libraries (IALL)

Address c/o Jennefer Aston, Secretary, POB 4460, Dublin 7 Tel.: +353 1-817-5121, Fax +353 1-817-5151, jaston@lawlibrary.ie; www.iall.org
Languages English, French, German, Spanish
Established 1959, New York, by European and American law librarians
Officers Pres: Jules Winterton; 1st VP: Richard A. Danner; Secr: Jennefer Aston; Treas: Ann Morrison
Staff None
General Assembly Entire membership meets annually
Membership Total members: Over 600 (420 individual, 180 institutional). 60 countries represented. Types of membership: Individual, institutional, life. Requirements: Any person or institution interested in the aims of the Association
Structure Governed by executive officers and Board of Directors meeting annually. Affiliations: FID, IFLA
Sources of Support Membership dues, private gifts
Major Fields of Interest Law libraries, international cooperation among legal resource libraries, acquisition and research of multinational legal material

Major Goals and Objectives To promote the work of individuals, libraries, and other institutions and agencies concerned with the acquisition and bibliographic processing of legal materials collected on a multinational basis, and to facilitate the research and use of such materials on a worldwide basis

Activities Establishment of regular channels of communication among law librarians in 60 countries; dissemination of information through the official journal; establishment of the IALL Courses in Law Librarianship. Sponsors seminars, sessions within the IFLA General Council meetings, annual course on international law librarianship, annual website award

Publications Official Journal: International Journal of Legal Information. Editor: Mark Engsberg (mark.engsberg@yale.edu). Free for members. subscripton for individuals: 60$, for institutions: 95$, Sustaining (assosciste) 250$ The IALL Messenger. No. 1 (1986). IALL Newsletter. No. 1 (Mar. 1975) – no. 25 (Dec. 1979). International Association of Law Libraries Bulletin. No. 1–29/30 (Sept. 1960 – Dec. 1972). International Journal of Law Libraries. Vol. 1–9 (1973–1981). Sloan, Irving J. Chronology of American Constitutional History and Law. Dobbs Ferry, NY: Oceana, 1987. Membership Directory, Proceedings and papers of meetings and courses

Bibliography Kavass, I. and Vlasman, G.W., "The International Association of Law Libraries," Juridische Bibliothecaris 3 (1982):12–14 (in Dutch); Sipkov, I., "International Association of Law Libraries," in ALA World Encyclopedia of Library and Information Services. 2nd ed., pp. 367–368. Chicago: American Library Association, 1986; Sipkov, I., "International Association of Law Libraries," Library of Congress Information Bulletin 46 (May 11, 1987):198–199 (review of 1986 meeting, Tokyo, during IFLA conference); "International Association of Law Libraries," in The Bowker Annual: Library and Book Trade Almanac. 34th Edition 1989–90. p. 729. New York: R. R. Bowker, 1989. Dahlmanns, Gerhard, J. "The International Association of Law Libraries." The Law Librarian 4(3) (Dec. 1973/Mar. 1974): 40–41. Dahlmanns, Gerhard J. "The International Association of Law Libraries: An Interim Account." IALL Bulletin No. 28 (June 1972): 7–12. Dahlmanns, Gerhard. "Serving Legal Information: Twenty-Five Years of IALL." In Courts, Law Libraries, and Legal Information in a Changing Society: 25th IALL Anniversary Meeting 4–23 (Freiburg, Germany: International Association of Law Libraries, 1984). Landheer, Bart. "Ten Years International Association of Law Libraries." International Association of Law Libraries Bulletin XXIII (June 1969):5–6. Schwerin, Kurt. "The International Association of Law Libraries: Its Beginnings." International Journal of Legal Information 12 (1&2) (Feb./April 1984): 1–6. Sprudzs, Adolf. "The International Association of Law Libraries and its Twenty-Five Years of Activities." The Law Librarian 15(3) (Dec. 1984): 50–53.Sprudzs, Adolf. "Thirty-Five Years of International Cooperation: The Case of the IALL." The Law Librarian 26(2) (June 1995): 321–326. [in PDF]. Wenger, Larry B. "IALL at 40." International Journal of Legal Information 27(1) (Spring 1999): 1–2

056 International Association of Music Information Centres (IAMIC)

Address Steenstraat 25, 1000 Brussels Tel.: +32 2 504 90 99, Fax +32 2 504 81 03, iamic@iamic.net; www.iamic.net

Officers Pres: Olga Smetanova; VP: Elisabeth Bihl; Treas: Eve O'Kelly; Gen Secr: Stef Coninx

General Assembly Annual meeting
Membership 43 members in 38 countries (organizations)
Structure Governed by Executive Board
Major Fields of Interest Organisations promoting new music
Major Goals and Objectives To enhance access to information, materials, and products provided by its members, and to encourage the performance, broadcast, and dissemination of music from members to encourage exchanges, collaborations, and the exchange of ideas, experiences and skills amongst its members
Activities Documentation activities, promotional and development projects; IAMIC network provides international access to the most comprehensive collections of new music information and materials

057 International Association of Orientalist Librarians (IAOL)

Address Moscow 103009 Tel.: +095 2028812, Fax +095 2029187; www.library.cornell.edu/wason/iaol
Languages English
Established August, 1967, at the 27th International Congress of Orientalists (now International Congress for Asian and North African Studies) in Ann Arbor, Michigan, USA
Staff None
General Assembly General membership meets every 3 years. 1989: Toronto, Canada. 2000: Montreal, Canada
Membership Total members: 250 (150 individual, 100 institutional). Dues (US Dollar): 10, individual; 12, institutional
Structure Governed by the 3 elected officers. Affiliations: IFLA, International Congress for Asian and North African Studies
Sources of Support Membership dues
Major Fields of Interest Oriental studies, librarianship
Major Goals and Objectives To promote better communication between Orientalist librarians and libraries and others in related fields throughout the world; to provide a forum for the discussion of problems of common interest; to improve international cooperation among institutions holding research resources for Oriental studies
Activities Centered in establishing better communication among librarians in Oriental collections throughout the world
Publications Official journal: IAOL Bulletin. 1967-. 2/yr. Free to members. Editor: Om P. Sharma. Address: South Asia Division, University of Michigan Library, Ann Arbor, MI 48109, USA. Circ: 250. English
Bibliography Tsuneishi, L., "International Association of Orientalist Librarians," Library of Congress Information Bulletin 45 (Dec. 8, 1986):400; "International Association of Orientalist Librarians (IAOL)," in The Bowker Annual: Library and Book Trade Almanac, 34th Edition 1989–90. pp. 731–732. New York: R. R. Bowker, 1989

058 International Association of School Librarianship (IASL)

Address POB 83, Zillmere, Queensland 4034 Fax +613 9428 7612; www.iasl-slo.org
Languages English

Established August, 1971, in Jamaica, at conference of the World Confederation of Organizations of the Teaching Profession (WCOTP)
Officers Exec Secr: Karen Bonanno
Staff 1 (paid), 1 (volunteer)
General Assembly General membership meets yearly. Conferences: 2003: Durban/South Africa; 2004: Dublin/Ireland; 2005: Hong Kong. Contact: Conference Sec Claire Johnston, Librarian, West Island School, 250 Victoria Rd, Pokfulam Hong Kong, Tel: (852) 28191962, Fax: (852) 28167257, email: cjohnston@wis.edu.hk
Membership Total members: 725 (700 individual and institutional, 25 associations). Sections: 1. 44 countries represented. Requirements: Interest in the development of school library services
Structure Governed by Board of Directors elected from 6 major geographic regions and officers. Affiliations: IFLA, WCOTP
Sources of Support Membership dues, sale of publications
Major Fields of Interest Development of school library services throughout the world
Major Goals and Objectives To encourage the development of school libraries and library programs in all countries; promote professional and continuing education of school librarians, teacher librarians, and media specialists; foster communication and research; promote publication and dissemination of information about school librarianship
Activities Annual Conferences, Committees and Special Interest Groups; Awards Programme: Ken Haycock Leadership Development Grant, Jean Lowrie Leadership Development Grant, IASL/Murofushi Research Fund; Support-a-Member Program; IASL/UNESCO co-operative action programme for books for school libraries in developing countries provides assistance to school libraries in Africa, Asia, the South Pacific, South America, and the Caribbean; IASL/SIRS International Commendation Award is given annually by SIRS Inc. for an innovative project related to school libraries; International School Library Day (4th of October); IASL–LINK (electronic forum on the Internet for members)
Publications Official journal: School Libraries Worldwide. Non-members US$30 00/yr or US$85.00/3 yrs. Add: Association Office at Dept 962, Box 34069, Seattle, WA 98124–1069, USA, iasl@rockland.com; IASL Newsletter. 1971-. 3/yr. Free to members. Other publications: Proceedings of conferences, monograph series, etc., Publications for sale, price lists available. Add same as association
Bibliography Cooke, M.J., "International Developments in School Librarianship: The Work of the IASL," Education Library Bulletin 24 (1981):44–47; Wright, S., "International Association of School Librarianship Hawaiian Conference 1984 – an Eyewitness Report". In: School Libraries in Canada 4 (1984):23+; Lowrie, J.E., "International Association of School Librarianship," in ALA World Encyclopedia of Library and Information Services. 2nd ed., pp. 370–371. Chicago: American Library Association, 1986; Wilslow, M., "IASL Jamaica Conference, 1985," IFLA Journal (1986):57–59; "IASL Meets in Halifax: 150 Delegates Attend," School Library Journal 33 (1986):80+; Suchy, K., "Report on the 15th Annual Conference of IASL," Catholic Library World 58 (1986):109–110; Lowrie, J.E., "The International Association of School Librarianship," Ohio Media Spectrum 39 (1987):5–7; Malhan, I.V, "18th Annual IASL Conference Report," Library Times International 6 (1989):44; "Report on 18th Annual Conference IASL, Kuala Lumpur July 22–26, 1989," International Leads 3 (Winter 1989):2–3; "International Association of

School Librarianship," in The Bowker Annual: Library and Book Trade Almanac. 34th Edition 1989–90. p. 732. New York: R. R. Bowker, 1989

059 International Association of Scientific and Technological University Libraries (IATUL)

Address c/o Paul Sheehan, IATUL Secretary, Dublin City University Library, Dublin 9 paul.sheehan@dcu.ie; www.iatul.org

Languages English

Established 1955, Düsseldorf, Federal Republic of Germany

Officers Pres: Maria Heijne; Treas: Reiner Kallenborn; Secr: Paul Sheehan

General Assembly Meets in annual conference

Membership Members from 45 countries. Requirements: Open "normally to libraries of academic institutions which offer courses in engineering or technology to the doctoral level;" institutional membership. Other types of membership available: Official observer, sustaining, nonvoting associate. Dues: Ordinary & Associate members EUR 107/yr, EUR 280/3 years, EUR 443/5 years; Sustaining Membership EUR 500/year

Structure Governed by Board of Directors and General Assembly of ordinary members. Affiliations: IFLA, FID, Scientific Associate of ICSU

Sources of Support Membership dues, sale of publications

Major Fields of Interest Librarianship, information science, information technology

Major Goals and Objectives To provide a forum for library directors to meet for an exchange of views on matters of current significance in the libraries of Universities of Science and Technology, and to provide an opportunity for them to develop a collaborative approach to problems

Activities Annual conferences, 2004: Krakow, 2005: Quebec; IATUL Diskussion List for members

Publications No official journal: IATUL News is no longer produced, back issues available on website; IATUL Alert (email bulletin for members). Other publications: Annual reports, proceedings of meetings, reports of seminars, workshops. Publications available for sale. Price lists issued. No publications exchange program

Bibliography Schmidmaier, D., "30th Anniversary of IATUL and Its 11th Conference," Zentralblatt für Bibliothekswesen 99 (1985):554–555 (in German); Shaw, D.F., "International Association of Technological University Libraries," in ALA World Encyclopedia of Library and Information Services. 2nd ed., p. 372. Chicago: American Library Association, 1986; Schmidmaier, D., "Tendenzen in der Arbeit der International Association of Technological University Libraries," (Trends in the Work of IATUL) Zentralblatt für Bibliothekswesen 101 (1987):170–173 (in German); Lucker, J.K., et al., "Report on the 1987 Meeting of the North American Regional Group of IATUL," IATUL Quarterly 2 (1988):72–77; Schmidmaier, D., "International Association of Technological University Libraries (IATUL) 1955–1988," LIBER News Sheet 24 (1988):30–34; "International Association of Technological University Libraries (IATUL)," in The Bowker Annual: Library and Book Trade Almanac. 34th Edition 1989–90. pp. 733–734. New York: R. R. Bowker, 1989

060 International Association of Sound and Audiovisual Archives (IASA)

Address c/o Ilse Assmann, Secretary General, PO Box 931, 2006 Auckland Park

Tel.: +27 11 714 4041, Fax +27 11 714 4419, assmanni@sabc.co.za; www.iasa-web.org
Languages English, German, French, Spanish
Established 1969, Amsterdam, during IAML Conference
Officers Pres: Kevin Bradley; Past Pres: Richard Green; VP: Jacqueline von Arb; Dafydd Pritchard; Pio Pellizzari; Secr Gen: Ilase Assmann; Treas: Anke Leenings; Edi: Dr. Janet Topp Fargion
Staff None
General Assembly General membership meets yearly. 2004: Oslo; 2005: Barcelona
Membership Total members: 420 (180 individual, 235 institutional, 4 honorary, 1 sustaining). Committees: 6 (Cataloguing & Documentation, Discography, Technical, National Archives, Radio Sound Archives, Research Archives). 60 countries represented. Types of membership: Full individual, Full institutional, Associate individual, Associate institutional, Sustaining, Honorary. Requirements: Open to individuals and institutions actively engaged in or having a serious interest in sound and audiovisual archive work and the goals of the Association. Dues EUR: 40 individual; 158 institutional; 198 sustaining
Structure Governed by Executive Board and General Assembly of members. Affiliations: IFLA, ARSC (Association for Recorded Sound Collections), IAML, FIAT (International Federation of Television Archives), FIAF (International Federation of Film Archives), ICA (International Council of Archives), AMIA (Association of Moving Image Archivists), SEAPAVAA (SouthEast Asia & Pacific Audiovisual Archives Association), CCAAA (Co-ordinating Council of Audiovisual Archives Associations), Unesco
Sources of Support Membership dues, publication sales
Major Fields of Interest Preservation, organization and use of sound and audiovisual recordings, techniques of recording, restoration and methods of reproducing sound and movind images. Archives of music, history, literature, drama, folklife, ethnomusicology, bio-acoustic and musical sounds, linguistics, dialect, radio and television archives, national archives, research archives
Major Goals and Objectives To promote the archival preservation and use of recorded sound and moving images; to promote international cooperation among archives which preserve recorded sound and audiovisual documents; to provide and promote the use of archival principles, recommendations and standards in sound and audiovisual archives and collections
Activities Supports the exchange of information and fosters international co-operation between audiovisual archives in all fields; annual conferences; Travel and research grants. Sponsors continuing education lectures, seminars, workshops
Publications Official journal: "IASA Journal" 2/yr. Add. same as association. Annual dues: Free for members; EUR 70 for subscribers. Other publications: "IASA Information Bulletin" 4/yr. "IASA Directory 2004" (directory of members). Bradley, K. ed., "Guidelines on the production and preservation of digital audio objects" (2004). Holst, P., ed., "Task force to establish selection criteria of analogue and digital audio contents for transfer to data formats for preservation purposes" (2003). Miliano, M., ed., "The IASA Cataloguing Rules: A manual for description of sound recordings and related audiovisual media" (1999). Harrison, H., ed., "Selection in Sound Archives" (1984); Lance, D., ed., "Sound Archives: A Guide to Their Establishment and Development" (1983). Publications available for sale via website. No publications exchange program
Bibliography "International Association of Sound Archives," IFLA Journal 9

(1983)370; "Report on the IAML/IASA Meeting," ibid.:371–372; Harrison, H.P., "International Association of Sound Archives (IASA)," in ALA World Encyclopedia of Library and Information Services. 2nd ed., p. 371. Chicago: American Library Association, 1986; Harrison, H.P., "Annual Conference of the International Association of Sound Archives (Berlin, 1985)." Fontes Artis Musicae 33 (1986):94–99; "News in the Field of Audio-visual Archives," Unisist Newsletter 17 (1989):66–67; "International Association of Sound Archives," in The Bowker Annual: Library and Book Trade Almanac. 34th Edition 1989–90. pp. 732–733. New York: R. R. Bowker, 1989

061   International Association of Users and Developers of Electronic Libraries and New Information Technologies (ELNIT Association)
Address   12 Kuznetski Most, 107999 Moscow   Tel.: +7 95 9284913, Fax +7 95 9219862, elnit@elnit.org; www.gpntb.ru
Established   1995
Officers   Pres: Yakow Shraiberg; Managing Dir: Boris Marshak

062   International Council for Scientific and Technical Information (ICSTI)
Address   5, rue Ambroise Thomas, 75009 Paris   Tel.: +33 1 45256592, Fax +33 1 42151262; www.icsti.org/icsti.html
Languages   English, French
Officers   Pres: Herbert Gruttemeier; Exec Secr: Elisabeth Maitre-Allain
General Assembly   Membership meets twice a year
Sources of Support   Sponsored by ICSU
Major Fields of Interest   Scientific and technical information
Major Goals and Objectives   Provide leadership in promoting recognition of the value of scientific and technical information to the world's economic, research, scholarly and social progress. Enhance access to and delivery of information for all constituencies in business, industry, academia, government and the public through the exchange of information and the sharing of experience among international peers. Be a forum for interaction among all participants in information flow
Activities   Recent projects: Digitisation and its effects on document archiving; Open Access and the future of STI; The future role of national STI centres
Publications   Official journal: Forum. Newletter, 4/yr. Other publications: Multilingual Thesaurus Of Geosciences, second edition (1995); Biotechnology Information Sources: North And South America (1994); Squaring The Information Circle, proceedings of an ICSTI symposium (1991); Numeric Databases: A Directory (1991); International Classification Scheme For Physics, third edition (1991), bilingual English-French

063   International Council on Archives / Conseil International des Archives (ICA; CIA)
Address   60 Rue des Francs-Bourgeois, 75003 Paris   Tel.: +33 140276306, Fax +33 142722065, ica@ica.org; www.ica.org
Languages   Documents: English, French; Congresses: English, French, German, Spanish, Russian
Established   1948, as provisional ICA; first congress held in 1950
Officers   Pres: Ian E. Wilson; Secr Gen: David Leitch

Staff   5 paid, permanent; more than 250 volunteers for the International Congress on Archives

General Assembly   Entire membership meets every 4 years. International Round Table Conferences on Archives, of leaders in the profession, dealing with major issues and problems, are held as Annual General Meeting

Membership   Individual, institutional, national administrations and associations. Regional Branches: 13 (Asociación Latinoamericana de Archivos (ALA), Arab Regional Branch (ARBICA), Caribbean Regional Branch (CARBICA), Central Africa Regional Branch (CENARBICA), East Asian Regional Branch (EASTICA), Eastern and Southern Africa Regional Branch (ESARBICA), Eurasia Regional Branch (EURASICA), European Regional Branch (EURBICA), North American Archival Network (NAANICA), Pacific Regional Branch (PARBICA), Southeast Asian Regional Branch (SARBICA), South and West Asian Regional Branch (SWARBICA), West African Regional Branch (WARBICA). Sections: 17 committees

Structure   Governed by Executive Board

Sources of Support   Membership dues, sale of publications, government subsidies (support of projects from various governments), subventions and contracts from Unesco or other partners

Major Fields of Interest   Archives, including records management

Major Goals and Objectives   To encourage and support the development of archives in all countries, in co-operation with other organisations, including international agencies, governmental and non-governmental; to promote, organise and co-ordinate best practice, the development of standards and other activities in the field of records and archives management; to establish, maintain and strengthen relations between archivists of all countries and between all institutions, professional bodies and other organisations, public and private, wherever located, which are concerned with the administration or preservation of records and archives, or with the professional training of archivists, especially through the exchange of information; to facilitate the interpretation and use of archives by making their content more widely known and by encouraging greater access to them

Activities   Past achievements: Production of 43 RAMP (Records and Archives Management Programme) studies for Unesco, published between 1981 and 1986; production of various guides; strengthening of the regional structures; organization of new sections, such as of municipal archives; of business and trade union archives, sports, architectural and notarial archives and professional education and training; conducting survey on the preservation of the world's archival and library heritage;Current priority areas: Professional training, conservation, automation, archival development and research in archives, administration (including records management). Approved a Code of Ethics in 1996. Approved in 2004 4 strategies and priority areas: Advocacy and promotion, Electronic Records and Automation, Preservation and protection, Education and Training

Publications   Official journal: Comma, International Journal on Archives (2001-); Flash (communicates news on ICA activities and highlights current issues in archives, publ. 3 times a year; 2003-); Archivum (1951–2000); Code of Ethics, Standards, Studies, FAQs, Bibliographies, CITRA Proceedings, UNESCO RAMP Studies. Most publications are published online

064 International Federation for Information Processing (IFIP)

Address Hofstr. 3, 2361 Laxenburg Tel.: +43 2236 73616, Fax +43 2236 736169, ifip@ifip.org; www.ifip.or.at

Established Jan. 1, 1960, at first International Conference on Information Processing, sponsored by Unesco

Officers Pres: Basie von Solms; Pres elect: Leon Strous; VP: Gerald Engel; Ramon Puigjaner; Lalit Sawhney; Treas: Chris Avram; Hon Secr: Roger Johnson

General Assembly Annual general assembly

Membership 48 organizations as Full Members, 3 Corresponding Members and 11 Affiliate Members, representing countries from all regions of the world. Requirements: Professional and technical organizations representing all branches of information processing

Structure Governed by the General Assembly and executive officers. Affiliations: IFLA, Unesco (Class B status), WHO (World Health Organization), ICSU (International Council of Scientific Unions), FIACC (Five International Associations Coordinating Committee)

Sources of Support Membership dues, sale of publications, Unesco

Major Fields of Interest All aspects of information processing

Major Goals and Objectives To promote all aspects of information science and technology by fostering international cooperation in the field of information processing; stimulating research, development, and the application of information processing in science and human activity; furthering the dissemination and exchange of information about the subject; encouraging education in information processing

Activities Major activities: biannual World Computer Congress (2000: Beijing, China; 2002: Montreal, Canada; 2004: Toulouse) Technical work is carried out in 16 program areas under Technical Committees: Foundations of Computer Science, Software:Theory and Practice, Education, Computer Applications in Technology, Communication Systems, System Modelling and Optimization, Information Systems, Relationship between Computers and Society, Computer Systems Technology, Security and Protection in Information Processing Systems, Artificial Intelligence, Human-Computer Interaction, Specialist Group on Entertainment Computing. Organizes triennial series on medical informatics (MEDINFO). Technical Committees sponsor international conferences on specialized topics

Publications Official journal: Information Bulletin. 1/yr.; IFIP Newsletter (pdf). Extensive publication program. Publishes conference proceedings, etc

Bibliography Glaser, G., "International Federation for Information Processing," in ALA World Encyclopedia of Library and Information Services. 2nd ed., pp. 376–377. Chicago: American Library Association, 1986

065 International Federation of Library Associations and Institutions (IFLA)*

Address c/o Royal Library/Koninklijke Bibliotheek, Prins Willem Alexanderhof 5, 2595 BE The Hague, POB 95312, 2509 CH The Hague Tel.: +31 70 3140884, Fax +31 70 3834827, IFLA@ifla.org; www.ifla.org

Languages Arabic, Chinese, English, French, German, Russian, Spanish

Established 1927, Edinburgh, Scotland, at the 50th Anniversary Conference of the British Library Association. Representatives of 15 countries signed resolution

Officers Pres: Ellen Tise; Pres-elect: Ingrid Parent; Treas: Barbara Schleihagen; Secr Gen: Jennefer Nicholson
Staff 14 (paid)
General Assembly General Assembly held annually 2009 Milan, Italy – 2010 Gothenburg, Sweden – 2011 San Juan, Puerto Rico – 2012 Helsinki, Finland
Membership More than 1700 members in over 150 countries. IFLA membership is comprised of International and National Associations, Institutions, and Personal and Student Affiliates. International and National Association Membership is open to associations of libraries and information centres, associations of librarians and library schools, and to associations of bibliographic and research institutes that are primarily concerned with the aims and activities of the Federation. Fees/yr divided into 12 bands, dependent on the country of residence of the majority of members of the association, band according to UNESCO Scale of Assessment figures and the United Nations list of Least Developed Countries.Band 12 countries: EUR 214, Band 1: EUR 21.162. Institutional members include library and information centres, library schools, bibliographic and research institutes, and other institutions or bodies that would like to contribute professionally to the activities of the Federation. Fees: For countries whose UNESCO assessment is 0.251 or higher, EUR 443. For countries that are assessed at 0.001 to 0.250, EUR 391. Countries which are included in the UN List of Least Developed Countries EUR 182. Institutional sub-units, One-person Library Centres, School Libraries. Fees differentiated in the same manner as Institutional members. The fee for Band 1 is EUR 224 per year; for Band 2 the fee is EUR 193; and for Band 3 it is EUR 104. Personal and Student Affiliates, Fees Personal Affiliates is EUR 130. For Student Affiliates the fee is EUR 57
Structure Governed by Council, composed of the representatives nominated by members, and meeting every year. The main IFLA steering bodies are the Governing Board, Professional Committee, and the Executive Committee. Affiliations: Unesco (consultative status), WIPO, ISO (International Organization for Standardization; observer status), ICSU (associate status), ICA, IBBY (International Board on Books for Young People)
Sources of Support Membership dues, sale of publications, government subsidies, foundation grants, Unesco
Major Fields of Interest International cooperation in all areas of librarianship and information services
Major Goals and Objectives The Federation shall be an independent international nongovernmental association, without profit motive, whose purposes shall be to promote international understanding, cooperation, discussion, research and development in all fields of library activity, including bibliography, information services and the education of personnel; and to provide a body through which librarianship can be represented in matters of international interest
Activities TThe activity of IFLA is accomplished through the six Core Activities (ALP, Action for Development through Libraries Programme; CLM Committee on Copyright and other Legal Matters; FAIFE, Committee on Free Access to Information and Freedom of Expression; ICABS, IFLA – CDNL Alliance for Bibliographic Standards; PAC, Preservation and Conservation; UNIMARC) and the 8 Divisions and 47 Sections
Publications Official journal: IFLA Journal. 1975-. 4/yr. Free to members.

065 International

Chair/Editorial Committee: Ramón Abad Hiraldo, Head Librarian, Instituto Cervantes, 102 Eaton Square, London SW1W 9AN, United Kingdom, Tel. +44 20 72010757, Fax +44 20 72350329. E-mail: biblon@cervantes.es. editor: Stephen Parker, E-mail: zest@bart.nl Other Publications: Sections newsletters, IFLA policies and procedures, Corporate Documents, Core Activities Newsletters, IFLA Professional Reports, Conference Proceedings, IFLA Saur Publications (www.saur.de). IFLA databases, directories, and indexes: IFLA Membership Directory, National Libraries of the World: an Address List, International Directory of Art Libraries, Directory of Union Catalogues, World Directory of National Parliamentary Libraries, IFLA Glossary

Bibliography "IFLA in 1982: Highlights," IFLA Journal 9 (1983):133–140; "IFLA 1983," VSB/SVD Nachrichten 59 (1983):367–381 (in French); "IFLA, What It Should Mean to U. S. Librarians," ed. R. Dougherty, Journal of Academic Librarianship 9 (1983):68–74; "IFLA in 1983: Highlights," IFLA Journal 10 (1984):189–198; Fang, J.R., "First IFLA in Africa Inspires Delegates," American Libraries 15 (1984):689–690; Vospler, R., "IFLA and the Recent Growth of Organized International Librarianship," in Advances in Librarianship. vol. 13, pp. 129–134. Orlando, FL: Academic Press, 1984; "IFLA in 1984: Highlights," IFLA Journal 11 (1985):147–156; IFLA and the Library World: A Review of the Work of IFLA. 1981–1985. comp. P. J. Swigchem. The Hague: IFLA, 1985; DeLoach, M.L, "An African Odyssey: A Report on the First African and African-American IFLA Pre-Conference Seminar in Nairobi, Kenya," Library Journal 110 (Mar. 1, 1985):57–62; Kaegbein, P., "IFLAs Medium-Term Programme 1986–1991," Library Times International 1 (1985):75; Sylvestre, J.J.G., "Canadians, Unesco and IFLA," Canadian Library Journal 42 (1985):219–220; Wijnstroom, M., "IFLA in the Eighties," Library Times International 2 (1985):1, 17; Avram, H.D., "The Importance of IFLA," ibid.:26, 40 guest editorial); Wijnstroom, M., "International Federation of Libary Associations and Institutions," in ALA World Encyclopedia of Library and Information Services. 2nd ed., pp. 377–381. Chicago: American Library Association, 1986; Fang, J.R., "IFLA Moves Towards the 21st Century: Chicago 1985 to Tokyo 1986," in The Bowker Annual of Library & Book Trade Information 1986. 31st ed., pp. 149–156. New York: R. R. Bowker, 1986; Lauster, A., "IFLA und Schulbibliotheken," (IFLA and School Libraries), Schulbibliothek Aktuell 1 (1986):56–61 (in German); Carroll, F.L., "Some Impressions of Former Presidents of IFLA 1963–79: Francis, Liebaers and Kirkegaard," International Library Review 18 (1986):147–152; Bourne, R., "The IFLA International Programme for Universal Bibliographic Control (UBC)," IFLA Journal 12 (1986):341–343; Hanitzsch, P., "Von Kopenhagen bis Chicago. Ein Rückblick auf die jüngste IFLA-Geschichte," (From Copenhagen to Chicago: Recent History of IFLA in Retrospect), Zentralblatt für Bibliothekswesen 100 (1986):482–488 (in German); Smith, M.A., "The IFLA Core Programme on Preservation and Conservation (PAC)," IFLA Journal 12 (1986):305–306; "Reports on the 51st Council and General Conference of IFLA, Chicago, Ill., Aug. 1985," Library of Congress Information Bulletin 45 (May 5, 1986):131–146, (May 12, 1986):151–169; "IFLA in 1982: Highlights," IFLA Journal 9 (1983):133–140; "IFLA 1983," VSB/SVD Nachrichten 59 (1983):367–381 (in French); "IFLA, What It Should Mean to U. S. Librarians," ed. R. Dougherty, Journal of Academic Librarianship 9 (1983):68–74; "IFLA in 1983: Highlights," IFLA Journal 10 (1984):189–198; Fang, J.R., "First IFLA in Africa Inspires Delegates," American Libraries 15 (1984):689–690; Vospler, R., "IFLA and the Recent Growth of Organized International

Librarianship," in Advances in Librarianship. vol. 13, pp. 129–134. Orlando, FL: Academic Press, 1984; "IFLA in 1984: Highlights," IFLA Journal 11 (1985):147–156; IFLA and the Library World: A Review of the Work of IFLA. 1981–1985. comp. P. J. Swigchem. The Hague: IFLA, 1985; DeLoach, M.L, "An African Odyssey: A Report on the First African and African-American IFLA Pre-Conference Seminar in Nairobi, Kenya," Library Journal 110 (Mar. 1, 1985):57–62; Kaegbein, P., "IFLAs Medium-Term Programme 1986–1991," Library Times International 1 (1985):75; Sylvestre, J.J.G., "Canadians, Unesco and IFLA," Canadian Library Journal 42 (1985):219–220; Wijnstroom, M., "IFLA in the Eighties," Library Times International 2 (1985):1, 17; Avram, H.D., "The Importance of IFLA," ibid.:26, 40 guest editorial); Wijnstroom, M., "International Federation of Libary Associations and Institutions," in ALA World Encyclopedia of Library and Information Services. 2nd ed., pp. 377–381. Chicago: American Library Association, 1986; Fang, J.R., "IFLA Moves Towards the 21st Century: Chicago 1985 to Tokyo 1986," in The Bowker Annual of Library & Book Trade Information 1986. 31st ed., pp. 149–156. New York: R. R. Bowker, 1986; Lauster, A., "IFLA und Schulbibliotheken," (IFLA and School Libraries), Schulbibliothek Aktuell 1 (1986):56–61 (in German); Carroll, F.L., "Some Impressions of Former Presidents of IFLA 1963–79: Francis, Liebaers and Kirkegaard," International Library Review 18 (1986):147–152; Bourne, R., "The IFLA International Programme for Universal Bibliographic Control (UBC)," IFLA Journal 12 (1986):341–343; Hanitzsch, P., "Von Kopenhagen bis Chicago. Ein Rückblick auf die jüngste IFLA-Geschichte," (From Copenhagen to Chicago: Recent History of IFLA in Retrospect), Zentralblatt für Bibliothekswesen 100 (1986):482–488 (in German); Smith, M.A., "The IFLA Core Programme on Preservation and Conservation (PAC)," IFLA Journal 12 (1986):305–306; "Reports on the 51st Council and General Conference of IFLA, Chicago, Ill., Aug. 1985," Library of Congress Information Bulletin 45 (May 5, 1986):131–146, (May 12, 1986):151–169; Erratum (May 26, 1986): 191; Negishi, M., "IFLA Tokyo Conference Report: A Japanese View," Library Times International 3 (Nov. 1986):35; Casey, D.W., "New Horizons of Librarianship Discussed at IFLA Conference," ibid.:33: "Africa at IFLA," African Research & Documentation 43 (1987):27–29; Matsumoto, S., "Post-Tokyo Conference of IFLA and Unesco's Expectation on Japan," Toshokan Zasshi 81 (1987):13–15 (in Japanese); Anuar, H., "The Library and Information Dimensions of the North-South Dialogue: Some Thoughts on the Threshold of the 21st Century," IFLA Journal 13 (1987):327–333; Molholt, P.A., "IFLA 1986: The New Horizons of Librarianship toward the 21st Century," Special Libraries 78 (1987):60–61; "IFLA Appoints Paul Nauta as New Secretary General," Library of Congress Information Bulletin 46 (Mar. 30, 1987):123; "Report on the 52nd General Conference of the IFLA, Tokyo, Japan," Library of Congress Information Bulletin 46 (Apr. 27, 1987):167–175; Kon, M., "Division of Regional Activities: Regional Section for Asia and Oceania," Toshokan-Kai 38 (1987):330–338 (in Japanese); Palmer, R., "Anatomy of an International Association Conference," (53rd, 1987, Brighton) Library Association Record 89 (1987):41–42; Spaulding, F.H., "IFLA 1987: Library and Information Services in a Changing World," Special Libraries 79 (1988):72–74; "IFLA 1987," Library Association Record 89 (1987):485–486, 513–522; Darrobers, M

066 International Group of Publishing Libraries (IGPL)*

Address c/o David Way, Secretary, 96 Guston Road, London NW1 2DB Tel.: +44 207 412 7532, david.way@bl.uk
Languages English
Established April, 1983, after inaugural meeting at the British Library
Officers Secr: David Way
Staff None
General Assembly General membership meets every 2 years
Membership Total members: 40 (30 individual, 10 institutional). 8 countries represented. Requirements: Members must belong to research and/or national libraries which are either active in publishing or are considering initiating publishing programs. No dues
Sources of Support Conference fees
Major Fields of Interest Library publishing
Major Goals and Objectives To share experience and explore the possibilities of active collaboration between research libraries which operate publishing programs
Activities Past achievements: Acted as a focus for international collaboration between national and research libraries for publishing, collaborated on mailings and joint publishing projects
Publications Official journal: IGPL Newsletter. 1986-. 1/yr. Free to members. Address same as Association. Circ: 150. English. Other publications: Reports of seminars and workshops. Publications available for sale
Bibliography "Library Publishing." British Library Occasional Paper 2, 1985; "Meeting of International Group of Publishing Libraries," Library of Congress Information Bulletin 46 (June 29, 1987):294
Comment No current information available

067 International Information Centre for Terminology (Infoterm)

Address Gymnasiumstrasse 50, 1150 Vienna Tel.: +43 1 4277 580-26, infopoint@infoterm.org; www.infoterm.info
Languages English, German, French
Established Infoterm was founded in 1971 under the auspices of UNESCO, the United Nations Educational, Scientific and Cultural Organization, with the objective to support and co-ordinate international co-operation in the field of terminology
Officers Pres: Albina Auksoriūtè; VP: Key-Sun Choi; A Min Tjoa; Alternate VP: Marietta Alberts
Staff 8 paid, 2 volunteers
General Assembly Meets every two years
Membership Members are national, international and regional terminology institutions, organizations and networks, as well as specialized public or semi-public or other kind of non-profit institutions engaged in terminological activities
Structure Infoterm Executive Board, meets once or twice every year
Sources of Support Infoterm is a non-profit association. There are no membership fees. Funding through projects
Major Goals and Objectives Infoterm promotes and supports the cooperation of existing and the establishment of new terminology centres and networks with the general

aim to improve domain communication, knowledge transfer and provision of content with a view to facilitating the participation of all in the global multilingual knowledge society
Activities Collecting information on terminological activities and their results; publishing these data in printed or computerized form so as to make them generally available; supporting the establishment of a world-wide network of terminology information and documentation centres; connecting these centres to other institutions or organizations collecting, creating or distributing terminological data; supporting the elaboration and use of harmonized methods and guidelines for terminology information and documentation centres on the one hand and for the generation of high-quality terminological data on the other hand
Publications Infoterm Newsletter (INL). 4/yr. 1976-; German/English/French, Biblioterm (BIB), 4/yr.; Terminology Standardization and Harmonization (TSH), 4/yr.; StandardTerm (STT), 4/yr
Bibliography Christian Galinski and Wolfgang Nedobity: 30 Years of Infoterm

068 International Network for the Availability of Scientific Publications (INASP)

Address 60 St Aldates, Oxford OX1 1ST Tel.: +44 1865 249909, Fax +44 1865 251060, inasp@inasp.info; www.inasp.info
Languages English
Established 1992
Officers Exec Dir: Tag McEntegart; Dir: Martin Bleicher; Sara Gwynn
Staff 16
General Assembly Annual general meeting
Membership Requirements: open to all interested organizations and individuals
Structure Advised by international council
Sources of Support Sponsored by British Medical Assn, Carnegie Corp of New York, ICSU/CDSI, CTA, Danida, Dept for Int Development (DFID, UK), French Ministry of Foreign Affairs, Nat Acad of Sciences (USA), NORAD, Reuters, Royal Swedish Acad of Sciences, Sida, UNESCO, WHO
Major Fields of Interest Flow of information within and between countries, especially those with less developed systems of publication and dissemination
Major Goals and Objectives To map, support and strengthen existing activities promoting access to and dissemination of scientific and scholarly information and knowledge; to identify, encourage and support new initiatives that will increase local publication and general access to quality scientific and scholarly literature; to promote in-country capacity building in information production, organization, access and dissemination
Activities Offers advice and support on all aspects of literature publication and dissemination, especially in response to and in partnership with institutions in developing and transitional countries; assists a number of funding and development agencies in the establishment and implementation of information-related programmes
Publications Official journal: INASP Newsletter. 3/yr. Address same as association. Editor: Pippa Smart. Other publications: resource books and directories in the area of information development. Many of these are available free online, and also in print, e.g.: The Use of ICTs in African Public Library Services. 2004, by Justin Chisenga; Reader Development and Reading Promotion: Recent experiences from seven countries in Africa.

2003, edited by Diana Rosenberg; Proactive Librarianship: Marketing and Public Relations: A Manual for Workshop Presenters. 2003, by Rheina Epstein

069 International Society for Knowledge Organization e.V. (ISKO)

Address c/o Peter Ohly, President, Lennestr. 30, 53113 Bonn Tel.: +49 228 2281142, exec@isko.org; www.isko.org
Languages English
Established July 22, 1989, Frankfurt, at the central railway station, by a group of interested specialists
Officers Past Pres/1st VP: María J. López-Huertas; 2nd VP: Claudio Gnoli
Staff None
General Assembly Membership meets every 2 years
Membership Types of membership: Individual, institutional. Requirements: Interest in goals and objectives of Society. Dues (US Dollar): 60, individual; 120, institutional
Structure Governed by Executive Board and the Scientific Advisory Council. 17 National Chapters (7 currently active)
Sources of Support Membership dues
Major Fields of Interest Conceptual organization of knowledge by classification, indexing, systematic terminology, concept analysis, etc
Major Goals and Objectives "To promote research, development and application of all methods for the organization of knowledge in general or of particular fields by integrating especially the conceptual approaches of classification research and artificial intelligence. The Society emphasizes philosophico-logical, psychological and semantic approachers of conceptual order." (Charter, Art. 4.1)
Activities International conferences every two years. 2002: Granada/Spain; 2004: London/England; 2006: Vienna/Austria. National and regional conferences on special topics
Publications Official Journal: Knowledge Organization. 4/yr. Editor-in-Chief: Richard P. Smiraglia, Palmer School of Library and Information Science, Long Island University, 720 Nothern Blvd., Brookville, NY 11548. e-mail: richard.smiraglia@liu.edu. Other publications: Conference proceedings (Ergon Verlag): http://www.ergon-verlag.de/index.html?information-_library-sciences_advances_in_knowledge_organization.htm)
Bibliography "International Society for Knowledge Organization (ISKO) Founded," Library Times International 6 (1989):47; "International Associations and Groups," Focus on International and Comparative Librarianship 20 (1989):57–59

070 Internationale Arbeitsgemeinschaft der Archiv-, Bibliotheks-, und Graphikrestauratoren (IADA)
(International Working Group of Archival, Library and Graphic Restorers)*

Address c/o André Page, Hallwylstr. 15, 3003 Bern Tel.: +41 31 325-0012, Fax +41 31 325-8463, andre.page@nb.admin.ch; www.iada-online.org
Languages English (60%), German (40%)
Established 1957, Marburg (D) as ADA (working group of Archives' conservators), merging with Library's and art on paper conservators, from 1967 name changed to IADA

Officers Pres: Andra Page; VP: Renate van Issem; Treas: Julia Bispinck; Edi: Birgit Reissland; Secr: Anna Buelow
Staff None
General Assembly General Assembly every 4th year. Copenhagen (Denmark), 1999, Goettingen (Germany), 2003, Vienna (Austria), 2007, Berne (Switzerland), 2011
Membership Total members: 548 from 24 countries. Requirements: Interest in the aims of the association. 109 extraordinary members (EUR 88.-/yr), 33 members in education (EUR 88.-/yr), 398 full members (EUR 100.-/yr)
Structure Executive board: 5 members. Extended board 5 members. Decisions taken according to the statutes. Modification of statutes by general assembly
Sources of Support Membership dues, sale of publications
Major Fields of Interest Preservation and conservation of paper-based objects (archives, books, art, photographs)
Major Goals and Objectives The IADA, which exclusively has non-profit-oriented goals and tasks, aims at continuing professional education of the conservators, promotion of the new generation, mutual exchange of experiences, representation of professional interests, and promotion of loyalty and helpfulness among colleagues. The association's sphere of activity is international, regardless of national or international borders. The association promotes the union with institutions working in the same field. The association fulfils its tasks through the co-operation of its members, by means of conferences and exhibitions, through expert committees and working groups as well as the publication of an information brochure. The association's publication organ is the information brochure "Mitteilungen der IADA".
Activities Seminars and other types of continuing education programs
Publications Official journal: Journal of Paper Conservation (PapierRestaurierung until 2008) – IADA Reports – Mitteilungen der IADA. 4 issues/yr (ISSN 1868–0860). Address: FotoText Verlag & Redaktionsbüro, Wolfgang Jaworek, Liststraße 7 B, 70180 Stuttgart, Germany, Tel. +49 711 609021, Fax +49 711 609024. jaworek@fototext.s.shuttle.de. For members as part of the membership. Online publications (pdf) on IADA's website http://www.iada-online.org/ : IADA-Beiträge / IADA Contributions in "RESTAURO" (1976–1999) München: Callwey. ISSN 0933–4017. IADA Congresses Preprints: 1967–2003. IADA Projects

071 Internet Chinese Librarians Club (ICLC)

Address c/o Xudong Jin, 43 Rowland Avenue, Delaware, OH 43015 Tel.: + 1 740 368-3250, xdjin@owu.edu; www.white-clouds.com/iclc/index.htm
Languages English
Established 1995
Membership Free
Major Goals and Objectives Providing an environment wherein we Chinese librarians, at home or abroad, can discuss at ease issues related to librarianship and information science. To make full use of the cyberspace and computer technology to cultivate scholarship among Chinese librarians and information specialists
Publications Chinese Librarianship: an International Electronic Journal; Critical Review of Library & Information Science Literature: an International Electronic Journal; Library and Information Science Research: an International Scholarly E-Journal

072 Legal Information Preservation Alliance (LIPA)*

Address PO Box 5266, Bloomington, IN 47407 Tel.: +1 812 822 2773, mkmaes@qmail.com; www.aallnet.org/committee/lipa

Languages English

Established March 8th, 2003, Washington, DC; conference at Georgetown University Law Center: Preserving Legal Information for the 21st Century: Toward a National Agenda

Officers Chair: Keith Ann Stiverson; Vice Chair: Janice Snyder Anderson; Secr/Treas: Judith Meadows; Board member: Janis Johnston; Rita Reusch

Staff 1 half-time paid

General Assembly Annual business meeting held during the American Association of Law Libraries annual conference. July 2009 in Washington, DC; July 2010 in Denver, CO; July 2011 in.Philadelphia, PA

Membership 82 institutional members; membership open to all interested law libraries; dues are $1,000 annually for U. S. academic law libraries and $500 annually for all other law libraries

Structure Illinois not-for-profit corporation with U. S. 501(c)(3) status

Sources of Support Financed primarily through membership dues plus annual support from the American Association of Law Libraries

Major Fields of Interest Preservation and authentication of print and digital legal information

Major Goals and Objectives To provide the leadership, the organizational framework, and the professional commitment necessary to preserve vital legal information by defining objectives, endorsing and promoting the use of appropriate standards and models, creating networks, and fostering financial and political support for long term stability

Activities LIPA commissioned a white paper on Preserving Legal Materials in Digital Formats and an inventory of existing and completed preservation projects; three member libraries implemented the Chesapeake Project to establish a regional digital archive, which is now a national effort called the Legal Information Archive under the auspices of LIPA; and established a print retention program to collect and maintain core U. S. primary law materials in several distributed storage repositories. LIPA sponsors educational programs and webinars on related topics

Publications All publications are available on the LIPA website and include the white paper, the preservation inventory, reports on the print retention project, Chesapeake Project reports, and minutes of annual meetings

Bibliography Special Features: Preserving Legal Information for the 21st Century: Toward a National Agenda. 96 Law Library Journal 579–668 (2004); Margaret K. Maes, Preservation and Collaboration: Ensuring the Future of Legal Information, 18 Trends in Law Library Management and Technology 49 (2008)

073 The Library Assembly of Eurasia (LAE)

Address c/o Nikonorova Ekaterina, General Director, Vozdvizhenka 3/5, 119019 Moscow Tel.: +7 95 2029482, Fax +7 95 2024964, mbs@rsl.ru; www.rsl.ru/SONEGOS/default.htm

Languages Russian (working language), English (language of international communication)

Established 1992 as union of non-governmental organizations, reorganized into Non-profit partnership in 2003
Officers Pres: Viktor Fedorov; Dir Gen: Ekaterina Nikonorova
Staff 2 paid, 4 volunteers
General Assembly Gathering once a year (usually in April) to decide on main guidelines of LAE activities. The general meeting is the supreme managing body of the Partnership. Main purpose of the general meeting is to provide the observance by the Partnership of objects for which it was established. The general meeting is entitled to resolve any questions of the Partnership's activity. The following questions fall within the exclusive competence of the general meeting: a) making amendments to these by-laws; b) determining the priority directions of the Partnership activity, principles of forming and using its property; c) election of the President of the Partnership; d) appointment of the Director-General and early termination of his office; e) election of the Revision commission (Reviser); f) approval of the time-limit of the general meeting; g) reorganization and liquidation of the Partnership; h) approval of annual report on financial and economic activity and annual balance sheet of the Partnership; i) approval of financial program of the Partnership and making amendments to it; j) approval of projects of the Partnership; k) establishing the affiliates and opening the representative offices of the Partnership; l) participation of the Partnership in other organizations
Membership Legal entities, national libraries of CIS countries, foreign national libraries and library associations that share the purposes and objects of the Partnership may become members of the Partnership. Membership fee for the year 2005 is 300 USD. Entrance fee is 100 USD
Structure The following bodies are managing bodies of the Partnership: the general meeting of members; the President; the Director-General
Sources of Support Membership fees, Entrance fees, contributions, donations, proceeds
Major Fields of Interest 1) Policy, Strategic and Legal Issues: Culture, education, science and information society. The socio-economic value of digital cultural, educational and scientific heritage. Licensing, Digital rights management. Access to information and legal issues. National strategies and information society. Common contribution to innovation. 2) Technology/Communication: Standards and metadata. Virtual reality. Digitisation and digital repositories. Preservation of digital objects. Access to diverse cultural, educational and research content. Application of existing technologies. Libraries in the system of educational and scientific communications. 3) Societal issues: Impact of culture, education and science on Life-long learning, Edutainment and cultural traditions. Linguistic and cultural diversity. Integration of information resources: New services for the citizen
Major Goals and Objectives The purposes of the Partnership's activity are as follows: consolidation of the efforts of BAE members, primarily the national libraries, to keep and develop the general library and information space, national assets of culture, to provide the possibility to appraise its funds, including the electronic databases, electronic libraries and catalogues, for mutual enrichment of national cultures, social protection and support of libraries, library staff and public unions; assistance in the development of library and information activity in CIS. The following are objects of the Partnership's activity: systematic promoting and informing work to reach the primary purposes of the Partnership; interrelation with the Russian, foreign and international institutions and

organizations on matters falling within the scope of activities of the Partnership, including the development and implementation of joint initiatives, projects, studies, programs and events; attracting voluntary donations, charitable contributions to reach the purposes and objects of the Partnership; participation in the working out of state and inter-state library policy; development and realization of joint programs, scientific researches and measures in the matters of library and book work, bibliography and information support work; realization of international, national, and regional programs to provide free access to cultural, scientific and information values, protect the memorials of book publishing and hand-writing culture, spiritual growth of individuals, especially the rising generation
Activities Magazine "Bulletin of the Library Assembly of Eurasia"; Eurasian Information and Library Congress; Consultation of Directors of National Libraries (CIS countries); E-library for Russian-Kazakhstan project; E-library for Russian-Belarusian project; International interlibrary loan
Publications Bulletin of the Library Assembly of Eurasia. 4/yr. International Model Codex 2004

074   Ligue des Bibliothèques Européennes de Recherche (LIBER) (League of European Research Libraries)

Address   P.O. Box 90407, 2509 LK The Hague   Tel.: +31 70 314 0767, Fax +31 70 314 0197, wouter.schallier@kb.nl; www.libereurope.eu
Languages   English, French, German
Established   1971 in Strasbourg at Council of Europe
Officers   Pres: Hans Geleijnse; Exec Dir: Wouter Schallier; Treas: Raymond Bérard; Secr: Peter K. Fox; Past Pres: Elmar Mittler
Staff   1
General Assembly   General membership meets once a year. 2002: Graz, 2003: Rome, 2004: St. Petersburg, 2005: Groningen, 2006: Uppsala
Membership   Research libraries of more than 30 countries, membership is restricted to the area of the Council of Europe
Structure   Governed by Executive Board. Affiliation: IFLA
Sources of Support   Membership dues, sale of publications, subsidies, gifts and bequests, ad hoc grants
Major Fields of Interest   Cooperation between European research libraries
Major Goals and Objectives   The aim of the foundation is to represent the interests of research libraries of Europe, their universities and their researchers. It promotes in particular: efficient information services, access to research information, in any form whatsoever, innovative end-user services for teaching, learning and research, preservation of cultural heritage, efficient and effective management in research libraries
Activities   Represents the interests of European research libraries; seeks to identify and define the needs for common effort and initiates activities in these areas, either alone or in co-operation with other organizations; supports the improvement of professional skills in research libraries through meetings, seminars, working groups, and publications; supports special projects and development schemes; promotes standardizations in areas vital for co-operations among libraries, such as library automation; plays an active role in shaping a long-term vision for the development of a European research library network, while representing the collective expertise of its member libraries

Publications Official journal: LIBER Quarterly: The Journal of European Research Libraries. Previous titles: (1972–1990) LIBER Bulletin; (1991–1997) European Research Libraries Cooperation (ERLC): the LIBER Quarterly. ISSN 1435–5205. Ed. by Bakker, Trix. For subscription contact: K. G. Saur Verlag GmbH A part of The Thomson Corporation, Ortlerstrasse 8, 81373 München, Germany, POB 701620, 81316 München. Tel. +49 89 769 02–0, Fax +49 (0)89 769 02–150. email: saur.info@thomson.com. Other publications: Annual reports, proceedings of meetings, reports of seminars and workshops
Bibliography Clavel, J.-P, "LIBER-a Brief Account of Its Origins," LIBER Bulletin 1 (1972):3–5; Kroller, E, "Harmonisierung der Konzeption und Realisierung der europäischen Bibliothek aus bibliothekarischer Sicht," (Harmonization and Realization of the Concept of the European Library from a Library Perspective) in Zur Internationalität wissenschaftlicher Bibliotheken. 76. Bibliothekartag in Oldenburg. 1986. (Zeitschrift für Bibliothekswesen und Bibliographie. Sonderheft 44) pp. 40–47 (in German); Schnelling, H., "New European Perspectives for LIBER," LIBER Bulletin 27 (1985):60–64; Munthe, G., "LIBER," in ALA World Encyclopedia of Library and Information Services. 2nd ed., p. 452. Chicago: American Library Association, 1986; Munthe, G., "LIBER-A Library Organization, Its Origin, Its Objectives and Its Achievements," Libri 38 (1988):45–50; Koch, H.-A., "The Ligue des bibliothèques européennes de recherche (LIBER) and International Library Co-operation," IATUL Quarterly 3 (1989):173–79

075 Major Orchestra Librarians' Association (MOLA)

Address c/o Patrick McGinn, President, 1530 Locust Street, Philadelphia, PA 19102 president@mola-inc.org; www.mola-inc.org
Languages English, with some things in print and on our website in German and French
Established 1983
Officers Pres: Tom Takaro
Staff 1 administrative officer, volunteer; occasional administrative assistance paid hourly; all other work done by volunteer members individually, on the Executive Board or through committees
General Assembly The Anunal meeting is required by Bylaws. 2005: Los Angeles
Membership Over 200 organizations and their librarians, including those of orchestras, opera and ballet companies, military bands and music conservatories. Membership includes musical organizations in Asia, Australia, Europe, the Mideast, North and South America
Structure MOLA is a federally-incorporated non-profit organization. Bylaws set out the governing structure to include Executive Board, committees appointed by the President and Board, terms of office, and membership requirements. President changes each year in a 3-year term of Vice-President, President, Past-President
Sources of Support Annual dues paid by member organizations; sponsorships and donations received through fund-raising
Major Fields of Interest Communication among orchestra librarians
Major Goals and Objectives To educate and assist librarians, present a unified voice in publisher relations and provide education, support, and information to performing arts and other music service organizations
Activities Annual conference; resource website both for members and the public; listserv for members' questions and data-sharing; collaboration with other industry

organizations, including the Music Library Association (MLA), Music Publishers Association (MPA), International Association of Music Libraries, Archives and Documentation Centers (IAML), American Symphony Orchestra League (ASOL), American Federation of Musicians (AFM), International Conference of Symphony and Opera Musicians (ICSOM), Regional Orchestra Players Association (ROPA), Organization of Canadian Symphony Musicians (OCSM), American Society of Composers, Authors and Publishers (ASCAP), Broadcast Music Incorporated (BMI), and Society of Composers, Authors and Music Publishers of Canada (SOCAN)

Publications Newletter: Marcato, 1984-, 4/yr. Editor: David Gruender. Address: Indianapolis Symphony, 45 Monument Circle, Indianapolis, IN 46204–2910, Fax 317–262–1129email: davidg@indyorch.org. Other publications: The Music We Perform; The Orchestra Librarian, A Career Introduction; MOLA Music Preparation Guidelines for Orchestral Music; What is MOLA? All available as pdf files

Bibliography Publications listed above. Mentioned as resource in many industry websites and publications. Articles about MOLA include October 1999 issue of Harmony Magazine; numerous articles since 1994 in the AFM journal International Musician; many music industry and general press articles in the fall of 2003 about worldwide donation of orchestral music to the Iraqi National Symphony Orchestra

076   Metropolitan Libraries Section

Address c/o Tay Ai Cheng, Secretary, 278 Marine Parade Road, 449282 Singapore Tel.: +62 63424555, Fax +62 63424222, aicheng@nlb.gov.sg; www.archive.ifla.org

Languages English

Established 1968 as Round Table of the International Association of Metropolitan Libraries in Liverpool, England; 1976, became a Round Table of IFLA, Transformation into a Section of IFLA since January 2004

Officers Chair: Liv Saeteren; Secr+Treas: Ai Cheng Tay; Information Coordinator: Vickie McDonald

Staff None

General Assembly Entire membership meets once a year. 2004: Singapore; 2005: Riga, Latvia; 2006: Paris, France; 2007: Seattle, Washington; 2008: Prague, Czech Republic

Membership Total members: Approx. 100. 40 countries represented. Types of membership: Institutional only. Requirements: Open to metropolitan city libraries all over the world, serving populations of 400,000 people or more, and national libraries, when appropriate

Structure Governed by executive officers, meeting twice a year. Affiliation: IFLA

Sources of Support Membership dues

Major Fields of Interest Libraries of cities with 400000 or more inhabitants

Major Goals and Objectives To serve as a platform for professional communication and information for public libraries of cities with 400,000 or more inhabitants; to assist the worldwide flow of information and knowledge by promoting practical collaboration in the exchange of books, exhibitions, staff, and information in all phases of metropolitan city public library service; to organize conferences where the exchange of experience and ideas takes place on library systems, library buildings, and library activities

Activities Initiating studies to investigate problems and solutions of metropolitan city library service in developing countries. Promoting public library progress in metropolitan

areas throughout the world. In accordance with the Medium-Term Programme, current activities focus on library networks in larger cities, library buildings, formation of special subject departments within city libraries, organization and use of catalogs, automation of circulation and catalogs, problems of library services to ethnic and linguistic minorities in large cities, research library work, and online information services
Publications   No official journal. INTAMEL Metro 2/yr newsletter. Free to members. English. Address same as Association. Annual reports appear in IFLA Annual. Papers of working party meetings appear in International Library Review. Issues Annual International Statistics of City Libraries (INTAMEL) and occasional monographs
Bibliography   Alison, W.A.G., "INTAMEL Meets in Hungary: Big City Concerns," Library Association Record 83 (1981):575; Harrison, K.C., "Origin, Development and Tasks of INTAMEL," in Metropolitan Libraries on Their Way into the Eighties, ed. M. Beaujean, pp. 101–108. Munich: K. G. Saur, 1982; Eyssen, J., "To Meet Again after 15 Years: INTAMEL in Gothenburg," Buch und Bibliothek 36 (1984):692–694 (in German); Cedergren, S., "International Association of Metropolitan City Libraries (INTAMEL)," in ALA World Encyclopedia of Library and Information Services. 2nd ed., pp. 368–369. Chicago: American Library Association, 1986; Cooke, C.B., "The Work of INTAMEL," IFLA Journal 14 (1988):252–254; "International Association of Metropolitan City Libraries," The Bowker Annual: Library and Book Trade Almanac. 34th Edition 1989–90. p. 730. New York: R. R. Bowker, 1989
Comment   Formerly: Round Table of the International Association of Metropolitan Libraries (INTAMEL)

077   Middle East Librarians Association (MELA)*

Address   c/o William J. Kopycki, 8 Kamal el-Din Salah St, Garden City, Cairo   Tel.: +20 2 2796-3564, Fax 0+20 2 2796-0233, secretary@mela.us; www.mela.us
Languages   English
Established   1972, Binghamton, New York, during annual meeting of the Middle East Studies Association of North America (MESA)
Officers   Pres: Anchi Hoh; Past Pres: Omar Khalidi; VP/Program Chair: Michael Hopper; Secr/Treas: William J. Kopycki; MELA Notes Edi: Marlis Saleh; Webmaster: Robin Dougherty; MELANET-L List Manager: Kristen Wilson
Staff   None
General Assembly   Entire membership meets once a year usually in November, just prior to the start of the Middle East Studies Association annual meeting
Membership   Anyone who is employed by an institution to service Middle East library materials in a professional capacity (selection, acquisition, cataloging, indexing, reference work, administration, and/or preparation of research tools), as well as any other person who has an interest in these aspects of Middle East library materials. Dues: US $30.00/yr
Structure   Governed by executive officers meeting at least once a year
Sources of Support   Membership dues, sale of publications, vendor sponsorship/contributions, membership fundraising
Major Fields of Interest   Middle East and North African studies, including the Arab world, Turkey, Israel, Iran; library collections all over the world concerned with this area
Major Goals and Objectives   To facilitate communication among members through meetings and publications; to improve the quality of area librarianship through the

development of standards for the profession and education of Middle East library specialists; to compile and disseminate information concerning Middle East libraries and collections and represent the judgment of the members in matters affecting them; to encourage cooperation among members and Middle East libraries, especially in the acquisition of materials and the development of bibliographic controls; to cooperate with other library and area organizations in projects of mutual concern and benefit; to promote research in and development of indexing and automated techniques as applied to Middle East materials

Activities MELA's George Atiyeh Prize offers financial aid to attend the annual meetings of MELA and of the Middle East Studies Association of North America (MESA); the annual David H. Partington Award grants public and tangible recognition to its members who have displayed a high standard of excellence and accomplishments in and contributions to the field of Middle East librarianship. The Committee for Cataloging is one of the more active committes, working to establish national standards and best practices for the cataloging of Middle East language materials, with particular emphasis on Arabic and Persian-script in shared MARC21 bibliographic and authority records

Publications Official journal: MELA Notes. 1973-. Annual. Free to members; also available on website. English. Indexed in Index Islamicus

Bibliography Minutes of the previous year's business meeting are published in MELA Notes

078 NORDBOK
(Nordic Literature and Library Committee)

Address P.O.Box 8145 Dep, 0033 Oslo Tel.: +47 23117500, Fax +47 23117501; www.nordbok.org

Languages Norwegian

Established 1989

Major Fields of Interest Nordic literature and librarianship

Major Goals and Objectives To encourage the propagation of Nordic literature; to strengthen public library cooperation in the Nordic countries; to ensure more inter-Nordic translations of books for children and adults; to contribute to the increased promotion of literature in Nordic minority languages; to support cooperation between Nordic public libraries; to protect the Nordic community of language; to strengthen cooperation in the library world and the world of literature between the Nordic countries, the Nordic localities and Europe; to ensure Nordic participation in international cooperation within the field of literature and libraries

Activities To initiate projects which will serve to extend the knowledge of Nordic literature and/or contribute to making Nordic literature in the original languages more accessible in the individual Nordic countries; to act as consultant to the Nordic Council of Ministers in the field of literature and libraries; inform about Nordic literature and library cooperation both within the Nordic countries and outside

079   Nordic Association for Medical and Health Information (NAMHI)

Address c/o Keiu Saarniit, Puusepa street 8, 51014 Tartu Tel.: +372 7318186, Fax +372 7318186, Keiu.Saarniit@kliinikum.ee; www.nordbalt.no

Established 1993

Membership Consists of the following associations: Bibliotekarforbundet, Faggruppen for Medicinsk Information, Denmark; Norsk Bibliotekforening, Spesialgruppen for Medisin og Helsefag, Norway; Svensk Biblioteksförening, Specialgruppen för vårdbibliotek, Sweden; Samtarfshópur Laeknisfraedibókavarda, Iceland and Bibliothecarii Medicinae Fenniae, Finland. The members of these five international organisations are collectively attached to the Association
Structure Governed by a Board consisting of two members from each country
Major Fields of Interest Medical and health information in Nordic countries
Major Goals and Objectives To increase collaboration between Nordic professional groups, thus strenghtening the specialist knowledge and encouraging development of Nordic librarians, specialising in bio-medical areas, or within the health services
Activities Organizes conferences and seminars; continuing education courses

080   North American Fuzzy Information Processing Society (NAFIPS)

Address c/o Dr. Joseph M. Barone, Treasurer, 321 East 43rd Street, Apt. 209, New York, NY 10017 president@nafips.org; www.nafips.ece.ualberta.ca
Languages English
Established 1981
Officers Pres: Joseph M. Barone; Past Pres: Dimitar Filev; Hon Pres: Loffi Zadeh; Pres-Elect: Marek Reformat
Staff 20 (volunteers)
General Assembly Entire membership meets once a year. 2010: Toronto, Canada, July 12th-14th
Membership Requirements: Interest in promoting the purpose of the Society. Dues (US Dollar): 19/yr
Structure Governed by the Board of Directors (elected 3 members per year for 3-yr. terms)
Sources of Support Membership dues. Budget (US Dollar): 1986/87: $3,000; 1987/88: $11,000
Major Fields of Interest Theory of fuzzy sets
Major Goals and Objectives Objectives: 1. Provide forums for the discussion and dissemination of quality research results and applications; 2. Contribute to the definition and development of intelligent systems; 3. Integrate diverse disciplines to solve real world problems; 4. Facilitate Technology Transfer; 5. Foster professional relationships with relevant national or international organizations; 6. Promote international collaboration within the North American Fuzzy Community; 7. Collaborate on Standard Activities
Activities Annual meetings, and publication of conference and workshop proceedings. Sponsors continuing education workshops, lectures, seminars
Publications Official journal: International Journal of Approximate Reasoning. 1986-. 6/yr. (US Dollar) 128. Free to members. Editor-in-Chief, Piero P. Bonissone, General Electric Corporate Research and Development. email: Bonissone@research.ge.com. Other publications: Annual reports, proceedings of meetings, Mailing list (updates about NAFIPS activities and related posting; email: listproc@listproc.gsu.edu)

081   North American Sport Library Network (NASLIN)

Address c/o Gretchen Ghent, 2500 University Drive NW, Calgary, Alberta T2N 1N4

Tel.: +1 403 2206097, Fax +1 403 2826837; http://libguides.ucalgary.ca/naslin
Established 1989
Membership Consists of librarians, archivists, and information specialists involved in the publication, acquisition, organization, retrieval and dissemination of information relating to all aspects of sport, physical education, and recreation. Membership is free
Structure Governed by Steering Committee
Major Fields of Interest Sport librarianship
Major Goals and Objectives To facilitate communication and resource sharing among sports librarians, archivists, and information specialists through conferences, educational programs and other cooperative projects. To communicate with related organizations, nationally and internationally regarding cooperative projects and programs. These organizations include, the International Association for Sports Information, Canadian Association for Sports Heritage, and the International Association of Sports Museums and Halls of Fame
Activities Holds conferences
Publications Official newsletter: NASLINE (Online edition) (ISSN 1480–5162, 2/yr); Conference Notes

082   Pacific Islands Association of Libraries, Archives and Museums (PIALA)

Address c/o RFK Library, University of Guam, UOG Station, Mangilao 96923   Tel.: +1 671 7352345, Fax +1 671 7346882, piala.org@gmail.com; http://sites.google.com/site/pialaorg
Languages English
Established 1991
Staff None
General Assembly Every year in November. Annual PIALA meetings rotate throughout the region
Membership Ca. 150. PIALA Membership is open to all individuals, institutions, and corporations interested in supporting its goals
Sources of Support Membership fees, conference regulations, publications
Major Fields of Interest Libraries, archives, museums, and related institutions of the Pacific Islands
Major Goals and Objectives Fostering awareness and encouraging cooperation and resource sharing among the libraries, archives, museums, and related institutions of the Pacific Islands. PIALA's goals are promoting knowledge of the functions, resources, services, and needs of regional collections; developing and promoting programs for the extension and improvement of services
Publications PIALA Newsletter, 2–3/yr. Free with PIALA membership. Union List of Serials in Libraries in Guam and Micronesia. October 2002 ed. Price: $14.50; PIALA 2000: Libraries and Archives: Where Information and Language Literacy Begin. Selected papers of the 10th PIALA Conference. Price: $25.00; PIALA '98: Libraries, Archives ard Museums: What's in Them for Us? Selected papers of the 8th PIALA Conference. Price: $25.00; PIALA '97: Place of Enlightenment. Papers of the 7th PIALA Conference. Price: $25.00; PIALA '96: Identifying, Using and Sharing Local Resources. Selected Papers from the 6th PIALA Conference. Price: $25.00; PIALA '95: Preservation of Culture through Archives ard Libraries. Selected Papers from the 5th PIALA Conference. Price: $20.00;

PIALA '94: Pacific Information Liberation: The Wave of the Future. Selected Papers from the 4th PIALA Conference. Price: $13.50; PIALA '93: Collecting, Preserving and Sharing Information in Micronesia. Selected Papers from the 3rd PIALA Conference. Price: $10. For information on PIALA pubitcaiions contact Arlene Cohen (acohen@uog9.uog.edu)
Bibliography FID News Bulletin, Vol. 42, No. 12 (Dec. 1992); InCite, Vol. 18, No. 12 (Dec. 1997); National Library of Australia News, Vol. VII, No. 7 (April 1997); Union List of Serials in Pacific Island Libraries, 2003; Directory of Libraries and Archives in the Pacific Islands, 2nd ed. 2003

083   Pacific Regional Branch of the International Council on Archives (PARBICA)*

Address   c/o Secretary-General Mark Crookston, PO Box 21025, Government Buildings, 6144 Wellington   Tel.: +64 4 496 1394, Fax +64 4 496 6210, Mark.Crookston@archives.govt.nz; www.parbica.org
Languages   English
Established   1980, London. Inaugural Conference, Suva, Fiji, Oct. 25–27, 1981
Officers   Pres: Setareki Take; VP: Dianne Macaskill; Secr Gen: Mark Crookston; Treas: Adrian Cunningham; Edi: Karen Brennan
Staff   Volunteers; secretarial staff as requested
General Assembly   Biennial General Conference. Recent Conferences – 1997: Noumea, New Caledonia; 1999: Suva, Fiji; 2001: Republic of Palau; 2003: Wellington, New Zealand; 2005: Nadi, Fiji; 2007: Noumea, New Caledonia; 2009: Brisbane, Australia; 2001: Apia, Samoa (planned)
Membership   34 institutional (government agencies, non-government organisations) and 19 individual members. Requirements: Archival institution, practicing archivist, or interest in aims of the Association
Structure   Voting members of the General Conference elect a Bureau consisting of a President, Vice-President, Secretary-General, Treasurer and 3 members. The Brueau has powers to co-opt additional expertise as required. Administration supported by a Secretariat. Parent organisation: International Council on Archives
Sources of Support   Membership dues and other subsidies. General Conference programmes are funded and supported from various sources including National Archives of Australia, Archives New Zealand, AusAid, NZAid, Commonwealth Foundation, UNESCO, Int. Council on Archives
Major Fields of Interest   Archives, records and information management, Culture and heritage sector activities
Major Goals and Objectives   1. establish, maintain and strengthen relations between archivists of the region and between all institutions, professional bodies and organisations which are concerned with the administration or preservation of records and archives, or with the professional training of archivists, especially through the exchange of information; 2. promote the management and use of records and archives and the preservation of the archival heritage of the region, through the sharing of experiences, research and ideas on professional archival and records management matters and on the management and organisation of archival institutions; 3. facilitate the use of archives in the region by encouraging public education and information, by making them more widely known, and by encouraging greater ease of access; 4. stimulate, organise and coordinate activities to support recordkeeping and archives in the region; 5. sponsor and/or certify

professional training of regional archivists and other recordkeeping professionals; 6. cooperate with other organisations or institutions concerned with the documentation of human experience and the use of that documentation for the benefit of mankind
Activities The PARBICA Recordkeeping for Good Governance Toolkit. A series of guidleines to assistgovernment organsiations create, maintain and dispose of their records. It developed for adaptation and use across institutional and jurisdictional boundaries. Support for the UNESCO Memory of the World Programme in the Pacific.Researching and publishing a Pacific Archives Reader
Publications Quarterly newsletter Panorama. Free to members or available for US$15/yr. PARBICA Recordkeeping for Good Governance Toolkit. 2007–2010. PARBICA Compendium of Pacific Archives Legislation. Compiled and edited by Nancy Lutton. Canberra, 2001; Education and Training for Records and Archives Management in Pacific Island Nations. A Needs Assessment and Report prepared for PARBICA. Laura Millar, International Records Management Trust, 2003; The Darwion Shipping Container Trial. Report and Results. Ted Ling, National Archives of Australia, 2002; Using Shipping Containers for Records Storage. Specification and Description. Ted Ling, National Archives of Australia, 2002; Building a Low Cost Archives in the Tropics. Specification and Description, Ted Ling, National Archives of Australia, 2003
Bibliography Cleland, L., PARBICA 1984–1985. Archives and Manuscripts 13 (1985):189–195.; PARBICA Constitution 2009. available from http://www.parbica.org/constitution1.htm; Tale, Setareki, Canoeing in Cyberspace: Recordkeeping in the Pacific. A Fiji Case Study. Australian Society of Archivists Conference 2006. Wickman, Danielle, Recordkeeping Legislation and its Impacts: The PARBICA Recordkeeping for Good Governance Toolkit. Archives and Manuscripts, 36(1) 2008; Wickman, Danielle, Measuring performance or performing measurements? Measuring the impact and sustainability of the PARBICA Recordkeeping For Good Governance Toolkit. Archives and Manuscripts, 37(2) 2009

084   Polski Zwiazek Bibliotek (PZB) (Association of Polish Libraries)*

Address ul. Toruriska 1, 87–140 Chelmza Tel.: +48 56 6545214, Fax +48 665 886 222, Pzb1@op.pl; www.pzb.org.pl
Languages Polish, English
Established 2000, Torun, new administrative division of a country
Officers Pres: Jan Krajewski
Staff 1
General Assembly Once of year, next meeting: 9th October 2010
Membership 105 libraries, public (-95%) and school, teaching, academic
Structure Executive Committee
Sources of Support Financed through membership dues, projects of conferences, seminary, workshops
Major Fields of Interest Integration of Polish libraries, make a permanent cooperation with organizations of libraries and librarians from other countries
Major Goals and Objectives To deepen the awareness of public knowledge about the needs and conditions of libraries in Poland; to initiating cooperation of libraries and other institutions and organizations related to the book, to supporting initiatives to promote

books and reading
Activities Organizing national and international conferences, training seminars, workshops, meetings of libraries and librarians, response to legislative changes in the area of books and reading
Publications Public Libraries to the European Union, Torun, 2001
Bibliography December – 2009: organize a nationwide protest of Polish libraries and monitoring of process Act legislation about organize and conducting cultural activity

085   Private Libraries Association (PLA)

Address   c/o Jim Maslen Honorary Membership Sectretary, 29 Eden Drive, Hull, hu8 8jq dchambrs@aol.com; www.plabooks.org
Languages   English
Established   1956, London, following a letter from Philip Ward to The Observer
Officers   Hon Memebership Secr: Jim Maslen
General Assembly   Entire membership meets once a year
Membership   Worldwide member representation. Requirements: Book collectors, i. e. collectors of rare books, fine books, single authors, special subjects and, above all, collectors of books for the simple pleasures of reading and ownership. Membership applications should be addressed to the Hon. Membership Secretary. Dues (Pound Sterling): 30 (US Dollar 55)
Structure   Governed by executive officers and council
Sources of Support   Membership dues, sale of publications
Major Fields of Interest   Book collecting
Major Goals and Objectives   To promote and encourage the awareness of the benefits of book ownership; to publish works related to this field; and to serve as a forum for the presentation of papers concerning book ownership
Activities   Publication of journal, member books, and annual check list 'Private Press Books'. Correspondence within the Association is encouraged, and the Association attempts to provide useful information to members through its journal and other publications
Publications   Official journal: The Private Library. 1957-. 4/yr. Free to members. English. Other publications: Newletter and Exchange List 4/yr; Series of illustrated books on specialized aspects of bibliophilia, issued free to members. Recent publications: Arnold, John, "The Fanfrolico Press" (2009); "A modest collection, the Private Libraries Association 1956–2006" (2007); Goldman, Paul, "Beyond decoration, the illustrations of John Everett Millais" (2005)
Bibliography   Ward, P. and Chambers, D.J., "Twenty-five Years of the PLA", The Private Library, 3rd Ser., Vol. 3:3 (Autumn 1980); 4 (Winter 1980). 3rd Ser., Vol. 4:2 (Summer 1981)

086   Red Latinoamericana de Información Teológica (RLIT)

Address   c/o Noemí Zuliani, Secretary, Ramon L. Falcon 4080, 1407 Buenos Aires Tel.: +54 11 46361737, Fax +54 11 46361741; www.ibiblio.org/rlit
Languages   Spanish
Established   1994

Membership Requirements: open to all denominations, even though the Protestant Christian presence is prevalent
Major Fields of Interest Theological librarianship
Major Goals and Objectives To unite the theological librarians of the Central Latin American region
Publications Official journal: Boletin del Bibliotecario Teológico Latinoamericano

087 Seminar on the Acquisition of Latin American Library Materials (SALALM)

Address c/o SALALM Secretariat, 7001 Freret Street, New Orleans, LA 70118–5549 Tel.: +1 504-247-1366, Fax +1 504-247-1367, salalm@tulane.edu; www.salalm.org
Languages English, Spanish
Established 1956 at Chinsegut Hill, Florida, under the auspices of the Columbus Memorial Library of the Pan American Union and the University of Florida Libraries, by Stanley, L. West and Marietta Daniels Shepard, who served as Permanent Secretary, 1956–68, and Executive Secretary, 1968–73. In 1968, Association was incorporated, and present constitution and bylaws adopted. Since 1973, the Secretariat has moved to designated academic member libraries with strong Latin American programs, every 3 to 5 years
Officers Pres: Fernando Acosta-Rodrígue; VP/Pres-elect: Nerea LLamas; Past Pres: Pamela Graham; Exec Secr: Hortensia Calvo; Treas: Jane Garner
Staff 1 (paid)
General Assembly Entire membership meets once a year; sometimes also mid-winter meetings. 2004: Ann Arbor/Michigan
Membership Total members: Approximately 500, including about 150 institutions. Requirements: any person, institution, or other organization interested in the aims of SALALM. Dues (US Dollar): Personal membership: $60, First-time membership: $50, Rate for members in Latin America, Caribbean, Puerto Rico: $30, Student membership: $30, Students in Latin America, Caribbean, Puerto Rico: $15, Emeritus: $30, Retired members in Latin America, Caribbean, Puerto Rico: $15, Institutional membership: $110, Supporting institutional membership: $500
Structure Governed by Executive Board and constitution
Sources of Support Membership dues, sale of publications, return on investments, support by host institution
Major Fields of Interest Latin American bibliography, acquisitions, networking, collection development, library operations and services in Latin America
Major Goals and Objectives Control and dissemination of bibliographic information about all types of Latin American publications; development of library collections of Latin Americana; promotion of cooperative efforts to improve library service for individuals and institutions; improving library service to the Spanish- and Portuguese-speaking population of the United States
Activities Various committees, Compilation of bibliographies, Annual José Toribio Medina Award in recognition of outstanding contributions by SALALM members to Latin American Studies
Publications Official journal: SALALM Newsletter. 1964-. 4/yr. Free to members, non-members may subscribe for $25/yr. Editors: Nerea Llamas, University of Michigan. Mary Jo Zeter, Michigan State University. Address same as Association. English, Spanish,

Portuguese, French. Other publications: Proceedings of meetings, and Bibliography and Reference Series, e.g., Ilgen, W. and Jakubs, D., An Acquisitions Manual/Manual de Adquisições (1988, Bibl. & Ref. Series, 21); Karno, H. and Block, D., Directory of Vendors of Latin American Library Materials (3rd ed., 1988, Series, 22); Loroña, L., ed., A Bibliography of Latin American and Caribbean Bibliographies. 1987-1988 (1988, Series, 23), etc. Issues annual Microfilming Projects Newsletter. Resources for Locating and Evaluating Latin American Videos. Latin American Information Series. Edited by Laura D. Shedenhelm, University of Georgia Libraries, University of Georgia Libraries, Main Library, Athens, Ga. 30602-1641, Tel. 706-583-0212, Fax 706-542-4144.e-mail: shedenhe@arches.uga.edu. Publications available for sale. Price lists issued. No publications exchange program

Bibliography "SALALM at Chapel Hill: A Time for Understanding Latin America," Library Journal 109 (1984):1274; Kahler, M.E., "Report on the Seminar on the Acquisition of Latin American Library Materials, SALALM XXX," Library of Congress Information Bulletin 44 (Sept. 2, 1985); Hazen, D. H., "Seminar on the Acquisition of Latin American Material," in ALA World Encyclopedia of Library and Information Services. 2nd ed., pp. 753-755. Chicago: American Library Association, 1986; "Report from the 23rd Seminar on the Acquisition of Latin American Library Materials," Library of Congress Information Bulletin 45 (Aug. 11, 1986):284-288; "SALALM and ACURIL Consider Strategies for Coping with Shrinking Budgets," Library of Congress Information Bulletin 46 (Nov. 16, 1987):483-491; Hodgman, S., "Seminar on the Acquisition of Latin American Library Materials," in ALA Yearbook 1989. pp. 223-224. Chicago: American Library Association, 1989

088 Sociedad Argentina de Información (SAI)*

Address Av. Pueyrredón 854, 11 A, 1032 Buenos Aires Tel.: +54 11 49610102, Fax +54 11 49610102, sai@sai.com.ar; www.sai.com.ar

Languages Spanish

Established 1997

Officers Dir: Raúl Escandar; Secr: Gerardo Barrionuevo; Daniel Jodor; Pablo Lopérfido

Staff 15 paid, 6 volunteers

Major Fields of Interest Research on information world

Activities Further education and training, symposia, conferences

Publications Journals: Revista Argentina de Bibliotecología. ISSN 0329-5265. Revista Argentina de Humanidades y Ciencias Sociales. ISSN 1667-9318. Boletín informativo electrónico. ISSN 1667-6351. Books: Bibliografía de Bibliografías Argentinas, por Horacio Zabala y Oscar Fernández. Dostoievsky: una bibliografía en español, por Laura Pérez Diatto. Catálogo Colectivo de Publicaciones Periódicas Biomédicas, por la Asociación de Bibliotecas Biomédicas Argentinas. CD-ROMs: Actas del Primer Simposio Electrónico Internacional: Conservación Preventiva en Bibliotecas, Archivos y Museos: desde el porqué hasta el cómo. Actas del Simposio electrónico Las 3 T (tesis, tesistas y tutores)

089 Société Internationale des Bibliothèques et des Musées des Arts du Spectacle (SIBMAS)
(International Society of Libraries and Museums of the Performing Arts)
Address c/o Secretary General: Sylvie François, 8400 2e Avenue, H1Z 4M6 Montréal Tel.: +39 06 6819471, Fax +39 06 68194727, sylvie.francois@cirquedusoleil.com; www.sibmas.org
Languages English, French
Established 1954, Zagreb, Yugoslavia. Originally founded as section of IFLA under name Section Internationale des Bibliothèques-Musées des Arts du Spectacle. Became autnomous association under present name in 1972
Officers Pres: Claire Hudson; Ex-Pres: Claudia Blank; 1st VP: Helen Adair; 2nd VP: Nicole Leclercq; Secr Gen: Sylvie François; Treas: Jan Van Goethem
Staff None
General Assembly Entire membership meets every 2 years. Sept. 2004: Barcelona, August 2006: Vienna
Membership Institutional members in 54 countries
Structure Governed by a Council. Affiliations: IFLA, ICOM, IFTR
Sources of Support Membership dues
Major Fields of Interest Theater libraries, theater documentation centers, theater museums, and dance
Major Goals and Objectives To promote research, practical and theoretical, in the documentation of the performing arts; establish international contacts between theater libraries and documentation centers, and coordinate the work of members
Activities Cooperative project of international theater bibliography. Holding congresses
Publications Online journal at http://www.firt-iftr.org/sibmas/site/index.jsp. Other publications: The World Directory on Theatre Museums and Libraries. 5th edition in spring 1996, and since March 7, 2002 is accessible in an online version. The International Bibliography of Theatre (IBT), published by the Theatre Research Data Centre at Brooklyn College of the City University of New York. The World Encyclopedia of contemporary Theatre, 6 vol. (1994–2000)

090 South and West Asian Regional Branch of the International Council on Archives (SWARBICA)
Address c/o Prince Abbas Khan, Secretary General, Administrative Block Area, Block 'N', 44000 Islamabad Tel.: +92 51 9202044, Fax +92 51 9206349, mail@swarbica.org; www.swarbica.org
Languages English
Established 1976, New Delhi
Officers Pres: Ali Akbar Ashari; VP: Sharif Uddin Ahmed; Gen Secr: Prince Abbas Khan; Treas: Saroja Wettasinghe
Staff None
General Assembly Entire membership meets every 2 years
Membership 11 national archives in 6 countries. Types of membership: Individual, institutional, honorary, national. Requirements: Individual: Interest in archives; institutional: Custody of archival materials, interest in archives by association

Structure Governed by executive officers and committee, meeting annually. Affiliations: A Regional Branch of the International Council on Archives (ICA)
Sources of Support Membership dues, sale of publications, private gifts, government grants, subsidies from ICA
Major Fields of Interest Archives
Major Goals and Objectives To promote conservation, administration, and utilization of archive material in South and West Asia; establish, maintain, and strengthen relations among all having such materials in their custody
Activities Sponsors seminars, workshops and other continuing education programs, e.g., on archival training requirements of the region and on records management. Participates in programs and meetings of ICA
Publications Official journal: SWARBICA Journal. 1977-. 1/yr. Free to members. Address same as Association. English. Circ: Membership. All transactions of the Association appear in the official journal. Newsletter published occasionally

091   Sri Lanka Library Association (SLLA)*

Address 275/75 Bauddhaloka Mawatha, Colombo 7 Tel.: +94 1 589103, Fax +94 1 589103, slla@sltnet.lk; www.nsf.ac.lk/slla
Languages English
Established 1960, Colombo
Officers Pres: Upali Amarasiri; Immediate Past Pres: P.B. Amarasiri; P. Ranasingha; VP: J. Rathnayake; Gen Secr: Pushpamala Perera; Treas: D.I.D. Andradi
Staff 5 paid
General Assembly Annually Last friday of Month of June in Colombo
Membership Total 392 members. Cooperate Membership: 213, Non Cooperate Membership: 149
Structure Governed by Executive Council. Affiliations: COMLA, IFLA
Sources of Support Financed through Membership and Professional Education. No govt. subsidies
Major Fields of Interest To organize, develop and regularize the study and teaching of Library Science, Documentation and Information Science, to support protect and maintain the status, interests and welfare of the profession of librarianship and information science for the advancement of the study and practice of Library,Documentation and Information Services and related subjects
Major Goals and Objectives According to Sri Lanka Library Association (Incorporation) (Amendment) Act, No. 7 of 2004 the objectives of SLLA are: to establish, maintain and promote the Library, Documentation and Information Services in Sri Lanka and to setup professional standards for such services; to co-ordinate and co-operate with authorities concerned with planning, programming and developing of all aspects of library, documentation and information services; to provide professional advice and to promote, facilitate and assist in the use of new technologies in the field of library science, documentation and information service; to organize discussions, meetings, conferences and seminars relating; to library science documentation and information service and encourage and facilitate the participation of person interested; to safeguard, protect and promote the rights, privileges, status, interests and welfare of the Librarians and Information Scientists; to organize, conduct and control the education and training of

persons desiring to qualify as professional librarians and information scientists and for that purpose prescribe, approve and accredit appropriate courses of study; to promote and facilitate the study, teaching and research on library science and information science and services; to co-operate and co-ordinate with other establishments and associations both national and international, having objects similar to the corporation; to unite all those engaged in library and information services and promote coordination and fellowship among them to promote co-ordination and cooperation between libraries in Sri Lanka; to collect literature pertaining to library information and documentation science and maintain a library and documentation center; to introduce a Code of Conduct and Ethics for the members of the Corporation and monitor the implementation of such Code; and to do all such other acts and things as are incidental or conducive to the attainment of the above objects

Publications   Official Journal: Journal-Sri lanka Library Review- Annually Rs. 200; Newsletter -SLLA Newsletter Quarterly Free of charge to all members. Editor: Mrs.Swarna Jayatilake. Main language use English but included sinhala & Tamil articles as received. Sri Lanaka Library Association Annual Report English. Free for members

Bibliography   Conference Proceedings: The National Conference on Libraary & Information Science. Freee for Participants Price Rs.500/= Main language use English

Comment   Sri Lanka Library Association is celebratng its Golden Jubilee Aniversary in 2010

092   Standing Conference of African National and University Libraries in Eastern, Central and Southern Africa (SCANUL-ECS)

Address   c/o Beatrice Sekabembe, Secretary SCANUL-ECS, P. O. Box 7062, Kampala Tel.: +256 41 541524, Fax +256 41 341975; www.scanul-ecs.org

Languages   English

Established   Has its origin in the Standing Conference of African University Libraries in the East African region (SCAULEA), founded in the mid 1960s, ceased to exit in 1977. In 1984, at a seminar in Botswana, the University Librarians in the region agreed to revive and expand SCAULEA and also to include national libraries. A constitution was made and the first SCANUL-ECS was held in Malawi as a pre-conference to the Standing Conference of Eastern, Central, and Southern African Librarians (SCECSAL). Re-established in 1994 in Malawi

General Assembly   Entire membership meets every 2 years. The following conferences have been held: 1994 Malawi, 1996 Lesotho, 1998 Kenya, 2000 Namibia, 2002 South Africa, 2004 Uganda. The seventh SCANUL-ECS will be held in 2006 in Tanzania

Membership   All national and university libraries in the SCANUL-ECS region are eligible members. Membership fee is US$ 100.00. Current membership close to 80. Over 100 institutions are eligible

Structure   Governed by conference membership that sits every 2 years

Sources of Support   Membership dues; funding through International Network for the Availability of Publications (INASP), and Electronic Information for Libraries Network (eIFL.net), and other local support from Organizations and Publishers/Booksellers

Major Fields of Interest   All areas that promote academic library development, eg., Funding, Consortia building and management, library standards, marketing, advocacy, etc

Major Goals and Objectives   To support and develop national and university library

services in the areas covered by East, Central and Southern Africa. To promote inter-change, content and cooperation among national and university libraries in the region
Activities To collect, coordinate and disseminate information on library activities. To encourage increased contact among members and the international library community. To organize and encourage conferences, seminars, workshops and subject meetings. To initiate and implement regional projects and resource sharing. To promote the participation of the information sector in the major socioeconomic activities in the region. Ongoing studies/projects: Directory of national and university libraries in the region; Tax Exemption on Educational materials in the SCANUL-ECS region; Standards for SCANUL-ECS libraries; User information literacy programmes
Publications SCANUL-ECS Newsletter; Conference Proceedings; Case Studies, namely: a. Willemse, J.: Library funding: adequate financial support for African university libraries, 2002; b. Sekabembe, B.: Library consortia in the SCANUL-ECS region: activities of existing and functioning library consortia in Eastern, Central, and Southern Africa, 2002; c. Simui, M. H. & Kanyengo, C.W.: An investigation into the funding of university libraries in Zambia, 2004
Bibliography Bankole, E. B., "Standing Conference of African University Libraries (SCAUL)," in ALA World Encyclopedia of Library and Information Services. 2nd ed., p. 785. Chicago: American Library Association, 1986

093 Standing Conference of African University Libraries, Western Area (SCAULWA)

Address c/o Bibliothèque centrale, BP 2006, Dakar Tel.: +221 824 69 81, Fax +221 824 23 79, hsene@ucad.sn
Languages English, French
Established 1972, Lagos, at Conference of University Librarians, as an area organization of SCAUL
General Assembly Entire membership meets every 2 years. Biennial Conferences 199, 2001, 2003, all held in Ghana
Membership Requirements: Membership in the West African Conference of the Association of African Universities
Structure Governed by conference membership meeting every 2 years
Sources of Support Membership dues, sale of publications. Funding and support through Danish International Development Agency (DANIDA) and International Network for the Availability of Scientific Publications (INASP)
Major Fields of Interest University libraries
Major Goals and Objectives (1) To keep members informed of each other's activities and, whenever possible, to correlate such activities in the common interest; (2) to support and develop university library services in Africa
Activities Holding conferences and other activities to carry out the goals of the Association. Past achievements: Established medium for exchange of ideas, sharing professional views and seeking solutions; established professional journal. Current: Journal publication; cooperative acquisition of African publications; organizing conferences and meetings. Future: Publication of books and reports; staff training and exchanges. Association sponsors continuing education seminars, lectures, and workshops

Publications Official journal: African Journal of Academic Librarianship (superseded SCAUL Newsletter. 1965–82). 1983-?. 2/yr. New newsletter with two issues a year since 2001. Other publications: Proceedings of meetings, two directories

Bibliography Bankole, E. B., "Standing Conference of African University Libraries (SCAUL)," in ALA World Encyclopedia of Library and Information Services. 2nd ed., p. 785. Chicago: American Library Association, 1986. S. N. Amanquah (ed.): African University Libraries in the 21st Century. Proceedings of the Revival Meeting of the Standing Conference of African University Libraries, Western Area, held in Achimota, Ghana, 2327 November 1999. Kumasi 2000

094   Standing Conference of Eastern, Central and Southern African Librarians (SCECSAL)

Address c/o Sekretariat Stella Naledi Madzigigwa, POB 60503, Gaborone Tel.: +267 3188 520, infomatrixbotswana@gmail.com; www.scecsal.org

Languages English

Established Derives its origins from the East African Library Association (EALA) (1957–1970), 1st SCECSAL Dar Es Salaam 1974

Staff Provided by host country of Conference

General Assembly General assembly takes place at the Conference/every 2 years. 2000: Windhoek, 2002: Johannesburg, 2004: Kampala

Membership Members: 11 National Library Associations. Requirements: Open to all independent countries in Eastern, Central and Southern Africa (Angola, Botswana, Burundi, Ethiopia, Kenya, Lesotho, Madagascar, Malawi, Mauritius, Mozambique, Namibia, Rwanda, Seychelles, Somalia, Swaziland, Tanzania, Uganda, Zambia, and Zimbabwe)

Structure Governed by decision of the general meeting during the Conference. Management of business of Standing Conference rests with Library Association of host country, which provides an acting Executive Committee that adheres to the policy guidelines of SCECSAL

Sources of Support Membership dues, conference fees, support by host country of conference; government and private subsidies

Major Fields of Interest Libraries and librarianship in region

Major Goals and Objectives Provide a forum through which members of the library and information profession in the region meet to discuss issues of mutual interest; establish, strengthen and spread information professionalism in all the countries of the region; promote regional and international understanding and co-operation in the area of library and information profession; collect, collate, publish, preserve, conserve and disseminate research information through publications to potential and prospective clientele in the region and beyond; encourage capacity building by promoting education and training of library and information professionals; encourage exchange of staff and students amongst institutions in the region, and solicit funds for the programme for capacity development; promote cooperation with other library and information profession organizations outside the SCECSAL Region in the areas of library and information work; promote the adoption and use of information and communication technologies in library and information work; and undertake such other activities as will promote the development of the information profession in the SCECSAL Region

Activities Center around the goals of the Association
Publications No official journal. Other publications related to SCECSAL: Sustainable Financing of National and University Libraries: Proceedings of the 4th Standing Conference of African National and University Libraries in Eastern, Central and Southern Africa (SCANUL-ECS), Government Office Park Auditorium, 10 – 11 April 2000, Windhoek, Namibia / Compiled and edited by Justin Chisenga. Windhoek: Namibian Information Workers Association, 2000 ISBN: 99916–752–3-X. [Copies available at: US$15:00 each. For orders contact: Ms Sandra Garises. email: sandra.garises@bon.com.na). Income generation: experiences from eight university libraries in Eastern, Central and Southern Africa / Tirong arap Tanui, Joseph J. Uta, Annie Pienaar, Jenny Raubenheimer, Hester G. Boltman, Julita Nawe, Elizabeth Kiondo, James Mugasha, C. B. M. Lungu; edited by Diana Rosenberg. Oxford: INASP, Sovenga: SCANUL-ECS, 2001. 90p. [Distributed by INASP free of charge to members of SCANUL-ECS; others ˇ.50.. For orders, contact: Diana Rosenberg. email: drosenberg@gn.apc.org
Bibliography "Regional Council Meeting for East, Central and Southern Africa," COMLA Newsletter 62 (Dec. 1988):3

095 Substance Abuse Librarians&Information Specialists (SALIS)

Address P.O. Box 9513, Berkeley, CA 94709–0513 Tel.: +1 510 883-5746, Fax +1 510 664-0594, salis@salis.org; www.salis.org
Languages English
Established 1978
Officers Chair: Julie Murphy; Chair-elect: Meg Brunner; Secr: Christine Goodair; Treas: Barbara S. Weiner
General Assembly Annual meetings. 2005: Chicago, Illinois; 2006: Reno, Nevada; 2007: Boston, Massachusetts
Membership Full, Associate, Institutional and Sponsoring Membership
Structure Governed by Executive Board. Affiliations: International Council on Alcohol and Addictions (ICAA)
Major Fields of Interest Exchange and dissemination of alcohol, tobacco, and other drug (ATOD) information
Major Goals and Objectives "(1) to provide an association of individuals and organizations having a professional, scientific, or technical interest in library and information science, especially as these are applied in the recording, retrieval and dissemination of knowledge and information in the area of alcohol, tobacco and other drugs; (2) to promote and improve the communication, dissemination and use of objective, accurate and timely information about alcohol, tobacco and other drugs; and (3) to encourage the national and international development, co-operation and linkage among SALIS members, organizations and other information resources." (1991 bylaws)
Activities Sponsors annual conferences, offers Listserv, cooperates with regional and international organizations to further its goals
Publications Official journal: SALIS News. 4/yr. Address same as Association

Part II

National Associations

Albania

096 Albanian Library Association

Address   c/o Buzo Tefta, Tirana Tel.: +355 42 57670, Fax +355 42 23843, buzot2001@yahoo.com
Languages   Albanian
Established   1993
Structure   Affiliations: IFLA since 1997

Angola

097 Biblioteca Nacional de Angola

Address   Largo António Jacinto, 2915 Luanda
Officers   Dir: Maria José Faria Ramos

Antigua and Barbuda

098 Library Association of Antigua and Barbuda

Address   PO Box 822, St John's Tel.: +1 268 462 3500, Fax +1 268 462 1537
Languages   English
Established   1983
Structure   Affiliation: IFLA since 1984
Major Fields of Interest   Library services in Antigua and Barbuda
Major Goals and Objectives   Committed to raising the level of professionalism among library/information personnel, improving library/information facilities, and making library facilities the pivotal centre of education in Antigua and Barbuda

Argentina

099 Asociación Bibliotecaria de Misiones (ABGRA)

Address   Paraná 918 2do. Piso, C1017AAT Ciudad de Bs. As Tel.: +54 11 4811-0043, info@abgra.org.ar; www.abgra.org.ar
Languages   Spanish

100 Asociación de Bibliotecarios, Archivistas, Documentalistas e Informáticos (ABADIN)

Address   Paraná 918 2do. Piso, C1017AAT Ciudad de Bs. As info@abgra.org.ar
Languages   Spanish

101 Asociación de Bibliotecarios Graduados de la República Argentina (ABGRA) (Association of Graduate Librarians of the Argentine Republic)

Address c/o Marta Andrade, Paraná 918, Piso 2º, C1017AAT Buenos Aires Tel.: +54 11 42715269, Fax +54 11 42730571, secretaria@abgra.org.ar; www.abgra.org.ar
Languages Spanish
Established Nov. 5, 1953, Buenos Aires, as Asociación de Bibliotecarios Graduados de la Capital Federal (Association of Graduate Librarians of the Federal Capital), succeeding the Centro de Estudios Bibliotecologicos del Museo Social Argentino, founded in 1943
Staff None
General Assembly Entire membership meets annually
Membership Total members: 800+ (individual). Types of membership: Individual, honorary. Requirements: Open to officially recognized professional librarians
Structure Governed by Executive Council in cooperation with other groups of the Association. Affiliations: Comisión Nacional Argentina para la Unesco, IFLA
Sources of Support Membership dues, private donations, government subsidies
Major Fields of Interest All areas of library science, documentation, and information; library education, particularly postgraduate level
Major Goals and Objectives To develop and maintain the librarian's profession by working for the professional status of librarians, defending their interests, and working toward solutions of problems encountered in the exercise of librarianship; to cooperate with the State in matters pertaining to libraries and librarians and maintain relations with other organizations with similar interests; to promote the annual conferences and to publish materials related to the activities of the library profession
Activities Annual National Meeting for Librarians, Special Library Conferences, Workshops, Seminars, Training courses, Periodicals, Technical advice, Special Library
Publications Official journal: REFERENCIAS (1994-). 4/yr. ISSN 0328–1507. email: secretaria@abgra.org.ar. Other publications: Bibliotecología y documentacíon (2/yr.); conference proceedings, annual reports, and others. Exchange of publications with other library associations and libraries in effect
Bibliography Gravenhorst, H. and Suarez, R. J. (tr. by E. S. Gleaves), "Argentina," in ALA World Encyclopedia of Library and Information Services. 2nd ed., pp. 76–78. Chicago: American Library Association. 1986

102 Asociación de Bibliotecarios Profesionales de Rosario

Address Corrientes 653 - 1er piso - Of. 4, 2000 Rosario, Santa Fé Tel.: +54 341 4112075, abprosarios@yahoo.com.ar
Languages Spanish
Established 1952
Membership Total members: Approx. 200 librarians with diploma
Sources of Support Membership dues
Major Fields of Interest Professional education and professional development of librarians
Major Goals and Objectives To promote professional status and further professional development of librarians
Activities Offering seminars, workshops, and other continuing education programs; professional evaluations at requesting institutions. Association sponsors cultural and

professional activities for members
Publications Official journal: Boletín: Asociación de Bibliotecarios Profesionales. Other publications: Manuals, guides, and others

103 Asociación de Bibliotecas Biomedicas Argentinas (ABBA) (Association of Argentine Biomedical Libraries)

Address Av. Pueyrredón 854, 11° A, 1032 Buenos Aires Tel.: +54 11 49610102, Fax +54 11 49629115, abba@sai.com.ar; www.sai.com.ar/abba
Languages Spanish
General Assembly Entire membership meets annually
Sources of Support Membership dues
Major Fields of Interest Biomedical librarianship
Major Goals and Objectives To promote the development of biomedical libraries in Argentina
Activities Sponsors conferences, seminars, workshops
Publications Official journal: Revista Argentina de Documentación Biomedica. Catálogo Colectivo de Publicaciones Periódicas Biomédicas. Published by EdicionesScientíficas Argentinas. Addres: Sociedad Argentina de Información, Av. Pueyrredón 854, piso 11, oficina A, 1032 Buenos Aires, Argentina, Tel. +54 11 49610102, Fax +54 11 49629115. email: abba@sai.com.ar

Armenia

104 Haykakan Gradaranayin Asotsiatsia (ALA) (Armenian Library Association)*

Address c/o Davit Sargsyan, President, 72, Terian Street, Yerewan, 0009 Tel.: + 3741 58 4259, Fax + 3741 52 9711, info@ala.am; www.ala.am
Languages 7th October, 1994, Yerevan, Republic of Armenia
Established 1994
Officers Pres: Davit Sargsyan; VP: Rafik Ghazaryan; Secr: Nazeni Arzumanyan
Staff Voluntary
General Assembly Membership meets annually
Membership Total number of members: 280. Sections: 2 (Inner-Republican and Foreign Relations). Requirements for joining: Any library worker and specialist over 18 years of age may become a member upon payment of the dues provided for in the Bylaw. Amount of dues: 1000 AMD
Structure Governed by Executive Board
Sources of Support Membership dues, grants, support from sponsors and state, voluntary contributions from organizations
Major Fields of Interest Development of libraries in Armenia
Major Goals and Objectives To use the specialized abilities of its members for the development of library work in Armenia, to improve access to services and resources by means of modern methods and technology
Activities Develops library programs, participates in approving government documents concerning library work, offers continuing education for librarians

Publications No official journal. Other publications: Annual Bulletin, Armenian Library Annual 8. Compiled and edited by: Nerses Hayrapetyan and Rafik Ghazaryan

Australia

105 Aboriginal & Torres Strait Islander Library & Information Resource Network (ATSILIRN)
Address GPO Box 553, Canberra, ACT 2601 tlane@nla.gov.au; home.vicnet.net.au/~atsilirn/
Languages English
Established Nov 1993
Officers Pres: Melissa Jackson; VP: Kathy Frankland; Treas: Ronald Briggs
Membership Membership includes students, individuals and organisations that provide information or resource services, with the majority of members coming from library and archival institutions Fees (Australian Dollars): 17,25; Students 11, 50; Oranizations 86,25
Major Fields of Interest Aboriginal & Torres Strait Islander people working in libraries and for those people servicing the information needs of Aboriginal & Torres Strait Islander peoples
Major Goals and Objectives To support Aboriginal and Torres Strait Islander peoples working in libraries, archives, and information or resource services. To support people providing library, archives and information or resource services to Aboriginal and Torres Strait Islander peoples. To educate Aboriginal and Torres Strait Islander peoples about what is happening in libraries, archives; the wider community about the library, archive and information needs of Aboriginal and Torres Strait Islander peoples; people who are in positions to effect changes to how library, archive, information and resource services are provided to Aboriginal and Torres Strait Islander peoples
Activities Eliectrnic discussion list, annual conferences
Publications Official journal: ATSILIRN Newsletter

106 Australian and New Zealand Map Circle (ANZMapS)
Address Parkes Place, Parkes ACT 2600 Tel.: +61 3 83448416, Fax +61 3 93470974, j.cain@unimelb.edu.au; http://australianmapcircle.org.au/
Languages English
Established 2009. A merger of the Australian Map Circle (founded 1973, following a meeting for map keepers at the National Library, Canberra, April 1973. Original name was Australian Map Curators' Circle) and the New Zealand Map Society (formed 1977)
Officers Pres: Dr. Martin Woods; VP: Adelle Edwards; Secr: Brian Marshall
Staff 4 (volunteers)
General Assembly Entire membership meets once a year. 2010 conference in Adelaide, State Library of South Australia, April 7th-9th
Membership Individual and institutional. Requirements: Interest in maps. Dues (Australian Dollar): 50, for individual and organizations, 30, for studentsincl. AMC journal, The Globe, and the occasional Newsletter
Structure Governed by membership and executive officers. Affiliation: IFLA
Sources of Support Membership dues, sale of publications

Major Fields of Interest The making, use and care of cartographic materials within the entire information milieu
Major Goals and Objectives To promote communication between producers, users and curators of maps; To improve the skills and status of persons working with map collections; To promote the development and effective exploitation of map collections throughout Australia
Activities Branch meetings and annual conference; mounting of a large remote sensing and map exhibit in the National Museum of Victoria for Map Week. Compilation of a publication on facsimile maps of Australia; holding first conference in Queensland. Association has been active in promoting library-related legislation by submission to the Attorney General's office on the implications of The Copyright Act and maps
Publications Official journal: The Globe. 1974-. 2/yr. Address same as association, attention Dr. Brendan White. Other publications: Newsletter 4/yr, to supplement The Globe, (email: bwhyte@unimelb.edu.au), also available online as pdf File; AMcircle (emaillist), Conference proceedings, Checklist of Australian Map Catalogues and Indexes, and others. Price lists issued

107 Australian and New Zealand Society of Indexers (ANZSI)*

Address PO Box 5062, Glenferrie South VIC 3122 Tel.: +61 3 9818 1760, ANZSIinfo@anzsi.org; www.anzsi.org
Languages English
Established 1976, replacing the Society of Indexers in Australia
Officers Pres: Mary Russell; VP: John Simkin; Secr: Michael Ramsden; Treas: Margaret Findlay
Staff Volunteers: committee members at state and national level; newsletter editor; membership secretary
General Assembly Annual general meeting
Membership Personal and corporate membership. Restrictions: Open to persons and institutions engaged in indexing, and to others interested in promoting the objects of the Society
Structure National Executive Committee, State branches in NSW, VIC, ACT, NZ, QLD
Sources of Support Membership fees (AUS$52 per year)
Major Fields of Interest Indexing in Australia
Major Goals and Objectives To improve the quality of indexing in Australia To further the training, continuing professional development, status and interest of indexers in Australia; to act as an advisory body on indexing; to provide opportunities for those interested in and connected with indexing to meet and exchange information, ideas and experiences
Activities Further education, workshops, biannual conference, seminars
Publications Newsletters

108 Australian Government Libraries Information Network (AGLIN)

Address GPO Box 1780, Canberra ACT 2601 aliaaglinexec@lists.alia.org.au; www.nla.gov.au/flin
Established 1993, as Federal Libraries Information Network (FLIN), 2003, name changed to AGLIN (Australian Government Libraries Information Network)

General Assembly Annual general meeting. Next conference: 1st-3rd September 2010
Membership Restricted to Australian Government information services; No fees for membership
Structure Independent organization managed by an executive
Major Fields of Interest Australian government libraries
Major Goals and Objectives Represent the interests and concerns of member libraries and information services in wider government forums; develop and implement co-operative schemes and resource sharing activities among Australian Government libraries and information services; serve as a forum to consider and reach consensus on issues and policies which affect Australian Government libraries and information services; promote improved access to information by Australian Government agencies and their staff, research and development in the application of new technologies and information systems relevant to Australian Government libraries and information services, and improvements in the management of Australian Government libraries and information services. Develop a capacity for the provision of expert advisory services. Foster and facilitate the dissemination of Australian Government publications to the wider community
Activities Workshops and seminars, Information Sharing Fora
Publications No official journal

109 Australian Law Librarians Association (ALLA)
Address c/o Cecily Adams, Secretary, GPO Box 1408, Brisbane QLD 4001 Tel.: +61 7 3360 5720, cecily.adams@ags.gov.au; www.alla.asn.au
Languages English
Established 1969, Sydney
Officers Pres: Leanne Cummings; VP: Naish Peterson; Secr: Cecily Adams; Treas: James Butler
Staff 2 (volunteers)
General Assembly Entire membership meets every two years
Membership Total members: over 700 (librarians, information workers and publishers working in all sectors of the legal industry including private law firms, universities, government departments, courts and tribunals and other private organisations). Requirements: Interest in objectives of Association
Structure Governed by National Board
Sources of Support Membership dues, sale of publications
Major Fields of Interest Law libraries; law librarianship; legal information
Major Goals and Objectives The primary objectives of ALLA are: To provide state and national network for law librarians in Australia; To provide a national focus for law librarianship and legal and business information; To act as a lobby group to promote the interests of law libraries, law collections and legal information services in the wider community; To benefit members and enhance the status of the profession by the further education and training of law librarians, legal information officers and others
Activities National survey of law libraries; publications; workshops and conferences. Email list allg-anz for members
Publications Official journal: Australian Law Librarian 1973-.4/yr. Editor: Petal Kinder, Federal Court of Australia, Tel. +61 3 8600 3561, Fax: +61 3 8600 3572, Email: petal.kinder.fedcourt.gov.au. English. IOther publications: Reports of seminars,

workshops; National Survey of Law Libraries in Australia (1984); Australian Legal Periodicals and Loose-leaf Services Abbreviations (1986); Executive Responsibility for the Administration of Commonwealth Statutes (1984), and others. Publications available for sale

110 Australian Libraries Copyright Committee (ALCC)

Address   PO Box E202, Kingston, ACT 2604   Tel.: +61 2 62621273, Fax +61 2 6245 6273, mdawes@nla.gov.au; www.digital.org.au
Languages   English
Officers   Chair: Tom Cochrane
General Assembly   Once or twice a year in the National Library of Australia
Membership   Members: 8
Structure   Cross-sectoral committee with representatives from the following organisations: Australian Council of Archives, Australian Library and Information Association, Council of Australian State Libraries, Council of Australian University Librarians, Federal Libraries Information Network, National Library of Australia
Major Fields of Interest   Acting on behalf of Australian libraries and archives on copyright
Major Goals and Objectives   Seeks to have the interests of users of libraries rand archives recognised and reflected in copyright legislation, and in so doing, help build and sustain a copyright regime which promotes learning, culture and the free flow of information and ideas in the interests of all Australians
Activities   Copyright advisor, Copy-Lib mailing list (email list devoted to copyright issues)
Publications   Official Journal: Copyright Bulletin 2/yr

111 Australian Library and Information Association (ALIA)

Address   POB 6335, Kingston ACT 2604   Tel.: +61 2 62158222, Fax +61 2 62822249, enquiry@alia.org.au;jennefer.nicholson@alia.org.au; http://alia.org.au/
Languages   English
Established   1937, as Australian Institute of Librarians. 1949 name changed to Library Association of Australia (LAA). Incorporated by Royal Charter, 1963. Present name adopted 1988
Officers   Pres: Jan Richards; Ecec Dir: Sue Hutley
Staff   20 (paid); 300 (volunteers, throughout Australia)
General Assembly   Annual general meeting, Biennial conference
Membership   Individual and institutional membership. Requirements: Open to all librarians and others interested in the goals of the Association. Professional membership for recognized librarians
Structure   Governed by Board of Directors. Affiliation: IFLA, ASLA
Sources of Support   Membership dues, sale of publications, continuing education conferences
Major Fields of Interest   Librarianship; library education; library management; library and information studies; related information technology
Major Goals and Objectives   (1) To promote the free flow of information and ideas in th interest of all Australians, a thriving culture, economy and democracy. (2) To promote and

improve the services provided by all kinds of library and information agencies. (3) To ensure the high standard of personnel engaged in information provision and foster their professional interests and aspirations. (4) To represent the interests of members to governments, other organisations and the community. (5) To encourage people to contribute to the improvement of library and information services through support and membership of the Association

Activities Conferences, e-lists, events, awards and fellowships. Sponsors exhibits and continuing education programs

Publications Official journal: Australian Library Journal. 1951-. 4/yr. ISSN 0004–9670. Editor: John Levett, POB 74, Middleton 7163 Maria Charlton MAP Marketing, Cnr Scott Street and Parnell Place, Newcastle 2300, Tel. 03 6292 1699, Fax 03 6292 1699, alj@alia.org.au. Other publications: inCite. newsletter, publ. monthly. Australian Academic & Research Libraries. Journal 4/yr. ISSN 0004–9670. Editor Dr Peter Clayton, Faculty of Communication, University of Canberra, POB 1, Belconnen ACT 2616, Tel. 02 6201 5431/2312, fx 02 6201 5119 email: aarl@alia.org.au

Bibliography Tilley, CM., "Australian Public Libraries, the Library Association of Australia and Literacy," International Library Review 16 (1984):143–156; Chou, M.P., "Seven Down Under: Synopsis of a Trip to New Zealand and Australia," (Joint LAA/NZLA Conference, Aug. 1984), Hawaii Library Association Journal 41 (1984):27–31; Bryan, H., "Australia," in ALA World Encyclopedia of Library and Information Services. 2nd ed., pp. 88–91. Chicago: American Library Association, 1986; Mackinnon, M., "Professionalism: The LAA Board of Education and the Decade Ahead," Australian Library Journal 34 (1987):5–13; Flowers, T, "To the Association's Credit," ibid.:226–228; Conochie, J., "AIL/LAA Major Achievements in the Area of Special Librarianship," ibid.:236–238; Bryan, H., "The Achievements of the LAA (and the AIL) over the First Fifty Years," ibid.:244–246; Horton, W., "Objectives for the Future," ibid.:261–263; Adams, J., "The Individual Member and the Future: The View from Head Office," ibid.:267–272; Judge, P., "The Professional Future," ibid.:272–278; Webb, M., "The Library Association of Australia's Library and Information Services for People with Disabilities," Link-up 50 (1988):24–25; "The Australian Libraries Summit: A Report by Warren Horton," InCite 9 (Nov. 1988):1,6–7; "ALIA's Royal Charter," InCite 10 (Feb. 1989):12–13

Comment Formerly: Library Association of Australia

112 Australian School Library Association (ASLA)*

Address POB 155, Zillmere Queensland 4034 Tel.: +61 7 36330510, Fax +61 7 36330570, asla@asla.org.au; www.asla.org.au

Languages English

Established 1969, Canberra

Officers Pres: Robert Moore; VP: June Wall; Marie Clarke; Treas: Chris Kahl; Secr: Lis Jorgensen

Staff (Contract:) Executive Officer: Karin Bonanno; Journal Editor; Rachael Hoare

General Assembly Biennial conference (every two years) 2011: Sydney 3–6 October

Membership Total members: 7 member associations. Requirements: Association is a federation of state school library associations

Structure Governed by National Council with representatives from the Associations in

each State and Territory, holding teleconference meetings about every 6 weeks. ASLA is a federation of State and Territory associations, each with its own constitution, objectives, membership conditions, and fees. Each State association has its own name, and often own acronym. ASLA is a coordinating body for over 2,000 teacher-librarians in Australia. Affiliations: ALIA, IASL, SLANZA
Sources of Support Membership dues, sale of publications, conferences
Major Fields of Interest School librarianship, teacher librarianship, school libraries
Major Goals and Objectives Professional development of school libraries and school librarianship; national forum of school libraries and school librarianship; Development of policies and standards for teacher librarianship
Activities Association involved in standards in school librarianship; professional development of school library personnel. Active in sponsoring research in school libraries and student achievement
Publications Official journal: ACCESS (formerly School Libraries in Australia. 1972–1987). 1987-. 4/yr. Membership subscription and direct subscription. Address same as Association. Circ: 3,000. English. Other publications: Teaching information skills: professional development CD-ROM. Learning for the future: developing information services in schools (Second edition), ISBN 1 86366 710 5, 82 pages $A32.95 + $A8.00 postage and handling fee. Available from Curriculum Corporation. Steps to Success: Information Literacy Video. Step to Success: Slide presentation; Online I: Constructing Communities of Learning and Literacy Conference Proceedings, ISBN 0975222309; Learning for the Future: a professional development kit; several conference proceedings CD-ROM format (information on web site)
Bibliography Lundin, R., "The Basis for an ASLA Manifesto," Australian School Librarian 20 (1983): 18–20; "Joint ALIA/ASLA Statement on Library and Information Services in Schools," InCite 10 (May 1989):2; Bonavita, J. H. Vella, "ASCIS, the Australian Schools Cooperative Information Service," COMLA Newsletter 64 (June 1989):8–9; Hunter, J., "Frontline (Editorial)," InCite 10 (Aug. 1989):2,4; Jeffrey, N.: "The Responsibility of Professional TL Associations". In: L. Hay and J. Henri (eds.): ITEC Virtual Conference '96 Proceedings, ASLA, ITEC, Australia. 1996, p. 119–121; Bonanno, K.: "The Role of the Professional Association in the Emergence of Information Literate School Communities". In: J. Henri and K. Bonanno (eds.): The Information Literate School Community: Best practice. Centre for Information Studies, Charles Stuart University, Wagga Wagga, NSW, Australia 199, p. 217–230

113 Australian Society of Archivists (Inc.) (ASA)

Address 11/388 Newman Road, Geeburg QLD 4034, POB 638, Virginia QLD 4014 Tel.: 1800 622 251 (free call), Fax +61 7 3633 5254, office@archivists.org.au; www.archivists.org.au
Languages English
Established 1975, Canberra
Officers Pres: Jackie Bettington; VP: Pat Jackson; Secr/Treas: Clive Smith; Managing Êdi: Shauna Hicks
Staff 1 part-time
General Assembly Annual general meeting and conference
Membership Total members: 802 (609 individual, 193 institutional). Branches: 7.

Requirements: No requirement for associate/institutional membership; professional membership: Graduate of university plus 2 years experience in recognized archival institution, or, graduate training in archives administration plus 1 year experience in recognized archival institution. Dues (Australian Dollar): 140–300, professional; 60–190, associate; 300–500, institution; 150
Structure Governed by Council consisting of 10 professional members of the Society elected every 2 years. Branches: 8. Affiliations: ICA
Sources of Support Membership dues, sale of publications
Major Fields of Interest Archives; archival material; recordkeeping standards
Major Goals and Objectives The Australian Society of Archivists aims to: promote a professional identity amongst archivists; promote the keeping care and use of archives and encourage research and development in all areas of archival practice; establish and maintain standards of archival practice and professional conduct amongst archivists, including standards of archival qualifications and professional training; encourage the responsible use of archives including cooperating with other organisations and groups with common interests and concerns; encourage communication and cooperation amongst archivists, their institutions and the users of archives; publish and disseminate information relevant to the archival profession
Publications Official journal: Archives and Manuscripts. 1955-.2/yr. (Australian Dollar) 150. Free to members. Address same as association. Indexed in Australian Public Affairs Information Service. LISA. Historical Abstracts. Other publications: Directory of Archives in Australia; conference proceedings, and others. Price lists available. Publications exchange program in effect
Bibliography Saclier, Michael: "Ten Years of the Australian Society of Archivists in Retrospect" In: Archives and Manuscripts 13 (1985), p.145–147; Berzins, Baiba: "Thoughts about the Next Decade" In: ibid., p.147–150

114 East Asian Library Resources Group of Australia (EALRGA)

Address POB 10, O'Connor, ACT 2602 sprentice@optusnet.com.au; http://coombs.anu.edu.au/SpecialProj/NLA/EALRGA/committee.html
Languages English
Established 8th Feb. 1995. Incorporates the Japanese Library Resources Group of Australia (JALRGA).
Officers Pres: Renata Osborne; Treas: Wan Wong; VP & Secr: Susan Prentice; Edi: Blick-har Yeung
Staff None
General Assembly Entire membership meets every 2 years
Membership Requirements: Any individual or institution interested in East Asian library services. Dues (Australian Dollar): 15, for all members
Structure Governed by members through executive officers
Sources of Support Membership dues
Major Fields of Interest East Asian librarianship in Australia
Major Goals and Objectives To promote standards of East Asian librarianship; to encourage exchange of information among members and similar organizations; to develop an effective bibliographic control of East Asian collections in Australia
Activities Electronic Forum

Publications Official journal: EALRGA Newsletter. (Australian Dollar) 15/yr. Free to members. Circ: 100. English. Editor: Bick-har Yeung. Adress: Bailieu Library, University of Melbourne, Parkville, VIC 3010, Australia, bhy@unimelb.edu.au
Comment No current information available

115 Friends of Libraries Australia Incorporated (FOLA)

Address Locked Bag 1315, Tullamarine Victoria 3043 Tel.: +61 3 93380666, Fax +61 3 93351903, dferguson@fairfieldcity.nsw.gov.au; www.fola.org.au
Languages English
Established Dec 1994, at a function in Queen's Hall, State Library of Victoria, by FOLA patron, the Honourable Justice Michael Kirby AC, CMG
Officers Pres: Dr. Alan Bundy; VP: Kristina Barnett; Exec Dir: Daniel Ferguson
Major Fields of Interest Interests and concerns of all library users
Major Goals and Objectives To encourage and assist the formation and development of Friends of Library groups in Australia. To promote the development of excellence for all people residing in Australian staes and territories. To provide a means for Friends of Library groups to have access to information and ideas that will prove useful to them in the operation of their organisations. To promote public awareness of the existence of Friends of Library groups, and of the services they support and provide. To liase with bodies with similiar aims to achieve goals
Publications Newsupdate (quarterly magazine)
Bibliography Daniel Ferguson (ed.): Friends of Libraries Resource Book. 1997, 2004

116 Health Information Management Association of Australia Ltd. (HIMAA)

Address 1st Floor, 51 Wicks Road, North Ryde NSW, Locked Bag 2045, North Ryde NSW 1670 Tel.: +61 2 98875001, Fax +61 2 9887 5895, himaa@himaa.org.au; www.himaa.org.au
Languages English
Established 1949, as the New South Wales Association of Medical Records Librarians and the Victorian Association of Medical Librarians
Staff 9
Membership Full members: 468; student members: 236; associate members: 90; organizational members: 19
Structure Controlled by an elected, voluntary 8 member Board of Directors
Sources of Support Membership fees, education programs, conference publications
Major Fields of Interest Health information management
Major Goals and Objectives Strives for the highest quality management of health information services
Activities Symposia, conferences, Clinical Coder Education
Publications Official journal: Health Information Management. Online, 4/yr. Publication list available: www.himaa.org.au

117 International Association of Music Libraries, Archives and Documentation Centres, Australian Branch (IAML-Australian Branch)

Address c/o Laurel Dingle, President, P.O. Box 3488, South Brisbane, Queensland 4101 Tel.: +61 7 3840 7835, Fax +61 7 3875 6325, musiclib@vicnet.net.au; www.iamlaust.org

Languages English

Established 1970, IAML-Australia and New Zealand Branch formed in Australia; 1982, two separate Branches established, IAML-New Zealand Branch, and IAML-Australian Branch

Officers Pres: Robyn Holmes; Treas: Bligh Glass

General Assembly Entire membership meets once a year

Membership 54 members. Dues (Australian Dollars): Corporate/Institutional Members 120.00/yr, Individual Members 60.00/yr, Student/Concessional Members 30.00/yr

Structure Governed by executive officers under the parent body. Affiliations: A branch of IAML

Sources of Support Membership dues, sale of publications

Major Fields of Interest Music bibliography; music librarianship

Major Goals and Objectives Encourage and promote the activities of music libraries, archives and documentation centres and to strengthen the cooperation among institutions and individuals in these fields of interest. To support and to facilitate the realisation of projects in music bibliography, music documentation and music library science and to explore effective means of accomplishing them. To promote the availability of all publications and documents relating to music, particularly to encourage international exchange and lending. To encourage and support the development of standards in all areas that concern the Branch. To further the bibliographical control of musical collections of the past and the present. To support the protection and preservation of musical documents of the past and the present.To co-operate with other organisations in the field of music, musicology, librarianship, archival science and documentation

Activities Sponsors conferences, seminars, workshops, and other continuing education programs

Publications Official journals: Continuo. 1982-. Intermezzo: Newsletter of the IAML (Australia Branch) 4/yr. (ISSN 1039–6241). Other publications: Annual reports, proceedings of conferences, seminars, etc. Address for all IAML publications and subscriptions: vigilante@lib.unimelb.edu.au

118   Records Management Association of Australia (RMAA)

Address PO Box 276, St Helens TAS 7216 Tel.: +61 7 32102171, Fax +61 7 32101313, kate.walker@rmaa.com.au; www.rmaa.com.au

Languages English

Officers Chair: David Pryde; Vice Chair: Debbie Prout

General Assembly International Conferences, 2004: Canberra

Membership Individual, corporate and vendor memebership, open to any person or organisation interested in Records Management services and committed to observing our Memorandums and Articles

Structure The Federal Board consists of 1 elected member from each region. The Board sets direction and manages the Business of the Association. The Board manages Standing Committees/Special Interest Portfolios which each have a Co-ordinator (who should also be Federal Board Member). Members are called upon, or can volunteer, for various activities as part of these Standing Committees/Special Interest Portfolios

Major Fields of Interest Management of Records

Major Goals and Objectives To enable records management professionals to develop and utilise their skills and experience to leverage the value of records as corporate assets and as evidence of business activities
Activities Development of standards for records management, advocacy on records management issues, delivery of courses, conventions and seminars at both federal and state level
Publications Official journal: INFORMAA Quarterly. 4/yr. Dues: 74, 80 (Australian Dollars). Other publications: newletters, Records Management List Serve

119 State Library of New South Wales, Collection Services

Address c/o Diana Richards, Macquarie Street, Sydney NSW 2000 echylewski@sl.nsw.gov.au
Languages English
Officers Dir: Regina Sutton

Austria

120 Büchereiverband Österreichs / formerly Verband Österreichischer Volksbüchereien und Volksbibliothekare (BVÖ) (Association of Austrian Public Libraries)

Address Museumstr. 3/B/12, 1070 Wien Tel.: +43 1 40697220, Fax +43 1 406359422, bvoe@bvoe.at; www.bvoe.at
Languages German
Established 1948, Vienna, as Verband Österreichischer Volsbüchereien; name changed to Verband Österreichischer Volksbüchereien und Volksbibliothekare
Officers Secr Gen: Gerald Leitner
Staff 10 (paid)
General Assembly Entire membership meets every 2 years
Membership Total members: 2,500. Types of membership: Individual, institutional. Requirements: Open to Austrian public libraries and librarians
Structure Governed by Executive Committee: Affiliations: IFLA
Sources of Support Membership dues, government subsidies
Major Fields of Interest Public libraries and librarianship
Major Goals and Objectives To serve the needs of public libraries and the training of librarians; to represent the interests of the public library community; to give guidelines regarding furnishing and equipment; to provide bibliographical services
Activities Development of public library plan to improve library education; publication of training material; promoting libraries; Future: To build a network of provincial libraries. Association has been active in promoting legislation, such as the Library Act. Offer of an online-service and of education seminars, workshops and librarian job training
Publications Official journal: Bücherei Perspektiven. 1984-. 4/yr. Address same as Association. Editor: BVÖ. German. Other publications: Österreichische Systematik für Öffentliche Büchereien. ed. F. Pascher. 1995; Bibliotheks(t)räume. ed. M. Pisarik. 1997; Öffentliche Büchereien in Österreich. ed. G. Leitner/F. Pascher. 1998

Bibliography Strassnig-Pachner, M.R., "Austria," in ALA World Encyclopedia of Library and information Services. 2nd ed., pp. 91–93. Chicago: American Library Association, 1986; Pascher, R, "Büchereien für morgen," (Public Libraries for Tomorrow) Erwachsenenbildung in Österreich 4 (1987): 1–3

121   Cultural Service Centre Austria (CSC)

Address   Klosterwiesgasse 32/I, 8010 Graz Tel.: +43 316 8112100, Fax +43 316 81121030, office@cscaustria.at; www.cscaustria.at
Languages   German
Established   1998
Major Goals and Objectives   Development of concepts, electronic provision of services and products for information technologies in archives, museums, libraries and similar institutions
Activities   Workshops, seminars; databasehosting for libraries, museums and archives; applicationhosting (eCommerce, Publishing Tools)

122   Media Archives Austria (MAA)

Address   Webgasse 2a, 1060 Wien Tel.: +43 1 5973669-53, info@medienarchive.at
Languages   German
Established   1976, as Arbeitsgemeinschaft Österreichischer Schallarchive, restructured 1987 to AGAVA. Present name adopted in 2004
Officers   Chair: Dr. Rainer Hubert; Vice Chair: Siegfried Steinlechner; Daniela Lachs; Thomas Ballhausen
Staff   2 (volunteer)
General Assembly   Entire membership meets at least every 3 years. 1987: Vienna, October 2
Membership   Total members: 40 (19 individual, 21 institutional). Requirements: Institutional: Audiovisual archive or collection; individual: Audiovisual archivist
Structure   Governed by executive officers. Affiliations: IASA (International Association of Sound Archives)
Sources of Support   Membership dues, sale of publications, government subsidies, sponsorships
Major Fields of Interest   Audiovisual archives
Major Goals and Objectives   Co-ordination of audiovisual archives in Austria; improvement of cooperation, cataloging, acquisition and distribution, conservation and restoration; training of audiovisual archivists and librarians
Activities   Past and current: Training courses for av-media archivists and librarians; widening of the scope of the former Arbeitsgemeinschaft Österreichischer Schallarchive to the entire field of audiovisual archive studies. Future: Improvement of funding for audiovisual archives by governmental authorities and private organizations; re-structuring of Austrian audiovisual archives. Association active in promoting related legislation, e.g., it took several initiatives to give audiovisual archives the same stature as libraries and museums. Sponsors continuing education programs
Publications   Official journal: Das audiovisuelle Archiv. 1988-. (formerly Das Schallarchiv. 1976–1987). 2/yr. Free to members. Address same as Association. Editor: Rainer Hubert. Address: c/o Österreichische Phonothek, Webgasse 2a, A-1060 Vienna.

Circ: 150. German, with English abstracts. Other publications: Annual reports, proceedings of meetings, and a monograph series: Holzbauer, R., Jagschitz, G., and Malina, P. Handbuch Audiovisueller Medien in Österreich (Handbook of Audiovisual Media in Austria) (1989). Publications available for sale
Bibliography Holzbaum, Jagschitz, Malina, Fachinformationsführer audiovisuelle Medien; "News in the Field of Audio-visual Archives," Unisist Newsletter 17 (1989):66–67

123 Österreichische Bibliothekenverbund und Service GmbH (Austrian Library Network)

Address Brünnlbadgasse 17/2a, 1090 Wien Tel.: +43 1 40351580, Fax +43 1 403515830, office@obvsg.at; www.obvsg.at
Languages German
Established 2002
Officers Manag Dir: Wolfgang Hamedinger
Membership 60 scientific libraries
Major Fields of Interest Automation concepts in scientific libraries, online catalogues
Activities Planing, coordinating and implementing of unified automation concepts; operative administration of the network and its online catalogues, lead-managing binding norms and standards; advising and supporting network members

124 Österreichische Gesellschaft für Dokumentation und Information (ÖGDI) (Austrian Society for Documentation and Information)*

Address Wollzeile 1–3, 1010 Vienna office@oegdi.at; www.oegdi.at
Languages German, (English)
Established 1951, as Österreichische Gesellschaft für Dokumentation und Bibliographie. Present name adopted 1971
Officers 1st Chair: Dr. Gabriele Sauberer; 2nd Chair: Dr. Bettina Schmeikal; 3rd Chair: Dr. Lorent Mikoletzky; Treas: Dr. Hermann Huemer; Prof. Dr. Christian Schlögel; Secr: Dr. Carola Wala; Dr. Herwig Jobst
Staff None
General Assembly Entire membership meets once a year. Special meetings take place irregularly
Membership Over 70 private and 8 corporate members. Requirements: Relationship with the documentation and information profession
Structure Governed by 3 executive officers. ÖGDI is a member of ASIS&T (European Chapter of the American Society for Information Science and Technology), BIS (Bibliothek Information Schweiz), DGI (Deutsche Gesellschaft für Informationswissenschaft und Informationspraxis e.V.), IFAP National Committee (Information for All Program of the Austrian UNESCO Commission), OCG (Oesterreichische Computergesellschaft), Termnet (International Network for Terminology), VWGÖ (Verband der Wissenschaftlichen Gesellschaften Österreichs).
Sources of Support Membership dues, dues from courses, and project funding
Major Fields of Interest Information and documentation science; information and communication technology; information management; knowledge management

Major Goals and Objectives Promotion of cooperation between LIS organisations; education and training of LIS personnel; national lobbying for the information professionals; establishment of an official "profile of the profession" for information professionals

Activities Annual course for information brokers. Promoting professional documentation and information in research, science, industrial projects, and particularly in innovations benefitting the Austrian economy. Enhancing and establishing contacts with foreign and international bodies with similar objectives. Association has been active in library-related legislation, such as intervening with regard to the Austrian law for personal data protection; sponsors training programs, lectures and workshops, master theses on current themes; provides forum for exchange of experiences among members; organizes bi-annual "ODOK" (in close cooperation with the Austrian Librarian Association)

Publications Proceedings of bi-annual meetings

Bibliography Hermann Huemer, Anke Weber (eds.), Vorsprung durch Informationskompetenz – Aus- und Weiterbildungsangebote für Informationsfachleute in Österreich. ÖGDI, 2007, ISBN: 978-3-9502337-0-4

125 Verband Österreichischer Archivarinnen und Archivare (VÖA) (Association of Austrian Archivists)

Address Postgasse 9, 1010 Vienna Tel.: +43 1 4000-84812 or -84821, Fax +43 1 40007238, sekretariat@voea.at; www.voea.at

Languages German

Established 1967, Linz

Staff Secretary: Heinrich Berg

General Assembly Entire membership meets once a year

Membership Types of membership: Individual, institutional. Requirements: Archivists and archives

Structure Governed by Executive Committee

Sources of Support Membership dues

Major Fields of Interest Archives; history

Major Goals and Objectives As a professional association, to promote Austrian archives and the interests of its members nationally and internationally

Activities Meetings, publication of journal

Publications Official journal: Scrinium: Zeitschrift des Verbandes Österreichischer Archivare. 1969-. 1/yr. Free to members. Address same as Association. Circ: Membership. German. Abstracted in Historical Abstracts

Bibliography Strassnig-Bachner, M.R., "Austria," in ALA World Encyclopedia of Library and information Services. 2nd ed., pp. 91–93. Chicago: American Library Association, 1986

126 Vereinigung Österreichischer Bibliothekarinnen und Bibliothekare (VÖB) (Association of Austrian Librarians)*

Address c/o Ortwin Heim, Fluherstr. 4, 6900 Bergenz Tel.: +43 5574 511 44099, Fax +43 5574 511 44095, Harald.weigel@vorarlberg.at; http://voeb.uibk.ac.at

Languages German

Established 1896, Vienna, as Österreichischer Verein für Bibliothekswesen, until 1919. Reorganized 1945 and named Vereinigung Österreichischer Bibliothekare. Present name adopted in 1993
Officers Pres: Harald Weigel; 1st VP: Maria Seissl; 2nd VP: Werner Schlacher; Secr: Ortwin Heim; Treas: Gerhard Zechner
Staff None
General Assembly Entire membership meets every 2 years
Membership Total members: over 1,000. Requirements: Open to persons who work in libraries, in documentation or information. Dues (Euro): 15 to 25, regular member; 100, sustaining member
Structure Governed by Executive Board (Präsidium). Affiliations: IFLA
Sources of Support Membership dues, sale of publications, bounties
Major Fields of Interest National and international librarianship
Major Goals and Objectives To promote librarianship in Austria; to represent the interests of Austrian librarians at home and abroad; to further advanced training of members
Activities International interlibrary loan; directives for professional education and training of librarians, documentalists, and information personnel. Publications to inform members. Cooperations with external professional associations
Publications Official journals: Mitteilungen der VÖB. 1950-. 3 to 4/yr. Free to members. Address same as Association. Circ: 1,000 (approx.). German. Other official publications: Conference proceedings, reports of seminars, workshops, and the scholarly series Biblos Schriften, e.g., Hirschegger, M., Geschichte der Universitätsbibliothek Graz 1918–1945 [History of the University Library Graz 1918–1945] (vol. 148, 1989); Oberhauser, O., Die Universitätsbibliothek der Technischen Universität Wien aus der Sicht ihrer Benutzer [The Technical University Library Vienna from the Users' Point of View] (vol. 149, 1989). Publications available for sale; price lists issued. Publications exchanged through the Austrian National Library
Bibliography Strassnig-Bachner, M.R., "Austria" in ALA World Encyclopedia of Library and Information Services. 2nd ed., pp. 91–93. Chicago: American Library Association, 1986

Azerbaijan

127 Azerbaijan Library Development Association
Address 3 H Hajiyev Street, Baku 37001 Tel.: +9 9412 300547, Fax +9 9412 470777, nazarova@uiuc.edu
Established 1999
Structure Affiliations: IFLA

Barbados

128 Library Association of Barbados (LAB)*
Address P.O. Box 827E, Bridgetown junior.browne@gmail.com

Languages English
Established 1968, Bridgetown
Officers Pres: Junior Browne; VP: Jillian Husbands; Secr: Caroline Woodroffe-Holder; Treas: Annemarie White; Asst Secr: Jessica Lewis
Staff None
General Assembly Entire membership meets at least 3 times a year
Membership Types of membership: Personal, associate, corresponding, institutional, honorary. Requirements: Individual: Open to all persons qualified in library and information science and related disciplines, and to other persons who by their services in the field of information management and dissemination in Barbados, are considered eligible by the Exec.Comm.; Associate: All other persons interested in the information profession; Corresponding: Persons living outside Barbados who otherwise meet the requirements for membership; Institutional: Libraries, other institutions or associations which may nominate a delegate as representative; Honorary: Persons who have rendered outstanding service to the information profession and are recommended by the Exec.Comm
Structure Governed by Executive Council. Affiliations: IFLA, ACURIL, COMLA
Sources of Support Membership dues
Major Fields of Interest Library and information science
Major Goals and Objectives (1) To unite qualified librarians, archivists and information specialists, and all other persons engaged or interested in information management and dissemination in Barbados, and to provide opportunities for their meeting together; (2) to promote the active development and maintenance of libraries and related institutions throughout Barbados, and to initiate and foster cooperation between these institutions; (3) to promote high standards of education and training for staffs of information services and to take such steps as are requisite to improve their status; (4) to consider any matter affecting information units, and to assist in the promotion of activities which would enhance their management, regulation and extension; (5) to promote a wide knowledge of information work
Activities Past achievements: Has been actively involved in educational programs; sponsored seminars and workshops in areas of major interest to libraries: 1986, Introduction to Library Automation; 1982, co-sponsored Seminar on Audio-visual Materials in Libraries; Association has also been involved in getting the Barbados Community College to offer a course for library assistants (technical staff) and assist in its coordination; Association co-sponsored with the Organization of American States (OAS) and the Department of Library Studies a regional workshop on the computer program CDS-ISIS (minimicro version) developed by Unesco for information storage and retrieval; sponsored Public Relations Seminar, and hosted a number of regional meetings. Current: Initiated regional quiz conducted over the University of the West Indies Distance Teaching Experiment (UWIDITE), a teleconferencing system linking Jamaica, Trinidad & Tobago, Barbados, Antigua, Dominica, Grenada and St. Lucia, which brings together young people of the Caribbean through the libraries; continuing fund raising efforts. Initiated relief efforts to donate children's books to Jamaican libraries devastated by Hurricane Gilbert in September 1988. Future: Improvement of professional image and status; provision of training opportunities at all levels; establishment of additional professional posts; realization and acceptance of the broadening role of the professional librarian. Sponsors

Book Week and continuing education programs
Publications Official journal: Bulletin of the Library Association of Barbados. 1968–1985. Irreg. Free to members. Address same as Association. Circ: 100. English; temporarily discontinued. Update: Occasional Newsletter of the Library Association of Barbados. There are plans for an Occasional Papers series
Bibliography Blackman, J., "Barbados," in ALA World Encyclopedia of Library and Information Services. 2nd ed., pp. 100–101. Chicago: American Library Association, 1986; Campbell, E.F., "Library Association of Barbados – 20 Years On," COMLA Newsletter 64 (1989):9 (gives an excellent overview of the Association by the current President)

Belarus

129 Belarusian Library Association
Address c/o MINSK Oblast Library, Igor Zaitsev, Gikalo str. 4, 220071 Minsk Tel.: +375 17 2095247, Fax +375 17 2095037; www.bla.by

Belgium

130 Archives et Bibliothèques de Belgique / Archief- en Bibliotheekwezen in België (ASBL/VZW)
(Belgian Association of Archives and Libraries)*
Address c/o Wouter Bracke, 4 boulevard de l'Empereur, 1000 Brussels Tel.: +32 2 5195743, Fax +32 2 5195735, wouter.bracke@kbr.be
Languages French, Dutch, English, German, Spanish, Italian
Established 1907, Brussels
Officers Pres: Frank Daelemans; Gen Secr: Wouter Bracke; Edi-in-chief: Marc Libert; Treas: André Vanrie
Staff 5 (voluntary)
General Assembly The executive board and the general assembly meet twice a year in Brussels (Royal Library of Belgium).
Membership Total members/subscribers: 500 (individual). Sections: 2 (librarians, archivists). Types of membership: Individual only. Requirements: Professional librarians and archivists. Dues (EUR): max. 250
Structure Governed by executive officers. Affiliations: IFLA, ICA
Sources of Support Membership dues, government subsidies, donations
Major Fields of Interest Libraries and archives
Major Goals and Objectives To promote study and research relating to archives, librarianship, and related disciplines, and to contribute publications in these areas
Publications Official journal: Archives et Bibliothèques de Belgique/Archief- en Bibliotheekwezen in België. 1923-. 2/yr. 450 (Belgian Franc). Address same as Association. EUR 30. French, Dutch. Publishes various specialized publications. Publishes also a series

Bibliography Vanderpijpen, W., "Belgium," in ALA World Encyclopedia of Library and Information Services. 2nd ed., pp. 103–105. Chicago: American Library Association, 1986

131 Association Belge de Documentation / Belgische Vereniging voor Documentatie (ABD/BVD) (Belgian Association for Documentation)*

Address Chaussée de Wavre 1683, 1160 Brussels Tel.: +32 2 6755862, Fax +32 2 6727446, info@abd-bvd.be; www.abd-bvd.be
Languages French, Dutch
Established 1947, Brussels
Officers Pres: Vincent Maes; VP: Marc Van den Berg; Secr: Christopher Boon; Treas: Didier Haas
Staff 19 volunteers
General Assembly yearly
Membership more than 600 professionals from both private and public sectors
Sources of Support Membership fees
Major Fields of Interest Information & Documentation
Major Goals and Objectives Studying and promoting information professions; informing its members on information management methods and techniques; creating networks of competence and experience exchange; training and professional improvement of its members; defending its members' interests on a federal, European and international level
Activities Organizing monthly meetings and an annual forum devoted to current topics in the field of information; editing several publications
Publications Official journal: Cahiers de la Documentation/Bladen voor Documentatie. 1949-. 4/y. Editor: Simone Jerome. Address same as Association. French, Dutch, English. Other official publications: ABD-BVD INFO, 10/y., reserved to members; Recueil de Stages Etudiants; Dossiers ABD-BVD: books collection (up to now: 4 issues)
Bibliography Vanderpijpen, W., "Belgium," in ALA World Encyclopedia of Library and Information Services. 2nd ed., pp. 103–105. Chicago: American Library Association, 1986

132 Association des Bibliothécaires Belges d'Expression Française (ASBL) (Belgian Association of French-Speaking Librarians)*

Address c/o Michel-C. Dagneau, rue Emile Vandevandel 39, 1470 Genappe Tel.: +32 67771477, Fax +32 67771477, abbef.be@gate71.be
Languages French
Established 1964, Namur. Earlier name: Association Nationale des Bibliothécaires d'Expression Française (ANBEF)
Staff 4 (volunteer)
General Assembly Entire membership meets once a year
Membership Total members: 1,900 (450 individual, 1,450 institutional). Requirements: Open to librarians, particularly those in public libraries. Dues (Belgian Franc): 75, individual; no dues, institutional
Structure Governed by executive officers. Affiliations: IFLA
Sources of Support Membership dues, sale of publications, government subsidies
Major Fields of Interest The status of librarians and public libraries

Major Goals and Objectives To assist members in professional development and professional status
Activities Past achievements: Effective in obtaining higher salaries for librarians; involved in a new law concerning public reading. Sponsors continuing education programs, lectures, seminars, workshops, to improve library services
Publications Official journal: Le Bibliothécaire: Revue d'Information Culturelle et Bibliographique. 1950-. 12/yr. 300 (Belgian Franc). Editorial Board. Address same as Association. French. Circ: 2,200. Indexed in Library Literature. LISA. ISA. Issues annual reports, conference proceedings, and other publications
Bibliography Vanderpijpen, W., "Belgium," in ALA World Encyclopedia of Library and Information Services. 2nd ed., pp. 103–105. Chicago: American Library Association, 1986

133 Association Professionnelle des Bibliothécaires et Documentalistes (APBD) (Professional Association of Librarians and Documentalists)*

Address Place de la Wallonie, 15, 6140 Fontaine-L'Eveque Tel.: +32 71 523193, Fax +32 71 522307, secretariat@apbd.be; www.apbd.be
Languages French
Established 1975, Namur
Officers Pres: Laurence Boulanger; VP: Marianne Bragard; Emmanuelle Plumat; Secr: Fabienne Gerard; Treas: Guy Tondreau
General Assembly Entire membership meets once a year, in February or March
Membership Ca. 300 members
Structure Governed by the President and executive officers. Affiliations: EBLIDA
Sources of Support Membership dues, government subsidies (ca. E4,000), subscriptions to our activities (conferences, seminars, etc.)
Major Fields of Interest All types of libraries, documentation centers
Major Goals and Objectives To unite professional librarians and documentalists of public, scientific, special, school, and research libraries; to promote the work of documentalists and librarians; to encourage professional development; to participate in scientific research; to create a general policy of the book and documentation (electronic documents included)
Activities Past achievements: Publication of works related to cataloging standards, author and title entries. Current and future: Continue publication of journal; organization of seminars and conferences. Association has been active in promoting library-related legislation, making proposals to the Culture minister and being present in various councils and committees. Sponsors continuing education programs
Publications Official journal: BLOC-Notes. 1978-. 4/yr. Membership only. Address: 35, rue Puits-en-Sock, B-4020 Liege. French. Selection of youth books and of science and information books for public and school libraries
Bibliography Vanderpijpen, W., "Belgium," in ALA World Encyclopedia of Library and Information Services. 2nd ed., pp. 103–105. Chicago: American Library Association, 1986

134 Vereniging van Religieus-Wetenschappelijke Bibliothecarissen (V.R.B) (Association of Theological Librarians)

Address Minderbroederstraat 5, 3800 Sint-Truiden www.theo.kuleuven.ac.be/vrb
Languages Dutch, French

Established 1965
General Assembly Entire membership meets twice a year
Membership Total members: 65 (individual and institutional). Requirements: Theological libraries and individuals interested in the aims of the Association
Structure Governed by Executive Council. Affiliations: Conseil International des Associations de Bibliothèques de Théologie (International Council of Theological Library Associations)
Sources of Support Membership dues
Major Fields of Interest Theological libraries and librarians
Major Goals and Objectives Establishment, development and promotion of librarianship and documentation services in the field of scientific-religious knowledge; improvement of the status and working conditions of personnel; discussion of problems concerning theological libraries
Activities Publication of reference sources; sponsoring of meetings
Publications Official journal: 'V.R.B.-Informatie. Free to members. Address same as Association. Dutch. Other publications for sale: Ooms, H. and Braive, G., Gids voor de kerkelijke wetenschappelijke bibliotheken in België (Guide to Theological Libraries in Belgium); Gide voor theologische bibliotheken in Nederland en Vlaanderen (Guide to Theological Libraries in the Netherlands and Flemish Belgium)
Bibliography Vanderpijpen, W., "Belgium," in ALA World Encyclopedia of Library and Information Services. 2nd ed., pp. 103–105. Chicago: American Library Association, 1986

135 Vlaamse Vereniging voor Bibliotheek-, Archief- en Documentatiewezen (VVBAD)
(Flemish Association of Librarians, Archivists and Documentalists)*

Address c/o Bruno Vermeeren, Statiestraat 179, 2600 Berchem Antwerp Tel.: +32 3 2814457, vvbad@vvbad.be; www.vvbad.be
Languages Dutch (with English abstracts in publications)
Established 1921, Gent, as Vlaamse Vereniging van Bibliotheek- en Archiefpersoneel (VVBAP). 1974, new statutes, and name changed to Vlaamse Vereniging van Bibliotheek-, Archief- en Documentatiepersoneel (VVBADP)
Officers Pres: Johan Vannieuwenhuyse; VP: Patrick Vanouplines; Secr: Myriam Lemmens; Treas: Simone De Landtsheer
Staff 4,5 paid
General Assembly Two General Assemblies each year
Membership Requirements: Working, studying or looking for employment in library, archive or documentation/information center. 4 sections, 2 commissions, ca. 12 workgroups
Structure Affiliations: ICA, IFLA, EBLIDA
Sources of Support Membership dues, publications and activities, subsidy from Flemish Min. of Culture
Major Fields of Interest Libraries, archives and information services
Major Goals and Objectives Advocacy, cross sectoral co-operation, profession and professional education, dissemination of information for and about the information sector
Activities Bi-annual conference 'Informatie', organized in September in uneven years; Bi-annual symposium 'Focus op ...', organized in September in even years. About 15

symposia or workshops every year. Bi-annual international study trip in even years. Involved in work on library and archival legislation
Publications   Official journal: Bibliotheek- en Archiefgids. 1983-. (formerly Bibliotheekgids. 1922–83). 6/yr. Circ: 1,200. Dutch, with English abstracts. Indexed in LISA, lib.Lit., ISA, Bull.Signal., etc. Other publications: Annual reports, series 'Archiefkunde' (monographies about archival issues), INFO. 12/yr. (formerly Bibinfo). a newsletter for members
Bibliography   Vanderpijpen, W, "Belgium," in ALA World Encyclopedia of Library and Information Services. 2nd ed., pp. 103–105. Chicago: American Library Association, 1986. F. Heymans (ed.): "Nu van hooger hand... 75 joar VVBAD". Antwerpen 1996

Benin

136   Association des Amis de la Lecture (ASSOCLE)
Address   BP 08-0353, Cotonou   ddeguenon@hotmail.com
Languages   French
Officers   Pres: Denis Togbé Deguenon

Bosnia and Herzegovina

137   Association of Information Professionals – Librarians, Archivists and Museologists
Address   c/o Biserka Sabljakovic, Trg oslobodenja - Alija Izetbegovic 1, 71000 Sarajevo   bam@bam.ba
Officers   Pres: Amra Residbegovic

138   Drustvo Bibliotekara Bosne i Hercegovine (DB BiH) (Association of Librarians of Bosnia and Hercegovina)
Address   c/o Amela Lalic, Zmaja od Bosne 8b, 71000 Sarajewo   Tel.: +387 33 275339, Fax +387 33 212435
Established   1949, Sarajevo
General Assembly   Entire membership meets irregularly, as necessary
Membership   Types of membership: Individual, honorary. Requirements: Open to any person working in a library or retired from the library profession
Structure   Governed by executive officers
Sources of Support   Membership dues, sale of publications, government subsidies
Major Fields of Interest   Library service, professional education of library workers
Major Goals and Objectives   To improve library and information services in Bosnia and Hercegovina; to establish a network of libraries and information services; to promote the professional education and development of members; to contribute to the cultural development of Bosnia and Hercegovina
Activities   Sponsors conferences, seminars, and other continuing education programs, to raise professional standards and improve library services in accordance with the goals and objectives of the Association

Publications Official journal: Bilten Drustva Bibliotekara Bosne i Hercegovine (Bulletin of the Association of Librarians of Bosnia and Hercegovina); Bibliotekarstvo Godisnjak Drustva Bibliotekara Bosne i Hercegovine (Library Science Annual of the Association of Librarians of Bosnia and Hercegovina). Both publications free to members. Address same as Association
Bibliography Kort, R.L., "Yugoslavia," in ALA World Encyclopedia of Library and Information Services. 2nd ed., pp. 864–865. Chicago: American Library Association, 1986

Botswana

139   Botswana Library Association (BLA)

Address c/o Stella Naledi Madzigigwa, PO Box 1310, Gaborone Tel.: +267 3552627, Fax +267 3158098, moahikh@mopipi.ub.bw; www.bla.0catch.com
Languages English
Established 1978
Officers Pres: Madzigigwa Radijeng
Staff None
General Assembly Entire membership meets annually
Membership Individual and institutional members. Requirements: Interest in aims of Association
Structure Governed by Executive Committee, Affiliations: COMLA, IFLA
Sources of Support Membership dues, sale of publications
Major Fields of Interest Library and information science
Major Goals and Objectives To unite persons interested in libraries; to promote development of libraries; to promote bibliographic research, studies in librarianship by means of articles, news briefs and reports on all aspects of library and information sciences, with emphasis on Southern Africa
Activities Past achievements: (1) Increase in membership from about 10 in 1978 to 50 in 1988; (2) regular publication of the BLA Journal; (3) Organizing SCECSAL VII (Standing Conference of Eastern, Central and Southern African Librarians) Conference in August, 1986 in Gaborone, attended by all library associations in the region. Current: Implementation of SCECSAL VII Conference resolutions, i. e. propagation with a view to the establishment of library and information centers in rural areas. Future: Organization of: (1) refresher courses and in-service training for library staff at various levels; (2) intensive courses for school teachers interested in becoming tutor-librarians. Association has been active in promoting library-related legislation, such as pursuing tightening up of legal deposit legislation. Sponsors Book Week, continuing education programs
Publications Official journal: Botswana Library Association Journal. 1979-. 2/yr. Free to members. Address same as Association. Circ: 200. English. Indexed in LISA. Other publications: Annual reports; reports of seminars, workshops
Bibliography African Book Publishing Record 10 (1984):31–32; Raseroka, K., "Botswana," in ALA World Encyclopedia of Library and Information Services. 2nd ed., pp. 132–133. Chicago: American Library Association, 1986

Brazil

140 Associaçao Brasileira de Educação em Ciência da Informação (ABECIN)
Address Av. Reitor Miguel Calmon S/N, 40.110-100 Salvador Tel.: + 55 71 3283-7746, mnassif@eci.ufmg.br; www.abecin.org.br
Languages Portuguese
Established 1967, Belo Horizonte, at the 5th Brazilian Library and Documentation Congress, as Brazilian counterpart to ALISE (formerly AALS), since 2001 ABECIN
Officers Pres: Lídia Maria Brandão Toutain; VP: Maria do Rosário de Fátima Portela Cysne; 1st Secr: Mōnica Erichsen Nassif; 2nd Secr: Marcos Luiz Cavalcanti de Miranda
General Assembly Entire membership meets annually
Membership Types and requirements: (1) Institutional: Library science and documentation schools represented by the head of each school and an elected delegate from each faculty; (2) individual: Faculty members of the Brazilian library science and documentation schools; (3) honorary: Individuals who have actively demonstrated their interest in the cause and development of librarianship; (4) cooperating: Individuals or organizations who demonstrate an interest in the training for and development of librarianship and make annual contributions to the Association
Structure Governed by Executive Board
Sources of Support Membership dues, subsidies
Major Fields of Interest Education for library and information science
Major Goals and Objectives "To provide an opportunity for the faculties of the Brazilian library science and documentation schools to meet for the discussion and resolution of common problems; to provide an opportunity for the development and improvement of education for librarianship in general through such measures and plans as may make possible the improvement of the faculties." (Chapter II, article 2 of Statutes)
Activities Sponsors conferences, seminars, and regional meetings of library educators; seeks to improve information service for library education and to promote attendance at library schools; aims at stronger cooperation at the international level
Bibliography Fonseca, Edson Nery da, "Brazil," in ALA World Encyclopedia of Library and Information Services. 2nd ed., pp. 137–139. Chicago: American Library Association, 1986

**141 Associaçao dos Arquivistas Brasileiros
(Association of Brazilian Archivists)**
Address Av. Presidente Vargas, 1733- Sala 903, 20.210-030 Centro Rio de Janeiro Tel.: +21 25072239, Fax +21 38522541, aab@aab.org.br; www.aab.org.br
Languages Portuguese
Established 1971
Officers Pres: Lucia Maria Velloso de Oliveira; Treas: Maria Celina Soares de Mello e Silva
Staff None
General Assembly Entire membership meets every two years
Membership Total members: 200 (individual and institutional)
Structure Governed by executive officers. Affiliations: ICA
Sources of Support Membership dues, sale of publications

Major Fields of Interest Archives
Major Goals and Objectives To promote the work of archives and the archival profession
Activities Sponsors continuing education lectures, seminars, workshops on current topics, such as new techniques in archival management; encourages cooperation between archivists and exchange of information
Publications Official Journals: Boletim 4/yr 1990-; Arquivo e administraçao. 1972-, 2/yr. Free to members. Address same as Association. Portuguese. Other publications: Annual reports, proceedings of conferences. Publications available for sale

142   Conselho Federal de Biblioteconomia (CFB) (Federal Council of Librarianship)

Address SRTVN Ed. Brasília Rádio Center. Salas 1079/2079, Brasília DF - CEP: 70.719-900 Tel.: +61 3282896, Fax +61 3282894, cfb@cfb.org.br; www.cfb.org.br
Languages Portuguese
Established 1962, Sao Paulo, by Laura García Moreno Russo, first president
Officers Pres: Nêmora Arlindo Rodrigues; VP: Regina Céli de Sousa; 1st Secr: Georgete Lopes Freitas; 2nd Secr: Celia Regina Simonetti Barbalho; Treas: Maria Elizabeth Baltar Carneiro de Albuquerque
Staff 6 (2 paid)
General Assembly Entire membership meets every two years
Membership Total members: 5,000+ (individual). Types of membership: Individual. Requirements: Open to all librarians
Structure Governed by Executive Council and officers. The Association comprises librarians from 10 different areas (estados)
Sources of Support Membership dues, sale of publications
Major Fields of Interest Economic status of the library profession
Major Goals and Objectives To promote the status of librarians and libraries in Brazil
Activities Sponsors courses, seminars, conferences, celebration of Book Week
Publications No publications program

143   Federaçao Brasileira de Associaçoes de Bibliotecários (FEBAB) (Brazilian Federation of Library Associations)

Address Rua Avanhandava 40 - conj. 110, 01306 Sao Paulo SP Tel.: +55 11 2579979, Fax +55 11 2830747, febab@febab.org.br; www.febab.org.br
Languages Portuguese
Established 1959, during the Second Brazilian Congress of Librarianship and Documentation, by Laura García Moreno Russo and Rodolpho Rocha, Jr
Staff 100 (paid)
General Assembly Entire membership meets every two years
Membership Total members: 24 associations. Commissions: 8 (University Libraries, Public and School Libraries, Agricultural Documentation, Biomedical Documentation, Social Sciences and the Humanities, Legal Documentation, Technological Documentation, and Technical Processes; each with their own organizational structure)
Structure Governed by Executive Committee and representatives of 8 specialized committees. Affiliations: IFLA

Sources of Support Membership dues, sale of publications, government and private subsidies
Major Fields of Interest Librarianship and documentation
Major Goals and Objectives To unite the library associations of the country; to promote the interests of professional librarians; to assist in the solution of problems in libraries and documentation centers; to assist the member associations in the Federation
Activities Activities center on improving state library associations, observing Book Week, sponsoring exhibits, conferences, and other continuing education programs. Sponsors the national specialized meetings of the eight standing committees of the Federation. Active in promoting library-related legislation
Publications Official journal: Revista Brasileira de Biblioteconomía e Documentaçao (Brazilian Review of Librarianship and Documentation). 1973-. 2/yr. (US Dollar) 30. Free to members. Editor: Francisco José de Castro Ferreira. Address same as Association. Circ: 1,000+. Portuguese, with English abstracts. Indexed in LISA, ISA, Lib.Lit., Other publications: Codigo de Catalogaçao Anglo-Americano (Anglo-American Cataloging Rules); proceedings of conferences, seminars, annual reports, etc. Publications available for sale
Bibliography McCarthy, C.M., "Achievements and Objectives in Brazilian Librarianship," International Library Review 15 (1983):131–145; Fonseca, Edson Nery da, "Brazil," in ALA World Encyclopedia of Library and Information Services. 2nd ed., pp. 137–139. Chicago: American Library Association, 1986

144 Federação Brasileira de Associações de Bibliotecários, Cientistas da Informação e Instituições (FEBAB)
(Brazilian Federation of Library Associations)
Address c/o Rua Avanhandava, 40 Conj. 108/110, CEP 01306-000 São Paulo - SP Tel.: +55 11 3257-9979, Fax +55 11 3257-9979, febab@febab.org.br; www.febab.org.br
Languages Portuguese
Established FEBAB was founded in 26th July 1959, from a proposal presented by the librarians Laura Russo and Rodolfo Rocha Junior, at the 2nd Brazilian Librarianship and Documentation Meeting (CBBD)
Officers Pres: Sigrid Karin Weiss Dutra; VP: Regina Célia Belluzo
Staff 1 paid, 10 volunteers
General Assembly Entire membership meets once a year. Meetings held during annual conferences of FEBAB and other organizations
Membership Profession Librarians Associations, Institutional, honorary
Structure Governed by executive officers. Affiliations: FEBAB
Sources of Support Membership dues, sale of publications, private gifts
Major Fields of Interest Information systems, Libraries, Knowledge management, Associations, Information Technologies, Information Society
Major Goals and Objectives To represent the interests of library profession. To assemble library entities as members and affiliated institutions. To encourage professional development. To promote libraries and their professionals. To support affiliate institutions' activities. To act as a documentation and memory center. To interact with national and international institutions. To develop and to support projects in the area. To contribute for the creation and development of committees and area groups activities

Activities Publication program. Sponsors conferences, workshops, and continuing education programs
Publications Official journal: Annual reports, proceedings of annual meetings, seminars, workshops, etc. Publications available for sale

145 Federaçao Brasileira de Associaçoes de Bibliotecários – Comissao Brasileira de Bibliotecas Centrais Universitárias (FEBAB/CBBCU)
(Brazilian Commission of University Libraries)
Address c/o Elaine Baptista de Matos Paula, Secretary, Campus Universitário, Lagoa Nova s/n, CP 1524, 59072-970 Natal Tel.: +55 21 2295-1595, Fax +55 21 2295-1397, elainebpt@sibi.ufrj.br; www.cbbu.org
Languages Portuguese
Established 1987
Officers Pres: Paul Maria Abrantes; VP: Marcia Valeria da Silva Brita Costa; Dir Planning/Marketing: Eneida de Oliveira; Financial Dir: Rosane da Silva Wendling Apparicio; Secr: Elaine Baptista de Matos Paula
Structure Governed by executive officers. Affiliations: FEBAB
Major Fields of Interest University libraries
Major Goals and Objectives To promote the development of university libraries in Brazil
Publications No official journal. Other Publications: Base de Dados de Bibliotecas de Instituições Brasileiras de Ensino Superior – BIBES. Guia de Bibliotecas de Instituições Brasileiras de Ensino Superior – 1º ed. 1994. Guia de Bibliotecas de Instituições de Ensino Superior – Guia BIBES – 2ª ed. revista e ampliada – 1998. Guia de Endereços Eletrônicos das Bibliotecas das IES 1ª ed. – 1998

146 Sistema Integrado de Bibliotecas da Universidade de São Paulo (USP/SIBi)
(University of São Paulo Integrated Library System)
Address Av. Prof. Luciano Gualberto, trav. J, 374 - 1 andar, 05508-900 Sao Paulo - SP Tel.: +55 11 3031-7448, Fax +55 11 3815-2142, dtsibi@org.usp.br; www.usp.br/sibi
Languages Portuguese
Established 1981, in São Paulo
Staff 757
Structure Composed of 39 libraries in São Paulo State; Technical Department and Supervisory Council
Major Fields of Interest Biological Sciene; Humanities; Technology and Exact Science
Major Goals and Objectives To create conditions for providing library services as a System, in order to support educational and research programs with appropriate access to information sources
Activities The USP/SIBi libraries develop their activities trough resource sharing, cooperative work and rational procedures and services
Publications Official journal: Boletim Annual do Departamento do SIBi/USP (annual); Dados Estatísticos do Sistema Integrado de Bibliotecas da USP (annual); Bibliotheca Universitatis-Acervo Bibliográfico da Universidade de São Paulo – Séc. XVII 2003; Cadernos de Estudos 9, 2003
Comment DEDALUS-USP OPAC available on web site

147 Sociedade da Informação
(Information Society in Brazil)
Address SAS, quadra 5, lote 6, bloco H, 8º andar, Brasilia DF – 70070-912 Tel.: +55 61 3211670, Fax +55 61 3211798; www.insoc.com.br
Languages Portuguese
Major Goals and Objectives To promote and coordinate information professionals

Brunei

148 Persatuan Perpustakaan Kebangsaan
(National Library Association of Brunei)
Address c/o Puan Nellie Dato Paduka Haji Sunny, Pres, Jalan Tungku Link, Gadong BE1410 Tel.: +673 2 249001, Fax +673 2 249504, chieflib@lib.ubd.edu.bn; www.ppknbd.org.bn/org/ppknbd
Languages Malay
Established 1986
Officers Pres: Puan Nellie Dato Paduka Haji Sunny; VP: Pg Haji Mohd Shahminan bin Pg Haji Sulaiman; Hon Secr: Haji Suhaimi bin Haji Abd. Karim; Hon Treas: Abu Hasrah bin Haji Kamis
Staff None
General Assembly Entire membership meets once a year
Membership Total members:160 (personal and institutional)
Structure Governed by Executive Council
Sources of Support Annual membership fees, donations and fund raising activities
Major Fields of Interest Libraries and library services
Major Goals and Objectives To promote the development of library services in Brunei Darussalam; to promote the education and training of professional staff
Activities Seminars
Publications Official newsletter: Wadah Pustaka. 1994
Bibliography "Brunei," COMLA Newsletter (Dec. 1987): 15; "Professional Education in Brunei Darussalam," Focus 20 (1989):28–29

Bulgaria

149 Bulgarian Library and Information Association (BLIA)*
Address c/o Snejana Ianeva, 4 Slavejkov Sqr., Sofia 1000 Tel.: +35 92 9870734, Fax +35 92 9870734, lib@fastbg.net; www.lib.bg
Languages Bulgarian, English
Established 1990, Sofia
Officers Pres: Vanja Grashkina; Secr: Krasimira Papazova
Staff 5 (paid)
General Assembly Annual meeting, 28th April 2010, Nat Conference 9–11 June
Membership 1093 individual members (12 lv. per year), 82 institutional members (40/80 lv. per year), 16 regional divisions, 5 sections

Structure Governed by Executive Board, Regional Divisions, Sections

Sources of Support Sponsors, memebership fees

Major Fields of Interest Library and Information Science from all types of Libraries

Major Goals and Objectives To participate in the development of a national library policy; to enhance the social status of library and information

Activities Projects, conferences, Events, Trainings

Publications Guidelines for development of public libraries (in Bulgarian), 2009. A handbook for library managers. Authors: Vanya Grashkina-Mincheva, Aneta Doncheva, Aleksandar Dimchev. University Publishing House "St. Kl. Ohridski", Sofia. ISBN: 978-954-07-2856-8; British Council – Bulgaria. ISBN: 978-954-92360-2-6; BLIA. ISBN: 978-954-9837-16-2 (The book is part of the project Management of public libraries financed by the British Council – Bulgaria); With modern libraries proud members of the European Union (in Bulgarian), 2008. Proceedings from the Sixteenth National Conference of BLIA – Sofia. ISBN 978-954-9837-15-5; The Library as a Community Information Center (in Bulgarian), 2006. A handbook for planning and building. Authors: Nancy Bolt, Bonnie McCune, James LaRue, Iskra Mihailova. 2-nd revised edition. ISBN-10: 954-9837-14-9 (The book is published by the ABLE Project, supported by the USA Department of State); Libraries and the Changes in Contemporary Bulgarian Legislation (in Bulgarian), 2004. Proceedings from the Fourteenth National Conference of ULISO – Varna, ISBN 954-9837-12-2; Library Collaboration – Present and Future. Ideas and Perspectives for Researches in the Field of Written Communications (in Bulgarian), 2003. Proceedings from the Thirteenth National Conference of ULISO – Sofia, ISBN 954-9837-10-6; Social Responsibility of Public Libraries and Their Role in Democratic Society (in Bulgarian), 2003. Proceedings from National Conference of ULISO – 2002, Evksinograd; ULISO in the Beginning of 21 Century (in Bulgarian), 2002. Proceedings from the Eleventh National Conference of ULISO – 2001, Sofia. ISBN 954-9837-06-08; Professional Ethics – Professional Perspectives (in Bulgarian), 2002. Proceedings from the Twelfth National Conference of ULISO – Sofia, ISBN 954-9837-07-6; Library System in Bulgaria (in Bulgarian), 2001. Proceedings from the Tenth National Conference of ULISO – 2000, Sofia. ISBN 954-9837-05-?; Libraries in New Millennium – Free and Equal Access to Information (in Bulgarian), 1999. Proceedings from the Ninth National Conference of ULISO with International Participation – Sofia. ISBN 954-9837-04-1; Librarianship in foreign countries: A Statute Book (in Bulgarian), 1998. ISBN 954-9837-02-5; Librarianship in Bulgaria: 1878–1998: A Statute Book (in Bulgarian), 1998. ISBN 954-9837-01-7; Library Legislation (in Bulgarian), 1998. Proceedings from the Eighth National Conference of ULISO – Sofia; Public Libraries and the challenge of the changes (in Bulgarian), 1998. Proceedings from the National Conference of ULISO – 1997, Blagoevgrad; Information Policy in Bulgaria – Formation and Current Development (in Bulgarian), 1997. Proceedings from the Seventh National Conference of ULISO; National Program for the Preservation of Library Collections (in English and Bulgarian), 1997. Published by ULISO and the Open Society Foundation – Sofia; Librarianship in Bulgaria (in English), 1997. Published by ULISO and Open Society Fund – Sofia; Library Collections – Current Status, Preservation and Development (in Bulgarian), 1996. Proceedings from the Sixth National Conference of ULISO – Sofia; The Chitalishte Library – Tradition and Future (in Bulgarian), 1996. Proceedings from a Jubilee Conference; Libraries and the Future (in Bulgarian), 1995.

Proceedings from the Fifth National Conference; Library – Information Services (in Bulgarian), 1994. Proceedings from the Fourth National Conference of ULISO

Burkina Faso

150   Association Burkinabé des Gestionnaires de l'Information Documentaire (ABGID)*
Address   11 BP, 1901 CMS Ouagadougou, 11   Tel.: + 226 70179720, aabgid@yahoo.fr
Languages   French
Established   Sept 7th 2004
Officers   Pres: Zoungo Ibrahim; Secr Gen: Kone Dilomama
Staff   7 volunteer
General Assembly   All 3 years, next meering: December 2010
Membership   200 members individual
Structure   Affiliations wirh: CIA, IFLA, BIBLIOTHEQUE SANS FRONTIERE, AIFDB
Sources of Support   Membership dues
Major Fields of Interest   Archives, Documentation. Library
Major Goals and Objectives   To promote the job of information science (archives, library, documentation)
Activities   Studies journey, promote activities, studies, meetings, seminars
Publications   ABGID-INFO

151   Association internationale francophone des bibliothécaires documentalistes (AIFBD)
Address   jhellema@ulb.ac.be
Languages   French
Officers   Treas: Jacques Hellemans

152   Panafrican Institute for Development
Address   01 BP, 1756 Ouagadougou
Officers   Manager: Diop Amadou

Cambodia

153   Association des Bibliothécaires et Documentalistes Cambodgiens (ABDC) (Cambodian Librarians and Documentalists Association (CLDA))
Address   c/o Bibliothèque Nationale, Thonevath Pou, 92 Christophe Howes Street 92, Daun Penh District, Phnom Penh   Tel.: +855 23 430609, Fax +855 23 430609, khlot.vibolla@bnc-nlc.info
Established   1996
Officers   Pres: Vibolla Khlot
Staff   5 volunteers+1 consultant Librarian
General Assembly   Meets every three years
Membership   140 personal members

Structure NGO
Sources of Support Membership fees: 5.000 Riel (=US$1,20) per year
Major Fields of Interest Training for librarians; publication of manual or handbook for librarians in Khmer (e.g. Library terminology); library cooperation, first international; cataloguing on-line
Major Goals and Objectives To improve the quality of librarianship and documentation in Cambodia; to defend the interest of libraries and documentation centres
Activities Training, basic and advanced; working group on cataloguing
Publications Official journal: Bulletin d' information de l'ABDC/CLDA Newsletter

Cameroon

154 Association des Bibliothécaires, Archivistes, Documentalistes et Muséographes du Cameroun (ABADCAM)
(Cameroon Association of Librarians, Archivists, Documentalists, and Museum Curators)*

Address B.P. 4609, Yaoundé Nlongkak Tel.: +237 99998608, 22060206, abadcama&gmail.com
Languages French, English
Established 1974
Officers Pres: Jerome Ndjock; VP: Rosemary Tchafack
Staff None
General Assembly Entire membership meets irregularly
Membership Total members: 40+
Structure Governed by executive officers
Sources of Support Membership dues, subsidies
Major Fields of Interest Libraries, archives, documentation centers, and museums
Major Goals and Objectives To encourage the establishment of libraries at all levels and in all parts of the country; to promote the training of personnel for libraries, archives, museums, and documentation centers
Activities Organizes conferences, general assemblies, seminars and workshops on various areas of librarianship, archival sciences, information sciences and museography
Publications Publishes Newsletter
Bibliography Chateh, Peter Nkangafack, "Cameroon," in ALA World Encyclopedia of Library and Information Services. 2nd ed., pp. 153–155. Chicago: American Library Association, 1986

Canada

155 Association for Media and Technology in Education in Canada (AMTEC)

Address 3-1750 The Queensway, Suite 1318, Etobicoke, ON M9C 5H5 Tel.: +1 902 457-6165, Fax +1 902 457-2618, Paul.Poirier@msvu.ca; www.amtec.ca/index2.html
Languages English

General Assembly Annual conference in late spring/early summer. 2004: Sudbury, Ontario
Membership Individual and institutional membership
Structure Governed by Board of Directors
Major Fields of Interest Media and Technology in Education
Major Goals and Objectives Works to facilitate and improve learning, in all sectors of education, through the appropriate application and integration of educational technology; committed to researching, developing, nurturing, supporting, evaluating and deploying educational technologies; promotes the professional development of educators in educational technology
Activities Conferences, AMTEC Listserv, awards
Publications Official journal: Canadian Journal of Learning and Technology (formerly: Canadian Journal of Educational Communication) 3/yr. Address: www.cjlt.ca/. Editor: Richrad F. Kenny. email: rick.kenny@ubc.ca

156 Association of Canadian Archivists (ACA)*

Address PO Box 2596, Station D, Ottawa ON KIP SW6 Tel.: +1 613 2346977, Fax +1 613 2348500, aca@archivists.ca; www.archivists.ca
Languages English, French
Established 1975
Officers Pres: Paul Banfield; Secr/Treas: Michele Dale
Staff 2
General Assembly Annual, May 17, 2009 in Calgary, AB; June 12, 2010 in Halifax, NS; June 4, 2011 in Toronto, ON
Membership 615 in 2009. Categories include Individual, Institutional, Student, Associate and Retired. Membership is for the calendar year, Jan 1 to Dec 31, annually. See http://www.archivists.ca/content/membership-form for current fees and forms
Structure Board of Directors and Committees; special interest sections and student chapters. Affiliated with ICA, SPA and Canadian archival organizations
Sources of Support Membership dues, journal subscriptions, conference registrations and publication sales
Major Fields of Interest Archives and archivists; development of the profession
Major Goals and Objectives The ACA currently has five Strategic Priorities: 1. Advocacy, 2. Communications, 3. Governance, 4. Outreach, 5. Professional Development
Activities Past achievements: Lobbying government for Access to Information, new National Archives legislation; successful yearly conferences, publishing Archivaria. Current: Planning 2005 through 2007 conferences, expanding web site and web services; developing descriptive standards; review of goals and priorities of the Association
Publications Official journal: Archivaria, Journal of the Association of Canadian Archivists. ACA Bulletin, a members newsletter
Bibliography Thompson, T., "Archivaria: A Brief Introduction to the Journal of the Association of Canadian Archivists," American Archivist 51 (1988):132–134

157 Association of Canadian Map Libraries and Archives/Association des Cartothèques et des Archives Canadiennes (ACMLA/ACACC)

Address c/o c/o Legal Deposit - Maps, 550, boulevard de la Cité, Gatineau, Quebec

K1N 0N4 Tel.: +1 403-220-5090, secretary@acmla.org; www.acmla.org
Languages English, French
Established 1967, as Association of Canadian Map Libraries
Officers Pres: Andrew Nicholson; 1st VP: Dan Duda; 2nd VP: Wenonah Van Heyst; Past Pres: Colleen Beard; Secr: Susan McKee; Treas: Susan Greeves
Staff 1 (part-time, paid), 7 (volunteers)
General Assembly General membership meets once a year
Membership Individual and institutional. Requirements: Affiliation with a map library or map archives
Structure Governed by executive officers. Affiliations: IFLA
Sources of Support Membership dues, sale of publications
Major Fields of Interest Maps and cartographic librarianship and archives
Major Goals and Objectives To promote interest in and knowledge of maps and map-related materials; to further the professional knowledge of its members; to encourage high standards in every phase of the organization, administration and development of map libraries
Activities Past achievements: Published three editions of Directory of Canadian Map Collections, two editions of Guide for a Small Map Collection, and 125 facsimiles of historic Canadian maps. Current and Future: Working on additions to the text and map publications. The Association has been active in promoting library-related legislation. Sponsors map exhibits
Publications Official journal: ACMLA Bulletin. 1967-. 3/yr. Free to members. Address same as Association. English and French. Circ: 300. Other publications: Facsimile maps, proceedings of conferences, annual reports, etc. Publications for sale (listed in journal), price lists available. Publications exchange program in effect with other library associations
Bibliography Rothstein, S., "Canada," in ALA World Encyclopedia of Library and Information Services. 2nd ed., pp. 155–165. Chicago: American Library Association, 1986

158 Association of Parliamentary Librarians in Canada/Association des Bibliothécaires Parlementaires au Canada (APLIC/ABPAC) (Association of Parliamentary Librarians in Canada)

Address 50 O'Connor St., Suite 1244, Ottawa, ON K1A 0A9 Tel.: +1 613 9968558, Fax +1 613 9479235, brodil@parl.gc.ca; www.ifla.org/VII/s3/proj/region-e.htm
Languages English, French
Established 1975
Officers Parliamentary Librarian: William R. Young; Secr: Lynn Brodie
Staff None
General Assembly General membership meets every two years at a different provincial capital. 2004: Edmonton
Membership 14. Requirements: Director of Canadian Parliamentary library
Structure Governed by executive officers (informal). Affiliations: IFLA
Major Fields of Interest Parliamentary librarianship; library services to Parliament
Major Goals and Objectives Communication among directors of Canadian parliamentary libraries.with the goal of bettering service to Canadian parliaments
Publications Publishes Bulletin 2/yr in april and december

Bibliography Rothstein, S., "Canada," in ALA World Encyclopedia of Library and Information Services. 2nd ed., pp. 155–165. Chicago: American Library Association, 1986

159 Association pour l'Avancement des Sciences et des Techniques de la Documentation (ASTED)
(Association for the Advancement of the Science and Technology of Documentation)*

Address 2065, rué Parthenais- bureau 387, Montreal, Quebec H2X 3T1 Tel.: +1 514 2815012, Fax +1 514 2818219, info@asted.org; www.asted.org
Languages French
Established Montreal, October 22, 1973
Officers Pres: Philippe Sauvageau; Exec Dir: Francis Farley-Chevrier
Staff 1 paid
General Assembly Yearly. in November, in Montreal
Membership 200 individual, 300 institutional; 6 sections. Individual membership fee is based on income; institutional memebership fee is based on type and size; no specific requirements
Structure General Assembly elects the Board of Directors; ASTED also operated a publishing company, Lee Editons ASTED
Sources of Support Membership fees, sale of publications, annual conference, annual government grant, occasional grant
Major Fields of Interest General advocacy, copyright, relationship with other publishers, authors, booksellers, professional development, government relations
Major Goals and Objectives Recognition of the excellence of Library and information professionals through advocacy, professional developemnt and strong relationships with partners
Activities ASTED has hosted the 2008 MLIC in Quebec City, and also played a piyotal role in the organization of the recent Joint conference of the library and information community of Quebec) 7 partners, close to 1000 attendants) in November 2009. ASTED is also involved in the preparation of the forthcoming conference. ASTED is also active in the field of access to digital content through public libraries
Publications Official journal: Documentation et Bibliothèques, current volume 56, quarterly, subscription: 110$. Editor: Michèle Hudon. Articles are in French, with summaries in English and Spanish. Circulation: 700; Newsletter: Les Nouvelles de l'ASTED, current volume: 29; sent by e-mail 10 times a year; other publications: French versions of AACR, books on thesauri, library policies, reading, infornation literacy. Publications are for sale. Catalogue available at www.asted.org, online sales. We also distribute French publishers in Canada; èditions du Cercle de la libraire, Éditions ADBS, Éditions ENSSIB
Bibliography Annual reports are available on our website

160 Bibliographical Society of Canada/La Société Bibliographique du Canada (BSC/SBC)

Address P.O. Box 575, Postal Station P, Toronto, ON M5S 2T1 gretagolick@rogers.com; www.bsc-sbc.ca
Languages English, French

Established May, 1946, at an inaugural meeting of librarians, bookmen, and editors, organized by Lorne Pierce
Officers Pres: Anne Dondertman; Past Pres: David McKnight; 1st VP: Paul Aubin; 2nd VP: Randall Speller; Janet Friskney; Treas: Tom Vincent; Secr: Great Golick
Staff None
General Assembly General membership meets once a year. 2010: May 31st, June 1st Montreal
Membership Requirements: Society welcomes as members all who share its aims and wish to support and participate in bibliographical research and publications. Dues (Canadian Dollar): 70/yr
Structure Governed by executive board according to constitution and by-laws. Affiliations: Canadian Library Association, Canadian Federation for the Humanities and Social Sciences
Sources of Support Membership dues, government subsidies
Major Fields of Interest Bibliography and bibliographical publications; print culture; history of the book and publishing
Major Goals and Objectives To promote the study and practice of bibliography: enumerative, historical, descriptive, analytical, and textual; To further the study, research, and publication of book history and print culture. To publish bibliographies and studies of book history and print culture. To encourage the publication of bibliographies, critical editions, and studies of book history and print culture. To promote the appropriate preservation and conservation of manuscript, archival, and published materials in various formats. To encourage the utilization and analysis of relevant manuscript and archival sources as a foundation of bibliographical scholarship and book history. To promote the interdisciplinary nature of bibliography, and to foster relationships with other relevant organizations nationally and internationally. To conduct the Society without purpose of financial gain for its members, and to ensure that any profits or other accretions to the Society shall be used in promoting its goal and objectives
Activities Association considers itself a publishing society, limited in scope only by the amount of money available
Publications Official journal: Papers/Cahiers. 1962-. 1/yr. Free to members. Address same as Association. Circ: Membership only. English, French. Other publications: Colloquium (series); Bulletin. 1973- (members only); price lists available

161   Bibliothèques publiques du Québec

Address 655 Chemin du Golf, J5W 1K2 Québec bibliotheque@ville.lassomption.qc.ca
Officers Pres: Suzanne Payette

162   Bureau of Canadian Archivists / Bureau Canadien des Archivistes (BCA)

Address bca@idrc.ca; http://bca.archives.ca
Languages English, French
Established 1976 by the Association of Canadian Archivists (ACA) and the Association des archivistes du Québec (AAQ)
Officers Pres: Nathalie Gélinas; Scott Goodine; VP: Linda Fraser; Secr Gen: Shelley Sweeney
Structure Governed by a board of six directors

Major Fields of Interest Represents archivists of Canada and the Association des archivistes du Québec
Major Goals and Objectives To ensure the professional development of Canadian archivists who are members of the Association des archivistes du Québec and the Association of Canadian Archivists
Activities Analysis of their needs, the ongoing exchange of information between the two constituent associations and the realization of joint projects in matters of training, development, standardization of archival practices, promotion and awareness to the social importance of the profession of archivist and of the safeguarding of the national archival heritage
Publications No official journal. Other publications: Rules for Archival Description (RAD) The Archival Fonds: from Theory to Practice (bilingual). An Introduction to Authority Control for Archivists (bilingual). Subject Indexing for Archives Developing Descriptive Standards: A Call to Action (Out of Stock). Authority Control: A Manual for Archivists (Out of Stock). Toward Descriptive Standards (Out of Stock)
Comment No address available

163 Canadian Association for Information Science / Association Canadienne des Sciences de l'Information (CAIS/ACSI)

Address c/o Catherine Johnson, President, North Campus Building Room 203, Faculty of Information & Media Studies, London, ON N6A 5B7 Tel.: +1 519 661-2111, cjohn24@uwo.ca; www.cais-acsi.ca
Languages English, French
Established 1970, Ottawa, at University of Ottawa Library School, to represent the specific problems of Canadians in the field of information science
Officers Pres: Carherine Johnson; VP: Nadia Caidi; Past Pres: Joan Bartlett; Dir/Membership: Clément Arsenault; Dir/Communications: Dinesh Rati; Secr: Heather L. O'Brian; Treas: Ali Shin; Ex-Officio Member: Heidi Julien
Staff 1 (paid)
General Assembly General membership meets once a year. 2010: June 2nd-4th Montreal
Membership Total members: 600. Requirements: Individuals and institutions actively engaged in the gathering, organization and dissemination of information. Dues (Canadian Dollar): 75, individual; 25, student, 40 senior citizen; 95, institutional. Address: University of Toronto Press Inc., Journals Dept, 5201 Dufferin St., North York, ON, Canada, M3H 5T8. Tel: +1 416 6677810 fax: +1 416 6677881. Fax Toll Free in North America: 1–800–221–9985. email: journals@utpress.utoronto.ca
Structure Governed by Board of Directors. Affiliations: None
Sources of Support Membership dues, sale of publications, government subsidies
Major Fields of Interest Transfer of information
Major Goals and Objectives To provide a forum for dialog and exchange of ideas concerned with the theory and practice of information transfer; to contribute to the advancement of information science in Canada
Activities Activities reflect the diverse membership of individuals and organizations involved in the production, manipulation, storage, retrieval, and dissemination of information in all formats. Association sponsors exhibits and continuing education

lectures, conferences, seminars, workshops and student award
Publications   Official journal: Canadian Journal of Information Science/Revue Canadienne des Sciences de l'Information. 1976-. 4/yr. (Canadian Dollar) 95 (110, foreign). Free to members. Editor: Heidi Julien. Address: School of Library and Information Studies, University of Alberta, 3–20 Rutherford South, Edmonton, Alberta, Canada T6G 2J4. Tél.: +1 780–492–3934, Fax: +1 780–492–2430. heidi.julien@ualberta.ca
Bibliography   Rothstein, S., "Canada". In: ALA World Encyclopedia of Library and Information Services. 2nd ed., pp. 155–165. Chicago: American Library Association, 1986; "Connexions: Linking Mind and Machine. 16th Annual Conference of the Canadian Association for Information Science, University of Ottawa, May 12–14, 1988" In: Canadian Journal of Information Science 13 (1988):3–119; "Canadian Association for Information Science (L'Association Canadienne des Sciences de l'Information)," in The Bowker Annual: Library and Book Trade Almanac. 34th Edition 1989–90, pp. 679–680. New York: R. R. Bowker, 1989

164   Canadian Association for School Libraries (CASL)

Address   c/o Diana Gauthier, Secr/Treas, 33 Burnview Cres., Ottawa, ON, K1B 3J2 Tel.: +1 613 824-3529, Fax +1 613 824-3645, diana.gauthier@opera.ncf.ca; www.cla.ca/AM/Template.cfm?Section=CASL2
Languages   English
Established   1961, at St.Andrews-by-the-Sea, at the Canadian Library Association Conference
Officers   Pres: Linda Shantz-Keresztes; Past Pres: Rcihard Beaudry; Secr/Treas: Diana Gauthier; Councillor: Dianne Leong-Fortier; Wendy Doucette; Cindy Matthews
Staff   None
General Assembly   General membership meets once a year at the conference of the Canadian Library Association
Membership   Requirements: Membership in Canadian Library Association and interest in school librarianship. Dues: Drawn from dues paid to Canadian Library Association
Structure   Governed by an Executive Council. Affiliations: A division of the Canadian Library Association. Member of IASL
Sources of Support   Membership dues drawn from dues paid to Canadian Library Association
Major Fields of Interest   School librarianship, including standards for school library programs; education for school librarianship; exchange of professional information; continuing education
Major Goals and Objectives   The objectives of the Division shall be: to provide a national voice for school libraries; to promote excellence in all aspects of school libraries; to provide members with opportunities for professional growth; to promote all forms of literacy including information literacy (skills and abilities in research, comprehension and dissemination) among; Canada's youth through the formal school system; to unite library and media personnel and other interested parties in furthering and improving school library media service throughout Canada; to provide for the exchange of ideas and experience among members; to co-operate with internal and external groups and organizations in the advancement of education and librarianship and library, information and media services;

and to support and promote the objectives of the Canadian Library Association
Activities Organizing professional development workshops; active awards program; successful conference sessions. Presents yearly awards (School Library Media Periodical Award, Margaret B. Scott Award of Merit); sponsors professional development workshops; various committees formed for publicity, education for school librarianship and professional development; revision of 1977 standards for school libraries, to be published as a series of position papers. Association has been active in lobbying federal government on legislation regarding copyright and pornography
Publications Official journal: School Libraries in Canada (SLIC) (formerly Mocassin Telegraph). 1961-. 4/yr. Address same as Association. Editor: Lilian Carefoot. Address: Waterloo School, 3519 Hallberg Road, Ladysmith, B. C. V9G 1K1, Tel.: +1 250 7543194. Fax: +1 250 7547869. email: lcarefoot@telus.net. English, occasionally French. Indexed in Canadian Periodical Index, Canadian Education Index. Canadian Magazine Index. Lib.Lit., etc. Other publications: Annual report, position papers, etc. Publications for sale, price lists available through Canadian Library Association. Publications exchange program in effect
Bibliography Burdenuk, E. and Hambleton, A.E.L., "CSLA Membership Profile: Fifty North and Forty West (Kipling's Danger Point)," School Libraries in Canada 3 (1982):4–6; Burdenuk, E., "Canadian School Library Association, 1961–1984," School Libraries in Canada 4 (1984):7–10; Neill, D.S., "Final Report of an Investigation of the Professional, Legal and Financial Implications of Forming an Independent National School Library Association (with discussion)," ibid.: 13–27; "Canadian School Library Association Will Stay within CLA," School Library Journal 30 (1984): 14; Rothstein, S., "Canada," in ALA World Encyclopedia of Library and Information Services. 2nd ed., pp. 155–165. Chicago: American Library Association, 1986; "A Year in Review [reports given at the 28th Annual General Meeting of the Canadian School Library Association, June 1988]," School Libraries in Canada 8 (1988):36–41

165 Canadian Association of Children's Librarians (CACL)

Address c/o Ann Foster, Secretary, Youth Services Manager, 806 Duchess St., Saskatoon, SK S7K 0R3 Tel.: +1 306 652-4183, Fax +1 306 -931-7611, sheinrich@wheatland.sk.ca; www.cla.ca
Languages English
Officers Pres: Lita Barrie; Secr/Treas: Ann Foster; Past Pres: Nancy Cohen
Staff None
General Assembly General membership meets once a year
Structure Governed by Executive Board. Affiliation: A section of CAPL (Canadian Association of Public Libraries), which is a division of the Canadian Library Association
Sources of Support Membership dues drawn from dues paid to the Canadian Library Association
Major Fields of Interest Library services to children
Major Goals and Objectives To further library services to children in Canada
Activities Carried out through various committees; presentation of two book awards (Book of the Year for Children Award, and Amelia Frances Howard-Gibbon Award)
Publications No official journal. CAPL divisional news (of which CACL is a section) appears regularly in Feliciter, the newsletter of the Canadian Library Association. A CLA Publications Committee is in charge of relevant publications for children's librarians.

Some of the publications: Storytellers' Encore: More Canadian Stories to Tell to Children (1984); Storytellers' Tape (1986); Subject Index to Canadian Poetry in English for Children and Young People (1986); Library Service to Children (series of pamphlets, 1988); Canadian Films for Children and Young Adults (1987), etc. Publications available through Canadian Library Association

166   Canadian Association of College and University Libraries / Association Canadienne des Bibliothèques de Collège et d'Université (CACUL/ACBCU)

Address   c/o Christine E. Sammon, Secretatry/Treasurer, 1407 14th Ave NW, Calgary, AB T2N 5R3 Tel.: +1 403 284-7630, christine.sammon@acad.ca; www.cla.ca/AM/Template.cfm?Section=CACUL

Languages   English, French

Established   1963, Winnipeg, Manitoba

Officers   Pres: Pam Ryan; Past Pres: Alison Nussbaumer; Secr/Treas: Christine E. Sammon; Dir-Grants: Carol Shepstone; Dir-Awards: Wendy Rodgers; Dir-Memebership: Gillian Byrne

Staff   None

General Assembly   Entire membership meets once a year at the Conference of the Canadian Library Association

Membership   Types of membership: Individual, institutional, student. Requirements: Members of Canadian Library Association with concern for and interest in college and university libraries. Dues: Drawn from dues paid to Canadian Library Association

Structure   Governed by executive officers who meet four times a year. Sections: 1 (Community and Technical College Libraries/CTCL). Standing Committees: 4 (Nominations, Award for Outstanding Academic Librarian, Innovation Achievement Award, CTCL/Micromedia Award of Merit) Affiliation: A division of the Canadian Library Association

Sources of Support   Funds from the parent body (through dues paid to the Canadian Library Association)

Major Fields of Interest   College and university libraries

Major Goals and Objectives   To provide a forum for cooperation and professional development of librarians at colleges and universities; to further the interests of the libraries of those institutions which offer education above the secondary level; to support the highest aims of education and librarianship

Activities   Sponsors conferences, seminars and workshops on relevant topics; provides standards and guidelines; implementation of CACUL's Strategic Plan, especially its continuing education goals through offering provincial/regional workshops

Publications   No official journal. Publishes a continuing series of peer-reviewed "Occasional Papers" covering topics of interest to members of the college and university library community. Dues: 10 $, free for members.Address: Member Services, Canadian Library Association, 328 Frank Street, Ottawa, Ontario K2P 0X8. Tel: +1 613 2329625, ext 301. Fax: +1 613 5639895. email: thesson@cla.ca

Bibliography   Rothstein, S., "Canada," ALA World Encyclopedia of Library and Information Services. 2nd ed., pp. 155–165. Chicago: American Library Association, 1986

167 Canadian Association of Family Resource Programs (FRP Canada)
Address   707 - 331 Cooper Street, Ottawa, ON K2P 0G5 Tel.: +1 613 2377667, Fax +1 613 2378515, info@frp.ca; www.frp.ca
Languages   English, French
Established   1975 as a national association of toy libraries, it became the Canadian Association of Family Resource Programs in 1994 and is now known under the name of FRP Canada
Officers   Pres: Crystal Elliott; VP: Natalie Chapman; Secr: Trish Plant; Treas: Stephanie Rivest
Staff   2 (paid), 6 (volunteer)
General Assembly   General membership meets once a year
Membership   Members include organizations that work with families such as child care programs, early intervention programs, community health centres, child protection agencies, Aboriginal family organizations, public health departments and national organizations with an interest in children and families
Structure   Governed by Board of Directors. Affiliations: International Association for the Child's Right to Play
Sources of Support   Membership dues, sale of publications, government subsidies, donations
Major Fields of Interest   Child development; parent education
Major Goals and Objectives   To advance social policy, research, resource development and training for those who enhance the capacity of families to raise their children
Activities   National projects to do research and produce resources for the field, regional professional development events, the development of advocacy tools, biennial national conference, general and members' web sites, the coordination of the Nobody's Perfect parenting program, a responsibility shared with the Canadian Institute of Child Health, A directory of family resource programs in Canada
Publications   Official journal: Play and Parenting Connections. Newsletter. 4/yr. Free to members. Address same as Association. Other publications: Publications list on the web http://www.frp.ca/g_PublicationsList.asp

168 Canadian Association of Law Libraries / Association Canadienne des Bibliothèques de Droit (CALL/ACBD)
Address   4 Cataraqui Street, Suite 310, PO Box 1570, Kingston ON K7L 5C8 Tel.: +1 613 5319338, Fax +1 613 5310626, office@callacbd.ca; www.callacbd.ca
Languages   English, French
Established   1963
Staff   None
General Assembly   General membership meets once a year
Membership   Total members: 500 (individual and institutional). Requirements: Law library or employment in a law library for individual membership Dues (Canadian Dollars): Active individual: 139.10/yr, Institutional (Corporate): 176.55/yr, Student: 47.08/yr
Structure   Governed by executive officers
Sources of Support   Membership dues, sale of publications
Major Fields of Interest   Law librarianship

Major Goals and Objectives   To promote law librarianship, develop Canadian law libraries, foster cooperation between them; provide a forum for meetings of persons interested in law librarianship, and cooperate with other associations with similar objectives or interests
Activities   Association's major purpose is to provide information exchange between members. This is accomplished through conferences, which include workshops and seminars, and through publications program
Publications   Official journal: Canadian Law Library Review. 5/yr. Dues: (Canadian Dollars) 96.30 for Canadian residents, 90 for non-residents. Address same as association. Other publications: Documents and reports related to law librarianship in Canada, Address same as association
Bibliography   Rothstein, Samuel, "Canada," in ALA World Encyclopedia of Library and Information Services. 2nd ed., pp. 155–165. Chicago: American Library Association, 1986; Tearle, B. and Hennessey, J., "CALL of the Wild/Far West: CALL/ACBD Annual Conference [Jasper, Alberta, 15–18 May 1988]," Law Librarian 19 (Aug. 1988):64–66

169   Canadian Association of Music Libraries (A Branch of the International Association of Music Libraries, Archives and Documentation Centres / Association Canadienne des Bibliothèques Musicales (CAML/ACBM)
Address   395 Wellington St., Ottawa, ON K1A 0N4 Tel.: +1 604 822-1408, Fax +1 604 822-1966, kirsten.walsh@ubc.ca; www.yorku.ca/caml
Languages   English, French
Established   1971
Officers   Pres: KIrstin Walsh
Staff   None
General Assembly   General membership meets once a year. 2004: Alberta
Membership   About 100 individual and institutional members. Requirements: Interest in music librarianship and the goals of the Association
Structure   Governed by Executive Board. Affiliations: Canadian University Music Society (CUMS), International Association of Music Libraries (IAML)
Sources of Support   Membership dues, sale of publications
Major Fields of Interest   Music librarianship
Major Goals and Objectives   To foster all aspects of music librarianship in Canada; to encourage the development of music libraries; to initiate and/or participate in projects dealing with music and musical resources; to foster the coming together of individuals or groups with kindred interests or problems; to cooperate with national, international, and other foreign organizations concerned with music in all its aspects; to encourage cooperation between libraries in sharing information about and access to printed music; to issue such publications as the Association deems useful
Activities   Association sponsors exhibits and continuing education lectures, seminars and workshops. Electronic mailling list: CANMUS-L. Contact Rob van der Bliek (bliek@yorku.ca)
Publications   Official journal: CAML review. 3/year. Editors: Desmond Maley (dmaley@laurentian.ca) and Denise Prince (denise.prince@mcc.gouv.qc.ca). Other publications: Toomey, K.M., ed., Musicians in Canada. A Bibliographical Finding List (2nd ed. 1981); Lewis, L.C., ed., Union List of Music Periodicals in Canadian Libraries

(2nd ed. 1981); Parker, C. P. G. and Emerson, D., eds., Title Index to Canadian Works Listed in "Roll Back the Years". Indes des titres d'oeuvres canadiennes énumérés dans "En Remontant les Années" by E. K. Moogk (1986). Directory of Music Collections in Canada. Compiled by Carol Ohlers, York University Libraries. email: carolo@yorku.ca
Bibliography "Canadian Association of Music Libraries," in Encyclopedia of Music in Canada, ed. by H. Kallman, G. Potvin, and K. Winters. Toronto: University of Toronto Press, 1981; Rothstein, S., "Canada," in ALA World Encyclopedia of Library and Information Services. 2nd ed., pp. 155–165. Chicago: American Library Association, 1986

170 Canadian Association of Public Libraries (CAPL)

Address 328 Frank Street, Ottawa, ON K2P OX8 Tel.: +1 613 232-9625, Fax +1 613 563-9895, info@cla.ca; www.cla.ca
Languages English
Established 1973, as a separate division of the Canadian Library Association
Officers Pres: John Teskey; VP: keith Walker; Past-Pres: Ken Roberts; Treas: Ingrid Langhammer
Staff None
General Assembly General membership meets once a year at the conference of the Canadian Library Association
Membership Requirements: Individuals and institutions belonging to Canadian Library Association and having interest in and concerns for Canadian public libraries. Dues: Drawn from dues paid to Canadian Library Association
Structure Governed by Executive Committee. Affiliations: A division of the Canadian Library Association
Sources of Support Funds from parent body (through membership dues paid to Canadian Library Association)
Major Fields of Interest Public libraries
Major Goals and Objectives To unite library personnel and other interested groups in furthering the welfare of public libraries in Canada; to promote and support freedom of access to public library resources and services, and to augment the ability of all individuals to use them
Activities Carrying out studies, sponsoring workshops and meetings in order to further the development of Canadian public libraries. CAPL/Brodart Outstanding Public Library Service Award. Sponsors Library Advocacy Now program (www.cla.ca/divisions/capl/advocacy/index.htm)
Publications Official journal: CAPL newletter. Available for members in pdf format. Other publications (available on the web): Information Service Training and Evaluation Kit, Dividends: The Value of Public Libraries in Canada, Selected Online Resources, CLA and CAPL Endorse UNESCO Public Library Manifesto
Bibliography Rothstein, S., "Canada," in ALA World Encyclopedia of Library and Information Services. 2nd ed., pp. 155–165. Chicago: American Library Association, 1986

171 Canadian Association of Research Libraries / Association des Bibliothèques de Recherche du Canada (CARL/ABRC)

Address Room 239, Morisset Hall, 65 University Street, Ottawa, Ontario K1N 9A5 Tel.: +1 613 56258003652, Fax +1 613 5625195, carl@uottawa.ca; www.carl-abrc.ca

Languages English, French
Established 1976, in Regina
Officers Pres: Leslie Weir; Exec Dir: Brent Roe
Staff 2 (paid, part-time)
General Assembly General membership meets twice a year
Membership Total members: 27 university libraries plus Library and Archives Canada, the Library of Parliament, and the Canada Institute for Scientific and Technical Information (CISTI). Requirements: Institutional membership only and limited to libraries of universities having doctoral graduate programs in the arts and sciences and to other such institutional libraries as approved by the Board of Directors. Dues: Not published
Structure Governed by the Board of Directors elected by and from the membership. Affiliations: AUCC (Association of Universities and Colleges of Canada)
Sources of Support Membership dues, grants from private corporations
Major Fields of Interest Research libraries and preservation of research library materials
Major Goals and Objectives To provide organized leadership for the Canadian research library community in the development of policies and programmes which maintain and improve the cycle of scholarly communication; To work toward the realization of a national research library resource-sharing network in the areas of collection development, preservation and access; and To increase the capacity of individual member libraries to provide effective support and encouragement to postgraduate study and research at national, regional, and local levels
Activities Committees: Effectiveness Measures and Statistics, Copyright, Terms of Reference, Government Policies and Legislation Committee, Scholarly Communication. CARL/ABRC Award for Distinguished Service to Research Librarianship
Publications No official journal. Other publications: CARL/ABRC Statistics. Address same as association
Bibliography Steele, C.R., "Conference: Research Libraries in the Online Environment," Australian Academic and Research Libraries 14 (1983):178–181; Rothstein, S., "Canada," in ALA World Encyclopedia of Library and Information Services. 2nd ed., pp. 155–165. Chicago: American Library Association, 1986

172 Canadian Association of Special Libraries and Information Services (CASLIS)

Address c/o Canadian Library Association, 328 Frank Street, Ottawa, ON K2P 0X8 Tel.: +204 6543086, mlis@mts.net; www.cla.ca/caslis/
Languages English
Established 1969, to replace the Research and Special Libraries Section of the Canadian Library Association
Staff None
General Assembly. General membership meets once a year at the conference of the Canadian Library Association
Membership Types of membership: Individual, institutional. Requirements: Individuals and institutions belonging to the Canadian Library Association and having an interest in special libraries and information services. Dues: Drawn from dues paid to Canadian Library Association
Structure Governed by Executive Council meeting 3 times a year. Affiliations: A division of the Canadian Library Association

Sources of Support Membership dues drawn from dues paid to the Canadian Library Association
Major Fields of Interest Special libraries and information sciences
Major Goals and Objectives To support and promote the objectives of the Canadian Library Association, to unite special libraries personnel, information specialists, documentalists and other interested parties in furthering and improving special library service throughout Canada, to provide for the exchange of ideas and experience among members and to co-operate with internal and external groups and organizations in the advancement of special librarianship and special library and information services
Activities CASLIS Ottawa Chapter has set up a job bank answering service at CLA headquarters, and there are plans for a national service of this type; workshops and seminars; various activities carried out by geographic chapters, sections (art libraries, health sciences, etc.). Offers CASLIS Award for Outstanding Special Librarianship in Canada
Publications Official journal: Special Issues: Bulletin of the Canadian Association of Special Libraries and Information Services. ISSN 1488–8661. Editorial Board: Tracey Palmer, Rebecca Richardson Beausejour (email: rebecca.beausejour@edu.gov.on.ca), Mia Yen
Bibliography Pandit, J., "CASLIS and SLA Joint Conference a Success," Library Times International 2 (1985):29–30; Rothstein, S., "Canada," in ALA World Encyclopedia of Library and Information Services. 2nd ed., pp. 155–165. Chicago: American Library Association, 1986

173 Canadian Council of Archives / Conseil Canadien des Archives (CCA)

Address 130 Albert Street, Rm 501, Ottawa, ON K1P 5G4 Tel.: +1 613 5651222, Fax +1 613 5655445, cca@archivescanada.ca; www.cdncouncilarchives.ca
Languages English, French
Established 1985
Officers Chair: Ian Forsyth; VChair: Leslie Latta-Guthrie; Dir: Robin Keirstead; Diane Baillargeon
General Assembly General assembly will be held November 6&7, 2004
Membership 18 Members: 1 representative from each of the 10 provincial councils and 3 territorial councils or their equivalent organizations, the Chairperson of the Council, the Vice-Chairperson of the Council, 1 representative of the Bureau of Canadian Archivists, 1 representative from the Association des archivistes du Québec and 1 representative of the Association of Canadian Archivists, one representative of the Library and Archives Canada
Major Fields of Interest Archives in Canada
Major Goals and Objectives Supports coordination and exchanges of views among archival institutions in Canada; preservation of the national heritage by improving the administration, effectiveness and efficiency of the archival system
Publications No official journal. Other publications e. g. Directory of Archives. 1999. Publications list on the web: www.cdncouncilarchives.ca/publications/public.pdf

174 Canadian Council of Information Studies/ Le Conseil Canadien des écoles de sciences de l'information

Address c/o School of Information Studies, 3459 McTavish St., Montreal, Quebec, H3A

1Y1 Tel.: +1 604 822-2404, Fax +1 604 822-6006, france.bouthillier@mcgill.ca
Languages English, French
Officers Pres: France Bouthiellier
Major Fields of Interest Library and Information Science Education

175 Canadian Health Libraries Association / Association des Bibliothèques de la Santé du Canada (CHLA/ABSC)

Address 39 River St., Toronto, ON M5A 3P1 Tel.: +1 416 6461600, Fax +1 416 6469460, info@chla-absc.ca; www.chla-absc.ca
Languages French, English
Established 1976
Officers Pres: Marlene Dorgan; VP: Orvie Dingwall; Past Pres: Dianne Kharouba; Treas: Shannon Long; Secr: Shauna-Lee Konrad; Dir/PR: Rebecca Raworth; Dir/CE-Coord: Lindsay Glynn
General Assembly General membership meets once a year. May 30-June 3, 2005: Toronto, ON
Membership Requirements: Individuals and institutions supporting the aims of the Association
Structure Governed by executive officers
Sources of Support Membership dues
Major Fields of Interest Health sciences library services
Major Goals and Objectives To improve health and health care by promoting excellence in access to information; to represent the interests of health libraries on issues involving governmental and private agencies
Activities Sponsors annual meetings with exhibits, and continuing education programs; provides placement service
Publications Official journal: Journal of the Canadian Health Libraries Association (JCHLA). Formerly known as Bibliotheca Medica Canadiana (BMC), 4/yr, electronic publication, starting with volume 25, issue 1, 2004. JCHLA is published by the National Research Council of Canada Research Press; ISSN: 1708–6892. Other publications: Membership directory (annual); CanHealth; occasional papers and course syllabi
Bibliography Groen, F., "Small is Beautiful," Canadian Library Journal 41 (1984):113; Rothstein, S., "Canada," in ALA World Encyclopedia of Library and Information Services. 2nd ed., pp. 155–165. Chicago: American Library Association, 1986; Harrison, C. and Conchelos, M., "Report on the CHLA Membership Survey and Continuing Education Needs Assessment," Bibliotheca Medica Canadiana 8 (1986):54–61

176 Canadian Library Association (CLA)

Address 328 Frank Street, Ottawa, ON K2P 0X8 Tel.: +1 613 2329625, Fax +1 613 5639895, info@cla.ca; www.cla.ca
Languages English
Established 1946, in Hamilton; incorporated 1947, in Ottawa as Canadian Library Association/Association Canadienne des Bibliothèques. French title dropped 1968, but bilingual programs kept in order to serve all libraries and librarians in Canada. New Constitution and By-Laws adopted in 1975; amendments passed in 1989
Officers Exec Dir: Kelly Moore

Staff 10 full and part-time staff
General Assembly General membership meets once a year. 2004: Victoria/BC
Membership Total members: 2410 (1,954 Personal and 456 Institutions). Requirements: Interest in the improvement of library and information services in Canada
Structure Governed by an elected Executive Council, which is advised by over thirty interest groups and committees. The Association's five constituent divisions are: Canadian Association of College and University Libraries (CACUL), including the Community and Technical College (CTCL) section; Canadian Association of Public Libraries (CAPL), including the Canadian Association of Childrens' Librarians (CACL) section; Canadian Association of Special Libraries and Information Services (CASLIS), with chapters in Calgary, Edmonton, Manitoba, Ottawa, Toronto and Atlantic Canada; Canadian Library Trustees Association; Canadian School Library Association, including the School Library Administrators' (SLAS) section. Affiliations: IFLA, ALA, ASTED, COMLA, OLA, and others
Sources of Support Membership dues, sale of publications, government subsidies, private gifts, and fees from conferences, meetings and seminars. Budget (Canadian Dollar): 1986/87: Approx. 1,901,700; 1989/90: Approx. 1,900,000
Major Fields of Interest Library service in general and type-of-library interests
Major Goals and Objectives To improve the quality of library and information services in Canada; to develop higher standards of librarianship; to develop active and meaningful communication among its members; to encourage and support high levels of professional conduct on the part of its members; to promote strong public support for library and information services
Activities Active in promoting legislation relating to copyright, postal regulations, pornography, and access to information. Activities are carried out by the divisions and the interest groups dealing with topics of current interest, such as access to government information, action for peace and security, preservation/conservation, technical services, information technology, multilingual services, services for persons with disabilities, online users, prison libraries, services for distance learning, Third World Libraries, literacy, and others. Active in professional issues on copyright and taxation. Association sponsors exhibits and continuing education lectures, seminars and workshops, awards and sholarships
Publications Official journal: Canadian Library Journal. 1947-. 6/yr. Free to members. Address same as Association. Other publications: Proceedings of meetings; Feliciter, newsletter of the CLA. 1956-. 6/yr. Free to members. email: publishing@cla.ca. Editor: Elizabeth Morton; CM: A Reviewing Journal of Canadian Materials for Young People (6/yr.); Canadian Periodical Index; The Canadian Library Yearbook; England, C, and Evans, K., Disaster Management for Libraries (1988); Hébert, F., Report on Photocopying in Canadian Libraries (1988); Interlibrary Loan Procedures Manual/Le Manuel de Pret entre Bibliothèques (1989); Weihs, J., with Lewis, S., Nonbook Materials: The Organization of Integrated Collections (3rd ed., 1989), and other monographs, microfilm, etc. Publications for sale; catalogs available
Bibliography Wedgeworth, R.F., "ALA-CLA – Ties That Bind But Don't Chafe," (Theme speech, CLA Conference, 1981) Canadian Library Journal 38 (1981):301–305; Horrocks, N., "Constant Change: 38th Annual Conference of the Canadian Library Association," Library Journal 108 (1983):1452–53; Havens, S., "At Its 39th Annual

Conference, the Canadian Library Association Considered ... Human Values in the Computer Age." Library Journal 109 (1984):1411–14; Rothstein, S., "Canada," in ALA World Encyclopedia of Library and Information Services. 2nd ed., pp. 155–165. Chicago: American Library Association, 1986; "A Membership Development Strategy for the Canadian Library Association," APLA Bulletin 50 (Nov/Dec. 1986): 1,7; Embey, S., "Canadian Library Association Conference: A Report," Library Times International 4 (1987):20; Miller, B.M.E., "Canadian Library Association," in ALA Yearbook 1988. pp. 90–93. Chicago: American Library Association, 1988; Owen, L., "Canadian Library Association Bites the Bullet in Halifax," American Libraries 19 (1988):563–564; Berry, J.N., "Government, Marketplace, & Association. Report on the June 16–20 Conference of the Canadian Library Association" In: Library Journal 113 (1988):48–50; Nelson, M.G., "Worrying about the Information Market Place in Halifax," Wilson Library Bulletin 63 (1988):37–39; "CLA '88 [conference]: Resource Sharing Comes of Age," Canadian Library Journal 45 (1988):265–266; Cooney, J., "Canadian Library Association," in ALA Yearbook 1989. pp. 83–84. Chicago: American Library Association, 1989; "Canadian Library Association," in The Bowker Annual: Library and Book Trade Almanac. 34th Edition 1989–90, pp. 680–681. New York: R. R. Bowker, 1989

177 Canadian Library Trustees Association (CLTA)

Address c/o Canadian Library Association, 328 Frank Street, Ottawa, ON K2P 0X8 Tel.: +1 613 232-9625, Fax + 1613 563-9895, info@cla.ca; www.cla.ca
Languages English
Staff None
General Assembly General membership meets once a year at the conference of the Canadian Library Association
Membership Requirements: Open to library trustees
Structure Governed by Executive Board meeting 4 times a year. Affiliations: A division of the Canadian Library Association
Sources of Support Membership dues drawn from dues paid to the Canadian Library Association
Major Fields of Interest Library trustees
Major Goals and Objectives To work towards the improvement of trustees and trusteeship through sharing ideas and information; promote trusteeship as the ideal form of public library governance
Activities Helps library trustees to understand the responsibilities that are involved in trusteeship; sponsors workshops; various committees. The task of the division is complex due to the diversity of members, who include trustees of large urban libraries, small rural libraries and other types of library service
Publications Official journal: CLTA Newsletter; discontinued 1975. Divisional news now appears in Feliciter, the newsletter of the Canadian Library Association. Publishes Canadian Library Trustees' Handbook. Address: Member Services, Canadian Library Association, 328 Frank Street, Ottawa, ON K2P 0X8, Tel.: +1 613 2329625 ext 301, Fax: +1 613 5639895

178 Canadian Urban Libraries Council

Address c/o Jefferson Gilbert, Executive Director, 2006 Queen Street EAst, No. 7,

Toronto, Ontario M4L 1J3 jgilbert@culc.ca
Languages French
Officers Chair: Jeff Barber; Exec Dir: Jefferson Gilbert

179 Corporation des bibliothécaires professionnels du Québec

Address 353, St-Nicolas, Suite 103, Montreal, Quebec H2Y 2P1 info@cbpq.qc.ca
Languages French
Officers Pres: Guylaine Beaudry; Exec Dir: Régine Horinstein

180 Council of Prairie and Pacific University Libraries (COPPUL)*

Address c/o Alexander Slade, Exec Dir, 2005 Sooke Road, Victoria, BC V9B 5Y2
Tel.: +1 250 3912554, Fax +1 250 3912556, coppul@royalroads.ca;
www.coppul.ca/index.html
Languages English
Established 1991; incorporated as a non-profit society in May 2000
Staff 1,5
Membership 21 university libraries located in Manitoba, Saskatchewan, Alberta and British Columbia
Structure Governed by Board of Directors
Sources of Support Membership fees
Major Fields of Interest University Libraries in Canada
Major Goals and Objectives Provides leadership in the development of solutions that meet the academic information resource needs of its member institutions
Activities Resource sharing, collective purchasing, document delivery
Publications No official journal

181 Ex Libris Association (ELA)*

Address c/o Faculty of Information Studies, University of Toronto, 140 St. George St, Toronto, ON M5S 3G6 ExLibris@ischool.utoronto.ca; http://exlibris.fis.utoronto.ca
Languages English
Established 1986
Officers Pres: Carroll Lunau; Past Pres: Janet Jacobson; Secr+Memeber Secr: Jean Weihs; Treas: Bob Henderson
Staff None
General Assembly General membership meets once a year
Membership 200+ personal and 5 organizational members. Requirements: Interest in objectives of Association. Dues: 25 Canadian Dollars
Structure Governed by Board of Directors. Affiliations: Ontario Library Association
Sources of Support Membership dues, donations, sales
Major Fields of Interest History of libraries, oral history, archival material
Major Goals and Objectives (1) Provide a forum for interested individuals; (2) provide a vehicle for collection of oral library history; (3) identify and ensure collection of materials relating to library history; (4) encourage identification of holdings of archival history; (5) provide a focus for intellectual and social activities of retired members of the library community

Activities Biographical project for prominent Canadian librarians, W. Kaye Lamb Award, Internet hook-up project in Addis Ababa, Ethiopia, school libraries
Publications Official journal: ELAN Ex Libris Association Newsletter (pdf format)

182 Federal Libraries Coordination Secretariat (FLCS)

Address 395 Wellington Street, Ottawa, ON K1A 0N4 Tel.: +1 819 934-7427, Fax +1819-934-7534, FLCS-SCBGF@lac-bac.gc.ca; www.collectionscanada.gc.ca/flcs-scbgf/index-e.html
Languages English, French
Established 1976, by the National Librarian of Canada
Staff FLLO staff
General Assembly Annual general meeting
Membership Total members: 58 (institutional). Requirements: Senior library officer of every department or agency having a centralized library system in the administrative branch of the federal government, and in those departments or agencies not having a centralized library system, the senior officer of each library
Structure Governed by a Senior Advisory Committee (under development), a Library Managers' Committee (under development), the Federal Libraries Forum and Ad Hoc working groups, such as one for Procurement
Sources of Support Government subsidies
Major Fields of Interest Coordination of federal library services
Major Goals and Objectives To advise and assist the National Librarian in coordinating library services in the Government of Canada and to improve communications among federal librarians
Activities Task forces and working groups carrying out a variety of projects in the interest of library services, Conservation of library materials, management information system on federal libraries, exchange of technical information on library automation, etc. The Council has a group monitoring and working on the revision of the Canadian Copyright Act
Comment formerly: Council of Federal Libraries / Conseil des Bibliothèques du Gouvernement Fédéral

183 Indexing and Abstracting Society of Canada / Société Canadienne d'indexation (ISC/SCI)*

Address P.O. Box 664, Station P, Toronto, On Can M5S 2Y4 info@indexers.ca; www.indexers.ca
Languages English, French
Established 1977
Officers Pres: Mary Newberry
Staff None
General Assembly Entire membership meets once a year. 2009: Toronto; 2010: Montreal
Membership There are currently 119 members; 109 individuals, 8 institutional, and 2 students. Requirements: Interest in indexing and abstracting. Dues (Canadian Dollar): 90 individual, 105 institutional, 60 student; outside Canada add 10

Structure Governed by Executive Board. Affiliations: Society of Indexers (UK), American Society of Indexers, Australian Society of Indexers, Association of South African Indexers and Bibliographers
Sources of Support Membership dues, sale of publications. Budget (Canadian Dollar): Approx. 20,000
Major Fields of Interest Indexing
Major Goals and Objectives To encourage the production and use of indexes; to promote the recognition of indexers; to improve indexing techniques; and to provide a means of communication among individual indexers in Canada
Activities Past achievements: Program meetings, publications. Current: Issuing a register of indexers. Future: Publication of the register; publishing standards for good indexing and establishing an award to recognize good indexing; promotion of the value of indexing among business people and the general public. Association sponsors continuing education lectures, seminars and workshops
Publications Official journal: ISC/SCI Bulletin. 1977-. 3 or 4/yr. Free to members of ISC/SCI and to members of affiliated indexing societies. Address same as Society's. Other publications: ISC / SCI Membership Directory annually (for members only). Register of Indexers Available annually
Comment Listserv for members only

184 Provincial and Territorial Library Directors Council (PTLDC)

Address P.O. Box 9831, Victoria BC, V8W9T1 Tel.: +1 250 3561791, Fax +1 250 9533125, PLSB@gov.bc.ca
Languages English

185 Regroupement des Archivistes Religieux

Address 1190, Rue Guy, Montréal, Québec H3H 2L4
Languages French
Established 1967

Chile

186 Colegio de Bibliotecarios de Chile CBC (Chilean Library Association)

Address Diagonal Paraguay 383, Torre 11, Depto. 122, Santiago 6510017 Tel.: +56 2 2225652, Fax +56 2 6355023, cbc@bibliotecarios.cl; www.bibliotecarios.cl
Languages Spanish
Established 1969, Santiago (Law decree N 17 161), superseding the Asociación de Bibliotecarios de Chile (established 1953)
General Assembly Entire membership meets twice a year
Membership Total members: 500 (individual). Types of membership: Individual. Requirements: To possess a university degree in library science
Structure Governed by Executive Committee meeting twice a month. Affiliations: Confederación de Colegios Profesionales de Chile, IFLA
Sources of Support Membership dues

Major Fields of Interest Library development, especially public and school libraries
Major Goals and Objectives To represent the interests of the library profession and the librarians of Chile; to further library services through public and school libraries
Activities Development of standards and publications program; protecting the rights of the library profession. Active in promoting library-related legislation
Publications Official journal: Boletín. irreg. Noticia Bibliotecarios. 12/yr. Both free to members. Address same as Association. Circ: Membership. Spanish. Other publications: Indices de Publicaciones Periodicas en Bibliotecología (Catalog of Periodical Publications in Librarianship); Micronoticias; Servicio de Alerta; a "Code of Professional Ethics;" "Standards for Chilean Public and School Libraries;" "Chilean Standards for Documentation," and others. Publications issued for sale, price lists available. Has publications exchange program with other associations and libraries
Bibliography Herrero de Alvarez, M. Teresa, "Chile," in ALA World Encyclopedia of Library and information Services. 2nd ed., pp. 188–190. Chicago: American Library Association, 1986

China

187 China Society of Indexers
Address c/o Ge Yong-Qing, 3663 Zhongshan Road (North), Shanghai Tel.: +86 21 63569074, Fax +86 21 62579196; www.cnindex.fudan.edu.cn(inchineseonly)
Languages Chinese, English

188 Chinese Archives Society
Address 21 Feng Sheng Hutong, Beijing 100032 Tel.: +86 10 66175130, Fax +86 10 66183636, sab@public3.bta.net.cn
Languages Chinese
Established Dec., 1981
Membership Total members: Approx. 400
Major Fields of Interest Archives
Major Goals and Objectives To further development of archives in China

189 Hong Kong Library Association (HKLA)
Address P.O. Box 10095, General Post Office, Hong Kong Tel.: +852 28597009, Fax +852 29152458, hkla@hkla.org; www.hklib.org.hk
Languages Chinese, English
Established 1958, Hong Kong; constitution was revised in 1987, with right to vote and hold office restricted to professionally qualified members
Officers Pres: Jim Chang; Secr: Iris Yuen
General Assembly Entire membership meets once a year, in December, in Hong Kong
Membership Types of membership: Individual, student, corresponding, institutional, honorary. Requirements: Open to those whose professional activities in library, information, or documentation work qualify them for membership. Dues (Hong Kong Dollar): 50–250, individual; 500, institutional
Structure Governed by Executive Committee. Affiliations: COMLA, IFLA

Sources of Support Membership dues, sale of publications
Major Fields of Interest Library services
Major Goals and Objectives To encourage the development of policies promoting the provision of information and library services in Hong Kong. This shall include the provision of guidelines and standards for such services. To provide for librarianship and information work, a focal point as well as a network of formal and informal communication within Hong Kong and with China and other countries. To unite and promote the interests of all persons engaged in library and information work in Hong Kong, and to ensure the effective representation of the interests of members. To encourage professional education and training for librarianship and information work in Hong Kong
Activities Sponsors annual conferences, continuing education seminars, workshops, lectures, exhibits, awards
Publications Official journal: Hong Kong Library Association Newsletter, Hong Kong Library Association Journal
Bibliography Pang, M.: Factors affecting the participation rate of professional librarians/information workers in joining the Hong Kong Library Association. In: Journal of the Hong Kong Library Association, Vol. 17 (1999), pp.27–59; Ladizesky, Kathleen: HKLA's visit to libraries in Guangzhou, March 1991. In: Focus on International and Comparative Librarianship, Vol. 22/2 (1991), pp. 55–57; Ladizesky, Kathleen: HKLAs visit to libraries in Shezhen, China. In: Focus on International and Comparative Librarianship, Vol. 21/1 (1990), pp. 3–6; Poon, Paul W.T.: Library research in Hong Kong: a review of the Journal of the Hong Kong Library Association 1969–1983. In: Journal of the Hong Kong Library Association, No. 8 (1984), pp. l-7; Kan, Lai-bing: Hong Kong Library Association annual report 1982. In: Journal of the Hong Kong Library Association, No. 7 (1983), pp. 123–127; Ho, Wen-Kuang: Silver Jubilee issue of the Hong Kong Library Association journal [In English and Chinese]. In: Journal of the Hong Kong Library Association, No. 7 (1983), pp. 1–145; Quinn, Malcolm: The status of librarians in Hong Kong. In: COMLA-Newsletter, No. 33, Sept 81, pp. ll-13; Quinn, Malcolm: The status of librarians in Hong Kong. In: Journal of the Hong Kong Library Association, No. 5 (1980), pp. 5–9; Quinn, M., Rydings, H.A., Kan, Lai-bing; Report of the Hong Kong Library Association Sub-committee on Professional Training for Librarians in Hong Kong. In: Journal of the Hong Kong Library Association, No. 3, July 75, pp.17–22; Kan, Lai-bing, Leong, Mary: Hong Kong Library Association. In: Encyclopedia of library and information science (ed. Miriam A. Drake), 2nd ed. New York 2003, pp. 1203–1207; O'Hara, Randolph: Hong Kong Library Association. In: Encyclopedia of library and information science, New York 1973, pp. 494–498

190 Hong Kong Teacher Librarians' Association (HKTLA)

Address POB 74493, Kowloon Central Fax +852 2579 0137, hktla@school.net.hk; http://hktla.school.net.hk
Languages Chinese, English
Established 1983
Structure Governed by executive officers
Sources of Support Membership dues
Major Fields of Interest Teacher librarians
Major Goals and Objectives To promote schoolwork in support of educational

development; to facilitate the exchange of work experience among members who had completed the first In-Service Training Course for School Librarians; to organize recreational activities for members and to look after their general welfare
Activities Librianship courses, Discussion forum
Bibliography Kan, Lai-Bing, and Yan, A.S.W., "Libraries in Hong Kong: Growth and Development," Singapore Libraries 18 (1988):65–74

191 Library Society of China

Address 33 Zhongguancun Nandajie, Beijing 100081 wuyue@nlc.gov.cn
Languages Chinese
Officers Pres: Wu Yue; Dir: Zhan Furui

192 Macau Library and Information Management Association (MLIMA)

Address P.O. Box 1422, Macau Tel.: +853 66976977, macau_mlima@yahoo.com.hk; www.mlima.org.mo(chineseonly)
Languages Chinese, English
Established 1995
Staff 1, paid
Membership Over 240 individual members from libraries and information centres
Major Fields of Interest Library professional and information work
Major Goals and Objectives To coordinate libraries and information centres in Macau. To help libraries and information centres to train staff. To provide and exchange information on library science area for members and library staff with better relationship among local and overseas libraries. To promote the functions of library to the public, developing the library professional in Macau, and increasing professional status. To set up rules and standardization for libraries as a reference and a guideline
Activities Macau Library Weeks
Publications Journal of Macau Library and Information Management Association

193 Macau Library and Information Management Association

Address P.O. Box 1422, Macau
Languages Chinese
Officers Pres: Raymond Wong; Secr: Yamaka Lam

194 Zhongguo Kexue Jishu Qingbao Xuehui (CSSTI) (China Society of Scientific and Technical Information)

Address c/o Mr. Zheng Yanning, 15, Fuxing Ave., Beijing 100038 Tel.: +86 10 68514024, Fax +86 10 68514024, zhengyn@istic.ac.cn; www.istic.ac.cn(chineseonly)
Languages Chinese, English
Established 1964
Officers Secr Gen: Zheng Yanning
General Assembly Entire membership meets 3 times a year
Membership Requirements: Individual: Members are elected; Institutional: Members of Science and Technology Information Associations of the provinces, municipalities, and autonomous regions. Dues: None
Structure Governed by Executive Board

Sources of Support   Government subsidies
Major Fields of Interest   Information science of Science and technology
Major Goals and Objectives   To develop information science; to promote information activities and to further the development of science, technology and economy in China
Activities   To organize and conduct the academic research and exchange of information science & technology in both of the theory and practice. To popularize and disseminate STI knowledge, advanced technology and S & T achievements. To provide information consultation and service including market survey to meet various information requirements of the Nation. As a national academic and intermediate institution, to increase links between central and local authorities in the field of S&T Information, to strengthen the communication and cooperation among information bodies and professionals, to create more channels and opportunities for the academic exchange and information cooperation at home and abroad. To recommend and award the works of excellence of articles and books of information science and technology, and outstanding-members with great academic and service achievements in the information circle. To publish books and periodicals of information science and service, and also of popular science books
Publications   Official journal: Journal of the China Society of Scientific and Technical Information (ISSN 1–000–135). 1982-. 6/yr. (Yuan Renminbi) 1.30. Address same as Association. Chief editor: Zhang Weiliang. Chinese, with English abstracts. Other publications: The Bulletin of CSSTI; China Information Review; Journal of Popsoft
Bibliography   "Organization Profile: 7. China Society of Scientific and Technical Information," Journal of Information Science 9 (1984):29–30; Khurshid, A., "Library Associations in Asia," Herald of Library Science 28 (1989):3–10

Colombia

195   Asociación Colombiana de Bibliotecologos y Documentalistas (ASCOLBI) (Colombian Association of Librarians)

Address   Calle 21 No. 6–58 oficina 404, Santa fe de Bogotá Tel.: +57 2823620, Fax +57 2825487, juntadirectiva@ascolbi.org; www.ascolbi.org
Languages   Spanish
Established   1956, at Biblioteca Nacional
Officers   Pres: Edgar Allan Delgado
Staff   9 (volunteers)
General Assembly   Entire membership meets once a year
Membership   Total members: 400 (390 individual, 10 institutional). Chapters: 4. Types of membership: Individual, institutional, student, honorary. Requirements: Individual: Professional librarians, assisting staff, students of library science, teachers of library science, or persons with experience in the library field; Institutions: All legally constituted organizations interested in the promotion of books, libraries, documentation, and information in general.
Structure   Governed by Executive Committee. Affiliations: FID, IFLA
Sources of Support   Membership dues, private gifts, sale of publications
Major Fields of Interest   Library profession
Major Goals and Objectives   To contribute to the cultural, economic, and social

development of the nation; to promote and make known the objectives of the library profession; to promote relationships between librarians and to improve the status of the members of the Association; to promote research and to provide technical assistance to the public and private sectors

Activities Past achievements: A major contribution was the implementation of Law 11, 1978, which recognized the library profession in Colombia, and the exercise of the bylaws of this legislation. Current and future: To improve the financial status of the Association; to improve the official journal; to strengthen the Association's work by creating a network of concerned professionals, and by publishing a national directory. Association continues to be active in promoting library-related legislation and its implementation

Publications Official journal: Carta al Bibliotecario (supersedes Boletín de la Asociación Colombiana de Bibliotecarios. 1957–79). 1979-. 4/yr. (US Dollar) 10. Free to members. Editors: Moisés Pedraza and Lucy Espinosa. Address same as Association. Circ: 1,200. Spanish

Bibliography Torres, A., "Colombia," in ALA World Encyclopedia of Library and Information Services. 2nd ed., pp. 213–215. Chicago: American Library Association, 1986

196 Sociedad Columbiana de Archivistas (SCA)

Address Cra. 4 no. 18–50, Of. 807-1, Bogotá, Distrito Capital Tel.: +57 3214582611, Fax +57 2840303, contactenos@scarchivistas.org; www.scarchivistas.org
Languages Spanish
Established 2000
Structure Governed by a board of directors
Major Fields of Interest Columbian archives
Major Goals and Objectives To promote the conditions of archives and professional archivists
Publications Electronic journal (www.sociedadcolombianadearchivistas.org/publica.htm)

Congo, Democratic Republic

197 Association des Bibliothecaires, Archivistes, Documentalistes et Museologues

Address c/o Desire Didier Tengeneza, BP 3182, Kinshasa didierteng@yahoo.fr
Languages French
Officers Pres: Desire Didier Tengeneza

Costa Rica

198 Colegio de Bibliotecarios de Costa Rica (Library Association of Costa Rica)

Address c/o Silvia Diaz Ruiz, Apartado 615-2070, 615-2070 San José Sabanilla Tel.: +506 234 9889, Fax +506 280 8386, cbibliotecariocr@racsa.co.cr; www.metabase.net/metarecursos/profesionales/colegio.shtml

Languages Spanish
Established 1949
Officers Pres: Silvia Diaz Ruiz
Membership 395 members
Structure Affiliated to Federación de Colegios Profesionales de Costa Rica
Major Fields of Interest Libraries and librarianship
Major Goals and Objectives To improve professional qualifications of members through courses, seminars, and various programs; to represent and protect professional interests of librarians
Activities Premio Nacional de Bibliotecologia Efraim Rojas Rojas
Publications Official journal: Revista de Bibliotecología y Ciencias de la Información
Bibliography Retana, P., "Costa Rica," in ALA World Encyclopedia of Library and Information Services. 2nd ed., pp. 230–231. Chicago: American Library Association, 1986

Croatia

199 Hrvatsko Arhivisticko Drustvo (HAD) (Croatian Archival Society)*

Address Marulicev trg 21, 10000 Zagreb Tel.: +385 1 4801981, Fax +385 1 4829000, had@arhiv.hr; www.had-info.hr
Languages Croatian
Established November 7, 1954, Zagreb
Officers Pres: Deana Kovacec; Sectretary: Ivana Prgin; Treasurer: Sanja Brlic; Member of the Exec Board: Silvija Babic; Ladislav Dobrica; Nela Kusanic; Drazen Kusen
Staff 4 members of the Executive Board, 2 voluntary (Secretary, Treasurer)
General Assembly General Assembly take place once every year. Last General Assembly that was also electoral, was held in Osijek on October 23, 2009. Next meeting will be in Slavonski Brod, October 21, 201
Membership Total number of members: 148. Annual dues: 100 kuna (ca. 14 Euros)
Sources of Support Association is financially supported by Ministry of Culture. Partly it is financed through membership dues and donations.
Major Fields of Interest Archives
Major Goals and Objectives To further the development of archives in Croatia; to represent the interests of Croatian archivists
Activities Organization of annual archival conference and every four years organization of archival congress. Association has already held 43 annual conferences and 3 congresses. Coordination of national celebration of International day of Archives. Cooperation with archival association of neighbour countries.
Publications Proceedings of annual conferences and congresses.

200 Hrvatsko knjiznicarsko drustvo (Croatian Library Association)

Address c/o National and University Library, Hrvatske bratske zajednice 4, 10000 Zagreb Tel.: +385 1 6159320, Fax +385 1 6164186, hkd@nsk.hr; www.hkdrustvo.hr(onlyCroatian)

Languages Croatian
Established 1948
General Assembly Entire membership meets annually
Membership Types of membership: Individual. Requirements: Librarians or persons interested in the promotion of librarianship
Structure Governed by Executive Council. Affiliations: IFLA
Sources of Support Membership dues, sale of publications, government subsidies
Major Fields of Interest Librarianship
Major Goals and Objectives To promote librarianship and library services in the country; to encourage the establishment and development of libraries in Croatia; to protect the interests, education and training of Croatian librarians
Activities Sponsors conferences, seminars, workshops, exhibits, and other continuing education programs
Publications Official journal: Vjesnik Bibliotekara Hrvatske (Croatian Librarians' Bulletin). 1951-. 2/yr. Free to members. Address same as Association. Croatian. Other publications: Knjiga i Citaoci (Books and Readers); professional monographs. Publications for sale. No publications exchange program in effect
Bibliography Kort, R.L., "Yugoslavia," in ALA World Encyclopedia of Library and Information Services, 2nd ed., pp. 864–865. Chicago: American Library Association, 1986

Cuba

201 Asociación Cubana de Bibliotecarios (ASCUBI) (Library Association of Cuba)

Address c/o Biblioteca Nacional "José Marti", Plaza de la Revolución, Aptdo 6881, Havana Tel.: +53 7 8817446, ascubi@bnjm.cu; www.bnjm.cu/ascubi
Languages Spanish
Established 1985, Havana
Officers Pres: Margarita Bellas Vilariño; VP: Miguel Viciedo Valdes; Marta Wong Cubelo; Felicia Perez Moya
Staff (provided by National Library)
Membership 2031 members
Structure Governed by executive officers. Affiliations: IFLA (since 1982). Sources of Support Government subsidies
Major Fields of Interest Libraries and library services
Major Goals and Objectives To further the development of libraries and librarians in the country
Publications Official journal: ASCUBI Informa. Bulletin
Bibliography Terry, M., "Cuba," in ALA World Encyclopedia of Library and Information Services. 2nd ed., pp. 231–235. Chicago: American Library Association, 1986

202 Sociedad Cubana de Ciencias de la Información (SOCICT)*

Address Tel.: +53 8603411-1204, eduardo@idict.cu; http://socict.idict.cu
Languages Spanish
Established 1985, Havana

Membership 500 members
Structure Governed by executive committee
Major Fields of Interest Information science and technique
Major Goals and Objectives To promote the development of information science and technique, to provide a forum for scientific exchange
Activities Meetings and seminaries
Publications No official journal. Other Publications: Revistas Electrónicas en Bibliotecología, Articles and directories
Comment no adress available

Curaçao

203 Fundashon Biblioteka Publiko Kòrsou
(Curaçao Public Library Association)

Address Abraham M. Chumaceiro Bulevar 17, Curaçao N.A. Tel.: +599 9 4345200, Fax +599 9 4656247, publiclibrary@onenet.an; www.curacaopubliclibrary.an
Languages Dutch, English
Established This Association was preceded by the Asociation di Biblioteka i Archivo di Korsow (ABAK) (Association of Libraries and Archives), whose President was Maritza F. Eustatia, and which existed from 1972 to 1978
Officers Chair: Shik-Tong Chan; Secr: M. Rojer; Treas: D. Pimentel
Structure Affiliations: IFLA (since 1983)
Major Fields of Interest Public libraries
Major Goals and Objectives To develop public libraries in the Netherland Antilles
Bibliography Foster, B., "Netherlands Antilles," in ALA World Encyclopedia of Library and Information Services. 2nd ed., pp. 599–600. Chicago: American Library Association, 1986

Czech Republic

204 Česká Archivní Společnost
(Czech Archival Society)

Address Podskalska 19, 128 00 Praha 2 cesarch@cesarch.cz; www.cesarch.cz
Established 1990
Membership More than 350 members
Major Fields of Interest Theory of archiving, archiving practice, historical auxiliary sciences
Major Goals and Objectives To support the specialised activities and interests of archivists in the Czech Republic
Activities Organizes conferences every 2 years
Publications Yearbook; Directory of Archives in the Czech Republik

205 Svaz knihovniku a informacních pracovniku CR (SKIP)
(Association of Librarians and Information Professionals)

Address Klementinum 190, 110 00 Prague 1 Tel.: +420 221663338, Fax +420 221663175, vit.richter@nkp.cz; http://skip.nkp.cz
Established Spring 1990; its activities are a continuation of a professional association of the same name which was established during the time of "Prague Spring" in 1968. At that time the association was dissolved in summer of 1970 by the Ministry of Interior
Officers Pres: Vít Richter; Secr: Zlata Houšková
Staff 4 (volunteers)
General Assembly Once in three years
Membership 918 personal (individual) members, 389 corporate members
Structure General Assembly, Executive Committee, EC Presidium, Supervisory Commission, 11 regional chapters, 4 sections, 1 commission, 2 round tables ("clubs")
Sources of Support Membership fees, government and privat (foundation) grants, sponsoring
Major Fields of Interest Library advocacy; participation in government policies and programmes of the library and information services development; programmes of advancement of literacy; library and copyright legislation; cooperation with memory institutions (AML); lifelong professional education; leisure activities; international cooperation
Major Goals and Objectives Extending public internet access in libraries; amendment of the Copyright Act, Library Act; funding of development programmes in the field of library and information services; advancement of reading competence and computer literacy
Activities Library Week (the first week of October); March – the month of Internet (in cooperation); Contemporary Libraries, conference (September, in cooperation); Automating Libraries, seminar (September, in cooperation); Archives, Libraries and Museums in Digital World, seminar (late autumn); A Night with Andersen (close to date of CA birth)
Publications Bulletin SKIP (Association Bulletin); professional publications

Denmark

206 Arkivforeningen
(Danish Association of Archivists)*

Address Rigsdagsgården 9, 1218 Copenhagen K Tel.: +45 33922399, cla@ra.sa.dk; www.arkivforeningen.dk
Languages Danish
Established 1917, Copenhagen
Officers Pres: Christian Larsen; Treas: Susanne Krogh Jensen
Staff 8–10 members of the board (voluntary)
General Assembly Entire membership meets once a year
Membership 46 institutions, 158 individuals
Structure Governed by Executive Committee
Sources of Support Membership dues

Major Fields of Interest Archives and archival studies
Major Goals and Objectives To be the forum for lectures and discussions on archival subjects and other activities of common interest to all employed in archives
Publications No official journal. Arkivforeningens Publikationer. Irreg. Issues proceedings of seminars, reports, manuals for archivists, and other publications. Price lists available. No publications exchange program. Activities Sponsors seminars and conferences
Bibliography Christian Larsen (ed.): Erindringer fra arkivvæsenet 1959–2004 : fra fire rigsarkivarers tid. Copenhagen : Arkivforeningen 2007, 228 p., ill.,
ISBN 978-87-990238-3-7; Elisabeth Bloch & Christian Larsen (eds.): At vogte kulturarven eller at slette alle spor : om arbejdet med den danske bevaringsstrategi, vol. I og II. Copenhagen: Arkivforeningen 2006, 149, 123 pp., ISBN 87-990238-1-4 (vol. I), ISBN 87-990238-2-2 (vol. II); Karsten Gabrielsen (ed.): Rapport fra et nordisk seminar om arkivformidling afholdt 14. marts 2003 i Eigtveds Pakhus, København af Arkivforeningen. Copenhagen : 2004, 109 pp., ISBN 87-990238-0-6

207 Bibliotekarforbundet: Forbundet for Informationsspecialister og kulturformidlere (BF)
(Danish Union of Librarians: Union of Information Specialists andCultural Intermediaries)*

Address c/o Bruno Pedersen, Lindevangs Alle 2, 2000 Frederiksberg Tel.: +45 38882233, Fax +45 38883201, bf@bf.dk; www.bf.dk
Languages Danish
Established 1924, Copenhagen
Officers Pres: Pernille Drost
Staff 24 (paid)
General Assembly All members meet every second year
Membership Total members: 5,000 (individual)
Structure Governed by Executive Committee. Affiliations: IFLA
Sources of Support Membership fees. Budget (Danish Kroner) 2005: 28,334,322; 2006: 28,807,106; 2007: 29.308.187; 2008: 30.370.619; 2009: 30.077.237
Major Fields of Interest Library affairs; cultural matters; union matters
Major Goals and Objectives To strenghten the further work in the professional field, to enforce the educational work, and make a special effort to secure employment and salaries of librarians
Activities As a trade union, BF is working with salaries and working conditions of professional librarians. Also working in the field of creating new job areas for lirbrarians: outside traditional library field, e-government etc
Publications Official journal: Bibliotekspressen, 1970-, 20/yr. Editor: Henrik Hermann. Circ. 6,573
Bibliography Kirkegaard, P., "Denmark," in ALA World Encyclopedia of Library and Information Services. 2nd ed., pp. 246–248. Chicago: American Library Association, 1986

208 Bibliotekslederforeningen (BLF)
(Association of Danish Public Library Managers)

Address Ludvig Feilbergs vej 7, 8210 ÅBYHØY Tel.: +45 65514400, Fax +45

65517337, bbi@bib.aarhus.dk; www.bibliotekslederforeningen.dk(onlydanish)
Languages Danish
Officers Manager: Britta Bitsch

209 Biblioteksstyrelsen (BS)
(Danish National Library Authority)

Address H.C. Andersens Boulevard 2, 1053 Kopenhagen V Tel.: +45 33733373, Fax +45 33733372, post@bibliotekogmedier.dk; www.bibliotekogmedier.dk
Languages Danish, English
Established former name: Statens Bibliotekstjeneste changed into present name in 1997
Major Goals and Objectives To ensure the optimal exploitation of resources and the development of the cooperative Danish library service across municipal and governmental sectors. To develop standards for electronic document delivery, choice of materials, interlibrary lending. To develop annual target and action plans for Denmark's Electronic Research Library
Activities Being responsible for collecting and preparing statistical information about Danish libraries and publishing the results which appear in two separate volumes, dealing with public library statistics and research library statistics respectively. Administrating the Danish public lending right scheme
Publications Danish library statistics 2002; The NAPLE Report: The public library in the Electronic World: A survey initiated by NAPLE. Ed. Niels Ole Pors. 2002

210 Danmarks Biblioteksforening (DB)
(Danish Library Association)*

Address c/o Michel Steen-Hansen, Farvergade 27D, 2.sal, 1463 Copenhagen Vartov Tel.: +45 33250935, Fax +45 33257900, dbf@dbf.dk; www.dbf.dk
Languages Danish
Established 1905, Copenhagen
Officers Pres: Vagn Ytte Larsen; 1st VP: Hanne Pigonska; 2nd VP: Kirsten Boelt; Exec Dir: Michel Steen-Hansen
Staff 7 (paid)
General Assembly Entire membership meets annually
Membership 90 (of 98) municipalities – the politicians representing the committee dealing with libraries. 2000 all in all including municipalities, personal, institutional and others
Structure Governed by Executive Committee. Affiliations: IFLA, EBLIDA etc.
Sources of Support Membership dues, sale of publications, government subsidies
Major Fields of Interest Public libraries and their development, library policies, lobby activities
Major Goals and Objectives To further public library development; to ensure that public libraries can further enlightenment, education and cultural activity to the highest standard for the good of the community and of the individual
Activities Various communication, information and lobby activities; active in promoting library-related legislation; sponsors publications, seminars, workshops; the oldest and main association in Denmark, with active branches in all five Danish regions

Publications Official journal: Danmarks Biblioteker (8 issues/year); Biblioteksvejviser (Library Directory, annual); and others. Publications for sale, price lists available from www.dbf.dk. Publications exchange program in effect with other associations, libraries, and institutions

Bibliography Most recent publication in English: Library Space. Inspiration for buildings and design. Edited: H. Niegaard, K. Schulz and J. Lauridsen, published by Danmarks Biblioteksforening, 2009. Other publications: Dyrbye, Ørum og Svane-Mikkelsen: Det stærke folkebibliotek : 100 år med Danmarks Biblioteksforening (about the first hundred years of the association and its fight for public libraries and free access to knowledge etc), published by Danmarks Biblioteksforening, 1985; Kirkegaard, P., "Denmark" In: ALA World Encyclopedia of Library and Information Services. 2nd ed., pp. 2.46–248. Chicago: American Library Association, 1986; Niegaard, H., "Danmarks Biblioteksforenigings Aarsmode 1985: Konsoliderigens time?" (The Danish Library Association's Annual Meeting 1985: Time to Consolidate?) In: Bibliotek 70 7 (1986):190–193 (in Danish); "Danmarks Biblioteksforenings arsmode i Nyborg den 19–21 marts 1986," (The Danish Library Association's Annual Meeting in Nyborg, 19–21 March 1986) Bogens Verden (1986): 193–244 (special issue, in Danish); Kajberg, L., "The Library of the Future Key Issue at the Annual Conference of the Danish Library Association," Library Times International 4 (1987):20

211 Danmarks Forskningsbiblioteksforening (DF) (Danish Research Library Association)*

Address c/o Ms Hanne Dahl, Tangen 2, 8200 Aarhus N Tel.: +45 89402207, df@statsbiblioteket.dk; www.dfdf.dk
Languages Danish
Established 1978
Officers Pres: Per Steen Hansen; VP: Eli Greve; Treas: Susanne Krag Dalsgaard; Secr: Hanne Dahl
General Assembly Entire membership meets once a year
Structure Governed by Executive Board. Affiliations: IFLA
Sources of Support Membership dues, government subsidies
Major Fields of Interest Research libraries and the library community
Major Goals and Objectives To further cooperation between research libraries; to promote research libraries and their viewpoints among the general public and the political decision-makers; to support and encourage cooperation with national and international organizations
Activities Sponsors conferences, seminars, meetings and other continuing education programs. Association has been active in promoting library-related legislation, such as working for a new administrative framework which resulted in the establishment of the new office of National Librarian
Publications Official journal: DF-Revy. 1978–2009 – REVY. 2010 -. 6/yr. Free to members. Address: DF Sekretariatet, Tangen 2, 8200 Aarhus N. Editor: René Steffensen. Address: Solbjerg Plads 2, 2000 Frederiksberg Circ: 1000. Scandinavian languages, occasionally English. Indexed in LISA. Nordisk BDI-index
Bibliography Birkelund, P., "Danish Research Librarianship Organizes Itself into a New Group," Nordinsk Tidskrift for Bok och Bibliotheksvasen 67 (1980):19–21 (in Danish);

Gregerson, K., "Association of Danish Research Libraries Wants to Keep a Low Profile," Bogens Verden 63 (1981):428–429 (in Danish); Gronbaek, J.H., "Stop the Discord: Danish Research Libraries Association's Renewed Potshots at the Danish Library Association Harms the Entire Library Cause," ibid.:464–466 (in Danish); Kirkegaard, P., "Denmark," in ALA World Encyclopedia of Library and Information Services. 2nd ed., pp. 346–348. Chicago: American Library Association, 1986

212 Danmarks Skolebibliotekarer (Danish School Librarians)

Address c/o Bjarne Thostrup, Måløvhøjvej 10, 2750 Ballerup Tel.: +45 2325 8165, info@emu.dk; http://www.emu.dk/gsk/skolebib/org/index.html
Languages Danish
Established Former name: Danmarks Skolebibliotekarforening; present name adopted in 2004
Membership 2,300 members
Major Fields of Interest School libraries and librarians
Major Goals and Objectives To further school libraries and the professional development of school librarians
Publications Official journal: Skole Biblioteket (The School Library). Address: Kongshvilebakken 10–12, DK-2800 Lyngby

213 Dansk Musikbiblioteks Forening (DMBF) (Danish Association of Music Libraries)

Address Aspegården 38, 2670 Greve fam.dujardin@image.dk; http://dmbf.nu
Languages Danish
Membership Requirements: Interest in music librarianship
Structure Affiliations: Association is the Danish Branch of the International Association of Music Libraries, Archives and Documentation Centres (IAML)
Sources of Support Membership dues
Major Fields of Interest Music libraries, music librarianship
Major Goals and Objectives To further the development of music libraries and music librarianship
Publications official journal: MusikBIB. Journal for Music Libraries. 4/y. Free for members
Bibliography Kirkegaard, P., "Denmark," in ALA World Encyclopedia of Library and Information Services. 2nd ed., pp. 246–248. Chicago: American Library Association, 1986

214 HK/KOMMUNAL Library Committee

Address c/o Güler Celik, Weidekampsgade 8, Postbox 470, 0900 Copenhagen C Tel.: +45 33304362, Fax +45 33304449, 44bbh@hk.dk; www.biblioteksassistent.dk(onlydanish)
Languages Danish
Established 1974
Officers Pres: Kirsten Westh; Secr: Güler Celik

Egypt

215 Central Bank of Egypt (Library Economic Research Sector)
Address   c/o Mohamed Ezzat, 54, Gomhoreya Str, Cairo, PO Box 11511, Cairo
Established   2002
Officers   Pres: Mohamed Ezzat
Membership   50 members

El Salvador

216 Asociación de Bibliotecarios de El Salvador (ABES) (Association of Salvadoran)
Address   Jardines de la Hacienda Block "D", pje. 19 No. 158. Ciudad Merliot, Antiguo Cuscatlan, La Libertad, El Salvador   Tel.: +503 2241-4464, Fax +503 2228-2956, junta_directiva@abc.edu.sv; www.abes.org.sv
Languages   Spanish, Portuguese, English
Established   1958, at the Biblioteca Nacional, San Salvador
Officers   Pres: Yensi Vides; VP: Olinda Gomez; Secr: Laura Aguilar; Treas: Angela Arèvalo
General Assembly   Entire membership meets once a year in July at the Biblioteca Nacional in San Salvador
Membership   Types of membership: Individual, institutional, life, honorary. Requirements: Open to those with at least two years experience in the library field, and to holders of the degree of Bachelor of Science and Letters, who work in libraries in El Salvador
Structure   Governed by Executive Committee. Affiliations: FID
Sources of Support   Membership dues
Major Fields of Interest   Libraries and library education
Major Goals and Objectives   To promote the education and economic status of librarians; to establish, organize, and maintain libraries at all levels; to create a school of librarianship and organize a curriculum for library science; to promote a national bibliography, and to maintain the exchange of professional experiences and ideas among the members of the association
Activities   Sponsors conferences, meetings and other activities to carry out the goals and objectives of the Association
Publications   Official journal: Informa: Boletín Mensual (newsletter). 1973-. 12/yr. Free to members. Address same as Association. Spanish, English, Portuguese. Circ: 150. Issues annual reports and other occasional publications
Bibliography   Fernández de Criado, Jeannette, "El Salvador," in ALA World Encyclopedia of Library and Information Services. 2nd ed., pp. 266–267. Chicago: American Library Association, 1986

217 Comité de Cooperación Bibliotecaria de El Salvador (CCBES)*
Address   Apartado Postal 67 - Multiplaza, Antiguo Cuscatlan   ccbes1@gmail.com; www.sites.google.com/site/ccbes1

Languages Spanish
Established Founded in 1996, in San Salvador
Officers Pres: Carlos R. Colindres; Treas: Aida Cabrales; Trustee: Marta Hernandez
Staff 5 (volunteers)
General Assembly Monthly; Extraordinary meetings when needed
Membership 25 members
Structure The president coordinates meetings with all members to plan for year activities. Any of the members in the Board of directors can establish contacts with local institutions to develop workshops, offer seminars or planned other activities
Sources of Support The only source of funding comes from workshops offered by the Committee
Major Fields of Interest Library development in El Salvador
Major Goals and Objectives To further the cooperation between libraries; to raise the professional standards of those who work in different information unities of the country
Activities Courses, digitalisation projects
Publications No official journal. Publishes bulletins. One of the most relevant CCBES publications is its Plan of Inter-library Cooperation (Plan de Cooperacion Inter Bibliotecaria, 1996), produced after a series of consultations with librarians from all over the country. CCBES maintains bulletins in its website (with local & international news, articles on library and information science)
Bibliography One of the most relevant CCBES publications is its Plan of Inter-library Cooperation (Plan de Cooperacion Inter Bibliotecaria, 1996), produced after a series of consultations with librarians from all over the country. CCBES maintains bulletins in its website (with local & international news, articles on library and information science). Most recently, one of its members published a book in Spanish called "Information science in the XXI century" (Author: Carlos Colindres, ISBN:978-99923-71-565; Year: 2009)

Eritrea

218 Library and Information Association of Eritrea

Address c/o Biniam Ghebretatios, PO box 7409, Asmara

Estonia

219 Eesti Raamatukoguhoidjate Ühing (ELA) (Estonian Librarians Association)

Address c/o Reet Olevsoo, Tonismägi 2, 10122 Tallinn Tel.: +372 6307429, Fax +372 6307429, ela@nlib.ee;
www.nlib.ee/ERY/;www.goethe.de/z/30/infomoe/estland/deest15.htm
Established 1923, refounded 1988
Officers Pres: Anneli Sepp
General Assembly General meeting at least once a year
Membership 3 institutional and 730 personal members, including 12 honorary members

Structure The ELA Board; Committees: Collection Management, Education, Classification and Indexing, Terminology, Antiquarian Book. Working Groups: Acquisition of Public Libraries; Distance Learning. Sections: Rural Libraries, School Libraries, Special Libraries; Club of Retired Librarians (Eks-klubi); Branches in Libraries, Towns and Counties
Sources of Support Entrance and membership fees; grants and financing of projects by public sector institutions
Major Fields of Interest Libraries and librarianship in Estonia
Major Goals and Objectives To develop librarianship; to enhance professional skills of librarians; to protect professional interests
Activities Congresses of Estonian librarians, annual meetings and forums, library days, summer camps, contests, information days, seminars
Publications Official journal: ELA Yearbook 1990-. Co-publisher of Estonian library journal Raamatukogu. Also conference, meeting and seminar materials and other professional publications

Fiji

220 Fiji Library Association (FLA)

Address c/o Treasurer, Gwen Mar, Laucala Campus, Suva Tel.: +679 3223-245; www.fla.org.fj
Languages English
Established 1972, Suva, at University of the South Pacific
Staff None
General Assembly Entire membership meets annually in Suva, in December
Membership 93 members (includes 6 schools). Type of membership: Individual, institutional, overseas, life. Requirements: Applicants for membership accepted under rules prescribed by the Association. Open to any person or institution maintaining libraries or archives. Dues: According to income
Structure Governed by FLA Council. Affiliations: COMLA, IFLA
Sources of Support Membership dues, sale of publications, fundraising
Major Fields of Interest Development and improvement of library services and training
Major Goals and Objectives To encourage and foster development of libraries, librarianship, archives and archivists and other associated activities within Fiji and the South Pacific; to unite all persons engaged or interested in library work; to promote the better administration of libraries, and the position and qualifications of library personnel; to assist in the promotion of legislation affecting libraries; to cooperate with other groups in promoting these aims
Activities Past achievements: Holding annual National Library Week since 1979; sponsoring workshops funded by the Asia Foundation; organizing an annual Fiji Certificate in Librarianship course for the training of paraprofessionals. Current: Continue professional staff training programs for government librarians; organize programs for National Library Week. Future: Prepare a compendium of community library experiences and resources in the Pacific countries with COMLA support; publish a collection of children's stories. Sponsors seminars, workshops, and other continuing education programs

Publications Official journal: Fiji Library Association Journal (formerly Newsletter). 1973-. irreg. Free to members. Address same as Association. Editor: Paula Jones. Circ: 130+. English. Indexed in LISA. Other publications: Proceedings of meetings, annual reports, Libraries and Archives in Fiji; Selection Guide for General References; Fiji Library Directory, and others. Publications for sale, price lists available. No publications exchange program in effect, but the Association would consider exchanging with other national associations; the University of the South Pacific Library buys 40+ copies of the Journal for exchange purposes
Bibliography Holdsworth, H., "Fiji," in ALA World Encyclopedia of Library and Information Services. 2nd ed., pp. 278–279. Chicago: American Library Association, 1986

Finland

221 Arkistoyhdistys r.y. – Arkivföreningen r.f. (AY-AF)
(Society of Finnish Archivists)

Address POB 755, 00101 Helsinki Tel.: +358 50 4000070, laura.ahoranta@arkistoyhdistys.fi; www.arkistoyhdistys.fi
Languages Finnish, Swedish
Established May 24, 1947, first organizational meeting in Helsinki
Officers Chair: Kenth Sjöblom; Secr: Laura Ahoranta; Treas: Karin Gref
Staff None
General Assembly Entire membership meets annually, with informal meetings on special themes 3 to 4 times a year
Membership Types of membership: Individual. Requirements: Archival staff of the state administration and private archives; research workers and others with professional interest in archival matters
Structure Governed by Executive Council
Sources of Support Membership dues, sale of publications
Major Fields of Interest Archives and professional development of archivists
Major Goals and Objectives To establish communication between all archivists and to promote knowledge in all essential questions in the archival field
Activities Sponsors annual meetings and special meetings; arranges excursions to major archives and other places of interest; continues publication program; sponsors continuing education seminars, workshops
Publications No official journal. Publishes series, Arkisto (Archives) in Finnish, with Swedish summaries

222 Bibliothecarii Medicinae Fenniae (BMF)
(Finnish Association of Medical Librarians)

Address Kivenhakkaajankatu 4 C 68, FI-20700 Turku Tel.: +358 9 47472384, Gunilla.Jansson@sydvast.fi; www.terkko.helsinki.fi/bmf
Languages Finnish, Swedish
Established Nov. 14, 1980, constitutive meeting
Officers Pres: Gunilla Jansson
Staff None

General Assembly Entire membership meets twice a year (statutory meetings)
Membership Types of membership: Individual. Requirements: Biomedical librarianship
Structure Governed by Executive Board. Affiliations: IFLA
Sources of Support Membership dues, sale of publications, occasional subsidies
Major Fields of Interest Medical librarianship and librarians
Major Goals and Objectives To be a connecting link between the personnel in medical libraries in Finland. This is done by developing medical libraries and professional skills of the personnel and making the medical libraries known. On the operational level, these goals are carried out by training, informing and publishing, by arranging meetings, by promoting bills and making statements, and by participating in international cooperative activities
Activities In accordance with the stated goals and objectives: Expanding the Association by bringing together medical librarians in Finland; sponsoring information exchanges, publishing, training; participating in activities of international medical librarianship; offering continuing education programs
Publications No official journal, but sends out membership letters. Other publications: Guide books; Pekkarinen, Päivi, and Toivari, Seija, eds., Lääketieteellinen kirjasto: Opaskirja. No publications exchange program

223 Finlands Svenska Biblioteksförening r.f.
(The Finnish-Swedish Library Association)

Address PB 4212, 00099 Helsinki Tel.: +358 2 2154040, robin.fortelius@biblioteken.fi; www.biblioteken.fi/page.asp?_item_id=1249
Languages Swedish, Finnish
Established Nov. 13, 1982, through a merger of two regional associations of Swedishlanguage librarians, Sodra Finlands svenska biblioteksförening (for Southern Finland) and Österbottens svenska biblioteksförening (for Ostrobothnia, i. e. west Finland)
Officers Chair: Robin Fortelius
Staff None
General Assembly Entire membership meets annually
Membership Dues: 20EUR, Students and pensioners 10EUR. Address: c/o Ulrika Nykvist, Vasa stadsbibliotek – landskapsbibliotek, PB 235, 65101 Vasa, Tel: +358 6 3253537
Structure Governed by Executive Council. Affiliations: IFLA (since 1987)
Sources of Support Membership dues
Major Fields of Interest Swedish-language librarianship
Major Goals and Objectives To promote the interests and professional development of Swedish-language librarians in Finland
Bibliography "Finlands Svenska Biblioteksforening," Kirjastolehti 75 (1982):627–628

224 Finnish Association of Information Studies *

Address 33014 Tampere sihteeri@informaatiotutkimus.fi; www.informaatiotutkimus.fi
Languages Finnish, Swedish
Established Dec. 1979, Tampere
Officers Secr: Outi Nivakoski
Staff 4 (volunteers)

General Assembly Entire membership meets twice a year
Membership Individual and institutional members
Structure Governed by Executive Board. Affiliations: IFLA
Sources of Support Membership dues, sale of publications, government subsidies
Major Fields of Interest Library Science and information research
Major Goals and Objectives To promote library science and informatics as a science and as a field of research
Activities Past achievements: Annual research seminars for scientists and librarians who are interested in library science and informatics. Current: Publishing the journal; sponsoring research seminars
Publications Official journal: Informaatiotutkimus (previous title: Kirjastotiede ja Informatiikka). 1981-. 4/yr. Free to members. Indexed in LISA. ISA. Publications exchange program in effect

225 Suomen Kirjastoseura – Finlands Biblioteksförening (FLA) (The Finnish Library Association)

Address Runeberginkatu 15 A 23, 00100 Helsinki Tel.: +358 9 6221399, Fax +358 9 6221466, fla@fla.fi; www.fla.fi
Languages Finnish
Established 1910, Helsinki
Officers Pres: Markku Laukkamen; Gen Secr: Sinikka Sipilä
Staff 6 (paid: 5 full-time, 1 part-time)
General Assembly Entire membership meets every two years
Membership About 1900 personal members. Requirements: Open to any library supporter, e.g., library staff, library committee members, and library users
Structure Governed by Executive Council. Affiliations: IFLA, EBLIDA
Sources of Support Membership dues, sale of publications, government subsidies, grants from private and public foundations. Budget: 550,000 euros
Major Fields of Interest Finnish library policy in general, including all types of libraries
Major Goals and Objectives To promote the development of library services, to make people aware of the libraries' social and academic roles and their cultural significance, and to enhance the professional skills of those involved in the library field
Activities Campaigns for the libraries, provides decision makers with expert information on the subject, further education courses and several theme days annually, and the nationwide Library Meeting every two years, runs projects with various partners, participates actively in topical debates; current discussions concern the role of libraries in the information society, the development of librarianship and information studies education, and the image and status of library work, arranges study trips to Finnish libraries for foreign scholarship-holders and study tours abroad for members
Publications Official journal: Kirjastolehti (Library Journal). 1908-. 8/yr. Address same as Association. Free to members. Circ: 4500. Indexed in LISA, KATI (includes Finnish articles and monographs). Other publications: Professional literature in Finnish, posters, brochures. Publications exchange program of journal only
Bibliography "Goals of the Finnish Library Association," Kirjastolehti 74 (1981):271–274 (in Finnish); Hamalainen, S., "library Organisations Demand a More Developed Library Network," Kirjastolehti 76 (1983): 198–200 (in Finnish); "Operational

Plan of the Finnish library Association for 1984," ibid.:201–203 (in Finnish); Koski, P., Suomen kirjastoseura 1910–1985. Helsinki: FLA, 1985 (ISBN 951-9025-40-5, includes English summary); "Suomen Kirjastoseura 1910–1985," Library Times International 2 (Sept. 1985):30; Sievänen-Allen, R., "Finland," in ALA World Encyclopedia of Library and Information Services. 2nd ed., pp. 280–282. Chicago: American Library Association, 1986

**226 Suomen koulukirjastoyhdistys ry
(School Library Association in Finland)**

Address c/o Johanna Hirmasto, Jousenkaari 8 a 5, 02130 Espoo
suomen.koulukirjastoyhdistys@gmail.com; www.suomenkoulukirjastoyhdistys.fi
Languages Finnish
Officers Pres: Johanna Hirmasto; VP: Seija Salminen
Major Fields of Interest School libraries and school librarianship
Major Goals and Objectives To changes ideas and experiences about developing and improving school libraries and school librarianship
Activities Organizes study trips to outstanding school libraries; provides information about local, national and international school library projects and developments; participates in the activities of international school library organisations

**227 Suomen Tieteellinen Kirjastoseura r.y. – Finlands Vetenskapliga Biblioteksamfund r.f.
(Finnish Research Library Association)***

Address PO Box 217, 00171 Helsinki Tel.: +358 9 191 21724, Fax +358 9 191 23956, kimmo.tuominen@parliament.fi; www.stks.fi
Languages Finnish, Swedish
Established 1929, Helsinki
Officers Library Dir: Pirjo Vatanen; Secr: Meri Kuula
Staff 2 (paid)
General Assembly Entire membership meets twice a year
Membership Individual and institutional membershsip. Requirements: Anyone working in the fields of research libraries and information services or related areas, or anyone interested in furthering the aims of the Association
Structure Governed by Executive Committee. Affiliations: IFLA, NVBF (Nordic Union of Research Librarians)
Sources of Support Membership dues, sale of publications, government subsidies
Major Fields of Interest Research libraries and information services
Major Goals and Objectives To promote research and information activities concerning research libraries and information services; to develop the professional skills of its members; to participate in national and international cooperation in the library field
Activities Sponsors conferences, seminars, educational courses, as well as regular monthly meetings on topics of current interest. The 6 sections of the Association also provide a variety of activities. Trips, organized by the Study Tour Section, offer an opportunity for visiting foreign libraries
Publications Official journal: Signum. 1968-. 8/yr. Free to members. Address same as Association. Circ: 1,500. Finnish, Swedish, English abstracts. Other publications: Guide to

Research Libraries and Information Services in Finland. Activities
Bibliography   Sievänen-Allen, R., "Finland," in ALA World Encyclopedia of Library and Information Services. 2nd ed., pp. 280–282. Chicago: American Library Association, 1986

228   Tietoasiantuntijat ry (TiAs)
(Society for Finnish Information Specialists)*

Address   Harakantie 2, 02650 Espoo   Tel.: +358 9 5418138, Fax +358 9 5418167, info@tietoasiantuntijat.fi; www.tietoasiantuntijat.fi
Languages   Finnish, English, Swedish
Established   5th of January1955, Helsinki, first registration
Officers   Pres: Narjut Kokko; VP: Marjukka Nyberg
Staff   2 part-time, the editor of the magazine gets a small fee
General Assembly   General Assembly meetings are held twice every year. Next meeting takes place on 4 May 2010 in Helsinki, the one before that took place on 10 December 2009 also in Helsinki
Membership   otal number of members (March 2010): 572, of which 535 individual members and 37 organisations. Chapters: 4 (Future, Public sector, Business, Eastern Europe). Types of membership available: Individuals, organisations, students, retirees. Requirements for joining: should work in the field of information science Fees: Individuals (70 EUR), organisations (550 EUR), students (30 EUR)
Structure   Governed by Executive Board. No official affiliations with other organizations, no existing parent organizations.
Sources of Support   Membership dues, sale of publications, government subsidies
Major Fields of Interest   Information services; information resources management; Enhance Reserach and publication
Major Goals and Objectives   To be the leading influential international actor its field in Finland; Bringing together information services providers as well as publishers, management and innovation consultants and scientists
Activities   The Association promotes information services, develops professional skills of its members, and enhances research and publishing in its area of expertise, and acts as a general liaison in the fields of information and knowledge management. The Association performs these functions by promoting general awareness of the knowledge management and information sector by arranging professional training and seminars, by supporting research, and by co-operating with Finnish and international organisations as well as by acting as a professional network. The Association is one the organisers of the global ICSTI conference (with the theme From Information to Innovation) in Helsinki, Finland 10 and 11 June in 2010. The conference features top speakers in the fields of scientific and technical information, both Finnish and foreign. The Association organizes seminars and shorter training sessions for both its members and the general public. The Association regularly gives its expert opinion on forthcoming legislation such as Copyright Act.
Publications   Tietoasiantuntija magazine (5/yr); E-mail newsletter is delivered to the members of the Association approximately 20 times per yr
Bibliography   Poisalo, Tiina: Laehdeluetteloista tietoverkkoihin : Tietopalveluseura 50 vuotta. Publication info: Espoo: Tietopalveluseura, 1997 (Tampere. Mainosmakasiini). Abstract in English and in Swedish. Summary: A solid grasp on information.

Resume: Grepp om informationen
Comment formerly Tietopalveluseura ry

France

229 Agence Bibliographique de l'Enseignement Supérieur (ABES)
Address 27 avenue Professeur-Jean-Louis-Viala, 34193 Montpellier Cedex 5 Tel.: +33 467548410, Fax +33 467548414; www.abes.fr
Languages French, English, Spanish
Established 1994
Staff 51
Publications Monthly news bulletin

230 Association des Archivistes Français (Association of French Archivists)
Address 9, rue Montcalm, 75018 Paris Tel.: +33 1 46063944, Fax +33 1 46063952; www.archivistes.org
Languages French
Established 1904, Paris
Officers Pres: Christine Martinez; VP: Brigitte Pipon; Laurence Üerry; Xavier de la Selle; Treas: Christian Perrot
Staff 6 (volunteers)
General Assembly Entire membership meets annually
Membership Total members: Approx. 550. Types of membership: Individual, institutional, honorary. Requirements: Interest in aims of Association
Structure Governed by Executive Board. Affiliations: ICA
Sources of Support Membership dues
Major Fields of Interest Archives management, preservation, and research
Major Goals and Objectives To promote the development of archives; to improve all aspects of archives management, preservation and research
Activities Special issues of the journal on business archives, audiovisual archives, municipal archives, and others
Publications Official journal: La Gazette des Archives. 1933-. 4/yr. Free to members. Available on the web: www.archivistes.org/Gazette/index.php. French. Publications exchange program with other associations in effect
Bibliography "Pour une politique documentaire nationale," Documentaliste 23 (1986):155–162

231 Association des Bibliothécaires de France (ABF) (Librarians association of France)*
Address 31, rue de Chabrol, 75010 Paris Tel.: +33 1 55331030, Fax +33 1 55331031, abf@abf.asso.fr; www.abf.asso.fr
Languages French
Established 1906 in Paris
Officers Pres: Pascal Wagner; VP: Marie Josée Rich; Dominique Lahary; Secr Gen: Maïté Vanmarque; Treas: Martine Itier-Coeur; Dep Secr Gen: Matthieu Rochelle;

Annick Guinery
Staff 6 (paid)
General Assembly The General Assembly meetings are annual. Next meetings: May 2010 in Tours, June 2010 in Lille
Membership 2,222 individual, 172 institutional. Dues for individual memebership: from 6 to 40 EUR per year, according to individual income
Structure ABF is divided in 22 regional groups. Each group elects its own executive board and regional president. The "National Council" (Conseil National, "CN") gathers all regional presidents. This national council elects the national executive board (Bureau national, "BN") and the national president. ABF is participating in a group of associations of librarians and archivists, IABD. This grouping is likely to evolve into a federation of associations
Sources of Support The association is financed through membership dues, sale of publications, and government subsidies
Major Fields of Interest Librarianship and library services
Major Goals and Objectives To assert the need to equip the libraries of human, technical and financial means to fullfill their missions; to represent the French Librarians with French, foreign and international institutions and organizations, and promote exchanges with colleagues from other countries; to establish a code of ethics and ensure its implementation, in accordance with the principles set out by UNESCO and IFLA; to encourage by any means and any form at both national and local level (coordination, membership, international organization ...) reconciliations with associations with similar vocations and goals
Activities Organisation of seminars and conferences; training of librarian clerks
Publications Official journal : Bibliothèque(s), five issues per year. Other publications: manuals about librarianship ('médiathèmes' series), see : http://www.abf.asso.fr/pages/publication.php; Le métier de bibliothécaire / Association des bibliothécaires de France; sous la direction d'Yves Alix. – 12éme éd. – Paris, Cercle de la Librairie, 2010. – 42 EUR. Annual reports and proceedings of conferences are avalaible in the website
Bibliography Lethève, J., "On the Occasion of the 75th Anniversary of the French Librarians Association: A Retrospective View," Bulletin d'Information de l'ABF 112 (1981):31–32 (in French); Chauveinc, M., "France," in ALA World Encyclopedia of Library and Information Services. 2nd ed., pp. 285–292. Chicago: American Library Association, 1986; "Pour une politique documentaire nationale," Documentaliste 12 (1986):155–162; Terrac, J.-C., "L'association 'Dialogue entre les cultures'," (The Association 'Dialogue between Cultures') Bulletin d'Informations de l'ABF 132 (1986):36–37 (in French); David, Philippe, "Droits de l'homme, solidarité professionnelle des bibliothécaires et relations internationales: l'activité de la commission de l'ABF," (Human Rights, Professional Solidarity of Librarians and International Relations: The Activity of the French Librarians Association commission), ibid.:48–49 (in French); Gascuel, J., "Assemblée générale: compte rendu d'activité," (The General Assembly: Report of Activities), Bulletin d'Informations de l'ABF 136 (1987):47–48; Antoine, D., "Travail sur le fichier des adhérents de l'ABF," (Analysis of the ABF Membership), ibid.:53–60
Comment formerly : Association des bibliothécaires français

232 Association des Bibliothèques Chrétiennes de France (ABCF) (Association of French Theological Libraries)

Address c/o Secrétariat ABCF, Sr Emmanuel Saint-Amand, Abbaye Notre-Dame, 6 rue Montmorin, 77640 Jouarre contact@abcf.fr; www.abcf.fr
Languages French
Established 1963, Paris
Officers Pres: Michèle Behr; VP: Odile Dupont; Secr/Treas: Sr. Emmanuel Saint-Amand
Staff Five volunteers, elected for four years
General Assembly Entire membership meets once a year for four days
Membership Total members: 220. Types of membership: Institutional. Requirements: Libraries of seminaries, monasteries, convents, universities, diocesan libraries or other similar institutions. Dues: EUR 32
Structure Governed by Executive Committee. Affiliations: Conseil International des Associations de Bibliothèques de Théologie (International Council of Theological Library Associations). Affiliation: BETH
Sources of Support Membership dues
Major Fields of Interest Theological libraries
Major Goals and Objectives To further the development of theological libraries through increased cooperation
Activities Commissions on technical services are charged with aiding members in their work; some cooperative activities with International Council of Theological Library Associations and first with Bibliothèques Européennes de Théologie (BETH)
Publications Official journal: Bulletin de Liaison de l'ABCF. 1971-. 3/yr. EUR 10. Free to members. Address same as Association. Circ: 250. French

233 Association des Conservateurs de Bibliothèques (ACB)

Address 16 rue Claude Bernard, 75231 Paris CEDEX 05 Tel.: +33 1 44081862; www.acb.asso.fr
Languages French
Established 1967, Paris, as successor to the Association des Titulaires des Diplômes Supérieures de Bibliothécaires (founded 1960), substitutes Association de l'École Nationale Supérieure des Bibliothécaires (AENSB)
Staff None
General Assembly Entire membership meets once a year
Membership Total members: 600 (individual). Types of membership: Individual, life, student, emeritus, honorary. Requirements: Diploma of the l'École Nationale Supérieure de Bibliothécaires (ENSB). Dues: 34 EUR, students: 17 EUR
Structure Governed by elected Council of 21 members and executive officers. Affiliations: IFLA
Sources of Support Membership dues, sale of publications
Major Fields of Interest Library and information science; professional education; new technology
Major Goals and Objectives To create and maintain a spirit of cooperation among members; to contribute to the development of the National School of Librarianship; to maintain placement services for library school graduates; to promote research in library science and the professional development of librarians through conferences, publications,

and other activities; to establish cooperative relationships with other organizations at a national and international level
Activities Organizes congresses, seminaries, study trips
Bibliography Chauveinc, M., "France," in ALA World Encyclopedia of Library and Information Services. 2nd ed., pp. 285–292. Chicago: American Library Association, 1986; "Pour une politique documentaire nationale," Documentaliste 23 (1986): 155–162

234 Association des Diplômés de l'École de Bibliothécaires-Documentalistes (ADEBD)
(Association of Graduates of the School of Librarians / Documentalists)

Address 43bis rue de la Glacière, 75013 Paris Tel.: +33 1 53631416
Languages French
Established 1936, by alumni of the École des Bibliothécaires-Documentalistes of the Catholic Institute in Paris
Officers Pres: Claudine Masse; Secr: Véronique Goulay
Staff Volunteers
General Assembly Entire membership meets once a year, in or near Paris
Membership Total members: 500+ (individual). Types of membership: Individual, honorary. Requirements: Alumni of the École de Bibliothécaires-Documentalistes
Structure Governed by Executive Council. Affiliations: IFLA, ADBS, ASLIB, Anciens Elèves de l'Institute Catholique de Paris
Sources of Support Membership dues
Major Fields of Interest Status of librarians and documentalists in France; new fields of library school curriculum
Major Goals and Objectives To improve communication among members; to provide latest information concerning the profession; to help new graduates of the School find employment; to establish communications with related organizations to promote librarianship
Activities Working for improvement of status of librarians; helping members in career placement and professional development; sponsoring meetings, lectures, workshops; providing scholarship aid to students
Publications Official journal: Bulletin d'Information de l'Association des Diplômés de l'École de Bibliothécaires-Documentalistes. 1971-. 2/yr. Free to members. Address same as Association. Circ: 500+. French. Also issues an Annuaire
Bibliography Chauveinc, M., "France," in ALA World Encyclopedia of Library and Information Services. 2nd ed., pp. 285–292. Chicago: American Library Association, 1986; "Pour une politique documentaire nationale," Documentaliste 23 (1986): 155–162

235 Association des directeurs des bibliothèques municipales et intercommunales des grandes villes de France (ADBGV)

Address c/o Alain Caraco, Pres, Carré Curial, BP 208, 73002 Chambéry Tel.: +33 4 79600420, Fax +33 4 79600444, a.caraco@mairie-chambery.fr; www.adbgv.asso.fr
Languages French
Established 2002
Officers Pres: Gilles Gudin de Vallerin
Staff equivalent of at least 50 full-time employees

General Assembly Annual general assembly
Membership Directors of municipal libraries in cities with more than 50000 inhabitants. Dues: 20 EUR
Structure Governed by administrative council
Major Goals and Objectives Cooperation and exchange of information and experiences between libraries which face the same problems
Activities Projects conducted by working groups

236 Association des Directeurs et des personnels de direction des Bibliothèques Universitaires et de la Documentation (ADBU) (Association of Directors of University Libraries)
Address 103, bd Saint-Michel, 75005 Paris Tel.: +33 1 44329227, Fax +33 1 44329228, pres.adbu@bnu.fr; www-sv.cict.fr/adbu/
Languages French
Established 1971. After the university reform of 1968 and the creation of new statutes for university libraries in 1970, directors of university libraries felt the need to organize and cooperate
Officers Pres: Albert Poirot; Secr: Laure Delrue
Staff None
General Assembly Entire membership meets once a year
Membership Total members: 178. Members are the directors of all university libraries, plus one section chief per library. No other members admitted
Structure Governed by Executive Board. Affiliations: IFLA
Sources of Support Membership dues
Major Fields of Interest Management of university libraries
Major Goals and Objectives Exchange of information and experiences on the guidance of university libraries
Activities Sponsors conferences, meetings; publications
Publications Official journal: La Lettre de L'ADBU. Publishes congress proceedings and occasional technical reports, such as a "Guide to Interlibrary Lending."
Bibliography Chauveinc, M., "France," in ALA World Encyclopedia of Library and Information Services. 2nd ed., pp. 285–292. Chicago: American Library Association, 1986; "Pour une politique documentaire nationale," Documentaliste 23 (1986):155–162

237 Association des Documentalistes de Collectivités Territoriales (Interdoc)
Address 101 rue de Sèze, 69006 Lyon f.bouvard@cg71.fr; www.interdoc.asso.fr
Languages French
Established 1993
Officers Pres: Michel Noguier; VP: Martine Lavoue; Secr: Franciane Bouvard; Treas: Isabelle Picchi
Membership 140 institutional members
Structure Governed by administrative council
Major Fields of Interest Documentation
Major Goals and Objectives To build a forum for practical exchange of professional problems; to offer advice and assistance

Publications No official journal. Other publications e.g.: Thesaurus. 2003; Plan de Classment. 1993; Ressources Documentaires en Action Sanitaire et Sociale. 1996; Guide d'Orientation de Documentation Européenne. 1996

238 Association des professionnels de l'information et de la documentation (ADBS)
(French Association of Information Scientists and Special Librarians)*

Address 25 rue Claude Tillier, 75012 Paris Tel.: +33 1 43722525, Fax +33 1 43723041, adbs@adbs.fr; www.adbs.fr
Languages French
Established 1963, Paris
Officers Pres: Elisabeth Gayon; Secr Gen: Carole Legrand
Staff 9 (paid)
General Assembly Entire membership meets every 2 years
Membership Types of membership: Individual, institutional, student. Requirements: To be an information specialist or librarian
Structure Governed by Council and executive officers. Affiliations: IFLA, WERTID (West European Round Table on Information and Documentation), AIESI (Association Internationale des Écoles en Sciences de l'Information)
Sources of Support Membership dues, grants
Major Fields of Interest Information systems; special libraries
Major Goals and Objectives To develop information exchanges among professionals; to improve professional development of members; to promote the status of the profession; to disseminate and develop new technologies
Activities Since 1974, organized the National Congress on Information and Documentation every 2 years: Le Congrès IDT (information, documentation, transfer des connaissances) with over 1,000 participants from France and abroad. Association acts as a communication link between the public and private sector in information work. Hosted and organized the IFLA Congress in Paris, August 1989. Signed exchange agreement with CSSTI (China Society for Scientific and Technical Information). Extensive system of continuing education courses and specialized offerings
Publications Official journal: Documentaliste-Sciences de l'Information. 1963-. 5/yr. (French Franc) 360; 420 foreign. Free to members. Director: E. de La Potterie; Chief Editor: Jean-Michel Rauzier. Address same as Association. Circ: 4,200. French. Indexed in LISA, ISA. Journal provides extensive abstracts of French-language professional periodicals and other current information, including latest technology. Issues monthly newsletter, ADBS-Informations. Editor: Paul-Dominique Pomart; annual Membership Directory (e.g., L'Annuaire 89). Extensive publication program on general and specialized topics, e.g., Répertoire des banques de données professionnelles (11th ed., 1989); Michel, Jean and Sutter, Eric, Valeur et compétitivité de l'information documentaire, l'analyse de la valeur en documentation (1988); Recherche en Sciences de l'Information (series); Dictionnaire de Sigles: Electronique-Télécommunications-Informatique (4th ed., 1986); proceedings of congresses, annual reports. Publications issued for sale, price lists available. Publications exchanged with other library associations and libraries
Bibliography Kellermann, L., "ADBS and Its Training Activities," Documentaliste 19 (1982):153–156 (in French); "ADBS Activities in the Field of Specialization Training for

Documentalists," IAALD Ouarterly Bulletin 28 (1983):239–242; Chauveinc, M., "France," in ALA World Encyclopedia of Library and Information Services. 2nd ed., pp. 285–292. Chicago: American Library Association, 1986; "Pour une politique documentaire nationale," Documentaliste 23 (1986):155–162; Robert, L.J., "L'Association Française des Documentalistes et des Bibliothécaires Spécialisés," (French Association of Information Scientists and Special Librarians), Special Libraries 79 (Fall 1988):332–335

239 Association Française des Sciences et Technologies de l'information (ASTI) (French Association for the Information Sciences and Technologies)

Address 4, place Jussieu, 75252 Paris cedex 05 Tel.: +31 1 47407544, asti@ibisc.univ-evry.fr; www.asti.ibisc.univ-evry.fr

Languages French

Established 1998

Membership 28 founding associations

Structure Governed by adminstrative council of 25 elected members

Major Fields of Interest Information science and technology

Major Goals and Objectives To unite the community of information science and technology

Activities Organizes congresses, work groups, summer school

Publications Official journal: ASTI-Hebdo. Online available

240 Association Nationale des Documentalistes de l'Enseignement Privé (ANDEP)

Address c/o Françoise Machebeuf, Secrétaire, 5, rue Fleury, 03200 Vichy Tel.: +33 4 70 59 80 40, francoise.machebeuf@wanadoo.fr; www.andep.org

Languages French

Officers Pres: Emmanuelle Mucignat; VP: Mathilde Leconte; Anne-Sophie Duval; Claire-Hélène Vigneron; Treas: Martine Robine

Major Fields of Interest Professional exchanges on the profession; protection and evolution of the profession of trader-librarian

Activities Meetings, congress (every 3 years), training courses

Publications Official Journal: Dec Info. 2/yr. Actes, 7e congrés ANDEP, Toulouse, 27–29 Octobre 2001. 2002

241 Association pour le Développement des Documents Numériques en Bibliothèques (ADDNB)

Address c/o François Michaud, Bâtiment A 60, rue de Wattignies, 75012 Paris Tel.: +33 1 53461584, Fax +33 1 53461590; www.addnb.org

Established 1996

Major Fields of Interest Numeric documents

Major Goals and Objectives To develop the use of numeric documents (software, CD.Roms, Internet), to encourage the cooperation between libraries

Publications No official journal. Other publications: Guide des documents multimédias en bibliothèques 1999-. email: docnum@addnb.org

242 Fédération des enseignants documentalistes de l'Éducation nationale (FADBEN)
(Federation of Associations of Documentalists-Librarians of National Education)

Address 25 rue Claude Tillier, 75012 Paris Tel.: +33 1 43724560, Fax +33 1 43724560, fadben@wanadoo.fr; www.fadben.asso.fr
Languages French
Established 1972
Officers Pres: Isabelle Fructus
Staff None
General Assembly Entire membership meets annually
Structure Governed by executive officers
Sources of Support Membership dues
Major Fields of Interest Information scientists, librarians
Major Goals and Objectives To further professional development of information scientists/librarians with educational training from public academic institutions
Activities Organizes congress, seminaries, summer university
Publications No official journal. Other Publications: Médiadoc, videos, congress proceedings, bibliographies
Bibliography "20.05.89. Strasbourg. Congrès de la FADBEN," ADBS-Informations 232 (June 1989):2

243 Société Française des Sciences de l'Information et de la Communication (SFSIC)

Address c/o Secrétariat de la SFSIC, 6, avenue Gaston-Berger, 35043 Rennes cedex Tel.: +33 2 99141592, Fax +33 2 99141588, secretariatgeneral@sfsic.org; www.sfsic.org
Languages French
Established 1974
Officers Pres: Alain Kiyindou; Gen Secr: Olivier Galibert; Treas: Claudine Batazzi
Membership 450 researchers, who work in the field of information or communication. Restrictions: Application for membership must be allowed by the administrative council. Dues/yr: 40 eur professional, 23 eur students or pensioners, 150 eur institutions
Structure Governed by administrative council consistiing of 12–20 members
Sources of Support Membership dues and subventions
Major Fields of Interest Research in the field of information or communication
Major Goals and Objectives To contribute to the development of information and communication sciences
Activities Organizes biannual congresses and seminaries
Publications Official journal: La lettre d'Inforcom. 2/yr

Gabon

244 Association des documentalistes du Gabon (ADG)

Address BP 17068, Libreville Tel.: +241 612273, Fax +241 763909, youmba@nomade.fr
Established 1984

Major Fields of Interest Documentation
Major Goals and Objectives To promote, establish, and apply the methods and standards of documentation; to foster the use of new technologies; to encourage research
Publications Official journal: Bulletin de Liaison de l'Association des Documentalistes du Gabon

Georgia

245 Association of Information Specialists (AIS)
Address 47, Kostava St. 5th Floor, Room 503, 380043 Tbilisi Tel.: +995 32 334310, Fax +1 801 681 8765; www.ais.org.ge
Languages English, Georgian
Established 1997
Officers Pres: Besiki Stvilia; VP: Irina Chanturishvili; Exec Dir: George Shatirishvili
Major Fields of Interest Libraries, Library and Information Science Education
Activities Offers training course of continuing professional education for librarians and information specialists; sponsors workshops and conferences
Publications Official journal: AIS newsletter. (distributed electronically. online from AIS Website or recieve by E-mail)

246 Georgian Library Association
Languages Georgian, English, Russian
Membership Memebers: 29
Structure Governed by Executive Board. Affiliations: IFLA
Major Fields of Interest Library management and preservation in Georgia
Major Goals and Objectives Co-operation, joint coordination of the activities, Strengthening the dialogue and exchange of ideas between the libraries and the society, Consciously developing the intellectual and creative potential of the members of the Association, encouraging the innovations, Taking advantage of the talent and energy of the young people, Stating the precise goals and objectives, supporting plausible discussions and implementing sensible practical tasks
Activities Organizes National Library Week, workshops and other events
Publications Official journal: Sakartvelos Biblioteka. 2000-. 4/yr. Since 2003 also in electronic form: www.library.ge. Chief Editor: Aleksanrer Loria
Comment No adress or contact information available

Germany

247 Arbeitsgemeinschaft der Archive und Bibliotheken in der Evangelischen Kirche (AABevK)
(Study Group of Archives and Libraries in the Evangelical Church)
Address c/o Dr. Bettina Wischhöfer, Lessingstraße 15 a, 34119 Kassel Tel.: +49 561 78876-0, Fax +49 561 78876-11, info@evangelische-archive.de; www.ekd.de/archive/index.htm

Languages German

Established 1936, as Arbeitsgemeinschaft landeskirchlicher Archivare; name changed into Arbeitsgemeinschaft für das Archiv- und Bibliothekswesen in der evangelischen Kirche in 1961; then changed into Arbeitsgemeinschaft für kirchliches Archiv- und Bibliothekswesen in 1970; present name adopted in 1990

General Assembly Entire membership meets every 3 years

Membership Sections: 2 (archives, libraries). Requirements: Archives and research libraries in the Evangelical Church, which are administered by at least 1 full-time worker. No dues

Structure Governed by Executive Committee, under the Evangelical Church. No affiliations

Sources of Support Sale of publications, support by the Evangelische Kirche in Deutschland (Evangelical Church in Germany)

Major Fields of Interest Religious/church archives and librarianship

Major Goals and Objectives To function as forum for professional concerns of archives of the Evangelical Church; to assist in basic methods of management; to publish professional material; to give assistance in the evaluation, exchange of experience, and consultation to members for the improvement of their archives; to represent Church archives and librarianship to the public; to communicate and cooperate with similar establishments and organizations; to promote interlending among Church archives and libraries; to establish standards and rules for the classification and cataloging of archival material

Activities Publication of research in the area of Church archives and librarianship, as well as on Church history. Sponsors continuing education courses, workshops for members working in Church archives and related institutions. Association has been active in promoting library-related legislation for the Evangelical Church in Germany, for regulations as to the use of Church archives and libraries, and others. Sponsors book week activities

Publications Official journal: Allgemeine Mitteilungen. 1969-. irreg. Free to members. Editor: Kirchenarchivdirektor Hermann Rückleben. Address: Postfach 2269, Blumenstrasse 1, D-7500 Karlsruhe. Circ: Membership only. German. Other publications: Veröffentlichungen der Arbeitsgemeinschaft der Archive und Bibliotheken in der evangelischen Kirche; Reports of seminars, workshops. Publications for sale. No publications exchange program

Bibliography Erbacher, H., Zeitschriften-Verzeichnis evangelisch-kirchlicher Bibliotheken (2nd ed., 1980); Bibliotheksführer der evangelischen Kirchen in der Bundesrepublik Deutschland (1982); Handbuch des kirchlichen Archivwesen. Band 1: Die zentralen Archive in der evangelischen Kirche (Handbook of Church Archives, v. 1: The Central Archives of the Evangelical Church) (3rd ed., 1986)

248 Arbeitsgemeinschaft der Bibliotheken und Dokumentationsstellen der Ost-, Ostmittel- und Südosteuropaforschung e.V. (ABDOS)
(Association of Libraries and Documentation Centers for Eastern, Eastern Central and Southeastern Europe Research)

Address c/o Dr. Jürgen Warmbrunn, Gisonenweg 5–7, 35037 Marburg Tel.: +49 6421 184-150, Fax +49 6421 184-139, warmbrun@herder-institut.de; www.abdos.de

Languages German
Established 1970
Officers Vice-Chair: Dr. Liliana Djekovic-Sachs
Staff None
General Assembly Entire membership meets once a year. 2002: Liberec, Czech Republic; 2003: Moscow, Russia; 2004: Kiel, Germany; 2005: Berne, Switzerland
Membership Ca. 35 individual and 15 institutional members. Requirements: To work in academic or other institutions specializing in research on Eastern, Eastern Central and Southeastern Europe
Structure Registered association of benefit to the public. Governed by Chair
Sources of Support Conference fees, membership fees
Major Fields of Interest Libraries with specialized collections of material on Eastern, Eastern Central and Southeastern Europe
Major Goals and Objectives To provide a forum for exchange of information; to cooperate with other national and international organisations
Activities Consist mainly of holding the annual conferences and publishing the proceedings and a relevant journal
Publications Official journal: ABDOS-Mitteilungen. 1981-. 2/yr. Free to members. Editor: Dr. Hans-Jakob Tebarth, Martin-Opitz-Bibliothek, Berliner Platz 5, 44623 Herne, Germany. Proceedings

249 Arbeitsgemeinschaft der Fachhochschulbibliotheken (Association of Libraries of Polytechnic Institutions)

Address c/o Sonja Peters, Friedrichstr. 57–59, 38855 Wernigerode Tel.: +49 39 43659170, Fax +49 39 43659174, speters@hs-harz.de; www.hs-harz.de
Languages German
Established 1977
Officers Chair: Sonja Peters
General Assembly Entire membership meets annually
Membership Open to libraries of polytechnic institutions (Fachhochschulen)
Major Fields of Interest Libraries of polytechnic institutions
Major Goals and Objectives To promote the development of polytechnic libraries and provide a forum for the exchange of ideas and cooperation
Activities Meetings are hosted by a member institution. Some current activities are in the area of library automation, user services, government support, etc

250 Arbeitsgemeinschaft der Großstadtbibliotheken (Association of Metropolitan City Libraries)

Address c/o Harald Pilzer M.A., Wilhelmstr. 3, 33602 Bielefeld Tel.: +49 521 512443, Fax +49 521 513387; www.vbnw.de/34.html
Languages German
Officers Chair: Harald Pilzer
General Assembly Entire membership meets annually
Membership Open to libraries serving metropolitan areas
Major Fields of Interest Metropolitan city libraries

Major Goals and Objectives To provide a forum for cooperation and exchange of information for metropolitan city libraries; to further the development of such libraries
Activities Sponsors conferences, seminars, etc. Issues are union catalogs, collection development, and continuing education

251 Arbeitsgemeinschaft der Kunst- und Museumsbibliotheken (AKMB) (Working Group Art and Museum Libraries)*

Address c/o Sonja Benzner, Ludwig Forum für Internationale Kunst / Bibliothek, Juelicher Str. 97–109, 52070 Aachen Tel.: +49 241 1807-118, sonja.benzner@mail.aachen.de; www.akmb.de
Languages German
Established 1995 in Berlin
Officers Chair: Sonja Benzner; Vice Chair: Volker Schuemmer; Secr: Sybille Hentze; Treas: Sabine Winter
Staff None
General Assembly Entire membership meets once a year
Membership Types of membership: Institutional and personal. Requirements: art or museum library or documentation department, art or museum librarian
Structure Governed by executive officers. Affiliations: ASpB (Arbeitsgemeinschaft der Spezialbiblitheken/Association of Special Libraries)
Sources of Support Membership fees, donations
Major Fields of Interest Cooperation and bibliographical activities of German art and museum libraries
Major Goals and Objectives Providing and enabling the exchange of information, communication and practical experience, promoting cooperation with other institutions and organisations, building and maintaining international contacts
Activities Lobbying for members interest, organizing professional lectures, advanced training and further educational courses, several subcommittees, "museums libraries", "software", "standards", "cataloguing advisory"
Publications AKBM-news, since 1995, 2 issues/yr
Bibliography Catherine Hilliard: Getting it all together. German art libraries in the year 2000. In: Art Libraries Journal Vol 26 (2001), no. 3, p. 27–32; Christiane Schaper: Die Arbeitsgemeinschaft der Kunst- und Museumsbibliotheken – AKMB. In: Spezialbibliotheken heute – Wettbewerb und Kooperation. 28. Arbeits- und Fortbildungstagung der AspB / Sektion 5 im DBV, Hannover 2001. Jülich 2001, p. 133–138; Carola Wenzel: Arbeitsgemeinschaft der Kunst- und Museumsbibliotheken (AKMB). In: ARLIS UK & Ireland: News-Sheet no. 148 (2000), p.7–8; Christiane Schaper: Neue Organisationsformen in Kunst- und Museumsbibliotheken. In: Deutscher Museumsbund. Bulletin (2000), no. 4., p. 13–14; Kunst- und Museumsbibliotheken: Schranken noch zu überwinden. In: Kolibri. Kongresszeitung zum 89. Deutschen Bibliothekartag an der Albert-Ludwigs-Universität Freiburg, no. 2 (5/26/1999), p. 1 + 3; Rüdiger Hoyer: Bericht über die Aktivitäten der 'Arbeitsgemeinschaft Kunst- und Museumsbibliotheken' (AKMB) im Rahmen des 89. Bibliothekartages in Freiburg i.Br. In: IFLA/Section of Art Libraries Newsletter No. 45 (1999), no. 2, p. 12–13; Scheuer, Bettina: Respektables Magazin. Rezension der AKMB-news. In: Buch und Bibliothek 51 (1999), p. 647–648; Christiane Schaper: ARLIS conference 1998 – experiences as a first time

overseas delegate. In: ARLIS News Sheet No. 134 (Sept. / Oct. 1998), p. 10; Lutz Jahre: Collaboration between artists and librarians in a German Magazine. In: Art Libraries Journal Vol. 23 (1998), no. 1, p. 22–25; Margret Schild: Kunstbibliotekssamarbejde i Tyskland. In: ARLIS/Norden Info (1998), no. 1, p. 38–39 [text in english]; Margret Schild: Working Group of Art and Museum Libraries in Germany. In: IFLA / Section of Art Libraries Newsletter No. 42 (1998), no. 1, p. 6 – 7; Margret Schild, Monika Steffens: Die Arbeitsgemeinschaft der Kunst- und Museumsbibliotheken (AKMB). Vorstellung einer jungen, sehr aktiven Vereinigung. In: Rundbrief Information & Bibliotheken Vol. 12 (1997), no. 66, p. 30–32; Monika Steffens, Margret Schild: The Arbeitsgemeinschaft der Kunst- und Museumsbibliotheken (AKMB). A review one year after its foundation. In: Art Libraries Journal Vol. 21 (1996), no. 4; Monika Steffens: Kunst- und Museumsbibliotheken – 1. Mitgliederversammlung der AKMB in Göttingen. In: Bibliotheksdienst Jg. 29 (1995), p. 1154–1157; for earlier background information see Arbeitsgemeinschaft der Kunstbibliotheken. Munich 1975; Laura held: The AKMB – Arbeitsgemeinschaft der Kunst- und Museumsbibliotheken. In: AKBM-news Vol. 9 (2003), no. 2, p. 3–6 IFLA special: German art libraries

252 Arbeitsgemeinschaft der Parlaments- und Behördenbibliotheken (APBB) (Association of Parliamentary and Administrative Libraries)

Address   c/o Dr. Jürgen Kaestner - Archiv, Bibliothek, Dokumentation, Schlossplatz 1–3, 65183 Wiesbaden Tel.: +49 611 350380, Fax +49 611 350379; www.apbb.de
Languages   German
Established   1955, Düsseldorf, as Commission of Parliamentary and Administrative Libraries of the Association of German Librarians (Verein Deutscher Bibliothekare). Present name adopted in 1957
Officers   Chair: Jürgen Kaestner
General Assembly   Entire membership meets once a year
Membership   Total members: 500 (institutional). Types of membership: Institutional. Requirements: Member institutions should be parliamentary or administrative libraries. No dues
Structure   Governed by executive officers
Sources of Support   Sale of publications
Major Fields of Interest   All activities of parliamentary and administrative libraries
Major Goals and Objectives   Representation of common interests towards third parties; improvement of cooperation between parliamentary and administrative libraries in Germany; counselling of the member libraries and their staff, e.g., with regard to the introduction of electronic data processing in libraries
Activities   congresses; current topics: organisation and management issues, data base and internet enquiries etc
Publications   Official journal: Mitteilungen (news bulletin in electronic form, pdf format). 1958-. 2/yr. Address same as Association. Indexed in Deutsche Bibliographie. Bibliotheksdienst. Issues Arbeitshefte (Working Papers) (annual). Leipziger Memorandum
Bibliography   Taube, Utz-Friedebert, "25 Jahre Arbeitsgemeinschaft der Parlaments- und Behordenbibliotheken,"(25 Years of APBB) Zeitschrift für Bibliothekswesen und Bibliographie 28(1981):76–79; Dietz, W., Kirchner, H., and Wenicke, K.G., eds., Bibliotheksarbeit für Parlamente und Behörden: Festschrift zum 25-jährigen Bestehen der

Arbeitsgemeinschaft der Parlaments- und Behördenbibliotheken (Library Work for Parliaments and Government Agencies: Festschrift for the 25th Anniversary of APBB). Munich: Saur, 1980 (all in German)

253 Arbeitsgemeinschaft der Regionalbibliotheken im Deutschen Bibliotheksverband
(Association of German Regional Libraries)

Address c/o Corinna Roeder, Pferdemarkt 15, 26121 Oldenburg Tel.: +49 441 799-2801, Fax +49 441 799-2865, roeder@lb-oldenburg.de; www.bibliotheksverband.de/fachgruppen/arbeitsgruppen/regionalbibliotheken.html
Languages German
Established 1971, Cologne, through a merger of the Arbeitsgemeinschaft Kommunaler Wissenschaftlichen Bibliotheken (Working Group of Municipal Research Libraries) and the Arbeitsgemeinschaft der Landesbibliotheken (Working Group of State Libraries)
Officers Chair: Corinna Roeder; 1st Vice Chair: Dr. Axel Halle; 2nd Vice Chair: Dr. Irmgard Siebert
General Assembly Entire membership meets once a year
Membership Total members: 60 (institutional). Types of membership: Institutional. Requirements: Libraries with predominant research collections, or central libraries of individual regions (states, districts, cities)
Structure Governed by Executive Board. Affiliations: VDB
Sources of Support Member contributions
Major Fields of Interest Regional libraries
Major Goals and Objectives (1) Promotion of librarianship outside the universities; (2) general exchange of knowledge and experience; (3) solution of problems in regional planning; (4) discussion of common projects; (5) mutual support in representing the interests of individual libraries
Activities Various activities cover the following areas: Analysis of use structure, common guidelines for acquisition policies, expansion of bibliographic services; maintenance of and access to collections, cooperation with universities and professional schools, cooperation with public libraries, and definition of cultural responsibilities

254 Arbeitsgemeinschaft der Spezialbibliotheken e.V. (ASpB)
(Association of Special Libraries)

Address c/o Jadwiga Warmbrunn, Gisonenweg 5–7, 35037 Marburg Tel.: +49 6421 184151, Fax +49 6421 184139, geschaeftsstelle@aspb.de; www.aspb.de
Languages German
Established 1946 as Arbeitsgemeinschaft der technisch-wissenschaftlichen Bibliotheken; present name adopted in 1967
Officers Chair: Dr. Jürgen Warmbrunn; 1st Vice Chair: Henning Frankenberger; 2nd Vice Chair: Michael Normann
Membership Total members: 1,000 (individual and institutional). Requirements: Open to libraries, documentation centers, institutions, business and lawyers and other interested persons. Dues: None. Members are obliged to purchase conference reports
Structure Governed by Executive Board. Affiliations: IFLA
Sources of Support Sale of publications

Major Fields of Interest   Cooperation among special libraries
Major Goals and Objectives   To promote the exchange of practical experience and the cooperation between special libraries, particularly with respect to lending and exchange of facilities
Activities   Carried out in accordance with the aims of the Association: Sponsoring conferences; publishing guidelines for special libraries; promoting information and documentation facilities in special libraries; training librarians in modern technologies for information management and information services; representing special libraries of the Federal Republic of Germany in international organizations and at meetings
Publications   Official journal: Bericht über die Tagung (Conference report). 1946-. Biennial. Address same as Association. Other publications: ASpB-Schriftenreihe, etc. Publications available for sale

255 Arbeitsgemeinschaft für juristisches Bibliotheks- und Dokumentationswesen (AjBD)
(German Law Libraries Association)

Address   c/o Dr. Hans-Peter Ziegler, Ismaninger Str. 109, 81675 München Tel.: +49 89 9231358, Fax +49 89 9231201; www.ajbd.de
Languages   German
Established   1971, Cologne
Officers   Chair: Hans-Peter Ziegler; Vice Chair: Sabine Lieberknecht
Staff   9 volunteers
General Assembly   Entire membership meets once a year
Membership   Requirements: Libraries with law collections and librarians working there
Structure   Governed by Executive Board. Affiliations: IALL (German Section)
Sources of Support   Sale of publications, membership dues
Major Fields of Interest   Law librarianship; legal documentation and information; legal bibliography
Major Goals and Objectives   To promote law librarianship and documentation; to provide exchange of information and mutual assistance to members
Activities   Sponsors continuing education programs (about 1–2 per year); publication of series and journal
Publications   Official journal: Recht, Bibliothek, Dokumentation (RBD): Mitteilungen der AjBD. 1971-. 3/yr. (Euro) 25,50. German. Other publications: Arbeitshefte der AjBD. a numbered series, irreg. Price lists available. No publications exchange program
Bibliography   Arbeitsgemeinschaft für juristisches Bibliotheks- und Dokumentationswesen (AjBD)/German Law Libraries Association. In: Lansky, R.: Handbuch der juristischen Bibliotheken/Handbook of Law Libraries, Berlin 1993, p. 271–314 (in German)

256 Arbeitsgemeinschaft für Medizinisches Bibliothekswesen (AGMB)
(Association for Medical Librarianship)

Address   c/o Dr. Diana Klein, Am Hubland, 97074 Würzburg Tel.: +49 931 31-85910, Fax +49 931 888-5970; www.agmb.de
Languages   German
Established   1970, Cologne

Officers Chair: Dr. Diana Klein; 1st Vice Chair: Dr. Eike Hnetschel; 2nd Vice Chair: Anna Schlosser; Treas: Christa Gieser
General Assembly General assembly meets once a year. 2010: 27th-29th September Mainz
Membership 454 members. Dues: none
Major Fields of Interest Medical librarianship
Major Goals and Objectives To promote medical libraries and medical librarianship; to offer to its members extensive information, exchange of experiences, personal contacts, mutual advice
Publications official journal: medizin-bibliothek-information. 2001-. 3/y
Bibliography For background information see Horstmann, W. and Hansen, U., Arbeitsgemeinschaft für Medizinisches Bibliothekswesen (Berlin: Deutscher Bibliotheksverband, 1975)

257   Arbeitsgemeinschaft Gefangenenbüchereien / Deutscher Bibliotheksverband (Sektion 8)

Address c/o Gerhard Peschers, Gartenstr. 26, 48147 Münster Tel.: +49 251 2374-116, Fax +49 251 2374201, gerhard.peschers@jva-muenster.nrw.de; www.gefangenenbuechereien.de
Languages German
Established 1995
Officers Speaker: Gerhard Peschers
General Assembly No regular meetings
Membership Working group consists of 4 members
Major Fields of Interest Prison Libraries in Germany
Publications Deutsches Bibliotheksinstitut (Ed.): Bibliotheksarbeit in Justizvollzugsanstalten. Berlin 1986; Gerhard Peschers, Klaus Josef Skopp: Bibliotheksarbeit im Strafvollzug in Nordrhein-Westfalen. In: Buch und Bibliothek Vol. 46/3 (1994), p. 256–262; Wilhelm Gröning, Gerhard Peschers: Gefangenenbücherei mit Modellcharakter, die Bibliothek der JVA Gelsenkirchen. In: Buch und Bibliothek, No. 3 (1999), p.196; Gerhard Peschers: Weiterentwicklung der Bibliotheksarbeit im Justizvollzug in NRW. In: Buch und Bibliothek Vol. 51 (1999), p. 254–256; Gerhard Peschers: Gefangenenbüchereien als Zeitzeugen: Streifzug durch die Geschichte der Gefangenenbüchereien seit 1850. In: Begleitbuch zur Ausstellung Ketten-Kerker-Knast: Zur Geschichte des Strafvollzugs in Westfalen im Gustav-Lübcke-Museum in Hamm 2000 (Ed.:Maria Perrefort), p. 123–141; Beate Möllers: Menschen brauchen Medien und Gefängnisse Bibliotheken. In: ProLibris No.2 (2001), p. 97–99; Gerhard Peschers: Die Bücherei der JVA Bielefeld-Brackwede II. In: ProLibris No, 2 (2001), p. 99–100

258   Arbeitsgemeinschaft Katholisch-Theologischer Bibliotheken (AKThB) (Association of Catholic Theological Libraries)

Address c/o Jochen Bepler, Domhof 30, 31134 Hildesheim Tel.: +49 5121 138331, Fax +49 5121 138313, dombibliothek@bistum-hildesheim.de; www.akthb.de
Languages German
Established 1947, Frankfurt am Main

Officers Pres: Jochen Bepler; VP: Dominikus OFM Göcking; Treas: Dr. Hermann-Josef Schmalor
General Assembly Entire membership meets once a year
Membership Total members: 160 (institutional). Types of membership: Institutional only. 5 countries represented. Requirements: Catholic theological libraries. Dues (Euro): 35
Structure Governed by Executive Board. Affiliations: Conseil International des Associations de Bibliothèques de Théologie (International Council of Theological Libraries)
Sources of Support Membership dues
Major Fields of Interest Catholic theological libraries
Major Goals and Objectives To promote and further theological librarianship and theological libraries within the Catholic Church in German-speaking regions; to promote cooperation among member libraries; to improve theological library collections
Activities To advance the cooperation between members and the (further) education of librarians; to cooperate with other libraries at home and abroad
Publications Official journal: Mitteilungsblatt der AKThB. 1952-. 1/yr. Membership. German. Other publications: Newsletter of the President; Handbuch der kirchlichen katholisch-theologischen Bibliotheken. etc. Publications for sale. No publications exchange program
Bibliography "35. Jahrestagung," (35th Annual Meeting) Bibliotheksdienst 8 (1982):693–694; Gilmont, J.-E and Osborne, T. P. "Les associations de bibliothèques de théologie," Revue théologique de Louvain 15 (1984):73–85 (in French). For background information see Reichert, F.R., "Kooperation im kirchlichen Bibliothekswesen Deutschlands. Die Arbeitsgemeinschaft Katholisch-Theologischer Bibliotheken," (Cooperation between Theological Libraries: The AKThB) Bibliotheksarbeit heute. ZfBB Sonderheft 16 (1973):176–184 (in German); Der innerkirchliche Leihverkehr – Beobachtungen und Tendenzen. Ed. Rita Warmbold. 1994

259 Arbeitsgemeinschaft Patientenbibliotheken im Deutschen Bibliotheksverband

Address c/o Brigitta Hayn, Schumannstr. 20–21, 10117 Berlin Tel.: +49 30 450573047, Fax +49 30 450573901, brigitta.hayn@charite.de
Languages German
Officers Chair: Brigitta Hayn
Major Goals and Objectives Exchange of information
Activities Educational activities for librarians

260 Berufsverband Information Bibliothek e.V. (BIB) (Association of Information and Library Professionals)*

Address c/o Michael Reisser (Secretary), Gartenstr. 18, 72764 Reutlingen, P.O. 1324, 72703 Reutlingen Tel.: +49 7121 34910, Fax +49 7121 300433, mail@bib-info.de; www.bib-info.de
Languages German
Established Founded 2000. Present name since 2000, absorbed 1997 the Verein der Bibliothekare an Öffentlichen Bibliotheken (VBB, founded 1949) and Bundesverein der Bibliotheksassistenten/innen und anderer Mitarbeiter/innen an Bibliotheken (BBA,

founded 1987), absorbed 2000 Verein der Diplom-Bibliothekare an wissenschaftlichen Bibliotheken (VdDB, founded 1948) and Verein der Bibliothekare und Assistenten (vba; founded 1997)
Officers Pres: Susanne Riedel; Secr: Michael Reisser
Staff 5 employees, including 2 editors of the journal "BuB (Buch und Bibliothek) – Forum für Bibliothek und Information"
General Assembly Every year, open to all members (no delegates): Deutscher Bibliothekartag, June 2011 in Berlin; Deutscher Bibliothekartag, May 2012 in Hamburg; Kongress für Information und Bibliothek, March 2013 in Leipzig
Membership 6,300 personal members
Structure General Assembly, Managing Committee, Office/Headquarter, 6 Committees, 15 State Divisions
Sources of Support Membership fees (25 to 97 Euros p.a.)
Major Fields of Interest IMembers: Librarians and library workers employed in public and academic libraries. BIB represents the interests of librarians; maintains professional standards. Stresses the importance of professional training and salaries that correspond to the level of training. Increases public awareness of the social and educational importance of libraries and professional standards
Activities Education and training of librarians, lobbying, professional help and support including publications
Publications Official journal: BuB – Forum für Bibliothek und Information. 10/y. Free to members
Bibliography vba: Die ersten 50 Jahre, 1999; Innenansichten-Außenansichten: 50 Jahre VdDB, 1998; H. J. Kuhlmann: Der Weg zum kritischen Bürger: 40 Jahre VBB, 1989

261 Bibliothek&Information Deutschland (BID)
(Federal Union of German Library and Information Associations)

Address c/o Barbara Schleihagen, Straße des 17. Juni 114, 10623 Berlin Tel.: +49 30 39001480, Fax +49 30 39001484, bid@bideutschland.de; www.bideutschland.de
Languages German
Established Sept. 20, 1989, by prominent librarians representing institutional and personal library associations of the Federal Republic of Germany, in order to centralize lobbying efforts on behalf of libraries and librarians; replaces the Deutsche Bibliothekskonferenz. In June 2004, associations for librarians and information professionals joined forces and form now the BID
Staff 1
General Assembly Whole membership meets once a year
Membership Total members: 7 associations: (1) Deutscher Bibliotheksverband (DBV); (2) Bertelsmann Stiftung; (3) Verein Deutscher Bibliothekare (VDB); (4) Goethe-Institut e.V.; (5) Deutsche Gesellschaft für Informationswissenschaft und Informationspraxis e. V. (DGI); (6) Berufsverband Information Bibliothek (BIB); (7) ekz.bibliotheksservice GmbH (ekz)
Structure Governed by Board of Directors
Sources of Support Membership fees
Major Fields of Interest Library associations; librarianship

Major Goals and Objectives Improving the representation of the library world to the general public of Germany; designing public relations more effectively; strengthening cooperation among library associations and information professional associations
Activities Advancement of libraries
Publications official journal: Bibliotheksdienst: Organ der Bundesvereinigung Deutscher Bibliotheksverbände. 12/y. Ed. Zentral- und Landesbibliothek Berlin; Other Publications: Entscheidungssammlung zum Bibliotheksrecht. Lehren und Lernen mit der Schulbibliothek. Manifest für Schulbibliotheken. etc
Bibliography "Germany: New Structure of Cooperation among Library Associations," Herald of Library Science 28 (1989):290–291; "Federal Federation of German Library Associations Founded," Library Times International 6 (1990):54

262 Deutsche Gesellschaft für Informationswissenschaft und Informationspraxis e.V. (DGI)
(German Association for Information Science and Practice)

Address Hanauer Landstraße 151–153, 60314 Frankfurt am Main Tel.: +49 69 430313, Fax +49 69 4909096, mail@dgi-info.de; www.dgi-info.de
Languages German
Established 1941, Berlin; reorganized 1948, Cologne
Officers Chair: Nadja Stein
General Assembly Entire membership meets once a year
Membership Total members: 1,900 (individual, corporate and sponsoring). Requirements: Open to individuals and institutions interested in the aims of the Association
Structure Governed by Executive Council. Affiliations: IFLA, ASLIB, EUSIDIC, ICR (International Council for Reprography), SVD, ÖGDI
Sources of Support Membership dues, government subsidies
Major Fields of Interest Advancement of information and documentation in theory and practice
Major Goals and Objectives Promotion of information science and practice; to be a communications forum for providers and consumers; promotion, image enhancement, and PR for the profession; the analysis and interpretation of policy and regulations governing the information profession; the planning and conducting of conferences; co-operating with national and international associations; conducting research projects; stimulating the use of electronic information media
Activities Conventions, conferences, workshops, publications, work groups, committees and specialist sub-committees
Publications Official journal: Since 1998 the journal is named Information – Wissenschaft und Praxis. 1998-. former name: Nachrichten für Dokumentation (NfD) (Documentation News). 1948–97. 6/yr. Free to members. Address same as Association. German, with English summaries. Indexed in Lib.Lit., LISA, ISA, etc. (A technical journal for information and documentation with an abstracts service in information science). Other publications: Annual reports, proceedings of conferences, seminars, workshops. Various monographs published in series DGI-Schriftenreihe. Publications issued for sale, price lists available, listed in official journal. Publications exchange program in effect with other library associations, libraries, and other institutions

Bibliography   Keren, C. and Schwuchow, W., "Economic Aspect of Information Services – Report on a Symposium," Journal of Informaion Science 3 (Nov. 1981):249–21; Pflug, Günther and Kaegbein, Paul, "Germany, Federal Republic of," in ALA World Encyclopedia of Library and Information Services. 2nd ed., pp. 306–309. Chicago: American Library Association, 1986; Schwuchow, W., "Deutsche Gesellschaft für Dokumentation (DGD) Conference (FRG, 1989)," International Forum for Information and Documentation 14, no. 4 (1989):31+
Comment   Name until 1999: Deutsche Gesellschaft für Dokumentation e. V. (DGD)

263   Deutsche Gesellschaft für Medizinische Informatik, Biometrie und Epidemiologie e.V. (GMDS)

Address   Bonner Str. 178, 50968 Köln   Tel.: +49 221 37994755, Fax +49 228 37994756, info@gmds.de; www.gmds.de
Languages   German
Officers   Pres: Prof. Dr. J. Haerting; 1st VP: Prof. Dr. H. Bickeböller; 2nd VP: K. Kuhn; Treas: Prof. Dr. H.G. Schweim
General Assembly   Entire membership meets once a year
Membership   1,670 members
Major Fields of Interest   Medical information
Major Goals and Objectives   Advancement of medical information, medical documentation, medical biometry and epidemiology in theory and practice
Comment   Name until 1991: Deutsche Gesellschaft für Medizinische Dokumentation, Informatik und Statistik e.V

264   Deutscher Bibliotheks- und Informationsverband e.V. (BID) (German Library and Information Association)

Address   c/o Dr. Monika Braß, Strasse des 17. Juni 114, 10623 Berlin   Tel.: +49 30 644 9899-20, Fax +49 30 644 9899-29, bid@bideutschland.de; www.bideutschland.de
Languages   German
Established   2004
Officers   Pres: Barbara Lison; Vice Pres: Gabriele Berger; Ulrich Hohoff
Membership   Total members: 7 (institutional). Types of membership: Institutional
Structure   Governed by a President and 15 Directors
Major Fields of Interest   Informaton and Know How, Networking
Major Goals and Objectives   Provide German libraries and librarians with international information, represent German libraries and German librarians in international committees, international cooperation between libraries and librarians, participate in all relevant committees
Activities   BID is the official representation of any international cooperation. The following tasks are either done or coordinated by the BID: To inform about international developments and topics in Germany, represent German libraries globally, transfer know-how via contributing to international committees as well as speeches and workshops, transfer know-how to Germany, inform about and advise to international sponsorship, promote international cooperation of libraries and librarians.
Publications   Official journal: Bibliotheksdienst: Organ von Bibliothek & Information Deutschland (BID)

265 Deutscher Bibliotheksverband e.V. (DBV) (German Library Association)

Address c/o Elke Dämpfert, Strasse des 17. Juni 114, 10623 Berlin Tel.: +49 30 39001-480, -482, Fax +49 30 39001484, dbv@bibliotheksverband.de; www.bibliotheksverband.de
Languages German
Established 1949, Nierstein, as Deutscher Büchereiverband e.V (DBV); 1961, founding of state library associations in the Federal Republic of Germany; 1973, new name adopted and membership expanded from public libraries to include research libraries
Officers Exec Dir: Barbara Schleihagen
Staff 4
General Assembly Entire membership meets once a year
Membership Total members: 2,000 (institutional). Types of membership: Institutional
Structure Governed by Board of Directors. Affiliations: IFLA, ALA, CLA (Canada), LA, Arbeitskreis für Jugendliteratur e.V (Munich), Deutsche Friedrich Schiller Stiftung e.V (Darmstadt), etc
Sources of Support Membership fees
Major Fields of Interest Public libraries; research libraries; library services
Major Goals and Objectives Promotion of library work and professional librarianship, cooperation between libraries, lobbying and advocacy
Activities DBV is the association of reference and lending libraries and other institutions concerned with library work, as well as the legal holders of libraries, such as parishes, boroughs, and other communities in so far as they maintain public libraries and give grants to libraries within their reach. The Association works for improvement of library services according to international standards through collective projects. Maintains the office for international cooperation, which is responsible for international communications and projects
Publications Official journal: Bibliotheksdienst (issued jointly with Bibliothek&Information Deutschland BID). 1949-. 12/yr. (Euro) 45. (34 for members). Circ: 3,000. German. Issues annual report, proceedings of annual meetings, and others

266 Deutscher Verband Medizinischer Dokumentare e.V. (DVMD e.V.)

Address c/o Sabine Kapsammer, P.O. Box 100129, 68001 Mannheim Tel.: +49 621 71761393, Fax +49 621 71761395, dvmd@dvmd.de; www.dvmd.de
Languages German
Established 1972 as Verein Medizinischer Dokumentationsassistenten
Officers Chair: Katharina Thorn; VP: Andrea Großer; Jens Knösel
Staff 1, paid
Membership 1,200 members
Major Fields of Interest Public relations activities, networking in the area of medical documentation
Major Goals and Objectives Quality assurance for professional training, representation of interests in the field of medical documentation
Activities congresses, publications
Publications official journal: mdi – Forum der Medizin-Dokumentation und Medizin-Informatik

Comment Official representative in the International Federation of Health Records Management (IFHRO)

267 Evangelisches Literaturportal e.V. (eliport)

Address Bürgerstr. 2a, 37073 Göttingen Tel.: +49 551 500759-0, Fax +49 551 500759-19, info@eliport.de; www.eliport.de
Languages German
Established 1952
Officers Manag Dir: Gabriele Kassenbrock
General Assembly Entire membership meets once a year
Membership Total members: 28 (institutional). Requirements: Libraries of the Lutheran Church. No dues
Sources of Support Sale of publications, Evangelische Kirche in Deutschland (Lutheran Church)
Major Fields of Interest Lutheran libraries
Major Goals and Objectives Support and organization of Lutheran libraries
Activities Developing and organizing Lutheran libraries open to the public. Sponsors Book Week and continuing education programs
Publications Official journal: Der Evangelische Buchberater. 1947-. 4/yr. (Deutsche Mark) 15. Editor: Andreas Schimkus. Address same as Association. Circ: Membership. German. Other publicaions: Buchauswahl für Evangelische Büchereien (annual book review); Handwörterbuch der evangelischen Büchereiarbeit (Handbook for Lutheran Libraries) (1980)
Comment formerly: Deutscher Verband Evangelischer Büchereien e.V.

268 Gesellschaft für Bibliothekswesen und Dokumentation des Landbaues – Fachliche Arbeitsgemeinschaft der ASpB (GBDL) (Association of Librarianship and Documentation in Agriculture)*

Address c/o Dr. Birgid B. Schlindwein, Maximus-von-Imhof-Forum 3, 85354 Freising, 85350 Freising Tel.: +49 8161 71-4029, Fax +49 8161 71-5309, schlind@weihenstephan.de; www.weihenstephan.de/GBDL
Languages German
Established 1958, Bad Godesberg
Officers Pres: Wolfrudolf Laux; VP: Werner Köglmeier; Secr/Treas: Dr. Birgit Schlindwein
General Assembly Entire membership meets every 2 years
Membership Total members: 52 (40 individual, 12 institutional), 3 countries represented. Requirements: Education in documentation or library affairs, agricultural sciences
Structure Governed by elected executive officers. Affiliations: IAALD, ASpB
Sources of Support Membership dues, sale of publications
Major Fields of Interest Agricultural libraries and documentation centers
Major Goals and Objectives Promotion and development of documentation and information in the field of agricultural sciences in the country; international cooperation with information and documentation centers and libraries; conferences

Activities Sponsors conferences, sometimes jointly with other agricultural associations; furthers international cooperation with information and documentation centers and libraries dealing with literature in the agricultural sciences; furthers the development of agricultural information and documentation in the Federal Republic of Germany

Publications Official journal: Mitteilungen der Gesellschaft für Bibliothekswesen und Dokumentation des Landbaues. 1958-. 2/yr. Free to members. Editor: Dr. B. Schlindwein, c/o TU München, TB Weihenstephan, 85350 Freising, Germany. German. Indexed in Schrifttum zur Informationswissenschaft und -praxis. Conference papers are published in official journal

Bibliography 10 Jahre Dachverband wissenschaftlicher Gesellschaften der Agrar-, Forst-, Ernährungs-, Veterinär- und Umweltforschung e. V. Munich, 1983. pp. 26–30. (in German)

269 Gesellschaft für Klassifikation e.V. (GfKl)
(German Classification Society)

Address c/o Prof. Dr. Claus Weihs, Vogelpothsweg 87, 44221 Dortmund Tel.: +49 231 7554363, Fax +49 231 7554387, vorstand@gfkl.de; www.gfkl.org

Languages German

Established 1977

Officers Pres: Prof. Dr. Claus Weihs; 1st VP: Prof. Dr. R. Decker; 2nd VP: PD Dr. B. Lausen; Treas: Prof. Dr. D. Baier

General Assembly Entire membership meets once a year

Membership 308 members

Major Fields of Interest Information and documentation

Major Goals and Objectives To develop research activities related to the classification and ordering of data, to the processing of statistical or conceptual information, and to the construction of databases and information (retrieval) systems. To foster the exchange of methods and the personal contacts between different disciplines. To promote the education in this domain

Publications Official journal: Briefe zur Klassifikation. 2/y. Other publications: Studies in Classification, Data Analysis, and Knowledge Organization; Datenanalyse und Klassifikation

270 Internationale Vereinigung der Musikbibliotheken, Musikarchive und Musikdokumentationszentren – Gruppe Bundesrepublik Deutschland (IVMB – Deutsche Gruppe/BRD; IAML-FRG)
(International Association of Music Libraries, Archives and Documentation Centres – German Branch/FRG)

Address c/o Thomas Kalk, Bertha-von-Suttner-Platz 1, 40227 Düsseldorf, 40200 Düsseldorf Tel.: +49 211 8992939, Fax +49 211 8932939, sekretaer@aibm.info; www.aibm.info

Languages German, English, French

Established 1976, as a national branch of IAML, to take over the activities of the Arbeitsgemeinschaft der Musikbibliotheken (Working Group of Music Libraries)

General Assembly Entire membership meets once a year

Membership Individual and institutional members. Requirements: Music libraries and

documentation centers or those with music collections and librarians working there; any other person or institution interested in supporting the work of the association
Structure Governed by executive officers. Affiliations: A national branch of IAML
Sources of Support Membership dues
Major Fields of Interest Music librarianship
Major Goals and Objectives To further the development of music libraries and documentation centers, and to be concerned with their practical problems
Activities Sponsors meetings, seminars, workshops
Publications Official international journal: Fontes Artis Musicae. Free for members. Associated national journal: Forum Musikbibliothek. Other publications: Regeln für die alphabetische Katalogisierung von Musikdrucken, Musiktonträgern und Musik-Bildtonträgern. 1997; series Lehrbriefe Musik. etc

271 Pharma Arbeitskreis Information und Dokumentation (P.A.I.D.) (Pharma working group for information and documentation)

Address c/o Dr. Jaroslava Paraskevova, Chair, Benzstraße 1, 61352 Bad Homburg Tel.: +49 6172 888-2522, Fax +49 6172 888-1244, jaroslava.paraskevova@medapharma.de; www.paid.de
Languages German
Established Founded in 1987 as a platform for discussions with professional colleagues
General Assembly Members meet twice a year
Membership 36 members (institutional and individual)
Structure Organisation of pharmaceutical companies
Sources of Support Membership fees
Major Fields of Interest Librarianship, documentation, information services, in-house databases, document management, archiving and record management, knowledge management, intranet design and administration
Major Goals and Objectives Take up and work on current topics in the field of information and documentation within a circle of experts
Activities 2 meetings of the working group per year; in addition various activities of 4 regional groups which focus on special subjects and report the results at the general meetings
Publications S. Bayer, T. Dahm, J. Paraskevova, S. Rehm, B. Reißland, M. Wesslowski: Decision support for knowledge management (KM). In: Information in Wissenschaft&Praxis, Vol. 55, No. 5 (2004), p. 273–274; B. Reißland: The sun always shines on PAID. In: Information in Wissenschaft&Praxis, Vol. 55, No. 6 (2004), p. 345–348

272 Verband der Bibloheken des Landes Nordrhein-Westfalen *

Address c/o Dr. Rolf Thiele, Universitätsstraße 33, 50931 Köln Tel.: +49 221 470-2404, Fax +49 221 470-5166, thiele@ub.uni-koeln.de; www.vbnw.de
Languages German
Major Fields of Interest Development of libraries and library services

273 Verein Deutscher Archivarinnen und Archivare e.V. (VdA) (Association of German Archivists)

Address Wörthstraße 3, 36037 Fulda Tel.: +49 661 29109-72, Fax +49 661 29109-74, info@vda.archiv.net; www.vda.archiv.net
Languages German
Established 1946. Former name: Verein Deutscher Archivare
Officers Chair: Dr. Michael Diefenbacher; 1st Vice Chair: Dr. Clemens Rehm; 2nd Vice Chair: Katharina Tiemann; Treas: Dr. Irmgard Christa Becker
General Assembly Entire membership meets once a year
Membership Total members: 2,200 (individual). Sections: 8. Type of membership: Individual, student, emeritus. Requirements: Trained archivists or staff of archives
Structure Governed by executive officers and general assembly
Sources of Support Membership dues
Major Fields of Interest Archives
Major Goals and Objectives Promotion of German archives and archival science; promotion of education and continuing education of archivists; promotion of exchange of experiences and improvement of cooperation between archives and archivists, and with related disciplines in the information and documentation field at the national and international level
Activities Mainly planning for annual congresses (Deutsche Archivtage); sponsors continuing education programs and workshops on specialized topics. Association has been active in promoting library-related legislation, such as archival legislation (Archivgesetzgebung) in Germany. Sale of publcations
Publications Official journal: Archivar. Zeitschrift für Archivwesen. 1947-. 4/yr. German. Issues proceedings of conferences. Other publications: Diplom-Archivarin, Diplom-Archivar – heute. 1993. etc. Publications for sale
Bibliography Eckhart, G. F, "Verein deutscher Archivare," Per Archivar 37 (1984):455–460 (in German)

274 Verein Deutscher Bibliothekare e.V. (VDB) (Association of German Librarians)

Address c/o Thomas Slöber, Universitaetsstraße 22, 86159 Augsburg sekr@bibliothek.uni-augsburg.de; www.vdb-online.org
Languages German
Established 1900; reactivated 1948, Munich
Officers Pres: Ulrich Hohoff; Secr: Thomas Slöber
General Assembly Entire membership meets once a year
Membership Total members: 1,600 (individual). Types of membership: Individual. Requirements: Academic and research librarians with university degree
Structure Governed by executive officers and Executive Council of 13 members
Sources of Support Membership dues
Major Fields of Interest Development of libraries and library services
Major Goals and Objectives The Association represents the academic and research librarians of Germany and promotes their professional interests, continuing education and training, and cooperation between librarians on a national and international level

Activities seminars, congresses, publications, cooperation with other organisations of librarianship
Publications Official journal: VDB-Mitteilungen. Free to members. 2/y. Other publications: Jahrbuch der Deutschen Bibliotheken. 1902-. Biennial. Address: Jahrbuch-Redaktion, c/o Corinna Haager-Lindeboom, P. O. Box 2620, 72016 Tübingen
Bibliography Hering, J. and Jopp, R.K., "Bericht über die 34. ordentliche Mitgliederversammlung am 3. Juni 1982 in der Technischen Hochschule Darmstadt," (Report of the 34th Annual Meeting in Darmstadt, June 3, 1982) Zeitschrift für Bibliothekswesen und Bibliographie 29 (1982):412–430 (in German); Bermann, H., "72. Deutscher Bibliothekartag, Darmstadt, 1.–5. Juni 1982," (German libary Conference, Darmstadt, June 1–5, 1982) Biblos 31 (1982):348–350; Pflug, G. and Kaegbein, P., "Germany, Federal Republic of," in ALA World Encyclopedia of Library and Information Services. 2nd ed., pp. 306–309. Chicago: American Library Association, 1986

275 Vereinigung deutscher Wirtschaftsarchivare e.V. (VdW)*

Address c/o MIchael Jurk, Jürgen-Ponto-Platz 1, 60301 Frankfurt a. Main Tel.: +49 69 26351393, Fax +49 69 26351539, vdwsekretariat@Dresdner-Bank.com; www.wirtschaftsarchive.de
Languages German
Established 1957
Officers Chair: Michael Jurk; Vice Chair: Dr. Detlef Krause; Treas: Dr. Eva Moser
General Assembly Annual conference, where the entire membership is invited
Membership over 350 members (institutional and individual)
Major Fields of Interest Archive management
Activities Educational training courses for members
Publications Official journal: Archiv und Wirtschaft. 1967-. 4/y. Address: Bertelsmann AG, Corporate History, c/o Dr. Helen Müller, 33311 Gütersloh. Other publications: VdW (Ed.), 50 Jahre Vereinigung deutscher Wirtschaftsarchivare 1957 – 2007, Stuttgart 2007; Kroker, Evelyn (Ed.), Handbuch für Wirtschaftsarchive. Theorie und Praxis, München 1998

Ghana

276 Ghana Library Association

Address c/o President, P.O. Box 4105, Accra Greater Accra Region Tel.: +233 21 764822, Fax +233 21 763523
Languages English
Established 1962, Accra, at the University of Ghana
Officers Pres: Valentina J.A. Bannerman
Staff None
General Assembly Entire membership meets annually
Membership Total members: 100+. Types of membership: Individual, institutional. Requirements: Open to all librarians and institutions having libraries. Dues scaled according to salary
Structure Governed by executive officers: Affiliations: IFLA, COMLA

Sources of Support Membership dues, subsidies
Major Fields of Interest Development of libraries; advancement of the professional status of librarians
Major Goals and Objectives To bring together people interested in libraries and librarianship; to promote and safeguard the professional interests of librarians
Activities Past achievements: Uniting all librarians in Ghana; achieving recognition for librarians from the central government. Current and Future: Working for the improvement of libraries relevant to the needs of Ghana
Publications Official journal: Ghana Library Journal. 1963-. 2/yr. Free to members. Address same as Association. English. Proceedings of annual meeting, workshops, and conferences appear in journal
Bibliography Dua-Agyemang, H. "Ghana," in ALA World Encyclopedia of Library and Information Services. 2nd ed., pp. 310–312. Chicago: American Library Association, 1986; Agyei-Gyane, L., "The Ghana Library Association: History and Development," Libri 36 (1985):113–118

277 Ghana Library Board

Address c/o Susannah Minyila, P.O. Box 663, Accra Greater Accra Region Tel.: +233 21 665083, Fax +233 21 247768, info@ghanalibraryboard.com; www.ghanalibraryboard.com
Languages English
Major Fields of Interest National libraries and archives libraries
Major Goals and Objectives To promote education through the provision of reading materials such as books, periodicals and other non-book materials; to act as a center for information dissemination for the general Public

Greece

278 Association of Greek Librarians and Information Scientists

Address c/o Eva Semertzaki, 52 Skoufa St., 10672 Athens Tel.: 30 (1) 3226625., info@eebep.gr
Officers Pres-elect: Christina Kyriakopoulou
Staff None
General Assembly Entire membership meets annually in Athens.
Membership Total members: 230+. Types of membership: Individual, institutional. Requirements: Library school degree or 6 months in library service.
Structure Governed by executive officers. Affiliations: IFLA
Sources of Support Membership dues, government subsidies.
Major Fields of Interest Libraries and library development in Greece
Major Goals and Objectives To promote library development in Greece; to promote librarianship as a science; to assist in legislation for better library service; to increase public awareness of the significance of libraries for cultural and technological development; to cooperate with other professional associations abroad.
Activities Various activities carried out by Committees, e. g. Documentation, Cataloging and Classification, Union Catalog of Books, Public Affairs, Communications, etc.

Sponsors conferences, seminars, workshops. Participates in international congresses and represents Greek librarianship.
Publications Official journal: Greek Library Association Bulletin. 1970-. Irregular. Free to members. Address same as Association.
Bibliography Papademetriou, George C, "Greece," in ALA World Encyclopedia of Library and Information Services. 2nd ed., pp. 315–316. Chicago: American Library Association, 1986.

279   Society of Hellenic Archives
Address B.P. 76072, 171 01 N.Smyrni Tel.: +30 210 8259875, Fax +30 210 8223093, eae@eae.org.gr; www.eae.org.gr
Languages Greek

Guatemala

280   Asociación Bibliotecológica de Guatemala (Library Association of Guatemala)
Address 7 Avenida 27–69 zona 8, Ciudad de Guatemala Tel.: +502 24717444, Fax +502 23384507, juntadirectivaabg@gmail.com; http://es.oocities.com/asociaciondebibliotecarios/contactenos.htm
Languages Spanish
Established 1948
General Assembly Once a month
Membership Type of membership: Individual. Requirements: Librarians with diploma, or others working in libraries
Structure Governed by executive officers
Sources of Support Membership dues, subsidies
Major Fields of Interest Libraries and library services in Guatemala
Major Goals and Objectives To promote libraries and library services in the country; to further the status of librarians and their professional development
Activities Sponsors meetings, seminars, workshops and other continuing education programs for librarians
Publications Official journal: Boletín de la Asociación Bibliotecoiógica de Guatemala. Irreg
Bibliography Palma R., G., "Guatemala," in ALA World Encyclopedia of Library and Information Services. 2nd ed., pp. 317–318. Chicago: American Library Association, 1986

Guinea-Bissau

281   Association Guineenne des Documentalistes, Archivistes et Bibliothecaires (AGDAB)
Address C.P. 104, Bissau Tel.: +245 251868, Fax +245 251125, i_djalo@hotmail.com; www.ica.org/members.php?pid=1681&plangue=eng

Established 1994
Officers Pres: Iaguba Djalo

282 Instituto Nacional de Estudos e Pesquisa (INEP) (National Institute for Studies and Research)

Address Complexo Escolar 14 de, CP 112, Bissau - Guiné-Bissau Tel.: +245 251 867, Fax +245 251 125; www.inep-bissau.org
Languages Portuguese, French, English, German
Established 1987
Staff 32 (paid), 5 (volunteers)
Structure Governed by Board according to a decree of the Council of Ministers. Affiliations: ICA, CODESRIA, IFS, CERDAS, AAPS
Sources of Support Government subsidies; consultancy
Major Fields of Interest Social sciences, natural sciences, archival studies
Major Goals and Objectives To conduct research in these fields and produce publications
Activities Past achievements: Organizing international Colloquium in 1986: "Sobre a Formação da Nação;" National and Technical Cooperation Assessments and Practical Programmes for Guinea Bissau. Current and future: Research activities and publications. Institute has been active in library-related legislation, such as Legal Deposit, and National Archives Law. Sponsors continuing education programs
Publications Official journal: Soronda. 1985-. 2/yr. Address same as Institute. Portuguese. Publishes annual reports, proceedings of meetings, reports of seminars, workshops. Other publications: Monograph series Kacu Martel; a Socio-Economic Information Bulletin (BISE); a Scientific Technological Information Bulletin. Publications available for sale and exchange
Bibliography St-Amant, R., "The Beginnings of the National Institute for Studies and Research in Guinea-Bissau," CAD Information (Paris: International Council on Archives, May, 1987), pp. 9–10 (available in French and English); Cruzeiro, M. M., "Guinea-Bissau," in ALA World Encyclopedia of Library and Information Services. 2nd ed., p. 319. Chicago: American Library Association, 1986

Guyana

283 Guyana Library Association (GLA)

Address c/o National Library, A.Postal 10240, Georgetown Tel.: +592 222486, Fax +592 223596
Languages English
Established 1963
Staff None
General Assembly Entire membership meets 3 times a year
Membership Total members: 62 (50 individual, 12 institutional). Sections: 6. Requirements: Open to all librarians regardless of professional rank, archivists, documentalists, and all other persons interested in the goals of the Association. Dues (Guyana Dollar): 500, institutional; 200, 100, 50.00

Structure Governed by Executive Committee. Affiliations: COMLA, ACURIL, Guyana Society
Sources of Support Membership dues, sale of publications, fund raising activities
Major Fields of Interest Development of libraries; training of library assistants; educating users on the value of libraries; documentation and information services
Major Goals and Objectives (1) To foster the close association of all persons and organizations in Guyana interested in the promotion of librarianship and related fields; (2) to publicize the role of libraries and librarians in national development and to make recommendations for the promotion of legislation affecting libraries and librarians; (3) to organize meetings, lectures, seminars, training courses, etc. for the purpose of promoting effective library services in Guyana; (4) to promote the recruitment, training and education of librarians and to improve their status; (5) to promote bibliographic activities in Guyana; (6) to advise on the organization of new libraries, the improvement of existing libraries, and to promote a high standard of library services in Guyana; (6) to publish a journal at regular intervals to record the activities of the Association and to publish articles of interest to members
Activities Training courses for Library personnel. Provides contact for persons with similar interests. Sponsors library-related seminars and workshops. Gives advice on building library collections and Documentation Centers. Staff training. Career Guidance. Exhibitions. Radio Talks
Publications Official journal: Guyana Library Association Bulletin. 1971-. 2/yr. (US Dollar) 25. Free to members. Address same as Association. English. Other publications: Guide to Library Services in Guyana (revised periodically); Union List of Scientific and Technical Periodicals held in the Libraries of Guyana; Newsbrief. 1985-. Irreg. Publications available for sale, some free
Bibliography Stephenson, Y.V., "Guyana," in ALA World Encyclopedia of Library and Information Services. 2nd ed., pp. 319–321. Chicago: American Library Association, 1986

Haiti

284 Association des Archivistes Haitiens

Address Boîte Postale 1299, Porte-au-Prince Tel.: +509 2 22728566
Languages French
Officers Pres: Jean-Yves Jason Muscadin

Hungary

285 Alliance of Libraries and Information Institutes

Address Budavári Palota F épület, 1827 Budapest iksz@oszk.hu

286 Magyar Könyvtárosok Egyesülete (MKE/AHL) (Association of Hungarian Librarians)*

Address Budavári Palota " F" épület 439 szoba, 1827 Budapest Tel.: +36 1 3118634, Fax +36 1 3118634, mke@oszk.hu; www.mke.oszk.hu

Languages Hungarian, English
Established 1935, Budapest
Officers Pres: Klára Bakos; VP: Agnes Hajdu Barát; Éva Bartos; Gábor Kiss; Gen Secr: Anikó Nagy
Staff 3
General Assembly 2 times a year
Membership 1814/84 members; Types of membership: individual and institutional. Regional branches: Bács-Kiskun County Branch, Békés County Branch, Borsod County Branch, Fejér County Branch, Hajdú-Bihar County Branch, Heves County Branch, Jász-Nagykun-Szolnok County Branch, Komárom-Esztergom County Branch, Nógrád County Branch, Pécs-Baranya County Branch, Pest County Branch, Somogy County Branch, Szabolcs-Szatmár-Bereg County Branch, Tolna County Branch, Vas County Branch, Veszprém County Branch, Zala County Branch, Zemplén County Branch. Special branches: Section of Bibliography, Section of Advanced Information, Technologies and Society, Section of Children's Librarians, Section of Local History Librarians, Section of Public Libraries, Section of Agricultural Librarians, Section of Museum Librarians, Section of Sci-Tech Librarians, Section of Reader Services Librarians, Section of Social Science Librarians, Section of Music Librarians
Structure Governed by Executive Board. Affiliations: IFLA
Sources of Support Association of Hungarian Librarians is financed through membership dues and our association used to apply for project money to the different foundations. AHL has the different Sponsors time to time
Major Fields of Interest General and comprehensive representation of LIS, librarians, education and culture
Major Goals and Objectives Objectives and tasks: to act with responsibility to preserve the intellectual heritage; to strengthen the role of libraries and librarians in society; to guarantee unlimited and equal access to information; to co-operate in enlarging and sharing information resources, to strengthen professiona relations; to support the creation of a harmony between library infrastructure and modern services; to raise the library profession onto the highest professional and moral niveau, to protect professional interests; to take a professional stand in determining the strategic directions of Hungarian librarianship, in formulating its vision
Activities Major activities: participation in preparing decisions relating to legislation, administrative society; participation in developing library education and extension training; building relations with professional and other organisations in Hungary and abroad; co-ordination of the relationship between libraries and librarians working in similar fields, in the same region, in communities and over the Hungarian borders; organisation of professional fora to get acquainted with modern theory and practice, to promote a higher standard of professional work; organisation of consultations, exchanges of experience, extension training events, conferences, lectures, study tours; supporting the activities of specialised professional cooperatives; organisation of annual conferences on the current issues of professional policy; presentation of the events and achievements of the profession; taking a stand in issues of professional ethics. Awards, prizes: memorial medal "For the Association of Hungarian Librarians"; "Young librarian of the year" prize; memorial medal in the honour of István Füzéki (for outstanding professional achievement); Fitz József book prize (for the most successful books); proposals for

decorations awarded by the state and local authorities.

Publications Articles, annual reports, proceedings of conferences, bibliographies. Novels, short stories and poems from librarians. Attitudes and declarations related to the standardization, library policy and other professional questions. Publishing the volume of essays for the 75 anniversary of AHL

Bibliography Ferencné, B., "The Hungarian Library Association," Library Association Record 88 (1986):294; Kiss, J., "Hungary," in ALA World Encyclopedia of Library and Information Services. 2nd ed., pp. 343–346; Slawinski, I., "21. Tagung der Vereinigung der Ungarischen Bibliothekare," (21st Conference of the Hungarian Library Association) Mitteilungen der Vereinigung Österreichischer Bibliothekare 42 (1989):33–34 (in German)

Comment International relations: membership of IFLA, associated member of EBLIDA, close relationship with Hungarian librarians living in the neighbouring countries, and with the library associations of European countries

287 Magyar Levéltárosok Egyesülete (MLE) (Association of Hungarian Archivists)*

Address c/o c/o Association of Hungarian Archivists, Magyar Levéltárosok Egyesülete, Budapest, Pf. 233., 1364 Budapest Tel.: +36 1 4116738, Fax +36 1 4116737, mle.titkarsag@gmail.com; www.leveltaros.hu

Languages Hungarian

Established 1986

Officers Pres: Tyekvicska Arpad; VP: László Szogi; Gyorgy Tilcsik; Secr: Anita Kiss

General Assembly Annually

Membership Ca. 670 personal members

Structure Presidency, Steering Committee, Sections, Working committees

Sources of Support Membership fee, sponsorship by archival institutions and firms, public applications

Major Fields of Interest Interests of Hungarian archival community and development of professional resources

Activities Lobbying, professional meetings and conferences, networking

Publications Official Journal: Levéltári Szemle, 4/yr. Volumes on the yearly conferences

288 Magyar Orvosi Könyvtárak Szövetsége (MOKSZ) (Hungarian Medical Library Association)

Address Ülloi út 26, Budapest lvasas@lib.sote.hu; www.lib.sote.hu/moksz

Languages Hungarian

Officers Pres: Dr. Lívia Vasas

Iceland

289 Félag skólasafnskennara

Address Hvassaleiti 68, 103 Reykjavík thorasjofn@langholtsskoli.is

290 Upplýsing – Félag bókasafns- og upplýsingafræða (Information – the Icelandic Library and Information Science Association)
Address PO Box 8865, 128 Reykjavik Tel.: +354 5337290, Fax +354 5889239, upplysing@upplysing.is; www.bokis.is
Languages Icelandic
Established November 26th 1999, in Reykjavík, from a merger of 4 Icelandic Library associations: Bókavardafélag Íslands (The Icelandic Library Association), Félag bókasafnsfraedinga (The Association of Professional Librarians), Félag bókavarda í rannsóknarbókasöfnum (The Association of Research Librarians), Félag um almenningsbókasöfn og skólasöfn (The Association on Public and School Libraries)
Officers Pres: Sigrun Klara Hannesdottir
General Assembly In May each year
Membership Primarily personal memberships (professionals and paraprofessionals), also hospitable to institutions and overseas members
Structure Affiliations: EBLIDA, IFLA, IASL, NVBF
Major Fields of Interest All aspects of library and information science work in Iceland
Major Goals and Objectives To strengthen cooperation amongst libraries and the professionals working in the information field; to encourage the development of Icelandic libraries; work for the recognition of the importance of the services of libraries and information centers within the Icelandic society; to work with other Icelandic organizations with similar objectives and to strengthen contacts with organizations with similar objectives in other countries as well
Activities Organizing conferences and seminars, providing training and publishing training materials, newsletter and periodical
Publications Newsletter Fregnir (three times a year); journal Bókasafnid (a yearbook of library and information science, language is Icelandic with summaries in English; www.bokasafnid.is)
Bibliography A Leid til Upplysing ar (History of Icelandic Library Associations). English Summary. Reykjavík 2004

India

291 Developing Library Network (DELNET)
Address c/o Dr. H. K. Kaul, Director, J.N.U Campus, Nelson Mandela Road, Vasant Kunj , New Delhi 110070 Tel.: +91 26471111, Fax +91 26741122, director@delnet.ren.nic.in; http://delnet.nic.in
Languages English
Established 1992, registered as society, in operation since jan 1988
Officers Pres: S. Varadarajan; VP: Dr. S.S. Murthy; Dir: H. K. Kaul; Treas: Dr. Hanish Chandra
Membership 748 Libraries (institutional and associate-institutional members). Dues: Admission Fee : Rs.5,000, Institutional membership: Rs.7500/ yr (For libraries with 10,000 or more book collection). Associate institutional membership Rs.10,000/yr (For libraries with less than 10,000 books). Overseas Institutions: Admission fee : US $100/-Annual Membership fee : US $500/-

Sources of Support Promoted by the National Informatics Centre, Department of Information Technology, Ministry of Communications and Information Technology, Government of India and India International Centre, New Delhi
Major Fields of Interest Development of a network of libraries
Major Goals and Objectives To promote sharing of resources among the libraries by developing a network of libraries, by collecting, storing and disseminating information and by offering computerised services to the users; To undertake scientific research in the area of Information Science and Technology, create new systems in the field, apply the results of research and publish them; To offer technical guidance to the member-libraries on collecting, storing, sharing and disseminating information; To coordinate efforts for suitable collection development and reduce unnecessary duplication wherever possible; To establish /facilitate the establishment of referral and /or research centres, and maintain a central online union catalogue of books, serials and non-book materials of all the participating libraries; To faciliate and promote delivery of documents manually or mechanically; To develop specialised bibliographic database of books, serials and non-book materials; To develop databases of projects, specialists and institutions; To possess and maintain electronic and mechanical equipment for speedy communication of information and delivery of electronic mail; To coordinate with other regional, national and international networks and libraries for exchange of information and documents
Activities ILL Online, Retro-conversion, Referral services, Creation and maintenance of bibliographic databases, Document Delivery Services, Training programmes, Lectures and Workshops
Publications No official journal. Other publications: Newsletter. Online Databases: Union Catalogue of Periodicals; Database of Periodical Articles; Indian Specialists: A Who's Who; CD-ROM Database; Union List of Video Recordings; Union List of Sound Recordings; Union List of Newspapers; Union List of Serials : Management Libraries; Union List of Serials : Petroleum and Natural Gas; Union Catalogue of Hindi Books; Multilingual Books : Sample Database; Urdu Manuscripts Database; Database of Theses and Dissertations; DEVINSA Database

292 Indian Association of Special Libraries and Information Centres (IASLIC)

Address P-291, CIT Scheme No. 6M, Kankurgachi, Kolkata 700 054, West Bengal
Tel.: +91 33 23529651; www.iaslic.org
Languages English
Established 1955, Calcutta
Officers Pres: Jatindra Nath Satpathi; Gen Secr: Arun K. Chakraborty
Staff 21 (7 paid, 14 volunteers)
General Assembly Entire membership meets once a year
Membership Types of membership: Individual, institutional, life, honorary. Requirements: Individuals admitted on receipt of subscription, into different categories. Institutions, both profit and nonprofit, admitted on receipt of subscription
Structure Governed by Executive Council. Affiliations: FID, IFLA, National Commission for Unesco in India
Sources of Support Membership dues, sale of publications, government subsidies
Major Fields of Interest Special librarianship; documentation and information services; translating and abstracting; reprography, management techniques

Major Goals and Objectives To promote library and information service; to coordinate activities and forst mutual cooperation among special libraries; to imprve technical efficiency and professional welfare; to act as a center of research and study
Activities Organizes conferences, special interest groups meetings, seminars, offers continuing education programs
Publications Official journal: IASLIC Bulletin. 1956-. 4/yr.Free to members. Fees: 800000 Indian Rp or 80 US Dollar/ yr. Editor: Dr. Arjun Dasgupta. Address same as Association; Circ: 1,200. English. Indexed in ILSA (Indian Library Science Abstracts). Other publications: Annual reports, proceedings of seminars, conferences, workshops; IASLIC Newsletter. 1966-. 12/yr. Editor: H. Basu; Indian Library Science Abstracts. 1967-. 4/yr; Directory of Special and Research Libraries in India, and many other monographs. Publications for sale, price lists available. Publications exchanged with other associations
Bibliography Das Gupta, R.K., "India," in ALA World Encyclopedia of Library and information Services. 2nd ed., pp. 350–353. Chicago: American Library Association, 1986; Subba Rao, C.V., "Professional Associations of India: IASLIC's Record of Service and Achievements," Herald of Library Science 26 (1987):192–201; Khurshid, A., "Library Associations in Asia," Herald of Library Science 28 (1989):3–10; Singh, Sewa, "Joint ILA/IASLIC Conference," ibid.:86–90; Kaula, P.N., "13th National Seminar of IASLIC," ibid.: 107–108; Subba Rao, G.V., "Some Obsevations on the Joint Conference of ILA and IASLIC at Calcutta," ibid.:212–218; Kaula, P.N., "Joint ILA and IASLIC Conference: Resolutions," ibid.:256–257

293 Medical Library Association of India (MLAI)

Address c/o Dr. R. P. Kumar, Secretary, K-43, Kailash Colony, New Delhi 110 048 drrpkumar@hotmail.com
Activities Annual convention

294 National Committee of Archivists (NCA)

Address c/o National Archives of India, Janpath, New Delhi 110001 Tel.: +91 23383436, Fax +91 23384127, archives@nic.in; www.nationalarchives.gov.in
Languages Mostly English, occasionally Hindi
Established 1953
Officers Dir: Shri S.M.R. Baqar
General Assembly Entire membership meets annually; meetings are hosted by member states
Membership Director of Archives, Director General of Archives, Government of India as Chairman & Convener. A representative each of all State Governments/Union Terriloties, being invariably the senior most professional archivist; Heads of Archives Offices of Union Territories placed under the National Archives of India. A Deputy Director of Archives/Assistant Director of Archives, Government of India as Member-Secretary. No membership fee
Major Fields of Interest Archival science, archival management
Major Goals and Objectives To discuss archival problems and to disseminate knowledge of their approved solutions; to achieve uniformity in professional practices; to draw attention to the advantages and disadvantages of new techniques and developments;

to co-ordinate activities of common interest among archives offices in the country; to consider and recommend measures to accelerate archival development in the country; to develop contacts and liaison with archival institutions in the Region as a whole; to solve problems by co-operative efforts at a professional level
Publications Proceedings of the meetings of the Committee are brought out from time to time

295 Society for Information Science (SIS)

Address c/o NK Wadhwa, Secretary, KS Krishnan Marg, New Delhi 110012 nkwadhwa@gmail.com; www.sis.org.in
Established 1975
Officers Pres: Dr. Naresh Kumar; VP: SC Dhawan; Dr. Ramesh Kundra; Secr: NR Wadhwa
Membership Membership restricted to Information professionals
Structure Governed by Executive Committee
Major Goals and Objectives To promote interchange of information in the discipline of information science and its subdivision amongst the specialists and between specialists and the public; To encourage and assist the professionals to maintain the integrity and competence of the profession; To foster a sense of partnership amongst the professionals engaged in these fields
Activities Organises annual Conferences on different themes and short-term courses on various topics every year; sponsors Young Information Scientist Award
Publications Official journal: SISCOM. Quarterly Newsletter of SIS. Other publications: SISTRANS (Society for Information Science Transaction). The proceedings and papers presented at various seminars and Annual conventions and conferences are published normally as SISTRANS. The Society was also responsible for bringing out NISSAT Newsletter on behalf of Department of Science and Industrial Research, Govt. of India

Indonesia

296 Ikatan Pustakawan Indonesia (IPI) (Indonesian Library Association)

Address Jalan Salemba Raya no. 28A, 10430 Jakarta Tel.: +62 21 3101472, Fax +62 21 3101472, pusnas@rad.net.id; www.pnri.go.id/beranda
Languages Indonesian, English
Established 1973, Ciawi-Bogor, through a merger of the existing library associations: Indonesian Association of Special Libraries (1969), and the Indonesian Library, Archive and Documentation Association. Before that, there was an Indonesian Library Association, founded in 1954
Staff 2 (paid)
General Assembly Entire membership meets every 4 years
Membership Types of membership: Individual, institutional, student, honorary. Requirements: Individuals must have a diploma in librarianship and interest in

librarianship, libraries, documentation. Institutions must have an interest in library information development.
Structure   Governed by executive officers. Affiliations: IFLA, CONSAL
Sources of Support   Membership dues, sale of publications, government subsidies
Major Fields of Interest   All types of libraries; education for librarianship; all aspects of information studies and development
Major Goals and Objectives   (1) To improve the status of librarians; (2) to enhance library activities in national development; (3) to develop, promote, and apply the principles of library science to further education, science, and social welfare; (4) to develop the professional qualities of librarians
Activities   Promoting the development and establishment of libraries, including a National Library and rural libraries; publications program, especially library manuals; sponsors continuing education workshops, seminars. Between the four-yearly congress, IPI is organizing a working meeting held in conjunction with a library seminar every year. Each province in the country take turns in holding the meeting and seminar. From time to time, smaller seminars in cooperation with other professional associations, NGOs or government institutions, are also held. If funding allows, executive members of IPI are urged to attend the yearly IFLA or the three-yearly CONSAL
Publications   Official journal: Majalah Ikatan Pustakawan Indonesia (Journal of the Indonesian Library Association). 1974-. 4/yr. Address same as Association. Circ: 3,600+. Indonesian. Indexed in Indonesian Learned Periodicals Index. Other publications: Berita Ikatan Pustakawan Indonesia (IPI) (Indonesia Library Association News); annual reports, proceedings of seminars, workshops, conferences, monographs. Publications available for sale. Publications exchange programs with other associations, libraries, and nonlibrary institutions
Bibliography   Pringgoadisurjo, Luwarsih, "Indonesia," in ALA World Encyclopedia of Library and Information Services. 2nd ed., pp. 353–354. Chicago: American Library Association, 1986; Khurshid, A., "Library Associations in Asia," Herald of Library Science 28 (1989):3–10

Iran

297   Iranian Library and Information Science Association (ILISA)
Address   PO Box 11-1391, Tehran   http://ilisa.org.ir
Languages   Persian
Established   1966, Tehran
Staff   None
General Assembly   Entire membership meets annually
Membership   Total members: Approx. 949 (914 individual, 35 institutional). Types of membership: Individual, institutional, student, honorary. Requirements: Professional or nonprofessional librarian status or a love for books and an interest in the aims and work of the organization
Structure   Governed by executive officers. Affiliations: IFLA
Sources of Support   Membership dues, sale of publications, government subsidies
Major Fields of Interest   Library and information science; books; reading; education

Major Goals and Objectives   To develop the essence and principles of modern library science in Iran; to make known to the people the importance of the library professions; to protect the rights of librarians and to increase their professional status
Publications   Official journal: ILA Bulletin (in Persian). 1970-?. 4/yr. No information, whether the journal is still being published
Bibliography   Sharify, Nasser, and Sharify, Homayoun Gloria, "Iran," in ALA World Encyclopedia of Library and Information Services. 2nd ed., pp. 386–387. Chicago: American Library Association, 1986; Khurshid, A., "Library Associations in Asia," Herald of Library Science 28 (1989):3–10

298   National Iranian Oil Company, NIOC Central Library

Address   NIOC New Building, Hafez Ave., 15875-1863 Tehran
Languages   Persian
Officers   Pres: A. Faezi

Ireland

299   Central Catholic Library Association, Inc. (CCL)

Address   74 Merrion Square, Dublin 2   Tel.: +353 1 6761264, Fax +353 1 6787618, catholiclibrary@imagine.ie; www.catholiclibrary.ie
Languages   English
Established   1922
Staff   1 paid, 25 volunteers
General Assembly   Entire membership meets once a year, in Dublin
Membership   Total members: 450 (individual). Types of membership: Individual. Requirements: No strict requirements. Annual subscription: EUR 25; concessions: EUR 10
Structure   Governed by Council
Sources of Support   Members' subscriptions, donations
Major Fields of Interest   Theology, scripture, spirituality, church history, also Irish history&culture, literature, biography, travel, art
Major Goals and Objectives   To make available a wide range of books and other materials on all aspects of life to which religion, especially catholicism, is relevant
Activities   Lecture series in spring&autumn, exhibitions, development of a website
Publications   Newsletter BIBLIO. 3/yr

300   Cumann Cartlannaíochta Éireann (ISA)
(Irish Society for Archives)

Address   isar@eircom.net; www.ucd.ie/archives/isa/isa-index.html
Languages   English, Irish
Established   1970
Officers   Chair: Raymond Refaussé; Hon Secr: Andrew White; Hon Membership Secr: Antoinette Doran; Hon Treas: Kerry Houston
Staff   None
General Assembly   Entire membership meets 7 times a year

Membership Requirements: Archivists and those interested in archives; archival institutions. Dues (Euro): 25, individual; 40, institutional; 10 Student
Structure Governed by executive officers. Affiliations: ICA
Sources of Support Membership dues, sale of publications, government subsidies
Major Fields of Interest Promotion and preservation of archives
Major Goals and Objectives To further the establishment and development of archives in Ireland; to promote the professional development of archivists. Specific objectives are: (1) To promote the preservation of archives and to aid in the rescue of material from destruction, neglect, or loss; (2) to increase public interest in archives and to promote greater use of and access to archives; (3) to coordinate the work of all authorities, institutions, and individuals concerned or interested in the custody, study, or publication of records; (4) to provide a center for the collection and dissemination of technical information of value to those engaged or interested in archives; (5) to publish informal news sheets of archival interest and to arrange for lectures on this and related subjects
Activities Sponsors meetings, conferences, workshops for the members, who are archivists, librarians, public servants, and professional and amateur historians
Publications Official journal: Irish Archives. 1/yr. Editors: Elizabeth McEvoy and John McDonough. Other publications: ISA newsletter 2/yr. Kate Manning, Archives Department, University College Dublin, Belfield, Dublin 4. email: kate.manning@ucd.ie
Bibliography Ellis-King, D., "Ireland," in ALA World Encyclopedia of Library and Information Services. 2nd ed., pp. 389–391. Chicago: American Library Association, 1986
Comment No address available

301 Cumann Leabharlann na h-Éireann (LAI) (The Library Association of Ireland)

Address 53 Upper Mount Street, Dublin 2 Tel.: +353 61 202193, Fax +353 61 213090, president@libraryassociation.ie; www.libraryassociation.ie
Languages English, Irish
Established 1928, at meeting held to re-establish the earlier, defunct Cumann na Leabharlann. Incorporated in 1952
Officers Pres: Deirdre Ellis-King; Secr: Michael Plaice
Staff 1 (part-time); Hon.officers and officers of sections and groups are volunteers
General Assembly Entire membership meets once a year, and at the Annual Joint Conference with the Library Association, Northern Ireland Branch
Membership Types of membership: Individual, institutional, life. Requirements: personal membership is open to persons employed in the profession of librarianship (including library assistants) while Associate membership is open to those with an interest in the work, progress and welfare of libraries but who are not employed in the profession
Structure Governed by Executive Board and honorary officers. Affiliations: IFLA; The Library Association, Northern Ireland Branch/LANI (with LANI joint annual conference, and joint publication of journal)
Sources of Support Membership dues, sale of publications, fees from conferences and seminars
Major Fields of Interest Librarianship in all its aspects, and information work
Major Goals and Objectives To promote and develop high standards of librarianship and of library and information services in Ireland; to maintain the profession of

librarianship in an appropriate status among the learned and technical professions

Activities   Past achievements: Maintaining close liaison with the Northern Ireland Branch of The Library Association; developing new special interest groups and sections within the Association; establishing Children's Book Week in the Republic of Ireland (through the Youth Library Group). Current: Campaigning for: (a) removal of charges for admission to public libraries; (b) acceptance of post-graduate professional qualification as the norm in Irish libraries; (c) improvement and extension of school library services. Association is working on a membership survey as a basis for planning future activity; preparing a new edition of the Directory. Future: Implementation of a nation-wide distance learning staff training scheme for libraries and information services; the provision of more and better opportunities and facilities for members to improve and extend their professional interests and expertise. Association has been active in promoting library-related legislation, such as the Public Libraries Act 1947. Currently involved in promoting new legislation for public libraries in Ireland. Sponsors Book Week activities, exhibits, continuing education programs

Publications   Official journal: An Leabharlann. The Irish Library. 1930-. 4/yr. Free to members. Editors: Mary Kintner South Eastern Education and Library Board, Windmill Hill, Ballynahinch, Co. Down, N. Ireland, BT24 8DH. Fax: +8 01238 565 072. Pat McMahon (Editor and Business Manager) Galway Public Library, Island House, Cathedral Square, Galway, Ireland. Tel. 00 353 91 562471. Fax. 00 353 91 565039. Circ: 5000. English. Indexed in LISA. Other publications: Annual reports, reports of seminars, workshops, Directory of Libraries and Information Services in Ireland. (available at http://www.libraryassociation.ie/directory/index.tmpl)

Bibliography   Ellis-King, D., "Ireland" In: ALA World Encyclopedia of Library and Information Services. 2nd ed., pp. 389–391. Chicago: American Library Association, 1986; Shorley, D., "Tree for All, Fee for All: Belfast 1988. The Joint Conference of the Northern Ireland Branch of the Library Association and the Library Association of Ireland: View from the Chair" In: Library Association Record 90 (May 1988):289

302   Cumann Leabharlannaithe Scoile (CLS)
(Irish Association of School Librarians)

Address   St. Andrew's College, Booterstown Avenue, Blackrock, Co. Dublin
smiller@st-andrews.ie
Languages   English
Established   1962, at University College, Dublin
Staff   None
General Assembly   Entire membership meets annually
Membership   Total members: about 130 (individual). Chapter: 1. Types of membership: Individual. Requirements: Interest in school libraries.
Structure   Governed by Executive Council. Branch of the School Library Association
Sources of Support   Membership dues
Major Fields of Interest   School libraries
Major Goals and Objectives   To promote the establishment, development, and use of school libraries in Ireland as instruments of education, both formal and informal; to provide school librarians with opportunities for mutual assistance and further education
Activities   Sponsors summer courses for school librarians and other continuing education

programs; active in obtaining official support for secondary school libraries from national and local government funds
Publications Official journal: C. L. S. Bulletin. 1962-. 1/yr. Free to members. Address same as Association
Bibliography Ellis-King, D., "Ireland," in ALA World Encyclopedia of Library and Information Services. 2nd ed., pp. 389–391. Chicago: American Library Association, 1986

Israel

303 Igud Ha'arkhiyy Yona Yim Be-Israel (IAA) (Israel Archives Association)

Address P.O.Box 39652, 61396 Tel-Aviv-Yaffo Tel.: +972 3 6406789, Fax +972 3 6408883, urialgom@bezeqint.net
Languages Hebrew
Established 1950
Staff Volunteers
General Assembly Entire members meet once a year
Membership 350 individual members. Membership is granted to individuals who work in archives
Structure General Assembly elects Council that elects Executive Committee, the latter appoints committees
Sources of Support Membership dues and grants
Major Fields of Interest Archives, Records Management and Information Science
Major Goals and Objectives a) Fostering members interrelationship and coordination of the activities. b) Intensified the public archival awareness. c) Intensified the status of the archivists. d) Encourage the discussion in professional issues. e) Promotion the professional training, Archival Research, Records Management and Information Science. f) Coordinate and assist to sight archival material of the history of the Jewish people around the world. g) Carry out the connections with the International Council on Archives and other International Organizations
Activities Organize Conferences, Seminars, Courses and Work Shops for its members
Publications Official Journal: ARKHIYYON. Reader in Archives Studies and Documentation, publicized once a year; MEIDA (Information). Quarterly Newsletter; Y'IUNIM BEARKHIYYONA'UTH (Studies in Archival Science). Twice a year; Dictionary of Archival Terminology 1993; A Guide for Maintenance of Records in Archival Depositories. 2nd ed. 2000 (all in Hebrew)
Bibliography Sever, S., "Israel," in ALA World Encyclopedia of Library and Information Services. 2nd ed., pp. 393–398. Chicago: American Library Association, 1986; Aloufi, Zohar: From Conference to Conference. The Israel Archives Association, June 1950-February 1993. In: ARKHIYYON. Reader in Archives Studies and Documentation. Hebrew, pp. 131–170, English abstract p. LIX. Nos.10–11, 1999

304 Igud Menahalei Archyyionim Ba-Rashuiot Ha-Mekomyiot (ADMA) (Association of Directors of Municipal Archives)

Address c/o Netanya City Archives, 8 Tel-Chai Street, Netanya 42403 Tel.: +972 9

8603438, Fax +972 9 8624246, zaloufi@hotmail.com; www.nlr.ru/prof/liborg/country.php?id=100
Languages Hebrew
Established 1996
Membership About 90 membersT. Member has to be a director
Structure The governing body is the General Assembly. ADMA is one of several associations within the Union of Local Authorities in Israel. Its activities are under the auspices of this Union. Affiliation: IAA
Sources of Support Membership fees, and funds from the Union of Local Authorities in Israel
Major Fields of Interest Archives, Records Management and Information Science
Major Goals and Objectives a) Intensified the archival awareness of other municipal departments and that of the public. b) Intensified the status of the archivists. c) Promotion of the professional training, Archival Research, Records Management and Information Science
Activities Organize Conferences, Seminars, Courses and Work Shops for its members, in coordination with the IAA

305   Information Processing Association of Israel (IPA)

Address P.O. Box 53113, Tel Aviv 61530 Tel.: +972 3 647 3023, Fax +972 3 647 3023, mosheg@mail.biu.ac.il; www.ifip.or.at/members/israel.htm
Languages English, Hebrew
Established 1956; originally founded as the Association of the Users of Unit-Record Equipment, new name adopted 1964
Staff 5 (paid)
General Assembly Entire membership meets annually
Membership Types of membership: Individual. Requirements: Open to anyone who has had at least 1 year of experience in data processing
Structure Governed by Executive Council. Affiliations: IFLA
Sources of Support Membership dues
Major Fields of Interest Information processing and technology
Major Goals and Objectives Advancement of information processing in all areas; raising and advancing the professional level of all people connected with information processing; development of public consciousness of the field of information processing
Activities Establishing societies in various areas and integrating computerization within their professions. Establishing Work Groups in various areas. Active as Professional Committees. Prizes and grants
Publications Official journal: Maase Hoshev (Action and Thought). 1972-. 4/yr. Membership only. Address same as Association. Hebrew, with some English translations. Other publications: Annual reports, proceedings of meetings, seminars, conferences, and others. Publications available for sale. Publications exchange program in effect. Activities Sponsors seminars, workshops, and other continuing education offerings; promotes the exchange and sharing of information on a broad international scale; promotes staff exchanges and studies abroad of Israeli professionals
Bibliography Khurshid, A., "Library Associations in Asia," Herald of Library Science 28 (1989):3–10

306 Israeli Center for Libraries

Address icl@icl.org.il; www.icl.org.il
Languages Hebrew
Established 1965, through the cooperation of the Department for Libraries in the Ministry of Education and Culture and Israel Librarians and Information Specialists Association and The School of Library, Archive and Information Studies at the Hebrew University in Jerusalem
Sources of Support Supported by the Ministry of Science, Culture and Sport
Major Fields of Interest National roof organization that looks after the joint interests of all the libraries
Major Goals and Objectives To advance and foster libraries, librarianship, information science and the culture of books and reading in Israel
Activities Guidance and in-service courses, annual conferences, Library depot (supplies furniture and additional equipment for libraries), Ascola (Round table forum for librarians Information Specialists, which serves as an interactive lever for the exchange of information and ideas and for support), Literary projects, assigns ISBN for books, ISSN for publications and ISMN for musical works
Publications Bibliographical databases, periodicals and professional literature on information and librarianship
Comment No address available

307 Israeli Society of Libraries and Information Centers (SEMEL ASMI)*

Address 8 Blum St., Kfar Saba 44253 Tel.: +972 77 2151800, Fax +972 77 4340509, asmi@asmi.org.il; www.asmi.org.il
Languages Hebrew, English
Established 1966
Officers Chair: Shahaf Hagafny
Staff 2 (paid), 7 (volunteers)
General Assembly Entire membership meets once a year
Membership Total members: about 400. Types of membership: Full, associate, institutional, student, honorary, supporting. Requirements: Education in librarianship and/or information work, and actual employment in one of these fields. Dues: 300 shekels; retired and students – 200 shekels; first-year students – free
Structure Governed by Executive Committee and Officers. Affiliations: IFLA
Sources of Support Membership dues, sale of publications, government subsidies
Major Fields of Interest Special libraries; information work
Major Goals and Objectives To promote professional standards; to facilitate oral and written communication among members; to promote professional training of members and of those wishing to join the profession by setting standards of professional education and initiating or administering professional examinations; to cooperate and affiliate with other bodies having similar or allied interests in Israel or abroad
Activities Sponsors courses, seminars, continuing education programs in library and information science
Publications Official journal: Information and Librarianship. 1993-

Bibliography Sever, S., "Israel," in ALA World Encyclopedia of Library and Information Services. 2nd ed., pp. 393–398. Chicago: American Library Association, 1986

Italy

308 Associazione Archivistica Ecclesiastica (AAE) (Ecclesiastical Archivists Association)

Address Piazza S. Calisto, 16, 00153 Rome Tel.: +39 06 68100822, info@archivaecclesiae.org; www.archivaecclesiae.org

Languages Italian, occasionally French, Spanish, English

Established Feb. 4, 1956, to help the ecclesiastical authorities and ecclesiastical archivists

Staff All volunteers

General Assembly Entire membership meets every 2 years

Membership Requirements: Archivist in some ecclesiastical institution or scholar of archival studies

Structure Governed by Executive Council, elected every 2 years

Sources of Support Membership dues, sale of publications, government subsidies, occasional donations

Major Fields of Interest All types of archives of the Catholic Church: Diocesan, Parochial, Cathedral Chapters (Capitoli Cattedrali), Houses of Religious Orders and Congregations, various ecclesiastical associations, Catholic laypersons' associations

Major Goals and Objectives To promote the development and effective management of ecclesiastical archives of all types

Activities Promoting good management of ecclesiastical archives, good reference services, and cooperation of members. Sponsored meetings in Brescia 1980, in Rome 1982, in Loreto 1984; publication of proceedings; continuing the journal, with one volume commemorating the 25 years of the Association (1982); beginning of a Guida degli Archivi Diocesani d'Italia (Guide to Diocesan Archives in Italy)

Publications Official journal: Archiva Ecclesiae. 1958-. Biennial. Price depends on number of pages. Editor: President of Association. Address same as Association. Italian. Other occasional publications

Bibliography References to the Association's activities and achievements may be found in the Guida Monaci for many years; in the Bibliography of Archivum Historiae Pontificiae since 1980, and in L'Osservatore Romano in the years of meetings or publication of the volumes of Archiva Ecclesiae

309 Associazione Bibliotecari Documentalisti Sanita (BDS)

Address V.le Regina Elena, 291, 00161 Rome Tel.: +39 6 49852216, Fax +39 6 49852216; biblio.area.cs.cnr.it/bibliotecario/bibliossn/

Languages Italian

Established 2000, Rome

Officers Pres: Gaetana Cognetti; VP: Maurizio Vaglini; Secr: Gaetano Grillo

310 Associazione dei Bibliotecari Ecclesiastici Italiani (ABEI)

Address   c/o Segreteria, Via Mons. Cambiaso 32/16, 17031 Albenga segreteria@abei.it; www.abei.it
Languages   Italian
Established   1978
Membership   Dues: 25 Eur
Major Fields of Interest   Church libraries
Major Goals and Objectives   To promote church librarianship and the conservation of church libraries
Publications   Official journal: Bolletino di Informacione. Other publications: Annuario delle biblioteche ecclesiastiche italiane 1990, a cura di A. Ornella, S. Bigatton, P. G. Figini. Milano, Editrice Bibliografica, 1990. VIII-103 p.; Biblioteche ecclesiastiche in Italia Meridionale. Atti del Convegno interregionale, Reggio Calabria, Laruffa Editore, 1992. 164 p.; Le biblioteche ecclesiastiche alle soglie del Duemila: situazione, bilancio, prospettive. Atti del Convegno, a cura di Mauro Guerrini. Palermo, L'Epos, 2000. 110 p
Comment   Headquarter: Roma, piazza S. Maria Maggiore n. 5

311 Associazione Italiana Biblioteche (AIB)
(Italian Libraries Association)*

Address   c/o Biblioteca nazionale centrale, viale Castro Pretorio 105, 00185 Rome, C.P. 2461, Ufficio Roma 158, 00185 Rome Tel.: +39 6 4463532, Fax +39 6 4441139, aib@aib.it; www.aib.it
Languages   Italian
Established   1930, Rome, at the First International Congress of Libraries and Bibliography; reorganized 1951
Officers   Pres: Mauro Guerrini; VP: Claudio Leombroni; Gen Secr: Giovanna Frigimelica; Treas: Palmira Maria Barbini
Staff   5 (paid)
General Assembly   General assembly meets at least once a year, usually in May and in October/November
Membership   Total members: 4000+ (individual and institutional). Types of membership: Individual, institutional, honorary, student. Requirements: Librarians, libraries, interested institutions and companies. Fees: EUR 55 individual, EUR 130 institution, EUR 25 student
Structure   Governed by National Executive Board on behalf of General assembly. Regional branches. Standing committees are established in order to put into practice the statutory aims of the Association. Affiliations: IFLA, EBLIDA, WIPO
Sources of Support   Membership dues, sale of publications, government subsidies, training courses and other kinds of sponsorship
Major Fields of Interest   Library policy, library science, library education
Major Goals and Objectives   To support the organization and development in Italy of libraries and of a library service taking more and more into account the needs of users; to act as a professional representative in all cultural, scientific, technical, legal and legislative spheres, on any matter which may concern a better organization of library and documentation services; to promote, support and develop any action useful to ensure a qualified professional education; to provide their own members with scientific and technical aids for continuing professional education; to contribute in every place to

directions and decisions of library policy; to promote the observance of the ethical principles of the library profession; to defend the dignity and the professional specificity of librarians

Activities   Active lobbying for libraries and librarians; international cooperation, for a new National Libraries Act; public campaign about reading to and by children, management of a Register of Italian professional librarians from 1998; Labour Observatory ("Osservatorio Lavoro"), devoted to lobbying and consultancy on labour relations, recruitment of librarians, etc.; study, field surveys, research, development of guidelines and professional tools, information and debate on any matter of interest for library and information services; training courses, conferences, special Library

Publications   Official journals: Bolletino AIB, founded 1955, 4/yr, circulation: 4000. AIB Notizie, founded 1989, Bi-monthly newsletter, circulation: 4000. Other publications: Agenda del bibliotecario, 1/yr. Various series and monographs, proceedings of conferences; reports of seminars, workshops. Publications available for sale (see the on line catalogue <http://www.aib.it/aib/editoria/catalogo.htm>). Publications exchange program in effect

Bibliography   Solimine, G., "Lo sviluppo dell'Associazione, le sue strutture, la sua organizzazione," (The Association's Growth, Its Composition, Its Organization), Bollettino d'Informazioni 25 (1985):435–441 (in Italian); Sotgiu, M.C.C., "The Association and Its Questioners," ibid.:527–530 (in Italian); Revelli, Carlo, "Considerazione tra un congresso e l'altro," (Some Reflections between Two Congresses), Bollettino d'Informazioni 26 (1986):421–429; Carpenter, Ray L., "Italy," in ALA World Encyclopedia of Library and Information Services. 2nd ed., pp. 398–400. Chicago: American Library Association, 1986; Mandillo, A.M., "Il gruppo nazionale sulla professione dell'AIB," (AIB's National Group on the Profession), Bollettino d'Informazioni 28 (1988):37–39; "Le interviste di Erasmus: un presidente allo specchio," (Erasmus' Interviews: A President in the Mirror), Biblioteche Oggi 6 (1988):33–41 (in Italian); Frigimelica, G., "Associazione italiana biblioteche. Italian library association: a brief presentation", AIB Notizie 21 (4):10–11 (http://www.aib.it/aib/editoria/n21/0410.htm3)

312   Associazione Italiana per la Documentazione Avanzata (AIDA) (Italian Association for Advanced Documentation)

Address   c/o CASPUR, via dei Tizii 6B, 00185 Rome   Tel.: +39 6 49910825, Fax +39 6 49910076, aida@aidaweb.it; www.aidaweb.it

Languages   Italian, English (for correspondence)

Established   1983

Staff   None

General Assembly   Entire membership meets every two years

Membership   Total members: about 400 (individual and collective bodies, plus 4 honorary). Fees: 26,00 EUR (students nonprofessional), 62,00 EUR (professionals – individual), 207,00 EUR (professionals – collective profit and non-profit)

Structure   Governed by executive officers

Sources of Support   Membership dues, fundings

Major Fields of Interest   Advanced documentation and information services

Major Goals and Objectives   To contribute, with other institutions, to the definition, knowledge and development of documentation and information science as a cultural area, peculiar for the exercise and treatment of documentation and information practice; to strenghten the 'documentalist' [information specialist] profession as an activity of a high specialised content, having as its object the transformation or reduction of the document into information units, the creation of documentary languages, information storing, retrieval and circulation

Activities Sponsoring workshops, seminars, meetings to give members opportunity for exchange of information and continuing education in the area of documentation

Publications Official journal: AIDA Informazioni 4/yr.(print and online). Free to members. Subscription: 103,00 EUR. Address same as Association. Italian. Other publications: AIDAlampi (newsletter). Issues proceedings of conferences and other occasional publications

313 Associazione Nazionale Archivistica Italiana (ANAI) (National Association of Italian Archivists)

Address Via Giunio Bazzoni, 15, 00195 Rome Tel.: +39 06 37517714, Fax +39 06 37517714, segreteria@anai.org; www.anai.org
Languages Italian, French
Established 1949, Orvieto
Officers Pres: Isabella Orefice; Secr national: Cecilia Pirola
Staff 1 paid, some volunteers
General Assembly Entire membership meets annually or biennially
Membership Total members: 1100+ (individual and institutions)
Structure Governed by Executive Board. Affiliations: ICA
Sources of Support Membership dues, government subsidies, private gifts
Major Fields of Interest Archival collections
Major Goals and Objectives To study problems concerning public and private archives; to contribute to the preservation and utilization of the holdings of Italian archives; to encourage cooperation between Italian and foreign archivists; to promote scientific and technical activities of archivists; to improve the standards of archive personnel and to protect their interests
Activities Sponsors conferences, workshops, seminars, and other continuing education programs; works for greater political and cultural unity in matters of scientific research and greater economic assistance for archival activities
Publications Official journals: Archivi per la Storia. 1988-. Anai Notizie. 1994–1999-. Il Mondo degli Archivi. 1999-. Other publications: Annual report, proceedings of workshops, seminars, conferences, and monographs. Publications for sale. Publications exchange program in effect with foreign countries

314 Gruppo Italiano Documentalisti dell'industria Farmaceutica e degli Istituti di Ricerca Biomedica (GIDIF-RBM)

Address via Tajani 3, 20133 Milano Tel.: +39 382380380, gidif-rbm@mondino.it; www.gidif-rbm.it
Languages Italian
Established 1983
Officers Pres: Giovanna Miranda; Treas: Silvia Molinari
General Assembly Annual meetings

Major Fields of Interest   Biomedical information and documentation
Major Goals and Objectives   To promote the professional image of documentalists; to promote the further education of documentalists in the field of biomedicine; to contribute to the development of the professions
Activities   Conventions, workshops, study groups
Publications   Official newsletter: Notizie. 4/yr

315   Sezione Italiana dell'International Association of Music Libraries, Archives and Documentation Centres (IAML Italia)
(International Association of Music Libraries, Archives and Documentation Centres – Italian Branch)
Address   c/o /o Biblioteca Civica Angelo Mai e Archivi Storici, piazza Vecchia, 15, 24129 Bergamo   Tel.: +39 35 399430, Fax +39 35 240655, presidente@iamlitalia.it; www.iamlitalia.it
Languages   Italian, English, German, French
Staff   None
General Assembly   Annual assembly. 2002: Brescia, 2003: Napoli, 2004: Bologna
Membership   Personal and institutional members. Dues: 68 Eur, institutions; 39 Eur, personal
Structure   Governed by executive officers. Affiliations: A national branch of IAML (Association does not have its own constitution)
Sources of Support   Membership dues
Major Fields of Interest   Music bibliography and librarianship
Major Goals and Objectives   To represent Italy within the IAML and to coordinate the activities of Italian IAML members
Activities   Association has participated in some IAML activities, especially in RISM, RILM, RIdIM and RIPMXIX. In 1984, organized the annual meeting of IAML in Como. In cooperation with the Ufficio Ricerca Fondi Musicali (Milan), Association established the rules for cataloging printed and manuscript music
Publications   Conference proceedings

Jamaica

316   Library and Information Association of Jamaica (LIAJA)
Address   POB 125, Kingston 5   Tel.: +1 876 927-1614, Fax +1 876 927-1614, liajapresident@yahoo.com; www.liaja.org.jm
Languages   English
Established   1949, Kingston, at Institute of Jamaica
Officers   Pres: Paulette Stewart; 1st VP: Pualine Nicholas; 2nd VP: Claudette Thomas; Immediate Past Pres: Mavis Williams; Secr: Odean Cole-Phoenix; Treas: Koren Witter-Thomas
Staff   None
General Assembly   Annual General Meeting in January
Membership   Types of membership: Full, Associate, Student, Corresponding, Institutional, Sustaining, Honorary. Requirements: Open to all library staff members, and

to those having an interest in libraries and library work.
Structure Governed by Executive Council. Affiliations: COMLA, ACURIL, IASL, IFLA, PSAJ
Sources of Support Financed by membership dues
Major Fields of Interest Library profession and library development
Major Goals and Objectives (1) To unite all persons engaged in or interested in library work in Jamaica, and to provide opportunities for their meeting together to discuss matters relating to libraries; (2) to encourage cooperation among libraries and to promote the active development and maintenance of libraries throughout Jamaica; (3) to promote a high standard of education and training of library staff and whatever may improve the status of librarians; (4) to promote a wide knowledge of library work and to form an educated public opinion on libraries
Activities Sponsors conferences, seminars, and other continuing education programs. The School Library Section and the Special Library Section carry out various activities, some jointly with the Department of Library Studies of the University of the West Indies. Association was greatly involved in relief efforts for Jamaican libraries devastated by Hurricane Gilbert in September 1988
Publications Official journal: JLA Bulletin. 1950-. Annual. Address same as Association. Other publications: JLA News. 4/yr.; occasional bibliographies and monographs, Directory of Jamaican Libraries. Brown, Hyacinth, ed., Disaster Planning in Jamaica. Safeguarding documents and vital data (1989)
Bibliography Iton, S.M., "Jamaica," in ALA World Encyclopedia of Library and Information Services. 2nd ed., pp. 402–403. Chicago: American Library Association, 1986; "Caribbean Generosity," COMLA Newsletter 66 (Dec. 1989):6

Japan

317 Ato Dokyumenteshon Kenkyukai (JADS) (Japan Art Documentation Society)

Address c/o Bureau:Hatano Labo, ?110-0007 Ueno-Kouen7-7, Taito Fax +81 03-3828-5797, ldt02307@nifty.ne.jp; wwwsoc.nii.ac.jp/jads/index-e.html
Languages Japanese
Established 1989

318 Daigaku Toshokan Mondai Kenkyukai (Society of Study on Academic Library Problems)

Address c/o H.Oishi, 3-4-1-606, Okusawa, Setagaya-ku, Tokyo 158-0083 Fax +81 3 37485390; www.daitoken.com(injapaneseonly)
Languages Japanese

319 IAML Nihon Shibu (Kokusai Ongaku Bunken-Kyokai Nihon Shibu) (International Association of Music Libraries, Archives and Documentation Centers – Japanese Branch)

Address c/o Documentation Centre of Modern Japanese Music, 1-18-14 Azabu-Dai, Minato-ku, Tokyo 106-0041 Tel.: +814 2396 1369, Fax +814 2396 1369;

http://www.iaml.info/organization/national_branches/japan
Languages Japanese, English
Established 1979, Tokyo
Officers Pres: Masakata Kanazawa; VP: Yasuko Todo; Secr: Hitoshi Matsushita; Treas: Yoshiko Mori
Staff None
General Assembly Entire membership meets once a year in Tokyo, May or June
Membership Total members: Approx. 70 (individual, institutional). Requirements: Payment of dues
Structure Governed by executive officers. Affiliations: IMC Japanese Committee
Sources of Support Membership dues
Major Fields of Interest Music libraries, archives, and documentation
Major Goals and Objectives To accomplish within a national framework all the tasks IAML undertakes on an international scale, and to collaborate in all of the fields the Association deems necessary
Activities Sponsors conferences, seminars, workshops, and other continuing education programs
Publications No official journal. Publishes newsletter
Bibliography Kon, Madoko, "Japan," in ALA World Encyclopedia of Library and Information Services. 2nd ed., pp. 403–408. Chicago: American Library Association, 1986

320 Japan Society for Information and Media Studies (JSIMS)

Address c/o Onodera, Natsuo, Kasuga 1–2, Tsukuba, Ibaraki, 305-8550 Tel.: +81 298 591364, Fax +81 298 591364, office@jsims.jp; www.jsims.jp
Languages Japanese
Established 2000
Staff 2 (part-time), volunteer
General Assembly Anually
Membership 350 personal, 6 institutional; requirements: to be engaged in research, or have an interest, in information and media studies
Structure Non-profit academic society
Sources of Support Membership fees
Major Fields of Interest Information and media studies
Major Goals and Objectives To contribute to progress and development of information and media studies
Activities Publication of a journal, holding conferences and meetings, other activities
Publications Journal of Information and Media Studies (Joho Media Kenkyu); JSIMS Newsletter

321 Joho Shori Gakkai
(Information Processing Society of Japan)

Address 1–5 Kanda-Surugadai, Chiyoda-ku, Tokyo 101-0062 Tel.: +81 3 35188374, Fax +81 3 35188375; www.ipsj.or.jp
Languages Japanese
Established April 1960

Major Goals and Objectives   To promote development of the arts, sciences, industry, and humanity through conducting various activities about information processing with computers and communications and providing resources for discipline and opportunities of cooperation with sister societies to members
Activities   Sponsors conferences

322   Jouhou Kagaku Gijutsu Kyokai (INFOSTA)
(Information Science and Technology Association)

Address   Sasaki Building, 2-5-7 Koisikawa, Bunkyo-ku, Tokyo, 112-0002 Tel.: +81 3 38133791, Fax +81 3 38133793, infosta@infosta.or.jp; www.infosta.or.jp/start-e.html
Languages   Japanese, English
Established   1950. Originally founded as the Japan Society for Universal Decimal Classification (UDC)
General Assembly   Entire membership meets annually
Structure   Governed by executive officers. Affiliations: FID
Sources of Support   Membership dues, sale of publications, private subsidies
Major Fields of Interest   Information science and technology; documentation
Major Goals and Objectives   To promote research on the theory and application of documentation; to promote dissemination of knowledge about the UDC system in Japan; to collect materials on documentation and its usage; to sponsor lectures, symposia and training courses
Activities   Sponsors conferences, symposia, training courses, seminars, workshops, and other continuing education programs
Publications   Official journal: Dokumenteshon Kenkyu (Journal of Information Science and Technology Association). 12/yr. Free to members. Address same as Association. Japanese. Other publications: Universal Decimal Classification Schedule; Infomanto (Informant). 2/yr.; Production of Documents and Databases, annual reports, proceedings of conferences, seminars, etc
Bibliography   Kon, Madoko, "Japan," in ALA World Encyclopedia of Library and Information Services. 2nd ed., pp. 403–408. Chicago: American Library Association, 1986; Librarianship in Japan, ed. by Editorial Committee of Librarianship in Japan, Japan Organizing Committee of IFLA Tokyo, August 1986, p. 71

323   Kango Toshokan Kyogikai
(Japan Nursing Library Association)

Address   c/o Nursing Library, Kitazato University, 2-1-1. Kitazato, Sagamihara 228-0829 Tel.: +81 24 5471684, Fax +81 24 5471996, shouko-f@fmu.ac.jp; wwwsoc.nii.ac.jp/kantokyo/index.html(japaneseonly)
Languages   Japanese

324   Keizai Shiryo Kyogikai
(Association for Documentation in Economics)

Address   c/o Faculty of Economics, Kyoto Keizai Univ., Yoshida Honmachi, Sakyo-ku, Kyoto 606-8501 Fax +81 75 7533490, sakurada@econ.kyoto-u.ac.jp; wwwsoc.nii.ac.jp/ade(japaneseonly)
Languages   Japanese

325   Knowledge Management Society of Japan

Address   international@kmsj.org; www.kmsj.org/english/kmsj.htm
Languages   Japanese
Established   1998
Officers   Manag Dir: Tom Takanashi; Pres: Matsutaro Morita
Membership   Individual and corporate; Restrictions: Everybody who aspires to study about knowledge management; those corporations who are ready to support the aims and activities of the Society
Structure   Governed by Executive Board
Major Fields of Interest   Knowledge Management
Major Goals and Objectives   Aims at engaging in extensive studies about knowledge management and at supporting developments of such studies
Activities   Holds annual convention and meetings of respective Study Groups; promotes views and opinions concerning knowledge management; engages in exchanges with relevant societies in and out of Japan
Publications   Annual Bulletin; Quarterly KM report
Comment   No address available

326   Kokkoshiritsu Daigaku Toshokan Kyoryoku Iinkai (The coordinating Committee for Japanese University Libraries)*

Address   c/o Library, Keio Univ, 2-15-45 Mita, Minato-ku, Tokyo 108-8345 Fax +81 3 5427-1645, x-somu@lib.keio.ac.jp
Languages   Japanese

327   Kokuritsu Daigaku Toshokan Kyogikai (Association of National University Libraries)

Address   c/o Library, Univ. of Tokyo, 7-3-1, Hongo, Bunkyo-ku, Tokyo 113-0033 Fax +81 3 3818 0146, wwwsoc@nii.ac.jp; http://wwwsoc.nii.ac.jp/anul/e/organization/regulations/bylaws.html
Languages   Japanese
Established   1954
General Assembly   Entire membership meets annually
Membership   Type of membership: Institutional. Requirements: libraries of academic institutions fully supported by the Japanese National Government
Structure   Governed by Executive Committee. Affiliations: Japanese University Libraries International Liaison Committee; Joint Committee for Library Cooperation of National, Public and Private Universities; Japan Library Association (JLA)
Sources of Support   Membership dues
Major Fields of Interest   Academic and research library and information services
Major Goals and Objectives   The Association shall aim at supporting the advancement of library functions through close coordination and cooperation among national university libraries, promoting inter-library use of scholarly information resources extensively, and contributing development of infrastructures for scholarly information distribution in order to help universities achieve their missions
Activities   Sponsors conferences, seminars, workshops, and other continuing education programs. Investigation and research activities carried out by various Committees and

Groups
Publications Official journal: Daigaku Toshokan Kenkyu (Journal of College and University Libraries). 1972-. 2/yr. Japanese. Indexed in LISA. Other publications: Annual reports, proceedings of conferences, seminars, etc
Bibliography Kon, Madoko. "Japan," in ALA World Encyclopedia of Library and Information Services. 2nd ed., pp. 403–408. Chicago: American library Association, 1986; Librarianship in Japan, ed. by Editorial Committee of librarianship in Japan, Japan Organizing Committee of IFLA Tokyo, August 1986, p. 71; Khurshid, A., "Library Associations in Asia," Herald of Library Science 28 (1989):3–10

328   Kouritsu Daigaku Kyokai Toshokan Kyogikai (KODAIKYO) (Public University Library Association)

Address   c/o Library, Kanazawa Bijutsu Kogei Univ., 5-11-1, Odateno, Kanazawa Kanazawa   Tel.: +81 03-3501-3336, Fax +81 03-3501-3337, jimu@kodaikyo.jp
Languages   Japanese
Established   1969
General Assembly   Entire membership meets annually
Membership   Requirements: Library of public university in Japan
Structure   Governed by executive officers
Sources of Support   Membership dues, sale of publications, government subsidies
Major Fields of Interest   Public university libraries
Major Goals and Objectives   To promote research and cooperation between public university libraries in Japan
Activities   Sponsors conferences, seminars, workshops, and other continuing education programs
Publications   Official journal: Kouritsu Daigaku Kyokai Toshokan Kyogikai Kaihou (KODAIKYO Bulletin). 1/yr.; Kouritsu Daigaku Toshokan Gaiyou (Public University Library Annual). 1/yr.; Kouritsu Daigaku Jittai Chosa. Fuzoku Toshokanhen (Public University States Report. Library Division). 1/yr.; Koudaikyo Toshokan Kyogikai Kenshu Houkokusho (KODAIKYO Study Report). 1/yr. Daigaku Toshokan Kenkyu (Journal of College and University Libraries). 1972-. 2/yr. Japanese. Indexed in LISA. Other publications: Annual reports, proceedings of conferences, seminars, etc
Bibliography   Kon, Madoko, "Japan," in ALA World Encyclopedia of Library and Information Services. 2nd ed., pp. 403–408. Chicago: American Library Association, 1986; Librarianship in Japan, ed. by Editorial Committee of Librarianship in Japan, Japan Organizing Committee of IFLA Tokyo, August 1986, p. 75

329   Mita Toshokan Joho Gakkai (Mita Society for Library and Information Science)

Address   c/o School of Library and Information Science, Keio University, 2-15-45 Mita, Minato-ku, Tokyo 108-8345   Tel.: +81 334534511, mslis@slis.keio.ac.jp; wwwsoc.nii.ac.jp/mslis/index.html(japaneseonly)
Languages   Japanese, English
Established   1963, Tokyo
Staff   1 (paid)
General Assembly   Entire membership meets annually

Membership Open to librarians and other interested persons and institutions
Structure Governed by Executive Committee
Sources of Support Membership dues, sale of publications
Major Fields of Interest Library and information science
Major Goals and Objectives To develop library and information science, and promote librarianship and information activities
Activities Sponsors conferences, seminars, workshops, and other continuing education programs
Publications Official journal: Library and Information Science. 1963-. 1/yr. Address same as Association. Japanese, English. Indexed in Lib.Lit., LISA. Other publications: Annual reports, proceedings of conferences (preprints), seminars, etc
Bibliography Kon, Madoko, "Japan," in ALA World Encyclopedia of Library and Information Services. 2nd ed., pp. 403–408. Chicago: American library Association, 1986; Librarianship in Japan, ed. by Editorial Committee of Librarianship in Japan, Japan Organizing Committee of IFLA Tokyo, August 1986, p. 74

330 Nihon Akaibuzu Gakkai (JSAS) (Japan Society for Archival Science)*

Address c/o Prof. Minoru Takahashi, 10-3 Midoricho,Tachikawa, Tokyo 190-0014 office@jsas.info; www.jsas.info
Languages Japanese
Established 2004, Tokyo, at meeting at Gakushuin University
Officers Pres: Minoru Takahashi; VP: Masahito Ando; Kazunori Ishihara; Secr: Kiyofumi Kato
General Assembly Entire membership meets once a year, around April
Membership Total members: As of Mar. 2010, 420 (individual and students); 17 (organizational). Membership: individual, students, organizational. Requirements: Open to any interested individuals, students and organizations interested in archives and archival science
Structure Governed by Executive Committee. Member of ICA and EASTICA
Sources of Support Membership dues, sales of publications
Major Fields of Interest Research on records and archives management; Research on topics such as the formation, structure and history of archives; Research on the education and training of archivists
Major Goals and Objectives To promote development of archival institutions, archival management as well as the education and training of archivists
Activities Holds symposia on major topics of archives and archival science at the annual meetings. Active in promoting relevant legislations, such as Public Records Management Act. Sponsors conferences, seminars, workshops and other relevant programs
Publications Official Journal: Akaibuzu Kenkyu (Journal of the Japan Society for Archival Science). 2004-. 2/yr. Yen 2000 per issue. Free to members. Address same as Association. Japanese with English abstracts. Other Publication: Nyumon Akaibuzu no Sekai (Introduction to Archival Science, an anthology of articles translated into Japanese). 2006. Compiled by the Records Management Society of Japan and the JSAS. On sale by Nichigai Associates, Inc.

Bibliography   Takayama, Masaya, et al. "Japan: Libraries, Archives and Museums," in: Encyclopedia of Library and Information Sciences, 3rd ed., pp. 3042–3059

331   Nihon Igaku Toshokan Kyokai (JMLA) (Japan Medical Library Association)

Address   Noguchi House 305 26 Daikyo-Cho, Shinjuku-Ku, Tokyo 160-0015 Tel.: +81 3 53686216, Fax +81 3 53686236, jmlajimu@sirius.ocn.ne.jp; wwwsoc.nii.ac.jp/jmla/index.html(japaneseonly)

Languages   Japanese

Established   1927

Staff   2 (paid)

General Assembly   Entire membership meets once a year

Membership   Requirements: Libraries attached to non-profit institutions, which possess a certain amount of holdings as provided in the Constitution and Bylaws

Structure   Governed by Executive Committee. Affiliations: IFLA, Japan Library Association (JLA)

Sources of Support   Membership dues, sale of publications, documents supplied from abroad to member libraries. Budget (Yen): 1986/87: 67,813,179; 1987/88: 59,192,927

Major Fields of Interest   Library and information science for medicine and dentistry

Major Goals and Objectives   (1) To promote the progress of medicine through the various activities of medical libraries; (2) to fulfill this mission, the Association carries out the following programs: (a) Research in medical library administration and management of information systems, (b) interlibrary loan and document supply services, (c) training and education of medical librarians, and (d) a variety of other activities

Activities   Past achievements: Changed the Association's fiscal year to the present system (beginning April and ending March); revised rules for regular membership and abolished associate membership in order to unify members. Current and future: Building an integrated network for supporting the nation's 1,000 hospital libraries in their activities and document supply. Sponsors conferences, seminars, workshops, and other continuing education programs

Publications   Official journal: Igaku Toshokan (Medical Library). 1954-. 4/yr. Free to members. Address same as Association. Japanese, with English abstracts. Other publications: Annual reports, proceedings of conferences, seminars, etc. Kaiho. 6/yr.; Genko Igaku Zasshi Shozai Mokuroku (Union List of Current Periodicals Acquired by the Japanese Medical, Dental and Pharmaceutical Libraries). 1/yr.; Igaku Yousho Sougou Mokuroku (Union Catalog of Foreign Medical Books). 4/yr., annual cumulation. Publications listed in journal; available for sale

Bibliography   Tonosaki, M., "The Activities of the Japan Medical Library Association" In: Az Orvosi Konyvtaros 25 (1985):223–235; Kon, Madoko, "Japan" In: ALA World Encyclopedia of Library and Information Services. 2nd ed., pp. 403–408. Chicago: American Library Association, 1986; Librarianship in Japan, ed. by Editorial Committee of Librarianship in Japan, Japan Organizing Committee of IFLA Tokyo, August 1986, p. 72; Khurshid, A, "Library Associations in Asia," Herald of Library Science 28 (1989):3–10

332 Nihon Nougaku Toshokan Kyogikai (NOTOKYO; JAALD)
(Japan Association of Agricultural Librarians and Documentalists)

Address c/o Library, Tokyo Nogyo Daigaku, 1-1-1, Sakuragaoka, Setagaya-ku 156-0054 Tel.: +81 3 5477-2776, Fax +81 3 5477-2776, JAALD@nifty.com; jaald.ac.affrc.go.jp(japaneseonly)
Languages Japanese
Established 1966, Tokyo
Staff 3 (paid), 17 (volunteers)
General Assembly Entire membership meets once a year in Tokyo
Membership Requirements: To be approved by the Executive Board of JAALD and pay the required dues
Structure Governed by Board of Directors. Affiliations: IAALD
Sources of Support Membership dues, sale of publications, translations (from Japanese to English), indexing and abstracting services.
Major Fields of Interest Agricultural librarianship and documentation (including forestry, fisheries, and veterinary science)
Major Goals and Objectives To promote agriculture, forestry, fisheries, and veterinary science, and to contribute to research and development in these fields
Activities Past achievements: Publication of the translations of four papers in International Agricultural Librarianship (1981); translation of Primer for Agricultural Libraries by O. Lendray (1983); translation of CAB/CAIN Evaluation Project by S. Harvey (1984). Current and future: Compilation of a Bibliography of Japanese Agricultural Bibliographies; publication of "How to Search for Information in the Agricultural Sciences." Sponsors conferences, seminars, workshops, and other continuing education programs
Publications Official journal: Nihon Nougaku Toshokan Kyogikai Kaiho (Bulletin of JAALD). 1966-. 4/yr. Free to members. Circ: Membership. Japanese. Indexed in Dokumenteshon Kenkvu; Japanese Agricultural Sciences Index (JASI). Other publications: Annual reports, proceedings of conferences, seminars, etc. JAALD Sirizu (JAALD Series). Irreg. Publications for sale. No publications exchange program in effect
Bibliography Makiyama, Shin-ichi, "Japan Association of Agricultural Librarians and Documentalists (JAALD)," Quarterly Bulletin of IAALD 26 (1983):100–101; Makiyama, Shin-ichi, "Japan Association of Agricultural Librarians and Documentalists," Igaku Toshokan 31 (June 1984):105–111 (in Japanese); Kon, Madoko,"Japan," in ALA World Encyclopedia of Library and Information Services. 2nd ed., pp. 403–408. Chicago: American library Association, 1986; Librarianship in Japan, ed. by Editorial Committee of Librarianship in Japan, Japan Organizing Committee of IFLA Tokyo, August 1986, p. 71–72; Khurshid, A., "Library Associations in Asia," Herald of Library Science 28 (1989):3–10

333 Nihon Toshokan Joho Gakkai (JSLIS)
(Japan Society of Library and Information Science)*

Address c/o University of Tsukuba, Tsukuba-Shi, Ibaraki-ken 305-8550 jslis-info@slis.tsukuba.ac.jp; www.soc.nii.ac.jp/jslis/aboutjslis_1_en.html
Languages Japanese, English
Established 1953, Tokyo

Officers Pres: Akira Nemoto; Exec Committee: Makiko Miwa; Hiroya Takeuchi; Shunsaku Tamura; Yuko Yoshida; Atushi Ikeuchi
General Assembly Entire membership meetstwice a year
Membership Members: 764, 714 individual, 50 institutional
Major Fields of Interest Library and information science
Major Goals and Objectives Promoting research activities and education on Library and Information Science mainly in Japan
Publications Official journal: Nihon Toshokan Joho Gakkaishi Journal of the Japan Society of Library and Information Science (english)

**334 Nihon Toshokan Kenkyukai (NITTOKEN; NAL)
(Nippon Association for Librarianship)**
Address 3-8-5-108, Toyosaki, Kita-ku, Osaka 531-0072 Fax +81 6 371 8739, CZS04500@nifty.ne.jp; wwwsoc.nii.ac.jp/nal/
Languages Japanese
Established 1946
General Assembly Entire membership meets annually
Membership 1100 personal and 800 institutional members. Requirements: Interested in goals and objectives of Association. Personal, institutional, honorary and supporting members
Structure Governed by Executive Board
Sources of Support Membership dues, sale of publications
Major Fields of Interest Library science
Major Goals and Objectives 1. Publication of the official scholarly journal Toshokan-Kai (The Library World) and other library related books and materials; 2. Grants to promote library research; Holding Annual Conventions, Annual Library Seminars and Monthly Study Meetings; 3. Holding training classes, seminars and lectures; 4. Advisory services about library management; 5. Other relevant enterprises
Activities Supports library studies; sponsors conferences, seminars, workshops, and other continuing education programs
Publications Official journal: Toshokan-Kai (Library World). 6/yr. Other publications: Daigakusei to Toshokan (College Student and Library) (1981); annual reports, proceedings of conferences, seminars, etc
Bibliography Kon, Madoko,"Japan," in ALA World Encyclopedia of Library and information Services. 2nd ed., pp. 403–408. Chicago: American Library Association, 1986; Librarianship in Japan, ed. by Editorial Committee of Librarianship in Japan, Japan Organizing Committee of IFLA Tokyo, August 1986, p. 75

**335 Nihon Toshokan Kyokai (NITOKYO; JLA)
(Japan Library Association)**
Address 1-11-14 Shinkawa Chuo-ku, Tokyo 104-0033 Tel.: +81 3 35230811, Fax +81 3 35230841, info@jla.or.jp; www.jla.or.jp/index-e.html
Languages Japanese
Established 1892, Tokyo, as Nihon Bunko Kyokai
Officers Chair: Noboru Shiomi; Secr Gen: Kaname Matsuoka
Staff 17 (paid)

General Assembly Entire membership meets annually at the All Japan Library Conference
Membership More than 2800 institutional and 5800 individual members. Types of membership: Individual, institutional, student, patron. Requirements: Open to librarians and any other interested persons
Structure Governed by Executive Board. Divisions: 6. Committees: 24. Affiliations: IFLA
Sources of Support Membership dues, sale of publications
Major Fields of Interest Libraries and librarianship
Activities As the only general association of Japan covering all types of libraries and subjects, activities span a wide range of areas. Acts as the representative association for Japanese librarianship at national and international library associations. Promotes the development of libraries in Japan by acting as a liaison and encouraging cooperation between various types of libraries and reading facilities. Works for improving the status of librarians. Promotes reading campaigns. Sponsors awards, conferences, seminars, workshops, and other continuing education programs
Publications Official journal: Toshokan Zasshi (Library Journal). 1907-. 12/yr. Free to members. Address same as Association. Principal publications: Nihon No Toshokan (Statistics on Libraries in Japan), published annually since 1952; Toshokan Handobukku (JLA Librarian's Handbook). 5th ed. 1990; Toshokan Yogoshu (JLA Librarian's Glossary). 1988, rev. ed. 2003; Toshokan'in No Tame No Eikaiwa Handobukku (English Conversation Handbook for Lib rarians). 1991; Librarianship in Japan. 1986, rev. Ed. 1994; Nippon Decimal Klassification (NDC); Nippon Cataloging Rules (NCR); Basic Subject Headings; Nihon No Sankotosho (Guide to Japanese Reference Books); Toshokan Nenkan (Library Yearbook), annualy since 1982; Sentei Tosho Somokuroku (Standard Catalog of Selected Books); Toshokan No Shigoto (Library Work); JLA Library and Information Science Text Series
Bibliography Kon, Madoko,"Japan," in ALA World Encyclopedia of Library and Information Services. 2nd ed., pp. 403–408. Chicago: American Library Association, 1986; Librarianship in Japan, ed. by Editorial Committee of Librarianship in Japan, Japan Organizing Committee of IFLA Tokyo, August 1986, p. 70; Khurshid, A., "Library Associations in Asia." Herald of Library Science 28 (1989):3–10; "Librarianship in Japan" in: Encyclopedia of Library and Information Science, New York 2003, pp.1553–1560

336 Nihon Yakugaku Toshokan Kyogikai (YAKUTOKYO; JPLA) (Japan Pharmaceutical Library Association)

Address c/o Business Center for Academic Societies Japan, 5-16-9 Honkomagome, Bunkyo-ku, Tokyo 113-8422 Tel.: +81 3 6287-4550, Fax +81 3 6287-4555, info@yakutoko.jp; www.yakutokyo.jp(onlyinJapanese)
Languages Japanese
Established 1955, Tokyo
Staff 1 (paid), 3 (volunteers)
General Assembly Entire membership meets once a year, in Tokyo
Membership Requirements: Open to libraries and librarians of pharmaceutical colleges and pharmaceutical firms
Structure Governed by Executive Committee.

Affiliations: Pharmaceutical Society of Japan
Sources of Support   Membership dues, sale of publications
Major Fields of Interest   Library services and documentation in the field of pharmacy and pharmaceutical sciences
Major Goals and Objectives   To develop pharmaceutical libraries and fulfill the library's mission as the special information center for research and education in the pharmaceutical sciences; to conduct research on the management, operation and technologies of pharmaceutical libraries; to facilitate cooperation between member libraries as well as other associations with similar interests
Activities   In accordance with the goals and objectives, encourages cooperation among members in such areas as expanding interlibrary loan, compilation of union catalogs, etc. Sponsors exhibits, conferences, seminars, workshops, and other continuing education programs
Publications   Official journal: Yakugaku Toshokan (Pharmaceutical Library Bulletin). 1956-. 4/yr. Free to members. Address same as Association. Japanese. Indexed in Dokumenteshon Kenkyu. Other publications: Annual reports, proceedings of conferences, seminars, Union List of Periodicals of Pharmaceutical Libraries (1980), and other monographs. Publications for sale. Publications exchange program in effect with other associations
Bibliography   Kon, Madoko,"Japan," in ALA World Encyclopedia of Library and Information Services. 2nd ed., pp. 403–408. Chicago: American Library Association, 1986; Librarianship in Japan, ed. by Editorial Committee of Librarianship in Japan, Japan Organizing Committee of IFLA Tokyo, August 1986, p. 72; Khurshid, A., "Library Associations in Asia," Herald of Library Science 28 (1989):3–10

337   Senmon Toshokan Kyogikai (SENTOKYO; JSLA) (Japan Special Libraries Association)

Address   c/o Japan Library Association, Blg, F6, 1-11-14, Shinkawa, Chuo-ku, Tokyo 104-0033   Tel.: +81 3 35378335, Fax +81 3 35378336, jsla@jsla.or.jp; www.jsla.or.jp
Languages   Japanese
Established   1952, Tokyo
Officers   Pres: Nobuo Yamaguchi; Secr Gen: Masanobu Nogoshi
Staff   1 (paid)
General Assembly   Entire membership meets once a year. 2003: Tokyo, 2003: Sendai, 2004: Hiroshima
Membership   Requirements: must be involved in research, reference, record management, and other special library activities; must be able to make a contribution to the JSLA; has to employ at least one full-time pension who is involved in the above activities
Structure   Governed by Executive Board and the Planning Board. Committees: 7. Affiliations: IFLA
Sources of Support   Membership dues, sale of publications.
Major Fields of Interest   Special libraries
Major Goals and Objectives   To promote cooperative activities between government libraries, local assembly libraries, nongovernmental organizations, research and other institutions, in order to stimulate their growth and development

Activities   Research, Continuing Education, Survey of special libraries in Japan (triennially), International networking, sponsors awards
Publications   Official journal: Senmon Toshokan (Bulletin of the Japan Special Libraries Association). 1960-. 6/yr. (Yen) 13,000. Free to members. Editor: Editorial Committee. Address same as Association. Circ: 1,500. Japanese. Other publications: Senmon Joho Kikan Soran (Directory of Special Libraries in Japan) Published triennial. 32,000 Yen. ISBN 4-88130-020-2; Senmon Toshokan to Chosakuken Q & A 2002. (Special Libraries and Copyright Issues : Q & A 2002) ed. by Copyright Committee, JSLA. 2002. White paper, workshop lectures, reports of delegation tours, and other items are published irregularly
Bibliography   Kon, Madoko,"Japan," in ALA World Encyclopedia of Library and Information Services. 2nd ed., pp. 403–408. Chicago: American Library Association, 1986; Librarianship in Japan, ed. by Editorial Committee of Librarianship in Japan, Japan Organizing Committee of IFLA Tokyo, August 1986, p. 73; Khurshid, A., "Library Associations in Asia," Herald of Library Science 28 (1989):3–10

338   Shiritsu Daigaku Toshokan Kyokai (JASPUL)
(Japan Association of Private University Libraries)

Address   3-3-35, Yamate-cho, Suita-shi, Osaka 564-8680 Tel.: +81 6 6368-1157, Fax +81 6 6368 0071, kyokai@jaspul.org; www.jaspul.org
Languages   Japanese, English
Established   1930, as Tokyo Private University Library Association
Staff   None
General Assembly   Entire membership meets once a year
Membership   Requirements: 4-year private university libraries in Japan.
Structure   Governed by general meetings, Board of Directors, and District Conference. Affiliations: IFLA, Kokkosiritu Daigaku Toshokan Kyoryoku Iinkai (Joint Committee for Library Cooperation of National, Public and Private Universities)
Sources of Support   Membership dues, sale of publications, donations
Major Fields of Interest   Libraries of private universities
Major Goals and Objectives   To promote the development of university libraries through (1) research and study of university libraries and their publications, (2) organizing conferences and lectures on research, (3) publishing an official journal, (4) liaison activities
Activities   Organizes annual general and research meetings on various themes concerning the private university library, such as the effects of computerization, the new media, the future, etc. Participated in the IFLA Tokyo Convention (1986). Sponsors conferences, seminars, workshops, and other continuing education programs
Publications   Official journal: Shiritsu Daigaku Toshokan Kyokai Kaihou (Bulletin of the Japan Association of Private University Libraries). 1952-. 2/yr. Free to members. Address same as Association. Japanese. Other publications: Annual reports, proceedings of conferences, seminars, etc. Official journal for sale
Bibliography   Kon, Madoko,"Japan," in ALA World Encyclopedia of Library and Information Services. 2nd ed., pp. 403–408. Chicago: American Library Association, 1986; Librarianship in Japan, ed. by Editorial Committee of Librarianship in Japan, Japan Organizing Committee of IFLA Tokyo, August 1986, p. 72; Khurshid, A., "Library Associations in Asia." Herald of Library Science 28 (1989):3–10

339 Shiritsu Tanki Daigaku Toshokan Kyogikai (SHITANTOKYO) (Junior College Library Association)

Address c/o Atomi Junior College Library, 1-5-2 Otsuka, Bunkyo-ku, Tokyo 112-8687 Tel.: +81 427421411, Fax +81 427 434916, taniguchi@nittai.ac.jp; www.shitantokyo.org
Languages Japanese
Established 1977
General Assembly Entire membership meets annually
Membership Requirements: Libraries of junior colleges in Japan
Structure Governed by Executive Board. Affiliations: IFLA
Sources of Support Membership dues, sale of publications
Major Fields of Interest Junior college libraries
Major Goals and Objectives To promote the development of junior college libraries; to conduct research on junior college libraries
Activities Conducts research on junior college libraries. Sponsors conferences, seminars, workshops, and other continuing education programs
Publications Official journal: Tanki Daigaku Toshokan Kenkvu (Journal of Junior College Libraries). 1/yr.; Shiritsu Tanki Daigaku Toshokan Kyogikai Kaihou (Bulletin of the Junior College Library Association). 2/yr. Other publications: Annual reports, proceedings of conferences, seminars, etc
Bibliography Kon, Madoko,"Japan," in ALA World Encyclopedia of Library and Information Services. 2nd ed., pp. 403–408. Chicago: American Library Association, 1986; Librarianship in Japan, ed. by Editorial Committee of Librarianship in Japan, Japan Organizing Committee of IFLA Tokyo, August 1986, p. 74; Khurshid, A., "Library Associations in Asia," Herald of Library Science 28 (1989):3–10

340 Société Franco-Japonaise des Bibliotecaires et des Documentalistes

Address 3-9-25, Ebisu, Sibuya-ku, Tokyo 150-0013 Tel.: +81 3 54217643, Fax +81 3 54217653; wwwsoc.nii.ac.jp/sfjbd/index-f.html
Languages Japanese, French
Established 1970
Publications Official journal: Bulletìn de la société franco-japonaise des bibliothécaires et des ducumentalistes

341 University Hospital Medical Information Network (UMIN)

Address c/o UMIN center, Hospital Computer Center, the University of Tokyo Hospital, 7-3-1 Hongo, Bunkyo-ku, Tokyo 113-8655 Tel.: +81 3 56890729, Fax +81 3 56890726, admin@umin.ac.jp; www.umin.ac.jp
Established 1989
Officers Chair: Tetsuya Igarashi
Membership 42 university hospitals
Sources of Support Sponsored by the Ministry of Education, Culture, Science, Sports and Technology (MEXT), Japan
Major Fields of Interest Cooperative organization for national medical schools
Major Goals and Objectives To provide up-to-date information to healthcare professionals. To foster communications between healthcare professionals. To support

collaborative work among university hospitals. To promote collaborative medical research. To standardize medical data and collect hospital statistics
Activities Provides databases and other information for medical professionals
Publications UMIN Brochure (online). Other publications e.g.: Kiuchi T, Takahashi T. High Speed Digital Circuits for Medical Communication; the MINCS-UH Project. Methods of Information in Medicine 39:353–5, 2000; Kiuchi T, Ohe K, Sakurai T. UMIN – Key information infrastructure for the Japanese Medical Community. MEDINFO 2001 IOS press 1359–63, 2001; Kiuchi T. Introduction of Information Infrastructure for Medical Academic Activities in Japan – UMIN and MINCS-UH. International Conference on Advances in Infrastructure for Electronic Business, Science, and Education on the Internet, 2002

342 Zenkoku Gakkou Kouritsu Toshokan Kyougikai (ZENKOKU SLA; JSLA) (Japan School Library Association)*
Address 2-7 kasuga 2-chome, Bunkyo-ku, Tokyo 112 Tel.: +81 3 38144317, Fax +81 3 38141790; www.j-sla.or.jp(japaneseonly)
Languages Japanese
Established 1950
Officers Pres: I. Suzuki; Exec Dir: M. Morita
Staff 17 (paid), 11 (volunteer councilors, working as teachers or librarians)
General Assembly Entire membership meets once a year, with national and regional conferences alternating
Membership Total members: 61 (prefectural school library associations). Divisions: 7. Sections: 5. Requirements: (1) Being a prefectural school library association; (2) Obtaining approval by the Board of Directors; (3) Paying membership dues. Dues: Amount decided on basis of scale of prefectural school library association
Structure Governed by Executive Committee. Affiliations: IASL
Sources of Support Membership dues, sale of publications. Budget (Yen): 2008: 285,000,000
Major Fields of Interest School libraries
Major Goals and Objectives To promote communication among prefectural school library associations; to promote the development of school libraries through seminars, surveys and research
Activities Past achievements: To hold National Conference of JSLA; publication of proposal "In Pursuit of Education from the Learner's Point of View;" awarding "School Library Prizes" to outstanding practitioners. Current: Awarding "The Japan Picture Book Prize;" organizing workshops and assemblies for each category of library employees; examining standards for selecting comic books for school libraries. Future: Examination of standards for school library facilities; publication of "School Library White Paper." Association has been active in promoting library-related legislation: The School Library Law was enacted in 1953. JSLA has been taking a leading role in the movement for a revision of this law. Sponsors exhibits, conferences, seminars, workshops, and other continuing education programs
Publications Official journal: Gakkou Toshokan (School Library). 1950-. 12/yr. (Yen) 9,000. Free to members. Editor: Yoshiro Kasahara. Address same as Association. Circ: 21,000. Japanese; Gakkou Toshokan Sokuhou-ban (School Library Newsletter). 1954-.

every 10 days. Free to members. Address same as Association. Circ: 21,000. Japanese. Other publications: Gakkou Toshokan Kihon Tosho Mokuroku (Masterpieces for the School Library). 1/yr.; Subject Headings for School Libraries; An Outline of Library Science; annual reports, proceedings of conferences, seminars, etc. Publications for sale; price lists available. Publications exchange program in effect
Bibliography Kon, Madoko,"Japan," in ALA World Encyclopedia of Library and Information Services, 2nd ed., pp. 403–408. Chicago: American Library Association, 1986; Librarianship in Japan, ed. by Editorial Committee of librarianship in Japan, Japan Organizing Committee of IFLA Tokyo, August 1986, p. 73; Khurshid, A., "Library Associations in Asia," Herald of Library Science 28 (1989):3–10

343 Zenkoku Rekishi Shiryo Hozon Riyo Kikan Renraku Kyogikai (Japan Society of Archives Institutions)

Address c/o Toshisuke Kumasaki, Vice-Pres, 150-1 Ushirogawara City, Yamaguchi-Shi Tel.: +81 83 924 2116, Fax +81 83 924 2117; www.jsai.jp(japaneseonly)
Languages Japanese

Jordan

344 Jordan Library and Information Association (JLIA)

Address POB 6289, Amman Tel.: +962 6 4629412, Fax +962 6 4629412; www.jordandevnet.org/search/search\%20results.php3?SEARCH=545
Languages Arabic, English
Established 1963, Amman
Officers Head: Fadil Klayb
Staff 3 (paid), 25 (volunteers)
General Assembly Entire membership meets once a year
Membership Total members: 543 (368 individual, 175 institutional). 20 countries represented. Types of membership: Individual, institutional, honorary, supporter. Requirements: (1) Academic degree in library science; (2) academic degree in the arts and sciences plus 5 years experience in libraries; (3) high school certificate plus 10 years experience.
Structure Governed by Executive Committee. Affiliations: IFLA; Ministry of Culture and Youth
Sources of Support Membership dues, sale of publications, social activities, fees from training courses.
Major Fields of Interest Librarianship, documentation, information, archives
Major Goals and Objectives (1) To unite the efforts of Jordanian librarians to promote library services in Jordan; (2) to promote and develop library services in the Arab countries; (3) to collect and publish studies in library science, information and documentation; (4) to encourage the public and private sectors to establish libraries in Jordan; (5) to provide training of personnel in order to establish and improve library services in Jordan and the Arab countries
Activities Offering courses in library science; participating in many cultural and social activities in Jordan and other countries; translating Dewey Decimal Classification, the

Anglo-American Cataloging Rules, and numerous books in library science; participating in Book Fairs. Association offers continuing education programs; sponsors the Jordanian National Bibliography and Cataloging in Publication Data
Publications   Official journal: Rissalat at-Maktaba (The Message of the Library). 1964-. 4/yr. Free to members. Address same as Association. Arabic, with English abstracts. Other publications: Annual reports, proceedings of meetings; Jordanian National Bibliography; Directory of Libraries and Librarians in Jordan (bilingual; updated every few years); various directories of libraries and periodicals in Jordan; publications related to library science practices. Price lists issued, publications listed in official journal
Bibliography   Nimer, R. E. and Akrush, A., "Jordan Library Association in Twenty Years 1963–1983," Rissalat-Al Maktaba 18 (Dec. 1983):3–7 (in English and Arabic); "The JLA Administrative Report for the Year 1984," Rissalat-Al Mataba 20 (1985):45–54 (in Arabic); El Hadi, Mohamed M., "Jordan," in ALA World Encyclopedia of Library and Information Service. 2nd ed., p. 415. Chicago: American Library Association, 1986

Kazakhstan

345   East-Kazakhstan Librarians Association

Address   102 Ushanov St., UST-KAMENOGORSK 492000   director@pushkinlibrary.kz
Established   1995
Officers   Pres: Khabiba Akzhigitova

346   Library Association of the Republic of Kazakhstan

Address   Levoberezhie, zdanie NABRK, 01000 Astana   Tel.: +7 327 2695829, Fax +7 327 2696586, bark@nabrk.kz
Established   1995
Officers   Pres: Rosa A. Berdigaliyeva; Exec Secr: Marina N. Yablonskaya
Major Goals and Objectives   To promote common library interests, organization and development of perfect library service system in East-Kazakhstan and establish friendly relations among librarians and those who are involved in library services

Kenya

347   Kenya Library Association

Address   PO Box 46031, Nairobi   Tel.: +254 733 732 799; www.klas.or.ke
Languages   English
Established   1956, Nairobi, as a branch of the East African Library Association (EALA), until it was dissolved late 1972. In 1973, the Kenya Library Association was established as an independent organization
Officers   Pres: Rosemary Gitachu; Secr: Esther K. Obachi; Treas: Elizabeth J. Yegon
Staff   None
General Assembly   Entire membership meets once a year

Membership Individual and institutional membership. Requirements: Librarians and those working in libraries; libraries and related institutions. Only professional librarians can vote.
Structure Governed by Executive Council. Affiliations: IFLA
Sources of Support Membership dues, government subsidies
Major Fields of Interest Library development and the library profession
Major Goals and Objectives To encourage the promotion, establishment, and improvement of libraries, library services, books, and book production in East Africa; to improve the standard of librarianship and the status of the library profession; to bring together all who are interested in libraries and librarianship
Activities Sponsors continuing education programs and works towards improving educational programs and training facilities for librarians
Publications Official journal: Maktaba (Libraries [in Kiswahili]). 1972-. 2/yr. Address same as Association. Newsletter: Kelias News. 6/yr. Other publications: Annual reports, proceedings of conferences
Bibliography Howe, V, "International Conference on Education and Training for Agricultural Library and Information Work, Nairobi, March 1983," Quarterly Bulletin of IAALD 28 (1983):19–23; Ndegwa, J., "Kenya," in ALA World Encyclopedia of Library and Information Services. 2nd ed., pp. 416–417. Chicago: American Library Association, 1986

Korea, Democratic People's Republic

348 Library Association of the Democratic People's Republic of Korea

Address PO Box 200, Pyongyang, Central District Tel.: +850 2 3215614, nsj@co.chesin.com
Languages Korean
Established 1953, Pyongyang
Officers Pres: Shin O. Sun; Secr: Kang Mi Hwa
Structure Affiliations: IFLA
Major Fields of Interest Library development and library services
Major Goals and Objectives To promote the development of libraries and library services in the country; to further the professional development of librarians
Bibliography Lee, Pongsoon, "Korea, Democratic People's Republic of," in ALA World Encyclopedia of Library and Information Services. 2nd ed., pp. 421–422. Chicago: American Library Association, 1986; Khurshid, A., "Library Associations in Asia," Herald of Library Science 28 (1989):3–10

Korea, Republic

349 Hanguk Tosogwan Hyophoe (TOHYOP; KLA) (Korean Library Association)

Address San60-1, Banpo-Dong, Seocho-Gu, Seoul 137-702 Tel.: +82 2 5354868, Fax +82 2 5355616, W3master@kla.kr,klanet@hitel.net; www.korla.or.kr(onlyinKorean)

Languages Korean
Established 1945, Seoul, as Chosun Library Association; renamed 1955
Officers Pres: Tae-Seung Kim; Secr: Kyung-Ku Lee
Staff 7 (paid)
General Assembly Entire membership meets annually at the National Library Convention
Structure Governed by Board of Directors. Affiliations: IFLA
Sources of Support Membership dues, government subsidies, private donations
Major Fields of Interest Library services
Major Goals and Objectives To promote and improve library services and facilities in Korea through mutual exchanges and cooperation among domestic and foreign libraries and librarians, with the ultimate purpose of contributing to the cultural and economic development of the Republic of Korea
Activities As the oldest library association in the country, KLA has been representing Korean libraries at international conferences, particularly at IFLA; sponsors workshops, seminars, conferences, Book Week, Library Week and numerous continuing education programs; and continues the extensive publication program of practical library tools and other reference works
Publications Official journal: Tohyop Wolbo (KLA Bulletin). 1969-. 12/yr. Free to members. Address same as Association. Korean. Other publications: Annual reports, bibliographies, proceedings of seminars, conferences; Library Research. 6/yr; Statistics on Libraries in Korea. 1965-, 1/yr; List of Selected Korean Books. 1964-; Korean Cataloging Rules, etc. Price lists available
Bibliography Lee, Pongsoon, "Korea, Republic of," in ALA World Encyclopedia of Library and Information Science. 2nd ed., pp. 422–424. Chicago: American Library Association, 1986; Khurshid, A., "Library Associations in Asia," Herald of Library Science 28 (1989):3–10

350 Korean Library and Information Science Society (KLSS)*

Address c/o Department of Library Science,Archives and Information Studies, Pusan 609-735 Tel.: +82 51 510-3494, Fax +82 51 510-6559, liss@pnu.edu; http://liss.jams.or.kr
Languages Korean
Established 1970, Seoul, at meeting at Ewha Woman's University Library, through sponsorship of the Asia Foundation and leading librarians
Officers Pres: Jae-Wohan Lee; Exec Secr: Durk Hyuan Chang; Treas: Eun Joo Lee
Staff 2 (volunteers)
General Assembly Entire membership meets once a year in Seoul
Membership Total members: 120 (individual). Types of membership: Individual. Requirements: Open to any professional librarian or to any interested person recommended for membership by any two members
Structure Governed by Executive Committee
Sources of Support Membership dues
Major Fields of Interest Library and Information Science
Major Goals and Objectives To exchange results of research and development in librarianship and information science carried out by members

Activities Sponsors seminars on development of library school curricula and other relevant topics in librarianship and information science. Offers continuing education programs
Publications Official journal: Tosogwan Hak (Studies in Library Science). 1970-. Annual. Free to members. Circ: 600. Korean, with English abstracts. Address: c/o Ewha Woman's University Library, 11–1 Dachyun-dong, Sudaemun-ku, Seoul 120. Other publications: Proceedings of seminars, conferences, workshops. Publications exchange program in effect with libraries
Bibliography Lee, Pongsoon, "Korea, Republic of," in ALA World Encyclopedia of Library and Information Services. 2nd ed., pp. 422–424. Chicago: American Library Association, 1986; Khurshid, A., "Library Associations in Asia," Herald of Library Science 28 (1989):3–10

351 Korean Medical Library Association

Address Tel.: +82 2 3225831, Fax +82 2 3225832, kmla@kmla.or.kr; www.kmla.or.kr(onlyinKorean)
Languages Korean
Comment No address available

352 Korean Society for Information Management (KOSIM)

Address kosim@kgu.ac.kr; www.kosim.or.kr
Languages Korean
Comment No address available

353 Research Institute for Korean Archives and Records (RIKAR)

Address 50-3 Namgajwadong, Seodaemungu, Seoul 120-728 Tel.: +82 31-300-1781, Fax +82 31-300-1915, rikar@rikar.org; www.rikar.org
Established 1998
Officers Chair: Young-Koo You; Pres: Hak-Joon Kim
Major Fields of Interest Management of Records
Major Goals and Objectives To promote scientific organization and preservation of records
Activities Research for the systematic administration of archives, research projects related to archival studies, program development and training for archivists, public relational activities to promote archival culture, printing and publication of important archival material
Publications Official journal: RIKAR Newsletter 4/yr. 1999-. Other publications: Series of Archival Studies

Latvia

354 Latvijas Bibliotekāru bierdrība (LBB, LAL) (Library Association of Latvia)

Address Terbatas iela 75, 1001 Riga Tel.: +371 7289874, Fax +371 7280851, silvija.tretjakova@lnb.lv

Established 1923
Officers Pres: Silvija Tretjakova; Secr: D. Ralla
Membership 400 members
Structure Organised in regional departments and in sections. Affiliations: IFLA
Sources of Support Budget: 18 200 euros
Major Fields of Interest Libraries and librarianship
Major Goals and Objectives Protection of librarians' interests; participation in working out and implementation of library laws; co-operation with library community and associations in other countries; organization of national and international seminars and conferences; participation at congresses, seminars, conferences abroad; exchange of professional experience in Latvia and abroad; co-ordination of the work of the LAL sections; supervision of the LAL regional departments
Activities Communicates with its members post, e-mail, individual contacts, conferences, seminars etc.International

355 Latvijas Skolu bibliotekāru asociācija (LSBA) (Latvian School Librarian Association)

Address Hanzas ielā 7, Riga Tel.: +371 7026803; www.liis.lv/lsba
Languages Latvian
Established 1996
Major Fields of Interest School librarianship
Major Goals and Objectives To work out and bring into practice a new conception of school library development; to manifes the interests of school librarians in different institutions; participate in the creation of documents referring to the development of school libraries; to develop professional training and further education system of school librarians

Lebanon

356 Association des Bibliothèques du Liban (ABL) (The Lebanese Library Association)

Address P.O. Box 11-5020, Beirut Tel.: +961 1 3500002606, Fax +961 1 744703, fabdalla@lau.edu.lb
Languages Arabic (some French, Armenian, English)
Established 1960, Beirut
Officers Pres: Fawz Abdallah; Secr: Rudaynah Shoujah
Staff None
General Assembly Entire membership meets once a year, in December, in Beirut
Structure Governed by Executive Board. Affiliations: IFLA, AFLI
Sources of Support Membership dues
Major Fields of Interest Development of libraries and professional standards for librarians
Major Goals and Objectives To raise the standards of libraries and librarians in Lebanon; to develop bibliographic research and facilitate cooperation in national and international fields; to urge the authorities concerned to organize courses in library science; to work for the formation of a union of Arab library associations

Activities Participation in IFLA; sponsors continuing education workshops, seminars, conferences; instrumental in developing a library science program at the Lebanese University
Publications Official journal: Newsletter of the Lebanese Library Association. 1975-. 4/yr. Free to members. Arabic
Bibliography Hanhan, L.M., "Lebanese Library Association: Past and Present," Library Times International 1 (1984):13–14; Hafez, Aida Kassantini, "Lebanon," in ALA World Encyclopedia of Library and Information Services. 2nd ed., pp. 446–447. Chicago: American Library Association, 1986; Khurshid, A., "Library Associations in Asia," Herald of Library Science 28 (1989):3–10

Lesotho

357 Lesotho Library Association (LLA)
Address Private Bag A26, Maseru 100 Tel.: +266 213420, Fax +266 340000, s.mohai@nul.ls
Languages English, Sesotho
Established 1978
Staff None
General Assembly Entire membership meets once a year
Membership Requirements: Professional librarian, or working in library; institution with library
Structure Governed by executive officers. Affiliations: IFLA
Sources of Support Membership dues, government subsidies
Major Fields of Interest Library development
Major Goals and Objectives To promote, safeguard and encourage the establishment and improvement of libraries and the professional interests of librarians in Lesotho
Activities Assisted in drafting of deposit law for Lesotho; active in areas of public, school, and special libraries, information services, and education and training. Sponsors continuing education workshops and seminars
Publications Official journal: Lesotho Books and libraries. 1/yr. Other publications: Annual reports, proceedings of conferences, e. g. Proceedings of SCECSAL (1980)
Bibliography Lebotsa, M.M., "Lesotho Library Association Annual General Meeting – Hlotse High School, 19th March, 1983," Lesotho Books and Libraries 3 (1982/83):1–9; Forshaw, V, "Lesotho," in ALA World Encyclopedia of library and Information Services. 2nd ed., pp. 451–452. Chicago: American Library Association, 1986

Lithuania

358 Lietuvos bibliotekininkų draugija (Lithuanian Librarians' Association)*
Address Sv. Ignoto 6-108, LT-01120 Vilnius Tel.: +370 5 262 5570, Fax +370 5 262 5570, lbd_sekretore@amb.lt; www.lbd.lt/eindex.htm
Languages Lithuanian

Established 1931, reestablished 1989
Officers Pres: Petras Zurlys; VP: Garunkstyte Vida; Dr. Birute Railiene; Regina Varniene; Secr: Zivile Svitraite
Staff Volunteers
General Assembly Annual meetings
Membership About 2500 individual members located in 76 departaments all over the country. Type of membership available is Personal and honorary members. Membership is available for any citizen of the Republic of Lithuania, who recognises the Statute of the association and pays the membership due
Structure Consists of departments, executive and control bodies. Affiliations: IFLA
Sources of Support Membership fees, grants
Major Fields of Interest Libraries and librarianship
Major Goals and Objectives To raise the reputation of librarians in Lithuanian society; to represent the social and professional rights of its members; to initiate and provide in-service training of librarians; to petition Lithuanian government and authorities for better recourses and equipment for libraries; to gain experience in the world practice of librarianship; to ensure the utmost professionalism in its members
Activities Librarian of the Year awards, Contest of the year Best Lithuanian Librarians Associations' departament, National Library Week, congresses
Publications Official journal: Tarp knygų (In the World of Books), 12/yr. Address: K.Sirvydo 4, 01504 Vilnius, Lithuania. Tel. +370 5 2398687, Fax. +370 5 2639111, e-mail: tk@lnb.lt or leidyba@lnb.lt. Other publications: Bulletin of the Lithuanian Librarians' Association. – Vilnius, 1994–1999. – No 1–6.; Libraries and Society : Proceedings of the II Nordic-Baltic Meeting of Librarians held in Birstonas, Lithuania. May 15–17, 1997. – Vilnius, 1997. – 91 p.; Library as Information Gateway to the New Millennium = Bibliotieka – informacionnye vorota novova tysiachiletiya : Proceedings of the 6th Congress of Baltic Librarians October 5–6, 2000 Vilnius, Lithuania. – Vilnius, 2000. – 277 p.; L ibrary Management and Information Technology : Proceedings of the Seminar held in Vilnius, Lithuania. May 27–29, 1996. – Vilnius, 1996. – 105 p.; Lietuvos bibliotekininku draugija : Str. ir dok. rink. / Sudaryt. ir spec. red. V.Rimsa. – Vilnius, 1990. – 136 p.; Lietuvos bibliotekininku draugija informuoja / Sudare Povilas Saudargas. – Vilnius, 1996. – 23 p.; Lietuvos didziosios bibliotekos = Biggest Libraries in Lithuania / Sudare Sigita Viksraitiene, Emilija Banionyte, Birute Butkeviciene. – Vilnius, 1997. – 42 p.; Uzsienio ir tarptautines bibliotekininku draugijos : Str. ir dok. rink. / Sudaryt. ir spec. red. V.Rimsa. – Vilnius, 1991

Luxembourg

359 Association Luxembourgeoise des Bibliothécaires, Archvistes et Documentalistes (ALBAD)
(Luxembourgish Librarians', Archivists' and Documentalists' Association)*

Address c/o Bibliothèque nationale de Luxembourg, 37 boulevard Roosevelt, 2450 Luxembourg Tel.: +352 260959-333, Fax +352 475672, michel.donven@bnl.etat.lu; www.albad.lu
Languages Luxembourgish, German, French and English

Established Founded the 16.12.1991 in Luxembourg-City, National Library. Invitation of all librarians, archivists and documentalists in the country by national library director, Jul Christophory
Officers Pres: Jean-Marie Reding; VP: Romain Reinard; Guy Theissen; Secr Gen: Dr. Michel Donven; Secr: Michéle Wallenborn; Treas: Agnès Poupart
Staff None
General Assembly One general assembly by year, normally in March, takes place in libraries in different regions of the country
Membership Ca. 100–110 members: ca. 50 full, 45 support and 10 institution members altogether. Full members have to be qualified persons and/or work in libraries / archives / documentation centers. Annual fee: 20 EUR for full and support members (since the 01.01.2010), 50 EUR for institution members (since the 05.02.2010)
Structure Structure: Governing board and members. Possibility of creating commissions. Affiliated to IFLA since June 2003 and to EBLIDA since Sept. 2008. Parent organizations: Luxembourgish Public Libraries' Association (ULBP – Union Luxembourgeoise des Bibliothèques Publiques – www.ulbp.lu), Luxembourgish Public Libraries' Community Foundation (FËB – Fir Ëffentlech Bibliothéiken)
Sources of Support Financial support only by membership fees
Major Fields of Interest National lobbying for libraries and librarians (since 2003), especially public libraries. More intensive cooperation with regional (Saarland (Germany) and Lorraine (France) and international organizations (IFLA & EBLIDA)
Major Goals and Objectives Constitution 2009, Art. 2: Advocacy for the librarian's, archivist's and documentalist's profession; training for members; development in the field of libraries, archives and documentation; collaboration between librarians, archivists and documentalists working in the Grand-Duchy of Luxembourg; collaboration with institutions following the same aims at international level; support of libraries, archives and documentation centers by all initiative
Activities Current: Creation and development of library infrastructures through free consulting services. Projected: lobbying for a professional library legislation. Accomplishments: Assisting the foundation of a public libraries' association (ULBP – founded the 31.01.2007), involving the engagement of parliament members, and a community foundation for public libraries (FËB – founded the 24.11.2009). Development of libraries' perception by political parties. Huge increase of library students by offering individual mentoring programs. Affiliation to international organizations (IFLA & EBLIDA)
Publications Newsletter "Feuille de liaison", normally 3 copies/year, only for members; Libraries in Luxembourg: Lëtzebuerger Bibliothéiksguide 2010. Published in February 2010. ISBN 978-2-87980-057-8. For free (and free shipping costs), available by order by E-Mail to the ALBAD-President. (online: http://www.albad.lu/librariesworld-guides/index.html)
Bibliography Overview: Reding, Jean-Marie: Das Bibliothekswesen Luxemburgs : ein Überblick. In: Bibliothek : Forschung und Praxis, Nr. 3/2008. – München : K. G. Saur, 2008. – P. 325–334; Lëtzebuerger Bibliothéiksguide 2010 = Librairies in Luxembourg 2010 = Bibliothèques au Luxembourg 2010 = Bibliotheken in Luxemburg 2010 / [éd.:] ALBAD; [ed. & coord. by: Jean-Marie Reding]. – Luxembourg : Éd. Saint-Paul, 2010. – 104 p. – Library facts, p. 85–87 & selective bibliography, p. 88–89. –

ISBN 978-2-87980-057-8
Comment   Annual budget: ca. 1,700 EUR

Macedonia

360   Bibliothkarsko Drustvo na Makedonija (Macedonian Library Association)
Address   Bld. Gotse Delchev, 6, 1000 Skopje   Tel.: +389 91 212736, Fax +389 91 226846, bdm@bdm.org.mk; www.bdm.org.mk
Languages   Macedonian, English
Established   1949
Officers   Pres: Suzana Kotovchevskai; Secr: Kiril Angelov

Malaysia

361   Medical Librarians Group of Malaysia (MLG)*
Address   c/o MLG Secretariat, Jln. Yaacob Latif, Bdr. Tun Razak, Cheras, 56000 Kuala Lumpur   Fax +603 91738610; 202.186.179.2/mlg/
Languages   Malay, English
Established   1998
Officers   Chair: Maimunah Kadir; Secr: Salizah Ali; Treas: Faizah Zain
General Assembly   Once a year – AGM. Meetings quarterly. Last meetings: 8th April 2010, next meeting 15th June 2010
Membership   Individual memebers: 80, institutional members: 28
Structure   Governed by executive board. Affiliation: PPM
Sources of Support   Librarians Association of Malaysia
Major Fields of Interest   Health information
Major Goals and Objectives   Promotes excellence and leadership of health information proffessionals through education, communication and resource sharing by utilizing the information systems and services, cooperation and networking among member libraries in support of informed health care decision making
Activities   Benchmarking/Library visits – Every two years. Product demo at every MLG meeting. Community of Practice Workshop (COP) 14th June 2010
Publications   Official journal: MLG newsletter. Standard for medical Libraries in Malaysia (to be published before end of 2010)

362   Persatuan Perpustakaan Malaysia (PPM) (Library Association of Malaysia)
Address   P.O. Box 12545, 50572 Kuala Lumpur   Tel.: +60 3 26922069, Fax +60 3 26947390, mai@mail.hukm.ukm.my; www.pnm.my/ppm
Languages   Malay, English
Established   1955, Singapore, as the Malayan Library Group; reorganized 1958, as the Library Association of Malaya and Singapore. When Singapore became an independent

republic in 1965, the library association changed into two separate organizations (1966), the Library Association of Singapore and the present Library Association of Malaysia
Staff 1 (paid)
General Assembly Entire membership meets annually in Kuala Lumpur in March
Membership Requirements: Open to persons or institutions interested in libraries in Malaysia
Structure Governed by an Executive Council. Standing Committees: 5. Affiliations: IFLA, CONSAL; maintains close cooperation with the Library Association of Singapore through a permanent Joint Liaison Council
Sources of Support Membership dues, government and private subsidies
Major Fields of Interest Development of libraries and the library profession
Major Goals and Objectives To unite all persons engaged in library work or interested in libraries in Malaysia; To promote a better administration of libraries; To encourage professional education and training for librarianship
Activities Sponsored national and international conferences; offers continuing education workshops, seminars, etc.; bestows awards of excellence for student from Schools of library and information science
Publications Official journal: Majallah Perpustakaan Malaysia. 1971-. 2/yr. Membership. Address same as Association. Circ: 500. Malay and English. Other publications: Berita PPM. 6/yr; Sumer Pustaka. newsletters, Malay and English. Issues annual reports, proceedings of meetings, workshops, seminars, in Malay and English. Publications available for sale
Bibliography Osman, Z.B., The Role of the Library Association of Malaysia in Providing Professional Leadership in Malaysia. Loughborough, England: Loughborough University of Technology, 1981; Wijasuriya, D.E.K., "Malaysia," in ALA World Encyclopedia of Library and Information Services. 2nd ed., pp. 510–512. Chicago: American Library Association, 1986; Khurshid, A., "Library Associations in Asia," Herald of Library Science 28 (1989):3–10

Maldives

363 Maldives Library Association *

Address c/o National Library, Biloorijehige, Majeedee Magu 20-04, Male Tel.: +960 7767707, info.malias@gmail.com; www.infomalias.wordpress.com
Languages Dhivehi, English
Established Feb. 22,1987, first inaugural meeting
Officers Pres: Aishath Shabana; VP: Fathimath Shiham; Secr: Aminath Shiuna; Advisor: Habeeba Husein Habeeb; Treas: Khadheeja Mohamed; Edi: Aminath Riyaz; Training Off: Athiyya Shakeel; PR Off: Guleyfa Mohamed
Staff 6 (volunteers)
General Assembly Entire membership meets 3 times a year
Membership 12 (individual and institutional). Requirements: Interest in library work. Dues (Ruliyea): 26
Structure Governed by executive officers and National library
Sources of Support Membership dues; National library (included in budget)

Major Fields of Interest Library development; library education; promotion of library use
Major Goals and Objectives To upgrade all libraries in the Maldives, to have training courses and workshops for staff, and to promote library use
Activities Past achievements: Establishment of the library association in order to improve and upgrade libraries, which are in the early stages of development. Current: Organizing meetings to discuss common problems. Future: Invite experts from overseas to advise on particular problems and to run workshops. Active in promoting library-related legislation, such as a constitutional law for the library association. Plans a series of films for local television
Publications No official journal; publishes newsletter. No publications exchange program

Mali

364 Association Malienne des Bibliothécaires, Archivistes et Documentalistes (AMBAD)
(Association of Librarians, Archivists and Documentalists of Mali)*

Address c/o Direction Nationale de la Documentation et des Bibliothèques, Hamdal Laye Aci 2000, BP E 4473, Bamako Tel.: +223 229 9423, +223 229 5393, Fax +223 229 9396, remadoc@gmail.com; www.ml.refer.org/remadoc
Languages French
Established 1978
General Assembly Twice a year
Membership Ca. 100 members
Sources of Support Membership dues (ca. CFA 3,000/US$ 6 anually)
Major Fields of Interest Archives, libraries, information services
Major Goals and Objectives To promote development of archives, libraries and documentation services in Mali
Activities Organizes seminars, conferences, exhibits; has contact with other national and international related organizations
Publications No official journal; some occasional publications
Bibliography Koita, Al Hadi, "Mali," in ALA World Encyclopedia of Library and Information Services. 2nd ed., pp. 513–514. Chicago: American Library Association, 1986; Repertoire des professionnels des bibliothéques, des archives et de la documentation au Mali. Bamako: AMBAD, 2004

Malta

365 Malta Library and Information Association (MaLIA)*

Address c/o University Library MSD2080, Msida Tel.: +356 79322054 (mobile), Fax +356 21249841, info@malia-malta.org; www.malia-malta.org
Languages Maltese, English
Established 1969, University of Malta

Officers Chair: Laurence Zerafa; Secr: Claudio Laferla; Hon Secr: Ruth Muscat; Treas: Josephine Spiteri; PRO/Int'national Secr: Martes Paris; Assist Hon Secr: Oliver Mamo; Edi: Anita Ragonesi; Co-Edi: Eman Grima
General Assembly Annual General Meeting: Yearly meeting in February. This meeting is held at the University of Library. Next meeting in February 2011
Membership Fee for membership: 12 Euro. Total number of members: 89; Life: 32
Structure Governed by Executive Council. Affiliations: IFLA, COMLA, EBILDA
Sources of Support Membership and publications; funds generated by organizing 'Library Courses' and 'sponsorship' of specific projects by private companies or banks.Membership dues, sale of publications
Major Fields of Interest Libraries, Librarianship, Reading, Copyright & The Book
Major Goals and Objectives To promote, encourage and assist bibliographical studies and research; to maintain a library collection for members of the Association in such location that the Association may decide; to hold courses in library and information studies; to maintain a register of library and information professionals
Activities Past achievements: First register of practicing qualified librarians opened in 1988, with 16 professionals. Worked for the improvement of Maltese librarians' salaries, status and working conditions; achieved recognition of teacher librarians by the Department of Education; promoted staff development and training; created public awareness of the need for library and information services and the necessary financial support; promoted a national information policy and the establishment of a National Council for Libraries, Archives and Documentation Centres; promoted a public library system, with the inauguration of the Public Library at Beltissebh in 1974; sponsored the establishment of a National Archives in 1987. Sponsored international conferences, such as, Conference of Mediterranean Librarians, 1983; COMLA Regional Workshop on Bibliography, 1984; COMLA Regional Council for Europe Meeting, 1984, etc. Current and Future: Diploma course in library and Information Studies, Faculty of Education, University of Malta; editing, designing and distributing COMLA Newsletter since 1986. A Major achievement has been the production of the Malta National Bibliography since 1984, which is compiled cooperatively by Association members. Association has been active in promoting library-related legislation through the work of the National Librarian. Sponsors annual Book Week and continuing education programs. Now involved Nationally regarding the current Library Legislation
Publications Newsletter every 3 months. Recent publications (all for sale): A mosaic of library and archive practice in Malta (2009); Report on the state of Maltese libraries (2006); Libraries and National Development (2000); A directory of libraries and information units in Malta (1996)
Bibliography www.facebook.com/group.php?gid=63097875928

Marshall Islands

366 Marshall Islands Library Association (MILA)

Address c/o John K. Pagolu (Advisor), P.O. Box 1258, Majuro 96960
Established 1991, in response to the White House Library Conference
Membership About 30 members

Structure Affliliation: PIALA
Activities Library training, sponsors Saturday story hours in several locations island wide and hosts' activities for Children's Book Week, National Library Week, and National Education Week. In the past we have had book-making sessions, MILA members and high school students have gone into schools for story telling, and poster and essay contests have been held
Publications No publications program

Mauritius

367 Association of Professional Librarians

Address c/o National Library, Fon Sing Blding, 12 Edith Cavell Street, Port Louis
Languages English
Established 1973
Officers Pres: Y. Chan Kam Lon

368 Mauritius Library Association

Address c/o Ministry of Education Public Library, Moka Road, Rose Hill rhauroo@yahoo.co.uk; ncb.intnet.mu/mcrl/mla.html
Languages English
Established 1973
Staff None
General Assembly Entire membership meets once a year
Membership Total members: Approx. 50 (individual). Requirements: Librarians and those interested in the aims of the Association.
Structure Governed by executive officers. Affiliations: Commonwealth Library Association; International Association of School Librarianship
Sources of Support Membership dues
Major Fields of Interest Library development
Major Goals and Objectives To promote the establishment and improvement of libraries in Mauritius; to raise the standard of libraries and the status of librarians; to unite all those who are interested in books
Activities Sponsors conferences, workshops, seminars
Publications Official journal: Mauritius Library Association Newsletter. 4/yr. Address same as Association. English
Bibliography Jean-François, S., "Mauritius," in ALA World Encyclopedia of Library and Information Services. 2nd ed., pp. 521–522. Chicago: American Library Association, 1986

Mexico

369 Asociación Mexicana de Archivos y Bibliotecas Privados, A.C. (AMABPAC)*

Address Plaza de las Vizcainas No.39, Col. Centro CP 06080, México, D.F. Tel.: +52 5 687-0657, Fax +52 5 687-0657, contacto@amabpac.org.mx; www.amabpac.org.mx

Languages Spanish
Established April, 1994 Mexico City Several private archives got together
Officers Pres: Manuel Ramos; Secr: Teresa Matabuena
Staff 22 voluntaries
General Assembly Every 3 months. On Mondays taken place on Plaza de las Vizcainas, meeting 2010: 24 th of May
Membership Total members: 22 One chapter on process North Part of the Republic Saltillo, Coahuila. Requirements to be a particular archive with public consultation. 300.00 US$ annually
Structure Board of Directors
Sources of Support Membership dues, donations
Major Fields of Interest Archives and Librarianship
Major Goals and Objectives Interchange of information, technical support, diffusion on our contents, publish catalogues, books,etc of our archives. Directories. Keep and care our archival resources.zz
Activities Conferences, exhibitions, further education, seminars, round tables
Publications 5 books called tour around the private archives

370 Asociación Nacional de Administradores de la Información Documental, A.C. (ANAID)

Address Av. Lopez Mateos Pte. #223, 3er Piso Col Centro, 20000 Aguascalientes AGS Tel.: +52 449 9169898, Fax +52 449 9169898
Languages Spanish
Activities Organizes congresses, events
Publications Publishes Boletin

371 Colegio Nacional de Bibliotecarios, A.C. (CNB)

Address Apd. Postal 70-150, México D.F. 04510 Tel.: +52 1 33 3134-2277, sergiolr@redudg.udg.mx; www.cnb.org.mx
Languages Spanish
Established 1980
Officers Pres: Sergio López Ruelas; Treas: Martha Ibánez Marmolejo
Membership 110 personal members. Requirements: Librarians with the title lic, master or doctor
Sources of Support Membership dues
Major Fields of Interest Professional development of librarians
Major Goals and Objectives To maintain groups of academical discussion; to disseminate the importance of the profession
Activities Sponsors award, organizes meetings, conferences, exhibtions, seminaries, further education, round tables
Publications Official journal: Informaciones del Colegio Nacional de Bibliotecarios. 3/yr. 1980

372 Sociedad Para el Desarollo Científico de la Archivistica S.C.

Address Calle Enrique Rebsamen n° 55 Col. Narvarte, México D.F. 03020 Tel.: +52 55 55184785, Fax +52 55 55184785

Languages Spanish

Moldova

373   Library Association of the Republic of Moldova
Address   c/o Mariana Harjevschi, Secretary, Str. 148, Stefan Cel Mare, Chisinau
Officers   Pres: Lidia Kulikovski

Montenegro

374   Associations of Montenegrin Librarians
Address   c/o Ruza Danilovic, Crnogorskih junaka 136, 81250 Cetinje
Officers   Pres: Branislav Borilovic

**375   Udruzenje bibliotekara Crne Gore
(Association of Librarians of Montenegro)**
Address   Bulevar crnogorskih junaka br. 163, Cetinje   Tel.: +382 41 231-143, info@cnbct.vbcg.me
Established   1960
General Assembly   Entire membership meets annually
Membership   70 individual members
Structure   Governed by executive officers
Sources of Support   Membership dues
Major Fields of Interest   Librarianship
Major Goals and Objectives   To maintain and enhance the professional standards; to promote the library profession; to develop libraries and library environment
Activities   Sponsors conferences, seminars, workshops, and other continuing education programs
Publications   Official journal: Le Courrier Bibliographique; Revue de l'Association des Bibliothécaires du Monténégro et de la Bibliothèque nationale de la R. S. de Monténégro à Cetinje
Bibliography   Kort, R.L., "Yugoslavia," in ALA World Encyclopedia of Library and Information Services. 2nd ed., pp. 864–865. Chicago: American Library Association, 1986

Morocco

**376   Association Nationale des Informatistes
(National Association of Information Specialists)**
Address   c/o Headquarters, Siège du Centre National de Coordination et de Planification de la Recherche Scientifique et Technique, Boîte postale 6580, Rabat-irfane, 10000 Rabat   Tel.: 212 (1) 74944/73131
Languages   Arabic, French
Established   1972

Officers Pres: Abdelhamid Miski
General Assembly Entire membership meets once a year.
Membership Total members: 221 (205 professional librarians, 16 other individuals). Types of membership: Individual.
Structure Governed by executive officers. Affiliations: IFLA
Sources of Support Membership dues; government subsidies
Major Fields of Interest Librarianship; information services; information studies; archival studies; professional development.
Major Goals and Objectives To unite information scientists and specialists; to improve the level of information science in Morocco through conferences, round tables, seminars, and continuing education programs; to represent the interests of librarians, archivists and information specialists.
Activities Carried out in accordance with goals and objectives.
Publications Official journal: Bulletin de l'Informatiste. 12/yr. Circ: Membership. Address same as Association. French. L'Informatiste. 2/yr.
Bibliography Hariki, G. and Lekbir, B., "Morocco," in ALA World Encyclopedia of Library and Information Services. 2nd ed., pp. 565–566. Chicago: American Library Association, 1986.

Myanmar

377 Myanmar Library Association

Address c/o National Library, 1st floor, 6 storeyed complex of Government Offices, Kannar Road, Yangon Tel.: +951 1 272058, Fax +951 1 532927
Established 1992
Officers Pres: U Khin Maung Tin; Secr: U Thein Shwe

Nepal

378 Nepal Community Library Association *

Address GPO 11995, Kathmandu Baluwatar Tel.: +977 4423141, Fax +977 4430017, ncla@live.com
Languages Nepal and English
Officers Chair: Basudev Dhungana; VP: Monan Kunari Sterchan; Rem Raj Aryal; Rajendra Chandnary; Gen Secr: Ganesh Prasad Neupaney
General Assembly General Assembly is conducted once a year
Membership 46 members (community libraries)
Structure Governed by executive committee consisting of 17 memebers out of whom 15 are elected and are nominated by the elected committee
Sources of Support READ Nepal, a NGO supporting community libraries in Nepal; memebership dues
Major Fields of Interest Promotion and Supporting of comunity libraries in Nepal
Major Goals and Objectives To develop coordination, harmonous relation and strenghthening network between the community libraries; exchanging information

opportunities and experiences among the community libraries; advocacy and research for prmoting community libraries

379 Nepal Library Association (NLA)
Address c/o Nepal National Library, GPO 2773, Kathmandu Tel.: +977 331316, nla-info@nla.org.np
Established 1979
Officers Pres: Bhola Kumar Shrestha; Secr: Prakash Thapa
Membership 200 members

Netherlands

380 Branchevereniging Archiefinstellingen Nederland (BRAIN) (Association for Dutch Archives)*
Address Spui 70, 2511 BT The Hague Tel.: +31 6 54714703, bureau@archiefbrain.nl; www.archiefbrain.nl
Languages Dutch
Established 26th June 2007, Amersfoort
Officers Pres: Jantje Steenhuis; Secr: Marteen Schenk; Treas: Daan Hertogs; Exec Officer: Ariela Netiv; Wim Reijnders; Lieuwe Zoodsma; Jan van der Meer
Staff 1 paid: office employee
General Assembly General Assembly: 2x a year, Meeting 2010: 8th of March
Membership 66 institutional members, 3 institutional supporters
Structure Board and operational knowledge sections
Sources of Support No governmental support, membership dues
Major Fields of Interest Representing the interests for the broad field of archives (municipal, state archives, business)
Major Goals and Objectives Promoting and organizing cooperation between associated members; organizing consultations, determining positions and organizing lobby for the field/members specifically and cultural heritage in general; organizing collaborative facilities and services for members; contribution to the development of expertise within the field of activity
Activities Implementing services (f. e. two yearly Quality Survey) for the benefit of the archives field of activity; – organizing study days and other (network) events for members and other dutch archives; development of promotional campaign to strengthen identity of dutch archives; development of online knowledge platforms for DIV and archives; Lobby and contributing to development of national policy on archives
Publications Boudestein, W.: Kwaliteitsmonitor Dienstverlening Archieven 2009: www.archiefbrain.nl/downloads/brain_kda2009_rap.pdf; Frommé, R.: De grijswaarde van het archiefwezen. 2009: www.archiefbrain.nl/downloads/arbeidsmarkt_uitstroom_logo.pdf. Newsletters (4x/yr); Annual reports; Conference proceedings, etc.
Bibliography BRAIN and KVAN; Archiveren = vooruitzien, june 2009. www.archiefbrain.nl/downloads/visiebinnenwerk.pdf

381 Federatie van Organisaties op het gebied van het Bibliotheek-, Informatie-en Documentatiewezen (FOBID)
(Federation of Organizations in the Fields of Library, Information, and Documentation Services)
Address Grote Marktstraat 43, 2511 BH The Hague, Postbus 16146, 2500 BC Den Haag Tel.: +31 70 3090115, Fax +31 70 3090200, fobid@debibliotheken.nl; http://sitegenerator.bibliotheek.nl/fobid/home
Languages Dutch
Established 1974, to serve the common interests of national associations of public libraries (NBLC), librarians (NVB and other organisations in the library and information fields
Staff 2 (paid)
Membership Umbrella organization for Dutch associations in library, information, and documentation services: NBLC, the Netherlands Public Library Association; NVB, the Netherlands Association for Library, Information and Knowledge Professionals; KB, National Library of the Netherlands, and UKB, the co-operative Association of Thirteen University Libraries, the National Library and the Library of the Royal Dutch Academy of Science, with the Open University as Associate member
Structure Governed by Executive Board. Affiliations: IFLA, EBLIDA
Sources of Support Contributions by constituent partners and additional funds by interested partners
Major Fields of Interest Professional associations in library, information, and documentation services
Major Goals and Objectives To coordinate the work of the professional associations in library, information, and documentation services in the Netherlands, to be a focal point for the whole profession, to have a framework for cooperation where desirable, and to unite the various fields of librarianship
Activities Providing coordination and unity among the associations in the Netherlands. Federation carries out tasks on behalf of the member associations, such as organizing the annual library congress, professional projects in the field of normalization, unification of cataloging rules according to ISBD, and publication of directories. 4 Committees: legal aspects, bibliographic issues, professional education and international/IFLA-issues
Publications No official journal. Other publications: Regels voor de titelbeschrijving; Geactualiseerde 'handleiding licentierechten van digitale bronnen' in het Nederlands. 2002. Address: www.surf.nl/fobid/licentie.htm
Bibliography Mathijsen, A.H.H.M., "Netherlands," in ALA World Encyclopedia of Library and Information Services. 2nd ed., pp. 596–599. Chicago: American Library Association, 1986; Mathijsen, A.H.H.M., "Professional Organizations," in Libraries and Documentation Centres in the Netherlands, ed. E. Z. R. Cohen et al., pp. 15–20. The Hague, Nederlands Bibliotheek en Lektuur Centrum, 1987

382 FOBID Netherlands Library Forum (FOBID)*
Address Prins Willem-Alexanderhof 5, 2595 BE The Hague, PB 90407, 2509 LK The Hague Tel.: +31 70 3140511, Fax +31 70 3140651, fobid@kb.nl; www.fobid.nl
Languages Dutch
Established 1974

Officers   Pres: Maria Heijne; Treas: Nol Verhagen; Exec Secr: Dr. Marian Koren
Staff   0,5 Fte paid and 0,2 fte support staff
General Assembly   3–4 Board meetings a year, 3–4 meetings a year for Committees and working groups
Membership   4 founding partners, 3–4 additional partnerships on various topics
Structure   Legal form: Foundation. 4 founding and core partners are: Netherlands Public Library Association (VOB); National Library of the Netherlands(KB); Dutch consortium of the thirteen university libraries and the National Library of the Netherlands(UKB), and the Netherlands Association for Library, Information and Knowledge Professionals (NVB)
Sources of Support   Core partners pay annual support contribution. Additional partners (SURF foundation, OCLC/Pica, Netherlands Institute for Public Libraries (SIOB) contribute annually for support of the secretariat and specific issues
Major Fields of Interest   Advocacy, legal matters, international relations and exchange, promotion of Libraries in the Netherlands, professional development and education, international surveys and statistics
Major Goals and Objectives   FOBID was founded in 1974 to improve the co-operation between different types of libraries and institutions for information and documentation services. Its aim is to defend the interests of these institutions and their professionals, and to enhance professional development. The main activities focus on advocacy of the library field's legal interests, on international networking and co-operation of professionals in the field of bibliographic matters, statistics and education. A division of tasks has been made into four Committees: legal aspects, bibliographic issues, professional education and international/IFLA-issues. The secretariat is executed by Dr. Marian Koren (employer of Netherlands Public Library Association) at the National Library of the Netherlands, based on an agreement of cooperation signed by The Netherlands Public Library association (VB), National Library of the Netherlands(KB); FOBID Netherlands Library Forum, and Netherlands Institute for Public Libraries (SIOB)
Activities   Legal aspects: The main issues focus on the implementation of the EU Directives on Copyright and Dutch law. The Legal Committee co-operates with a lobbyist, hired by FOBID, to achieve the best possible results for libraries. The Committee also advises on licenses, database protection legislation, digital rights management and other related issues. The Committee co-operates with EBLIDA (EGIL Expert group) and IFLA's CLM Committee in the field of intellectual property (WIPO) and World Trade (WTO) issues. Bibliographic issues: Setting up and maintaining standards is one of the main aspects of this Committee. Different forms of bibliographic control are analysed with a view to future international co-operation. The Committee advises on necessary decision-making in the bibliographic field, also related to international standards, (eg. RDA implementation). Professional Education: The Committee presented a report on future development in an aging professional field. Measures to be taken include pilot projects to recruit new staff and to improve professional curricula. Participation in European educational projects is another means to attract a flexible professional workforce and increase knowledgeable staff. A wiki of job descriptions is available: www.fobidwiki.nl. Statistics: A working group of relevant partners has been established to improve Dutch library statistics and present them internationally. FOBID International Office: FOBID International Office serves as one stop access point for international colleagues in search of library issues, visits, requests regarding libraries in The

Netherlands. (A dedicated website www.libraries.nl is forthcoming (end 2010). The International Office also serves for Dutch librarians to informa about international library issues. Efforts are made to increase the involvement of professionals in international library development and networking. For example through seminars, preparation of IFLA-issues and focused presentation of international issues in the library journals. About 25 colleagues from the Netherlands are involved in IFLA Standing Committees and bodies, a number of 40–50 persons visits the IFLA conferences annually. The Dutch library community supports both EBLIDA and IFLA in various ways, as they are located in Dutch national library institutions. FOBID also works for strengthening the network of international library organisations in The Hague, under the name: The Hague, World Library Capital. FOBID has a website www.fobid.nl with some information in English and encourages Dutch library institutions to be accessible in other languages

383 International Association of Music Libraries, Archives and Documentation Centres, Australian Branch (IAML-Australian Branch)

Address c/o Roger Flury, Postbus 125, 1200 AC Hilversum roger.flury@natlib.govt.nz
Languages English
Established 1970, IAML-Australia and New Zealand Branch formed in Australia; 1982, two separate Branches established, IAML-New Zealand Branch, and IAML-Australian Branch

384 Koninklijke Vereniging van Archivarissen in Nederland (KVAN) (Royal Dutch Society of Archivists)

Address c/o May Scheepers, Markt 1, 6811 CG Arnhem Tel.: +31 26 3521605, Fax +31 26 3521699, bureau@kvan.nl; www.kvan.nl
Languages Dutch
Established 1891, Haarlem
General Assembly Entire membership meets twice a year
Membership Types of membership: Individual. Requirements: Open to all natural persons who want to support the work of the KVAN, are working in archives, those who have graduated form or are taking part of an archive education school or course. It has also corresponding members abroad
Structure Governed by executive officers. Affiliations: ICA, DIVA, FIAT, FIAF
Sources of Support Membership dues
Major Fields of Interest Archives and records management
Major Goals and Objectives To promote the development of archives and records management in the Netherlands
Activities Sponsors meetings, continuing education programs, publication of journal, etc
Publications Official journal: Archievenblad. 1892-. 10/yr. Free to members. Dutch. Other publications: Almanak van het Nederlands Archiefwezen (directory of Archives in the Netherlands) annually; Jaarboeken (Yearbooks)

385 Landelijke Werkgroep Schoolmediathecarissen Voortgezet Onderwijs (LWSVO) (Dutch Association of School Librarians)*

Address c/o Mirjam Brugts, Secretariaat, Sandinostraat 12, 1069 NJ Amsterdam

Tel.: +3136 5472727, m.brugts@meergronden.nl; www.lwsvo.nl
Languages Dutch
Established 1982
General Assembly Twice a year, in April and November
Membership Over 400 personal members, working as a school librarian or in relation with school librarians
Major Fields of Interest School librarianship
Major Goals and Objectives To promote the interests of professionals who work in school libraries
Publications Official journal: Nieuwsbrief. Editor: Annette Faber. Tel. +31 317 465855. email: annettefaber@hetnet.nl; Other publications: Opzet voor een beleidsnota; Poster "Laat me de mediatheek zien..." (A2); Katoenen tasje met LWSVO; Werklijst Wereldliteratuur (1999); Themalijst Nederlands Basisvorming (2000); Naslagwerkenlijst (2000); Themalijst Nederlandse literatuur (2001)

386 Nederlandse Bibliotheek Dienst (NBLC) (Netherlands Library Supply Service)*

Address Veursestraatweg 280, 2265 CL Leidschendam, Postbus 437, 2260 AK Leidschendam Tel.: +31 70 3377733, Fax +31 70 3377899, info@nbdbiblion.nl; www.nbdbiblion.nl
Languages Dutch, English
Established 1972, Amsterdam; based on The Central Association for Public Libraries, founded 1908, and combining denominational public library groups, such as the Katholiek Lectuur Centrum (KLC) (Catholic Centre for Libraries and Literature) and the Christelijk Lektuur Centrum (CLC) (Christian Centre for Literature), into one unified national organization of public library work
General Assembly Entire membership meets twice a year.
Membership Requirements for membership in association: Public library; for membership in section: Working in public library.
Structure Governed by the Executive Board. Affiliations: IFLA, NVB, ROTNAC, VBC (Flemish Library Centre)
Sources of Support Membership dues, sale of publications, government subsidies; Central Services.
Major Fields of Interest Public library work; ethnic minorities; education; technical innovations in library work; literacy and reading promotion
Major Goals and Objectives To promote optimal functioning of public librarianship; to cooperate with other organizations and institutions active in the field of books and information; to establish contact with organizations concerned with education and training
Activities Past achievements: library work for ethnic minorities, mentally handicapped and adult education integrated into Association's activities and in many public libraries. Current: Information technology; user friendly library work; promotion of reading. Future: Development of local community centers in public libraries, and continuing current activities. Association has been active in promoting library-related legislation, e. g. a draft Library Act was made when the present one was abolished, but without success, and library work is now regulated by the Welfare Act, but rather poorly. Association receives occasional grants from government for special activities, apart from regular subsidies.

Association participates in the 'Nederlandse Bibliotheek Dienst' (Netherlands Library Service), which supplies public libraries with already processed and bound Dutch publications. Various working groups are concerned with library building, mobile libraries, standards, automation, Literature Information Service, etc
Publications   Official journal: Bibliotheek en Samenleving (library and Society). 1972-. 12/yr. Free to members. Address same as Association. Dutch, with English summaries. Publishes professional publications on various subjects, for specific readers' groups, including adult education and minorities. Price lists available. Publications listed in a weekly Information Bulletin
Bibliography   Spruit, E.M., "National Service to Public libraries in the Field of Audiovisual Media: The Situation in the Netherlands." INSPEL 16 (1982): 103–109; Hersch-van-der Stoel, F., "The 10th Anniversary of the Dutch Centre for libraries and literature," Bibliotheek en Samenleving 10 (1982):39–42 (in Dutch); Mathijsen, A.H.H.M., "Netherlands," in ALA World Encyclopedia of library and Information Services. 2nd ed., pp. 596–599. Chicago: American library Association, 1986; Riesthuis-Groenland, M.-L., "Het NBLC: structuur en taken," (The NBLC: Its Structure and Services), Open 18 (1986):291–298 (in Dutch); Mathijsen, AH.H.M., "Professional Organizations," in Libraries and Documentation Centres in the Netherlands, ed. E. Z. R. Cohen et al., pp. 15–20, The Hague: NBLC, 1987; Boulogne, G., "Structuurwijziging van het NBLC: vergroting van de slagvaardigheid met behoud van een gewaarborgde beroepsinhoudelijke inbreng," (Structurai Reform of the NBLC: Increasing the Effectiveness while Retaining the Guaranteed Professional Contribution), Bibliotheek en Samenleving 15 (1987)323–324; Riesthuis-Groenland, M.-L., "Hoe en waarom een nieuwe NBLC-structuur?: Enkele antwoorden op eerste reacties," (How and Why a New NBLC Structure?: Some Comments on the First Reactions), ibid.:337–338; "Literatuurlijst structuur NBLC," (Bibliography on the Reform of the NBLC), ibid.:341–342
Comment   Nederlands Bibliotheek en Lektuur Centrum war forerunner to VOB

387   Nederlandse Vereniging van Beroepsbeoefenaren in de Bibliotheek-, Informatie- en Kennissector (NVB)
(Netherlands Association for Library, Information and Knowledge Professionals)

Address   c/o Verenigingsbureau, Hardwareweg 4, Postbus 1466, 3800 Amersfoort BL Tel.: +31 30 2311263, Fax +31 30 2311830, info@nvbonline.nl; www.nvbonline.nl
Languages   Dutch
Established   1912, as Nederlandse Vereniging van Bibliothecarissen; new name adopted in 1974, reflecting the expansion of membership to include documentalists and information specialists
General Assembly   Entire membership meets annually
Membership   Total members: 3200+ (approximately 2500 individual and 700 institutional members). Requirements: Individuals and institutions engaged in library, documentation or information work outside the public library field. Fees: for individuals EUR 29,00, per chapter EUR 7,50. For institutions the fee varies dependant on the number of staff employed in the information section
Structure   Governed by Executive Board. Organized in chapters reflecting the type of library or a particular interest. Affiliations: IFLA
Sources of Support   Membership dues; donations

Major Fields of Interest Research libraries; special libraries; public libraries; professional staff
Major Goals and Objectives To stimulate library and information science and documentation research; to promote the status and represent the interests of members
Activities Various activities according to the goals and objectives of the Association. Organizes workshops, seminars, conferences, training courses and study trips
Publications Official journal: NVB Nieuwsbrief. 1985-. 6/yr. Free to members. Editor: Mw. A. D. Kuipers-Beukman. Address same as Association. Circ: Membership. Dutch. Other publications: Open (published jointly with other Dutch library associations; see FOBID entry); annual reports, proceedings of meetings. Publications available for sale, listed in Open
Bibliography Mathijsen, A.H.H.M., "Netherlands," in ALA World Encyclopedia of Library and Information Services, 2nd. ed., pp. 396–399. Chicago: American Library Association, 1986; Mathijsen, A.H.H.M., "Professional Organizations," in Libraries and Documentation Centres in the Netherlands, ed. E. Z. R. Cohen et al., pp. 15–20, The Hague: Nederlands Bibliotheek en Lektuur Centrum, 1987; Van Swigchem, P.J., "Vijf en zeventig jaar NVB," (75 Years of NVB), Bibliotheek en Samenleving 15 (1987):192–193; Wijnstroom, M., "Nederlanders op het internationale bibliotheek vinkentouw," (The Dutch at the International library Helm), Open 19 (1987):409–413; "De NVB een huis voor velen," (The NVB as a House for Many; Conference to Celebrate the 57th Anniversary of the NVB; special issue), ibid.:381–413 (in Dutch)

388   Nederlandse Vereniging van Gebruikers van Online Informatiesystemen (VOGIN)
(Netherlands Association of Users of Online Information Systems)

Address c/o NVB-verenigingsbureau, Nieuwegracht 15, 3512 LC Utrecht Tel.: +31 33 4546 653, Fax +31 33 4546 666, info@nvbonline.nl; www.nvb-online.nl/index.html?pagina=353
Languages Dutch, English
Established 1977, Delft
General Assembly Entire membership meets twice a year
Membership Requirements: Individuals and institutions engaged in online work or interested in the topic
Structure Governed by Executive Board. Independent department of NVB
Sources of Support Membership dues, government subsidies
Major Fields of Interest Online information systems
Major Goals and Objectives To increase the knowledge of its members about computer readable databases and to foster the use of these; to collect and exchange experiences in this field; to cooperate with other related organizations, both in the Netherlands and abroad; to influence policy-making bodies in this field
Activities Sponsors awards (Molsterprijs), conferences, online training and continuing education courses for members
Publications Online opsporen van informatie. 6e herziene druk, ISBN 90-5483-099-9. (NBLC, 's-Gravenhage 1996)
Bibliography Mathijsen, A.H.H.M., "Netherlands," in ALA World Encyclopedia of Library and Information Services. 2nd ed., pp. 596–599. Chicago: American Library

Association, 1986; Mathijsen, A.H.H.M., "Professional Organizations," in Libraries and Documentation Centres in the Netherlands, ed. E. Z. R. Cohen et al., pp. 15–20, The Hague: Nederlands Bibliotheek en Lektuur Centrum, 1987

389 NVBA, vereniging van en voor personen werkzam in het beheer van organisatie

Address c/o K.C. Laurijssen-van der Kolk, Groeneveld 2, 5653 PC Eindhoven info@nvba-info.nl; www.nvba-info.nl
Languages Dutch
Established 1947, The Hague, as Nederlandse Documentalistenkring (NDK); formerly: Nederlandse Vereniging van Bedrijfsarchivarissen (NVBA), since 2001 NVBA
General Assembly Entire membership meets twice a year, usually in May/June and November/December
Membership Types of membership: Individual. Requirements: Active in archives/documentation.
Structure Governed by executive officers
Sources of Support Membership dues, private subsidies.
Major Fields of Interest Archival studies; records management; library and office automation
Major Goals and Objectives (1) To promote the professional skills of members; (2) to provide professional contacts and promote cooperation among members; (3) to represent the members' interests regarding their profession
Activities Past achievements: Information exchanges concerning office automation. Current: The place of a company/business archive in today's offices. Future: Protect the name of company/business archives as related to Records Management
Publications Official journal: Repeat. 1987-. 11/yr. Free to members. Dutch. Other publications: Bewaartermijnerlijst in een Bedrijfsarchief (1986), etc

390 Sectorinstituut Openbare Bibliotheken (Netherlands Institute for Public Libraries)*

Address Grote Marktstraat 43, 2511 BH Den Haag, Postbus 16146, 2500 BC Den Haag Tel.: +31 70 3090222, Fax +31 70 3090299, infosiob@siob.nl; wwww.siob.nl

391 UKB (Samenwerkingsverband van de Universiteitsbibliotheken, de Koninklijke Bibliotheek en de Bibliotheek van de Koninklijke Nederlandse Akademie van Wetenschappen)
(Association of the University Libraries, the Royal Library and the Library of the Royal Netherlands Academy of Arts and Sciences)

Address PO Box 90407, 2?09 LK Den Haag Tel.: +31 10 4081208, Fax +31 10 4089049, hans.wilbrink@kb.nl; www.ukb.nl/index.htm
Languages Dutch
Established 1977, as successor to the Rijkscommissie van Advies inzake het Bibliotheekwezen (Advisory Council on Library Affairs), abolished in 1975
Officers Pres: M.A.M. Heijne
General Assembly Entire membership meets 6 times a year

Membership The 13 University Libraries, the Royal Library and the Library of the Royal Dutch Academy of Science. As from 2001 there is also an associate member: the Open University. Requirements: Members are represented by chief librarians of the institutions (university libraries and national library)
Structure Governed by Executive Board. Affiliations: IFLA
Sources of Support Membership dues.
Major Fields of Interest Library cooperation
Major Goals and Objectives Promote mutual consultation and cooperation among member libraries; coordination of inter-library loan, collection development, subject accessing, preservation or library material, etc
Activities Sets up study groups to reach its goals, organizes conferences
Publications No official journal. Occasional publications
Bibliography Brak, J.A.W., "Library Consortia," in Libraries and Documentation Centres in the Netherlands, ed. E. Z. R. Cohen et al., pp. 21–30, The Hague: NBLC, 1987

392 Vereniging Openbare Bibliotheeken in Nederland (The Netherlands Public Library Association)*

Address c/o Thea van Lankvelt, Grote Marktstraat 43, 2511 BH The Hague, P.O. Box 16146, 2500 The Hague, BC Tel.: +31 70 3090500, Fax +31 70 3090599, vereniging@debibliotheken.nl; www.debibliotheken.nl
Languages Dutch, English
Established 8th April 1972, The Hague
Officers Chair: Prof. E.C.M. Jürgens; Secr/Treas: M.M.B. Mertens
Staff 10
General Assembly 2 meetings, 17th June and 9th Dec 2010
Major Fields of Interest Public libraries

393 Vereniging van Pers- en Omroepdocumentalisten (VPOD) (Association of Press and Broadcasting Documentalists)

Address c/o Jost Brinks, Secretary, Elzenlaan 4, 2665 DE Bleiswijk Tel.: +31 10 4067746, Fax +31 10 4066942; www.vpod.nl
Languages Dutch
Established 1977
Major Fields of Interest Press and broadcasting documentation
Major Goals and Objectives To promote the profession of press and radio documentalists

394 Vereniging voor het Theologisch Bibliothecariaat (VTB) (Theological Library Association)

Address c/o Secretary, Kloosterlaan 24, 5435 XD St Agatha VTB-request@nic.surfnet.nl; http://theo.kuleuven.be/beth/page/25/
Languages Dutch
Established 1947, Tilburg, as Vereniging voor het Godsdienstig-wetenschappelijk Bibliothecariaat (VSKB) (Association for Seminary and Monastery Libraries); new name adopted 1973 and membership no longer restricted to Catholic institutions
Staff None

General Assembly Entire membership meets annually
Membership Total members: 69 (libraries and/or librarians). Requirements: To subscribe to the aims of the Association and to be admitted by the governing authorities
Structure Governed by executive officers. Affiliations: Conseil Interational des Associations des Bibliothèques de Théologie
Sources of Support Membership dues, private subsidies
Major Fields of Interest Theology and auxiliary sciences
Major Goals and Objectives To promote librarianship in the fields of the theological sciences
Activities Cooperation among theological research libraries. When founded, the organization was intended for Catholics only, but now has effectively expanded to include librarians of all denominations in the field of theology. Activities carried out through several working groups
Publications Official journal: Medelingen van de VTB (Communications of the VTB) (supersedes Medelingen van de VSKB. 1948–73). 1973-. 4/yr. Free to members. Dutch. Other publications: Gids van Theologische Bibliotheken in Nederland en Vlaanderen, 1983, Voorburg: Protestantse Stichting tot Bevordering van het Bibliotheekwezen en de Lectuurvoorziening in Nederland; XXXIV; Bibliografie Doctorale Scripties Theologie (BDST): annual list of the 'doctoral' theses by the student of the theological faculties in the Netherlands from 1977 -, of the faculty K. U. Leuven from 1984, and of the protestant faculty Brussels from 1985-.
Bibliography Mathijsen, A.H.H.M., "Professional Organizations," in Libraries and Documentation Centres in the Netherlands, ed. E. Z. R. Cohen et al., pp. 15–20, The Hague: Nederlands Bibliotheek en Lektuur Centrum, 1987

New Zealand

395 Archives and Records Association of New Zealand, Inc. (ARANZ)*

Address P.O. Box 11-553, Manners Street, Wellington www.aranz.org.nz
Languages English
Established 1976, Wellington
General Assembly Entire membership meets once a year
Membership membersindividual and institutional. 25 countries represented. Requirements: Interest in the aims of the Association
Structure Governed by Council. Affiliations: ICA, PARBICA
Sources of Support Membership dues, annual conference profits
Major Fields of Interest All aspects of archives and records management, including standards, education and training, employment, preservation, research, users and their interests, changing technology etc., publications
Major Goals and Objectives Promoting the understanding and importance of records and archives in New Zealand; Preservation of archives and records; training of archival personnel. To foster the care, preservation and use of archives and records, both to public and private, and their effective administration. To maintain and increase public awareness of the importance of archives and records in all matters affecting their preservation and use. To cooperate or affiliate with any other bodies in New Zealand or elsewhere with like

objects. To promote professional competence in the administration and preservation of archives and records; by providing advice to the appropriate authorities on levels and standards of professional education and training, and by promoting the training of archivists, records keepers, curators, librarians and others by the dissemination of specialised knowledge

Activities To publish a journal and other publications in furtherance of these objects

Publications Publication of a bi-annual journal, Archifacts, organisation of annual conferences, promotion of the value of archives and records to the public, reviewing and commenting on national standards, branch network to support archivists and records managers, joint projects with Australian Society of Archivists and Records Management Association of Australasia

Bibliography Patterson, B., "The Anatomy of an Interest Group," Archifacts 2 (June 1986): 1–5

396 Council of New Zealand University Librarians (CONZUL)

Address PO Box 11915, Manners Street, 6142 Wellington Tel.: +64 4 381 8500, Fax +64 4 381 8501; www.nzvcc.ac.nz/contact

Staff 1

General Assembly Membership meets three times a year

Membership Requirements: Limited to top management of New Zealand's university libraries

Major Fields of Interest Improve access for students and staff of New Zealand universities to the information resources required to advance teaching, learning and research

Major Goals and Objectives Providing leadership on library and information issues across the sector; Striving for innovative solutions in teaching, learning and research; Collaborating for the common benefit of library users Developing partnerships with professional colleagues

Publications No official journal. Other publications: reports

397 Health Information Association of New Zealand (HIANZ)

Address c/o The Secretary, Christopher Deane, PO Box 40183, Glenfield Auckland Tel.: +64 9 4151863, Fax +64 9 4159610, cdeane@crownworldwide.com; www.hianz.org.nz

Languages English

Established 1989. Formerly, the Health Libraries Section of NZLA Members decided to form a separate Association to preserve and enhance the section's work and projects

Officers Pres: Chris Sorensen; VP: Maggie Mackenzie; Secr: Christopher Deane; Treas: Nicola Brandsen

Membership Including Coding and Health Librarians

Structure Executive

Major Fields of Interest Health Information, Consumer Health Information, Drug information, Health Information Systems, Health and Medical Libraries, Health Management, Health Promotion, Mental Health Sector, Patient Information, Records Management, and the Voluntary Health Sector

Major Goals and Objectives   To further the work of health sciences information services in New Zealand
Activities   To promote an awareness of health information issues through newsletter and other publications, seminars and conferences and lobbying at appropriate levels. To develop and promote standards and codes of practice for health information professionals, and the publishing of them. To support and assist the development of Health Information professionals by offering an active continuing education, regular conferences, seminars, and scholarships
Publications   HIANZ Dictionary of Clinical Abbreviations
Bibliography   "Health Information Association of New Zealand (HIANZ)," Library Times International 6 (Jan. 1990):55

398   International Association of Music Libraries, Archives and Documentation Centres, New Zealand Branch, Incorporated (IAML-NZ)
Address   c/o Marilyn Portman, Wellesley Street, Auckland, PO Box 4138, Auckland Tel.: +64 9 3077761, Fax +64 9 3077741, portmanm@akcity.govt.nz; www.iaml.info/IamlNZ
Languages   English
Established   1970, IAML – Australia and New Zealand formed in Australia; 1974, New Zealand Division formed; 1982, IAML – New Zealand Branch formed
General Assembly   Entire membership meets once a year
Membership   Requirements: Interest in goals of the Association
Structure   Governed by executive officers under the parent body, the International Association of Music Libraries, Archives and Documentation Centres (IAML). Affiliations: IFLA, National Music Council of New Zealand, New Zealand Library Association
Sources of Support   Membership dues, sale of publications, private grants
Major Fields of Interest   Music bibliography; music librarianship
Major Goals and Objectives   To bring together people and music (literature, scores, recordings and music information) through the library system or other suitable channels in New Zealand; and to establish and maintain international links through the parent body, the International Association of Music Libraries, Archives and Documentation Centres (IAML)
Activities   Major accomplishments of the Association are the publications. Association has been active in promoting library-related legislation, such as Submission on the New Zealand Copyright Act
Publications   Official journal: Crescendo: Bulletin of the International Association of Music Libraries (New Zealand Branch). 1982-. 3/yr. Other publications: New Zealand music libraries newsletter. Orchestral scores. Ed. Freed, Dorothy and Seaman, Gerald, comp. 1978. Directory of New Zealand music organisations. Ed. Freed, Dorothy. 1983
Bibliography   Freed, D., "Music in New Zealand," New Zealand Libraries 43 (1982):184–185

399   Library and Information Association of New Zealand Aotearoa (LIANZA)*
Address   P.O. Box 12-212, Wellington, 6144   Tel.: +64 4 4735834, Fax +64 4 4991480, alli@lianza.org.nz; www.lianza.org.nz

Languages English
Established 1910, Dunedin, New Zealand
Officers Pres: Barbara Garriock; Pres Elect: Carolyn Robertson; Immediate Past Pres: Glen Walker
Staff 4 full-time equivalents
General Assembly Entire membership meets once a year, next meeting Tuesday 30th November 2010, Dunedin
Membership Institutional members: 397, personal Memberships: 1884, regions: 6, special Interest Groups: 11
Structure Membership organisation run by a Council. Partnership with Te Roopu Whakahau, Affilliations with, SLANZA, NZLLA, National Library APLM
Sources of Support Membership fees, Professional Development, Conference Profit, Sponsorship
Major Fields of Interest Librarianship and information services
Major Goals and Objectives LIANZA works (i) for library and information professionals in New Zealand Aotearoa by building communities to represent their professional interests and provide professional development services to them; (ii) with library and information organisations to support the delivery of library and information services that are vital to the economic, social, and cultural wellbeing of New Zealand Aotearoa
Activities Professional Registration, Submissions on Copyright, Professional development
Publications New Zealand Library & Information Management Journal – biennial publication. October 2006. Editor: Alison Fields, free to members $30. Annual Report is no longer printed, available on LIANZA website
Bibliography Porter, K., "Dunedin Conference Marks 75th Anniversary of New Zealand Library Association." Library Times International 2 (1985):44–45; McKeon, B., "New Zealand," ALA World Encyclopedia in Library and Information Services. 2nd ed., pp. 600–603. Chicago: American Library Association, 1986; "NZLA Splashes Out on Libraries Promotion Campaign." Library Times International 3 (1987):71–72; Wooliscroft, M., "Libraries in the Marketplace: The New Zealand Library Association Conference, February 1988," COMLA Newsletter 60 (June 1988):7; Thompson, J. et al., "Price Waterhouse Report: New Zealand Library Association Submission," New Zealand Libraries 45 (1988):211–214; Johnston, S., "Education for Librarianship," ibid.:226–230; Caudwell, J., "1989 Presidential Address: Winners and Losers," New Zealand Libraries 46 (1989):3,5; "NZ Library Group in Financial Crisis," library Times International 6 (1989):39; "NZLA Survives Liquidation Threat," COMLA Newsletter 66 (Dec. 1989):2

400 New Zealand Law Librarians Inc. (NZLLA)

Address PO Box 25062, Wellington paula.robinson@justice.govt.nz; www.nzlla.org.nz
Languages English
Officers Pres: Alistair Jenkin; VP: Angela McLuckie; Treas: Therese Duffin; Secr: Paula Robinson
Structure Managed by a National Executive, elected annually by a ballot of all members
Major Fields of Interest Legal information in New Zealand

Major Goals and Objectives   To promote the interests of our members, the legal profession and the public around issues of access to legal information
Publications   Official newsletter: NZLLG News

401   New Zealand Society of Archivists (NZSA)

Address   Marion Street, POB 27 057, Wellington   Tel.: +64 4 2338155; www.archivists.org.nz
Languages   English
Established   1990
Staff   6 volunteers
General Assembly   Annual General Meeting, conferences
Membership   120 personal members
Structure   Governed by a council
Sources of Support   Membership fees
Major Fields of Interest   Representative organisation for those working with archives in New Zealand
Major Goals and Objectives   Promote professional identity; provide an authoritative voice on archival matters; establish and maintain professional standards, including a code of ethics; establish training standards; advocate for conditions of employment; establish and maintain communication between archivists, institutions and users; cooperate with other organisations with complementary objectives
Activities   Holds conferences, symposia, hires out a basic training kit, supports the National Register of Archives and Manuscripts in New Zealand (NRAM)
Publications   Official journal: New Zealand Archivist. 4/yr. Editorial address: P O Box 27–057, Wellington, NZ. A Directory of Archivist in New Zealand, 1992

402   School Library Association of New Zealand Aotearoa (SLANZA)

Address   PO Box 631, 4440 Palmerston North   Tel.: +61 6 345 8952, slanza@xtra.co.nz; www.slanza.org.nz
Languages   English
Established   2000
Officers   Pres: Senga White; Exec Officer: Frances Gibbons
Major Fields of Interest   school libraries and librarianship
Major Goals and Objectives   To strengthen and promote the role of the school library; to enable all school communities to become information literate; to provide a national voice for the school library community; to advocate the critical role of school libraries in teaching and learning; to represent all school library staff: Teacher Librarians, Teachers with Library Responsibility: School Librarians, and support staff; to lobby for improved funding to provide better library facilities and services; to create opportunities to recognise excellence within the school library field; to improve the professional standing, working conditions and qualifications for all staff involved with school libraries; to support professional development through biennial conferences, regular newsletters and Web site; to develop links with associated national and international professional organisations

Nicaragua

403   Asociación Nicaragüense de Bibliotecarios y Profesionales Afines (ANIBIPA) (Nicaraguan Association of Librarians and Related Professionals)
Address   Bello Horizonte, tope Sur de la Rotonda $\frac{1}{2}$ cuadra abajo J-II-57, Managua info@metabase.net; www.metabase.net/metarecursos/profesionales/anibipa.shtml
Languages   Spanish
Established   1965, as Asociación Nicaragüense de Bibliotecarios (ASNIBI)
Officers   Pres: Yadira Roque; VP: Dalia Centeno
General Assembly   Entire membership meets once a year
Membership   Dues: (US Dollar) 10/yr
Structure   Governed by executive officers. Affiliations: IFLA (since 1974)
Sources of Support   Membership dues, government subsidies
Major Fields of Interest   Librarians; professional development
Major Goals and Objectives   To improve libraries and the status and professional development of librarians in Nicaragua
Activities   Sponsors conferences, workshops, and other continuing education programs
Publications   No official journal. Publishes newsletter, Novedades
Bibliography   Cárdenas Perez, L., "Nicaragua," in ALA World Encyclopedia of Library and Information Services. 2nd ed., p. 603. Chicago: American Library Association, 1986

Niger

404   Association des Spécialistes Nigériens de l'Information Documentaire (ASNID)
Address   B.P. 873, Niamey   asnid_niger2001@yahoo.fr
Established   1991

Nigeria

405   Nigerian Library Association (NLA)*
Address   c/o National Library of Nigeria HQ, Sanusi Dantata House, Central Business District, PMB 1 Garki GPO 900001, Abuja   Tel.: +234 803 334-8817, nlanationalsec@yahoo.com; www.nla.ng.org
Languages   English
Established   1962
Officers   Pres: Victoria Okojie
Staff   None
General Assembly   Entire membership meets once a year
Membership   Total members:more than 5000 individual members. Requirements: Must be a qualified librarian, paraprofessional or library student.
Structure   Governed by Council. Affiliations: IFLA
Sources of Support   Membership dues, sale of publications, government subsidies.
Major Fields of Interest   ICT, University, Schoil & Public Libraries

Major Goals and Objectives   To unite persons interested in Libraries, Librarianship and Information services; to safeguard and promote the professional interests pf librarians; to promote the establishment and development of libraries and to assist in the promotion of such legislation as may be considered necessary for the establishment, regulation and management of libraries in Nigeria; to watch legislation affecting and to assist in the promotion of such legislation as may be considered necessary for the establishment, regulation and management of libraries in Nigeria; to promote and encourage bibliographical study, research and library cooperation

Activities   Organizes conferences, workshops and seminars on special subjects of interest to members. Association has been active in promoting libraryrelated legislation, such as the State Library Board in Bendel, Benue, Anambra, Imo, Cross River, Rivers. Sponsors Book Week, exhibits, continuing education programs, and a literacy campaign to promote adult readership

Publications   Official journal: Nigerian Libraries. 1964-. 2/yr. ISSN 0029–0122, Editor-in-Chief: Dr S Olajire Olanlokun. Address: University Library, University of Lagos, Akoka, Yaba, Lagos. E-mail: library@unilag.edu; Annual Subscription Rates: Nigeria N300, OAU Countries US$65, Other countries US$60. English. Indexed in Lib.Lit.; LISA. Other publications: Proceedings of meetings, reports of seminars, workshops, etc. Publications available for sale through Mrs. O. Jegede, Librarian, Institute of Advanced Legal Studies, University of Lagos, Lagos. No publications exchange program

Bibliography   Dosunmu, J.A., "Nigeria," in ALA World Encyclopedia of Library and Information Services. 2nd ed., pp. 605–606. Chicago: American Library Association, 1986; Dosunmu, J.A., "Preservation and Conservation of Library Materials in Nigeria: A New Awareness," COMLA Newsletter 64 (June 1989):3–4

Norway

406   ABM-utvikling – Statens senter for arkiv, bibliotek og museum (Norwegian Archive, Library and Museum Authority)*

Address   Observatoriegt. 1b, 0254 Oslo, Box 8145 Dep, 0033 Oslo   Tel.: +47 23117500, Fax +47 23117501, post@abm-utvikling.no; www.abm-utvikling.no
Languages   Norwegian
Established   2003
Officers   Dir Gen: Stein Slyngstad
Staff   about 65 employees
Major Fields of Interest   Archives, libraries and museums
Major Goals and Objectives   To work towards the improved development, preservation, and use of our cultural and knowledge based assets; to improve the ability of the sectors and the institutions to meet the new challenges posed to our society, today and tomorrow
Activities   TTo promote partnerships and collaboration between the three sectors (archive, library, museum), in addition to addressing sector specific challenges; to encourage the sectors and their institutions to find improved solutions to specific tasks and to engage in meeting new societal challenges; to grant funds for projects, in addition to supporting measures directed by the institutions themselves; to administer governmental subsidies to the sector and may be delegated additional administrative tasks; to act in a

consultative capacity vis-à-vis public authorities
Publications ABM-Skrift; Scandinavian Public Library Quarterly (SPQL)

407 Arkivarforeningen
(Association of Archivists)

Address c/o Synne Stavheim, P.O. Box 4015 Ullevål Stadion, 0806 Oslo Tel.: +47 22022657, post@forskerforbundet.no; www.arkivarforeningen.no
Languages Norwegian
Established 1936, Oslo
General Assembly Entire membership meets every year
Membership Total members: about 100. Types of membership: Individual. Requirements: Position and qualifications as an archivist within the state archival system
Structure Governed by Executive Board. Affiliations: ICA, Norsk Forskerforbund, Akademikernes Fellesorganisasjon
Sources of Support Membership dues
Major Fields of Interest Archives and archival personnel
Major Goals and Objectives To improve the professional and economic standards of members, such as wages, working conditions, and professional development
Activities Past achievements: Significant improvements in the wage level and some improvements regarding working conditions of members. Current and future: Continue working for better wages, working conditions, and opportunities for professional development of members
Publications Official journal: Norsk Arkivforum. 1980-. Biennial. (Norwegian Krone) 60. Free to members. Address same as Association. Circ: 300–400. Norwegian

408 ARLIS/Norden – Norge. Forening for Kunstbibliotekarbeid
(Art Libraries Society Norden)*

Address c/o Eva Eide, P.O. Box 8196 Dep., 0034 Oslo Tel.: +47 22940543, Fax +47 22940406, eva.eide@ra.no; www.arlisnorden.org/norge/norge.html
Languages Norwegian
Established 1983, Oslo
General Assembly Entire membership meets annually.
Structure Affiliations: IFLA.
Sources of Support Membership dues
Major Fields of Interest Art libraries and librarianship
Major Goals and Objectives To promote art librarianship in Norway.
Activities Organizing annual meetings and conferences on special topics, such as the new Norwegian Art Bibliography, new media, especially video and microfiche, etc. Sponsors continuing education programs
Publications Official journal: ARLIS-Nytt (News from ARLIS/Norge). 1983-. 4/yr. Free to members. Address same as Association. Norwegian.
Bibliography Rabben, A. L. and Bonafede, C.W., "ARLIS/Norge: Art Librarianship in Norway and the Literature of Norwegian Art," Art Libraries Journal 11(1986):25–27. Text of paper presented to the IFLA Section of Art Libraries at the IFLA Conference, Chicago, August 1985.

409 Forskerforbundets Bibliotekforening (FBF)

Address c/o Lisbeth Eriksen, Postboks 5003, 1432 Ås Tel.: +47 64 96 50 58, Fax +47 64 94 76 70, lisbeth.eriksen@umb.no; www.forskerforbundet.no
Languages Norwegian
Membership 400 members

410 Norsk Arkivråd (NA)
(Norwegian Archives Council)

Address Postboks 812 Sentrum, 0104 Oslo Tel.: +47 22 202890, Fax +47 22 208506, postmottak@arkivrad.no; www.arkivrad.no(onlyinNorwegian)
Languages Norwegian
Established 1961
General Assembly Members meet once a year

411 Norsk Bibliotekforening (NBF)
(Norwegian Library Association)

Address PO Box 6540, N-0606 Oslo, Etterstad Tel.: +47 90660423, Fax +47 35535551, tore.andersen@norskbibliotekforening.no; www.norskbibliotekforening.no
Languages Norwegian
Established 1913
Officers Pres: Tore K. Andersen
Staff 8
General Assembly Last held March 2004
Membership Total members: 3,800 (individual and institutional). Sections for various types of libraries and types of librarians. Requirements: Open to all, no special requirements
Structure Governed by Executive Board. Affiliations: IFLA, EBLIDA
Sources of Support Membership dues, sale of publications, distribution of periodicals
Major Fields of Interest All topics of interest to libraries and librarians
Major Goals and Objectives To encourage and promote the development of all kinds of Norwegian library activities, including documentary and information activities
Activities Sponsors meetings, conferences and continuing education programs; participates in international activities
Publications Official journal: Bibliotekforum 1995-. Approx. 10/yr. (Norwegian Krone) 260. Free to members. Editor: Ingrid Stephensen, Sec./Treas. Address same as Association. Circ: Membership. Norwegian. Other publications: Annual reports, proceedings of beetings; Reports etc
Bibliography Granheim, E., "Norway," in ALA World Encyclopedia of Library and Information Services. 2nd ed., pp. 608–609. Chicago: American Library Association, 1986; Granheim, E., "NLA Conference Report: Libraries for the Future Discussed," (1986 Meeting in Stavanger, Norway) Library Times International 3 (1986):32

412 Norsk Fagbibliotekforening (NFF)
(Norwegian Association of Special Libraries)

Address c/o Tove Haavi Johnsen, P.b. 164 Sentrum, 3502 Hømefoss Tel.: +47 32117128, tove.haavi-johnsen@hibu.no; www.fagbibliotek.no

Languages Norwegian
Established 1948; merged with Norske Forskningsbibliotekarers Forening (NFF) (Association of Norwegian Research Librarians)
Officers Pres: Kristin Røijen; Secr: Tove Haavi Johnsen
General Assembly Entire membership meets once a year
Membership Total members: 554 (526 individual, 28 institutional). Requirements: Employee of a special library; special library
Structure Governed by Executive Board. Affiliations: IFLA, NBF
Sources of Support Membership dues
Major Fields of Interest Special and academic libraries, especially in areas of automation and cooperation
Major Goals and Objectives To strengthen the role of special libraries in society, research, education, business and industry
Activities Seminars, courses, meetings; information work, publications; national, nordic and international collaboration
Publications Official journal: NFF-Informasjon. 4/yr. Free to members. Editor: Hans Martin Fagerli. Address: Universitetsbiblioteket i Oslo, Planardelingen, Drammensveien 42, N-0255 Oslo 2. Circ: 900. Norwegian. Other publications: Reports of seminars, workshops; NFF-Skrifter, occasional series
Bibliography Granheim, E., "Norway," in ALA World Encyclopedia of Library and Information Services. 2nd ed., pp. 608–609. Chicago: American Library Association, 1986

413 Norwegian Union of Municipal and General Employees
Address PO Box 7003, 0130 Oslo post@fagforbundet.no
Languages Norwegian
Officers Pres: Jan Davidsen

414 Skolebibliotekarforeningen i Norge
(Norwegian Association of School Librarianship)
Address c/o Marit Aasbren, Bjørndalsveien 47, 1605 Fredrikstad maasbren@online.no; www.skolebibliotekarforeningen.no
Languages Norwegian
Established 1978
General Assembly General meeting every two years
Membership 502 members
Structure Six of our twenty counties have their own regional association who have meetings and arrange courses that are open for non-members. We have a national board which contains 5 members
Major Fields of Interest School libraries and librarianship
Major Goals and Objectives To improve the working conditions for teachers who are responsible for the school library; to strengthen the school library as an educational tool and an area for presentation of literature; to work for the local councils to establish school libraries, so that every pupil can use a library close to their home; to work for better education for teachers who work as school librarians; to create a professional forum for

school library issues arranging meetings, courses and seminars, by giving out a magazine and presenting a website; to collect and publish relevant literature on school library issues
Publications Official Journal: Skolebiblioteket (4 issues/yr)

Pakistan

415 Library Promotion Bureau (LPB)*
Address c/o Dr. Ghaniul Akram Sabzwari; Pres, 1239/9 Dastgir Society, Federal B Area, Karachi, PO Box 8421, Karachi Tel.: +92 21 857-6301, Fax +92 21 857-6301, lpb_pakistan_66@yahoo.com; www.lpbpk.com
Languages English,
Established 1965, Karachi, Pakistan
Officers VP: Dr. Rais Ahmed Samdani; Secr Gen: Abdul Samad Ansari; Finance Secr: Prof. Liaquat Ali Khan; Asst Secr: Aman Khatoon; Nasreen Shagufta
Staff 9, volunteers
General Assembly Entire membership meets once a year, Executive Board holds quarterly meetings
Membership Total Membership 180 (120 individual, 60 institutions). Dues Pakistan Rupees: Individual Rs. 500; Institutions Rs. 800; Foreign US$ 120
Structure Governed by Board of Directors
Sources of Support Membership dues, sale of publications, private donations
Major Fields of Interest Library and information science
Major Goals and Objectives 1. To publish and promote professional literature; 2. to introduce Pakistan Librarianship abroad; to encourage professional librarians to produce professional literature; to reduce dependency on foreign literature by producing professional literature in the country; to publish professional literature in Urdu and other languages of Pakistan; to publish reference books on various subjects; 7. Pakistan Library & Information Science Journal, quarterly journal, is being published since 1968. It is devoted to publish research articles of the senior and junior professional librarians and scholars of other fields; to publicize researches made by scholars in the country; 9. to update professional librarians with the changes and developments taking place in the country; 10. to exhibit Bureau's publications; 11. to participate in professional conferences, seminars and workshops; 12. To encourage research activities in the field of Library and Information science; 13. To extend cooperation to professional associations and groups
Activities Past achievements: Extensive publications program. Current: To publish journal regularly and also books on library and information science, Future: A Manual on the Library of Congress Classification Scheme (by G. A. Sabzwari); Bureau has been active in promoting library-related legislation
Publications Pakistan Library & Information Science Journal, 4/yr. Annual Subscriptions for individuals Rs. 500, Institutions Rs. 800 and Foreign US$120. Founder Patron: M. Adil Usmani; Chief Editor Dr. G. A. Sabzwari; Editors: Nasim Fatima, Wasil Usmani, Rais A. Samdani. Circulation: 500. Address: Karachi University Campus, P. O. Box 8421, Karachi 75270, Pakistan. Phone & Fax: 857–6301. E-mail: jpb_pakistan_66@yahoo.com English, Urdu. Indexed in Library Literature & Inforamtion Science Index; Readers' Guide to Periodical Literature. Abstracted in: Library & Lirary &

Inforamtion Science Abstracts (LISA), Historical Abstracts, etc. English Publications: 1. Bibliographical Services and Resources in Pakistan.Rs. 200.00, $20.00. Akhtar H. Siddiqui and Nasim Fatima (1993); 2. Bibliographical Services throughout Pakistan. M. Adil Usmani. Rs. 40.00, $ 5.00; 3. Bibliographical Sources on Islam. Rais A. Samdani (1993). Rs. 100.00, $ 10.00; 4. Document Procurement Service. Akhtar H. Siddiqui (1972), Rs. 15.00; $ 3.00; 5. Dr. Abdul Moid and Pakistan Librarianship. Nasim Fatima and Rais A. Samdani (1981). Rs. 60.00, $ 6.00; 6. Guidelines for Archive Management in Pakistan. Nasim Fatima. Rs. 250.00, $ 25.00; 7. Guidelines for Researchers and Authors. Nasim Fatima (2004). Rs. 60.00, $ 6.00; 8. Index of Pakistan Library Bulletin 1968–1994 (1996). Rs. 125.00, $ 12.00; 9. Library and Information Science Research in University of Karachi. Nasim Fatima (1999). Rs. 200.00, $ 20.00; 10. Library Science: For Bachelor Classes. Ghaniul Akram Sabzwari (2004). Rs. 200.00, $20.00 (for Students Rs.150); 11. Library and Information Science: For M. A. Classes Library ed. Ghaniul Akram Sabzwari (2005). Paperback ed. Rs.250.00 for Students; 12. List of Theses submitted to the Dept. of Library and Information Science, Univ. of Sindh. Nisar Subphoto (1995). Rs. 30.00, $ 3.00; 13. Muhammad Adil Usmani: A Bio-bibliographical Study. Rais A. Samdani (2004), Rs. 250.00, $25.00; 14. Private Libraries in Makkah Al-Mukarrammah. Abdul Latif A. Dohaishm (1993), Rs. 60.00, $ 6.00; 15. Secondary School Library Resources and Services. Nasim Fatima. Rs. 60.00, $ 6.00; 16. Standard of Children Libraries in Pakistan. Nasim Fatima. Rs. 50.00, $ 5.00; 17. Subject Index to Pakistan Library Bulletin. 1968–1984. Nasim Fatima. Rs. 45.00, $ 5.00; 18. University Librarianship in Pakistan. Akhtar Hanif and Nasim Fatima (1986). Rs. 100.00, $10.00; 19. Pakistan Library & Information Science Journal. Quarterly. Rs. 500.00, $150.00, Annual Subscription. (Foreign $150.00) Students. Rs. 400; 20. Reality of Death. Abdur Rahman Aajiz. Tr. By G. A. Sabzwari (2002). Rs. 250.00, $ 20.00; 21. Who's Who in Library and Information Science in Pakistan. G. A. Sabzwari (2004), 3rd ed. Rs. 250.00, $ 10.00. Also 21 books in Urdu Language. Bureau is struggling to produce books on Library and Information Science specially Reference books but due to lack of support and poor response from libraries, library schools and professional librarians publishing activities are limited. Association is facing great hardship in continuing publishing our quarterly journal PLISJ due to very few subscriptions in country and abroad (only 6 abroad, 2 Univ. libraries and 4 individual)

Bibliography Khurshid, A, The State of Library Resources in Pakistan (1982); Khurshid, A., "Pakistan," in ALA World Encyclopedia of Library and Information Services. 2nd ed., pp. 629–633. Chicago: American Library Association, 1986

416 Pakistan Library Association (PLA)

Address c/o Farhat Hussain, Secretary, Stadium Road, Ground Floor, Karachi
Tel.: +92-0333-2658156, plasindh@gmail.com; http://pla-sindhbranch.weebly.com
Languages English, Urdu
Established 1957, Karachi
Officers Pres: Malahat Kaleem Sherwani; VP: Mumtaz Memon; Nuzhat Yasmeen; Secr: Riaz Ali Khaskeli
Staff 2 (volunteers)
General Assembly Entire membership meets once a year
Membership Total members: 650+ (individual and institutional). Divisions: 5 (Public Libraries, College & University Libraries, Special Libraries and Documentation, Library

Services for Children and Young People, Library Education)
Structure   Governed by Executive Council. Affiliations: IFLA
Sources of Support   Membership dues, subsidies
Major Fields of Interest   Library development and the library profession
Major Goals and Objectives   To promote the better organization of libraries by arranging technical advice and assistance to library authorities. To improve study and research in library and information science and to disseminate information about current trends, theories and practices in the field of librarianship. To improve the status and professional standing of library professional and to safeguard their interests.
Activities   seminars, conferences and workshops
Publications   Official journal: PLA Newsletter. 12/yr. Circ: Membership. Address same as Association. Other publications: Code of Ethics for Librarians (1982); Public Library Facilities in Pakistan; Standards of College Libraries in Pakistan (1983); Standards of Special Libraries; Standards of University Libraries, etc. Publications available for sale
Bibliography   Khurshid, A., "Pakistan," in ALA World Encyclopedia of Library and Information Services. 2nd ed., pp. 629–633. Chicago: American Library Association, 1986; Sabzwari, G.A., "Pakistan Library Association," Pakistan Library Bulletin 19 (Dec. 1988): i-v; Khurshid, A., "Library Associations in Asia," Herald of Library Science 28 (1989):3–10

417   Pakistan Library Automation Goup (PakLAG)*

Address   IIMC Medical Complex, 7th Avanue, G-7/4, Islamabad Tel.: +92 514327776, 3214106248, majmalkhan@gmail.com; wwwe.paklag.org
Languages   English
Established   October 2000, Lahore, Pakistan, Informal Meeting
Officers   Pres: Khalid Mehmood; VP: Nadeem Siddique; Secr Gen: Muhammad Ajmal Khan; IT Consultant: Mohsin Ali; IT Manager: Asif Ali Kamal; Joint Secr: Nosheen Fatima Warriach; Treas: Aamir Rasul; Joint Secr: Saima Qutab
Staff   10, volunteers
General Assembly   Only Executives Meetings, 2010: 14th February, Frequency monthly, no General Assembly Meeting
Membership   2694 4 chapters, 1. Executive members 2. General members. No Membership Fee
Structure   Pakistan Library Association
Sources of Support   Contribution of Executive members, training fees and pakLAG Koha's sale
Major Fields of Interest   Library Automation, Research in Library and Information Science, Efficient USe of ICT in Library and Information Centres
Major Goals and Objectives   To provide professional and technical advice to libraries, information centers and documentation centers in their development programs; to recommend training programs for librarians so as to help them to develop, update and automate their libraries and documentation centers; to develop library automation and capacity building programs; to coordinate library development activities in the country with national as well as international development agencies and institutions; to provide information and conduct research studies on library development; to provide platform to the information professionals for the exchange of views, sharing of experiences,

networking among libraries as well as to develop consensus upon the common issues faced by the profession; to provide research support and policy recommendations to government at all levels and to legislate bodies in the formation of policies regarding the libraries and information services

Activities Designing and providing of software, training and support; proding indexes online; virtual catalog; a multilingual web OPAC (more than 10,000 entries so far); Library Software Directory; Open Access Periodical Directory; Vendors Catalogs: Resources (Presentations, Manuals, etc). PakLAG uploads presentations given by various LIS experts and other material useful for LIS students and professionals; training: keeping in view the emerging trends and technological developments, PAKLAG is actively engaged in the capacity building and human resource development activities. PakLAG organized training on state of the art library tools and technologies including LIMS, Zebra Server, MarcEdit, Data Converter, Endnote, PakLAG Web OPAC and Digital Library Software and Greenstone. Many workshops, seminars, lectures, internships and short term attachments have been arranged for LIS professionals; professional lobs. PakLAG has been uploading job advertisements of professional posts. It covers job information appeared in national dailies, sent by employers and LIS professionals in Pakistan and abroad; PakLIS News. Pak-LIS News is the first online newsletter of the library profession published in Pakistan; Publication Program: A PhD dissertation has been published. Some software user manuals have also been electronically published on CD-ROM; Survey of ICT Training Needs: Conducted a survey of Pakistani librarians to design future training program. The results were published in an international journal

Publications PakLIS News (Newsletter, Frequency Irregular) Managing Editor Muhammad Ajmal Khan; Book: Aletrbative Funding Model for Libraries in Pakistan. Dr. Khalid Mahmood (2005), 400 p, hardback. ISBN 969-8885-00-5. Rs. 700

Bibliography A Study of the Usefulness of Pakistan Library Automation Group's (PakLAG) Services by Muhammad Ajmal Khan. Librarian, National University of Computer and Emerging Sciences, Lahore. Email: ajmal.khan@nu.edu.pk and Dr. Khalid Mahmood, Professor & Chairman, Department of Library & Information Science, University of the Punjab, Lahore. Email: khalid@dlis.pu.edu.pk (Accepted at Library Philosophy and Practice and it will be appeared in April 2010); Volunteer endeavors to promote ICT in a developing country: the case of the Pakistan Library Automation Group; Mahmood, K.; Khan, M.A.; Siddique, N. Information Development (2008), vol. 24 issue 2, p135–142; Pakistan Library Automation Group: A review of achievements [Electronic Version]; Khan, M. A. Pak-LIS News (2004); The Role of Mailing Groups in the Development of the Library Profession in Pakistan: the case of plagpk. Citation Only Available, by: Siddique, Nadeem; Mahmood, Khalid. Information Development, Aug 2009, vol. 25 issue 3, p218–223

Palestine

418 Palestinian Library and Information Association (PLIA)

Address c/o Hani W. Jaber, POB 007, Nablus Tel.: +972 9 2394983, Fax +972 9 2345982, plia@najah.edu

Officers Pres: Hani Jaber

Paraguay

419 Asociación de Bibliotecarios Graduados (ABGRA)
Address Campus Universitario, 1408 San Lorenzo Tel.: +595 21 585620, Fax +595 21 585546, info@abgra.org.ar
Languages Spanish

Peru

420 Colegio de Bibliotecólogos del Perú (CBP)
Address Av. Dos de Mayo 1545, Oficina 218, San Isidro, LIma Tel.: +51-1 442-7513, cbperu@cbperu.info; www.cbperu.info
Languages Spanish
Established 1990, Lima
Officers Pres: Norma Magan de Hurtado
General Assembly 79+42
Membership 232 individual members. Requirements: the title licenciado from a peruvian university
Sources of Support Membership dues
Major Goals and Objectives To disseminate the profession
Activities To defend the profession, to look for work, to organize congresses, seminaries, exhibitions, further education
Publications Official journal: Boletín Informativo del CBP. 1990- irr.

421 Colegio de Bibliotecologos del Peru
Address Av. Dos de Mayo 1545, Of. 218 Lima 27 cbperu@gmail.com
Languages Spanish
Officers Pres: Norma Málan de Hurtado

Philippines

422 Agricultural Librarians Association of the Philippines (ALAP)*
Address c/o University Library, College, Laguna Tel.: +63 49 5362326, Fax +63 63 49 4362326, asvaldez@uplb.edu.ph; www.alapph.blogspot.com
Languages Filipino, English
Established 1972, by librarians from the Association of Colleges of Agriculture in the Philippines (ACAP) as a national association for all types of agricultural librarians
Officers Pres: Conception DL. Saul; VP: Elaine E. Joshi; Secr: Andriette S. Valdez; Treas: Lina C. Copioso; Auditor: Imelda B. Veluz; PRO: Emeralda L. Lansangan
Staff None
General Assembly General Assembly once a year. June 5th, 2009, Main Library Bldg., University of the Philippines Los Baños, College, Laguna. June 4th, 2010, College of Engineering and Agro-Industrial Technology Library, UPLB, College, Laguna

Membership Total number of Members: 198. Type of Membership: individual. Requirements for Joining: librarian or information specialists or information provider or any information professionals in an institution dealing with agriculture, natural resources and related fields. Annual dues: P100.00 (US$ 2.25)
Structure Governed by executive officers. Affiliations: IAALD
Sources of Support Membership dues, projects
Major Fields of Interest Agricultural libraries and information services
Major Goals and Objectives (1) To promote understanding the nature, scope and importance of agricultural research libraries, (2) to promote better cooperation and coordination among member libraries, (3) to encourage professional interests and growth of agricultural librarianship, (4) to actively encourage the establishment and development of agricultural libraries and the improvement of their services, and (5) to enhance and uphold the dignity of the library profession and to observe professional ethics at all times
Activities ALAP has a Standing Committee on Conferences and Workshops, which organizes meetings and continuing education programs. Provides financial support to members in the conduct of their theses/dissertations and attendance to conferences. The Association also served as an instrument in the establishment of the Philippine Agricultural Libraries and Information Services Network (PhilAgriNet)
Publications No official journal. Publishes newsletter, ALAP News. Irreg
Bibliography Sacchanand, C, "Training Programs of Library Associations in the Philippines," Journal of Philippine Librarianship 7 (1983): 11–26; "Agricultural Libraries Association of the Philippines," Bulletin of the PLAI 16 (New Series) (1984): 138a-138f; Quiason, S., "Philippines," in ALA World Encyclopedia of Library and Information Services. 2nd ed., pp. 645–647. Chicago: American Library Association, 1986; Khurshid, A., "Library Associations in Asia," Herald of Library Science 28 (1989): 3–10

423 Association of Special Libraries of the Philippines (ASLP)

Address T.M. Kalaw St., 1000 Ermita, Manila Tel.: +63 2 552-6763; +63 2 552-6601 Local 3322, 3323, Fax +63 2 552-6855, luz.fsilib@yahoo.com
Languages Pilipino, English
Established 1954, Manila
General Assembly Entire membership meets once a year in Manila
Membership Individual members shall be professional librarians or college-degree holders, with at least eighteen (18) units in library or information science, and working in special libraries. Life members are limited to former and present members of the ASLP Board. Associate members are those working in special libraries without the required library or information science units
Structure The Board of Directors is composed of nine members and shall have the power and authority to manage the Association's property and to regulate and govern its affairs. The Board, with the exception of the president, shall elect from among themselves a vice-president and president-elect, a treasurer, an auditor and a P. R. O. The immediate past president shall automatically become an ex-officio member of the Board for the year following his/her term. The secretary shall be appointed by the president with the concurrence of the Board. All officers and members of the Board of the Board of Directors shall serve for a period of one year
Sources of Support Membership dues, sale of publications, donations

Major Fields of Interest Trends and issues relating to the library and information profession, with emphasis on various specialized fields of research

Major Goals and Objectives (a) To promote understanding of the nature, scope and importance of the work of special libraries. (b) To foster cooperation, fellowship, and closer relations among the Association's members. (c) To encourage the establishment of special libraries in the country, as well as to help librarians improve their services. (d) To stimulate professional growth of members through the Association's continuing education program. (e) To uphold the dignity of the library profession through the members' observance of professional ethics at all times

Activities Hold seminars, conferences, fora, workshops and other similar activities that will provide venue for sharing and exchange of ideas between the participants and the experts in the field of library and information science invited as resource speakers; undertake outreach programs for libraries and librarians that need support and guidance in organizing and setting up their libraries

Publications Official journal: ASLP Bulletin. 1954-. 4/yr. Free to members. Address same as Association. English. Indexed in LISA. Other publications: Annual reports, proceedings of conferences; Directory of Special Library Resources and Research Facilities in the Philippines, etc. Publications available for sale

Bibliography Sacchanand, C., "Training Programs of Library Associations in the Philippines," Journal of Philippine Librarianship 7 (1983):11–26; "Association of Special Libraries of the Philippines," Bulletin of the PLAI 16 (New Series) (1984):80–87; Quiason, S., "Philippines," in ALA World Encyclopedia of Library and Information Services. 2nd ed., pp. 645–647. Chicago: American Library Association, 1986; Khurshid, A., "Library Associations in Asia," Herald of Library Science 28 (1989):3–10

424 Medical and Health Librarians Association of the Philippines (MAHLAP)*

Address T.M. Kalaw St., Manila info@mahlap.org; www.mahlap.org

Languages English

Established 1988, Manila. The idea of organizing an association of medical and health librarians was conceived at the seminar-workshop on "Current Management Trends for Health Care Libraries," Cebu, 3–7 November 1986; MAHLAP was formed at the Department of Science and Technology (DOST), in May 1987 during an organizational meeting supported by Philippine Council for Health Research and Development

Officers Pres: Ma. Lutgarda M. Dorado; VP: Mark Bendo; Treas: Rita P. Yusi; Auditor: Ma. Lindie D. Masalinto; P.R.O.: Jeanette Z. Burillo

Membership More than 180 professionals and institutions in the health and medical field

Structure Governed by Board of Directors composed of 9 persons. Parent organization: Philippine Librarian's Association of the Philippines

Sources of Support Membership fees, sponsorships and sale of publications

Major Fields of Interest Medical and Health Librarianship; Health Information Management; Health/Medical Informatics

Major Goals and Objectives To encourage and promote the collection, organization, and dissemination of medical/health information and library service

Activities Conducts seminars, workshops, fora, symposia, lectures and medical missions. MAHLAP Union List, MAHLAP Net (proposal), MeSH training, ICD-10 training

Publications Official journal: MAHLAP Newsletter. 1988-; Other publications:

Directory of Medical and Health Libraries in the Philippines, 1988, 1991, 1996, 2000, 2005, 2008; Proceedings Series of MAHLAP seminars and workshops – 1988, 1989, 1990, 1991, 1992, 1993, 1994, 1995, 1996

425 Philippine Association of Academic and Research Librarians (PAARL)

Address   T.M. Kalaw St., Ermita 1000 Manila Tel.: +632 524 4611 local 640, Fax +632 524 8835; www.dlsu.edu.ph/library/paarl/default.asp
Languages   English
Established   1972, Manila
Staff   Volunteers
General Assembly   Entire membership meets once a year
Membership   Regular, Associate, Institutional and Honorary Members. Dues (Philippine Peso): 150, individual; 500, institutional
Structure   Governed by Board of Directors. Affiliations: PLAI (Philippine Library Association, Inc.)
Sources of Support   Membership dues, fund raising
Major Fields of Interest   Academic and research libraries
Major Goals and Objectives   Represents the librarians of institutions supporting scholarly, research and/or formal education on the collegiate level and above. The Association shall encourage and promote the collection, organization and dissemination of information on research and academic library work; develop the usefulness and efficiency of these types of library service and librarianship; enhance the professional welfare and mutual aide among its members; and cooperate with other organizations of similar aims
Activities   Holds conferences and seminar-workshops, forums and symposia for the Continuing Professional Education (CPE) requirements of licensed and non-licensed librarians; Awards granted for the following: Academic Librarian of the Year, Professional Service Award, Participation in the annual celebration of The National Book Week, November 24–30, Scholarships designed to assist academic or research librarians to acquire a master's degree in library science and fellowship awarded to graduate students engaged in thesis research and writing, Awards granted to two member-librarians to attend local or international conferences/seminars, Advocacy in promoting the interests of academic and research librarians and those of the association, Research activities and collaborative research projects, Participation in the annual Philippine Book Fair and other book fairs, Holding of an annual Fellowship Luncheon, anniversary celebrations, etc., Fund-raising activities for the association's projects, Networking activities among institutional member-libraries in the area of interlending, document- delivery and other resource-sharing projects
Publications   Official journal: PAARL Newsletter. 1973-. 4/yr. Free to members. Address same as Association. Circ: Membership. English. Indexed in Index to Philippine Periodicals. Other publications: Annual reports, proceedings of conferences, workshops, seminars; PAARL Directory, etc. Publications available for sale. Publications exchange program in effect with libraries
Bibliography   Sacchanand, C, "Training Programs of Library Associations in the Philippines," Journal of Philippine Librarianship 7 (1983): 11–26; "Philippine Association of Academic and Research Libraries," Bulletin of the PLAI 16 (New Series) (1984):124–126; Quiason, S., "Philippines," in ALA World Encyclopedia of Library and

Information Services. 2nd ed., pp. 645–647. Chicago: American Library Association, 1986; Khurshid, A., "Library Associations in Asia," Herald of Library Science 28 (1989):3–10

426 Philippine Association of School Librarians (PASL)

Address c/o PLAI, T.M. Kalaw St., Ermita, 2801 Manila Tel.: +63 523 0068, Fax +63 525-9401
Languages English
Established 1977, Quezon City, at the Thomas Jefferson Cultural Center, at the end of a seminar on current trends in school librarianship
General Assembly Entire membership meets once a year in May
Membership Requirements: Individual: College degree with credits in library science and/or working in a school library; Institutional: Firms, agencies, and/or institutions interested in school librarianship.
Structure Governed by Executive Committee
Sources of Support Membership dues, private donations
Major Fields of Interest School librarianship
Major Goals and Objectives The main objectives of the association are: to encourage the creation of school libraries throughout the country especially in rural areas; to foster and maintain among its members high ideals of integrity, learning, professional competence, public service and conduct; to encourage and foster a continuing program of library education and research and make recommendations; and, to provide a forum for the discussion of school librarianship, library reforms, and relations of librarians to other professions and to the public
Activities Carried out under the guidance of a Committee on Professional Development. Sponsors seminars, conferences, workshops and other continuing education programs, as well as in-service training to upgrade skills of school librarians and to make them aware of current trends in school librarianship; organizing of regional chapters (10 possible regions). Active in promoting library-related legislation. Sponsors Book Week, exhibits
Publications No publications program
Bibliography Sacchanand, C., "Training Programs of Library Associations in the Philippines," Journal of Philippine Librarianship 7 (1983): 11–26

427 Philippine Association of Teachers of Library Science (PATLS)

Address 3/F Gonzales Hall, UP Main Library, UP Diliman, 1101 Diliman, Quezon City Tel.: +981 85-00 loc. 2869; www.patls.org
Languages English
Established 1964, Manila
General Assembly Entire membership meets once a year
Membership Types of membership: Individual. Requirements: Any librarian or other professional who is teaching or has taught library and information science.
Structure Governed by Executive Board. Affiliations: PLAI
Sources of Support Membership dues, sale of publications, income from training seminars and other fund-raising activities. Budget (Philippine Peso): 1986/87: 40,000; 1987/88: 50,000

Major Fields of Interest Library and information science education; teaching and training

Major Goals and Objectives To improve library education in the Philippines; to initiate and promote cooperative programs in education for librarianship among schools in the Philippines; to plan and implement a program for the accreditation of library schools; to provide a forum for discussion and publication of issues, trends, and other matters in library education

Activities Past achievements: (1) Seminars and workshops on new trends and techniques in teaching library science courses; (2) Participation in the IFLA Working Committees during IFLA Conference held in Manila, 1980; (3) Revision of the undergraduate library science curriculum and publication of Syllabi of Library Science Courses for use by all library science schools in the Philippines; (4) Publication of Directory of Teachers of Library Science; (5) Organized CONSAL VII in the Philippines in 1987. Current: Seminar on methods and techniques in teaching cataloging and reference; attracting more library science education students. Future: To actively participate in the library networking activities of the Philippine Library Association, Inc. Association has been active in promoting library-related legislation; it co-sponsored the proposed legislation for the professional status of librarians in the country. Sponsors Book Week, exhibits, continuing education programs, and standardization of the library science curriculum for undergraduate programs

Publications Official journal: PATLS Newsletter. 1976-. Irreg. Free to members. Circ: Membership. English. Other publications: The Annual National Book Week Program

Bibliography Retrospective sources: Agcaoili, C, "The Philippine Association of Teachers of Library Science and Its Objectives," Bulletin of the PLAI 1 (June 1965); Mercado-Tan, E, "Philippine librarianship: The Present and the Future," Bulletin of the PLAI 12 (1978–79): Nos. 1–4; "Philippine Association of Teachers of Library Science," Bulletin of the PLAI 16 (New Series) (1984):126–130; Khurshid, A., "Library Associations in Asia," Herald of Library Science 28 (1989):3–10

428 Philippine Group of Law Librarians, Inc. (PGLL)

Address Bldg.T. M. Kalaw Street, Ermita Manila Tel.: +63 2 5249740, pgll.org@gmail.com

Established 1980

Major Fields of Interest Law libraries

Activities Seminars

429 Philippine Library Association, Inc., Headquarters (PLAI)

Address c/o Lourdes C. Roman, Secretary, T. M. Kalaw Street, Room 301, Ermita Manila Tel.: +63 523 0068, lilia.echiverri@up.edu.ph; http://www.dlsu.edu.ph/library/plai/index.htm#DIRECT

Languages English

Established 1923, by 32 librarians, in Manila

Officers Pres: Lilia F. Echiverri

General Assembly Entire membership meets once a year

Membership Total members: Approx. 1,000

Structure Governed by a House of Delegates. Affiliations: IFLA, CONSAL

Sources of Support Membership dues
Major Fields of Interest Library and information services
Major Goals and Objectives To uphold the dignity and ethics of the library profession as well as of library service at high professional levels; to promote the establishment of libraries throughout the country; to promote cooperation, cordiality and fellowship among librarians; to encourage continuing programs of library education and research; to establish and encourage professional contacts among librarians in the Philippines and with other countries
Activities The PLAI functions as umbrella organization for all professional library associations in the country (about 28), and represents Philippine librarianship at IFLA (sponsored the 1980 IFLA Conference in Manila). Association plays an important role in organizing and conducting regular training programs, seminars, workshops, conferences, etc., at the local, regional and national levels, and is instrumental in promoting and developing library science and librarianship throughout the country
Publications Official journal: Bulletin of the Philippine Library Association. Inc., 4/yr. Free to members. English. Indexed in Ind.Phil.Per., Other publications: Newsletter; annual reports, proceedings of meetings, etc
Bibliography Sacchanand, C., "Training Programs of Library Associations in the Philippines," Journal of Philippine Librarianship 7 (1983):11–16; Vallejo, R.M., ed., "The PLAI: Its Involvement and Commitment. Diamond Anniversary Issue, 1923–1983," Bulletin of the Philippine Library Association. Inc. 16 (New Series) (1984) Nos. 1–2; Quiason, S.D., "Philippines," in ALA World Encyclopedia of Library and Information Services. 2nd ed., pp. 645–647. Chicago: American Library Association, 1986; Khurshid, A., "Library Associations in Asia," Herald of Library Science 28 (1989):3–10

430 Philippine Public Librarians League, Inc. (PPLL)

Address c/o PLAI Headquarters, T. M. Kalaw Street, Manila pgll.org@gmail.com
Languages English
Established 1959, at the Bureau of Public Libraries, Manila, by Laureana Villanueva, Chief of the Extension Division of the National Library
General Assembly Entire membership meets once a year
Membership Public librarians (civil servants) at all levels
Major Fields of Interest Public library services
Major Goals and Objectives To promote public library services, to promote unity and cooperation among public librarians, to know and understand their library problems, and to provide for a meaningful interchange of ideas among members
Activities Conducts Librarians' Conference-Workshops with the National Library every 2 years
Publications No publications program
Bibliography Sacchanand, C., "Training Programs of Library Associations in the Philippines," Journal of Philippine Librarianship 7 (1983):11–26; "Public Libraries Association of the Philippines," Bulletin of the PLAI 16 (New Series) (1984):130–134; Khurshid, A., "Library Associations in Asia," Herald of library Science 28 (1989):3–10

431 Society of Filipino Archivists, Inc

Address U.P. Diliman P. O. Box 171, Quezon City Tel.: +63 2 920 9060, Fax +63 2 920

6773; www.sfaonline.sphosting.com
Established 1991
Membership Institutional and individual membership. Requirements: Open to archivists, records officers/personnel, librarians and other personnel working in: Academic archives, Business and corporate archives, Government archives, Hospitals and medical archives, Religious and ecclesiastical archives, Personal and private archives, Audiovisual and film archives. Dues (Philippine Pesos): 100.00, individuals; 200.00 for institutions
Major Fields of Interest Committed to the advancement of the archives and records management profession
Major Goals and Objectives To promote and advance archives administration through education, research and study; To disseminate professional knowledge and techniques through national and international sharing of experience and knowledge related to archives administration; To develop, improve and advance standards appropriate to archives administration; To establish and maintain communication and cooperation among archivists, the institutions in which they work, and archives users; To promote the adoption of sound principles and standards by all agencies, public and private, that have responsibility for the preservation and administration of archival materials; To maintain and strengthen relations with records managers, historians, librarians, educators and others in allied disciplines; To cooperate with other professional organizations, cultural, educational and religious institutions having mutual interests in the preservation and use of cultural treasures/heritage; to purchase, lease, own, hold, acquire, or otherwise accept such property, real or personal, as may be necessary, convinient or appropriate to serve the purposes herein expressed
Activities Training courses for archivists, records managers, librarians and other information specialists

Poland

432 Polskie Towarzystwo Informacji Naukowej (Polish Society of Scientific Information)

Address Plac Sejmu Sląskiego 1, pokój 311, 40-032 Katowice uranos.cto.us.edu.pl/~ptin/
Languages Polish

433 Stowarzyszenie Archivistów Polskich (SAP) (Association of Polish Archivists)

Address c/o Zarzad Glówny, ul. Bonifraterska 6 lok. 21, 00213 Warsaw Tel.: +48 22 6358768, Fax +48 22 8313171, sap@sap.waw.pl; www.sap.waw.pl
Languages Polish
Established 1965
General Assembly Entire membership meets once a year
Membership Total members: Approx. 800
Structure Governed by executive officers
Sources of Support Membership dues
Major Fields of Interest Archives and records management

Major Goals and Objectives To promote the development of archives in Poland; to promote the profession of archivists; to represent the professional interests of archivists
Activities Sponsors conferences, workshops, continuing education programs
Publications Official journal: Archiwista. Free to members. Address same as Association. Circ: Membership. Polish. Other publications: Materialy Szkoleniowe

434 Stowarzyszenie Bibliotekarzy Polskich (SBP; PLA) (Polish Librarians Association)

Address al. Niepodleglosci 213, 02086 Warsaw   Tel.: +48 22 8258374, Fax +48 22 8255349, e.stefanczyk@bn.org.pl; ebib.oss.wroc.pl/sbp/
Languages Polish, English, Russian
Established 1917, Warsaw, as Union of Polish Librarians and Archivists; present name adopted 1953
Officers Pres: Elzbieta Stefanczyk
Staff 12 persons paid: 1. The PLA General Board Office, al. Niepodleglosci 213, 02086 Warsaw. Phone number: +48 22 8258374, +48 22 8259705. Dir: Mieczyslaw Szyszko. 2. The PLA Publishing House, ul. Konopczynskiego 3/5, 00335 Warsaw. Phone number: +48 22 8270847
Membership Total members: 8,300 (individual). Types of membership: Individual, emeritus. Requirements: Employment in library or information center; employment in library school or in offices connected with librarianship. Dues: Individual, scaled according to salary; supporting membership for institutions or organizations
Structure Governed by Executive Council and Executive Board. A Conference of Delegates meets every 4 years. Affiliations: IFLA
Sources of Support Membership dues, sale of publications; government subsidies only when needed
Major Fields of Interest Library and information services
Major Goals and Objectives To participate in legislative work relating to libraries and information resources; to foster and encourage research interests and professional development of its members; to represent librarians' opinions to the authorities, central administration, local government and other organizations and associations; to promote the humanist tradition of Polish culture; to contribute to the preservation and promotion of Polish and world literature; to foster high-profile publications market and public access to the books; to advocate activities for the sake of integration of the total librarians community
Activities publications; cooperation with the Ministry of Culture, National Library, science libraries, public libraries and related associations working among the librarians
Publications Official journal: Przeglad Biblioteczny (Library Review). 1927-. 4/yr. Editor: Barbara Sosinska-Kalata. Address: Konopczynskiego 5/7, PL-00335 Warsaw. Circ: 750+. Polish, with English summaries. Other publications: Bibliotekarz (The Librarian), 1934-. 12/yr.; Poradnik Bibliotekarza (Librarian's Advisor), 12/yr.; Zagadnienia Informacji Naukowej (Science Information Issues), 2/yr

435 Towarzystwa Nauczycieli Bibliotekarzy Szkól Polskich

Address ul. Nowy Swiat 21 A, 00-029 Warszawa   Tel.: +48 22 8264785, Fax +48 22 8264785; www.tnbsp.prv.pl

Languages Polish
Established 1992
Major Goals and Objectives to active participation in creating proper conditions for school libraries' activities, to integration of the teachers librarians' professional circles, to protection of professional interests of teachers librarians, activities for raising the prestige of school libraries and teachers librarians, formation of a creative professional attitude, supporting librarians' pprofessional development

Portugal

436 Associação Portuguesa de Documentação e Informação de Saúde (APDIS)

Address c/o Secretariado, Av. República - EAN, 2784-505 Oeiras Fax +351 214 407 972, secretariado@apdis.org; www.apdis.org(onlyPortuguese)
Languages Portuguese
Established 1991
General Assembly Pres: Maria do Rosário Gonzalez Barbosa Leitão; Sec: Orísia Maria da Silva Martins Pereira and Rosa Margarida Umbelino
Membership Associates can be staff professionals and institutional members interested in the goals of the association. 150 members to date
Structure Board of Directors, Financial Council and General Assembly
Sources of Support Membership fees, revenue from publications
Major Fields of Interest Development of documentation and information of health in Portugal and articulation with national systems on international systems
Major Goals and Objectives To contribute to the development of health care, resear and development; to teach professionals
Activities Workshops, teaching, work groups for indexing, promotion of quality, etc
Publications Lista de Publicações Periódicas existentes em Bibliotecas e Serviços de Documentação da área da Saúde em Portugal, last ed. 2004

Puerto Rico

437 Sociedad de Bibliotecarios de Puerto Rico (SBPR) (Puerto Rico Librarians Society)

Address P.O. Box 22898, Rio Piedras, PR 00931-2898 Tel.: +1809 787 7640000, ext. 7395, Fax +1809 787 7721479, ivan@calimano.org
Languages Spanish, English
Established 1961, at the University of Puerto Rico by a group of librarians interested in problems related to the profession
Officers Pres: Ivan Calimano
Staff None
General Assembly Entire membership meets twice a year in San Juan
Membership 400 members. Types of membership: Individual, institutional, student, honorary. Requirements: Master or Bachelor degree in library/Information Science, information professionals, or full-time library science students.

Structure Governed by executive officers. Affiliations: ACURIL, ALA, IFLA
Sources of Support Membership dues
Major Fields of Interest Librarianship, information science
Major Goals and Objectives To advance the cause of librarians in Puerto Rico; to gain recognition for the profession; to improve qualifications of members; to recruit the best talent available for the profession; to provide opportunities for professional development of individual members
Activities Was instrumental in the establishment of the Graduate School of Librarianship at the University of Puerto Rico. Continues working for the improvement of library and information services in Puerto Rico. Active in promoting library-related legislation. Sponsors conferences, seminars, and other continuing education programs
Publications Official journal: Acceso: revista puertoriqueña de bibliotecología y documentacion. 1999-. Free to members. Address same as Association. Circ: 400. Spanish, English. Indexed in Latindex. Newsletter: Informa, irregular. Other publications: Cuadernos Bibliotecologicos; Cuadernos Bibliograficos; etc. Publications for sale. Publications exchange program in effect with other library associations and libraries
Bibliography Ortiz, O.R., and Delgado, R.R., "Puerto Rico," in ALA World Encyclopedia of Library and Information Services. 2nd ed., pp. 685–687. Chicago: American Library Association, 1986

Romania

438 Asociatia Bibliotecarilor din România (ABR) (Romanian Library Association)*

Address Str. Boteanu nr. 1, sector 1, 010027 Bucuresti Tel.: +40 21 3123205, Fax +40 21 3120108, infoabr@gmail.com; www.abr.org.ro
Languages Romanian, English
Established 1990, Bucharest
Officers Pres: Mircea Regneala; VP: Adriana Szekely; Mihaela Zecheru; Gabriela Dumitrescu; Liliane Lazia; Valentina Lupu; Secr Gen: Robert Coravu; Corina Apostoleanu
Staff 2/2
General Assembly Once a year. 19–21 September 2007, Brasov; 17–19 September 2008, Pitesti; 10–12 September 2009, Constanta; 9 – 11 September 2010, Bucharest; 2011, Sibiu
Membership Total members: Approx. 2500 (individual and institutional). Departamental branches; various committees (cataloging&indexing, statistics, information literacy, reference services, automation, prezervation, library legislation, manuscripts and rare books etc.). Types of membership: Individual/Institutional
Structure Governed by executive officers. Affiliations: IFLA
Sources of Support Membership dues, sales of publications, sponsorships
Major Fields of Interest Library profession and status of library workers
Major Goals and Objectives To promote libraries and library services in Romania; to further the professional development of librarians
Publications Official journals: Revista Romana de Biblioteconomie si Stiinta Informarii/Romanian Review of Library and Information Science (2005-). 4/yr. 60

RON/15 EURO/yr. Director: Mircea Regneala, editor-in-chief Robert Coravu. Languages: Romanian (2005–2009), Romanian&English (from 2010). Other publications: Proceedings of conferences, seminars, and other professional monographs. Publications for sale. Active in promoting library-related legislation. Represents Romanian librarians at international activities

439 Asociatia Generala a Arhivistilor din Romania
(General Association of the Romanian Archivists)

Address B-dul Elisabeta, 49, 70602 Bucarest Tel.: +40 1 2229630, Fax +40 1 3125841
Languages Romanian

440 Biblioteca Metropolitan Bucaresti (BMB)
(Metropolitan Library of Bucharest)*

Address Take Ionescu Street, no. 4, sector 1, 010352 Bucharest Tel.: +4 021 3167300, Fax +4 021 3163625, florinrotaru@bmnms.ro; www.bmms.ro
Languages Romanian
Established 1831, Bucharest
Officers Gen Dir: Florin Rotaru
General Assembly Four times a year
Membership 222 members
Structure Executive Leadership, Consultance, Professional Personal and Adminsitrative Personal
Sources of Support The BMB is financed by the Bucharest City Hall but can also receive Finance through cultural programs, sponsorship
Major Fields of Interest Public Reading
Major Goals and Objectives Information, Documentation, Training, Research
Activities The BMB's main purpose is to organize the Public Library Service in Bucharest and in the ILvof District. Also this Library organizes the legal Depository and provides information and assistance for the RCEF of the Libraries in the country. Designer and Organizer of the National Digital Library of Romania
Publications Biblioteca Bucurestilor (monthly); the Literatorul-Review (monthly); The Journal of the French Libraries (Romanian version); The Yearbook of the internationsal Symposium "Book Romania Empore"

441 National Association of Public Libraries and Librarians in Romania (ANBPR)*

Address 15 Dr. Staicovici D. Nicolae Street, District 5, 050556 Bucharest Tel.: +40 21 4110277, anbpr_ro@yahoo.com; www.anbpr.org.ro
Languages Romanian
Established March 19, 1990, Bucharest, on the founders' initiative
Officers Pres: Popa Doina; Senior Deputy-Pres: Dragos Adrian Neagu; Deputy-Pres: Liviu Iulian Dediu; Sorin Burlacu; Gen Secr: Silvia Nestorescu
Staff Paid – only 2 – Operational Department staff. Voluntary – 11 members of the Executive Board
General Assembly The General Assembly has two annual meetings and every time it is required

Membership ANBPR has a total number of 3317 active members, legal and individual entities. ANBPR activity is based, in most of the cases, on the voluntary work of its members. The Association members are professional librarians with different specializations in librarianship, with a rich professional experience. Through their adherence to the goals and the mission of ANBPR, they are represented and supported, at an organizational level, according to the interests and the needs of this branch. ANBPR has the following categories of members: a) active members, individuals and legal entities interested in the objectives of the Association, which require the membership and act in accordance with the Statute; b) honorary members, persons form the country and abroad who have merits particulary in the fields of culture, science and art; c)Patron members, individual or legal persons who through their acts of patronage support in different forms,the Association objectives. New members can join the Association by writing a request to the Executive Board of the Branch were they are located (individuals) or to the Executive Board of the Association (legal persons). The members of the Board are the ones who approve the request of the new members with a simple majority of votes. The annual fee is 15 RON

Structure ANBPR has been concerned with its international recognition, establishing cooperative relationships with professional associations from United States of America (ALA) and Europe (IFLA and EBLIDA). ANBPR is member of IFLA since 2009. Currently, ANBPR collaborates also with some professional associations from Poland, Moldavia Republic and Bulgaria

Sources of Support The National Association of Public Libraries and Librarians in Romania is financed trough membership fees, tax participation at the Annual Conference of the Association and sponsorship.Since July 2009, ANBPR benefits, for a period of 4 years, by a grant

Major Fields of Interest Public libraries

Major Goals and Objectives Aims to involve all its valuable members into the strengthening and refining of the policy of the Association; to bring together thee public librarians of Romania and to promote the crucial role of the library in the community

Activities For the future, ANBPR aims to determine the development and optimization of the library services and librarianship profession. The Association, also, wants to promote the best practices in the librarianship field. The main directions of the ANBPR activity are the following: to organize training courses in the librarianship field as a partner of authorized institutions; to translate and publish books and directories of specialty; to organize conferences and symposium for solving the major problems of the librarianship professionals; to contribute to the development of legal norms which statuettes the librarianship profession; to vary the services offered by public libraries; to stimulate librarians to value their human and professional potential; to improve the social status of the librarian, in order to obtain higher material and social rights for this profession

Publications Newsletter BiblioMAGAZIN, which is delivered for free to all its member contacts. Is a quarterly publication, which first appeared in December 2009. Editor: Dr. Liviu-Iulian Dediu

Russia

442 Council of PCLI Programme Coordinators *
Address P.O.B. 44, 121096 Moscow pcpi@ifap.ru; www.ifap.ru/pcpi
Languages Russian
Established April 21st, 2008, Moscow
Officers Chair: Alexei Demidov; Secr: Irina Komarova; Exec Off of Dep of Educ Technologie: Ekaterina Ignatova; Deputy PR-officer: Igor Andreev
Staff 0/5
General Assembly Annual, last: November 24, 2009; next: to be assigned
Membership Approx 1,350 institutional members, 0 individuals. 3 regional divisions. Free membership, no special requirements
Structure Affilations: Garant Co., Ltd., Consultant Plus Co., Ltd., Civil Club. Parent organization: ICO "Information for All"
Sources of Support ICO "Information for All"
Major Fields of Interest Public access to the socially-significant information (e.g. legal, governmental, consumer, ecological, etc.)
Major Goals and Objectives Coordination for the contry-wide network of Pulic Centers of Socially-Significant Information
Activities Publishing the methodical, informational, analytical, etc. papers
Publications Monthly e-newsletter "PCLI Programme Newsletter". Founded in 2008, free of charge. Editor-in-Chief: Eugene Altovsky. Russian. Approx 1,500 subscribers. Annual report of the PCLI Programme. Recent publications: 2010 Report "Authorities' Websites in the Light of requirements set by Federal Law "On Ensuring Access to the Information on Activity of the Federal and Municipal Authorities". 2009 Articles Collection "10 Years of the PCLI Programme: Advances and Perspectives"; Booklet "Observatory of the Information Society: Russian Segment. The Start Point" (2009 revised issue); Booklet "How to Develop a Website Friendly for Visually Impaired Persons?"; Booklet "PCLI Programme" (2009 revised edition); Booklet "How the Visually Impaired Persons Accessed the Websites: What Other Persons Should to Know?" etc.

443 Rossiiskaya Bibliotechnaya Assotsiatsiya (RBA, RLA) (Russian Library Association)
Address 18, Sadovaya st, St. Petersburg 191069 Tel.: + 7 812 1188536, Fax + 7 812 1105861, rba@nlr.ru; www.rba.ru:8101
Languages Russian
Established 1994
Officers Pres: Vladimir N. Zaitsev; Exec Secr: Dr. Maya Shaparneva
Staff Headquarters: 5 (2 paid, 3 volunteers)
General Assembly Annual conference
Membership 462 members (11 associations, 451 institutions)
Structure Governed by Board. 35 Sections. Type of library sections: 01. Section of Regional Universal Research/Public Libraries, 02. Section of Art Libraries, 03. Section of Invalid Servicing Libraries, 04. Section of University Libraries, 13. Section of Medical and Hospital Libraries, 14. Section of Public Libraries, 15. Section of Musical Libraries, 16.

Section of Children Libraries, 17. Section of National Libraries (Subjects of Russian Federation), 19. Section of School Libraries, 22. Section of Agricultural Libraries, 26. Section of Rural Libraries, 33. Section of Junior Libraries, 35. Section of Science and Technology Libraries. Type of activity sections: 05. Section on Library Policy and Legislative Activity, 06. Section on Preservation and Conservation, 07. Section on Library History, 08./11. Sections on Library Automation, Formats and Cataloguing, 23-K. Interregional Committee for Cataloguing, 09. Section on Library Personnel Resources and Continued Professional Education, 10. Round Table on Librarian Communication and Professional Ethics, 12. Section on Acquisition and Collection Development, 18. Round Table on Management of Library Associations and Societies, 20. Section on Local Library Studies, 21. Section on Electronic Resources and Library Information Services, 24. Section on Bibliography, 25-K. Russian Committee on the IFLA, 27. Section on "New Generation of Librarians", 28. Section on International Contacts, 29. Section on Publishing and Bookselling, 30. Round Table on Reading, 31. Section on Research Work, 32. Section on Library management and Marketing, 34. Section on Rare Books and Manuscripts, 35. Section on Document Delivery and Interlending. Affiliation: IFLA
Major Fields of Interest   Libraries and Librarianship
Major Goals and Objectives   Consolidation, support and coordinating of libraries, library associations and schools activities; Representation and defense of librarians; Increment of the social status and prestige of the library profession; Defense of library user's rights
Activities   Library legislation improvement; Research work in library and information science field; Implementation the research results in practice; Library education. Core Programs: Creation the National Format of bibliographic records in machine-readable form for Russian libraries (RUSMARC; National Program for Library Collections Preservation; Preservation and Access to Newspapers
Publications   Official journal: RLA Information Bulletin. Contact: Dr. Maya Shaparneva. Address same as Association

444   Russian School Libraries Association

Address   Moscow 109012 s-bibl@mail.ru

445   Russian Society of Historians and Archivists

Address   12 Il'inka Ulitsa, 103132 Moscow Tel.: +7 95 3348297, Fax +7 95 3348297
Languages   Russian
Structure   Affiliations: SPA, EURASICA

Samoa

446   Library Association of Samoa (LAS)

Address   c/o NUS Library, Papaigalagala Campus, Toomatagi St., P.O.Box 1622, Apia Tel.: +685 2007 Ext. 166, Fax +685 22440, library@nus.edu.ws; www.nus.edu.ws
Languages   Samoan, English
Established   1986; revived 2001
Staff   All volunteers

General Assembly Entire membership meets once a year
Membership Total members: 21, representatives of special libraries and institutions
Structure Governed by executive officers. Affiliations: COMLA, Fiji Library Association (FLA), LIANZA (New Zealand), PIALA
Sources of Support Membership dues
Major Fields of Interest Libraries and library services, funding for associations, free subscription services and book donations from wealthy donors and international agencies
Major Goals and Objectives To promote library services in Western Samoa as well as to develop collections and preserving them
Activities Organizing conferences, workshops, training courses (with assistance from Unesco). There is now a LAP (Libraries of Asia in the Pacific) directory compiled by ANU. Book drives, Net Day and other promotional activities with schools
Publications Official journal: Library Association of Samoa Newsletter. Togi A. Tunupopo, c/o NUS Library
Bibliography "Library Association of W. Samoa," In: COMLA Newsletter 55 (Mar. 1987), p. 7; Article in the Fiji Library Association Newsletter, Dec. 2000; Tunupopo, A. Togi: 2000. Library Education in Samoa: Developing Collections and Library Services for the Twenty First Century (chpt. 11). In: Measina a Samoa 2000: Papers presented to the Measina a Samoa 2000 and beyond Conference 11.–14. December, Lepapaigalagala National University of Samoa, Apia. 2001 (ISBN 982 9003 167)

Senegal

447 Association Sénégalaise des Bibliothécaires, Archivistes et Documentalistes (ASBAD)
(Senegal Association of Librarians, Archivists and Documentalists)

Address c/o EBAD-UCAD, BP 3252, Dakar Tel.: +221 8642773, Fax +221 8242379; http://www.ebad.ucad.sn/sites_heberges/asbad
Languages French
Established July 9,1988. Dakar, at EBAD, through the merger of 2 professional associations in Senegal, ANABADS and ASDBAM
Officers Pres: Djibril Ndiaye; VP: Khady Kane Touré; Secr Gen: Bernard Dione; Treas: Oumar Guèye
General Assembly Entire membership meets twice a year
Membership Members are the combined membership of the former associations ANABADS and ASDBAM. Regional Branches. Committees: 7 (Archives, Libraries, Documentation, Statutes and Education, Social and Cultural Affairs, Finance, Public Information). Types of membership: Individual, associate, honorary, institutional. Requirements: Individual: Persons engaged in professional work in libraries, archives, or documentation centers; Associate: Persons interested in the development of libraries, archives, and documentation centers, and in the promotion of reading and culture; Institutional: Any institution supporting the goals and objectives of the Association. All subject to payment of membership dues, which are regularly set by Council. No dues for honorary members, who are elected by the Congress

Structure Governed by Congress and National Council, consisting of Executive Board and representatives of the Regional Branches and Committees. Affiliations: IFLA
Sources of Support Membership dues, various subsidies
Major Fields of Interest Libraries, archives, and documentation services
Major Goals and Objectives (1) To unify librarians, archivists and documentaliste and all those interested in libraries, archives and other centers of documentation; (2) to study all questions of a scientific, technical or administrative nature concerning libraries, archives, documentation centers and their staff; (3) to promote the development of libraries, archives and documentation centers; (4) to encourage scientific research
Activities By unifying the financial and personnel resources in the country, the Association hopes to become a strong national voice for the improvement of libraries, archives and documentation centers. It recognized the contributions of the following professionals by electing them to honorary membership at the constitutional congress in 1988: Amadou Mactar Mbow (Honorary President), Amadou Bousso, Samba Ndoucoumane Gueye, Emmanuel Dadzie, Raphaël Ndiaye, Saliou Mbaye, Théodore Ndiaye. The Association functions as the single representative of Senegal at IFLA
Bibliography "Procès Verbal du Congrès Constitutif de l'Association Sénégalaise des Bibliothécaires, Archivistes et Documentalistes (ASBAD), tenu à Dakar le 9 Juillet 1988." 3 pp. Typescript; ASBAD, "Statuts." Dakar, 9 July 1988. 5 pp. Typescript

Serbia

448 Bibliotekarsko društvo Srbijé (SLA) (Society of Serbian Librarians)*

Address Skerliceva 1, 11000 Beograd Tel.: +381 18 532 816, Fax +381 18 532 816, crvesna@sezampro.yu; www.bds.rs
Languages Serbian, English
Established 14.12.1947, Belgrade
Officers Pres: Zeljko Vuckovic; VP: Jasmina Ninkow; Secr: Vesna Crnogorac
Staff 1 Secretary (paid)
General Assembly Two regular assemblies per year, every February and December. On December 14th, the celebration of the Librarians Day
Membership 1752 individual members. 15 divisions and 6 sections
Structure Assembly (100 members), Executive Board (15 members), Supervising Board (3 members). Related organizations in the country: The Parent Library Community of Serbia, Serbian Academic Library Association – we cooperation in preparing the new law, the promulgation of standards and alike.
Sources of Support Association is financed through membership dues and through different mechanisms such as projects and donations
Major Fields of Interest Library and information services, education and training
Major Goals and Objectives Association's goal and objective is to gather and connect library staff, in order to realize and protect their professional, social and financial interests. The Association gathers in a unique professional organization the employees and other individuals who are in any way involved in or contribute to the development of library and information profession. The Association was established to promote and improve library

profession in Serbia, as well as protect the integrity of the professional staff in library and information services.

Activities Preparation of a new issue of the journal; prepares the annual international scientific conferences;participation in the committee for drafting a new Library Law (Commission of the Ministry of Culture); work on passing the new Statute of Association; the expansion of the membership of the Association and other current activities. Quality performance and the improvement of library and information services; permanent education and training; encouragement of theoretical development of library and information science; promotion of library services to the public; stimulation of creative work by awards and other forms of motivation; publication of professional literature; cooperation with related or similar organizations at home and abroad; participation in the preparation of laws and other normative acts and standards; protection of professional ethics in library activities; efforts to protect the professional integrity of staff in library and information services; participation in the international library and information organizations, programs and projects

Publications BIBLIOTEKAR (Librarian) – journal for the theory and practice of librarianship, published since 1948. Published regularly until 1997. Wasn't published from 1997 to 2006. Re-issued in 2006 and since then has been published in continuity with the support of the Ministry of Culture of the Republic of Serbia. Published four times a year. Since 2010 it will be published twice a year. Waiting for the decision by the Ministry of Science that it a scientific journal. For now, it is not for sale. There is a plan to sell it

449   Parent Library Community of Serbia

Address   Skerliceva 1, 11000 Beograd
Officers   Pres: Sreten Ugricic

Sierra Leone

450   Sierra Leone Association of Archivists, Librarians and Information Scientists (SLAALIS)

Address   c/o COMAHS Library New England, Freetown   Tel.: +232 22 220758
Languages   English
Established   1970, as Sierra Leone Library Association (SLLA); present name adopted to reflect the expansion in membership and fields of interest
Staff   None
General Assembly   Entire membership meets 3 times a year
Membership   Types of membership: Individual, institutional, honorary. Requirements: An interest in libraries, archives, and information science
Structure   Governed by Executive Council. Affiliations: COMLA, IFLA
Sources of Support   Membership dues, sale of publications, government subsidies
Major Fields of Interest   Libraries, archives, and information centers
Major Goals and Objectives   To promote the development of libraries, archives and information services in Sierra Leone; to represent the interests of members and further their professional development
Activities   Works for the improvement and development of libraries, archives, and

information services in Sierra Leone, concentrating on rural libraries and resource centers. Sponsors continuing education workshops, seminars, etc
Publications   Official journal: Sierra Leone library Journal. 1974-. 2/yr. Free to members. Address same as Association. English. Indexed in LISA. Other publications: Directory of Libraries and Information Services; annual reports, proceedings of meetings, seminars. Publications for sale
Bibliography   Jusu-Sheriff, G.M., "Sierra Leone," in ALA World Encyclopedia of Library and Information Services. 2nd ed., pp. 764–765. Chicago: American Library Association, 1986

Singapore

451   Library Association of Singapore (LAS)

Address   100 Victoria Street, #14-00, Singapore   Tel.: +65 6749 7990, Fax +65 6749 7480, president@las.org.sg
Languages   English, Chinese, Malay
Established   1955, as the Malayan Library Group; when Singapore became an independent republic in 1965, it divided into two associations, the Library Association of Malaysia, and the Library Association of Singapore; in 1972, the English name was adopted as the official one
Officers   Pres: Puspa Yeow
Staff   None
General Assembly   Entire membership meets annually in Singapore, in March
Membership   Types of membership: Individual, institutional, life, honorary, associate, teacher-librarian. Requirements: Open to professional librarians, those engaged in full-time library work, teacher librarians, interested persons not in the library field, libraries, and institutions interested in the aims of the Association. Dues vary to the monthly income earned
Structure   Governed by Executive Council. Affiliations: COMLA, CONSAL, IFLA
Sources of Support   Membership dues, sale of publications
Major Fields of Interest   Librarianship and library development, education for librarianship, professional conduct and ethics
Major Goals and Objectives   To unite and promote the interests of all those interested in Singapore libraries and those actively engaged in library work; to encourage the establishment and development of libraries, library administration, and the professional education of librarians; to publish information that will prove of service to members
Activities   Sponsors seminars, celebration of Book Week, exhibits, regular continuing education programs
Publications   Official journals: Singapore Journal of Library and Information Management. Editor: Narayanan Rakunathan. Address: sjlim@las.org.sg. Singapore Libraries Bulletin. Editor: Zarinah Mohamed. Address: slb@las.org.sg. Other publications: LAS Newsletter. 4/yr; Directory of Libraries in Singapore; Standards for Bibliographical Compilations; annual reports, proceedings of conferences, and other occasional publications. Price lists available. Publications exchanged with other associations
Bibliography   Wee, J.G., "Library Association of Singapore on the Move," Singapore

Libraries 11 (1981):3-9; Seng, C.T., "Point of View: IFLA and LAS," Singapore Libraries 15 (1985):39-44; Anuar, H., "Singapore," in ALA World Encyclopedia of Library and Information Services. 2nd. ed., pp. 365-367. Chicago: American Library Association, 1986; Zaiton, O., "The Role of the Professional Association in Preparing Its Members for New Trends," in Singapore-Malaysia Congress of Librarians and Information Scientists [1986; Singapore]. The New Information Professionals, pp. 32-45. Gower, 1987; Khurshid, A, "Library Associations in Asia," Herald of Library Science 28 (1989):3-10; Thuraisingham, A, "Library Association of Singapore," COMLA Newsletter 65 (Sept. 1989):13-14

Slovakia

452 Spolok slovenskych knihovnikov (SEK) (Slovak Librarians Association)*

Address Michalská 1, 814 17 Bratislava Tel.: +42 1904694054, silvia.stasselova@gmail.com; www.infolib.sk

Languages Slovak

Established 12th February 1946 in Bratislava, Slovakia (the first national professional librarians association)

Officers Pres: Silvia Stasselová

Staff staff (paid): 1, volunteers: 15 members of the Executive Committee, 8 regional branches committee members

General Assembly General Assembly meeting and Elections – at the end of current election period, various cities; INFOS / International Conference on Information Technologies in Libraries – in April each second year, Congress Center Academia, Vysoké Tatry / High Tatra Mountains Resort, next in April 2011, see www.infolib.sk

Membership 8 regional branches (Bratislava, Trnava, Trencín, Žilina, Banská Bystrica, Prešov, Košice), 1000 individual members (librarians and information specialists), 70 institutional members (national library, research /public / academic / special libraries)

Structure Governed by President, Vice-President, Executive Committee, 8 regional branches, 3 special interest groups, Secretary

Sources of Support Association is financed through membership dues only. Additional income from conferences, grants, sponsors.

Major Fields of Interest Libraries, library services, librarians and information specialists, new trends in library and information science, information technologies in libraries, life-long education of librarians and users, marketing of libraries, international cooperation.

Major Goals and Objectives Main goals: to support the development of libraries and library services; to increase the prestige of librarian profession; to support cooperation of all Slovak librarians community; to support cooperation with other professional associations worldwide; to represent Slovak librarianship under the framework of IFLA

Activities -INFOS / International Conference on Information Technologies in Libraries – since each second year in April, Congress Center Academia, Vysoké Tatry / High Tatra Mountains Resort, next in April 2011; InfoLib – portal of Slovak libraries and librarians community: www.infolib.sk; Top WebLib – best Slovak Library Website Award /

each year; Noc s Andersenom / Night with Andersen – children sleep / spend all night in libraries; Slovak Librarians association coordinates Slovak libraries during this international event held each year last Friday in March (main coordination center in Czech Republic); Rozprávkové Rádio Slovensko / Fairy Tail Radio Slovakia; since 2008 during the event Night with Andersen main Slovak radio offers special 24 hours programme on libraries, on the importance of reading, reports from the night childrens event on-site, fairy tails, discussions with children literature writers

Publications Publication program – IFLA official documents / manifestos / guidelines translated to Slovak language and published by Slovak Librarians Association, national associated member of IFLA; Proceedings – INFOS / International Conference on Information Technologies in Libraries – in April each second year, Congress Center Academia, Vysoké Tatry / High Tatra Mountains Resort, next in April 2011; Jubilee publications on the history of Slovak Librarians Association (55th, 60th Anniversary)

Bibliography Zväz slovenských knihovníkov (ZSK) founded on 12th February 1946 in Bratislava as the first national professional librarians association; Zväz slovenských knihovníkov, bibliografov a informacných pracovníkov (ZsKI) since 1968; Zväz slovenských knihovníkov a informatikov (ZKI) since 1973; Spolok slovenských knihovníkov (SSK)/ Slovak Librarians Association since 1990

Slovenia

453 Arhivsko Drustvo Slovenije (Archival Society of Slovenia)

Address Zvezdarska 1, 1127 Llubljana Tel.: +386 1 2414200, Fax +386 1 2414269, ars@gov.si; www.arhivsko-drustvo.si

Languages Slovene, German, English

Established 1954

Officers Pres: Mirjana Kontestabile Rovis

Staff 3 volunteers

General Assembly Anually

Membership 224 personal members

Structure Professional association. Affiliation: SPA

Sources of Support Membership fees, funding (government), donations

Major Goals and Objectives Development of archival science; promotion of the use of archival materials; professional training of staff members;organising professional seminars; international cooperation

Activities Publishing, seminars, awards

Publications Official journal: ARHIVI (Archives). The Gazette of the Archival Society and Archives of Slovenia, 1978-; VIRI (Documents). Collection of historical documents with commentaries; 1980

Bibliography Arhivsko Drustvo Slovenije – 40 let. Ljubljana 1995; Proceedings of the 50th anniversary of the Archival Society of Slovenia. ARHIVI Vol. 27,1 (2004)

454 Zveza Bibliotekarskih Drustev Slovenije (ZBDS) (Library Association of Slovenia)*

Address Turjaska 1, 1000 Ljubljana Tel.: +386 1 2001207, Fax +386 1 4257293, melita.ambrozic@nuk.uni-lj.si; www.zbds-zveza.si

Languages Slovenian

Established 1947, December 21, Ljubljana, first – general assembly of association

Officers Pres: Melita Ambrozic; VP: Sabina Fras-Popovic; Spela Razpotnik

Staff All voluntary

General Assembly General Assembly meetings are at least once per year (2010: May)

Membership Union of 8 regional library associations, with a total of approx. 1.300 individual members. Types of membership available: individual, institutional (associations)and honorary members. Divisions (sections): 10. No requirements for joining, a member should respect association's Statute and Code of Ethics. Fees: employed – 15 EUR / year; retired and students: 11 EUR / year; honorary members don't pay fees

Structure Governed by executive officers. Affiliations: IFLA, EBLIDA

Sources of Support Membership dues, sale of publications, government subsidies, training and educational fees, sponsorships, donations

Major Fields of Interest Librarianship

Major Goals and Objectives To develop librarianship; to promote professional education; to protect professional interests; to develop professionalism; to promote free access of information; to develop information literacy

Activities Carried out according to the goals and objectives of the Association. Sponsors conferences, seminars, workshops, and other continuing education programs

Publications Official journal: Knjiznica: Revija za podro?je bibliotekarstva in informacijske znanosti (The Library: Journal for Library and Information Science). 4/yr + special editions(printed version), electronic version: http://revija-knjiznica.zbds-zveza.si/index.html Founding: 1957. Price: for members of Slovenian Library Association – free; for non-members – 32,60 EUR, for institutions – 35,50 EUR, for students and retired – 7,00 EUR, for abroad – 68,00 EUR. Chief editor: Branka Badovinac. Responsible editor: Primož Južni?. Circulation: 1.450. Language: Slovenian, abstracts in English. Other major publications: proceedings of conferences, IFLA guidelines translations, annual reports, monograph publications, etc. All data and information (including a price list) concerning publications are online available: www.zbds-zveza.si/publikacije_zbds.asp. Publication exchange programme: is a part of National and University Library publication exchange programme (association donate publications, national library take care for an exchange)

Bibliography Kort, R.L., "Yugoslavia," in ALA World Encyclopedia of Library and Information Services. 2nd ed., pp. 864–865. Chicago: American Library Association, 1986; Segbert, M., The Evolving Library Scene in Slovenia, 1996, http://cordis.europa.eu/libraries/en/cee/slovenia.html; Bahor, S., Sešek, I., Union of Associations of Slovene Librarians. In: Encyclopedia of Library and Information Science, 2nd ed. Miriam Drake, 2003; Jakac-Bizjak, V. Il sistema bibliotecario sloveno (The Slovenian library system). BollettinoAIB, 2003, n. 4, pp. 443–453; Kodric-Dacic, E.

The Library System in Slovenia : the Identity Card (August 2004), available: www.nuk.uni-lj.si/dokumenti/pdf/slovenian_librarianship.pdf

South Africa

455 Association of South African Indexers and Bibliographers (ASAIB)*

Address c/o Department of Information Science, University of South Africa, PO Box 392, Unisa 0003 Tel.: +27 12 4296792, Fax +27 12 42932221, preezm@unisa.ac.za; www.asaib.org.za
Established 1994
Officers Pres: Marlene Burger; Secr: Madely du Preez
Membership Requirements: open to any person engaged in indexing and bibliographic work, or any person interested in the objectives of ASAIB. Membership fees: R60 individual membership, R120 corporate membership
Sources of Support Membership fees
Major Fields of Interest Indexing and bibliography
Major Goals and Objectives To serve the interests of Southern African indexers and bibliographers and to promote all aspects of indexing and bibliographic activity
Activities Compiles and maintains a register of free-lance indexers and bibliographers, which it disseminates to the publishing industry; liaises with the publishing industry to ensure the maintenance of standards as well as appropriate fees for indexers and bibliographers; offers short courses, meetings and workshops on indexing and bibliography; functions as an advisory bureau and information clearing centre, including information on recommended books, computerised indexing programs, and university and other courses in indexing and bibliography offered in South Africa
Publications Publishes guides such as basice manuals, conference proceedings and a newsletter. All publications are available from the secretary

456 LIASA Interest Group for Bibliographic Standards (IGBIS)*

Address c/o National Library of South Africa, PO Box 397, Pretoria, 0001 Tel.: +27 12 4296792, preezm@unisa.ac.za; liasa.org.za/interest_groups/igbis.php
Established 2001
Officers Chair: Madely du Preez
Membership LIASA Membership and practicing cataloguers and classifiers
Structure Affiliation: LIASA
Major Fields of Interest Bibliographic standards
Major Goals and Objectives Support and promote the aim and objectives of LIASA. Support and promote the aim and objectives of IGBIS at branch level. Promote standardisation in bibliographic work nationally amongst a united group of library and information workers, and other interested parties. Provide for the exchange of ideas and experiences with regard to the application of bibliographic standards among members. Address issues which affect the application of bibliographic standards. Identify training needs in respect of bibliographic standards. Conduct continuing education for information workers by arranging talks, meetings and workshops. Support academics, researchers,

students and the community through the provision of information about bibliographic standards
Activities Bibliographic standards workshops, training, conferences
Publications Publishes a newsletter

457 Library and Information Association of South Africa (LIASA)*

Address P.O. Box 1598, Pretoria 0001 Tel.: +27 12 4812870, Fax +27 12 4812873, karin@liasa.org.za; www.liasa.org.za
Languages English
Established 1997 as a unification of all existing library organisations in South Africa
Officers Pres: Tommy Matthee; Deputy: Tshidi Makhafola; Secr: Karlien De Klerk; Treas: Dr. Brian Brink; PR Off: Rene Schoombee
Staff Office Manager: Karin Kitching (karin@liasa.org.za); Secretarial Administrator: Ina van Straten (liasa@liasa.org.za); Membership Administrator: Mariëtte van Dyk (mariette@liasa.org.za, Tel: +27 12 481 2870)
General Assembly Entire membership meets once a year
Membership Members: individual and institutional
Major Fields of Interest Libraries and Librarianship
Major Goals and Objectives To promote the transformation of LIS into equitable and accessible services for all the people in South Africa; to unite all persons engaged or interested in library and information work and to actively safeguard and promote their dignity, rights and socio-economic status; to support and promote the democratic rights of LIS workers in their endeavour to create, acquire, organise and disseminate information without interference; to promote and provide education and training of LIS workers in co-operation with other institutions; to promote an ethical delivery of LIS to all the people in South Africa through a code of conduct for its members; to publicly recognise the contributions and achievements of members; to engage in, promote, facilitate and encourage activities including meetings, conferences and publications that will result in networking among members, and contact and liaison with the broader LIS sector; to encourage promotion of service standards and acceptable good practice especially extending services to disadvantaged/unserved communities; to facilitate and promote research and development in LIS; to act as one voice, to market, to lobby for and to represent the LIS sector at local, provincial, national and international levels on all aspects of LIS, including legislation; to facilitate cooperative activities within the broad LIS sector; to engage in any other activities that will promote the interest of LIS and LIS workers
Activities Representation of the interests of and promotion of the development and image of library and information workers and agencies
Publications Official journals: South African Journal of Libraries & Information Science. 2/y.; LIASA-IN-TOUCH. 4/y

458 Organisation of South African Law Libraries (OSALL)*

Address c/o c/o Selma Savitz, Treasurer, P.O. Box 783779, SANDTON 2146 Tel.: +27 11 242-8016, Fax +27 11 242-6447, hheij@bclr.com; www.osall.org.za
Established July 1976
Officers Chair: Fanus Olivier; Secr: N.N.; Treas: Gill Rademeyer
Staff 8, volunteers

General Assembly Annual AGM
Membership Requirements: Open to anyone interested in Law Librarianship. Dues: R174, institutional; R75, personal; R40, students/retired
Structure Governed by elected commmittee
Sources of Support Membership fees, sponsorship
Major Fields of Interest Law Librarianship in South Africa
Major Goals and Objectives To co-ordinate the activities of law libraries and legal collections by promoting co-operation between law libraries and legal information workers; to promote the interchange of bibliographical information, and other information relevant to law libraries and legal collections; to encourage the pooling, comparison and interchange of ideas on the handling and solution of problems common to law libraries and legal collections; to arrange and conduct meetings, discussions, courses and visits and to employ other forms of communication with a view to furthering the objects of the Organisation; to foster the study and application of library management tools and techniques for improving the effective utilisation of legal information; to promote the status of those engaged in law librarianship and to support the training and further education of librarians
Activities Organizes conferences an other events, offers listserv
Publications OSALL newsletter. 4/yr. Editor: Fiona Rennie. Address: Deneys Reitz, PO Box 784903, Sandton 2146, email: renn0708@deneysreitz.co.za

459 Suid-Africaanse Vereniging van Archivarisse (SASA) (South African Society of Archivists)*

Address P O Box 931, Auckland Park 2006
Established 1960
Officers VChair: Idelette Beute; Secr: Anri van der Westhuizen
Membership Requirements: open to all who are interested in the archival profession and the management and preservation of records and archival and manuscript sources. Dues: Individual membership – R80; Pensioners & full-time students – R70; Institutional Membership – R300
Major Fields of Interest Archives in Southafrica
Major Goals and Objectives The development of Archival Science and the promotion of the archival profession in South Africa
Activities Organizes congresses, seminars and other events
Publications Official journal: SASA Journal. Editorial Address: P O Box 931, Auckland Park, 2006. Other publications: Newsletter, Listserv

Spain

460 Asociación de Titulados Universitarios en Documentación y Biblioteconomía (ADAB)

Address Apartado 1115, 24080 Léon est.unileon.es/~adab/
Languages Spanish
Established 1987
Membership Requirements: Students and graduates in librarianship and documentation

Major Fields of Interest Librarianship and documentation
Major Goals and Objectives To faciliate the entrance into professional life for the graduates in library and information science
Activities To provide information on further education, congresses, seminaries etc
Publications Official journal: Cosas de la ADAB

461 Asociación Española de Archiveros, Bibliotecarios, Museólogos y Documentalistas (ANABAD)
(Spanish Association of Archivists, Librarians, Museologists and Documentalists)

Address c/ Recoletos 5, 3º Izqda., 28001 Madrid Tel.: +34 91 5751727, Fax +34 91 5781615, anabad@anabad.org; www.anabad.org
Languages Spanish
Established 1949, Madrid, as Asociación Nacional de Bibliotecarios, Archiveros y Arqueólogos (ANABA); 1978, new statutes and new name, Asociación Nacional de Bibliotecarios, Archiveros, Arqueólogos y Documentalistas, to expand membership to documentalists, and later to museum curators
Officers Pres: Maria Pilar Gallego Cuadrado; Secr: Jose Maria Nogales Herrera
General Assembly Entire membership meets annually in Madrid
Membership Total members: 1,700 (individual and institutional). Types of membership: Individual. Requirements: University graduates working in a library, archive, museum or documentation center
Structure Governed by Executive Council. Consists of 5 regional associations. Affiliations: FESABID, IFLA (through FESABID)
Sources of Support Membership dues, sale of publications, government and private subsidies
Major Fields of Interest Libraries, archives, museums, documentation
Major Goals and Objectives To improve the services of libraries, archives, museums, and documentation centers by means of professional personnel; to defend the professional interests of the members; to produce research studies and projects especially related to the practices of librarianship; to issue professional publications, catalogs, bibliographies; to maintain an information center; to cooperate with other organizations of a similar nature, particularly those in Latin American countries
Activities Publication of Bulletin and other professional monographs; organizing the national conferences; establishing committees concerned with certain special professional problems; professional education, both basic education and continuing education programs for members; cooperation with other institutions and organizations sharing common interests. Representation of the professions at the international level has been assumed by FESABID since 1989
Publications Official journal: Boletín ANABAD. 1949-. 3/yr. Free for members. Address same as Association. Spanish. Other publications: Hoja Informativa bimonthly, on the web, address: www.anabad.org/documentos/index.shtml. Annual reports, proceedings of conferences; series of monographs on special topics of current professional interest. Publications for sale
Bibliography Escolar-Sobrino, H., "Spain," in ALA World Encyclopedia of Library and Information Services. 2nd.ed., pp. 770–772. Chicago: American Library Association, 1986

462 Federación Española de Sociedades de Archivística, Biblioteconomía, Documentación y Museística (FESABID)
(Federation of Spanish Archival, Library, Documentation, and Museum Associations)
Address Sta. Engracia 17, 13°, 28010 Madrid Tel.: +34 91 5912013, Fax +34 91 5912013, gerencia@fesabid.org; www.fesabid.org
Languages Spanish
Established 1988, Madrid. Statutes signed by 4 associations: (1) La Asociación Andaluza de Bibliotecarios (AAB) (Andalusian Library Association), (2) La Asociación Española de Archiveros, Bibliotecarios, Museólogos y Documentalistas (ANABAD) (Spanish Association of Archivists, Librarians, Museologists and Documentalists), (3) La Sociedad Española de Documentación e Información Científica (SEDIC) (Spanish Society for Scientific Information and Documentation), and (4) La Societat Catalana de Documentació i Informació (SOCADI) (Catalanian Society for Documentation and Information)
Officers Pres: Gloria Perez Salmeron; Secr: Jose Maria Nogales Herrera
Staff 1, paid
General Assembly Entire membership meets twice a year
Membership Total members: 12 library associations
Structure Governed by General Assembly consisting of representatives of member associations, and Executive Board. Affiliations: IFLA, EBLIDA, ICA
Sources of Support Membership dues, government subsidy
Major Fields of Interest Professional organizations in the fields of archives, libraries, documentation centers, and museums
Major Goals and Objectives (1) Promote and develop professional activities in Spain, and contribute to the improvement of conditions for member associations to carry out their activities; (2) promote the cooperation between member associations and fadlitate the exchange of information about their respective activities, as well as their expertise and experiences; (3) publicize the functions and further the professional image and status of those who work in the fields with which the Federation is concerned
Activities Created 4 work groups: Caucus Iberoamericano IFLA, Comisión para la nueva titulación de Biblioteconomía y Documentación, Comité 50 de AENOR, Grupo BPI: Bibliotecas y Propiedad Intelectual

463 Red de Bibliotecas Universitarias Españolas
Address Plaza de las Cortes n.2, 28036 Madrid idoia.barrenechea@rebiun.org
Officers Pres: Idoia Barrenechea

464 Sociedad Española de Documentación e Información Científica (SEDIC)
(Spanish Society for Scientific Information and Documentation)
Address C/ Santa Engracia 17, 3°, 28010 Madrid Tel.: +34 915 934059, Fax +34 915 934128, sedic@sedic.es; www.sedic.es
Languages Spanish
Established 1976, Madrid; first Assembly, June 28,1977
Staff 4, paid
General Assembly Entire membership meets once a year

Membership Requirements: To be a professional information manager, librarian, or archivist; students and interested persons as associate members.
Structure Governed by General Assembly and Executive Council. Affiliations: FESABID, ASEDIE, CEDE, IFLA, ECIA
Sources of Support Membership dues, training, subsidies
Major Fields of Interest Information science, librarianship, archival studies, information management, knowledge management
Major Goals and Objectives To further education, training and professional development of information managers, librarians and archivists
Activities The Association is active in the following areas: (1) Education and training: Organization of formal professional studies in documentation, and continuing education seminars, etc.; (2) Publications: Professional journal and expanding professional publications program; (3) National and international relations: Collaboration with all Spanish organizations concerned with documentation, particularly in the field of application of new technologies; (4) Research and studies: Supporting various projects, such as survey of the current situation of documentalists in Spain; and a study of the needs in documentation in Spain; (5) Relations with members: Organizing conferences, study visits, seminars and various continuing education programs; expanding membership; (6) ACTIVA (labour exchange), Knowledge Management working group, Dublin Core working group, Health Science Libraries working group; (7) e-learning; (8) Certification Service of Information and Documentation Professionals. It is working since 1997. The Certification Commission, its directive board, is composed by 17 members, all of them renowned Spanish I+D professionals, professors and employers. Through this Service SEDIC is an active member taking part in the CERTIDoc Project settled in the frame Leonardo Da Vinci Programme of the European Union
Publications Official journals: Revista española de documentación. 1977–3/yr. Editor: Centro de Información y Documentación Científica (CINDOC) of the Consejo Superior de Investigaciones Científicas (CSIC). Boletín CLIP. Boletin de Novedades. electronic newsltter 12/yr. Other publications: Directorio español de empresas de servicios documentales 2003

Suriname

465 Stichting Cultureel Centrum Suriname (CCS) (Cultural Centre Suriname)

Address Henck Arronstraat 112–114, Paramaribo
Officers Chair: Ilse Vreugd; Secr: Joyce P. Linger

Swaziland

466 Swaziland Library Association (SWALA)

Address Elwatini Building, Corner of Market & Warner Streets, P.O. Box 2309, H100 Mbabane Tel.: +268 4042633, Fax +268 4043863, fmkhonta@uniswacc.uniswa.sz; www.swala.sz

Languages English
Established 1984, April 28, at Mbabane Library
Officers Chair: Faith Mkhonta; Vice Chair: Queeneth Fakudze; Secr: Jabulile Dlamini; Treas: Esther Nxumalo
Staff None
General Assembly Entire membership meets once a year, usually the first week of June
Membership 4 membership categories: individual, institutional, corresponding, and honorary. Requirements: Librarians, libraries, and other individuals and institutions interested in the aims of the Association. Dues (Emalangeni): 100.00, individual; 500.00, institutional
Structure Governed by Executive Committee. Affiliations: COMLA, IFLA, LA (Community Services Group)
Sources of Support Membership dues
Major Fields of Interest Libraries and librarianship
Major Goals and Objectives To promote the establishment and development of library and information services. To unite all persons engaged or interested in library and other information work, by holding conferences, meetings, seminars, and workshops for the discussion of matters affecting libraries and other information centres. To promote whatever may tend to the improvement of the position and qualifications of Librarians and other information personnel. To safeguard and promote the professional interests of Librarians and other information personnel. To monitor any legislation affecting libraries and other information centres and to assist in the promotion of such legislation as may be considered necessary for the regulation and management or extension of libraries and other information centres. To promote and encourage bibliographical study and research and library co-operation through networking. To collect and publish information to its members, for the promotion of the aims and objectives of the Association. To collect and publish information to its membership
Activities Organizes workshops, conferences, meetings and seminars. Association has been active in promoting library-related legislation, such as drafting the National library Service Act of 1985
Publications Official journals: SWALA Journal. 1984-. 1/yr. Free to members. Editor: Fred Onyango. Circ: Membership. English. Other publications: SWALA Newsletter; SWALA Member Directory; Proceedings of meetings, reports of seminars, workshops
Bibliography Kuzwayo, A.W.Z., "Swaziland," in ALA World Encyclopedia of Library and Information Services. 2nd. ed., pp. 788–789. Chicago: American Library Association, 1986; "Swaziland Library Association Executive Committee 1986/87," COMLA Newsletter 55 (Mar. 1987):15

Sweden

467 Arkivradet (AAS)

Address Virkesvägen 26, 12030 Stockholm Tel.: +46 8 55606142; www.arkivradet.org
Languages Swedish
Membership 800 personal members
Structure Non-proit-organization. Affiliation: SPA

Sources of Support Membership fees
Major Fields of Interest Archives, journal (diary), document management
Major Goals and Objectives Arkivradet AAS covers the development within the archives sector
Activities Archives and journal (diary) conference – two occasions every year
Publications Tema arkiv

468 DIK
(DIK Association – Documentation, Information & Culture)

Address P.O. Box 760, 13124 Nacka Tel.: +46 8 4662400, Fax +46 8 4662413, ake.lindstrom@dik.se; www.dik.se
Languages Swedish
Established 1972, as the professional organization/union for those employed in the fields of documentation, information and culture (DIK = Dokumentation, Information, Kultur) with an academic degree
Officers Pres: Åke Lindström
Staff 20
General Assembly General assembly meets every third year. Member associations have their own annual general meetings. Delegates meet once a year in a representative assembly
Membership Total members: 20,000 (individual). Requirements: University degree or qualified employment in documentation, information or cultural fields
Structure Affiliations: Swedish Confederation of Professional Associations, SACO
Sources of Support Membership dues
Major Fields of Interest Documentation, information, culture; conditions of employment, salaries, education
Major Goals and Objectives All members should receive a salary which is commensurate with their education, their qualifications, and their responsibilities. Higher quality of education and training
Activities Past achievements: The organization has expanded and is now known among employers of all fields. Current: Through negotiation activities and promotion seeks to improve salaries and working conditions of members. Members include archivists, librarians, administrators, curators, etc. Works towards pay equality for employees in the municipal, governmental and private sectors, and for a six-hour working day for all employees. Quality education and training are considered most important areas, both basic and continuing education. Federation collaborates with other professional associations and trade unions. Carries out negotiations on behalf of members and gives general, professional and legal advice on interpretation of agreements and other matters of employment. Through the journal keeps members up-to-date on the labor market. Offers members a voluntary group insurance. Active in promoting legislation of concern to members
Publications Official journal: DIK-forum. 1984-. 20/yr. (Swedish Krona) 125. Free to members. Address same as Federation. Circ: 11,000+. Swedish. Other occasional publications: A manual for new members, etc

469 Göteborgs University Library

Address Box 222, 405 30 Göteborg agneta.olsson@ub.gu.se

Languages Swedish
Officers Library Dir: Agneta Olsson

470 Svensk Biblioteksförening (Swedish Library Association)*

Address World Trade Center, D5, Klarabergsviadukten 70 or Kungsbron 1, 11122 Stockholm, P.O. Box 703 80, 10724 Stockholm Tel.: +46 8 54513230, Fax +46 8 54513231, info@biblioteksforeningen.org; www.biblioteksforeningen.org
Languages Swedish
Established 2000 as a result of a merger between Sveriges Almanna Biblioteksförening (SAB), founded in 1915, and Svenska Bibliotekarieforbundet (SB), founded in 1921
Officers Pres: Inga Lundén; Secr Gen: Niclas Lindberg
Staff Association: 5, paid. Journal Biblioteksbladet: 2, paid
General Assembly Entire membership meets once a year
Membership Total members: 3,500 (individual and institutional). Requirements: Individual: Interest in library matters; Institutional: Institutions/organizations dealing with library matters, research, or school/educational matters
Structure Governed by executive officers and membership. Affiliations: EBLIDA, NAMHI, IFLA, LIBER
Sources of Support Membership dues, sale of publications, conference fees
Major Fields of Interest Library and librarianship
Major Goals and Objectives The Swedish Library Association is a non-profit organisation which is independent of political parties and a free agent. The Association unites and works in support of all types of libraries by disseminating information on libraries and their activities, initiating public discussion and creating public opinion, performing lobbying, and promoting research and development
Activities Courses, conferences and annual meetings
Publications Official journal: Biblioteksbladet (BBL) (Library Journal). 1916-. 10/yr. SEK 500. Free to members. Editor: Henriette Zorn. Tel: +46 8 54513246. Circ: 5,500. Swedish. Other publications: Annual reports, proceedings of seminars, workshops. Some publications for sale. No publications exchange program in effect
Bibliography "The Future of the Swedish Library Association," Biblioteksbladet 70 (1985): i-xvi (insert, in Swedish); Tell, B., "Sweden," in ALA World Encyclopedia of Library and Information Services. 2nd ed., pp. 789–791. Chicago: American Library Association, 1986; Andersson, L.G., "SAB – den oandliga historian," (SAB – a Story without an End), DF-Revy 9 (1986):38–41 (in Swedish)
Comment Former name: Sveriges Allmänna Biblioteksförening. The Swedish Library Association was founded in 2000 as a result of a merger between Sveriges Allmänna Biblioteksförening, SAB (founded 1915), and Svenska Bibliotekariesamfundet, SBS (founded in 1921)

471 Svensk förening för informationsspecialister (TLS) (Swedish Association for Information Specialists)

Address Osquars Backe 25, 10044 Stockholm Tel.: +46 8 6782320, Fax +46 8 6782301; www.tls.se
Languages Swedish and other Scandinavian languages

Established 1936, Stockholm. Former name: Tekniska Litteratursällskapet (Swedish Society for Technical Documentation)
General Assembly Entire membership meets once a year
Membership Total members: individual and institutional. Requirements: Open to all those working in the field of technology and documentation
Structure Governed by Executive Board. Affiliations: IFLA
Sources of Support Membership dues, sale of publications, government subsidies
Major Fields of Interest Documentation in industry
Major Goals and Objectives To promote documentation and to stimulate research and development in this field; to improve the professional skills of its members, enabling them to attain the objectives of their organisations
Activities Training, conferences, publications, marketing, co-operation with other national and international organisations
Publications Official journal: Tidskrift för Dokumentation (TD) ("The Nordic Journal of Documentation") (until 1948, Teknisk Dokumentation). 1945-. 4/yr. Scandinavian languages or English. Other publications: Newsletter, TLS Information (membership only); annual reports, proceedings of seminars, conferences; handbooks, bibliographies, scholarly works of documentation. Publications available for sale. Publications exchange program in effect
Bibliography Bergsten, G., "Swedish Society for Technical Documentation. Fall Conference 1983." Tidskrift för Dokumentation 39 (1983):113–115 (in Swedish); Tell, B., "Sweden," in ALA World Encyclopedia of Library and Information Services. 2nd ed., pp. 789–791. Chicago: American library Association, 1986

472   Svenska Arkivsamfundet
(The Swedish Archival Association)*

Address Box 22063, 10422 Stockholm www.arkivsamfundet.se
Languages Swedish
Established 1952
Officers Pres: Sara Naeskind; VP: Berndt Fredriksson; Secr: Gunika Nordström; Treas: Birje Sjöman
General Assembly Entire membership meets once a year
Membership Total members: 735. 5 countries represented. Requirements: Interest in goals and objectives of Association. Dues (Swedish Krona): 60
Structure Governed by executive officers. Affiliations: ICA
Sources of Support Membership dues, sale of publications, research subsidies
Major Fields of Interest Archives and archival studies
Major Goals and Objectives To create and keep alive interest in public and private archives; to promote development of the care and maintenance of archives, and to spread information about archival matters
Activities Promoting the development of Swedish archives, records preservation and management, and making information on archival matters available to the public; publishing of journal. Association sponsors discussions and meetings
Publications Official journal: Arkiv, samhälle och Forskning. Free to members. Swedish

473 Svenska Musikbiblioteksföreningen (SMBF)
(Swedish Branch of the International Association of Music Libraries, Archives and Documentation Centres / IAML-Swedish Branch)
Address c/o Kerstin Carpvik, Box 16326, 10326 Stockholm Tel.: +46 8 51955426, arkivdok@muslib.se; www.smbf.nu
Languages Swedish, English, German
Established 1953, Stockholm. Name until 1980: Svenska Sektionen av AIBM
General Assembly Entire membership meets once a year
Membership Requirements: Any person or institution wishing to further the goals of the Association
Structure Governed by Executive Committee. Affiliations: A national branch of IAML
Sources of Support Membership dues, government subsidies
Major Fields of Interest Music librarianship
Major Goals and Objectives To encourage and promote the activities of music libraries, archives and documentation centers and to strengthen the cooperation among institutions and individuals in these fields of interest
Activities Carried out in coordination with those of IAML. Collaborated on Swedish cataloging rules and classification scheme for music and sound recording

Switzerland

474 Association genevoise des bibliothécaires et professionnels diplômés en information documentaire *
Address Case Postale 3494, 1211 Geneva comite@agbd.ch; www.agbd.ch/comite.php
Languages French
Established 9th of March, 1972, Geneva, Switzerland
Officers Pres: Pierre Boillat; VP: Jean-Philippe Accart
Staff 7 (voluntary)
General Assembly General Assembly held once a year (last one: 16th of Feb. 2010)
Membership 300 members; individual and corporate memberships; joining AGBD: only professionals living in the Geneva County; fees: 40 Swiss Francs (20 Swiss Francs for a retired person)
Structure Committee structure, participative government, name: 'Comité AGBD'. Affiliation with the national Swiss association BIS, and affiliation with IFLA
Sources of Support Membership dues and sales of the publication 'Hors-Texte'. No government subsidies
Major Fields of Interest Information Science in general
Major Goals and Objectives Defense of the profession at a local and national level. Representation at an international level. Collaboration with other local associations
Activities 3 or 4 lunch talks a year with the venue of an author; Study trip once a year (visits of libraries in Switzerland); Publication of a review (print) 'Hors-Texte'; Official declarations on different matters (politics...); Publication of a Code of Ethics; Annual Award in Librarianship; Training course (once a year)
Publications Official Journal: Hors-Texte; founded 30 years ago; published 3 times a year (March, June and November); part of the AGBD membership; non-member:

subscription 25 Swiss Francs a year; language: French. Editor: Eric Monnier, Rédaction Hors-Texte CP 3494, CH 1211 Genève 3 – Switzerland

475 Bibliothèque Information Suisse (BIS)

Address Hallerstraße 58, 3012 Bern info@bis.info
Officers Pres: Andreas Brellochs; Secr Gen: Barbara Kraeuchi
Major Fields of Interest Networking, Representing, Providing Information

476 Vereinigung der juristischen Bibliotheken der Schweiz / Association des bibliothèques juridiques suisses (JBS)

Address c/o Jean-Paul Rebetez, President, Av. Europe 20, 1700 Fribourg Tel.: +41 26 300 80 10, Fax +41 26 300 97 77, jean-paul.rebetez@unifr.ch; www.lawlibraries.ch
Languages German, French
Officers Pres: Jean-Paul Rebetez; Kerstin Reiher; Treas: Christoph Wegenast
General Assembly Annual General Assembly
Sources of Support Membership dues, donations
Major Fields of Interest Juridical Librarianship
Major Goals and Objectives To promote and represent the interest of the members; to foster the co-operation and development of juridical libraries
Activities Further education

477 Vereinigung Schweizerischer Archivare Associazione degli Archivisti Svizzeri / Uniun da las archivarias e dals archivaris svizzers (VSA/AAS/AAS/UAS) (Association of Swiss Archivists)*

Address c/o Sekretariat, Solothurnstrasse 13, Postfach, 3322 Urtenen-Schönbühl Tel.: +41 31 3122666, Fax +41 31 3122686, info@vsa-aas.org; www.vsa-aas.org
Languages German, French, Italian
Established 1922, in Lenzburg
Officers Pres: Anna Pia Maissen; VP: Gregor Egloff; Secr: Paolo Ostinelli; Treas: Regula Nebiker
Staff Secretarial services (paid)
General Assembly Entire membership meets annually. General Assembly 2009: Zurich; General Assembly 2010: Vaduz / FL
Membership Total members: Approx. 650 (110 institutional). Types of membership: Individual, institutional. Requirements: Open to archivists and archives.
Structure Supreme body: Annual General Assembly. Operative and strategic management: Executive Board
Sources of Support Membership dues
Major Fields of Interest Archives and records management
Major Goals and Objectives To promote the development of archives in Switzerland; to facilitate contact among archivists; to promote their cooperation and to assist in their professional activities; to promote their professional development and status; to promote archival training and advanced training
Activities Organizes colloquia on current problems in archives; disseminates information on archival matters and archival studies in Switzerland and abroad through

publications; maintains contact and exchanges information with other associations of similar interests, both Swiss and foreign. Offers further education possibilities
Publications   Official journal: arbido. 1986-. (supersedes Mitteilungen der Vereinigung Schweizerischer Archivare); print and newsletter, published jointly by 2 Swiss associations, VSA and BIS (Bibliothek Information Schweiz). Annual reports published online (www.vsa-aas.org). Issues monographs on archival and records management best practices (Publication series "Kultur für Profis: Archivwissenschaft"). Activities carried out according to goals and objectives of Association; organizes and sponsors courses, conferences, seminars, workshops; proceedings mostly published in arbido
Bibliography   Coutaz, G., Huber R., Kellerhals, A et al., Archivpraxis in der Schweiz – Pratiques archivistiques en Suisse. Baden: hier+jetzt 2007; Clavel, J.-P. and Médioni, J., "Switzerland," in ALA World Encyclopedia of Library and Information Services. 2nd ed., pp. 792–793. Chicago: American library Association, 1986

Syria

478   The Libraries and Documents Association of Syria

Address   Malki Street, Damascus, PO Box 3639, Damascus Tel.: +963 334294, 3320806, 3320278, Fax +963 3320804, fair2010@alassad-library.gov.sy; www.alassad-library.gov.sy
Languages   Arabic
Established   1984
Staff   390 (paid)
Structure   Governed by Ministry of Culture and National Guidance. Affiliations: IFLA (since 1986)
Sources of Support   Government subsidies. Budget (Syrian Pound): Approx. 11.4 million
Major Fields of Interest   Syrian publications, Arabic manuscripts, selected Arabic and foreign works in all fields
Major Goals and Objectives   Compilation and documentation of national works; promotion of librarianship in Syria; establishing the foundation for a national information network and its subsequent supervision
Activities   (1) Legal Deposit Law for all Syrian publications; (2) organize courses for technical services in the Library; (3) supervise the Library Association in Syria; (4) hold general cultural lectures and symposia; (5) supervise the establishment of the National Information Network; (6) preservation and restoration of manuscripts. Has been active in promoting library-related legislation. Contributed to establishment of the Arab Federation for Libraries and Information (AFLI). Sponsors exhibits and continuing education programs. "International Book Fair" and "Child Book Fair". Updating, re-installing and supplying all necessary to accomodate all facilities to the public for online use
Publications   No official journal. Publishes National Bibliography. 1/yr.; Analytical Index of Syrian Periodicals. 4/yr.; Internal Bulletin. 2/yr. Publications exchange program in effect
Bibliography   El Hadi, Mohamed M.,"Syria," in ALA World Encyclopedia of Library and Information Services. 2nd ed., pp. 794–795. Chicago: American Library Association,

1986; Khurshid, A., "Library Associations in Asia," Herald of Library Science 28 (1989):3–10

Taiwan

479   Chinese Information Literacy Association (CILA)
Address   100 Wenhwa Road, Seatewn, Taichung   Tel.: +886 4 22846644, Fax +886 4 24516453; www.cila.org.tw(chineseonly)
Established   2003
Structure   Governed by Board of Directors and steering committee
Major Fields of Interest   Preparing members for the demands of today's information society
Major Goals and Objectives   To make aware to educators and the general public that information literacy is a fundamental competency skill for lifelong learning. To incorporate information literacy into the education and the work place. To provide educators and practitioners a significant public access point and activities such as seminars, workshops, and events to acquire information literacy resources. To disseminate knowledge of information literacy through publications and advocacy groups. To provide government with an information literacy developing model and assessment systems
Activities   Provides training and consulting services, holds conference

480   Chung-kuo t'u-shu-kuan hsüeh-hui (LAC) (Library Association of China)
Address   c/o Teresa Wang Chang, 20 Chungshan South Road, Taipei 100-40   Tel.: +886 2 23312475, Fax +886 2 23700899, lac@msg.ncl.edu.tw; www.infolit.org/members/china.htm;http://lac.ncl.edu.tw
Languages   Chinese, English
Established   1925; reorganized in 1953
General Assembly   Entire membership meets annually in Taipei in December
Membership   Total members: 1,790.Requirements: Open to anyone who has studied library science or is interested in library work
Structure   Governed by Executive Board. Affiliations: IFLA
Sources of Support   Membership dues, government subsidies
Major Fields of Interest   Librarianship
Major Goals and Objectives   To promulgate professional education and training of librarianship and information science, to advocate ethics in professional practice, to strengthen the establishment of library and information networks, to improve the communication and cooperation among libraries and academic institutes both in the Republic of China and abroad, to promote the development and utilization of library resources, and to promote the reading interests of the general public. Dedicated to promoting Chinese culture, to enhancing studies and research in library and information sciences, and expediting the development and advancement of the profession through the joint efforts of library professionals
Activities   Sponsorship of continuing education programs, such as summer workshops, seminars; formulation of library standards; working for general improvements of library

services. Association is involved in joint library automation projects with the National Central Library, and Chinese language bibliographies
Publications   Official journal: Bulletin of the Library Association of China/Chung-kuo t'u-shu-kuan hsüeh-hui hui-pao. 1954-. 1/yr. (New Taiwan Dollar) 40. Address same as Association. Chinese, English. Other publications: Library Association of China Newsletter. 1975-. 6/yr. Chinese; proceedings of conferences, seminars. Publications for sale
Bibliography   Wang, Chen-Ku, "China, Republic of (Taiwan)," in ALA World Encyclopedia of Library and Information Services. 2nd ed., pp. 192–194. Chicago: American Library Association, 1986; Khurshid, A., "Library Associations in Asia," Herald of Library Science 28 (1989):3–10

Tanzania

481   Tanzania Library Association (TLA)

Address   P.O. Box 33433, Dar es Salaam Tel.: +255 744 296124, amcharazo@hotmail.com; www.tlatz.org
Languages   English, Kiswahili
Established   1973, after the dissolving of the East African Library Association (EALA). Originally was a branch of EALA (1971–1972)
Officers   Chair: Dr. Alli Mcharazo
General Assembly   Entire membership meets once a year
Membership   Requirements: Individuals working in libraries and documentation centers; institutions having libraries and documentation centers
Structure   Governed by Executive Committee and Annual General Meeting of all members. Affiliations: COMLA, FID, IFLA, SCESCAL, Tanzania Professional Centre, East African Book Development Council, Tanzania Book Development Council
Sources of Support   Membership dues, sale of publications, course and seminar fees, private donations
Major Fields of Interest   Librarianship and information science
Major Goals and Objectives   To promote reading and literacy; to improve standards and level of library development; to increase competence of members; to conduct research and produce publications
Activities   Offers sholarship, workshops, short courses film programmes, short talks, conferences
Publications   Official journal: Someni. 1973-. 2/yr. Free to members. Editor: Dr. D. Katundu. Address same as Association. English, Kiswahili. Indexed in LISA. Other publications: Series on library Development; newsletter; annual reports, proceedings of meetings, reports of seminars, workshops. No publications exchange program in effect
Bibliography   Kaungamno, E.E., "The Case of Tanzania Library Services," Canadian Library Journal 42 (1985):185–187; Kaungamno, E.E., "Tanzania," in ALA World Encyclopedia of Library and Information Services. 2nd ed., pp. 796–797. Chicago: American Library Association, 1986

Thailand

482 The Association of Thai Archives
Address Bangkok 10200 Tel.: +66 2 6133840, Fax +66 2 2220149, thaiarchives@yahoo.com

483 Thai Library Association (TLA)
Address 1346 Akarnsongkrau Road, Sukhapibal 1, Klongchan, Bangkapi, Bangkok 10240 Tel.: +66 2 7348023, Fax +66 2 7348024; tla.tiac.or.th
Languages Thai
Established 1954, Bangkok, with the aid of a grant from the Asia Foundation
General Assembly Entire membership meets annually, in November or December, in Bangkok
Membership Types of membership: regular, associate, honorary, contributing, institutional. Requirements: For each category, specific requirements as to library education, job status, contributions to librarianship, etc
Structure Governed by Executive Council. Affiliations: CONSAL, IFLA
Sources of Support Membership dues, subsidy from the Asia Foundation
Major Fields of Interest Library services
Major Goals and Objectives To encourage cooperation and assistance among members; to promote library education; to help with the growth and development of libraries throughout the country; to share professional knowledge and experiences with colleagues at home and abroad; to improve the status of librarians and safeguard their welfare; to help supervise the organization of any library upon request; to serve as a center to receive assistance from any source so as to obtain the objectives of the association
Activities Continuing education programs, e. g. workshop, conference, seminars, etc.; Organization of broadcast programs for the promotion of readership, book production and library development; Establish library standards for school libraries, special libraries, public libraries and vocational education and technology libraries; Organization of library week and National Book Week
Publications Official journal: TLA Bulletin. 1957–4/yr. Free to members. Address same as Association. Other publications: Annual reports, proceedings of conferences, seminars, and other professional publications
Bibliography Dhutiyabhodi, Uthai, "Thailand," in ALA World Encyclopedia of Library and information Services. 2nd ed., pp. 799–801. Chicago: American Library Association, 1986; Khurshid, A., "Library Associations in Asia," Herald of Library Science 28 (1989):3–10
Comment under the Patronage of H. R. H. Princess Maha Chakri Sirindhorn

Tonga

484 Tonga Library Association (TLA)
Address PO Box 278, Nuku'alofa Tel.: +676 29240, Fax +676 23960
Languages Tongan, English
Established 1987/88

General Assembly Entire membership meets once year
Structure Affiliations: COMLA
Sources of Support Membership dues
Major Fields of Interest Library services
Major Goals and Objectives Promote library services in Tonga
Activities Sponsors meetings and various library-oriented projects, such as furnishing kindergartens in the Kingdom with writing and drawing materials
Publications Official journal: Tonga Library Association Newsletter
Bibliography "Tonga Library Association Appeal," COMLA Newsletter 55 (Mar. 1987):6

Trinidad and Tobago

485 Library Association of Trinidad and Tobago (LATT)

Address P.O. Box 1275, Port of Spain Tel.: +1 868 6870194; www.latt.org.tt
Languages English
Established 1960
Officers Pres: Ernesta Greenidge; Secr: Sheryl Washington
Staff None
General Assembly Entire membership meets annually in Trinidad between January and March 31
Membership Types of membership: Individual, institutional, honorary, associate. Requirements: Open to librarians and all persons, groups, and organizations connected with and interested in the promotion of librarianship
Structure Governed by executive officers. Affiliations: COMLA, IFLA, ACURIL
Sources of Support Membership dues
Major Fields of Interest Librarianship
Major Goals and Objectives To unite all qualified or practicing librarians and any persons or organizations connected with and interested in the promotion of librarianship and its related fields in Trinidad and Tobago
Activities Sponsors conferences, seminars, and other continuing education programs, sometimes jointly with the Department of Library Studies of the University of the West Indies
Publications Official journals: BIBLIO. Newsletter, 4/yr. Free for members. BLATT: Bulletin of the Library Association of Trinidad and Tobago. 1961-. 1/yr. Address same as Association
Bibliography Jordan, A., and Comissiong, B., "Trinidad and Tobago," in ALA World Encyclopedia of Library and Information Services. 2nd ed., pp. 803–804. Chicago: American Library Association, 1986; Williams, G. and DeFour-Sanatan, C, "Challenge to the Information Specialist in the Caribbean," COMLA Newsletter 57 (Sept. 1987):10, 12

Turkey

486 Türk Kütüphaneciler Dernegi (TKD) (Turkish Librarians' Association)*

Address Necatibey Cad. Elgun Sok., 8/8, 06440 Ankara Tel.: +90 312 2301325, Fax +90 312 2320453, TKD.dernek@gmail.com; www.kutuphaneci.org.tr/web/node.php

Languages Turkish

Established 19th November 1949, Ankara

Officers Chair: Ali Fuat Kartal; Deputy: Ebru Kaya; Ahmet Karatas; Mehmet Soluk; Controller: Ahmet Emre Aydin

Staff 2 employees as voluntary

General Assembly Entire membership meets every 2 years

Membership Types of membership: Individual, institutional, student, honorary. Requirements: Professional librarians and others interested in the aims of the Association

Structure Governed by Executive Committee. Affiliations: IFLA

Sources of Support Membership dues, sale of publications, professional projects

Major Fields of Interest Information management, library development, public libraries, archives, special libraries, library laws etc.

Major Goals and Objectives Mission: a. Preparing scientific and vocational studies and publications on librarianship, information science and archives, and announcing them to all segments of the society; b. Raising the awareness of the public on the importance of information and documentation services which have become multi-disciplinary; c. Following new developments and informing the society and members of profession about them; d. Ensuring solidarity and compatibility among colleagues; e. Ensuring the implementation of code of professional ethics and intellectual freedom statement; f. Disseminating our studies all over the world by collaborating with national and international organizations of librarianship or other related fields; g. Pioneering in solving problems of information centers

Activities Organizing conferences, seminars and workshops on library and information science, documentation and archives; sponsoring annual Turkish Library Week

Publications Official journal: Türk Kütüphaneciligi (Turkish Librarianship). 1986- Quarterly (formerly: Bulletin of Turkish Librarian's Association 1952–1985). Free to members. Abstracted by LISTA. Address same as Association. Turkish/ English abtsracts and summaries. Other publications: Proceedings of conferences, seminars, and professional monogaphs. Publications for sale

Bibliography Taner, S., "Turkey," in ALA World Encyclopedia of Library and Information Services. 2nd ed., pp. 807–809. Chicago: American Library Association, 1986; Khurshid, A., "Library Associations in Asia," Herald of Library Science 28 (1989):3–10

487 Üniversite ve Arastirma Kütüphanecileri Dernegi (ÜNAK) (University and Research Librarians Association)

Address 06532 Beytepe/Anakara Tel.: +90 312 2992111, Fax +90 312 2992111, unak@unak.org.tr; www.unak.org.tr(onlyinTurkish)

Languages Turkish

Uganda

488 Consortium of Uganda University Libraries (CUUL)

Address c/o Beatrice Sekabembe, Secretary CUUL, P.O. Box 7062, Kampala Tel.: +256 41 541524, Fax +256 41 341975, info@iucea.org; www.iucea.org
Languages English
Established Has its origins in the resolutions of the workshop for university librarians, organized by the Inter University Council for East Africa (IUCEA) at Moi University, Kenya in May 2000, which emphasized library cooperation. As a follow up, in a workshop organized at Makerere University in August 2000, librarians agreed to form a consortium for all university libraries of both public and licensed private universities in Uganda. The Constitution and Memorandum of Cooperation were inaugurated in December 2001, and CUUL was formally registered as an association in August 2004
General Assembly Entire membership meets once every 2 years
Membership All university libraries in Uganda (state owned and licensed private) are eligible members. Membership fee is US$ 150.00. Current membership is 16 universities' libraries
Structure Governed by General Assembly which elects a CUUL Council formed of: Chairperson, Vice Chairperson, Secretary, Treasurer, Publicity Secretary, and 5 committee members
Sources of Support Membership fees of about US$150.00; funding support from Inter University Council for East Africa, Electronic Information for Libraries Network (eIFL.net), and local universities support
Major Fields of Interest All areas that promote academic library development, eg., funding, quality assurance, resource sharing, ICT infrastructure and skills development, library standards, marketing, and advocacy
Major Goals and Objectives Sharing of skills, information materials, and physical resources. Applying modern management skills. Introducing the use of ICT in member university libraries. Cooperative acquisition and processing. Developing competent library human resources. Widening financial resource base for libraries in Uganda through economies of scale
Activities Regular meetings to strategize on the way forward for CUUL. Information resource sharing of both traditional and electronic resources. Human resource skills development. Workshops/seminars for capacity building in ICT. Continuous lobbying of relevant authorities for support both at national, regional, and international levels. Partnership with key organization such as the Electronic Information for Libraries Network (eIFL.Net). Ongoing studies/projects: New developments include arrangements to formalize the adoption of CUUL as a member of the eIFL.NET. CUUL to spearhead the formation of a consortium of university libraries in East Africa. This is expected to include the Consortium of Tanzania University Libraries (COTUL) and one expected to be formed in Kenya
Publications Still in planning stages. Have official binding documents such as: CUUL Constitution, CUUL Memorandum of Cooperation

489 Uganda Library and Information Association (ULIA)

Address P.O. Box 5894, Kampala Tel.: +256 77 580287 (Secretary); +256 77 495592 (Chairman), Fax +256 41 348625, library@imul.com;

www.ou.edu/cas/slis/ULA/ula_index.htm
Languages English
Established 1957, Nairobi, as a Regional Branch of the East African Library Association (EALA); when EALA was dissolved in order to enable strong national associations to develop, the present association was formed in 1972
Officers Pres: Innocent Rugambwa; Secr Gen: Sarah Kaddu
Staff One paid Administrative Officer
General Assembly Entire membership meets once every year
Membership Types of membership: Individual, institutional. Requirements: Interest and involvement in libraries.
Structure Governed by executive officers. Affiliations: COMLA, FID, IFLA, SCECSAL
Sources of Support Membership dues, grants, paid for conferences and workshops
Major Fields of Interest Establishment and development of libraries and information services
Major Goals and Objectives Evolving a policy for School Libraries in Uganda. Evolving a policy on Library and Information Science in Uganda. A mop up campaign to uplift the image of Library and Information Services in Uganda. Building rapport with government, donors and the international community on issues pertaining Library and Information Science. Building of a culture of reading amongst youngsters
Activities Sponsors conferences, seminars and other continuing education programs; advises Government on establishing and developing more effective library and information services; establishes contacts with associations in other countries sharing similar goals and objectives; undertakes outreach activities such as children's reading tents
Publications Official journals: Uganda Information Bulletin (Newsletter) 4/yr; Library and Information Science Journal for Uganda. Other publications: Annual reports, proceedings of conferences, seminars. Publications for sale
Bibliography Siddique, M., comp., "Library Associations in the Muslim World," in Librarianship in the Muslim World 1984. vol. 2, ed. by Anis Khurshid and Malahat Kaleem Sherwani, p. 99. Karachi: University of Karachi, 1985; Kawesa, B.M., "Uganda," in ALA World Encyclopedia of Library and Information Services. 2nd ed., pp. 811–813. Chicago 1986; Charles Batambuze, Dick Kawooya: Librarianship and professional ethics: the case for the Uganda Library Association. In: Robert Vagaan: The Ethics of Librarianship: An International Survey. Berlin: 2002; Charles Batambuze: Uganda Library Association. In: The Encyclopedia of Library and Information Science, 2nd ed. New York 2003

Ukraine

490 Ukrainska bibliotechna asociacia (ULA) (Ukrainian Library Association)*

Address Turgenivska Str. 83/85, 04050 Kiev Tel.: +380 44 486-50-92, Fax +380 44 482-13-34, u_b_a@ukr.net; www.uba.org.ua
Languages Ukrainian
Established February 1, 1995, Kyiv, Ukraine
Officers Pres: Iryna Shevchenko

General Assembly The General Conference meeting takes place once in 3 years. The last meeting was in December 2009
Membership 1500 individual members, 20 institutional members and 18 regional divisions
Structure Form of government – All-Ukrainian public professional organization, names of governing bodies – the General Conference members and the Presidium. ULA cooperates with Ministry of Culture and Tourism of Ukraine, Ukrainian and foreign non-governmental organizations, publishers, etc.
Sources of Support Association is financed through membership dues, charitable contributions and grants
Major Fields of Interest Library services, librarianship and library profession in general
Major Goals and Objectives To guarantee access of citizens to the whole volume of knowledge and information accumulated in libraries; to shape in the society the understanding of the library priority as a centre of culture, drawing the society attention to its problems; to promote the improvement of library legislation, organization and management of librarianship
Activities Exercises public control of librarianship, bibliographic and informational activities; participates in the independent expertise of the plans and programs related to development of librarianship in the country; organizes public discussions of priority problems facing librarianship; informs public of the problems emerging in the sector and the ways of their solution; supports initiatives of public movements, institutions and organizations, programs of people's deputies aiming to develop culture and librarianship; helps to satisfy professional interests of the ULA members including expansion of international contacts; enhances professional level of ULA members, forms the environment for professional communication; promotes professional and social development of librarians, bibliographers and informational workers, improves the system of their continuous education; joins international non-governmental organizations, maintains direct international contacts and ties; encourages theoretical research and practical studies in the aria of librarianship, bibliographic and informational activities; holds conferences, seminars, workshops and other events on the issues of library and informational activities; encourages exchange of experience and professional development through preparing curricula, organizing courses, study visits etc.; provides for social protection of librarians, bibliographers and informational workers, improves conditions of their work and domestic life, helps to establish appropriate labor remuneration and retirement pensions for them, fosters professional solidarity; determines personal bonuses, prizes and other forms of moral and material incentives; performs necessary administrative, economic and other commercial activities through setting up self-supporting institutions and organizations with a status of a legal person, establishes enterprises
Publications Collections of documents, results of some researches, learning programs, methodological materials in Ukrainian language. Their distribution is free of charge
Bibliography see www.uba.org.ua

United Kingdom

491 Art Libraries Society of the United Kingdom & the Republic of Ireland (ARLIS/UK & Ireland)*

Address c/o Lorraine Blackman, Business Manager, Cromwell Road, South Kensington, London SW7 2RL Tel.: +44 207 9422317, Fax +44 207 9422394, arlis@vam.ac.uk; www.arlis.org.uk

Languages English

Established 1969, Inaugural meeting held at Central School of Art, London

Officers Chair: Pat Christie; Hon Treas: Stephanie Silvester; Hon Secr: Nicola Salliss

General Assembly General membership meets once a year in february

Membership Types of membership: Individual, institutional, student, honorary. Requirements: Open to all individuals and institutions interested in art librarianship, persons working in art libraries and institutions such as museums and galleries

Structure Directed by an Executive Committee which meets not less than 3 times a year and consists of not less than 6 or more than 20 members. Affiliations: IFLA

Sources of Support Membership dues, sale of publications

Major Fields of Interest Art and design librarianship

Major Goals and Objectives The Society is established to promote, maintain, improve and advance education by the promotion of all aspects of librarianship of the visual arts including architecture and arts

Activities Seminars, courses, conferences, visits, representation on committees (e.g., CILIP, British Library). The Association has been active in promoting library-related legislation

Publications Official journal: Art Libraries Journal. 1976-. 4/yr. Free to members. Gillian Varley. Address: 10 Prevetts Way, Aldeburgh, Suffolk 1P15 5LI1, Tel: +44 1728 451948, Fax: +44 1728 452460. Email: g.varley@arlis2.demon.co.uk. Other publications: ARLIS News-sheet. 1976-. 6/yr. Editor: Liz Lawes. Address: Chelsea College of Art and Design, Library, Manresa Road, London SW3 6LS. Circ: Membership. English; ARLIS Union List of Periodicals on Art & Design and Related Subjects; ARLIS Directory, 1/yr

Bibliography Pacey, P., "ARLIS, the Art Libraries Society in the United Kingdom," Inspel 15 (1981):46–49

492 Aslib Informatuion Ltd (ASLIB)

Address Howard House, Wagon Lane, Bingley, Bradford, BD16 IWA Tel.: +44 20 72533349, Fax +44 20 74900577, aslib@aslib.com; www.aslib.com

Languages English

Established 1924, Hoddesdon, Hertfordshire, at the first conference of representatives of UK special libraries and information bureaus, as Association of Special Libraries and Information Bureaux (Aslib); present name adopted in the 1980s

Officers Accounts Clerk: Ann Piacquadio; Training Manager: Nicole Adamides

General Assembly General membership meets once a year

Membership Total members: 2,200 (200 individual, 2,000 institutional). 70 countries represented. Types of membership. Corporate Membership, Affiliate Membership, Student Membership. Requirements: Interest in information management.

Structure Governed by Council. Affiliations: IFLA, FID

Sources of Support Membership dues, sale of publications, fees from courses, conferences, seminars.

Major Fields of Interest Provision and management of information, including librarianship and information science

Major Goals and Objectives To stimulate awareness of the benefits of good management of information resources and its value; to represent and lobby for the interests of the information sector on matters and networks which are of national and international import; to provide a range of information related products and services to meet the needs of the information society

Activities Four main functions within the Association: consultancy, publications, training and recruitment. Specialized activities are further carried out by the various Groups and Branches (Electronics, Engineering, Biosciences, Technical Translating, Social Sciences, Economic and Business Information, Midlands Branch, etc.). Past achievements: Developed new range of publications, courses, seminars and advisory services. Current: Publishing, courses, conferences and seminars, and an advisory service for members on subjects such as online information retrieval, networking and library automation; Extensive continuing education offerings are coordinated by the Aslib Training Programme Manager

Publications Official Journal: Managing Information. 10 issues/yr. Website: www.managinginformation.com. £ 169 + vat within the UK or + postage in other countries. Other Journals: Journal of Documentation. 61 issues available; Library Hi Tech News. 83 issues available. Other publications: a variety of titles on information management and knowledge, produced by Emerald and Aslib / Europa Publications. e. g. Assessing Information Needs: tools, techniques and concepts for the Internet age. 2nd Edition 2000, by David Nicholas. Business information at work. by Michael Lowe. 1999. Copyright made easier. 3rd Edition. 2000. Raymond A. Wall in collaboration with Sandy Norman, Paul Pedley and Frank Harris. Members get 20% discount on all publications. Aslib Corporate members are entitled to two complimentary subscriptions.

Bibliography Vickers, P.H., "Work of the Aslib Research Department," Aslib Proceedings 33 (Sept. 1981):368–371; "Renaming Proposed for Aslib," Library Association Record 84 (1982):281; "Big Changes at Aslib," New Zealand Libraries 43 (1982):209; "Changes at Aslib," Unesco Journal of Information Science. Librarianship and Archives Administration 5 (1983):68–69; Lewis, D.A., "Role of the Professional Organisation," Aslib Proceedings 35 (1983):108–120; "Aslib, the Association for Information Mangement: Some Recent Developments," Indexer 14 (1985): 154; Lewis, D.A., "Aslib Development Plan," Library Association Record 87 (1985):381; "Information '85: Aslib/IIS/LA/Society of Archivists/SCONUL Conference," ibid.:382–383+; Harrison, K.C., "United Kingdom," in ALA World Encyclopedia of Library and Information Services. 2nd ed., pp. 823–830. Chicago: American Library Association, 1986; Sippings, G., "The Use of Information Technology by Information Services: The Aslib Information Technology Survey 1987," The Electronic Library 5 (1987):354–357; "60th Aslib Annual Conference. The Information Business: Directions Forward," Aslib Proceedings 40 (1988):207–226

Comment (formerly The Association of Special Libraries and Information Bureaux)

493 Association of British Theological and Philosophical Libraries (ABTAPL)

Address c/o Carol Reekie, Honorary Secretary, Jesus Lane, Cambridge, CB5 8BJ

Tel.: +44 1223 741043, cr248@cam.ac.uk; www.abtapl.org.uk
Languages English
Established 1954, as the UK representative for the proposed International Association of Theological Libraries, which was not realized at that time
Officers Chair: Alan Linfield; Hon Secr: Carol Reekie; Hon Treas: Ian Jackson; Hon Edi: Humeyra Ceylan; Conference Secr: Rachel Eichhorn
Staff None
General Assembly General membership meets twice a year
Membership Requirements: Interest in the bibliography and librarianship of the subject fields.
Structure Governed by a committee. Affiliations: Library Association, BETH
Sources of Support Membership dues, sale of publications
Major Fields of Interest Bibliography and librarianship of theology and philosophy
Major Goals and Objectives Promote the cause of librarianship in these special fields and disseminate information about techniques, collections and publications relevant to members
Activities Helds day conference including a visit to a library in the specialisation in the Autumn, residential weekend held in the Spring
Publications Official journal: Bulletin of the Association of British Theological & Philosophical Libraries. 1974-. (new series). 3/yr. Free to members. Other publications: Bibliographies and guides, e. g. A Guide to the Theological Libraries; Union List of Periodicals
Bibliography Collison, R.L., "SCOTAPL and ABTAPL: The Early Years," Bulletin of the Association of British Theological and Philosophical Libraries 34/35 (1986):13–15

494 Association of Librarians in Land-Based Colleges and Universities (ALLCU)

Address c/o Christine Barclay, Carslogie Road, Cupar, Fife KY15 4JB jkeightley@warkscol.ac.uk; www.allcu.org.uk
Languages English
Established 1978
Officers Chair: Melanie Fisher; Secr: Jane Keightley; Treas: Margaret Patterson
General Assembly Entire membership meets once a year
Membership Dues: 10 English Pound/yr
Structure Governed by executive officers. Organization within CILIP
Major Fields of Interest Agricultural librarianship at academic libraries
Major Goals and Objectives To promote agricultural librarianship at college and university libraries; to provide a forum for exchange of information for agricultural librarians at such institutions; to improve the services of agricultural librarians at institutions of higher education
Activities ALLCU exists to provide an opportunity to discuss problems of mutual interest and their solutions; to keep abreast with new developments and techniques in agricultural and horticultural information with special reference to its organisation, dissemination and exploitation for college members; to see the functioning and operation of specialist libraries and research centres; to establish contacts with colleagues for assistance, co-operation and exchange; to act as a focus and forum for liaison with national and regional specialist information groups

Publications Official journal: ALLCU Bulletin
Bibliography "ALCU Conference 1989," Aslib Information 17 (1989):245
Comment Formerly: Agricultural Librarians in Colleges and Universities

495 Association of Librarians in Land-Based Colleges and Universities (ALLCU)

Address c/o Christine Barclay, Chair, Carslogie Road, Cupar Fife KY15 4JB Tel.: +44 1334 658998, cbarclay@elmwood.ac.uk; www.allcu.org.uk/index.html#anchor135040
Languages English
Established 1978
General Assembly Members meet once per year at the conference
Membership Dues (Pound Sterling): 10/yr
Structure Affiliation: CILIP
Major Goals and Objectives 1) To discuss problems of mutual interest and their solutions; 2) to keep abreast with new developments and techniques in agricultural and horticultural information with special reference to its organisation, dissemination and exploitation for college members; 3) to see the functioning and operation of specialist libraries and research centres; 4) to establish contacts with colleagues for assistance, co-operation and exchange; 5) to act as a focus and forum for liaison with national and regional specialist information groups
Activities Offers Margaret Whiteman Bursary, annual conferences: 2008: Wadham College, Oxford; 2009: Hadlow College, Kent
Publications Official journal: ALLCU Bulletin

496 Association of Senior Children's and Education Librarians (ASCEL)

Address John Dryden House 8–10 The Lakes, PO Box 216, Northampton Northamptonshire NN4 7DD Tel.: +44 1604 237954, helen.boothroyd@suffolk.gov.uk; www.ascel.org.uk(passwordrequired)
Languages English
Membership Librarians who have senior-management responsibility for providing library services to children and young people in England and Wales
Major Fields of Interest Network of children's and education librarians
Major Goals and Objectives To promote the value of library services for children
Activities Training, annual conference
Publications No official journal, regular newsletters

497 Association of UK Media Librarians (AUKML)

Address c/o Membership Secretary, PO Box 14254, London SE1 9WL Tel.: +44 207 2617792, membership@aukml.org.uk; www.aukml.org.uk
Languages English
Established 1986
Officers Chair: Richard Nelsson; Chair-elect: N.N.; Meeting Secr: Caroline White; Treas: Gertrud Erbach
Membership Dues (Pound Sterling): Full Member 25; Associate Member 20; Student/Unwaged 15
Structure Governed by executive board

Major Fields of Interest Create links between librarians and information workers in all areas of the media industry
Major Goals and Objectives To improve the professional standing of information workers through exchanging knowledge and experience
Activities Organizes meetings, events and conferences to keep members up-to-date with emerging techniques in information management
Publications Official journal: Deadline. Editor: Richard Nelsson. Address: richard.nelsson@guardian.co.uk

498 The Bibliographical Society

Address c/o The Honorary Secretary, Malet Street, London WC1E 7HU Tel.: +44 20 7862-8679, Fax +44 20 7862-8720, Secretary@BibSoc.org.uk; www.bibsoc.org.uk
Languages English
Established 1892, London
Officers Pres: John Barnard; Vice-Pres: David Pearson; Hon Secr: Meg Ford; Hon Librarian: Robin Myers
Staff Admin: Wim Van Mierlo
General Assembly The annual general meeting is held on the 3rd Tuesday in October
Membership Requirements: Membership is international and is open to all who, by reason of profession or private interest, are concerned with bibliography. It is conditional upon election by the Council. Candidates for membership should be proposed by a member and their names submitted through the Hon.Sec. Dues (Pound Sterling): 33.00 (overseas 37.00), a reduced rate of 25 for full-time students and anyone over the age of 65. Life membership for those over 60: 300.00
Structure Governed by Executive Council and executive officers
Sources of Support Membership dues, sale of publications, grants from British Library, bequests, donations
Major Fields of Interest Historical and textual bibliography
Major Goals and Objectives To promote and encourage study and research in the fields of historical, analytical, descriptive and textual bibliography, and the history of printing, publishing, bookselling, bookbinding and collecting; to hold meetings at which papers are read and discussed; to print and publish a journal and books concerned with bibliographical library, from time to time to award a medal for services to bibliography; to support bibliographical research by awarding grants and busaries
Activities Monthly Lecture Programme, sponsors grants and Gold Medal
Publications Official journal: The Library. 1892-. 4/yr. Free to members. English. Indexed in Abstracts of English Studies. Year's Work in English Studies. Index of Selected Bibliographical Journals (1935–70). Extensive past and current publications program in accord with the aims of the Society includes monographs, small and large quartos, facsimiles, and folio monographs. Issues annual report, occasional papers, list of members. Price lists available. Publications listed in journal. Publications exchange program in effect. Recent Publications: Gameson, R., "The Earliest Books of Canterbury Cathedral", London (2008); Shell, Alison/Emblow, Alison (Ed.), "Index to the Court Books of the Stationers' Company, 1679–1717 (2007); Foot, Mirijam, "Eloquent Witnesses: Bookbinding and Their history" (2004)
Bibliography Retrospective sources: The Bibliographical Society: Studies in Retrospect.

London: The Society, 1945 (covers 1892–1942); Myers, R., "The First Fifty Years of the Bibliographical Society, 1892–1942," Antiquarian Book Monthly Revue 5

499 Britain and Ireland Association of Aquatic Sciences Libraries and Information Centres (BIASLIC)

Address c/o Sarah Carter, Pakefield Road, Suffolk NR33 0HT www.ife.ac.uk/biaslic
Languages English
Established 1969 in Plymouth
Officers Chair: Ian McCulloch; Secr: Sarah Carter; Treas: Alison Bethel
Membership Members from all types and sizes of library – government, university research institute, learned society. Membership is free
Structure Governed by executive board
Major Fields of Interest Brings together librarians and information workers in marine biology, oceanography, fisheries, aquatic ecology and freshwater scientific and technological research
Major Goals and Objectives To provide a forum for the exchange of information, and a discussion of issues relevant to aquatic science librarianship and to librarianship as a whole
Activities Were instrumental in founding EURASLIC (European Association of Aquatic Science Libraries and Information Centres) and contribute to the activities of EURASLIC and IAMSLIC (International Association of Aquatic and Marine Science Libraries and Information Centers). Provide input for the Aquatic Sciences and Fisheries Abstracts database. Serve on advisory groups and working committees on aquatic information set up and sponsored by the FAO (Food and Agriculture Organization of the United Nations) and IOC (the Intergovernmental Oceanographic Commission of UNESCO). Exchange information via the BIASLIC email discussion list; organizes annual conferences
Publications No official journal. Other publications: Union serials lists. Directory of Marine and Freshwater Scientists and Research Engineers in the United Kingdom

500 British and Irish Association of Law Librarians (BIALL)

Address c/o Susan Frost, BIALL Administrator, 26 Myton Crescent, Warwick CV34 6QA contact@biall.org.uk; www.biall.org.uk
Languages English
Established 1969, Harrogate, Yorkshire, on the occasion of the Secon Law Librarianship sponsoed by Leeds Polytechnic
Officers President: Daniella King; Pres-Elect: David Will; Hon Secr: Blaine Bird; Treas: Alden Bowers
Staff 1
General Assembly Annual Conference and AGM in June each year
Membership Total members: over 850 (individual and institutional). Requirements: The individual/institution should be engaged using legal or related materials and legal information. Associate membership available for those not directly engaged as above.
Structure Governed by the Council, which consists of 4 officers assisted by a committee of five members, all annually elected
Sources of Support Membership dues, sale of publications
Major Fields of Interest Law librarianship

Major Goals and Objectives To promote the better administration and exploitation of law libraries and legal information units, principally in Britain and Ireland. The Association shall represent all jurisdictions in Britain and Ireland. The Association is formed for the benefit of members and to enhance the status of the profession by the further education and training of law librarians, legal information officers, documentalists and others, through the organisation of meetings and conferences, the publication of information of interest to members, the encouragement of bibliographical study and research in law and librarianship, the promotion of cooperation with other organisations or societies, and all other such things as are incidental or conducive to the attainment or furtherance of these objects

Activities Holds annual conferences, organises training courses

Publications Official journal: Legal Information Management. Formerly: The Law Librarian. 1970-. 3/yr. Address same as Association. Editor: Editor: Christine Miskin. Address: Information Consultant High Hall Steeton Keighley West Yorkshire BD20 6SB. Other publications: Directory of British and Irish Law Libraries. 7th ed. 2003; SLS/BIALL Academic Law Library Survey 2001/2002; E-Newsletter; Sources of Biographical Information on Past Lawyers. Guy Holborn, 1999; History of the British and Irish Association of Law Librarians 1969–1999. Mary Blake, 2000; Legal Research Training Packs 2007

Bibliography Moys, E.M., "BIALL Landmarks of the First Ten Years," The Law Librarian 11 (1980):3–5; Maiden, C., "BIALL – the 18th Annual Study Conference [Aberystwyth, 11–14 Aug. 1987]," Law Librarian 18 (1987):97–98; 19 (1988):33 (Addendum); Mineur, B.W., "Law and Librarianship," Law Librarian 19 (1988): 1–4; Fletcher, V. A. A. and Francis, C., "BIALL Course: Teaching Law Students to Use Full Text Online Databases [Institute of Advanced Legal Studies, London, Mar. 16, 1988]," Law Librarian 19 (1988):66–68

501 British Association for Information and Library Education and Research (BAILER)

Address c/o Professor John Feather, Chair, Loughborough Leicestershire LE11 3TU Tel.: +44 1509 223050, Fax +44 1509 223053, s.m.corrall@sheffield.ac.uk; www.bailer.org.uk

Languages English

Established 1992, superseding the Association of British Library and Information Schools (ABLISS), whose membership had been restricted to Heads of Departments, new association includes all teaching and research staff in the 18 Information and Library Schools in the United Kingdom and Ireland

Officers Chair: Sheila Corrall; Secr: Gaynor Eyre; Treas: Paul Matthews

General Assembly Entire membership meets four times a year, twice in London, twice in other areas

Membership Total members: 18 (institutional)

Sources of Support Membership dues

Major Fields of Interest Education for librarianship and information studies

Major Goals and Objectives To formulate and express the educational policy and attitudes of the LIS departments of the United Kingdom and Ireland; to maintain contact with other bodies concerned with education for librarianship and information work

Activities Lobbies on behalf of the sector; works with professional bodies; sponsors workshops for teachers in library schools
Publications No official journal. Occasional publications

502 British Records Association (BRA)

Address c/o Finsbury Library, 245 St John Street, London EC1V 4NB Tel.: +44 20 78330428, Fax +44 20 78330416, brrecass@btconnect.com; www.britishrecordsassociation.org.uk
Languages English
Established 1932, Nov., at conference of record and allied societies
General Assembly General membership meets once a year
Membership Institutional and individual membership. Requirements: Everybody who is interested in archives. Dues: (Pound Sterling): Full Member (institutional: 55/yr; individual, 25; retired/student/unwaged, 15); Affiliate Member (Institutions only – 20 per year). Affiliate members get all the benefits of full membership, but do not receive Archives
Structure Governed by Council. Affiliations: International Council on Archives, Commonwealth Archivists Association
Sources of Support Membership dues, sale of publications, government subsidies, institutional donations
Major Fields of Interest Preservation and use of records
Major Goals and Objectives To coordinate and encourage the work of all those individuals and bodies interested in the preservation and use of records, and to rescue records threatened with destruction or dispersal
Activities Maintains Records Preservation Section; Sponsors annual conferences, exhibits and continuing education lectures
Publications Official journal: Archives. 1949-. 2/yr. Free for members. Subscription: 50 Pound Sterling /yr. Address same as Association. English. Other publications: Newsletter, 2/yr; Archives and the User. (A series of books aimed at providing clear, comprehensive introductions to various classes of records and their publication); Guidelines (leaflets).
Bibliography "Private Archives and Public Funding. British Records Association, Hatfield House Conference, 1981," Archives 15 (1982):13M47, 170–174; Davies, J., "Report of the Annual Conference 1985," Archives 19 (1986):41–42

503 Business Librarians Association (BLA)

Address c/o Ann-Marie Ashby, Liaison Librarian, Edgbaston, Birmingham, B15 2TT Tel.: +44 1865 288883, emma.cragg@sbs.ox.ac.uk; www.bbslg.org
Languages English
Officers Chair: Andy Priestner; Secr: Nicole Dennis; Hon Treas: David Clare
General Assembly Annual General Meeting. 2006: Manchester – Manchester Business School, 2007: Northhampton – University of Northhampton, 2008: Leeds – University of Leeds, 2009: Dublin – Irish Management Institute
Membership Requirements: Open to those institutions in the UK and Ireland which offer courses in management education at Masters level or above. Library staff from these member institutions, with sufficient involvement in business information provision, are encouraged to contribute to the group

Major Goals and Objectives Intends to be a forum for discussion and exchange of ideas
Activities lis-business mailing list for the information exchange between members; annual conference

504 The Chartered Institute of Library and Information Professionals in Ireland (CILIP in Ireland)

Address c/o Exec Secreatry, 100 Craigbrack Road, Eglinton BT47 3BD Tel.: +44 7777 691726, elga.logue@btinternet.com; http://www.cilip.org.uk/ireland
Established 2002, as the Northern Ireland branch of CILIP
General Assembly Annual Joint Conference with the Library Association of Ireland
Structure Branch is governed by officers and a committee
Major Fields of Interest Libraries in Ireland
Major Goals and Objectives To set, maintain, monitor and promote standards of excellence in the creation, management, exploitation and sharing of information and knowledge resources; to support the principle of equality of access to information, ideas and works of the imagination which it affirms is fundamental to a thriving economy, democracy, culture and civilisation; to enable its Members to achieve and maintain the highest professional standards in all aspects of delivering an information service, both for the professional and the public good
Activities 1) Publication and communication: Communication is conducted with the membership through the Branch newsletter CILIP News; An Leabharlann – The Irish Library – which contains substantial articles and reviews and is published in co-operation with the Library Association of Ireland; CILIP in Ireland Branch Annual Report; Annual Members' Day and Annual CILIP Presidential Visit. 2) Education and Training is directed towards the educational and training needs of the profession. These include an annual conference which takes place in April and is held in co-operation with the Library Association of Ireland, one-day educational courses on specific topics and the import of CILIP Ridgmount Street building speakers. 3) Links with other Bodies both domestic and international are sustained with the Career Development Group and Colleges of Further and Higher Education, while international links have been developed especially through the Branch's long established links with the Library Association of Ireland. 4) Policy Forming includes submissions to appropriate government bodies on policy issues directly affecting library and information provision, and on professional issues, to CILIP, Ridgmount Street. Such submissions to, and meetings with Ministers, always stress the importance of maintaining the quality of the library service in Ireland and sustaining a healthy communication channel between Government and CILIP
Publications Branch newsletter CILIP News; The Irish Library (published in co-operation with the Library Association of Ireland); CILIP in Ireland Branch Annual Report

505 Chartered Institute of Library and Information Professionals in Scotland (CILIPS)

Address 1st Floor Building C, Brandon Gate, Leechlee Road, Hamilton ML3 6AU Tel.: +44 1698 458888, Fax +44 1698 283170, slic@slainte.org.uk; www.slainte.org.uk
Languages English
Established 1908, Edinburgh as Scottish Library Association, reformed in 2002 by the

amalgamation of the Library Association and the Institute of Information Scientists

Officers Pres: Moira Methven; VP: Ivor Lloyd; Asst Dir: Rhona Arthur; Cathy Kearney

Staff Dir: Elaine Fulton; Ass Dirs: Rhona Arthur, Cathy Kearney; Network Proj. Officer: Hazel Lauder; Information Officer: Emma Jones; Admin. Assist.: Ann Steele

General Assembly Yearly annual conference in May or June

Structure Governed by Council elected by membership. Four regional branches

Sources of Support Membership dues, sale of publications, conferences and courses

Major Fields of Interest To support the principle of equality of access to information, ideas and works of the imagination, as fundamental elements of Scotland's economy, democracy, culture and civilisation. To enable members to achieve and maintain the highest professional standards in all aspects of delivering library and information services for the good of the people of Scotland. To work with relevant Scottish organisations and the Library Association to set, maintain, monitor and promote standards of excellence in the creation, management, exploitation and sharing of information and knowledge resources within Scotland

Major Goals and Objectives 1) Library and information community: Influence the development of policies relating to the provision of information and library services at national and local level. Promote guidelines for the provision of services and provide advise on matters relating to the development of library and information services. Ensure the effective representation of the interests of members in the wider library and information community. Market and promote the role and value of library and information services to all sections of the community in Scotland. 2) Individual members: Unite all persons engaged or interested in library and information work. Promote and develop an effective infrastructure for the professional development of individual members and ensure provision of services and facilities according to changing needs and interests. Provide and disseminate information to members. Provide advice on matters relating to career development

Activities Representing library/information service interests at national and local level; developing and promoting standards; advising individual members; annual Conference; continuing Educational Development Programme; Publications Programme; bi-monthly journal Information Scotland

Publications Official journal: Information Scotland (formerly: Scottish Libraries) 1950-. 6/yr. Free to members. Editor: Debby Raven. email: debbyraven@btconnect.com. English. Indexed in LISA, Lib.Lit, etc. Other publications: Annual reports, proceedings of conferences and seminars; Scottish Library and Information Resources ISBN 0 954 1160 38; Publications for sale, price lists available. Publications exchange program in effect

Bibliography Ed. McElroy, R. et al.: "Advocating Libraries: Essays presented to Robert Craig"; Craig, R.: "Pace of Change: SLA 1908–1983". In: SLA News 177 (Sept/Oct. 1983), p. 7; "Council Capers" In: SLA News 178 (Nov/Dec. 1983), p. 5; "Robert Craig," (Executive Secretary to the SLA). In: SLA News 187 (May/June 1985), p.21–22

506 Chartered Institute of Library and Information Professionals (CILIP)

Address 7 Ridgmount St, London WC1E 7AE Tel.: +44 20 72550500, Fax +44 20 72550501; www.cilip.org.uk

Languages English

Established 2002, following the unification of the Institute of Information Scientists

(IIS) and The Library Association (LA)
Officers Pres: Biddy Fisher; Vice-Pres: Brian Hall; Immediate Past Pres: Peter Griffiths
Membership Categories: Corporate, student, affiliated, supporting, overseas, and institutional membership
Structure Governed by a council
Major Fields of Interest Library and information professionals
Major Goals and Objectives To promote and develop librarianship, to provide acces to information
Activities Offers further education, training and development programme, workshops, E-bulletin service, conferences, information services, professional support; sponsors medals and awards
Publications Official magazine: Update, 10 issues/yr

507 Cymdeithas Llyfrgelloedd Cymru (WLA) (Welsh Library Association)

Address Llanbadarn Fawr, Aberystwyth SY23 3AS Tel.: +44 1970 622174, Fax +44 1970 622190, hle@aber.ac.uk; www.dils.aber.ac.uk/holi/wla/wla.htm
Languages Welsh, English
Established A Branch of The Library Association (LA) (founded 1877); became Wales and Monmouthshire Branch of the Library Association in 1933, and assumed present name in 1971
General Assembly Entire membership meets three or four times a year
Structure Governed by executive officers within the LA structure. Affiliations: A national branch of LA; member of IFLA through LA
Sources of Support Membership dues, sale of publications
Major Fields of Interest Librarianship and information science
Major Goals and Objectives To promote the professional development of individual members; to provide and disseminate information to members; to represent the views of its members; to unite all persons engaged in or interested in library and information work
Activities To unite all persons engaged in or interested in library and information work; to co-operate with other agencies to promote the development of library and information services nationally and internationally; to support the interests of members working in specific areas; to publishe books, journals and other materials
Publications Official journal: Y Ddolen: Cylchgrawn Cymdeithas Llvfrgelloedd Cymru/Journal of The Welsh Library Association. 1970-. 3/yr. Free to members. Welsh, English. Other publications: Jones, B., A Bibliography of Anglo-Welsh Literature 1900–65 (1970); Huws, G., Ffynonellau gwybodaeth am Gymru a'r iaith Gvmraeg: Rhestr ddethol/Information Sources Relating to Wales and the Welsh Language: Select List (1984); WLA Index Series. WLA Bibliographies Series, annual reports, proceedings of meetings, conferences, etc. Publications available for sale from Honorary Secretary. No publications exchange program in effect

508 Early Years Library Network (EYLN)*

Address 7 Ridgmount Street, London WC1E 7AE Tel.: +44 20 7255 0500, hannah.plom; www.cilip.org.uk/eyln/index.html
Languages English

Established 2003
Staff 1, paid
Sources of Support Funded by a partnership between the Chartered Institute of Library and Information Professionals (CILIP) and the Esmee Fairbairn Foundation
Major Fields of Interest Library services for pre-school children and their families/parents
Major Goals and Objectives Seeks to raise the quality of library services to pre-school children and their families
Comment Due to a funding change the Early Years Library Network expects dramatic changes in the future. Please note that existing entry is partly out date.

509 International Association of Music Libraries, Archives and Documentation Centres – United Kingdom and Ireland Branch (IAML (UK&Irl))*
Address c/o Geoff Thomason, General Secretary, 124 Oxford Road, Manchester M13 9RD Tel.: +44 161 9075245, Fax +44 161 2737611; www.iaml.info
Languages English
Established 1953, London
Officers Pres: Richard Chesser; Immediate Past Pres: Liz Hart; Gen Secr: Geoff Thomason; Treas: Claire Kidwell
Staff None
General Assembly Entire membership meets once a year
Membership Types of membership: Individual and institutional. Requirements: none
Structure Governed by Executive Committee. Affiliations: A national branch of IAML; CILIP
Sources of Support Membership dues, sale of publications, courses
Major Fields of Interest Music libraries and librarianship
Major Goals and Objectives To represent the interests of music libraries and librarianship; to coordinate the work of music libraries and music librarians and to promote their status; to study and make effective music bibliography and music library science; to make available all the resources of British music libraries; to cooperate with other national and international organizations in related fields; to send delegates to conferences and to cooperate with the parent body in all possible ways
Activities Training, Courses, Education and Conferences, Awards and Grants
Publications Official Journal: BRIO. 1964-. 2/yr.Free to members. Editor: Katharine Hogg Katharine@foundlingmuseum.org.uk. English. Indexed in Lib.Lit., USA. RILM. Other publications: Newsletter. 2/yr. Free to members. Editor: Anna Pensaert amljp2@cam.ac.uk. Annual Survey of Music Libraries; IAML(UK&Irl) Annual Report; The Availability of Printed Music in Great Britain: a report (1988); Library and Information Plan for Music: written statement (1993); IAML(UK) Music Sets Survey 1997; The British Union Catalogue of Music Periodicals, 2nd edition, complied by IAML(UK&Irl)'s Documentation Committee (1998: ISBN 1-85967-133-8), available direct from the publishers, Ashgate; Working in a music library by IAML(UK&Irl)'s Courses & Education Committee: 1997 & 2002; Richard Turbet, ed., Music Librarianship in the United Kingdom (2003: ISBN 0-7546 0572-8), available direct from the publishers, Ashgate; Thompson, Pam & Lewis, Malcolm, Access to music information & collections: a plan for music libraries & archives in the UK & Ireland, 2003: ISBN 0-95451-700-8;

Ridgewell, Rupert, Concert programmes in the UK & Ireland: a preliminary report (2003: ISBN 0-95207-039-1). Publications Officer: Almut Boehme, Music Division, National Library of Scotland, George IV Bridge, Edinburgh, EH1 1EW. Tel. 0131 623 3880.

510 Japan Library Group (JLG)*

Address c/o Hamish Todd, Chair, 96 Euston Road, London NW1 2DB Tel.: +44 20 74127662, Fax +44 20 74127641, hamish.todd@bl.uk; www.jlgweb.org.uk
Established 1966
Officers Chair: Hamish Todd; Secr: Fujiko Kobayashi
General Assembly 2 meetings per year
Membership 16 academic libraries in the UK
Major Fields of Interest Material on Japanese studies in University Libraries in the UK
Major Goals and Objectives To pool experience and resources together in the development of holdings of Japanese language materials for Japanese Studies in national and university libraries in Britain; to enhance communication between librarians and the academics
Activities Various projects e. g. the UK Union Catalogue of Japanese Books

511 Librarians' Christian Fellowship (LCF)

Address c/o Graham Hedges, Secretary, 34 Thurlestone Avenue, Ilford, Essex, IG3 9DU Tel.: +44 20 85991310, secretary@librarianscf.org.uk; www.librarianscf.org.uk
Languages English
Established 1976
Officers Pres: Gordon A. Harris; Secr+Publ Off: Graham Hedges; Chair: Louise Manners; Treas: Nick Horley
Staff None
General Assembly Entire membership meets once a year
Membership Full membership open to all Christians who work in any professional or clerical position in any library, archive or information service, or who have worked in such a position in the past, or who are training to take up such a position, or have trained. Associate membership open to all Christians who desire to identify with, support and promote the work of the Fellowship but who are not working in the field of library, archive and information work
Structure Governed by membership Council. Affiliations: CILIP, Christian Book Promotions, Christian Research Association, Christians at Work, Evangelical Alliance, Universities' and Colleges' Christian Fellowship
Sources of Support Membership dues, donations
Major Fields of Interest Christian librarianship – the application of the Christian faith to library and information work
Major Goals and Objectives (a) The provision for all Christians engaged in or about to enter upon library work of the opportunity to examine their profession from a specifically Christian standpoint; (b) The positive presentation of our Lord Jesus Christ to the library world and through the library world to the general public, especially in the United Kingdom and Eire; (c) The promotion of the fellowship and unity between Christians engaged in library work; (d) The provision of opportunities for Christian librarians to make their professional training and experience available to the wider Christian community

Activities   Annual conferences, annual public lectures, library development programme within the UK and overseas (advice and practical help to Christian organisations unable to pay for professional staff for their library or information services)
Publications   Official journals: LCF Newsletter. 3/yr; Christian Librarian 1/yr. Other publications: Issues in Librarianship
Bibliography   Graham Hedges, Serving Christ in the Library. In: Impact Magazine Vol 1 (March 2003), p. 30; Graham Hedges, Twenty-two Year's Service in the Library and the Curch. In: Librarians's World, Vol. 7, No. 2 (1998), p. 22–24; Graham Hedges, Serving the Community. In: New Christian Herald, 30. Nov. 1996, p. 8

512   The Library Campaign *

Address   22 Upper Woburn Place, London WC1H OTB   Tel.: +44 845 450 5946, Fax +44 845 450 5947, librarycam@aol.com; www.librarycampaign.com
Languages   English
Established   1984
Officers   Dir: Jill Wight
Structure   Governed by an Executive Committee
Sources of Support   Donations, membership subscriptions and affiliations
Major Fields of Interest   Library and information services
Major Goals and Objectives   To advance the lifelong education of the public by the promotion, support, assistance and improvement of libraries through the activities of friends and user groups
Publications   Official journal: Library Campaigner. 3/yr. Free to members

513   Museum Librarians and Archivists Group *

Address   c/o Martin Flynn, London SW7 2RL   Tel.: +44 207 9422291, m.flynn@vam.ac.uk; http://mlagblog.wordpress.com/
Languages   English
Officers   Chair: Chris Mills
Staff   None
General Assembly   Group meets quarterly
Membership   Approximately 30 members, no fees involved
Structure   Informal group with minimal bureaucracy
Sources of Support   None
Major Fields of Interest   Museums, Libraries and Archives
Major Goals and Objectives   Share views, experiences and innovative ideas with librarians and archivists working in the museum sector
Activities   Biennial conferences, group visits to our own institutions, regular half-day seminars

514   Museums, Libraries and Archives Council (MLA)

Address   Grosvenor House, 14 Bennetts Hill, Birmingham B2 5RS   Tel.: +44 121 345 7300, Fax +44 121 345 7303, info@mla.gov.uk; www.mla.gov.uk
Languages   English
Established   2000, replaces the Museums and Galleries Commission (MGC) and the Library and Information Commission (LIC)

Officers Chief Exec: Roy Clare; PA to Chief Exec: Helen Abate
Staff 70
Membership We have not got members
Structure Governed by Executive Board
Sources of Support No membership fees, sponsored by DCMS
Major Fields of Interest Museums, Libraries and Archives
Major Goals and Objectives 1. To assist the funders of museums, libraries and archives to oversee constant improvement and increased responsiveness to local needs; 2. To enable museums, libraries and archives increase their contribution to learning and skills in order that individuals have improved life and employment opportunities; 3. To enable museums, libraries and archives to make an increasing contribution to their local economies and communities; 4. To be a highly effective organisation providing clear leadership and strong advocacy for the sector, respected and valued by all that we work with
Activities Major strategic initiatives: Renaissance in the Regions (revitalisation of regional museums in England); the People's Network (project to link all public libraries to the internet); Archives Task Force to investigate the future of archives in the UK; responsible for implementing Framework for the Future, the government's 10-year strategy for public libraries
Publications No official journal. Other publications available via: www.mla.gov.uk/information/publications/00pubs.asp

515 National Association of Toy and Leisure Libraries (NATLL)

Address 1 A Harmood Street, London NW1 8DN Tel.: +44 20 72554600, Fax +44 20 72554602, admin@playmatters.co.uk; www.natll.org.uk
Languages English
Established 1972 as the Toy Libraries Association (TLA), it became the National Toy Libraries Association (NTLA) and in 1993 was renamed the National Association of Toy & Leisure Libraries (NATLL). It has used the campaign title Play Matters since 1983
Staff 8 (paid)
General Assembly Entire membership meets once a year
Membership Requirements: Open to any interested individual, local authority, or toy library.
Structure Governed by elected Council of management
Sources of Support Membership dues, sale of publications, government grants, donations from charitable trusts and other sources
Major Fields of Interest Child development through play
Major Goals and Objectives To support existing toy and leisure libraries, to promote the development of new toy and leisure libraries, and to raise awareness of the importance of play
Activities Offers training courses covering toy and leisure library practice, child development, learning through play, and special needs provision; provides Helpline, a free Telephone information service available for anyone planning, setting up or running a toy or leisure library
Publications No official journal. Other publications: Good Toy Guide (2008/98); A guide to choosing and using Musical Instruments; Games Pack to Extended Schools games club; Learning to Share; More Playsense Acitivity Cards; Networking and Getting

together; Nuts and Bolts; PLay Helps Video; Playing to Learn Activity Pack with Game Cards (2002); Playing and Learning at Home (2002); Playsense Activity Cards for Babies and Young Children (2000); The Most Excellent Toy Guide (2001)
Bibliography Atkinson, P., "The Role of ACTIVE within PLAY MATTERS," Ark: Journal of Toy Libraries Association (Summer 1988):4–5

516 Network of Government Library and Information Specialists (NGLIS)

Address c/o Kate Pritchard, Secretary, Defra, Ergon House, 17 Smith Square, London, SWIP 3JR Tel.: +44 20 74388483, Fax +44 20 74389160; www.nglis.org.uk
Languages English
Established 1925
Officers Chair: Lorna Goodey; VChair: Diana Murgatroyd; Secr: Kate Pritchard; Treas: William Mead
Staff None
General Assembly General membership meets once a year
Membership Requirements: staff at all levels, particularly welcomes administrative officers, assistants and other library support grades who are often excluded from other professional organisations. Dues (Pound Sterling): 7,50/yr
Structure Governed by Committee of 16 members
Sources of Support Membership dues, sale of publications
Major Fields of Interest Government libraries and librarians
Major Goals and Objectives To cultivate a common interest in the cost-effective management of information among all staff working in UK government libraries, and to foster cooperation within the government service environment
Activities Runs courses, organises annual conferences and library visits, helds Summer Social
Publications Official journal: State Librarian. 1953-. 3/yr. English. Indexed in LISA. Lib.Lit. Publications exchange program in effect
Bibliography "Circle of State Librarians Conference on Government Libraries and the Challenge of Change," State Librarian 30 (1982):01–21; Driels, J., "Circle of State Librarians [1987] Conference on How to Manage More on Less: Cost Effective Management and Publicity for Today's Library and Information Services," State Librarian 36 (1988):2–13,16–18; Willsher, M.J.D., "Comments on the 1987 Circle [of State Librarians] Conference," ibid.:25

517 Records Management Society of Great Britain (RMS)

Address 14 Blandford Square, Newcastle upon Tyne NE1 4HZ Tel.: +44 191 2442839, Fax +44 191 2453802, info@rms-gb.org.uk; www.rms-gb.org.uk
Established 1983
Officers Chair: Mattew Stephenson; Vice Chair: David Bridge; Exec Secr: Paul Duller; Treas: Alison North
Membership Requirements: All those concerned with records and information, regardless of their professional or organisational status or qualifications; Organisations wishing to develop records or information systems and those which provide services in these fields. Dues (Pound Sterling): 60, individual; 250 corporate; 12, student; 30, retired
Major Fields of Interest Records management

Major Goals and Objectives The objects of the Society are to further knowledge of the management and administration of records, in whatever media, created during the course of the business activities of any organisation, and to promote fellowship and co-operation amongst individuals working in this field

Activities Helds regular meetings, develops training program, 13th annual conference 2010: Manchester

Publications Official journal: Records Management Bulletin. 6/yr. Other publications: reports, surveys and guidelines

518 Research Council Libraries&Information Consortium (RESCOLINC)

Address c/o Debbie Franks, Chair, Daresbury Science and Innovation Campus, Warrington WA4 4AD Tel.: +44 1925 603189, Fax +44 1925 603779, debbie.franks@stfc.ac.uk; www.rcuk.ac.uk

Languages English

Established 2002

Officers Chair: Debbie Franks

Structure Governed by steering group. Each Research Council LIS community has representatives on the Steering Group. This Group acts as the central point of contact for other organisations within the academic research sector and the information industries

Major Fields of Interest Library & Information Services (LIS) of the UK Research Councils

Major Goals and Objectives To obtain optimum information service supply benefits in support of researchers across the entire research council sector

519 Research Libraries UK (RLUK)

Address c/o RLUK Office, Edgbaston, Birmingham, B15 2TT Tel.: +44 121 4158108, Fax +44 121 4158109, helpdesk@rluk.ac.uk; www.rluk.ac.uk

Languages English

Officers Chair: Mark Brown; Treas: Sheila Cannell; Exec Dir: Dr. Mike Mertens

Staff 3, paid

General Assembly Annual meetings. 2007: Manchester; 2008: Cambridge; 2009: London

Membership 28 research libraries

Major Fields of Interest To increase the ability of research libraries to share resources for the benefit of the local, national and international research community

Major Goals and Objectives Provide strong leadership to find research-centred solutions to common problems. Influence change and provide a seedbed for innovative projects and services. Provide practical tools for finding information. Engage its membership to improve support for researchers. Foster synergies through strategic alliances and collaborative partnerships that will benefit research support in the UK, Ireland and worldwide. Help to shape the wider debate at national and international levels

Activities Helds conferences; Ongoing projects: Archives Hub (collaborative service which provides a single point of access to descriptions of archive collections held in universities and colleges throughout the United Kingdom); Britain in Print (to enhance electronic access to the pre-1700 British books collections of 8 CURL libraries; CoFoR

(Collaboration For Research); Monograph-Inter-Lending project; SHERPA (e-print institutional repositories); survey of outstanding material for cataloguing in CURL libraries

520 School Library Association in Scotland

Address Tel.: +44 131 347 5766, info@sla.org.uk; www.sla.org.uk
Languages English
Established 1937
Major Fields of Interest School libraries
Major Goals and Objectives To promote the establishment and improvement of school libraries in Scotland

521 School Library Association (SLA)

Address Unit 2 Lotmead Business Village, Wanborough, Swindon SN4 0UY Tel.: +44 1793 791787, Fax +44 1793 791786, info@sla.org.uk
Established 1937, incorporated 1955
Officers Pres: Miranda McKearney; Chair: Alec Williams; VChair: Eileen Armstrong; Treas: Pat Williams
Staff 6 staff members
General Assembly General membership meets once a year
Membership Requirements: Any individual, establishment, or organization with an interest in school libraries. Dues: 70 EUR
Structure Governed by Executive Officers and Executive Committee. Affiliations: IFLA, IASL; Joint Standing Committee with CILIP
Sources of Support Membership dues, sales of publications and training
Major Fields of Interest Development of school libraries (primary and secondary); training for school library work; information literacy; children's literature
Major Goals and Objectives Recognition of the school library as the center of the curriculum; increase training opportunities for teachers and librarians in school library work; take action to prevent the decline in funds for school library resources; provide an information/advisory service from national headquarters and through publications
Activities Centre for advice for school library staff, running advisory service, training courses and annual conference. Series of publications also support this advisory service. 2001–2004 part of Dept. for Education and Skills Working Party on School Libraries
Publications Official journal: School Librarian. 1937-. 4/yr. Free to members. Address same as the Association. English. Indexed in Lib.Lit., LISA. Other publications: Guidelines, Primary School Classification Scheme. Publications for sale and listed in journal; price lists available
Bibliography King, E.J., "The School Library Association of Great Britain: Its First Fifty Years," International Review of Children's Literature and Librarianship 2 (1987):82–94; Fea, V, "Change and Challenge – the School Library Association at Fifty," Education Libraries Bulletin 31 (Spring 1988):7–15

522 Scottish Health Information Network (SHINE)

Address c/o Ruth Robinson, Secretary, Corsebar Road, Paisley, PA2 9PN Tel.: +44 141 7178, ruth.robinson@uws.ac.uk; www.shinelib.org.uk
Languages English

Established 1975, Edinburgh, as Association of Scottish Health Sciences Librarians
Officers Chair: Joanna Ptolomey; Secr: Ruth Robinson; Treas: Margaret Theaker
Staff None
General Assembly Annual General Meeting
Membership Types of membership: Individual, institutional, associate. Requirements: Open to all health sciences librarians and libraries in Scotland.
Structure Governed by executive officers. Affiliations: The Library Association
Sources of Support Membership dues
Major Fields of Interest Committed to sharing services, sources and skills for health information across Scotland
Major Goals and Objectives To seek opportunities to inform and influence relevant policy-making and funding bodies on issues relating to health care library and information services; to act as a forum for exchange of views and information; to promote collaborative effort and partnership between health care library and information services in all sectors. This will include sharing of resources and expertise; shared problem-solving; and networking by both electronic and other means; to facilitate quality improvement in health care library and information services through promotion of recognised/approved guidelines and standards
Activities Providing opportunities for members to meet for continuing education (some members often isolated); participating in surveys, etc., in an ongoing attempt to improve services in facilities. Active in promoting library-related legislation. Association is represented at the Library Association's consultative meetings on the document "Guidelines for Library Provisions in the Health Service" and gives guidance on the differences between the Scottish Health Service and that for England and Wales. Sponsors, seminars, workshops and other continuing education programs
Publications Official journal: Interim. 1977-. 2/yr. Free to members. Editor: Michelle Kirkwood, Clinical Effectiveness Librarian, North Glasgow Univ. NHS Trust, Glasgow Royal Infirmary Alexandra Parade Glasgow G31 2ER. Tel: 0141 211 1239. Email: interimeditor@hotmail.com. List of other publications: shona.mcquistan@northglasgow.scot.nhs.uk

523   Sefydliad Siartredig Llyfrgellwyr a Gweithwyr Gwybodaeth Cymru (CILIP Wales)
(Chartered Institute of Library and Information Professionals Wales)

Address c/o CILIP Cymru Wales, Llanbadarn Fawr, Aberystwyth SY23 3AS Tel.: +44 7837 032536, Fax +44 7837 032536, mdp@aber.ac.uk; www.cilip.org.uk/get-involved/regional-branches/wales-cymru/about/pages/structure.aspx
Languages English, Gaelic
Established 2002, following the unification of the Library Association and the Institute of Information Scientists
Officers Chair: Mandy Powell
Major Fields of Interest Libraries in Wales

524   Society of Archivists *

Address Prioryfield House, 20 Canon Street, Taunton Somerset, TA1 1SW Tel.: +44 1823 327030, Fax +44 1823 271719; www.archives.org.uk

Languages English
Established 1947, as Society of Local Archivists
Officers Chair: Katy Goodrum; VChair: Martin Taylor; Hon Secr: Jenny Moran; Hon Treas: Larysa Bolton
Staff 2
General Assembly Entire membership meets twice a year, once in London and once at another place
Membership Total members: about 2200 (Registered Members, Members, Student Members, Honorary Life Members and Institutional Affiliates) Requirements: To be primarily occupied in the care or administration of archives and records. Dues: Vary according to salary
Structure Governed by Council. Affiliations: No formal affiliations, but has links through representation with a number of organizations in the information field, including FID
Sources of Support Membership dues, sale of publications, conference/seminar fees
Major Fields of Interest Archival collections
Major Goals and Objectives The preservation of archives and records; training and professional standards of archivists, records managers and conservators
Activities Active in promoting legislation, provides training and further education opportunities
Publications Official journal: ARC Magazine (Archives, Records Management and Conservation). 12/yr. Contact: sales@societymediasales.co.uk; Tel: +44 117 923 2951, Fax: +44 117 923 2467; Journal of the Society of Archivists. 1947-. 2/yr. Free to members. Other publications: Annual report, proceedings of meetings, reports of seminars, workshops, and others. Publications for sale, price lists available
Bibliography Hull, E, "The [British] Society of Archivists," Janus 2 (1985):7–9

525 Society of Chief Librarians (SCL)

Address Tel.: +44 7891 056114
Languages English
Officers Pres: Fiona Williams; Secr: Cath Anley; Hon Treas: Simon May
Structure Governed by National Executive Committee. Meetings are held five times a year
Major Fields of Interest Public librarianship in England, Wales and Northern Ireland

526 Society of College, National and University Libraries (SCONUL)

Address 102 Euston Street, London NW1 2HA Tel.: +44 20 73870317, Fax +44 20 73833197, info@sconul.ac.uk; www.sconul.ac.uk
Languages English
Established 1950, as the Standing Conference of National and University Libraries; 1994 merger with COPOL, the Council of Polytechnic Librarians; 2001 name change to the Society of College, National and University Libraries, having welcomed colleges of higher education into membership
Officers Chair: Jane Core; VChair: Fiona Parsons; Treas: Alun Jenkins
General Assembly Entire membership meets twice a year, in spring and fall.

Membership Members are: all universities in the United Kingdom and Ireland, many of the UK's colleges of higher education; also members are the major national libraries both sides of the Irish Sea
Structure Governed by Council (elected by full Conference of member institutions). Affiliations: IFLA
Sources of Support Membership dues.
Major Fields of Interest All aspects of university and national library administration including library buildings, performance improvement, access to information systems and services, scholarly communication, health services and information literacy
Major Goals and Objectives To promote the sharing and development of good practice; to influence policy makers and encourage debate; to raise the profile of higher education and national libraries
Activities Representing academic libraries at various national committees. Sponsoring conferences, and other continuing education programs. Active in promoting library-related legislation, e. g. Copyright Law, Public Lending Right, Quality Assurance, etc. Bestows the Library Design Award for new Major building or extension
Publications No official journal. Other publications: Information support for eLearning: principles and practice (joint paper with UKeUniversities Worldwide); SCONUL vision: academic information services in the year 2005; Newsletters, Statistics, Working papers, Briefing papers.
Bibliography Bowyer, T.H., "SCONUL: The Contribution of Geoffrey Woledge," Journal of Documentation 40 (1984):92–93; Munthe, G., "SCONUL/SCANDIA Meeting at the University of Sussex," Synopsis 15 (1984):84; Loughridge, B., "The SCONUL Graduate Trainee Scheme as Preparation for Professional Education in Librarianship and Information Work: Results of a Survey," British Journal of Academic Librarianship 2 (1987):191–203; Loveday, A.J., "Statistics for Management and Trend Analysis: A SCONUL Experiment," IFLA Journal 14 (1988):334–342

527 Society of Indexers (SI)

Address Woodbourn Business Centre, 10 Jessell Street, Sheffield S9 3HY Tel.: +44 114 244 9561, Fax +44 114 244 9563, info@indexers.org.uk; www.indexers.org.uk
Languages English
Established 1957
Officers Hon Pres: John Sutherland; Chair: Ann Kingdom; Secr: John Silvester; Treas: Sally Roots
General Assembly Annual general meeting and conference. 2008: Winchester, 2009: York; 2010: Middelburg, Netherlands
Structure Governed by executive council. Committees: 7
Major Fields of Interest Indexing, the quality of indexes and the profession of indexing
Major Goals and Objectives Promotes improved standards and techniques in all forms of indexing; provides, promotes and recognizes facilities for the initial training of new indexers and for further training at more advanced levels; establishes criteria for assessment of conformity of indexes to recognized standards; establishes and maintains procedures for conferring upon members recognized professional status; conducts and promotes research into indexing and related matters; publishes and disseminates guidance, information and ideas concerning indexing; promotes among indexers, authors, publishers

and other interested persons and organizations relationships conducive to the advancement of good indexing; enhances awareness and recognition of the role of indexers in the analysis, organization and accessibility of recorded knowledge and ideas
Activities Services for publishers and authors, training opportunities, workshops, established award
Publications Official journal: The Indexer. 2/yr. Exec Editor: Maureen MacGlashan. +44 (0) 1475 790577; editor@theindexer.org

528 Standing Conference on Library Materials on Africa (SCOLMA)*

Address c/o Lucy McCann, South Parks Road, Oxford OX1 3RG Tel.: +44 1865 270908, scolma@hotmail.com; www2.lse.ac.uk/library/scolma
Languages English
Established 1962
Officers Chair: Barbara Spina; Secr: Lucy McCann; Treas: Ian Cooke; Edi: Terry Barringer; Programme Secr: Marilyn Glanfield; Webmaster: Clive Wilson
Staff 1 (volunteer)
General Assembly General membership meets once a year, usually in London
Membership Open to institutions and libraries concerned with library materials on Africa. Dues: `3.00/yr
Structure Governed by Executive Committee
Sources of Support Membership dues, sale of publications
Major Fields of Interest Materials for African studies
Major Goals and Objectives Provides a forum for librarians and others concerned with the provision of materials for African studies in libraries in the United Kingdom
Activities Monitors, co-ordinates and improves the acquisition of library materials on Africa, especially through its co-operative Area Specialisation Scheme for the acquisition of materials from Africa, sponsors bibliographical projects, publishes bibliographical works and a journal, organises conferences and seminars on African bibliographical topics
Publications Official journal: African Research & Documentation. 1973-. 3/yr. Addres same as association. Circ: 500. English. Publications available for sale: Images of Africa: the pictorial record. Papers presented at the SCOLMA conference, London, 9–10 June 1994 ed. J. Pinfold, T. Barringer & C. Holden. SCOLMA, 1995. ISBN 0 905450 89 2. ˝.50; SCOLMA directory of libraries and special collections on Africa in the United Kingdom and Europe 5th ed., comp. T. French. Oxford: Zell, 1993. ISBN 0 905450 89 2. ˝2.00; Theses on Africa 1976–1988 ed. H. C. Price, C. Hewson and D. Blake. Oxford: Zell, 1993. ISBN 1 873836 35 X. ˝8.00; New directions in African bibliography ed. P. M. Larby. (Proceedings of the SCOLMA Silver Jubilee Conference) SCOLMA, 1988. ISBN 0 904090 06 X. ˆ.75; Maps and mapping of Africa ed. P. M. Larby. (Papers of the SCOLMA/BRICMICS Conference), SCOLMA, 1988. ISBN 0 904090 05 1. `.50; African studies. Papers presented at a colloquium in January 1985 British Library Occasional Paper no. 6, British Library Publications in Association with SCOLMA, 1986. ISBN 0 7123 0050 3. ´4.95; African population census reports: a bibliography and checklist ed. J. Pinfold. Oxford: Zell, 1985. ISBN 0 905450 19 1. «.00

529 UKOLN

Address c/o University of Bath, Bath BA2 7AY Tel.: +44 1225 386580, Fax +44 1225

386838, ukoln@ukoln.ac.uk; www.ukoln.ac.uk
Languages English
Established 1992
Officers Dep Dir: Paul Walk
Sources of Support Jointly funded by JISC and MLA (Museums, Libraries&Archives Council)
Major Fields of Interest Digital information management, providing advice and services to the library, information, education and cultural heritage communities
Major Goals and Objectives To influence policy and informing practice; to promote community-building and consensus-making by actively raising awareness; to advance knowledge through research and development; to build innovative systems and services based on Web technologies; to act as an agent for knowledge transfer
Activities see: www.ukoln.ac.uk/activities
Publications Official journal: UKOLN Newsletter; annual reports; electronic journal Ariadne. Recent publications: Criddle, S., McNab, A., Ormes, S. and Winship, I., "The Public librarian's guide to the Internet. London (2000), ISBN 1856043282; Russell, R. (Ed.), "Making sense of standards and technologies for serials management", London (2000), ISBN 185604338X

530 University Health and Medical Librarians Group (UHMLG)

Address c/o Maurice Wakeham, Secretary, Bishop Hall Lane, Chelmsford, Essex CM1 1SQ Tel.: +44 20 7794 0500, Fax +44 20 7794 3534, maurice.wakeham@anglia.ac.uk; www.uhmlg.ac.uk
Languages English
Established 2007. The University Health Sciences Librarians Group (UHSL) merged with the University Medical Schools Librarians Group (UMSLG) to form the University Health and Medical Librarians Group (UHMLG).
Officers Chair: Betsy Anagnostelis; Vive Chair: Iain Baird; Treas: Joanne Dunham
Major Fields of Interest Health sciences information
Major Goals and Objectives To liaise with appropriate bodies and organisations; to develop and co-ordinate library and information services in the Group by the exchange of expertise and information; to promote the provision and use of library and information services; to engage in common activities; to support research into best practice
Publications Reports

531 University Medical School Librarians Group (UMSLG)

Address c/o Betsy Anagnostelis, Secretary, Rowland Hill Street, London NW3 2PF library@medsch.ucl.ac.uk; www.umslg.ac.uk/group.html
Languages English
Major Fields of Interest Librarians of undergraduate and postgraduate medical schools in the United Kingdom and the Republic of Ireland
Major Goals and Objectives To develop and co-ordinate library and information services in the Group by the exchange of expertise and information; to promote the provision and use of library and information services; to liaise with other libraries, organisations or information services as appropriate; to engage in common activities

Activities Holds a minimum of two full meetings a year. One of these is a national one-day annual forum with invited speakers and open to all who wish to attend, at which major topical issues are reviewed and debated. Other open meetings are held from time to time; maintains discussion lists

532 Virgin Islands Library Association / St. Croix Library Association (SCLA)*

Address c/o St. Croix Library Association, P.O. Box 446 Kingshill, St. Croix 00851 Tel.: +340-778-1600 x7507, sallick@stx.k12.vi; www.crucianschoollibraries.wikispaces.com
Languages English
Established Christiansted, St. Croix 1968
Officers Pres: Susan K. Allick; VP: William Pollard; Secr: Edna Recana; Treas: Patricia Oliver
General Assembly Monthly from September to June
Membership 40
Structure Parent organization ALA
Sources of Support Membership dues
Major Fields of Interest At the present time most of our members are school librarians and our major mission is to advocate for best practices in teaching information literacy and promotion school library resources
Major Goals and Objectives The St. Croix Library Association, hereinafter referred to as SCLA, was created for the following purposes: to promote quality library service for library patrons in St. Croix and the wider Virgin Islands community, and to assist in the provision of such service; and to promote librarianships as a profession, and to assist individuals in the performance of the duties and responsibilities of that profession; and to develop and promote quality library programs for all libraries and patrons; and to assist in the adherence to ALA standards for the establishment and operation of academic, private, public, medical, school, and other special libraries in the territory; and to promote the generation and publication of local research materials
Activities Last five years "Learning Community" with the Caribbean Museum for the Arts that promoted literacy through the arts; Digitization project with VI Division of Libraries, Archives & Museums (DLAM) to preserve Virgin Island documents; Collaborations between the University of the Virgin Islands and the University of Pittsburgh to provide nearly thirty scholarships to students completing a Master of Library Science degree; Connecting to Collections "Statewide Planning Grant" that SCLA has agreed to support by identifying precious resources in collections throughout St. Croix public schools that are in need of preservation
Comment n conjunction with the St. Thomas Library Association the St. Croix Library Association makes up the Virgin Islands Libray Association

United States of America

533 Africana Librarians Council (ALC)

Address 3420 Walnut Street, Philadelphia, PA 19104-6206 Tel.: + 1 215 898-7555, library@pobox.upenn.edu; www.library.upenn.edu/collections/africa/ALC

Languages English
Established 1957
General Assembly Members meet twice yearly, once during the annual meeting of the African Studies Association and once in the spring at the home institution of a member
Membership Requirements: Members of ASA whether they are librarians, archivists or documentalists working with materials from and about Africa or scholars interested in the preservation of or access to Africana
Structure Governed by Executive Board. 3 standing committees: Bibliography, Cataloging, and Book Donation. Affiliations: a part of African Studies Association (ASA)
Sources of Support Sponsored by ASA
Major Fields of Interest Africana librarianship
Major Goals and Objectives Provide information related to acquiring resources for those whom the members serve; encourage research and publication with the intent of making Africana resource materials in all formats more accessible; provide for panel discussions and informative programs at the meetings of the African Studies Association; promote and publicize its activities by encouraging and supporting a newsletter, web sites, and other initiatives by members; promote improvements in the processing and cataloging of Africana so that those materials are made more quickly and easily accessible; foster cooperation and contacts with those in other countries, particularly in Africa, with similar concerns
Activities Presents Conover-Porter Award
Publications Official journal: Africana Libraries Newsletter. Other publications: Electronic Journal of Africana Bibliography. Editor: Afeworki Paulos. Address: 209 Harlan Hatcher Graduate Library, The University of Michigan, Ann Arbor, MI 48109–1205, email: apaulos@umich.edu

534 American Association of Law Libraries (AALL)*

Address 105 W. Adams Street, Suite 3300, Chicago, IL 60603 Tel.: +1 312 9394764, Fax +1 312 4311097; www.aallnet.org
Languages English
Established 1906, Narraganset Pier, Rhode Island
Officers Pres: Joyce Manna Janto; VP: Darey Kirk; Sevr: Ruth S. Hill; Treas: Susan Lewis-Somers; Past Pres: Catherine Lemann
General Assembly Entire membership meets annually. 2004: Boston; 2005: San Antonio
Membership Total members: over 5000. Type of membership: Individual, institutional, life, student, honorary, associate. Requirements: Persons officially connected with a law library, state library, or a general library maintaining a law section may become active individual members on payment of dues. Any library may become an institutional member.
Structure Governed by executive officers and council meetings. Affiliations: IFLA
Sources of Support Membership dues, sale of publications
Major Fields of Interest Law librarianship
Major Goals and Objectives To promote law librarianship, to develop and increase the usefulness of law libraries, to cultivate the science of law librarianship, and to foster a spirit of cooperation among the members of the profession

Activities   13 Special interest sections to deal with specialized areas of law librarianship; holds online discussion center; sponsors conferences, seminars, workshops, and other continuing education programs
Publications   Official journal: Law Library Journal. 1908-. 4/yr. Free to members. English. Indexed in Lib.Lit., LISA. Other publications: AALL Spectrum. 9/yr. Free to members; Law Librarians: Making Information Work (PLL SIS Resource Guide Series); AALL Biennial Salary Survey; Universal Citation Guide; Law Library Insights (four-part series of Resource Guides)
Bibliography   Bibliography Rempel, S.P., "Quo Vadis?" Law Library Journal 77 (1985):151–156; Howes, R., "American Association of Law Libraries," Law Librarian 16 (1985):121; Marke, J.J.,"Law Libraries," in ALA World Encyclopedia of Library and information Services. 2nd ed., pp. 430–433. Chicago: American Library Association, 1986; "American Association of Law Libraries Special Committee on the Future of AALL 1983–1985: Final Report Nov. 1985," Law Library Journal 78 (1986):351–361; Berring, R.C., "Dyspeptic Ramblings of a Retiring Past President," Law Library Journal 79 (1987):345–350; "Reports from the 80th Annual Meeting of the American Association of Law Libraries, Held in Chicago," Library of Congress Information Bulletin 46 (Nov. 30, 1987): 512–518; Pyrah, A., "'We the People' – 80th Annual Meeting of the AALL," Law Librarian 18 (1987):94–95; Wallace, M., "Statistics: Management and Political Tool [Future AALL-sponsored survey of private law libraries]," Law Library Journal 80 (1988):329–338; Leary, M.A., "American Association of Law Libraries," in ALA Yearbook 1989. pp. 21–22. Chicago: American Library Association, 1989; "American Association of Law Libraries," in The Bowker Annual: Library and Book Trade Almanac. 34th Edition 1989–90. pp. 631–633. New York: R. R. Bowker, 1989

535   American Association of School Librarians (AASL)

Address   50 E. Huron St., Chicago, IL 60611–2795 Tel.: + 1 312 280-4382, Fax + 1 312 280-5276, aasl@ala.org; www.ala.org/aasl
Languages   English
Established   1951, Chicago, during meeting of the American Library Association
Officers   Exec Dir: Julie Walker
Staff   11 (paid)
General Assembly   Entire membership meets once a year during ALA Annual Conference. In addition, members meet at separate National Conferences every 3 years
Membership   Types of membership: Individual, institutional, life, student. Requirements: Open to all those interested in school library media programs and services. Individual membership: $ 53–115$
Structure   Governed by Board of Directors and ALA Council. Affiliations: A Division of ALA, NCATE (National Council for the Accreditation of Teacher Education), IASL, and others
Sources of Support   Membership dues, government subsidies (grants, project proposals).
Major Fields of Interest   Library media services in schools, from kindergarten to 12th grade
Major Goals and Objectives   To establish a forum and voice for school librarians at the national level; to plan a program of study and service for the improvement and extension

of library media services in elementary and secondary schools as a means of strengthening the educational program; evaluation, selection, interpretation, and utilization of media as used in the context of school programs; stimulation of continuous study and research in the library field and to establish criteria of evaluation; synthesis of the activities of all units of the American Library Association in areas of mutual concern; representation and interpretation of the need for the function of school libraries to other educational and lay groups; stimulation of professional growth, improvement of the status of school librarians, and encouragement of participation by members in appropriate type-ofactivity divisions

Activities Sponsors awards, grants and scholarships, conferences, seminars, workshops, and other continuing education programs

Publications Official journal: AASL Hotlinks (Official Monthly E-mail Newsletter, access restricted to members).

Bibliography Pond, P.B., American Association of School Libraries: The Origin and Development of a National Professional Association for School Libraries. 1896–1951. Unpubl. doctoral dissertation. University of Chicago, 1982; "AASL Studies Options for Future: Secession from ALA a Possibility," School Library Journal 30 (1984):9–10; "AASL's Report Listing ALA Constraints Offers These Options for Resolution," ibid.:8–9; Flagg, G., "AASL Answers the Challenge: Programs Take Precedence over Politics at the Division's Third National Conference in Atlanta," American Libraries 15 (1984):785+; Robb, F.C., "Future Connections: AASL and Main Trends," School Library Media Quarterly 12 (1984):120–126; Miller, M.L., "What Next, AASL?" School Library Journal 31 (1984):28–30; Lowrie, J.E.,"School Libraries/Media Centers," in ALA World Encyclopedia of Library and Information Services. 2nd ed., pp. 733–736. Chicago: American Library Association, 1986; Mancall, J. C. and Bertland, L.H., "Step One Reported: Analysis of AASL's First Needs Assessment for Continuing Education," School Library Media Quarterly 16 (1988):88–98; Hand, D., "Information Power Arrives in School Library/Media Centers [AASL/AECT Guidelines for School Library Media Programs]," Ohio Media Spectrum 40 (Spring 1988):4; "School Library Media Guidelines 1988 Define Elements of Effective Programs," School Library Journal 34 (1988): 12; Weeks, A.C., "Information Power: Guidelines for School Library Media Programs," in ALA Yearbook 1988. pp. 27–28. Chicago: American Library Association, 1988; Kahler, J., "Information Power: Guidelines for School Library Media Programs: A Commentary," Texas Library Journal 64 (1988):69–70; Whitney, Karen A., "American Association of School Librarians," in ALA Yearbook 1989. pp. 22–25. Chicago: American Library Association, 1989; "American Library Association. American Association of School Librarians," in The Bowker Annual: Library and Book Trade Almanac. 34th Edition. 1989–90, pp. 637–639. New York: R. R. Bowker, 1989; Gaughan, T., "AALS Conference: Rugged Individuals Making Common Cause," American Libraries 20 (1989):1042–43

536 American Library Association (ALA)

Address 50 E. Huron Street, Chicago, IL 60611 Tel.: 1800 5452433, Fax +1 312 9443897, kfiels@ala.org; www.ala.org

Languages English

Established 1876, Philadelphia. ALA has influenced the course of American libraries since its inception in 1876, when such early library luminaries as Melvil Dewey and Justin Winsor issued a call to libraries to form a professional organization

Officers Pres: Jim Rettig; Exec Dir: Keith Michael Fiels
General Assembly Entire membership meets annually in June/July. 2004: Orlando/FL
Membership Total members: 64000+ (individual and institutional). 11 membership divisions. Requirements: Open to any person, library or organization interested in library service and librarians.
Structure Governed by an elected Council, and an Executive Board, which "acts for the Council in the administration of established policies and programs." Policies and programs are proposed by standing committees, designated as committees of the Association or committees of Council. Affiliations: IFLA, American Association of Law Libraries, American Society for Information Science, Canadian Library Association, Medical Library Association, Laubach Literacy International, etc
Sources of Support Membership dues, sale of publications, conference revenues.
Major Fields of Interest High quality library and information services
Major Goals and Objectives The mission of the American Library Association is to provide leadership for the development, promotion, and improvement of library and information services and the profession of librarianship in order to enhance learning and ensure access to information for all
Activities Besides a wide range of activities carried out by the Divisions, Sections, Committees and other ALA groups, many projects are initiated by ALA Headquarters Offices, e. g. the Office for Intellectual Freedom (OIF), Office for Research and Statistics (ORS), Office for Literacy and Outreach Services (OLOS), and others. Sponsors numerous conferences, meetings, forums, institutes, library promotions and other events
Publications Official journal: American Libraries. 1907-. 11/yr. ISSN 0002–9769. Subscription to institutions only: $60; $70 outside USA & Canada. Free to members. Editor: Leonard Kniffel. email: lkniffel@ala.org. English. Indexed in CUE. Education Index, ISA. LISA. Lib.Lit., Magazine Index, DIALOG, etc. Other publications: extended publishing programme e.g.: Power Research Tools. (2002) by Joyce Kasman Valenza, ISBN: 0-8389-0838-1; NEW Planning for Results, (2001) by Sandra Nelson, ISBN: 0-8389-3504-4; Disaster Response and Planning for Libraries, 2nd Ed. 2003, by Miriam B. Kahn, ISBN: 0–8389-0837-3; Literacy and Libraries (2001), by GraceAnne A. DeCandido, and OLOS, ISBN: 0-8389-3516-8; Ultimate Digital Library (2003), by Andrew K. Pace, ISBN: 0-8389-0844-6
Bibliography Galvin, T.J., "ALA, Unesco and NWICO (New World Information and Communication Order)," Newsletter on Intellectual Freedom 33 (1984):63–64; Kraske, G.E., Missionaries of the Book: The American Library Profession and the Origins of United States Cultural Diplomacy. New York: Greenwood Press, 1985; Holley, E.G.: "American Library Association" In: ALA World Encyclopedia of Library and Information Services. 2nd ed., pp. 43–49. Chicago: American Library Association, 1986; Wiegand, W.A., The Politics of an Emerging Profession: The American Library Association 1876–1917. New York: Greenwood Press, 1986; Sullivan, P., "ALA and Library Education: A Century of Changing Roles and Actors, Shifting Scenes and Plots," Journal of Education for Library and Information Science 26 (1986):143–153; "Strategic Plans for ALA and ACRL: A Comparison," College and Research Libraries News 47 (1986):709–712; Carroll, F.L., "International Relations of the American Library Association and R. Wedgeworth 1972–85," International Library Review 18 (1986):153–159; Kimmel, M.M., "The Committee on Accreditation: What It Can and

Cannot Do," Top of the News 43 (1987):143–148; Cassell, K.A., "The Women's Rights Struggle in Librarianship: The Task Force on Women," in Activism in American Librarianship. 1962–1973. ed. by M. L. Bundy and F. J. Stielow, pp. 21–29. New York: Greenwood Press, 1987; "ALA and Its Divisions: Relationships Past, Present and Future," College & Research Libraries News 48 (1987):318–320; Melton, E.,"American Library Association," in ALA Yearbook 1989. pp. 27–28. Chicago: American Library Association, 1989; Chisholm, M.E., "American Library Asociation," in The Bowker Annual of Library and Book Trade Information. 1988. pp. 152–166. New York: R. R. Bowker, 1988; Wiegand, W. A. and Steffens, D.L, "Members of the Club: A Look at One Hundred ALA Presidents." University of Illinois at Urbana-Champaign. Grad. School of Libr. & Info. Science, 1988; Schuman, P.G., "ALA and Its Divisions," College & Research Libraries News 49 (1988):27–31; Sorensen, R.J., "Continuing Education in the American Library Association," School Library Media Quarterly 16 (1988):119–121; "ALA Urges Use of Permanent Paper," Wilson Library Bulletin 62 (1988): 12; "News from Annual Conference in New Orleans: Big But Not So Easy," American Libraries 19 (1988):658–660, 662–668, 701–708; "Information Literacy is Focus of ALA Report," Library Journal 114 (1989):20–21; Gerhardt, L.N., "That Motto of ALA (The Best Reading, for the Largest Number, at the Least Cost')," School Library Journal 34 (1988):4; Summers, F. W., "American Library Association," in The Bowker Annual: Library and Book Trade Almanac. 34th Edition 1989–90, pp. 142–146; 634–637. New York: R. R. Bowker, 1989; Flagg, G. et al., "Issues of Reach and Grasp: ALA Faces up to Success," American Libraries 21 (1990):252–261 (Midwinter Meeting, Jan. 6–11, 1990, Chicago)

537 American Society for Information Science and Technology (ASIS&T)

Address 1320 Fenwick Lane, Suite 510, Silver Spring, MD 20910 Tel.: +1 301 4950900, Fax +1 301 4950810, asis@asis.org; www.asis.org

Languages English

Established 1937, Washington, D.C., as American Documentation Institute (ADI)

Officers Pres: Donald Chase; Pres-elect: Linda Smith; Treas: Vicky Gregory

General Assembly Entire membership meets annually, in fall. Next meeting: October 2010, Pittsburgh

Membership Requirements: Any interested person who applies for membership and pays the prescribed dues. Institutional memberships are available to both profit and nonprofit organizations. Dues (US Dollar): 140, regular; 40, student; 70, retired; 650, institutional

Structure Governed by Board of Directors, elected by membership. Affiliations: FID, NFAIS, and some 40 other organizations

Sources of Support Membership dues, sale of publications, revenues from meetings, continuing education seminars.

Major Fields of Interest Information science and technology; information storage and retrieval; information policy

Major Goals and Objectives Organized for scientific, literary and educational purposes, and dedicated to the creation, organization, dissemination and application of knowledge concerning information and its transfer. Specifically, the Society aims to provide knowledge, education, training and awareness to, for and about information and its transfer; to provide a forum for the discussion, publication, and critical analysis of work

dealing with the design, management, and use of information systems and technology
Activities Society provides a Placement Service, and bestows annual awards. Sponsors conferences, seminars, workshops, etc. as part of an extensive continuing education program
Publications Official journal: Journal of the American Society for Information Science and Technology (JASIST). Editor: Donald H. Kraft, Department of Computer Science, Louisiana State University, Baton Rouge, LA 70803–4020, Tel: +1 225 5781495, Fax: +1 225 5781465, e-mail: kraft@bit.csc.lsu.edu. Other publications: Bulletin of the American Society for Information Scienceand Technology; ARIST Annual Review of Information Science and Technology
Bibliography Resnik, L., "American Society for Information Science Approaching 50 Years Young," Library Times International 3 (1986):17, 19; Elias, A.W., "Historical Note: Fifty Years of ASIS – Thirty-Eight Years of JASIS," Journal of the American Society of Information Science 38 (1987):385–386; Berry, J.N., "A New Social Concern at ASIS [technology is not ethically neutral]," Library Journal 112 (1987):79–81; Davis, M., "ASIS Mid-Year Meeting on Artificial Intelligence," LASIE 19 (1988):20–24; "ASIS Celebrates Its 50th Anniversary," Bulletin of the American Society of Information Science 14 (1988):10–13; Resnik, L., "ASIS Celebrates 50 Years of Services [anniversary conference]," ibid.:58–60; Resnik, L.,"American Society for Information Science," in ALA Yearbook 1989, pp. 42–44. Chicago: American Library Association, 1989; Resnik, L., "American Society for Information Science," in The Bowker Annual: Library and Book Trade Almanac. 34th Edition 1989–90. pp. 160–163. New York: R. R. Bowker, 1989; Sherwood, D., "Annual ASIS Meeting Looks to the 90's," Information Today (The Newspaper for Users and Producers of Electronic Information Services) 6 (Dec. 1989): 1, 14; "Inside ASIS: ASIS Members Share Insights and Knowledge on Management of Information and Technology [ASIS Annual Meeting, Washington, DC, Oct. 1989]," Bulletin of the American Society for Information Science 16 (1990):4–8

538 American Society of Indexers (ASI)

Address 10200 West 44th Avenue, Suite 304, Wheat Ridge, CO 80033 Tel.: +1 303 4632887, Fax +1 303 4228894, info@asindexing.org; www.asindexing.org/site
Languages English
Established 1968
Officers Pres: Kate Mertes; Exec Dir: Annette Rogers
General Assembly Annual meetings. 2010: Minneapolis, MN; 2011: Providence, RI; 2012: San Diego, CA
Membership Individual and institutional. Requirements: open to all interested persons: professional indexers, editors, publishers, librarians, and anyone else curious about indexing. Dues: Regular $150; New member $130; Retired $130; Organizational $500; Sustaining Organizational $1,000
Structure Governed by Executive Board
Major Fields of Interest Indexing and indexes
Major Goals and Objectives To promote excellence in indexing and to increase awareness of the value of well-written and well-designed indexes
Activities Organizes conferences and trade shows, courses and workshops, online discussion groups

Publications   Official journal: Key Words, (Bulletin) 6yr. Free for members, $40 for nonmembers. Editor: LJudy Reveal, email: t keywords@asindexing.org. Other publications e.g.: Indexer Locator (online database). Recent publications: Index It Right! Advice from the Experts, Volume 1, Edited by Enid L. Zafran, 2005; Indexing Specialties: Web Sites, by Heather Hedden, 2007; Starting an Indexing Business, 4th Ed., edited by Enid L. Zafran & Joan Shapiro, 2009; Indexing Specialties: Cookbooks, edited by Alexandra Nickerson, Fred Leise, and Terri Hudoba, 2009; Index It Right! Advice from the Experts, Volume 2, Edited by Janet Perlman & Enid L. Zafran, 2010
Comment   formerly The American Society of Indexers

539   American Theological Library Association (ATLA)

Address   300 South Wacker Drive, Suite 2100, Chicago, IL 60606-6701 Tel.: +1 312 4545100, Fax +1 312 4545505, atla@atla.com; www.atla.com/atlahome.html
Languages   English
Established   1947, Louisville, Kentucky, at a special joint meeting of the ALA Religious Books Round Table and the American Association of Theological Schools (now ATS)
Officers   Pres: David R. Stewart; VP: Roberta A. Schaafsma; Secr: Ellen Crwaford
General Assembly   Entire membership meets once a year.
Membership   Total members: 800+ (individual, and institutional). Requirements: Open to persons actively engaged in professional library or bibliographic work in theological or related religious fields. Institutional membership for libraries or institutions with membership in the Association of Theological Schools in the U. S. and Canada.
Structure   Governed by Board of Directors. Affiliations: ALA, Association Forum of Chicagoland, ATS, BETH, NFAIS, RLIT
Sources of Support   Membership dues, sale of publications.
Major Fields of Interest   Theological librarianship in general; theological bibliography; microreproduction of theological material; indexing of religious journals; theological library development; preservation of theological materials
Major Goals and Objectives   To bring theological libraries into closer working relationships with each other; to improve theological libraries, and to interpret the role of such libraries in theological education; developing and implementing standards of library service; promoting research and experimental projects; encouraging cooperative programs that make resources more available; publishing and disseminating literature and research tools and aids; cooperating with organizations having similar aims; and otherwise supporting and aiding theological education
Activities   Provides a wide range of services and products for its members. Professional development opportunities are designed by the Professional Development Committee and include a variety of workshops, classes, and programs that benefit both individual and institutional members, holds annual conferences
Publications   Official journal: ATLA Newsletter. 1947-. 4/yr. Free to members. Address same as Association. Circ: Membership. English. Other publications: Summary of Proceedings, 1/yr; Theology Cataloging Bulletin, 4/yr; Annual Report; ATLA has produced bibliographic indexes in theology and religion for more than fifty years. Developed and maintained by professional indexers, editors, and support staff, ATLA's indexes are issued in one or more of three different formats: print, CD-ROM, and MARC. The ATLA Religion Database combines ATLA's three primary indexes (Religion Index

One: Periodicals, Religion Index Two: Multi-Author Works, and the Index to Book Review in Religion, and is available from ATLA on CD-ROM or in MARC format, or may be ordered through several online vendors

Bibliography Myers, S., "American Theological Library Association," in ALA Yearbook 1988. pp. 46–47. Chicago: American Library Association, 1988; Myers, S.,"American Theological Library Association," in ALA Yearbook 1989. p. 44. Chicago: American Library Association, 1989; "American Theological Library Association," in The Bowker Annual: Library and Book Trade Almanac. 34th Edition 1989–90, pp. 663–664. New York: R. R. Bowker, 1989

540   Asian Pacific American Librarians Association (APALA)

Address c/o Gary Colmenar, Executive Director, PO Box 1669, Goleta, CA 93116-1669
Tel.: +1 310-825-1639, Fax +1 310-825-3777, lpendse@library.ucla.edu; www.apalaweb.org
Languages English
Established 1980
Officers Pres: Sherise Kimura; VP/Pres-elect: Florante Peter Ibanez; Treas: Angela Boyd; Secr: Liladhar R. Pendse; Immediate Past Pres: Michelle Baildon
General Assembly Entire membership meets annually in conjunction with the ALA conference in summer, for the program meeting. Officers and members also meet during the ALA Midwinter meetings
Membership Requirements: Open to all librarians/information specialists of Asian/Pacific descent working in US libraries/information centers and related organizations, and to others who support the goals and purposes of APALA. Asian/Pacific Americans are defined as those who consider themselves Asian/Pacific Americans. They may be Americans of Asian/Pacific descent, Asian/Pacific people with the status of permanent residency, or Asian/Pacific people living in the United States.
Structure Governed by executive officers, committees, membership at-large. Affiliations: ALA
Sources of Support Membership dues, advertisers' fees for conference publication
Major Fields of Interest Asian/Pacific American librarians
Major Goals and Objectives (1) To provide a forum for discussing problems and concerns of Asian/Pacific American librarians; (2) to provide a forum for the exchange of ideas by Asian/Pacific American librarians and other librarians; (3) to support and encourage library services to the Asian/Pacific American communities; (4) to recruit and support Asian/Pacific Americans in the library/information science professions; (5) to seek funding for scholarships in library/information science schools for Asian/Pacific Americans; (6) to provide a vehicle whereby Asian/Pacific American librarians can cooperate with other associations and organizations having similar or allied interests
Activities Annual award program "to an individual for distinguished service and outstanding contributions to the better understanding of Asian/Pacific Americans and their contributions in America." Dissemination of information of value to the membership. Sponsors conferences, seminars, workshops, and other continuing education programs. Cooperates with like-minded organizations in promoting library-related legislation
Publications Official journal: APALA Newsletter. 1980-. 4/yr. Free to members. English. Other publications: Annual reports, proceedings of conferences, seminars,

bibliographies, e. g. "Books for Asian/Pacific Americans' Human Rights;" APALA Membership Directory (1/yr.); Collantes, Lourdes Y., ed., Asian/Pacific American Librarians Association: A Cross Cultural Perspective. Papers of the 1984 Program. June 25. 1984. Dallas. Texas (1985), etc. No publications exchange program

Bibliography   Har Nicolescu, S. and Collantes, A., "Asian/Pacific American Librarians Association," Ethnic Forum: Journal of Ethnic Studies and Ethnic Bibliography 6 (1986):138–140; "Asians as 'Model Minority:' Myth, Reality, or Both," American Libraries 19 (1988):667; Pineda, C.J.,"Asian/Pacific American Librarians Association," in ALA Yearbook 1989. pp. 48–49. Chicago: American Library Association, 1989; "Asian/Pacific American Librarians Association," in The Bowker Annual: Library and Book Trade Almanac. 34th Edition 1989–90. pp. 667–668

541   Association for Federal Information Resources Management (AFFIRM)

Address   400 North Washington Street, Suite 300, Alexandria, VA 22314 Tel.: + 1 703-778-4646, Fax + 1 703-683-5480, info@affirm.org; www.affirm.org

Languages   English

Established   1979

Officers   Pres: Casey Coleman; VP: Peter Tseronis

Staff   None

General Assembly   There are monthly program meetings with luncheon-speakers, at the George Washington University's Marvin Center, 21 Street, NW, Washington, DC; and annual one-day seminars in Information Resources Management, generally in fall

Membership   Requirements: Professionals currently or formerly employed by the federal government in some capacity related to IRM. Other persons interested may join as associate members.

Structure   Governed by officers and Executive Board

Sources of Support   Membership dues

Major Fields of Interest   Information systems and resources in the Federal government

Major Goals and Objectives   To provide a forum for information resources management professionals in order to exchange ideas and to express opinions not subjected to official approval; to promote and advance the concept and practice of information resources management (IRM) in the government of the United States; to provide a forum for exploring new techniques to improve the quality and use of federal information systems and resources; to advocate effective application of IRM to all levels of the federal government, to enhance the professionalism of IRM personnel, and interact with state and local governments on IRM issues

Activities   To explore new concepts and techniques to improve the quality and use of federal information systems and resources. Sponsors conferences, seminars, workshops, and other continuing education programs

Publications   Official journal: The AFFIRMation, newsletter. 1979-. 12/yr. Free to members. English. Other publications: AFFIRM White Papers – Emerging Issues Forum

Bibliography   "Association for Federal Information Resources Management (AFFIRM)," in The Bowker Annual: Library and Book Trade Almanac. 34th Edition 1989–90, p. 669. New York: R. R. Bowker, 1989

542 Association for Information and Image Management (AIIM)

Address 1100 Wayne Avenue, Suite 1100, Silver Spring, MD 20910 Tel.: +1 3015878202, Fax +1 301 5872711, aiim@aiim.org; www.aiim.org

Languages English

Established 1943, as National Microfilm Association. Name changed to reflect the expansion into other imaging technologies

Officers Pres: John Mancini; VP: Atle Skjekkeland; Peggy Winton

General Assembly Entire membership meets annually.

Membership Requirements: Member of the information and image processing community. Members are companies and individuals active in the design, creation, sale, and use of products and services for information and image management.

Structure Governed by a Board of Directors, composed of prominent individuals in the imaging disciplines

Sources of Support Membership dues, sale of publications, annual conference and exposition revenues.

Major Fields of Interest Imaging technology, including information transfer, storage and retrieval on optical disk, computer imaging, document digitization, micrographics and data transmission

Major Goals and Objectives To provide a forum which contributes to the effective development and application of information and image management systems through a Trade Association to benefit companies, and a Professional Society to benefit individuals; to provide opportunities, via the Annual Conference and Exposition and other meetings, for the interaction between trade and professional membership; to update membership on latest industry technology

Activities Provides educational opportunities, professional development, reference and knowledge resources, networking events, and industry advocacy

Publications Official journal: INFORM: The Magazine of Information and Image Management. 1987-. 12/yr. (formerly JIIM: Journal of Information and Image Management and Journal of Micrographics. 1967–1986). Free to members. English. Other publications: FYI/IM Newsletter. 12/yr. Free to members. Editor: Gregory E. Kaebnick. Address same as Association. Circ: 8,000. English. Extensive publication program of professional monographs, e.g., Information and Image Management: The State of the Industry. 1989; Saffady, W., Optical Storage Technology 1989: A State of the Art Review; Hardy, J., Introduction to Micrographics; Micrographic Film Technology (3rd ed.); Saffady, W., Micrographic Systems (3rd ed.); 1989 Information Management Sourcebook (annual Buying Guide and Membership Directory); Schantz, H.F., OCR/Imaging Systems in the Next Decade; Zakon, S., The Electronic Document; AIIM Standards Sets; Jordahl, G., Plugging into the Fax Track; Electronic Document Systems: User Evaluations; annual reports, proceedings of conferences, seminars, etc. Publications catalog available upon request

Bibliography Munro, K.G., "1985 Will be a Busy Year for Government Affairs," (AIIM legislative priorities) Journal of Information and Image Management 18 (1985):7; Steiger, B.A, "A Central Fact of Our Personal and Organizational Lives – Information Explosion Means Ever-Increasing Variety of Jobs," Washington Post. Sunday, Oct. 5, 1986, High Technology Supplement; "Association for Information and Image Management," in The

Bowker Annual: Library and Book Trade Almanac. 34th Edition 1989–90. p. 670. New York: R. R. Bowker, 1989

543 Association for Library and Information Science Education (ALISE)

Address 65 East Wacker Place, Suite 1900, Chicago, IL 60601-7246 Tel.: +1 865 4250155, Fax +1 865 4810390, contact@alise.org; www.alise.org
Languages English
Established 1915, Albany, New York, as Association of American Library Schools (AALS)
Officers Exec Dir: Kathleen Combs
General Assembly Entire membership meets once a year
Membership Requirements: Any library school with a program accredited by the ALA Committee on Accreditation, may become an institutional member. Any school that offers a graduate degree in librarianship or a cognate field, but whose program is not accredited, may become an associate institutional member. Any school outside the United States and Canada offering a program comparable to that of institutional or associate institutional membership, may become an international affiliate institutional member. Any faculty member, administrator, librarian, researcher, or other individual employed full-time may become a personal member. Any retired or part-time faculty member, student, or other individual employed less than full-time, may become an associate personal member.
Structure Governed by Board of Directors. Affiliations: IFLA, ALA, ASIS, SLA, MLA
Sources of Support Membership dues, sale of publications.
Major Fields of Interest Education for librarianship and information science
Major Goals and Objectives Promote excellence in education for library and information science, as a means of increasing the effectiveness of library and information services. To effect this goal, the objectives shall be: To provide a forum for the active interchange of ideas and information among LIS educators, and to promote research related to teaching and to LIS; to formulate and promulgate positions on matters related to LIS education; to cooperate with other organizations in matters of mutual interest
Activities Awards and Honors Program; Active in promoting library-related legislation, whenever feasible. Sponsors conferences, seminars, workshops, and other continuing education programs, particularly conferences that pertain to the interests of the Association. Supports National Library Week; cooperates with other library associations
Publications Official journal: Journal of Education for Library and Information Science (JELIS) (formerly Journal of Education for Librarianship). 1960-. 4/yr. $150 ($175, foreign). Free to members. Address same as Association. English. Indexed in Current Contents. Education Index. ISA. LISA, Lib.Lit., etc. Other publications: The Statistical Report (1/yr.); annual reports, proceedings of conferences, seminars, etc. Publications available for sale. No publications exchange program in effect
Bibliography "AALS Changes Its Name," Wilson Library Bulletin 57 (1983):552; Berry, J. et al., "The Washington Week That Was: A Report on the Meetings of ALA ALISE and the Urban Libraries Council, Jan. 5–12 [1984] in Washington, D.C.," library Journal 109 (1984):537–543; Summers, F.W., "The Role of the Association for Library and Information Science Education," Library Trends 34 (1986):667–677; Berry, J., "Tension, Stress and Debate at the 1986 Annual Conference of ALISE," Library Journal 111 (1986):29–31; Berry, J., "Protecting Our Turf at the January 14–16 ALISE Conference,"

Library Journal 112 (1987):43–46; Estabrook, L.,"Association for Library and Information Science Education," in ALA Yearbook 1989. pp. 49–50. Chicago: American Library Association, 1989; "Association for Library and Information Science Education," in The Bowker Annual: Library and Book Trade Almanac. 34th Edition 1989–90. pp. 670–671. New York: R. R. Bowker, 1989; Berry, J.N., "ALISE in Washington (1989 Conference)," Library Journal 114 (1989):37–38; Berry, J. and De Candido, G.A., "Challenges and Concerns Confront ALISE," Library Journal 115 (1990):57–58

544 Association for Library Collections and Technical Services (ALCTS)

Address 50 E Huron Street, Chicago, IL 60611-2795 Tel.: 800 5452433-5037, Fax +1 312 2805033, alcts@ala.org; www.ala.org/alcts
Languages English
Established 1957, as Resources and Technical Services Division of ALA; new name adopted in 1989 to reflect the expansion of activities
Officers Pres: Mary Case; Pres-elect: Cynthia Whitacre; Past Pres: M. Dina Giambi
Staff 4 (paid)
General Assembly Entire membership meets annually during ALA Conference
Membership Total members: almost 5000 (individual, and institutional). Requirements: Open to members of the American Library Association who elect membership in this division according to the provisions of the bylaws
Structure Governed by Board of Directors and Executive Committee. Affiliations: A division of ALA
Sources of Support Membership dues, sale of publications
Major Fields of Interest Library collections and technical services
Major Goals and Objectives To ensure access to information by improving the development and management of collections and the bibliographic organization within libraries; to promote research and publication in areas of divisional interest; to provide forums for discussion and to advance the professional interests of librarians engaged in the development of library collections and in technical services; to cooperate with other units of the American Library Association and with other national and international organizations in areas of mutual interest
Activities Acquisition, identification, cataloging, classification, and preservation of library materials; development and coordination of the country's library resources; and those areas of selection and evaluation involved in the acquisition of library materials and pertinent to the development of library resources
Publications Official journal: Library Resources and Technical Services. 4/yr. Free to members. Address same as Association. English. Indexed in Lib.Lit., LISA. Other publications: ALCTS Newsletter Online. 6/yr; 4 monographic series: Acquisitions Guides, Collection Management & Development Guides, Serials Guides, ALCTS Papers on Technical Services and Collections; Catalog: www.ala.org/ala/alcts/alctspubs/catalog/catalog.htm
Bibliography Reid, M.T.,"Resources and Technical Services Division," in ALA Yearbook 1989, pp. 216–217. Chicago: American Library Association, 1989; "American Library Association. Resources and Technical Services Division," in The Bowker Annual: Library and Book Trade Almanac. 34th Edition 1989–90, pp. 658–659. New York: R. R. Bowker, 1989; Hirshon, A., "ALCTS Five-Year Financial Plan," RTSD Newsletter 14

(1989):60–63; "Mission and Priorities Statement [Revised Draft, Nov. 1989]: Introduction" by Marion T. Reid (Chair, ALCTS Strategic Long Range Planning Task Force) ALCTS Newsletter 1 (1990):5; Muller, K., "Division Financial Results," ibid.:6–7

545 Association for Library Service to Children (ALSC)

Address 50 E Huron St, Chicago, IL 60611 Tel.: 1800 545 24332163, Fax +1 312 280 5271, alsc@ala.org; www.ala.org

Languages English, some publications in Spanish

Established 1957, as Children's Services Division of ALA; present name adopted in 1977

Officers Exec Dir: Aimee Strettmatter

General Assembly Entire membership meets once a year during annual ALA conference

Membership Total members: over 3800 (individual, and institutional). Requirements: An interest in or a commitment to providing the best library service to children in all types of libraries.

Structure Governed by Board of Directors (13 members). Affiliations: A division of ALA

Sources of Support Membership dues, sale of publications, private grants for projects.

Major Fields of Interest Services to children in all types of libraries

Major Goals and Objectives Improvement and extension of library services to children in all types of libraries. Responsible for the evaluation and selection of book and nonbook library materials for, and the improvement of techniques of, library service to children from preschool through eighth grade or junior high school age, when such materials or techniques are intended for use in more than one type of library

Activities Carrying out projects within its area of responsibility. Cooperation with all units of ALA whose interests and activities have a relationship to library service to children. Interpretation of library materials for children and of methods of using such materials with children, to parents, teachers, and other adults, and representation of the librarians' concern for the production and effective use of good children's books to groups outside the profession. Stimulation of the professional growth of its members and encouragement of participation in appropriate type-of-library divisions. Planning and development of programs of study and research in the area of selection and use of library materials for children for the total profession. Development, evaluation, and promotion of professional materials in its area of responsibility. Presents a number of distinguished awards, such as the (Randolph) Caldecott Award (most distinguished American picture book for children), (John) Newbery Award (most distinguished contribution to American literature for children), Notable Children's Books (annual listing of notable children's books published), (Laura Ingalls) Wilder Award (author or illustrator who made a substantial and lasting contribution to literature for children), (Mildred L.) Batchelder Award (American publisher of the most outstanding children's book published in the US during preceding year, which was originally published abroad), etc. Sponsors conferences, seminars, workshops, and other continuing education programs

Publications Official journal: Children and Libraries (CAL). 3/yr. Free to members. Dues (US Dollar): 40 (.50 for international subscribers). Address same as Association. Editor Sharon Korbeck, E1569 Murray Lane, Waupaca, WI 54981, 715–258–0369, or e-mail: toylady@athenet.net. Other publications: ALSConnect, newletter, 4/yr; 60 Years of Notable Children's Books; Bare Bones Children's Services; Building a Special Collection of Children's Literature in Your Library; New Books Kids Like; Newbery and Caldecott Awards, 2004 Ed.; Newbery and Caldecott Medal Books, 1986–2000: A Comprehensive Guide to the Winners; Special Collections in Children's Literature: An International Directory. Address: POB 932501, Atlanta, GA 31193–2501, Tel: 1–866–746–7252, International Callers: +1 312 9446780, Fax: +1 770 4429742

Bibliography Karrenbrock, M.H., "A History and Analysis of Top of the News. 1942–1987." Journal of Youth Services in Libraries 1 (1987):29–43; Jenkins, C. and Odean, K., "Recently Challenged Children's and Young Adult Books," Journal of Youth Services in Libraries 1 (1988):283–289; "Conference Highlights: Major Actions of the ALSC Board [and] YASD Board," Journal of Youth Services in Libraries 2 (1988):4–6; Somerville, M.R., "Association for Library Service to Children," in ALA Yearbook 1989. pp. 50–51. Chicago: American Library Association, 1989; "American Library Association. Association for Library Service to Children," in The Bowker Annual: Library and Book Trade Almanac. 34th Edition 1989–90, pp. 641–643. New York: R. R. Bowker, 1989

546 Association for Library Trustees, Advocates, Friends and Foundations (ALTAFF)

Address 109 S. 13th Street, Suite 3-N, Philadelphia, PA 19107 Tel.: + 1 312 280-2161, Fax +1 215 545-3821, altaff@ala.org; www.ala.org/ala
Languages English
Established 2009 with the merger of Friends of Libraries U. S. A. (FOLUSA) and ALTA
Officers Pres: Rose Mosley; Pres-elect: Rodrigue Gauvin; Secr / Treas: Robin Hoklotubbe
Staff Kerry Ward (Exec Dir, email: kward@ala.org); Gretchen Kalwinski (Program Assistant, email: gkalwinski@ala.org)
General Assembly Entire membership meets once a year at ALA Annual Conference. 2004: Orlando/FL
Membership Individual and institutional members. Requirements: Open to all interested persons and organizations.
Structure Governed by Board of Directors. Affiliations: A division of ALA
Sources of Support Membership dues, sale of publications
Major Fields of Interest Library policies and services
Major Goals and Objectives To educate and empower library trustees to advocate for and adopt library policies that promote the highest quality library and information services and ensure access to information for all
Activities Offers professional education opportunities, annual conferences, awards for distinguished service to library development and literacy
Publications No official journal. Issues occasional publications, bibliographies, pamphlets, such as, "A Questionnaire to Evaluate Your Library and Library Board" " Major Duties, Functions, and Responsibilities of Public Library Trustees – An Outline," and "Library Boards – Who Are They and How Do They Get There? A Survey." Automating your library: a planning book. By Kathleen Colson Mulroy and Elizabeth Steckman. 1994. No publications exchange program. Price lists available
Bibliography Miller, R.T., "ALTA's Workshop in Library Leadership," Show-Me

Libraries (Missouri State Libraries) 35 (1984):9–11; Jordan, S.L., "American Library Trustee Association," in ALA Yearbook 1989. pp. 41–42. Chicago: American Library Association, 1989; "American Library Association. American Library Trustee Association," in The Bowker Annual: Library and Book Trade Almanac. 34th Edition 1989–90. pp. 640–641. New York: R. R. Bowker, 1986

547 Association for Recorded Sound Collections (ARSC)

Address c/o Peter Shambarger, Executive Director, P.O. Box 543, Annapolis, MD 21404-0543 Tel.: +1 410 757-0488, execdir@arsc-audio.org; www.arsc-audio.org
Languages English
Established 1966, Syracuse, New York
Membership Over 1000 members from 23 countries. Dues (US Dollar): 36, individual, 20 student, 40 institutional, 72 sustaining, 200 donor, 500 patron, 1000, benefactor
Structure Governed by Executive Board. Affiliations: IASA, Music Library Association
Sources of Support Membership dues
Major Fields of Interest Management and preservation of audio collections
Major Goals and Objectives To promote the organization, management and preservation of audio collections; to encourage and participate in research and development, exchange of information, and cooperative projects and programs having preservation of audio materials as their goal
Activities Sponsors conferences, seminars, workshops, and other continuing education programs
Publications Official journal: ARSC Journal. 2/yr. Editor: Barry R. Ashpole. Address: 384 Main Street West, Grimsby, Ontario, Canada L3M 1T2 barry.ashpole@sympatico.ca. Other publications: ARSC Newsletter. Editor: Barry R. Ashpole; ARSC Bulletin 1/yr, ARSC Membership Directory, updated yearly

548 Association of Academic Health Sciences Libraries (AAHSL)

Address 2150 N 107th Street, Suite 205, Seattle, WA 98133 Tel.: +1 206 3678704, Fax +1 206 3678777, aahsl@sbims.com; www.aahsl.org
Languages English
Established 1978, Washington, D.C., as Association of Academic Health Sciences Library Directors
Officers Pres: Connie Poole; Immediate Past Pres: Julia Sollenberger; Pres-elect: Pat Thibodeau; Secr/Treas: Paul Schoening
General Assembly Entire membership meets once a year, usually in November.
Membership Types of membership: Institutional, associate. Requirements: Educational institutions which have an academic health sciences library
Structure Governed by Board of Directors
Sources of Support Membership dues.
Major Fields of Interest Biomedical information; medical education; medical librarianship
Major Goals and Objectives To promote, in cooperation with educational institutions, other educational associations, government agencies, and other non-profit organizations, the common interests of academic health sciences libraries located in the United States and elsewhere, through publications, research, and discussion of problems of mutual interest

and concern; to advance the efficient and effective operation of academic health sciences libraries for the benefit of faculty, students, staff, administrators, and practitioners
Publications No official journal. Other publications: Library Director Recruitment Guide (pdf); Annual Statistics of Medical Libraries
Bibliography "Association of Academic Health Sciences Library Directors," in The Bowker Annual: Library and Book Trade Almanac. 34th Edition 1989–90. pp. 671–672. New York: R.R.Bowker, 1989

549 Association of Architecture School Librarians (AASL)

Address c/o Gilda Santana, Secretary, 1223 Dickinson Drive, Coral Gables, FL 33146 Tel.: +1 305 284-5282, gsantana@miami.edu; www.architecturelibrarians.org
Languages English
Officers Pres: Edward H. Teague; VP/Pres-elect: Catherine Essinger; Secr/Treas: Gilda Santana; Past Pres: Janine Henri
General Assembly Annual meeting. 2004: Miami, FL
Membership Requirements: Open to anybody who is interested in the aims of the association
Structure Governed by Executive Board. Affiliations: ACSA, ARCLIB, ARLIS/NA, NAAB, VRA, EPIC connection
Major Fields of Interest Architectural school librarianship
Major Goals and Objectives To advance academic architectural librarianship, to develop and enhance the roll of architecture school librarians in the advancement of architectural education, and to promote a spirit of cooperation among members of the profession
Activities Holds listserv, sponsors meetings and conferences
Publications Official journal: Association of Architecture School Librarians Newsletter. (pdf: www.library.njit.edu/archlib/aasl/newsletters/index.html)

550 Association of Christian Librarians (ACL)

Address POB 4, Cedarville, OH 45314 Tel.: + 1 937-766-2255, Fax + 1 937-766-5499, info@acl.org; www.acl.org
Languages English
Established 1957
Officers Pres: Don Smeeton; VP: Alice Ruleman; Secr: Carrie Beth Lowe; Treas: Sheila O. Carlblom; Exec Dir: Janelle Mazelin
Staff 1 (paid)
General Assembly Entire membership meets once a year, usually during second week of June. 2004: Evangel University in Springfield, Missouri
Membership More than 500 individual and 80 institutional members. Requirements: A full member shall be a Christian librarian subscribing to the aims of the Association, who is affiliated with an institution of higher learning. Associate members include those who are in agreement with the purposes of the Association, but who are not affiliated with institutions of higher learning, e. g. librarian at publishing houses or church libraries, or those who are nonlibrarians
Structure Governed by Board of Directors and Executive Committee. Affiliations: Council of National Library and Information Associations (CNLIA)

Sources of Support   Membership dues, sale of publications
Major Fields of Interest   Religion; Christian education; library work as related to Bible Colleges, Institutes, Christian Liberal Arts Colleges, and Christian Day Schools
Major Goals and Objectives   To communicate official business of the ACL and news of the membership; to publish information regarding ACL conferences, teams, meetings, and activities; to publish articles on research, methods, trends, issues, theories, findings, and reviews of current books; to provide a forum for the ACL and its members; to print editorials and position statements of the ACL; to encourage scholarly writing
Activities   Sponsors Emily Russel Award in recognition of outstanding contributions to Christian librarianship, established Commission for International Library Assistance (CILA), Address: Ferne Weimer (CILA General Secretary), Billy Graham Center Library, Wheaton College, Wheaton, IL 60187–5593; holds conferences, seminars, workshops, and other continuing education programs
Publications   Official journal: The Christian Librarian. 4/yr. $16. Free to members. Address same as Association. Editor-in-chief: Anne-Elizabeth Powell. English. Indexed in Christian Periodical Index. Social Sciences and Religion Index. Other publications: Christian Periodical Index (CPI); annual reports, proceedings of conferences, seminars, etc. Publications available for sale
Bibliography   "Association of Christian Librarians," in The Bowker Annual: Library and Book Trade Almanac. 34th Edition 1989–90. pp. 672–673. New York: R. R. Bowker, 1989

551   Association of College and Research Libraries (ACRL)

Address   c/o American Library Association, 50 East Huron Street, Chicago, IL 60611-2795 Tel.: +1 312 2802523, Fax +1 312 2802520, acrl@ala.org; www.ala.org/acrl
Languages   English
Established   1938, Kansas City, at the ALA Conference, replacing the College and Reference Section of ALA, founded in 1889
Officers   Pres: Lori Goetsch
Staff   14 (paid)
General Assembly   Entire membership meets annually during ALA Conference and every 3 years at ACRL National Conference
Membership   Total members: more than 12000 (personal and institutional). Requirements: Membership in ALA.
Structure   Governed by Board of Directors. Affiliations: Largest division of the American Library Association
Sources of Support   Membership dues, sale of publications.
Major Fields of Interest   Academic and research librarianship; higher education
Major Goals and Objectives   The Association is a forum for and an advocate of academic and research librarians and library personnel. The object of the Association is to provide leadership for the development, promotion, and improvement of academic and research library resources and services, and to facilitate learning, research, and the scholarly communication process
Activities   Holds awards program; sponsors exhibits, conferences, seminars, workshops, and other continuing education programs; promulgates standards and guidelines to help libraries, academic institutions, and accrediting agencies understand the components of an excellent library

Publications Official journal: College and Research Libraries 1939-. 6/yr. Free to members. Address same as Association. Editor: William Gray Potter, University of Georgia Libraries, Athens GA 30602–1641, e-mail: wpotter@arches.uga.edu. English. Indexed in Lib.Lit., Current Index to Journals in Education. LISA. ISA. Social Sciences Citation Index, ERIC, etc. Official news magazine: College and Research Libraries News. 1966-. 11/yr. Free to members. Address same as Association. Other publications: Choice: Current Reviews for Academic Libraries; Academic Library Statistics; RBM: A Journal of Rare Books, Manuscripts, and Cultural Heritage (formerly Rare Books and Manuscripts Librarianship, RBML). 2/yr, no membership journal, subscriptions: $40 for U.S.; $45 for Canada, Mexico, or other PUAS Countries; and $55 for other foreign countries; White papers, reports; Monographs to assist academic librarians in developing their professional careers, managing their institutions, and increasing their awareness of developments in librarianship

Bibliography Jones, W. G. and Ford, B.J., "Values and ACRL: What Do Our Leaders Report?" in Academic Libraries: Myths and Realities, pp. 141–145. Chicago: ACRL, 1984; Hogan, S. A. and Koyama, J.T., "ACRL Issues for the 80s," College & Research Libraries News 45 (1984):178, 181; Havens, S., "Academic Libraries: Myths and Realities: The ACRL's Third National Conference," Library Journal 109 (1984):1419–21; Segal, J.S., "The Association of College and Research Libraries: What It Can Do for Academic Librarians in the 80's," Show-Me Libraries 36 (1984):8–12; Segal, J.S., "The Association of College and Research Libraries," Library Times International 2 (1986):74–75; Eswe, H.B., "ACRL Issues – An Action Agenda," (guest editorial) ibid.:76; "Strategic Plans for ALA and ACRL: A Comparison," College & Research Libraries News 47 (1986):709–712; "ACRLs Strategic Plan [Mission, Goals and objectives]," College & Research Libraries News 48 (1987):21–23, 25; "Strategic Planning for ACRL [first of a series of annual strategic planning reports]," College & Research Libraries News 49 (1988):292–294; Hilker, E., "Survey of Academic Science/Technology Libraries," ibid.:375–376; "Report from the ACRL Conference in Florence of Western Europeanists [April 4–8,1988]," Library of Congress Information Bulletin 47 (July 11, 1988):293–294; Wand, P.A., "The Budget Process and ACRL Financial Issues," College & Research Libraries News 49 (1988):757–760; Euster, J.R., "Association of College and Research Libraries," in ALA Yearbook 1989. pp. 51–53. Chicago: American Library Association, 1989; "American Library Association. Association of College and Research Libraries," in The Bowker Annual: Library and Book Trade Almanac. 34th Edition 1989–90, pp. 644–647. New York: R. R. Bowker, 1989; Gordon, L., "'Futurists or Fossils?' is the Question for ACRL/NY," Library Journal 114 (1989):114; Segal, J.S., "The State of the Association," College & Research Libraries News 50 (1989): 693–696; "The Strategic Plan in Action: ACRL Looks to the Future," ibid.:711–712

552 Association of Independent Information Professionals (AIIP)

Address 8550 United Plaza Blvd., Suite 1001, Baton Rouge, Louisiana 70809 Tel.: +1 225 4084400, Fax +1 225 9224611, office@aiip.org; www.aiip.org
Languages English
Established June 4, 1987, Milwaukee, Wisconsin
Officers Pres: Marcy Phelps; Past Pres: Edward Vawter; Pres-elect: Mragaret King; Secr: Vada Repta; Treas: Cliff Kalibjian

United States of America 553

Staff None
General Assembly Entire membership meets annually
Membership Requirements: Independent information professionals
Structure Governed by executive officers
Sources of Support Membership dues
Major Fields of Interest Information services
Major Goals and Objectives To advance the knowledge and understanding of the information profession; to promote and maintain high professional and ethical standards among its members; to encourage independent information professionals to assemble to discuss common issues; to promote the interchange of information among independent information professionals and various organizations; to keep the public informed of the profession and of the responsibilities of the information professional
Activities Sponsors AIIP Referral Program, AIIP Speakers Bureau; presents a number of awards
Publications No publications program

553 Association of Information and Dissemination Centers (ASIDIC)

Address P.O. Box 3212, Maple Glen, PA 19002-8212 Tel.: +1 215 6549129, Fax +1 215 6549129; www.asidic.org
Languages English
Established 1969, Columbus, Ohio, as Association of Scientific Information and Dissemination Centers. Present name adopted 1976
Officers Immediate Past Pres: Mike Walker; Pres: Tim Ingoldsby; Secr: Judy Luther; Treas: Jeff Massa
General Assembly Entire membership meets twice a year (spring and fall). Last meeting: March 2010, Philadelphia
Membership Requirements: Database vendor, database producer, or Major online searcher. Dues: $400, full member; $150, associate member
Structure Governed by Executive Committee
Sources of Support Membership dues, fees from meetings.
Major Fields of Interest Computerized databases
Major Goals and Objectives To foster, encourage, and improve the development, production, processing, storage, retrieval, dissemination and use of electronic information
Activities Sponsors conferences. Association is mainly involved in education and keeping track of developments in the industry affecting information centers and databases
Publications Official journal: ASIDIC Newsletter. For members only
Bibliography Granick, L.W., "Emergence and Role of Common Interest Groups in Secondary Information," Journal of the American Society for Information Science 33 (1982):175–182

554 Association of Information Systems Professionals (AISP)

Address c/o Kathy McCord, 4267 Grainger Hall, 975 University Avenue, Madison, WI 53706 aisp@bus.wisc.edu; aisp.bus.wisc.edu
Languages English
Established 1972
Officers Pres: Ben Carr; VP: Matt Edminster; Secr: Ryan Etten; Treas: Logan Buntrock

General Assembly Entire membership meets annually
Membership Requirements: University of Wisconsin-Madison students interested in information technology. Information systems, computer science, and electrical and computer engineering students are encouraged to join. Membership is free
Structure Governed by executive officers
Sources of Support Membership dues, sale of publications.
Major Fields of Interest Information processing methods and systems
Major Goals and Objectives To promote the development and dissemination of methods and techniques relating to the processing and flow of information in the automated office environment; to encourage those who design, manage, and implement various types of information systems; to encourage exchange of ideas and experiences among members and the business community; to provide an innovative support system for information systems professionals through information on changes and advancements in the field, promotion of personal and professional growth, and lending active support to members

555 Association of Jewish Libraries (AJL)

Address c/o NFJC, 330 Seventh Avenue, 21st Floor, New York, N.Y. 10001, P.O. Box 1118, Teaneck, NJ 07666 Tel.: +1 212 725 5359, ajlibs@osu.edu; www.jewishlibraries.org
Languages English, Hebrew, Yiddish
Established 1965, by merger of 2 groups, the Jewish Librarians Association (New York, 1946), and the Jewish Library Association (Cleveland, 1962). They now form the Association's 2 divisions: Research and Special Library Division (R&S) and Synagogue School & Center Division (SSC)
Officers Pres: Susan Dubin; Past Pres: Laurel Wolfson; VP/Pres-elect: David Hirsch; VP/membership: Laurie Haas; VP/publications: Deborah Stern; Recording Secr: Elena Gensler; Treas: Sheryl Stahl
General Assembly Entire membership meets once a year.
Membership Requirements: Anyone interested in Judaica librarianship and Judaica libraries. Dues: $50, individual and institutional; $30, students and retirees
Structure Governed by the Executive Board. Affiliations; Council of National Library and Information Associations (CNLIA); Cataloging Committee of ALA
Sources of Support Membership dues, sale of publications, private endowment (for book awards and manuscript competition)
Major Fields of Interest Judaica librarianship
Major Goals and Objectives To inform, educate, and serve as a means of communicating the most advanced techniques in Judaica librarianship; to promote the improvement of library services and professional standards in all Jewish libraries and collections of Judaica; to serve as a center of dissemination of Jewish library information and guidance; to encourage the establishment of Jewish libraries and collections of Judaica; to promote publication of literature which will be of assistance to Jewish librarianship; and to encourage people to enter the field of librarianship
Activities Sponsors conferences, seminars, workshops, and other continuing education programs. Sponsors several awards for excellence in Jewish book publishing and in Judaica librarianship
Publications Official journal: Judaica Librarianship. 1983-. irr. Free to members. Editor: Linda Lerman, Co-Editor: Leah Adler. English, some Hebrew. Indexed in Genealogical

Periodical Annual Index. Index of Articles on Jewish Studies. Index to Jewish Periodicals. ISA. LISA. Internationale Bibliographie der Zeitschriftenliteratur. etc. Other publications: AJL Newsletter. 4/yr. Free to members. Miscellaneous publications, such as, bibliographies, classification scheme, subject headings, basic library collections, reference material, library handbook, Index to Jewish Holiday Stories in Collections; Index to Jewish Values in Children's Literature, etc.; annual reports, proceedings of conferences, seminars, etc

Bibliography Wiener, T., "Report from the Convention of the Association of Jewish Libraries," Library of Congress Information Bulletin 45 (Oct. 20, 1986):353–356; Wiener, T., "Report from the Association of Jewish Libraries," Library of Congress Information Bulletin 46 (Dec. 14, 1987):547–550; Kaganoff, N.M., "The American Jewish Historical Society as an Archival Agency," Judaica Librarianship 4 (1987/88):38–39; Posner, M., "Association of Jewish Libraries," in ALA Yearbook 1988. pp. 58–60. Chicago: American Library Association, 1988; Lerman, L.P., "Association of Jewish Libraries," in ALA Yearbook 1989. pp. 54–55. Chicago: American Library Association, 1989; "Association of Jewish Libraries," in The Bowker Annual: Library and Book Trade Almanac. 34th Edition 1989–90, p. 673. New York: R. R. Bowker, 1989; Wiener, T., "Association of Jewish Libraries Meets in Washington, DC," Library of Congress Information Bulletin 48 (Oct. 9, 1989):351, 352–354

556 Association of Librarians in the History of the Health Sciences (ALHHS)

Address c/o Arlene Shaner (ALHHS Secretary/Treasurer), 1216 Fifth Avenue, New York, NY 10029 Tel.: +1 212-822-7313, ashaner@nyam.org; www.alhhs.org

Languages English

Established 1975, at annual meeting of the American Association for the History of Medicine (AAHM)

Officers Pres: Lisa A. Mix; Pres-elect: Stephen J. Greenberg; Treas/Secr: Arlene Shaner

Staff None

General Assembly Entire membership meets meets annually in conjunction with the American Association for the History of Medicine; 2010: Rochester, Minnesota, April 28th-29th

Membership Requirements: Persons who have professional responsibilities for library and archives collections and services in the history of the health sciences (voting member); persons interested in the aims of the Association, e. g. booksellers, retired members, friends (non-voting member). Dues: 15$/yr.

Structure Governed by officers and steering committees in annual meeting. Affiliations: AAHM, Medical Museums Association

Sources of Support Membership dues. Budget: No fixed amount

Major Fields of Interest History of medicine; rare book librarianship; medical librarianship; preservation; computer application to the history of medicine

Major Goals and Objectives a. to identify and make contact with persons similarly engaged; b. to provide opportunities to hold meetings on appropriate occasions; c. to issue a newsletter and such other materials as may seem appropriate; d. to cooperate with other similar organizations in projects of mutual concern; e. to provide opportunities for educational and professional growth programs

Activities Sponsors conferences, continuing education programs, awards

Publications Official journal: The Watermark. 1975-. 4/yr. Free to members. Linda A. Lohr (lalohr@buffalo.edu), University of Buffalo Health Sciences Library. Circ: Membership. English
Bibliography "Association of Librarians in the History of the Health Sciences," in The Bowker Annual: Library and Book Trade Almanac. 34th Edition 1989–90, p. 674. New York: R. R. Bowker, 1989

557 Association of Mental Health Librarians (AMHL)

Address c/o Stuart Moss, President, 140 Old Orangeburg Rd., Orangeburg, NY 10962 Tel.: +1 845-398-6576, Fax +1 845-398-5551, moss@nki.rfmh.org; www.mhlib.org
Languages English
Established 1964, as Society of Mental Health Librarians, inactive between 1978–79, reorganized under present name, 1980, in Boston, during informal meeting with the Institute on Hospital & Community Psychiatry
Officers Pres: Stuart Moss; Program Chair / Pres-elect: Joseph Tally; Past Pres: Gary McMilian; Treas: Arlene Krizanic
Staff None
General Assembly Entire membership meets once a year
Membership Requirements: Employed in a mental health library or information center. Dues: 15$
Structure Governed by executive officers. Affiliations: Institute on Hospital & Community Psychiatry of the American Psychiatric Association (APA)
Sources of Support Membership dues, sale of publications, meeting registrations
Major Fields of Interest Mental health librarianship
Major Goals and Objectives To provide mental health librarians with an opportunity for exchange of information, continuing education, and collegiality
Activities Sponsors conferences, seminars, workshops, continuing education programs, Small Grants Program (established to enhance opportunities for members of AMHL to engage in research, scholarship and creative endeavors), offers MHLIB Listserv (discussion forum for mental health librarians)
Publications No official journal. Other publications: Policy Information Exchange (PIE) (web-based source for information related to mental health, substance abuse, and disability policy, incl. database of over 5,000 docs); Guidelines for Working with Persons with Mental Illnesses; Report To Congress on the Treatment and Prevention of Co-Occurring Substance Abuse and Mental Disorders (available online: www.samhsa.gov/news/cl_congress2002.html)

558 Association of Moving Image Archivists (AMIA)*

Address 1313 N Vine Street, Hollywood, CA 90028 Tel.: +1 323 4631500, Fax +1 323 4631506, amia@amianet.org; www.amianet.org
Languages English
Established 1991
Staff 3 full-time staff members
General Assembly Annual Conference: 2009 – St. Louis, Missouri. 2010 – Joint conference with IASA in Philadelphia, PA

Membership Over 950 individual and institutional members worldwide. Dues: Dues (US Dollar): 75 individual, 35 student, 250 non-profit institutional, 500 for-profit institutional
Structure Volunteer Board of Directors and volunteer committee structure. AMIA is a member of the Coordinating Council of Audiovisual Archives Association (CCAAA), the North American Archival Network (NAANICA), the US Council of the Blue Shield (USCBS) and is part of the Digital Promise Coalition
Sources of Support The Association is supported through membership dues, donations and sponsorship
Major Fields of Interest Preservation of moving images, education, training
Major Goals and Objectives To advance the field of moving image archiving by fostering cooperation among those concerned with the acquisition, preservation, exhibition and use of moving image materials
Activities Events include an annual conference, workshops, screenings, and technical symposia. Publications include The Moving Image journal, a quarterly Newsletter, and Newsbriefs. Our scholarship program offers four annual scholarships, an internship, and fellowship. International programs include a fellowship and annual institutional memberships program for archivists in emerging nations for archives from emerging areas. In addition, our committees work to develop and promote standards, encourage fieldwide communication through our listservs, and honor the work of archivists and archival organizations. We collaborate internationally with other institutions and organizations to further the field
Publications Official journals: The Moving Image. 2001-. Editors: Marsha & Devin Orgeron. AMIA Newsletter. 4/yr, ISSN 1075–6477. Other publications: Membership Directory, the AMIA Tech Review
Bibliography In 2010 AMIA joins with the International Association of Sound and Audiovisual Archives for our first joint conference. The AMIA/IASA Conference will be a forum to discuss where convergence is possible, to communicate standards and to share mutual solutions and opportunities
Comment AMIA is open to, and encourages participation from, anyone working with moving images in their collections. AMIA's members range from those who work solely with moving images to organizations where moving images are only a small part of their collection

559 Association of Research Libraries (ARL)

Address 21 Dupont Circle, Suite 800, Washington, DC 20036 Tel.: +1 202 2962296, Fax +1 202 8720884, clowry@arl.org; www.arl.org
Languages English
Established 1932, Chicago, by chief librarians of 43 research libraries
Officers Pres: Marianne Gaunt; Exec Dir: Charles Lowry
Staff 28 (paid)
General Assembly Entire membership meets twice a year
Membership Total members: 123 (institutional). Types of membership: Institutional. Requirements: Membership eligibility is determined by membership criteria adopted by the ARL membership
Structure Governed by officers and Board of Directors. Affiliations: ALA, IFLA
Sources of Support Membership dues, sale of publications, research grants.

Major Fields of Interest Issues confronting large research libraries (university and nonuniversity libraries), such as development, organization, management, and access to information sources
Major Goals and Objectives To initiate and develop plans for strengthening research library resources and services in support of higher education and research
Activities Sponsors conferences, seminars, workshops, and other continuing education programs; helds career resources service, consulting service; provides electronic news resources and discussion lists
Publications Official journal: ARL: A Bimonthly Report on Research Library Issues and Actions from ARL, CNI, and SPARC. Address same as Association. English. Publications report on current issues of interest to academic and research library administrators, staff and library education professionals; more information: ARL Publications Distribution Center Tel. 301–362–8196, e-mail <pubs@arl.org
Bibliography Welsh, W.J., "ARL Holds 50th Anniversary Meeting," Library of Congress Information Bulletin 40 (June 18, 1982):183–184; Molyneux, R., "Growth at ARL Member Libraries 1962/63 to 1983/84," Journal of Academic Librarianship 12 (1986):211–216; Hewitt, J. A. and Shipman, J.S., "Cooperative Collection Development among Research Libraries in the Age of Networking: Report of a Survey of ARL Libraries," in Advances in Library Automation and Networking v. 1. pp. 189–232. Jai Press, 1987; "Joint ARL–Library of Congress Project to Produce Machine-Readable National Register of Microform Masters," Library of Congress Information Bulletin 47 (Jan. 4, 1988):2; Dougherty, R. M. and Barr, N.E., "Paying the Piper: ARL Libraries Respond to Skyrocketing Journal Subscription Prices," The Journal of Academic Librarianship 14 (1988):4–9; Stubbs, K., "Apples and Oranges and ARL Statistics [library statistics invite the unwary to draw illicit conclusions from mismated numbers]," Journal of Academic Librarianship 14 (1988):231–235; Gyeszly, S., "Reserve Departments and Automation: A Survey of ARL Libraries," Information Technology and Libraries 7 (1988):401–410; "ARL Receives Preservation Grant," Wilson Library Bulletin 63 (1989):13; Daval, N., "Association of Research Libraries," in ALA Yearbook 1989. pp. 55–61. Chicago: American Library Association, 1989; Daval, N., "Association of Research Libraries," in The Bowker Annual: Library and Book Trade Almanac. 34th Edition 1989–90, pp. 155–159. New York: R. R. Bowker, 1989; "ACRL," ibid.:674–676

560 Association of Specialized and Cooperative Library Agencies (ASCLA)

Address 50 East Huron St., Chicago, IL 60611 Tel.: 1800 5452433, ascla@ala.org; www.ala.org/ala/mgrps/divs/ascla/ascla.cfm
Languages English
Established 1977, through a merger of 2 ALA Divisions: Association of State Library Agencies, and Health and Rehabilitative Library Services Division
Staff 4 (paid)
General Assembly Entire membership meets annually during ALA conference
Membership Total members: more than 1000 (individual and institutional). Requirements: Membership in ALA. Dues: 40$ plus ALA membership
Structure Governed by Executive Board. Affiliations: A division of ALA
Sources of Support Membership dues.
Major Fields of Interest State library agencies,

specialized library agencies, and multitype library cooperatives

Major Goals and Objectives To represent state library agencies, specialized library agencies, and multitype library cooperatives and assist in the development and evaluation of their plans, and to coordinate activities with other appropriate ALA units. The specific objectives are: (1) Development and evaluation of goals and plans for member groups to facilitate the implementation, improvement and extension of library activities designed to foster improved user services, coordinating such activities with other appropriate ALA units; (2) representation and interpretation of the role, functions, and services of these agencies and cooperatives within and outside the profession, including contact with national organizations and government agencies; (3) development of policies, studies, and activities in matters affecting these agencies and cooperatives; (4) establishment, evaluation, and promotion of standards and service guidelines relating to the concerns of the association; (5) identifying the interests and needs of all persons, encouraging the creation of services to meet these needs within the areas of concern of the association, and promoting the use of these services provided by the agencies and cooperatives; (6) stimulating the professional growth and promoting the specialized training and continuing education of library personnel at all levels in the areas of concern of the association; (7) assisting in the coordination of activities of other units within ALA with related concerns; (8) granting recognition for outstanding library service; (9) acting as a clearinghouse for the exchange of information and encouraging the development of relevant materials, publications and research

Activities Carried out through the sections and committees, covering a wide range of issues in accordance with the goals and objectives of the Association. Some activities deal with matters involving state and local library legislation, state grants-in-aid and appropriations, and relationships among state, federal, regional, and local governments. Much attention is given to the development of standards, such as preparing revisions of Standards for Juvenile Correctional Institutions, the Library Standards for Jails and Detention Centers, and Standards for Adult Correctional Institutions. Sponsors conferences, seminars, workshops, and other continuing education programs, on topics such as consulting skills, automation activities, youth services, services to the impaired elderly, AIDS information, bibliotherapy, health care, managing effective programs for disabled persons, etc.; helds awards program

Publications Official journal: Interface. 4/yr. $10. Free to members. Editor: Sara Laughlin. Address: 1616 Treadwell Lane, Bloomington, IN 47408, Tel: +1 812 3348485; Fax: +1 812 3362215, email: laughlin@bluemarble.net. Other publications e. g. Library Services to the Sandwich Generation and Serial Caregivers. Linda Lucas Walling, compiler. 2001. ISBN: 0-8389-8139-9. $20. ASCLA member: $18; Planning for Library Services to People with Disabilities. by Rhea Joyce Rubin. 2001. ISBN: 0-8389-8168-2. $30. ASCLA members: $27; Library Networks in the New Millennium: Top Ten Trends. ed by Sara Laughlin, 2000. ISBN: 0-8389-8122-4. $25. ASCLA members $22.50; Strategic Planning for Library Multitype Cooperatives. 1997. ISBN: 0-8389-7914-9. $30. ASCLA members, $28; Strategic Planning for Multitype Library Cooperatives.1998. ISBN: 0-8389-7926-2. $28. ASCLA members, $25; The Functions and Roles of State Library Agencies. Compiled by Ethel E. Himmel and William J. Wilson. GraceAnne A. DeCandido, ed. 2000. ISBN: 0-8389-8105-4, $20 ($19 for ASCLA members)

Bibliography "ALA Unit [ASCLA] Awarded $.9 Million for Literature Project,"

American Libraries 14 (1983):696+; Daniels, B.E., "Association of Specialized and Cooperative Library Agencies," in ALA Yearbook 1989. pp. 61–62. Chicago: American Library Association, 1989; "American Library Association. Association of Specialized and Cooperative Library Agencies," in The Bowker Annual: Library and Book Trade Almanac. 34th Edition 1989–90. pp. 647–648. New York: R. R. Bowker, 1989

561 Association of Vision Science Librarians (AVSL)

Address c/o Elaine Wells, Chair, 33 West 42nd Street at Bryant Park, New York, NY 10036 goren@med.umich.edu; www.lhl.uab.edu/avsl
Languages English
Established 1968, Beverly Hills, California
Officers Chair: Gale Oren; Secr/Chair-elect: D. J. Matthews; Treas: Judith Schaeffer Young
Staff None
General Assembly Entire membership meets once a year, in December, in conjunction with the annual meeting of the American Academy of Optometry. 2010: Nov 17th-20th San Francisco, CA
Membership More than 100 individuals and over 75 institutions. Requirements: An interest in some aspect of the literature of vision. Dues: None
Structure Governed by executive officers and members. Affiliations: Special Interest Group of both the Association of Schools and Colleges of Optometry and the Medical Library Association
Sources of Support Sale of publications. No specific budget
Major Fields of Interest Vision science
Major Goals and Objectives To foster development of individual libraries; encourage cooperative activities among the member libraries; develop mechanisms for improving access to vision information; develop services, particularly reference and bibliographic services, for all individuals having frequent vision information needs; promote standards for academic vision science libraries; assist new vision science librarians
Activities Sponsors conferences
Publications No official journal. Other publications: Standards, Guidelines, Union List, Opening Day Books, Core AV List, Publication Considerations in the Age of Electronic Opportunities
Bibliography "Association of Vision Science Librarians," in The Bowker Annual: Library and Book Trade Almanac. 34th Edition 1989–90. pp. 676–677. New York: R. R. Bowker, 1989

562 Bibliographical Society of America (BSA)

Address c/o Michèle E. Randall, Exec Secretary, P. O. Box 1537, Lenox Hill Station, New York, N.Y. 10021 Tel.: +1 212 4522710, Fax +1 212 4522710, cmelish@fas.harvard.edu; www.bibsocamer.org
Languages English
Established 1904, New York City
Officers Pres: John Neal Hoover; VP: Claudia Funke; Secr: Caroline Douselle-Melish; Treas: G. Scott Clemens; Exec Secr: Michèle E. Randall
General Assembly Entire membership meets once a year, in late January in New York

Membership Majority of the Society's members are from the United States and Canada, but most European countries, Japan, Korea, Australia, and New Zealand are also represented, together with institutions in Brazil, India, Israel, Saudi Arabia, and ZimbabweRequirements: Open to all individuals and institutions interested in bibliographical problems and project. Dues: $65, individual, $75 institutional; $100, contributing; $250, sustaining; $1250, personal life, $20, student

Structure Governed by Council. Affiliations: American Council of Learned Societies

Sources of Support Membership dues, sale of publications, endowed funds

Major Fields of Interest Descriptive and analytical bibliography; printing, publishing, bookselling and other book trade history; textual editing; codicology and related manuscript studies

Major Goals and Objectives To support bibliographical inquiry in all areas listed above

Activities In accordance with the aims of the Society, activities promote bibliographical research and relevant publications. Initiated fellowship program. Continuing publication of quarterly journal and preparing manuscripts for publication as monographs. Some projects are being carried out jointly with related associations, e. g. a comprehensive survey of repositories of printing and publishing archives to result in the publication of a guide to the resources for bibliographical research in the US. Active in promoting library-related legislation, e.g., participated with other constituents of the American Council of Learned Societies in supporting re-authorization of the National Endowment for the Humanities. Awards short-term fellowships to encourage scholarship in bibliography. Sponsors regional meetings (lectures and exhibitions) with other bibliographical institutions

Publications Official journal: Papers of the Bibliographical Society of America. 1904-. 4/yr. Address: 233 E. 70th Street, 5P, New York, NY 10021. Subscriptions are available only through membership in the Society. Dues: $50, $20 per year for students providing proof of eligibility (a $15 postage surcharge is added for all non-US memberships). Back numbers are available from Periodicals Service Company, 11 Main Street, Germantown, NY 12526; e-mail: <psc@backsets.com or directly from the PSC website at www.backsets.com. English. Publishes monographs and contributed many Major bibliographical works. e.g.: Gatch, Milton McC.: Leander Van Ess and the Earliest American Collections of Reformation Pamphlets. Forthcoming, 2004; Huttner, Sidney F., and Elizabeth Stege Huttner: A Register of Artists, Engravers, Booksellers, Bookbinders, Printers and Publishers in New York City, 1821–42. New York 1993; Christianson, C. Paul: A Directory of London Stationers and Book Artisans, 1300–1500. New York 1990

Bibliography Wiegand, A.A., "Library Politics and the Organization of the Bibliographical Society of America," The Journal of Library History, Philosophy and Comparative Librarianship 21 (1986):131–157; "Bibliographical Society Meets," Antiquarian Bookman (AB) 81 (1988):1496–98; "Bibliographical Society of America," in The Bowker Annual: Library and Book Trade Almanac. 34th Edition 1989–90. p. 679. New York: R. R. Bowker, 1989; The Bibliographical Society of America, 1904–79: A Retrospective Collection. Charlottesville 1980; Mayo, Hope: The Bibliographical Society of America: A Centennial History. New York: The Bibliographical Society of America, 2004.(A record of the origins, activities, and contributions of the Society with a bibliography of its publications and lists of its officers and members)

563 Catholic Library Association (CLA)

Address c/o Jean R. Bostley, SSJ, Exec Dir, 100 North Street, Suite 224, Pittsfield, MA 01201-5178 Tel.: +1 413-443-2252, Fax + 1 413-442-2252, cla@cathla.org; www.cathla.org
Languages English
Established 1921, Cincinnati, Ohio. Originally founded as a section of the National Catholic Educational Association, becoming independent in 1931 and legally incorporated in 1955
Officers Pres: Nancy Schmidtmann; VP: Malachy McCarthy; Past Pres: Catherine Fennell; Exec Dir: Jean R. Bostley
General Assembly Entire membership meets once a year
Membership Requirements: Open to anyone interested in the aims of the Association
Structure Governed by Executive Board, assisted by Advisory Council. 4 sections (Academic Libraries, Archives, and Library Education Section, Children's Library Services Section, High School and Young Adult Library Services Section, Parish and Community Library Services Section)
Sources of Support Membership dues, sale of publications
Major Fields of Interest Catholic library and information science fields
Major Goals and Objectives The promotion and encouragement of Catholic literature and library work through cooperation, publications, education, and information
Activities The Association strives to initiate and foster any activity or library program that will promote literature and libraries not only of a Catholic nature, but also of an ecumenical spirit. Maintains representation to other professional associations having library/information service interests. Active in promoting library-related legislation, such as, obtaining Federal aid for Catholic school libraries, etc. Provides 2 scholarships annually to encourage promising students to enter the library profession, and presents other awards. Current and future: Increase of publications program to meet membership needs; computerization of membership services and publications; sponsorship of the American Catholic Heritage project; cooperative activities with other similar associations; increase of continuing education programs for members. Sponsors conferences, seminars, workshops, and exhibits
Publications Official journal: Catholic Library World. 1929-. 4/yr. $60. Free to members. Contact: Mary E. Gallagher, SSJ, Alumnae Library Elms College 291 Springfield Street Chicopee, MA 01013–2839, Tel: +1 413 265–2354, Fax +1 413 5947418, e-mail gallagherm@elms.edu. Other publications: CLA Handbook and Membership Directory; The Catholic Periodical and Literature Index 4/yr. (subscription); print, CDROM, online
Bibliography Lynch, Sister M.F., "Structuring CLS's Mission for the Future," Catholic Library World 56 (1985):270–271; Corrigan, J.T., "Catholic Library Association," in ALA Yearbook 1989. pp. 87–88. Chicago: American Library Association, 1989; "Catholic Library Association," in The Bowker Annual: Library and Book Trade Almanac. 34th Edition 1989–90. pp. 682–683. New York: R. R. Bowker, 1989

564 Center for Research Libraries (CRL)

Address 6050 S Kenwood Avenue, Chicago, IL 60637-2804 Tel.: +1 800 6216044, Fax +1 773 9554339; www.crl.edu

Languages English
Established 1949, as Midwest Inter-library Center, with grants from the Carnegie Corporation and Rockefeller Foundation. Organized under new name in 1966
Officers Pres: Bernard Reilly; VP: Melissa Trevvett; Chair: Fred Heath; Vice-Chair: Edward S. Macias
General Assembly Entire membership meets once a year. 2004: Chicago
Membership Total members: 192 (institutional). Requirements: Any institution supporting research or having a research library. Dues: Depend on size of library acquisitions expenditures over 5 years and number of volumes held
Structure The Center is a nonprofit organization operated and maintained by its member institutions. Members are represented on the Council by two persons, the head librarian (ex officio) and a nonlibrarian appointed by the president of the member institution. Associate members are not represented
Sources of Support Membership dues
Major Fields of Interest Library cooperation in research materials
Major Goals and Objectives To supplement and complement Major American research collections by maintaining a collection of important research materials
Activities Preservation projects e. g. the microfilming of government archives in Vietnam and Senegal, digitization of documents and publications from Brazil and South Asia, and the collecting of endangered newspapers and political materials from Europe and the developing regions of the world
Publications Official journal: Focus (online newsletter); 1980-. 4/yr. Available on CRL website. Contact:Yvonne Jefferson, email: jefferso@crl.edu, English. Other publications: bibliographies, annual reports, proceedings of conferences, seminars, etc
Bibliography "Center for Research Libraries: Meeting the Opportunity to Fulfill the Promise: A Symposium," Journal of Academic Librarianship 9 (1983):258–269; "Center for Research Libraries is Newest Member of CONSER Program," Library of Congress Information Bulletin 46 (June 22, 1987):286

565 Chief Officers of State Library Agencies (COSLA)*

Address 201 E. Main Street, Ste. 1405, Lexington, KY 40507 Tel.: +1 859 5149151, Fax +1 859 5149166, Lsingler-adams@amrms.com; www.cosla.org
Languages English
Established November 1973, Washington D.C.
Officers Pres: Susan McVey; Treas: Ann Joslin; VP/Pres-elect: Lamar Veatch; Secr: Donna Jones Morris; Dir: Jan Walsh; Robert Maier
Staff Staff/Management Services provided by Association Management Resources, Inc
General Assembly The Chief Officers meet three times a year. The annual meeting is held in the fall, and working sessions are scheduled in conjunction with the mid-winter and Library Legislative Days of the American Library Association
Membership Membership consists solely of the chief library officers of the 50 states and Washington D.C.
Structure Governed by Board of Directors. Affiliations: ALA, IMLS, the Gates Foundation
Sources of Support Membership dues

Major Fields of Interest Concerns of COSLA include effective statewide planning and action to ensure library service adequate to meet the needs of all communities; the strengthening of state library agencies, library systems and effective networks; federal appropriations for library services; national library service programs; use of new technology for library and information service; state library services; availability of state and federal documents; improved library statistics programs; continuing library education programs; and state-federal responsibilities for talking book service to blind and handicapped persons throughout the nation
Major Goals and Objectives Its purpose is to identify and address issues of common concern and national interest; to further state library agency relationships with federal government and national organizations; and to initiate cooperative action for the improvement of library services to the people of the United States
Activities Various committees carry out liaison activities with government agencies and other organizations
Publications No publications program
Bibliography Miller, R.T., "Cherry Blossoms, Chief Officers of State Library Agencies and Congress," Show-Me Libraries 37 (1986):3–4; "Chief Officers of State Library Agencies," in The Bowker Annual: Library and Book Trade Almanac. 34th Edition 1989–90, pp. 683–684. New York: R. R. Bowker, 1989

566 Chinese-American Librarians Association (CALA)

Address c/o Holly Yu, 5151 State University Dr, Los Angeles, CA 90032-8300 sctseng888@yahoo.com; www.cala-web.org
Languages English
Established 1973, as Mid-West Chinese American Librarians Association, a regional organization in Illinois. A year later, Chinese Librarians Association was formed in California in 1974. In 1976, Mid-West Chinese American Librarians Association was expanded to a national organization as Chinese American Librarians Association
Officers Pres: Xudong Jin; VP/Pres-elect: Zhijia Shen; Incoming VP/Pres Elect: Min Chou; Exec Dir: Haipeng Li; Treas: Shuyong Jiang
General Assembly Entire membership meets once a year during the annual ALA conference
Membership Requirements: Any individual or corporate body interested in the goals of the Association
Structure Governed by Executive Board members elected by the general membership. Seven chapters. Affiliations: ALA. In 1988, CALA established sister relations with the Library Association of Central Governments Units and Scientific Research Networks of Beijing, and with the Library Association of China in Taipei. CALA also exchanges publications with the East Asian Library Resources Group of Australia and many others.
Sources of Support Membership dues, sale of publications
Major Fields of Interest Sino-American librarianship; international exchanges of information and library personnel
Major Goals and Objectives To provide a medium through which Chinese-American librarians may cooperate with other associations and organizations: (1) To promote better communication among Chinese-American librarians; (2) to serve as a forum for the discussion of mutual problems and professional concerns among Chinese-American

librarians; (3) to promote the development of Chinese and American librarianship
Activities Sponsors awards and scholarships, Book Week, exhibits, conferences, seminars, workshops, and other continuing education programs, and promotes writers, publishers and book sellers so that they can reach a larger audience
Publications Official journal: Journal of Library and Information Science. 1975-. 2/yr. 20$. Free to members. (Published jointly with the Department of Social Education, National Taiwan Normal University, Taiwan). Editor: Zhijia Shen. Address: East Asian Library, University of Pittsburgh, 207L Hillman Library, Pittsburgh, PA 15260; Tel: +1 412 6488185; Fax: +1 412 6487683; e-mail: zjs2+@pitt.edu. English, Chinese. Indexed in Lib.Lit., Index to Chinese Periodicals. ISA, LISA, PAIS. etc. Other publications: Chinese American Librarians Association Newsletter (ISSN: 0736–8887) CALA E-Journal; CALA Listserv (current list owner is Shixing Wen, email: shwen@umich.edu); Children's Books by Chinese American Authors: An Annotated Bibliography, Compiled by Zheng Ye Yang
Bibliography Wan, W.W., "Chinese American Librarians Association: An Overview," Ethnic Forum: Journal of Ethnic Studies and Ethnic Bibliography 6 (1986):141–143; Seetoo Wilson, A., "Chinese-American Librarians Association (CALA)," in ALA Yearbook 1989. p. 98. Chicago: American Library Association, 1989

567 Church and Synagogue Library Association (CSLA)
Address 2920 SW Dolph Ct., Ste. 3A, Portland, OR 97219-4055 Tel.: +1 503 2446919, Fax +1 503 9773734, csla@worldaccessnet.com; http://cslainfo.org
Languages English
Established 1967, Philadelphia, during ALA conference, by Protestant, Catholic and Jewish librarians
Officers Pres: Rusty Tryon; Past Pres: J. THeodore Anderson; 1st VP/Pres-elect: Marjorie Smink; 2nd VP/Membership Chair: Marianne Stowers; Treas: Bill Anderson
General Assembly Entire membership meets once a year at three-day-conference
Membership Requirements: Interest in aims of Association and payment of dues. Dues: $25, individual; $45, church or synagogue; $70, affiliated; $175, institutional
Structure Governed by Executive Board. 29 active chapters. Affiliations: seven regional library associations
Sources of Support Membership dues, sale of publications.
Major Fields of Interest Church and synagogue librarianship
Major Goals and Objectives To provide educational guidance in the establishment and maintenance of library service in churches and synagogues; to act as a unifying core for the many existing church and synagogue libraries; to provide the opportunity for a mutual sharing of practices and problems; to inspire and encourage a sense of purpose and mission among church and synagogue librarians; to study and guide the development of church and synagogue librarianship toward recognition as a formal branch of the library profession
Activities Training sessions offered at regional and national workshops, provides counseling and guidance for individual libraries through its Library Services Committee, establishes chapters to provide ongoing service and fellowship in local areas; sponsors annual conference
Publications Official journal: Church & Synagogue Libraries. 1967-. 6/yr. Free to members. English. Indexed in Christian Periodical Index. Other publications: A numbered series of Guides to aid in the establishment and operation of congregational libraries, e.g.,

Pritchett, J. Providing Reference Service in Church and Synagogue Libraries (1988; No. 15); Archives in the Church or Synagogue Library (No. 10); Standards for Church and Synagogue Libraries (No. 6); Ward, L. Developing an effective library! Ways to promote yourcongrgational library (2004 No.19); Snyder, Susan Cataloging and classifying (2004, No. 20), etc.; A Basic Book List for Church Libraries (3rd ed., B. E. Deitrick); Church and Synagogue Library Resources (4th ed., R. Kohl & D. Rodda); Simple Steps to a Successful Workshop. Dottie Lewis. 2003. $8.50, members $7. Bibliographies: e. g. Church and Synagogue Library Resources: Annotated Bibliography; annual reports, proceedings of conferences, seminars, etc. Publications available for sale; Carol Campbell Classic Religions Book For Children, 2004; Patricia P. Dole Helping Children Through Books, 2004

Bibliography   Harvey, J.F., ed., Church and Synagogue Libraries. Metuchen, NJ: Scarecrow Press, 1980; Hannaford, C.,"The Church and Synagogue Library Association: Fifteen Years of Ecumenical Concern for Quality Service in Religious Libraries," Special Libraries 74 (1983); "Church and Synagogue Librarians Meet," Library Times International 2 (1985):3; Vanderhoof, A., "Church and Synagogue Library Association in Texas," Texas Library Journal 62 (1986):32–33; Karabinus, K., "Ohio Welcomes CSLA's Annual Conference," Church and Synagogue Libraries 21 (1988):1, 51; "Church and Synagogue Library Association," in The Bowker Annual: Library and Book Trade Almanac. 34th Edition 1989–90. pp. 684–685. New York: R. R. Bowker, 1989

568   Coalition for Networked Information (CNI)

Address   21 Dupont Circle, Suite 800, Washington, DC 20036   Tel.: +1 202 2965098, Fax +1 202 8720884, info@cni.org; www.cni.org

Languages   English

Established   1990

Officers   Exec Dir: Clifford A. Lynch; Assoc Exec Dir: Joan K. Lippincott

General Assembly   Memebership meeting once a year. 2010: Fall Membership Meeting, Washington, DC, December 13th-14th; 2011: Fall Membership Meeting, Washington, DC, December 12th-13th

Membership   About 200 institutions representing higher education, publishing, network and telecommunications, information technology, and libraries and library organizations

Structure   Governed by a Steering Committee

Sources of Support   Sponsored by ARL and EDUCAUSE

Major Fields of Interest   Dedicated to supporting the transformative promise of networked information technology for the advancement of scholarly communication and the enrichment of intellectual productivity

Major Goals and Objectives   To share knowledge about architectures and standards for networked information; to improve scholarly communication; to study the economics of networked information; to advance Internet technology and infrastructure; to enhance teaching and learning; to understand the institutional and professional implications of the networked environment; to expand government information on the Internet

Activities   Program structured around three central themes: Developing and Managing Networked Information Content; Transforming Organizations, Professions, and Individuals; Building Technology, Standards, and Infrastructure;

co-sponsors conferences and workshops
Publications   No official journal

569   Committee on South Asian Libraries and Documentation (CONSALD)

Address   c/o Mary Rader, South Asia Bibliographer, 728 State St., Madison, WI 53706-1494   mrader@library.wisc.edu; www.lib.virginia.edu/area-studies/SouthAsia/Lib/consald.html
Languages   English
Established   1970, as Committee of the Association for Asian Studies, Inc
Officers   Chair: Tim Bryson; Secr/Treas: Andrea Singer
Staff   None
General Assembly   Entire membership meets once a year at the annual meeting of the Association for Asian Studies
Membership   Requirements: open to all who are concerned with South Asian library resources and who are members of the Association for Asian Studies, Inc
Structure   Governed by Executive Board of the Committee shall consist of four librarians elected by the membership-at-large, three faculty members appointed by the South Asian Council and three ex-officio librarian members. Affiliations: Association for Asian Studies
Sources of Support   Membership dues (through the Association for Asian Studies)
Major Fields of Interest   South Asian studies
Major Goals and Objectives   The primary objective of the Committee is the development of North American library resources on South Asia. The Committee shall facilitate library cooperation, collection development, bibliographic control, access and preservation to benefit the use of South Asian research and teaching materials
Activities   Coordination and cooperation between South Asia research collections in the USA

570   Council on East Asian Libraries, Inc. (CEAL)

Address   c/o Ai-lin Yang, CEAL Treasurer, Stanford, CA94305-6004   Tel.: +1 650 736-7676, Fax +1 650 724-2028, ayang1@stanford.edu; www.eastasianlib.org
Languages   English
Established   1963, as a Committee of the Association for Asian Studies, Inc
Officers   Pres: Joy Kim; VP/Pres-elect: Peter Zhou; Secr: Dawn Lawson; Treas: Ai-lin Yang
Staff   None
General Assembly   Entire membership meets once a year during the annual meeting of the Association for Asian Studies
Membership   Requirements: Open to members of the Association for Asian Studies, Inc. A member of the AAS may become a CEAL member by subscribing to the Journal of East Asian Libraries. However, a subscriber shall have the option of not becoming a member of CEAL if he/she so desires. Dues (US Dollar): 30, individual
Structure   Governed by Executive Group consisting of 3 faculty members and 6 librarians, serving staggered terms of not more than 3 years. Affiliations: Association for Asian Studies
Sources of Support   Membership dues (through the Association for Asian Studies)
Major Fields of Interest   East Asian librarianship

Major Goals and Objectives (1) To further the profession of East Asian librarianship; (2) to serve as a faculty librarians' forum for the discussion of problems of common concern and to recommend programs for the improvement of library facilities; (3) to promote the development of library resources and bibliographic controls; (4) to improve interlibrary and international cooperation and services

Activities Initiated Chinese Cooperative Catalog, issued monthly by the Library of Congress. Activities carried out through subcommittees (Committee on Chinese Materials, Committee on Japanese Materials, Committee on Korean Materials, Committee on Library Technology, Committee on Publications, Committee on Technical Processing). Projects involving institutional cooperation are voted on by institutional members only

Publications Official journal: Journal of East Asian Libraries (JEAL). 3/yr. Address same as Association. Other publications: CEAL Online Directory (password required); Eastlib Listserv

571 Council on Library and Information Resources (CLIR)*

Address 1752 N Street, NW, Suite 800, Washington, DC 20036-2609 Tel.: +1 202 9394750, Fax +1 202 9394765, jwade@clir.org; www.clir.org

Languages English

Established 1956, by the Ford Foundation "for the purpose of aiding in the solution of the problems of libraries generally, and of research libraries in particular

Officers Pres: Henry Charles; Chair: Stephen Nichols; VChair: Wendy Pradt Lougee; Secr: James Williams; Treas: Herman Pabbruwe

Staff 11

Structure Governed by Board of Directors

Sources of Support Grants from public and private foundations, contracts with federal agencies, fees from sponsoring organizations, and donations from individuals

Major Fields of Interest Cyberinfrastructure, The Next Scholar, Preservation, The Emerging Library, Leadership, New Models

Major Goals and Objectives CLIR works at the intersection of libraries, scholarship, and technology, in partnership with organizations and individuals representing multiple disciplines and professions to address issues facing scholarly communication and higher education; fosters new approaches to the management of digital and nondigital information resources so that they will be available in the future; expands leadership capacity in the information professions; analyzes changes in the information landscape and help practitioners prepare for them

Activities Publications, Cataloging Hidden Special Collections and Archives: Building a New Research Environment, Postdoctoral Fellowship Program in Academic Libraries, Mellon Fellowships for Dissertation Research in Original Sources, Frye Leadership Institute, Rovelstad Scholarship in International Librarianship, Scholarly Communication Institute, Emerging Disciplines Symposium, Faculty Research Behavior Workshops, Undergraduate Research Practices Workshops

Publications Official journal: CLIR Reports (many are available online and free, address: www.clir.org/pubs/reports/reports.html). Other publications: CLIR Issues, CLIR Executive Summaries, Annual Reports, Press Releases

United States of America 573

572 Evangelical Church Library Association (ECLA)

Address   P.O. Box 353, Glen Ellyn, IL 60138   Tel.: +1 630 3757865, Judi@eclalibraries.org; www.eclalibraries.org
Languages   English
Established   1970
Officers   Pres: Donna Waln; Secr: Judi Turek; Recording Secr: Mary Clapp; Treas: Paul Trautwein
General Assembly   Entire membership meets once a year. 2010: Wheaton, IL, October 22nd-23rd
Membership   Requirements: Open to interested individuals and institutions or organizations. Dues: US membership fee of $30.00 includes a subscription to Church Libraries, Canadian membership is $40.00, other foreign memberships are $50.00 and publisher memberships are $100.00
Structure   Governed by Board of Directors
Sources of Support   Membership dues, sale of publications
Major Fields of Interest   Church libraries
Major Goals and Objectives   The establishment and growth of church libraries in evangelical churches
Activities   Encouraging church librarians by means of the quarterly journal, an annual conference in fall, and assistance with problems through Bulletin Board, letters and phone calls
Publications   Official journal: Church Libraries. 4/yr. Editor: Lin Johnson

573 Federal Library and Information Center Committee (FLICC)

Address   101 Independence Avenue, S.E., Washington, DC 20540-4935   Tel.: +1 202 7074800, Fax +1 202 7074818, tbro@loc.gov; www.loc.gov/flicc
Languages   English
Established   1965, by the library of Congress and the Bureau of the Budget to provide leadership in policy issues affecting the provision of information to government employees and the general public. Established as Federal Library Committee. Reorganization in 1984 brought changes in name (FLICC), mission, and membership
Officers   Exec Dir: Charles V. Stanhope
Staff   36 paid, 204 volunteers
General Assembly   Entire membership meets four times a year for FLICC, and twice a year for FEDLINK
Membership   Federal departments and agencies, and FEDLINK participants and members. Requirements: FLICC membership: predesignated federal departments and agencies as listed in the Federal Register notice. FEDLINK: Any library or organization in the US Federal Government that uses one of FEDLINK services. Dues: Users fees for FEDLINK
Structure   Governed by Executive Advisory Committee and FLICC membership. Affiliations: FLICC is administratively under the Library of Congress
Sources of Support   Government appropriations and FEDLINK membership users fees
Major Fields of Interest   Library information
Major Goals and Objectives   To achieve better utilization of library and information center resources and facilities; to provide more effective planning, development, and

operation of federal libraries and information centers; to promote an optimum exchange of experience, skill, and resources; to promote more effective service to the nation at large; to foster relevant educational opportunities
Activities Carried out by Working Groups, each group focuses on an area of importance to federal librarians and information specialists, incl. information policy issues, information technology, education, content management, preservation and binding, personnel, and cooperative endeavors. Activities FLICC's operating network is FEDLINK (the Federal Library and Information Network), the nation's largest library network. FLICC makes recommendations on federal library and information policies, programs, and procedures to federal agencies and to others concerned with libraries and information centers
Publications Official journal: FLICC Newsletter. 1965-. 4/yr. Free upon request. Address same as FLICC. English. Other publications: Online Video Library; FEDLINK Technical Notes; New Handbook on Federal Librarianship
Bibliography "FLICC to Hold Forum on Federal Information Access Policy," Library of Congress Information Bulletin 45 (Jan. 27, 1986):43–44; "FLICC to Hold Technology Seminars around the Country," ibid. (Mar. 31, 1986):94; "FLICC Sponsors Session on Laser Disk Technology," ibid. (Apr. 28, 1986):125; Zirps, C, "1986 FLICC Forum Considers Federal Information Policies," ibid. (May 19, 1986):177–178; "FLICC Cosponsors Seminars with USDA to Brief Federal Librarians on New Trends," ibid. (Aug. 11, 1986):281–282; "FLICC Issues New Publication," Library of Congress Information Bulletin 46 (Feb. 9, 1987):59–60; "Federal Library and Information Center Committee (FLICC)," in The Bowker Annual: Library and Book Trade Almanac. 34th Edition 1989–90. pp. 688–689. New York: R. R. Bowker, 1989; "Librarian Backs Interagency Cooperation: FLICC Elevated in Reorganization Plans," FLICC Newsletter 150 (1989): 1–2; "Access is the Key: Forum Explores Future of Federal Information Policies," FLICC Newsletter 151 (1990):7

574 Independent Research Libraries Association (IRLA)

Address c/o Dr. William M. Geiswold, Director, 225 Madison Avenue, New York, NY 10016-3405 Tel.: +1 212 685-0008, Fax +1 212 768-5605, wgriswold@themorgan.org; irla.lindahall.org
Languages English
Established 1972, at the Newberry Library, Chicago
Staff None
General Assembly Entire membership meets once or twice a year at various locations
Membership Total members: 18 (institutional). Foreign corresponding member: Herzog August Bibliothek Wolfenbüttel/Germany. Requirements: Library must be an independent institution, not subordinate to another organization; must have a collection of international importance with emphasis on specialized research materials; must be used by a national, or preferably, international group of readers
Structure Governed by members and Chair; an informal body. Affiliations: Informal affiliations with ACLS (American Council of Learned Societies), ARL, and other relevant groups
Sources of Support Membership dues
Major Fields of Interest Research libraries; humanities, science&technology

Major Goals and Objectives To strengthen the programs of member institutions
Activities Meetings at least once a year to exchange ideas and discuss issues of common interest; joint fund raising; no formal program
Publications No official journal. Issues IRLA Handbook, a membership directory

575 International Association of Music Libraries, Archives, and Documentation Centres – United States Branch (IAML-US)

Address c/o Manuel Erviti, Secretary, Berkeley, CA 94720-6000 Tel.: +1 510 642-2428, Fax +1 510 642-8237, merviti@library.berkeley.edu; www.iamlus.org
Languages English
Established 1951
Officers Pres: Judy Tsou; Past Pres: Mary Wallace Davidson; Secr: Manuel Erviti; Treas: Michael Colby
Staff None
General Assembly Entire membership meets once a year
Membership Individual and institutional. Requirements: Interest in aims of Association
Structure Governed by executive officers and Executive Board. Affiliations: IAML, IFLA
Sources of Support Membership dues
Major Fields of Interest Music librarianship; music bibliography
Major Goals and Objectives Development of music libraries, music librarianship, and music bibliography
Activities Donated Music Materials Program (facilitates the donation of music, books, journals, and recordings to libraries in East-Central and Southeast Europe, republics of the former Soviet Union, Africa, Asia, Latin America, and Pacific Ocean countries)
Bibliography Brook, B. S. and Ratliff, N., "International Association of Music Libraries, Archives and Documentation Centres (IAML)," in ALA World Encyclopedia of Library and Information Services. 2nd ed., pp. 369–370. Chicago: American Library Association, 1986

576 Library and Information Technology Association (LITA)

Address c/o American Library Association, 50 East Huron Street, Chicago, IL 60611-2795 Tel.: 800 54524334270, Fax +1 312 2803257, lita@ala.org; www.lita.org
Languages English
Established 1966, at ALA Midwinter Conference in Chicago
Officers Exec Dir: Mary Taylor
General Assembly Entire membership meets twice a year during the ALA Midwinter and annual conference. In addition, there are LITA National Conferences
Membership Requirements: Open to members of ALA.
Structure Governed by Board of Directors, with authority specified by the ALA Council. Affiliations: A division of ALA, National Information Standards Organization (NISO), ASIS
Sources of Support Membership dues, sale of publications, fees from conferences, institutes
Major Fields of Interest Information dissemination in the areas of library automation, video and cable communications, telecommunications, and audiovisuals

Major Goals and Objectives Concerned with the planning, development, design, application, and integration of technologies within the library and information environment. Major focus is on interdisciplinary issues and emerging technologies. Within these areas, LITA encourages and fosters research, promotes the development of appropriate technical standards, monitors new technologies with potential applications in information science, develops models of library systems and networks, examines the effects of automation on people, disseminates information, and provides a forum for the discussion of common concerns. The Association views itself as a source of leadership linking librarians and information specialists to technology for access to information

Activities LITA's activities were reorganized several years ago around an interest group structure, involving more members in programming and other activities. Interest groups successfully promote discussion and present programs on topics of current interest, such as on-line catalogs, expert systems, authority control, retrospective conversion, telecommunications, distributed systems, library consortia sharing automated systems, use of technology to fight illiteracy, etc. Presents awards. Sponsors exhibits, conferences, seminars, workshops, and other continuing education programs

Publications Official journal: Information Technology and Libraries (ITAL) (formerly Journal of Library Automation. 1968–81). 1982-. 4/yr. Free to members. 55$/ yr. English. Indexed in ISA, Lib.Lit., CompuMath Citation Index, etc. Other publications: Technology Electronic Reviews (ISSN: 1533–9165); various monographs and packets; annual reports, proceedings of conferences, seminars, etc. Publications available for sale. Limited publications exchange program in effect

Bibliography Berry, J.N., "Constant Change: The LITA Message [first national conference]," Library Journal 108 (Oct. 15, 1983):1898; Brandenhoff, S.E., "First National LITA Conference: Library Technology on Stage," American Libraries 14 (Nov. 1983):672+; Fenly, C., "Report on the Institute on Technology at the Library of Congress in the 1980's," Library of Congress Information Bulletin 45 (Aug. 4, 1986):276–278; "Interest Groups Two Years Later: How They are Working," LITA Newsletter 9 (Winter 1988):11–13; Boydston, J.M.K., "On the Conference Circuit: Whose Computer Revolution is It? – A Review [of LITA program]," Technicalities 8 (Nov. 1988):10–11; "Library Service, New Products Focus of LITA's Conference," Library Journal 113 (Dec. 1988):24; Welsch, E.K., "The LITA Conference: Digitized Images," Computers in Libraries 9 (Jan. 1989):32–33; Potter, W.G.,"Library and Information Technology Association," in ALA Yearbook 1989. p. 144. Chicago: American library Association, 1989; "American Library Association. Library and Information Technology Association," in The Bowker Annual: Library and Book Trade Almanac. 34th Edition 1989–90, pp. 651–653. New York: R. R. Bowker, 1989

577   Library Leadership and Management Association (LLAMA)

Address c/o American Library Association, 50 East Huron Street, Chicago, IL 60611-2795 Tel.: 800 54524335032, Fax +1 280 2169, lama@ala.org; www.ala.org/ala/mgrps/divs/llama/index.cfm

Languages English

Officers Pres: Gina Millsap

General Assembly Entire membership meets once a year. 2010: Washington, DC

Structure Governed by a Executive Committee

Major Fields of Interest Administration and management in all types of libraries
Major Goals and Objectives To encourage and nurture current and future leaders, and to develop and promote outstanding leadership and management practices

578 Library Public Relations Council (LPRC)

Address c/o Joan Kuhn, President, 195 S. Greeley Avenue, Chappaqua, NY 10514 Tel.: +1 914 2384779, Fax +1 914 2383597, librarypr@ssdesign.com; www.ssdesign.com/librarypr/content/aboutlprc.shtml
Languages English
Established 1940
Staff None
General Assembly Entire membership meets once a year during annual ALA conference, and 3 times a year in Metropolitan New York
Membership Total members: 284 (individual and institutional). 3 countries represented (USA, Australia, Canada). Requirements: Interested in aims of Association
Structure Governed by elected Board
Sources of Support Membership dues
Major Fields of Interest Public relations; marketing; communications
Major Goals and Objectives Professional development for library staff members in the fields of public relations and communications
Activities Offers outstanding speakers on all aspects of library public relations; shares speaker's tips with all members through mailings of summaries, hand-outs and other material; sponsors Two National Competitions; sponsors conferences, seminars, workshops, and other continuing education programs
Publications Official journal: Library Media & PR: Contact: librarypr@ssdesign.com. Publishes proceedings of meetings, reports of seminars, workshops
Bibliography Eldredge, J., "Public Relations and Marketing," in ALA Yearbook 1989. pp. 191–194. Chicago: American Library Association, 1989

579 The Manuscript Society

Address 14003 Rampart Ct., Baton Rouge, LA 70818 Tel.: +1 908 459-0155, sands@manuscript.org; www.manuscript.org
Languages English
Established 1948
Officers Pres: Edward N. Bomsey; VP: Barton L. Smith; Treas: Anthony Loscalzo; Exec Dir: Edward Oetting
Staff None
General Assembly Entire membership meets once a year
Membership Over 1800 individual and institutional members. Requirements: Interest in manuscripts. Dues (US Dollar): 45/yr
Structure Governed by Executive Board
Sources of Support Membership dues, sale of publications
Major Fields of Interest Autographs and manuscripts
Major Goals and Objectives To foster an interest in manuscripts
Activities Chief activity: Three-day annual meeting, held in a community offering good manuscript resources for viewing. Programs feature panel discussions, speakers of note,

exhibitions, etc. 2004: Chicago/IL
Publications   Official journals: Manuscripts. 1948-. 4/yr. Free to members. English. The Manuscript Society News. 4/yr. Other publications: Autographs and Manuscripts: A Collector's Manual, 1978; Directory; George Washington's Expence Account (facsimile); Manuscripts: The First 20 Years; annual reports, proceedings of conferences, seminars, etc
Bibliography   Fields, J.E., "Founding the Manuscript Society," AB Bookman's Weekly 73 (1984):785–786; Sifton, P.G., "Manuscript Society Meeting," Library of Congress Information Bulletin 43 (July 9, 1984):238–239; Filby, P.W., "Manuscript Society Views Rhode Island Treasures," AB Bookman's Weekly 76 (1985):240–242

580   Medical Library Association Inc. (MLA)

Address   65 East Wacker Place, Suite 1900, Chicago, IL 60601-7298 Tel.: +1 312 4199094, Fax +1 312 4198950, funk@mlahq.org; www.mlanet.org
Languages   English
Established   1898, Philadelphia; incorporated 1934
Officers   Pres: Carla J. Funk
General Assembly   Entire membership meets once a year. 2004: Washington, DC
Membership   More than 5000 individual and institutional members. Requirements: Persons actively engaged in professional library or bibliographic work in medical or allied scientific fields or who hold the Association's Certificate of Medical Librarianship; other persons interested in medical or allied scientific libraries may become associate members. Institutional members are medical and allied scientific libraries
Structure   Governed by Board of Directors and Executive Committee. Affiliations: ALA, IFLA
Sources of Support   Membership dues, sale of publications
Major Fields of Interest   Medical librarianship
Major Goals and Objectives   To influence the quality of available health information resources and provide timely, accurate, and relevant information; to improve the knowledge and skill of members; to develop and maintain information systems and resources; to broaden health information research; and to promote a legislative agenda that supports access to the world's health sciences information
Activities   Initiated strategic planning; strengthened and integrated all association programs: professional development, including continuing education, credentialling, honors & awards, information services and annual meeting; publications; information issues & policy; standards & practices. Developed and installed a computer system to handle membership, annual meeting, continuing education, and accounting functions. Providing programs and services in the following areas: Professional development, publications, standards and practices, and information issues and policy. Developing new and revised programs and services to support the design, development, and management of information systems; creation and provision of information services and education for health information users; research in health information science. Active in promoting library-related legislation. Sponsors exhibits, conferences, seminars, workshops, and other continuing education programs. The Continuing Education Committee is responsible for high quality courses, covering topics such as preserving endangered collections, designing expert systems, managing microcomputers, writing procedures manuals, offering workshops, etc. Presents a number of annual awards and scholarships; contributes to ALA

National Library Week

Publications Official journal: Journal of the Medical Library Association (JMLA). 4/yr. Editor: T. Scott Plutchak, AHIP, UAB Lister Hill Library (1), 1530 3rd Avenue South, Birmingham, AL 35294–0013 Tel: +1 205 9345460; Fax: +1 205 9343545, email: tscott@uab.edu. Other publications: MLA News. 1961-. 10/yr. Free to members. Contact: Barbara Redmond, email: mlacom2@mlahq.org; A variety of publications on health sciences librarianship, information management, and consumer health, current copublisher is Neal-Schuman Publishers

Bibliography Echelman, S., "Role of the Medical Library Association in Education, Standards and Other Support Services for Members," Inspel 16 (1982):49–57; Poland, U.H., "Reflections on the Medical Library Association's International Activities," Medical Library Association Bulletin 70 (1982):359–368; Shafer, R., "Equal Opportunities for Health Sciences Librarians: A Report on the 1986 Medical Library Association Annual Meeting," Library Journal 111 (1986):42–45; "Medical Libraries," in ALA World Encyclopedia of Library and Information Services. 2nd ed., pp. 522–541. Chicago: American Library Association, 1986; Love, E., "The Science of Medical Librarianship: Investing in the Future," Bulletin of the Medical Library Association 75 (1987):302–309; Mayfield, M. K. and Palmer, R.A., "Organizational Change in the Medical Library Association: Evolution of the Continuing Education Program," ibid.:326–332; "Medical Library Association Launches Credentialing Academy [of Health Information Professionals]," American Libraries 19 (1988):433; Walter, P.L., "MLA: Strategic Planning and All That Jazz," Library Journal 113 (1988):51–55; Palmer, R.A.,"Medical Library Association," in ALA Yearbook 1989. pp. 159–161. Chicago: American Library Association, 1989; "Medical Library Association," in The Bowker Annual: Library and Book Trade Almanac. 34th Edition 1989–90. New York: R. R. Bowker, 1989

581 Mountain Plains Library Association (MPLA)

Address c/o Judy Zelenski, Exec Secretary, 14293 W. Center Drive, Lakewood, CO 80228 Tel.: + 1 303.985.7795, mpla_execsecretary@operamail.com; www.mpla.us

Languages English

Established 1948

Officers Pres: Eileen Wright; VP/Pres-elect: Elvita Landau; Past Pres: Robert Blanks; Recording Secr: Robin Brooks Clark

General Assembly Members meet annually in a joint conference. 2010: April

Membership Member states: Arizona, Colorado, Kansas, Montana, Nebraska, Nevada, New Mexico, North Dakota, Oklahoma, South Dakota, Utah and Wyoming

Structure Governed by an elected board of representatives from each member state and a number of sections and roundtables representing interests and types of libraries

Major Fields of Interest Libraries in Arizona, Colorado, Kansas, Montana, Nebraska, Nevada, New Mexico, North Dakota, Oklahoma, South Dakota, Utah and Wyoming

Major Goals and Objectives To promote the development of librarians and libraries by providing significant educational and networking opportunities

Activities Offers grants, awards, continuing education opportunities, conferences

Publications Official journal: MPLA Newsletter. Bi-monthly. Address: same as association

582 Music Library Association, Inc (MLA)
Address 8551 Research Way, Suite 180, Middleton, WI 53562-3567 Tel.: +1 608 8365825, Fax +1 608 8318200, mla@areditions.com; www.musiclibraryassoc.org
Languages English
Established 1931, at Yale University School of Music library. Initial meeting to found association was held to discuss the common problems facing librarians and musicologists
Officers Pres: Ruthann B. Mc Tyre
General Assembly Entire membership meets once a year in winter or early spring. 2005: Vancouver, BC
Membership Individual and institutional members. Requirements: All persons or institutions actively engaged in library work or interested in the purposes of the Association
Structure Governed by Board of Directors. 11 Regional chapters. Affiliations: ALA, CNLIA, American Musicological Society, Music Publishers Association, IAML
Sources of Support Membership dues, sale of publications
Major Fields of Interest Music librarianship, bibliography
Major Goals and Objectives To promote the establishment, growth, and use of music libraries; to encourage the collection of music and musical literature in libraries; to increase the effectiveness of music library services; to further studies in music bibliography
Activities Sponsors exhibits, conferences, seminars, workshops, and other continuing education programs. Presents 4 awards at annual meeting
Publications Official journal: Notes. 1945-. 4/yr. Free to members. Linda Solow Blotner, University of Hartford, Hartt Library, West Hartford, CT 06117; Tel: +1 860 7684492; fax: +1 860 7685295; email: blotner@mail.hartford.edu. English. Indexed in LISA, Lib.Lit., Music Index. RILM Abstracts, etc. Other publications: MLA Newsletter. 4/yr. Free to members. Stephen Mantz, Davidson College, POB 7200, Davidson, N. C. 28035, email: stmantz@davidson.edu; Music Cataloging Bulletin. 12/yr, 25$/yr. Editor: Michelle Koth, Catalog Librarian, Yale University Music Library, PO Box 208240, New Haven, Ct. 06520–8240; Tel: +1 203 4320494; email: michelle.koth@yale.edu; Basic Manual Series; Index and Bibliography Series; Technical Reports
Bibliography Bradley, C.J., "Music Library Association: The Founding Generation," Music Library Association Notes 37 (1981):763–822; 39 (1982):490–491; Coral, L., "Music Library Association," in ALA Yearbook 1988. pp. 214–215. Chicago: American Library Association, 1988; Sommer, S.T., "Music Library Association," in ALA Yearbook 1989. pp. 162–163. Chicago: American Library Association, 1989; "Music Library Association," in The Bowker Annual: Library and Book Trade Almanac. 34th Edition 1989–90. pp. 695–696. New York: R. R. Bowker, 1989

583 National Association of Government Archives and Records Administrators (NAGARA)
Address 90 State Street, Suite 1009, Albany, NY 12207 Tel.: +1 518463-8644, Fax +1 518463-8656, nagara@caphill.com; www.nagara.org
Languages English
Established 1984, as successor to the National Association of State Archives and Records Administrators, established in 1974

Officers Pres: Tracey Berezansky; VP: Paul R. Bergeron; Secr: Caryn Wojcik; Treas: Nancy Fortna; Immediate Past Pres: Mary Beth Herkert
Staff None
General Assembly Entire membership meets once a year. 2010: Washington, DC August 10th-15th
Membership Individual and institutional members. Requirements: Open to local governments, federal agencies, and to any individual or organization interested in improved government records programs. State archival and records management agencies are sustaining members
Structure Governed by executive officers. Affiliations: Adjunct member of the Council of State Governments, Lexington, Kentucky
Sources of Support Membership dues, grants, revenues from annual meetings
Major Fields of Interest Government archival and records management
Major Goals and Objectives To unite local, state, and federal archivists and records administrators, and others interested in improved care and management of government records; to promote public awareness of government records and archives management programs; to encourage interchange of information among government archives and records management agencies; to develop and implement professional standards of government records and archival administration; to encourage study and research into records management problems and issues
Activities Publications program. Active in promoting library-related legislation, e.g., the appointment of the Archivist of the USA. Sponsors conferences
Publications Official journals: Clearinghouse. 1982-. 4/yr. Free to members. Editor: Stacie Byas, NARA Mid-Atlantic Region, Tel: +1 215 5970921, fax: +1 215 5972303, email: stacie.byas@nara.gov. Circ: Membership. English. Crossroads: Developments in Electronic Records Management and Information Technology. (newsletter) 4/yr. Editor: Scott Leonard, email: sleonard@kshs.org. Other publications: Records Management Technical Bulletins. Editor: Grace Lessner; available as HTML and PDF files (www.nagara.org/publications.html), for printed sets address same as association
Bibliography "National Association of Government Archives and Records Administrators (NAGARA)," in The Bowker Annual: Library and Book Trade Almanac. 34th Edition 1989–90, p. 696. New York: R. R. Bowker, 1989

584 National Association of State Information Resource Executives (NASCIO)

Address c/o AMR Management Services, 201 East Main Street, Suite 1405, Lexington, KY 40507 Tel.: +1 859 514 9156, Fax +1 859 514 9166, skarrick@AMRms.com; www.nascio.org
Languages English
Established 1969, as the National Association of State Information Systems (NASIS). In 1989, the membership voted to undertake a major realignment for the association, including a change in name to the National Association of State Information Resource Executives (NASIRE). This new name reflected an expansion of membership and the role of the members. In 2001, name change to the National Association of State Chief Information Officers
Officers Pres: Stephen Fletcher; VP: Kyle Schafer; Secr/Treas: Kenneth Theis; Past Pres: Gopal Khanna

Structure Governed by Executive Board
Major Fields of Interest Information resource management
Major Goals and Objectives To promote government excellence through quality business practices, information management, and technology policy
Activities Offers awards, educational programs, online services
Publications No official journal. Publishes annual online directory of contacts for information resource management functions and periodic reports on information resource management policies and practices

585 National Church Library Association

Address 275 South Third Street, Suite 204, Stillwater, MN 55082 Tel.: +1 651 430-0770, Info@churchlibraries.org; www.churchlibraries.org
Languages English
Established 1958, Minneapolis, at a special meeting of all interested church librarians
Officers Pres: Chuck Mann; Secr: Chris Magnusson
General Assembly Entire membership meets once a year
Membership Requirements: Open to church libraries, individuals, libraries, church organizations, and to any congregation that is planning to start a church library. Dues (US Dollar): 35, Individual or Church with 500 or fewer members; 50, Church with more than 500 members; 175, Businesses/Religious organizations/Ministry partners; 75–99, Contributor; 100–499, Donor; 500–999, Patron; 1000, Guarantor
Structure Governed by executive officers and Executive Council meeting at least twice a year. Affiliations: CNLIA
Sources of Support Membership dues, private donations, grants from Lutheran churches
Major Fields of Interest Church libraries
Major Goals and Objectives To encourage, inspire, and offer personalized support to you if you are setting up a new library; to provide direction, new ideas and education in organizing, promoting, and maintaining your library, especially if you have no previous library experience; to help you respond to trends in resources and technology; to support you in promoting a Christian ethic in your library; to provide you with a local support network in areas where chapter membership is available
Activities Sponsors conferences, seminars, workshops, and other continuing education programs
Publications Official journal: Libraries Alive. 4/yr. Contact: saburrowes@earthlink.net. Other publications: A Handbook for Church Librarians, 2002 revised edition, by Linda Beck; Annual reports, proceedings of conferences, seminars, basic booklists, service bulletins, etc. Publications exchanged with other library associations
Bibliography "Lutheran Church Library Association," in The Bowker Annual: Library and Book Trade Almanac. 34th Edition 1989–90, pp. 691–692. New York: R. R. Bowker, 1989

586 National Federation of Abstracting and Information Services (NFAIS)

Address 1518 Walnut Street, Suite 1004, Philadelphia, PA 19102-3403 Tel.: +1 215 8931561, Fax +1 215 8931564; www.nfais.org
Languages English

Established 1958, Washington, DC; (formerly National Federation of Abstracting and Indexing Services)
Officers Pres: Judith Russell; Pres-elect: Thomson Reuters; Past Pres: Terence Ford; Secr: Barbara Dobbs Mackenzie; Treas: Suzanne BeDell
General Assembly Entire membership meets once a year. 2010: Philadelphia, PA
Membership Total members: 50+ (institutional). Requirements: Open to all organizations involved in activities related to the creation, distribution and access of information
Structure Governed by Board of Directors and Member Assembly. Affiliations: ASIS, SLA, EUSIDIC etc
Sources of Support Membership dues, sale of publications, meeting registration fees
Major Fields of Interest Indexing; abstracting; databases; electronic publishing; information industry
Major Goals and Objectives To provide a common ground within the global Information community for the discussion and resolution of issues related to the creation, distribution and access of information. To promote the value of abstracting and indexing services and the technology that supports information access and retrieval
Activities Sponsors conferences, seminars, workshops, and other continuing education programs
Publications Bimonthly electronic newsletter; biweekly news alert for members only. Other publications: White Papers; Codes of Practice; Miles Conrad Lectures; conference proceedings; Guide to Database Distribution II (1995) by Joseph P. Bremner; Flexible Workstyles in the Information Industry 1993) edited by Ann Marie Cunningham & Wendy Wicks; Impacts of Changing Production Technologies (1995) edited by Dick Kaser; Beyond Boolean (1997); Computer Support to Indexing (1999); BIOSIS – Championing The Cause (2001) By Richard T. Kaser and Victoria Cox Kaser
Bibliography "New Name: NFAIS is Now the National Federation of Abstracting and Information Services," Indexer 13 (1982):82; Keenan, S.V., "NFAIS Silver Anniversary," Indexer 14 (1983):251–252; Neufeld, N. F. et al., eds. Abstracting and Indexing Services in Perspective; Miles Conrad Memorial Lectures. 1969–1983; Commemorating the 25th Anniversary of the National Federation of Abstracting and Information Services. Washington, DC: Information Resources Press, 1983 (contains bibliography); Neufeld, M. L. and Cornog, M., "Abstracting and Indexing," in ALA World Encyclopedia of Library and Information Services. 2nd ed., pp. 1–4. Chicago: American Library Association, 1986; Unruh, B.L., "Abstracting and Indexing," in ALA Yearbook 1989. pp. 13–14. Chicago: American Library Association, 1989

587 NorthEast Research Libraries Association (NERL)*

Address c/o NERL office, PO Box 208240, New Haven, CT 06520-8240 Tel.: +1 203 432 2897, Fax + 1 203 432 8527, nerl@yale.edu; www.library.yale.edu/NERLpublic
Languages English
Established July 1996, New Haven, CT USA (Yale University)
Officers Coordinator: Ann Okerson; Program Librarian: Joan Emmet
Staff 3
General Assembly 1–2 per year; location varies

Membership 27 'core' members (voting), 70+ smaller, affiliate members. Fees vary depending on type and activity level
Structure Headquartered and staffed at Yale University Library. 27 members have voting rights
Sources of Support Dues and fees
Major Fields of Interest Licensing of academic digital resources; may partner with other consortia to achieve its aim of cost effectiveness and money-saving for members
Publications No publications program

588 Progressive Librarians Guild (PLG)

Address 2083 Lawrenceville Rd., Lawrenceville, NJ 08648 libr.org/PLG
Languages English
Established 1990
Membership Requirements: Open to library workers and users who agree with PLG's Statement of Purpose. Dues (US Dollar): 20 for individuals, 10 for low income
Structure Administrated by Coordinating Commitee
Major Fields of Interest Recognition of the idea that libraries for the people has been one of the principal anchors of an extended free public sphere which makes an independent democratic civil society possible
Major Goals and Objectives to provide a forum for the open exchange of radical views on library issues; to conducting campaigns to support progressive and democratic library activities locally, nationally and internationally; to support activist librarians as they work to effect changes in their own libraries and communities
Activities Has sponsored several programs at the annual conference of the American Library Association and at the annual Socialist Scholars Conference in New York; local chapters also host gatherings, programs, and events; offers email discussion list
Publications Official journal: Progressive Librarian. irreg. Managing Ed.: Elaine Harger. email: eharger@agoron.net

589 Public Library Association (PLA)*

Address 50 E Huron Street, Chicago, IL 60611 Tel.: +1 800 54524335PLA, Fax +1 312 2805029, pla@ala.org; www.pla.org/ala/pla/pla.htm
Languages English
Established 1944
Officers Pres: Sari Feldman; Pres-elect: Audra Caplan; Past Pres: Carol Sheffer
Staff 8 (paid)
General Assembly Membership meets at the PLA National Conference every 2 years. ALA offers additional opportunites twice a year during the ALA Midwinter Meeting and the annual ALA conference
Membership More than 10,000 individual and institutional members. Requirements: Open to ALA members with an interest in public libraries. Dues: Regular member: $50 Student, member: $10, other member: $40 (this category is for inactive, retired, or unemployed, or for full or part-time in a library service position at a salary less than $25,000 a year). International member: $50, Trustee and associate members: $50 (this category includes those who are not employed in library and information services or related activities, but through their personal commitment and support, promote library and

information services). Members of governing boards, advisory groups, Friends organizations, and special citizen caucuses, and/or individuals interested in participating in the work of PLA

Structure Governed by Board of Directors. Affiliations: A division of ALA, IFLA (through ALA)

Sources of Support Membership dues, sale of publications, conference fees, grants and sponsorships

Major Fields of Interest All concerns shared by public librarians and others about public libraries

Major Goals and Objectives PLA is a member-driven organization that exists to provide a diverse program of communication, publication, advocacy, continuing education, and programming for its members and others interested in the advancement of public library service. PLA's core values are: Provides visionary leadership ever open to new ideas; Dedicated to lifelong learning; Focused on and responsive to member needs; Committed to a free and open exchange of information and active collaboration; Respects diversity of opinion and community needs; Committed to excellence and innovation

Activities Official bimonthly journal: Public Libraries. Free to members. Feature Editor: Kathleen Hughes email: khughes@ala.org. English. Other publications: publiclibrariesonline.org, Electronic newsletter; Libraries Prosper with Passion, Purpose and Persuasion: A PLA Toolkit for Success; Field Guide to Emergency Response: A Vital Tool for Cultural Institutions; Collection Development and Resource Access Plan for the Skokie Public Library; Forming and Funding Public Library Foundations, 2nd Edition; The PLA Reader for Public Library Directors and Managers; Public Library Data Service Statistical Report; Public Library Service Responses, 2007; Defending Access with Confidence: A Practical Workshop on Intellectual Freedom; Weeding Manual; A Guide to Research @ Your Library; The Public Librarian's Guide to Providing Consumer Health Information; Managing Facilities for Results: Optimizing Space for Services; Creating Policies for Results From Chaos to Clarity; Staffing For Results: A Guide to Working Smarter; The New Planning for Results: A Streamlined Approach; Managing for Results: Effective Resource Allocation for Public Libraries; Planning for Results: A Public Library Transformation Process; 100 Best books to Read in Kindergarten; 75 of the Best Books for Young Children; Nursery Rhymes, Songs and Fingerplays; Bare Bones Young Adult Services: Tips for Public Library Generalists; Customer Service: Balancing Rights and Responsibilities (Train the Trainer Series-Electronic Publication); Libraries Prosper: A Guide to Using the PLA Advocacy Toolkit (Train the Trainer Series-Electronic Publication); A Library Board's Practical Guide to Finding the Right Library Director; Trustee Facts File, 3rd Edition

Publications Official journal: Public Libraries, 1961-. 6/yr. (4/yr. until 1988). Free to members. Feature Editor: Renee Vaillancourt McGrath, 248 A N. Higgins Ave. #145, Missoula, MT 59802, email: publiclibraries@aol.com. English. Indexed in Lib.Lit., Current Index to Journals in Education. LISA. Other publications: Electronic newsletter; A Planning Process for Public Libraries (ALA, 1980); Planning and Role Setting for Public Libraries (ALA, 1987); Output Measures for Public Libraries (ALA, 1982, 1987); Public Library Data Service Statistical Report (PLA, published annually 1987 – present); Planning for Results: A Public Library Transformation Process (ALA, 1998); Wired for the Future: Developing Your Library Technology Plan (ALA, 1999); Managing for Results:

Effective Resource Allocation for Public Libraries (ALA, 2000); The New Planning for Results: A Streamlined Approach (ALA, 2001); Staffing for Results: A Guide to Working Smarter (ALA, 2002); Creating Policies for Results: From Chaos to Clarity (2004)
Bibliography see website

590 REFORMA (National Association to Promote Library Services to the Spanish Speaking)

Address c/o Siobhan Champ-Blackwell, Secretary, 2500 California Plaza, Omaha, NE 68178 Tel.: +1 402 280-4156, Fax +1 402 280-5134, SiobhanChamp-Blackwell@creighton.edu; www.reforma.org
Languages English
Established 1971, Dallas, Texas, during ALA conference
Officers Pres: Loida Garcia Febo; VP/Pres elect: Lucia González; Immediate Past Pres: Luis Chaparro; Secr/Recorder: Siobhan Champ-Blackwell
General Assembly Entire membership meets twice a year during ALA Midwinter and annual conference
Membership Requirements: Open to all interested persons and institutions
Structure Governed by Executive Board. Chapters: 21. Affiliations: ALA
Sources of Support Membership dues
Major Fields of Interest Library service and programs to Latinos and the Spanish speaking
Major Goals and Objectives Improve the full spectrum of library and information services for the approximately 19 million Spanish-speaking and Hispanic people in the United States, promote the development of library collections to include Spanish-language and Hispanic-oriented materials, recruit more bilingual and bicultural library professionals and support staff, develop library services and programs which meet the needs of the Hispanic community, establish a national information and support network among individuals who share our goals, educate the US Hispanic population regarding the availability and types of library services, and lobby to preserve existing library resource centers serving the interests of Hispanics
Activities Awards a number of scholarships to library school students that express interest in working with Latinos; sponsors conferences, seminars, workshops, and other continuing education programs which focus on service to Hispanics
Publications Official journal: Newsletter. 4/yr. Free to members. Other publications: Membership Directory; annual reports, proceedings of conferences, seminars, etc
Bibliography Gloriod, B., "Latin American Books and Hispanic Immigrants are Subjects of REFORMA Meeting," Library of Congress Information Bulletin 46 (Feb. 2, 1987):52; Betancourt, I., "REFORMA," in ALA Yearbook 1989. pp. 206–208. Chicago: American library Association, 1989

591 Society of American Archivists (SAA)

Address 17 North State Street, Suite 1425, Chicago, IL 60602-3315 Tel.: +1 312 606-0722, Fax +1 312 606-0728, servicecenter@archivists.org; www.archivists.org
Languages English
Established 1936, at a meeting in Providence, Rhode Island
Officers Exec Dir: Nancy Beaumont

Staff 10 (paid)
General Assembly Entire membership meets once a year in summer. 2004: Boston, MA
Membership More than 3900 individual and institutional members. Requirements: Persons and institutions interested in the preservation and use of archives, manuscripts, current records and machine-readable records, films, maps, etc
Structure Governed by Officers and Council
Sources of Support Membership dues, sale of publications, education offerings, grants
Major Fields of Interest Archives
Major Goals and Objectives To promote sound principles of archival economy and to facilitate cooperation among archivists and archival agencies. Through its publications, annual meetings, workshops, and Sections, the Society provides a means for contacts, communication, and cooperation among archivists and archival institutions
Activities SAA bestows several annual awards. Active in promoting relevant legislation, such as independent status of the National Archives. Sponsors conferences, seminars, workshops, and other continuing education programs, and has an extensive publishing program
Publications Official journal: The American Archivist. 1937–1997. 4/yr. 1998–2/yr. Free to members. Editor: Philip B. Eppard, State University of New York at Albany, School of Information Science & Policy, 135 Western Ave./113 Draper, Albany, NY 12222, +1 518 4425128, Fax: +1 518 4425367, email: pbe40@csc.albany.edu. English. Indexed in Lib.Lit. Other publications: Archival Outlook Newsletter. Address same as Association; Online Professional Resources Catalog (www.archivists.org/catalog/index.asp)
Bibliography Quinn, P.M., "Regional Archival Organizations and the Society of American Archivists," American Archivist 46 (1983):433–440; Brown, T.E., "Society of American Archivists Confronts the Computer," in American Archivist 47 (1984):366–382; Neal, D.C., "The Society of American Archivists," Illinois Libraries 69 (1987):538–542; Davis, S.E., "Development of Managerial Training for Archivists," American Archivist 51 (1988):278–285; Ericson, T.L., "Professional Associations and Archival Education: A Different Role, or a Different Theater?" ibid.:298–311; "Guidelines for Graduate Archival Education Programs," ibid.:380–389; "Archival Research Agendas [special issue]," American Archivist 51 (1988):16–105; Neal, D.C., "Archives," in ALA Yearbook 1989. pp. 44–46. Chicago: American Library Association, 1989; Neal, D.C., "Society of American Archivists," in The Bowker Annual: Library and Book Trade Almanac. 34th Edition 1989–90, pp. 152–154. New York: R. R. Bowker, 1989; "Society of American Archivists," ibid. p. 699

592 Society of School Librarians International (SSLI)

Address c/o Stephan & Jeanne Schwartz, 19 Savage Street, Charleston, SC 29401
Tel.: +1 843-577-5351, sbssteve@aol.com; http://societyofschoollibrarians.webs.com
Languages English
Established 1985
General Assembly Membership meets annually. 2010: Key West, FL, October 13th-16th
Major Fields of Interest Development of school library programs
Major Goals and Objectives To promote the selection and utilization of technology in education; to encourage continued professional development opportunities for school

librarians through its newsletters and conferences; to provides opportunities for building-level professionals to develop leadership skills and contributes to the advancement of the profession; to recognizes excellence in children's publications through its annual book awards program
Activities Organizes national conference, gives annual awards in various categories to outstanding trade books for young people

593 Special Libraries Association (SLA)

Address 331 South Patrick Street, Alexandria, VA 22314-3501 www.sla.org
Languages English
Established 1909, Brettenwoods, New Hampshire, during July meeting of ALA, with 56 charter members
Officers Exec Dir: Janice R. Lachance
General Assembly Entire membership meets once a year. 2004: Nashville, TN; 2005: Toronto, ON; 2006: Baltimore; 2007: Denver, CO; 2008: Seattle, WA
Membership More than 12,000 members in 83 countries in the information profession, including corporate, academic and government information specialists. Requirements: Individual: MLS or equivalent degree or 3 years of professional experience in special libraries; faculty members with 7 years experience in educating students in topics relating to special librarianship; Institutional (sustaining): Institutions and organizations wishing to support the objectives and programs of the Association
Structure Governed by Board of Directors. Affiliations: IFLA, CNLIA, etc
Sources of Support Membership dues, sale of publications, annual conference, exhibits, and advertising revenue from publications
Major Fields of Interest All aspects of special librarianship and information science
Major Goals and Objectives To strengthen the roles as information leaders in our organizations; to respond to clients' needs, adding qualitative and quantitative value to information services and products; to embrace innovative solutions for the enhancement of services and intellectual advancement within the profession; to deliver measurable results in the information economy; to provide opportunities to meet, communicate, collaborate, and partner within the information industry and the business community
Activities Presents annual awards and scholarships. Active in promoting library-related legislation, e.g., supported changes in the US copyright law, and monitors copyright law in Canada, opposed tariffs on information products and privatization of NTIS. Sponsors conferences, seminars, workshops, and other continuing education programs, particularly the Annual Conference and Exhibit, and the annual Winter Education Conference
Publications Official journal: Information Outlook. 12/yr. Free to members. Address same as Association. email: magazine@sla.org. Other publications: SLA Guide Series; SLA Research Series: From the Top: Profiles of U. S. and Canadian Corporate Libraries and Information Centers (1989V Survey of SLA Software Users (1988). SLA Triennial Salary Survey 1989. Valuing Corporate Libraries: A Senior Management Survey (1990), Powering Up: A Technological Assessment of the SLA Membership (1990), etc.; SLA Information Kits: Disaster Planning and Recovery (1989), Managing Small Special Libraries (1988). Perspectives on Special Library Automation (1989), Ladner, S., comp., Networking and Special Libraries (1990), etc.; numerous monographs, e.g., Tools of the Profession (1988), Winning Marketing Techniques: An Introduction to Marketing for

Information Professionals (1990), Mount, E., Special Libraries and Information Centers: An Introductory Text (2nd ed., 1990), Masyr, C., Space Planning for Special Libraries (1990), Jorensen, M.A., comp., Directory of Selected Research and Policy Centers Working on Women's Issues (5th ed., 1989), Rix, S.E., The American Woman 1990–91: A Status Report (1990), 2003 SLA Annual Salary Survey; etc. annual reports, proceedings of conferences, seminars, etc. Annual publications catalog with price list available upon request. Publications exchange program in effect

Bibliography Molholt, P., "75 Years of [SLA] Service: Reconsider, Redefine, Reconfirm," Special Libraries 74 (1983):298–301; Williams, R. N. and Zachert, M.J.K., "Knowledge Put to Work: SLA at 75," ibid.:370–382; Arterbury, V.J., "SLA's Long Ranging Objectives: A Vision for the Future," Special Libraries 75 (1984):61–68; Christianson, E.B., "Special Libraries," in ALA World Encyclopedia of Library and Information Services. 2nd ed., pp. 772–782. Chicago: American Library Association, 1986; Avallone, S., "The SLA Success Story: Annual Conference in Boston, June 7–12, 1986," Library Journal 111 (1986):55–60; "Transcending Its Specialism," American Libraries 17 (1986):586–588; Arterbery, V.J., "Accreditation: A Blueprint for Action," Special Libraries 77 (1986):230–234; Malinak, D., "SLA: A History Rich in Tradition: A Future Bright with Promise," Library Times International 3 (1987):81–82; Bender, D.R., "SLA: Prepared to Meet the Future," (Guest Editorial) ibid.:82; Shaw, R.V, "Report from the 78th Annual Conference of SLA in Anaheim, Calif.," Library of Congress Information Bulletin 46 (Nov. 23, 1987):501–503; Mobley, E.R., "Special Libraries Association," in ALA Yearbook 1988. pp. 313–315. Chicago: American Library Association, 1988; DeCandido, G.A., "SLA: High Energy & Social Concerns," Library Journal 113 (1988):43–47; Scheeder, D., "The SLA Government Relations Program," Special Libraries 79 (1988):184–188; Shaw, R.V, "Report from the Special Libraries Association Annual Conference, Denver, June 11–15," Library of Congress Information Bulletin 47 (Sept. 12, 1988):370–371; Clifton, J.A., "Special Libraries Association," in ALA Yearbook 1989. pp. 232–234. Chicago: American Library Association, 1989; Malinak, D., "Special Libraries Association," in The Bowker Annual: Library and Book Trade Almanac. 34th Edition 1989–90. pp. 147–151. New York: R. R. Bowker, 1989; "Special Libraries Association," ibid. pp. 699–700; "A Visionary Framework for the Future: SLA's Strategic Plan 1990–2005," SpeciaList 13 (1990), insert; Scheeder, D., "Special libraries – The International Scene," Special Libraries 81 (1990): 1–2; Spaulding, F.H., "Internationalism of SLA and IFLA 1989," ibid,:3–9

594 Theatre Library Association (TLA)

Address c/o c/o The New York Public Library for the Performing Arts, 40 Lincoln Center Plaza, New York, NY 10023 info@tla-online.org; www.tla-online.org
Languages English
Established 1937, New York City
Officers Pres: Kenneth Schlesinger; VP: Susan Brady; Exec Secr: David Nochimson; Treas: Colleen Reilly
Staff None
General Assembly Entire membership meets once a year
Membership Requirements: Interest in collections about the performing arts
Structure Governed by Board of Directors and officers. Affiliations: ALA, American

Society for Theatre Research, International Federation for Theatre Research, SIBMAS (International Association of Libraries and Museums of the Performing Arts)
Sources of Support Membership dues, sale of publications, donations from members
Major Fields of Interest Theater, film, television, radio, and all other performing arts except classical music
Major Goals and Objectives To advance the interests of all those involved in collecting and preserving theatrical materials and in utilizing those materials for purposes of scholarship
Activities Representation in SIBMAS (Societe Internationale des Bibliotheques et des Musees des Arts du Spectacle; Sponsors conferences, seminars, workshops, and other continuing education programs; presents awards
Publications Official journal: Broadside (The Quarterly Newsletter of the Theatre Library Association). 1940-. 4/yr. Free to members. Editor: Angela Weaver, email: aw6@u.washington.edu. Circ: Membership. English. Other publications: Performing Arts Resources (PAR) 1/yr; annual reports, proceedings of conferences, seminars, etc. Publications available for sale
Bibliography Buck, R.M., "Theatre Library Association," in ALA Yearbook 1989. pp. 239–241. Chicago: American Library Association, 1989; "Theatre Library Association," in The Bowker Annual: Library and Book Trade Almanac. 34th Edition 1989–90. p. 701. New York: R. R. Bowker, 1989

595   U.S. National Commission on Libraries and Information Science (NCLIS)

Address 1800 M Street NW, Suite 350, North Tower, Washington, DC 20036-5841 Tel.: +1 202 6069200, Fax +1 202 6069203; www.nclis.gov/index.cfm
Languages English
Established 1970
Major Fields of Interest advising the executive and legislative branches and other public and private organizations on national library and information policies and plans
Major Goals and Objectives Equal opportunity of access to information for all citizens through interconnecting services and a central control core of information
Activities Reports directly to the White House and the Congress on the implementation of national policy, conducts studies, surveys and analyses of the nation's library and information needs, promotes research and development activities, conducts hearings and issues publications as appropriate develops overall plans for meeting national library and informational needs and for the coordination of activities at the federal, state and local levels and provides policy advice to IMLS Director regarding financial assistance for library services
Publications Annual reports

596   Urban Libraries Council (ULC)

Address 125 S. Wacker Drive, Suite #1050, Chicago, IL 60606 Tel.: +1 847 8669999, Fax +1 847 8669989, jlazar@urbanlibraries.org; www.urbanlibraries.org
Languages English
Established 1971, Chicago, during annual ALA conference
Staff 7, paid

General Assembly Entire membership meets once a year in conjunction with annual ALA conference
Membership Total members: about 150 (institutional). Requirements: Urban libraries serving the cities of 100,000 or more individuals in a Standard Metropolitan Statistical Area
Structure Governed by Executive Board (16 members). Affiliations: ALA
Sources of Support Membership dues, sale of publications
Major Fields of Interest Legislative and financial support for urban public libraries
Major Goals and Objectives To identify and make known the problems relating to urban libraries serving the cities of 100,000 or more individuals located in a Standard Metropolitan Statistical Area. To provide information on state and federal legislation affecting urban library programs and systems. To facilitate the exchange of ideas and programs of member libraries and other libraries
Activities Conducts research and educational programs which will benefit urban libraries
Publications Official journal: The ULC Exchange (formerly The Lamp. 1975–1983). 1984-. 11/yr. Free to members. Address same as Association. Other publications: Gallup Surveys; Frequent Fast Facts Surveys; Public Libraries as Partners in Youth Development: Tools For Success; Information Technology Management in Urban Public Libraries
Bibliography Berry, J. et al., "The Washington Week That Was: A Report on the Meetings of ALA, ALISE and the Urban Libraries Council, Jan. 5–12 [1984] in Washington, DC," Library Journal 109 (1984):537–543; Doms, K., "Urban Libraries Council," in ALA Yearbook 1989. p. 245. Chicago: American Library Association, 1989

597 Visual Resources Association (VRA)

Address c/o Marcia Focht, Secretary, 0615 S. W. Palatine Hill Rd, PO Box 6000, Binghamton, NY 13902 Tel.: + 1 607-777-2215, Fax + 1 607-777-4466, mfocht@binghamton.edu; vraweb.org/index.html
Languages English
Established 1983, Philadelphia
Officers Pres: Maureen Burns; VP: Brian Shellburne; Secr: Marcia Focht; Treas: Billy Kwan; Past Pres: Allan T. Kohl
Staff Membership Services Coordinator, paid
General Assembly Annual meeting. 2005: Miami, FL
Membership Membership includes information specialists; digital image specialists; slide, photograph, microfilm and digital archivists; art, architecture, film and video librarians; museum curators; architectural firms; galleries; publishers; image system vendors; rights and reproductions officials; photographers; art historians; artists; and scientists
Structure Affiliations: ArLIS, AASL, ACRL, CAA, CIMI, cni, Digital future association
Major Fields of Interest Image Management
Major Goals and Objectives To further research and education in the visual resources profession and to promote a spirit of cooperation among members of the profession. The purposes of this Association are to establish a continuing forum for communication of information and ideas, and for the advancement of matters of mutual interest to the membership
Activities Sponsors conferences and awards; project: Cataloguing Cultural Objects

Publications Official journal: Visual Resources Association Bulletin. 4/yr. Editor: John J. Taormina, Duke University.Other Publications: Image Stuff. (newsletter). Co-editors: Corey Schultz (email: coreys@stanford.edu) and Kristin Solias (email: Kristin.Solias@umb.edu); VRA Special Bulletins. Editor: Wendy Holden, Senior Associate Curator, Asian Art Archives University of Michigan; Image Collection Guidelines:The Acquisition and Use of Images in Non-Profit Educational Visual Resources Collections

598 Women's National Book Association inc. (WNBA)

Address c/o Susannah Greenberg Public Relations, P.O. Box 237, NY 10150-0231 Tel.: +1 212 2084629, Fax +1 212 2084629, publicity@bookbuzz.com; www.wnba-books.org
Languages English
Established 1917
Officers Pres: Joan Geifand; VP/Pres-elect: Mary Gey James; Treas: Margaret E. Auer; Secr: Ruth Light; Past Pres: N.N.
General Assembly Entire membership meets for a breakfast program meeting during annual ALA conference; Chapters design their own programs and meetings
Membership Total members: 927 (900 individual, 27 institutional). Requirements: Individuals interested in aims of Association; institutions willing to support the Association. Dues: Each chapter has its own dues schedule, e.g., $15–35, individual, depending on income; $250, sustaining institutions
Structure Governed by Board of Directors. Local chapters: 9. Affiliations: National Library Week Partner of ALA; Non-Governmental Organization member of the United Nations
Sources of Support Membership dues
Major Fields of Interest Books, publishing and retailing, women's affairs, libraries, education
Major Goals and Objectives Advancement of women in the world of books; education of women and men about the book world, especially publishing; education of members of allied organizations about the way publishing works; study of the role of the publisher in society
Activities Presentation of awards: The biennial WNBA Award, honoring an American bookwoman "for an outstanding contribution to the world of books and, through books, to the society in which we live;" the annual Lucile Michels Pannell Award to a creative children's bookstore. Chapters carry out extensive programs of interest to the diverse membership of writers, editors, designers, book and magazine producers, booksellers, librarians, educators, and readers. Chapters sponsor conferences, seminars, workshops, lectures, and other continuing education events, often jointly with other groups sharing common interests, e.g., Women in Scholarly Publishing, Modern Language Association, American Booksellers Association, etc.
Publications Official journal: The Bookwoman. 3/yr. Free to members. English. In addition, chapters produce their own newsletters
Bibliography Rentschler, C., "Women's National Book Association," in ALA Yearbook 1989. p. 254. Chicago: American Library Association, 1989

599 Young Adult Library Services Association (YALSA)
Address 50 East Huron Street, Chicago, IL 60611 Tel.: +1 800 5452433 ext. 4390, Fax +1 312 6647459, YALSA@ala.org; www.ala.org/yalsa/
Languages English
Established 1957, as Young Adult Services Division (YASD), changed its name in 1992 and became known as the Young Adult Library Services Association (YALSA)
Officers Pres: Linda W. Braun; VP/Pres-elect: Kim Patton; Past Pres: Sarah Cornish Debraski
Staff 3, paid
Membership 5500
Structure Affiliation: ALA
Major Fields of Interest Library services to young adults (12–18)
Major Goals and Objectives To advocate, promote, and strengthen service to young adults as part of the continuum of total library services
Activities Sponsors awards and grants, offers Professional Development Center
Publications Young Adult Library Services

Uruguay

600 Asociación de Bibliotecólogos del Uruguay (ABU) (Uruguayan Library Association)
Address c/o Alicia Ocaso, Eduardo Victor Haedo 2255, 11.200 Montevideo Tel.: +59 82 4099989, Fax +59 82 4099989, aocaso@adinet.com.uy
Languages Spanish
Established 1978
Officers Pres: Alicia Ocaso
General Assembly Entire membership meets annually
Membership Total members: 390 (individual). Requirements: Librarians with a professional diploma/degree
Structure Governed by executive officers. Affiliations: IFLA
Sources of Support Membership dues
Major Fields of Interest Libraries and library profession
Major Goals and Objectives To promote the development of libraries and library science in Uruguay; to promote the professional status and professional development of members; to participate in national and international professional activities
Activities Sponsors conferences, continuing education programs, and other activities according to the goals and objectives of the Association
Publications Official journal: Actualidades Bibliotecológicas. 2/yr.; Boletín. 12/yr. Panel de Noticias
Bibliography Acerenza, E., "Uruguay," in ALA World Encyclopedia of Library and Information Services. 2nd ed., pp. 838–839. Chicago: American Library Association, 1986

Uzbekistan

601   Uzbekistan Library Association (ULA)

Address   16, Sharaf Rashidov av, Tashkent, 700017   Tel.: +998 139 16 58, Fax +998 133 09 08, ulapost@uzsci.net; www.ula.uzsci.net
Officers   Chair: Umarov Absalom; Prov Exec Dir: Irgashev Dzuma; Asst: Zaynutdinova Sevara
Membership   29 institutions
Major Fields of Interest   Libraries and librarianship in Uzbekistan
Major Goals and Objectives   Assistance in democratic transformations in Uzbekistan, by means of libraries development, providing of free access to their information resources, wide recognizing of importance of library and information services excellence in the state and public sectors
Activities   Organizes congresses, seminars, exhibitions and other events. Provides the members of Association with information about: Activity of library associations and leading libraries of Uzbekistan and foreign countries; New achievements in the field of library business and information technologies; The laws and normative documents on library business developed and is being developed in Uzbekistan and abroad; The new editions, electronic catalogues, databases

Zambia

602   Zambia Library Association (ZLA)

Address   c/o The Chairperson, POB 38636, Lusaka 10101
Languages   English
Established   1967, at the headquarters of the Zambia Library Services in Lusaka. The history of the Association is linked with the political history of the area. 1962–63, there was a Library Association of Rhodesia and Nyasaland, which became the Library Association of Central Africa in 1964, when the Federation of Rhodesia and Nyasaland was dissolved. With the creation of an independent Zambia, the Association became the Zambia Branch of the Library Association of Central Africa in 1965. This Association was replaced by the independent Zambia Library Association in 1967
General Assembly   Entire membership meets once a year for the Annual General Meeting, and also at the monthly lecture series
Membership   Total members: Approx. 250 (individual, institutional). Requirements: Open to all individuals interested in librarianship, upon payment of dues. No formal application required. Open to all institutions upon payment of prescribed fee
Structure   Governed by Executive Council. Affiliations: Adult Education Association of Zambia, COMLA, IFLA
Sources of Support   Membership dues
Major Fields of Interest   Development of librarianship in Third World nations, especially Africa. Appropriate library technology for developing countries
Major Goals and Objectives   (1) To unite all persons engaged in library work or interested in libraries in Zambia; (2) to encourage the establishment and development of libraries and library cooperation in Zambia; (3) to improve standards in all aspects of

librarianship, bibliography, and documentation in Zambia; (4) to act as an advisory and public relations body in all matters pertaining to libraries, bibliography, and documentation in Zambia; (5) to stimulate an awareness among central and local government bodies and other institutions of their responsibilities in providing adequate library services and facilities; (6) to promote whatever may tend to the improvement of the position and qualifications of librarians; (7) to undertake activities (e.g., meetings, conferences, publications) that will further the above objectives

Activities Advises on the establishment of library and information centres as well as offering training workshops in various areas of information management

Publications Official journal: Zambia Library Association Journal (ZLAJ). 1968-. Free to members. Address same as Association. Circ: Membership. English. Indexed in LISA. Zambia Library Association Newsletter (ZLAN). 1979-. 6/yr. Other publications: Annual reports, proceedings of conferences, and Occasional Publications Series. Publications for sale. Publications exchange program in effect

Bibliography Phiri-Zilole, M.K., "Performance of the Library Profession in Zambia," International Library Review 18 (1986):259–266; Mohamedali, O.N.,"Zambia," in ALA World Encyclopedia of Library and Information Services. 2nd ed. pp. 867–869. Chicago: American library Association, 1986; Lundu, M. C, "National Information Policy for Zambia Proposals," COMLA Newsletter 57 (Sept. 1987):5

Zimbabwe

603 Zimbabwe Library Association (ZLA)

Address POB 3133, Harare Tel.: +263 4 745365

Languages English

Established 1947, as the Central African Branch of the South African Library Association (CABSALA); 1959, established as the Library Association of Rhodesia and Nyasaland (now Zimbabwe, Zambia and Malawi); 1964, became the Library Association of Central Africa; 1967, Rhodesia Library Association, and 1980, Zimbabwe Library Association, when the country's name changed from Rhodesia to Zimbabwe

Staff None

General Assembly Entire membership meets once a year. Branches of Mashonaland and Matabeleland meet monthly

Membership Types of membership: Individual, institutional, life, student. Requirements: Open to all persons or institutions engaged in library or documentation work and interested in the aims of the Association

Structure Governed by Executive Council. Affiliations: FID, IFLA

Sources of Support Membership dues, sale of publications

Major Fields of Interest Libraries and librarianship

Major Goals and Objectives To unite all persons engaged in library services; to encourage the establishment and development of libraries; to improve standards in librarianship; to make governing bodies aware of their responsibility to provide adequate library and documentation services

Activities Improvement of library services to all through the establishment of Culture Houses (district libraries) throughout the country; promotes education and training of more qualified personnel. Acted as pressure group for governmental recognition of librarianship as a profession; works for improved library services and literacy programs. Sponsors conferences, seminars, workshops, and other continuing education programs

Publications Official journal: Zimbabwe Librarian (formerly Rhodesia Librarian. 1969–79). 1980-. 2/yr. Free to members. Address same as Association. English. Indexed in LISA. Other publications: Annual reports, proceedings of conferences, seminars, workshops; Chiware, E. R. T. and Matsika, K., A Handbook for Teacher-Librarians in Zimbabwe (1989). Publications for sale

Bibliography Mazikana, P.C., "Towards an Association for Librarians, Archivists and Other Information Scientists," Zimbabwe Librarian 14 (1982):51–53; Barnshaw, A., "Establishing and Maintaining Professional Standards in Zimbabwe Libraries," Zimbabwe Librarian 16 (1984):8–9; Johnson, N., "Zimbabwe," in ALA World Encyclopedia of Library and Information Services. 2nd ed., pp. 869–870. Chicago: American Library Association, 1986; Pakkiri, D., "The Zimbabwe Library Association: From CABSALA to ZLA," COMLA Newsletter 65 (Sept. 1989):8–9,11

Indexes

Index of Associations

ABM-utvikling – Statens senter for arkiv, bibliotek og museum (Norway), 406
Aboriginal & Torres Strait Islander Library & Information Resource Network (Australia), 105
Africana Librarians Council (United States of America), 533
Agence Bibliographique de l'Enseignement Supérieur (France), 229
Agricultural Librarians Association of the Philippines (Philippines), 422
Albanian Library Association (Albania), 096
Alliance of Libraries and Information Institutes (Hungary), 285
American Association of Law Libraries (United States of America), 534
American Association of School Librarians (United States of America), 535
American Indian Library Association (United States of America), 001
American Library Association (United States of America), 536
American Society for Information Science and Technology (United States of America), 537
American Society of Indexers (United States of America), 538
American Theological Library Association (United States of America), 539
Arab Club for Information (Syria), 002
Arab Federation for Libraries and Information (Tunisia), 003
Arab Regional Branch of the International Council on Archives (Algeria), 004
Arbeitsgemeinschaft der Archive und Bibliotheken in der Evangelischen Kirche (Germany), 247
Arbeitsgemeinschaft der Bibliotheken und Dokumentationsstellen der Ost-, Ostmittel- und Südosteuropaforschung e. V. (Germany), 248
Arbeitsgemeinschaft der Fachhochschulbibliotheken (Germany), 249
Arbeitsgemeinschaft der Großstadtbibliotheken (Germany), 250
Arbeitsgemeinschaft der Kunst- und Museumsbibliotheken (Germany), 251
Arbeitsgemeinschaft der Parlaments- und Behördenbibliotheken (Germany), 252
Arbeitsgemeinschaft der Regionalbibliotheken im Deutschen Bibliotheksverband (Germany), 253
Arbeitsgemeinschaft der Spezialbibliotheken e. V. (Germany), 254
Arbeitsgemeinschaft für juristisches Bibliotheks- und Dokumentationswesen (Germany), 255
Arbeitsgemeinschaft für Medizinisches Bibliothekswesen (Germany), 256
Arbeitsgemeinschaft Gefangenenbüchereien / Deutscher Bibliotheksverband (Sektion 8) (Germany), 257
Arbeitsgemeinschaft Katholisch-Theologischer Bibliotheken (Germany), 258
Arbeitsgemeinschaft Patientenbibliotheken im Deutschen Bibliotheksverband (Germany), 259
Archival Society of Slovenia (Slovenia), 453
Archives and Records Association of New Zealand, Inc. (New Zealand), 395
Archives et Bibliothèques de Belgique / Archief- en Bibliotheekwezen in België (Belgium), 130
Arhivsko Drustvo Slovenije (Slovenia), 453
Arkib Negara Malaysia (Malaysia), 005
Arkistoyhdistys r.y. – Arkivföreningen r. f. (Finland), 221

Index of Associations

Arkivarforeningen (Norway), 407
Arkivforeningen (Denmark), 206
Arkivradet (Sweden), 467
ARLIS/Norden (Finland), 006
ARLIS/Norden – Norge. Forening for Kunstbibliotekarbeid (Norway), 408
Armenian Library Association (Armenia), 104
Art Libraries Society Norden (Norway), 408
Art Libraries Society of North America (Canada), 007
Art Libraries Society of the United Kingdom & the Republic of Ireland (United Kingdom), 491
Arts Libraries Society of Australia and New Zealand (Australia), 008
Asian Pacific American Librarians Association (United States of America), 540
Aslib Informatuion Ltd (United Kingdom), 492
Asociación Bibliotecaria de Misiones (Argentina), 099
Asociación Bibliotecológica de Guatemala (Guatemala), 280
Asociación Colombiana de Bibliotecologos y Documentalistas (Colombia), 195
Asociación Cubana de Bibliotecarios (Cuba), 201
Asociación de Bibliotecarios, Archivistas, Documentalistas e Informáticos (Argentina), 100
Asociación de Bibliotecarios de El Salvador (El Salvador), 216
Asociación de Bibliotecarios Graduados (Paraguay), 419
Asociación de Bibliotecarios Graduados de la República Argentina (Argentina), 101
Asociación de Bibliotecarios Profesionales de Rosario (Argentina), 102
Asociación de Bibliotecas Biomedicas Argentinas (Argentina), 103
Asociación de Bibliotecólogos del Uruguay (Uruguay), 600
Asociación de Estados Iberoamericanos para el Desarrollo de la Bibliotecas de Iberoamérica (Venezuela), 009
Asociación de Titulados Universitarios en Documentación y Biblioteconomía (Spain), 460
Asociación Española de Archiveros, Bibliotecarios, Museólogos y Documentalistas (Spain), 461
Asociación Hispana de Documentalistas en Internet (Spain), 010
Asociación Interamericana de Bibliotecarios, Documentalistas y Especialistas en Información Agrícola (Peru), 011
Asociación Latinoamericana de Archivos (Colombia), 012
Asociación Mexicana de Archivos y Bibliotecas Privados, A. C. (Mexico), 369
Asociación Mexicana de Bibliotecarios, A. C. (Mexico), 013
Asociación Nacional de Administradores de la Información Documental, A. C. (Mexico), 370
Asociación Nicaragüense de Bibliotecarios y Profesionales Afines (Nicaragua), 403
Asociatia Bibliotecarilor din România (Romania), 438
Asociatia Generala a Arhivistilor din Romania (Romania), 439
Associaçao Brasileira de Educação em Ciência da Informação (Brazil), 140
Associaçao dos Arquivistas Brasileiros (Brazil), 141
Associaçâo Portuguesa de Bibliotecários, Arquivistas e Documentalistas (Portugal), 014
Associação Portuguesa de Documentação e Informação de Saúde (Portugal), 436

Association Belge de Documentation / Belgische Vereniging voor Documentatie (Belgium), 131
Association Burkinabé des Gestionnaires de l'Information Documentaire (Burkina Faso), 150
Association des Amis de la Lecture (Benin), 136
Association des Archivistes Français (France), 230
Association des Archivistes Haitiens (Haiti), 284
Association des Bibliothécaires, Archivistes, Documentalistes et Muséographes du Cameroun (Cameroon), 154
Association des Bibliothecaires, Archivistes, Documentalistes et Museologues (Congo, Democratic Republic), 197
Association des Bibliothécaires Belges d'Expression Française (Belgium), 132
Association des Bibliothécaires de France (France), 231
Association des Bibliothécaires et Documentalistes Cambodgiens (Cambodia), 153
Association des Bibliothèques Chrétiennes de France (France), 232
Association des Bibliothèques du Liban (Lebanon), 356
Association des Conservateurs de Bibliothèques (France), 233
Association des Diplômés de l'École de Bibliothécaires-Documentalistes (France), 234
Association des directeurs des bibliothèques municipales et intercommunales des grandes villes de France (France), 235
Association des Directeurs et des personnels de direction des Bibliothèques Universitaires et de la Documentation (France), 236
Association des Documentalistes de Collectivités Territoriales (France), 237
Association des documentalistes du Gabon (Gabon), 244
Association des professionnels de l'information et de la documentation (France), 238
Association des Spécialistes Nigériens de l'Information Documentaire (Niger), 404
Association for Documentation in Economics (Japan), 324
Association for Dutch Archives (Netherlands), 380
Association for Federal Information Resources Management (United States of America), 541
Association for Health Information and Libraries in Africa (Mali), 015
Association for Information and Image Management (United States of America), 542
Association for Information Management Professionals (United States of America), 016
Association for Information Systems (United States of America), 017
Association for Library and Information Science Education (United States of America), 543
Association for Library Collections and Technical Services (United States of America), 544
Association for Library Service to Children (United States of America), 545
Association for Library Trustees, Advocates, Friends and Foundations (United States of America), 546
Association for Media and Technology in Education in Canada (Canada), 155
Association for Medical Librarianship (Germany), 256
Association for Population/Family Planning Libraries and Information Centers – International (United States of America), 018
Association for Recorded Sound Collections (United States of America), 547

Index of Associations 398

Association for the Advancement of the Science and Technology of Documentation (Canada), 159
Association Française des Sciences et Technologies de l'information (France), 239
Association Francophone d'Informatique en Agriculture (France), 019
Association genevoise des bibliothécaires et professionnels diplômés en information documentaire (Switzerland), 474
Association Guineenne des Documentalistes, Archivistes et Bibliothecaires (Guinea-Bissau), 281
Association Internationale des Archives Francophones (Canada), 020
Association Internationale des Bibliothèques, Archives et Centres de Documentation Musicaux/Internationale Vereinigung der Musikbibliotheken, Musikarchive und Musikdokumentationszentren (New Zealand), 021
Association Internationale des Écoles des Sciences de l'Information (Romania), 022
Association internationale francophone des bibliothécaires documentalistes (Burkina Faso), 151
Association Luxembourgeoise des Bibliothécaires, Archvistes et Documentalistes (Luxembourg), 359
Association Malienne des Bibliothécaires, Archivistes et Documentalistes (Mali), 364
Association Nationale des Documentalistes de l'Enseignement Privé (France), 240
Association Nationale des Informatistes (Morocco), 376
Association of Academic Health Sciences Libraries (United States of America), 548
Association of Architecture School Librarians (United States of America), 549
Association of Archivists (Norway), 407
Association of Argentine Biomedical Libraries (Argentina), 103
Association of Austrian Archivists (Austria), 125
Association of Austrian Librarians (Austria), 126
Association of Austrian Public Libraries (Austria), 120
Association of Brazilian Archivists (Brazil), 141
Association of British Theological and Philosophical Libraries (United Kingdom), 493
Association of Canadian Archivists (Canada), 156
Association of Canadian Map Libraries and Archives/Association des Cartothèques et des Archives Canadiennes (Canada), 157
Association of Caribbean University, Research and Institutional Libraries (Puerto Rico), 023
Association of Catholic Theological Libraries (Germany), 258
Association of Christian Librarians (United States of America), 550
Association of College and Research Libraries (United States of America), 551
Association of Commonwealth Archivists and Records Managers (United Kingdom), 024
Association of Danish Public Library Managers (Denmark), 208
Association of Directors of Municipal Archives (Israel), 304
Association of Directors of University Libraries (France), 236
Association of French Archivists (France), 230
Association of French Theological Libraries (France), 232
Association of German Archivists (Germany), 273
Association of German Librarians (Germany), 274
Association of German Regional Libraries (Germany), 253

Index of Associations

Association of Graduate Librarians of the Argentine Republic (Argentina), 101
Association of Graduates of the School of Librarians / Documentalists (France), 234
Association of Greek Librarians and Information Scientists (Greece), 278
Association of Hungarian Archivists (Hungary), 287
Association of Hungarian Librarians (Hungary), 286
Association of Independent Information Professionals (United States of America), 552
Association of Information and Dissemination Centers (United States of America), 553
Association of Information and Library Professionals (Germany), 260
Association of Information Professionals – Librarians, Archivists and Museologists (Bosnia and Herzegovina), 137
Association of Information Specialists (Georgia), 245
Association of Information Systems Professionals (United States of America), 554
Association of Jewish Libraries (United States of America), 555
Association of Librarians, Archivists and Documentalists of Mali (Mali), 364
Association of Librarians and Information Professionals (Czech Republic), 205
Association of Librarians in Land-Based Colleges and Universities (United Kingdom), 495
Association of Librarians in the History of the Health Sciences (United States of America), 556
Association of Librarians of Bosnia and Hercegovina (Bosnia and Herzegovina), 138
Association of Librarians of Montenegro (Montenegro), 375
Association of Librarianship and Documentation in Agriculture (Germany), 268
Association of Libraries and Documentation Centers for Eastern, Eastern Central and Southeastern Europe Research (Germany), 248
Association of Libraries of Polytechnic Institutions (Germany), 249
Association of Mental Health Librarians (United States of America), 557
Association of Metropolitan City Libraries (Germany), 250
Association of Moving Image Archivists (United States of America), 558
Association of National University Libraries (Japan), 327
Association of Parliamentary and Administrative Libraries (Germany), 252
Association of Parliamentary Librarians in Canada (Canada), 158
Association of Parliamentary Librarians in Canada/Association des Bibliothécaires Parlementaires au Canada (Canada), 158
Association of Parliamentary Libraries of Australasia (New Zealand), 025
Association of Polish Archivists (Poland), 433
Association of Polish Libraries (Poland), 084
Association of Press and Broadcasting Documentalists (Netherlands), 393
Association of Professional Librarians (Mauritius), 367
Association of Research Libraries (United States of America), 559
Association of Salvadoran (El Salvador), 216
Association of Senior Children's and Education Librarians (United Kingdom), 496
Association of South African Indexers and Bibliographers (South Africa), 455
Association of Special Libraries (Germany), 254
Association of Special Libraries of the Philippines (Philippines), 423
Association of Specialized and Cooperative Library Agencies (United States of America), 560
Association of Swiss Archivists (Switzerland), 477

Association of the University Libraries, the Royal Library and the Library of the Royal Netherlands Academy of Arts and Sciences (Netherlands), 391
Association of Theological Librarians (Belgium), 134
Association of UK Media Librarians (United Kingdom), 497
Association of Vision Science Librarians (United States of America), 561
Association pour l'Avancement des Sciences et des Techniques de la Documentation (Canada), 159
Association pour le Développement des Documents Numériques en Bibliothèques (France), 241
Association Professionnelle des Bibliothécaires et Documentalistes (Belgium), 133
Association Sénégalaise des Bibliothécaires, Archivistes et Documentalistes (Senegal), 447
Associations of Montenegrin Librarians (Montenegro), 374
Associazione Archivistica Ecclesiastica (Italy), 308
Associazione Bibliotecari Documentalisti Sanita (Italy), 309
Associazione dei Bibliotecari Ecclesiastici Italiani (Italy), 310
Associazione Italiana Biblioteche (Italy), 311
Associazione Italiana per la Documentazione Avanzata (Italy), 312
Associazione Nazionale Archivistica Italiana (Italy), 313
Ato Dokyumenteshon Kenkyukai (Japan), 317
Australian and New Zealand Map Circle (Australia), 106
Australian and New Zealand Society of Indexers (Australia), 107
Australian and New Zealand Theological Library Association Ltd (Australia), 026
Australian Government Libraries Information Network (Australia), 108
Australian Law Librarians Association (Australia), 109
Australian Libraries Copyright Committee (Australia), 110
Australian Library and Information Association (Australia), 111
Australian School Library Association (Australia), 112
Australian Society of Archivists (Inc.) (Australia), 113
Austrian Library Network (Austria), 123
Austrian Society for Documentation and Information (Austria), 124
Azerbaijan Library Development Association (Azerbaijan), 127
Belarusian Library Association (Belarus), 129
Belgian Association for Documentation (Belgium), 131
Belgian Association of Archives and Libraries (Belgium), 130
Belgian Association of French-Speaking Librarians (Belgium), 132
Berufsverband Information Bibliothek e. V. (Germany), 260
Beta Phi Mu (International Library Science Honor Society) (United States of America), 027
Bibliographical Society of America (United States of America), 562
Bibliographical Society of Australia and New Zealand (Australia), 028
Bibliographical Society of Canada/La Société Bibliographique du Canada (Canada), 160
Biblioteca Metropolitan Bucaresti (Romania), 440
Biblioteca Nacional de Angola (Angola), 097
Bibliotekarforbundet: Forbundet for Informationsspecialister og kulturformidlere (Denmark), 207

Bibliotekarsko društvo Srbijé (Serbia), 448
Bibliotekslederforeningen (Denmark), 208
Biblioteksstyrelsen (Denmark), 209
Bibliothecarii Medicinae Fenniae (Finland), 222
Bibliothek&Information Deutschland (Germany), 261
Bibliothèque Information Suisse (Switzerland), 475
Bibliothèques Européenne de Théologie (Belgium), 029
Bibliothèques publiques du Québec (Canada), 161
Bibliothkarsko Drustvo na Makedonija (Macedonia), 360
Botswana Library Association (Botswana), 139
Branchevereniging Archiefinstellingen Nederland (Netherlands), 380
Brazilian Commission of University Libraries (Brazil), 145
Brazilian Federation of Library Associations (Brazil), 144
Britain and Ireland Association of Aquatic Sciences Libraries and Information Centres (United Kingdom), 499
British and Irish Association of Law Librarians (United Kingdom), 500
British Association for Information and Library Education and Research (United Kingdom), 501
British Records Association (United Kingdom), 502
Büchereiverband Österreichs / formerly Verband Österreichischer Volksbüchereien und Volksbibliothekare (Austria), 120
Bulgarian Library and Information Association (Bulgaria), 149
Bureau of Canadian Archivists / Bureau Canadien des Archivistes (Canada), 162
Business Librarians Association (United Kingdom), 503
Cambodian Librarians and Documentalists Association (CLDA) (Cambodia), 153
Cameroon Association of Librarians, Archivists, Documentalists, and Museum Curators (Cameroon), 154
Canadian Association for Information Science / Association Canadienne des Sciences de l'Information (Canada), 163
Canadian Association for School Libraries (Canada), 164
Canadian Association of Children's Librarians (Canada), 165
Canadian Association of College and University Libraries / Association Canadienne des Bibliothèques de Collège et d'Université (Canada), 166
Canadian Association of Family Resource Programs (Canada), 167
Canadian Association of Law Libraries / Association Canadienne des Bibliothèques de Droit (Canada), 168
Canadian Association of Music Libraries (A Branch of the International Association of Music Libraries, Archives and Documentation Centres / Association Canadienne des Bibliothèques Musicales (Canada), 169
Canadian Association of Public Libraries (Canada), 170
Canadian Association of Research Libraries / Association des Bibliothèques de Recherche du Canada (Canada), 171
Canadian Association of Special Libraries and Information Services (Canada), 172
Canadian Council of Archives / Conseil Canadien des Archives (Canada), 173
Canadian Council of Information Studies/ Le Conseil Canadien des écoles de sciences de l'information (Canada), 174

Canadian Health Libraries Association / Association des Bibliothèques de la Santé du Canada (Canada), 175
Canadian Library Association (Canada), 176
Canadian Library Trustees Association (Canada), 177
Canadian Urban Libraries Council (Canada), 178
Caribbean Archives Association – Regional Branch of the International Council on Archives (Martinique), 030
Catholic Library Association (United States of America), 563
Center for Research Libraries (United States of America), 564
Central Bank of Egypt (Library Economic Research Sector) (Egypt), 215
Central Catholic Library Association, Inc. (Ireland), 299
Česká Archivní Společnost (Czech Republic), 204
Chartered Institute of Library and Information Professionals (United Kingdom), 506
Chartered Institute of Library and Information Professionals in Scotland (United Kingdom), 505
Chartered Institute of Library and Information Professionals Wales (United Kingdom), 523
Chief Officers of State Library Agencies (United States of America), 565
Chilean Library Association (Chile), 186
China Society of Indexers (China), 187
China Society of Scientific and Technical Information (China), 194
Chinese-American Librarians Association (United States of America), 566
Chinese Archives Society (China), 188
Chinese Information Literacy Association (Taiwan), 479
Chung-kuo t'u-shu-kuan hsüeh-hui (Taiwan), 480
Church and Synagogue Library Association (United States of America), 567
CILIP in Ireland (United Kingdom), 504
Coalition for Networked Information (United States of America), 568
Colegio de Bibliotecarios de Chile CBC (Chile), 186
Colegio de Bibliotecarios de Costa Rica (Costa Rica), 198
Colegio de Bibliotecólogos del Perú (Peru), 420
Colegio de Bibliotecologos del Peru (Peru), 421
Colegio Nacional de Bibliotecarios, A. C. (Mexico), 371
Colombian Association of Librarians (Colombia), 195
Comité de Cooperación Bibliotecaria de El Salvador (El Salvador), 217
Comité français IFLA (France), 031
Committee on South Asian Libraries and Documentation (United States of America), 569
Commonwealth Library Association (Jamaica), 032
Conference of Directors of Directors of National Libraries of Asia and Oceania (Australia), 033
Conference of Directors of National Libraries (Australia), 034
Conference of European National Librarians (Switzerland), 035
Congress of South-East Asian Libraries (Vietnam), 036
Conselho Federal de Biblioteconomia (Brazil), 142
Consortium of Uganda University Libraries (Uganda), 488
Corporation des bibliothécaires professionnels du Québec (Canada), 179
Council of Australian University Librarians (Australia), 037

Council of New Zealand University Librarians (New Zealand), 396
Council of PCLI Programme Coordinators (Russia), 442
Council of Prairie and Pacific University Libraries (Canada), 180
Council on Botanical and Horticultural Libraries, Inc. (United States of America), 038
Council on East Asian Libraries, Inc. (United States of America), 570
Council on Library and Information Resources (United States of America), 571
Council on Library/Media Technicians (United States of America), 039
Croatian Archival Society (Croatia), 199
Croatian Library Association (Croatia), 200
Cultural Centre Suriname (Suriname), 465
Cultural Service Centre Austria (Austria), 121
Cumann Cartlannaíochta Éireann (Ireland), 300
Cumann Leabharlann na h-Éireann (Ireland), 301
Cumann Leabharlannaithe Scoile (Ireland), 302
Curaçao Public Library Association (Curaçao), 203
Cymdeithas Llyfrgelloedd Cymru (United Kingdom), 507
Czech Archival Society (Czech Republic), 204
Daigaku Toshokan Mondai Kenkyukai (Japan), 318
Danish Association of Archivists (Denmark), 206
Danish Association of Music Libraries (Denmark), 213
Danish Library Association (Denmark), 210
Danish National Library Authority (Denmark), 209
Danish Research Library Association (Denmark), 211
Danish School Librarians (Denmark), 212
Danish Union of Librarians: Union of Information Specialists andCultural Intermediaries (Denmark), 207
Danmarks Biblioteksforening (Denmark), 210
Danmarks Forskningsbiblioteksforening (Denmark), 211
Danmarks Skolebibliotekarer (Denmark), 212
Dansk Musikbiblioteks Forening (Denmark), 213
Deutsche Gesellschaft für Informationswissenschaft und Informationspraxis e. V. (Germany), 262
Deutsche Gesellschaft für Medizinische Informatik, Biometrie und Epidemiologie e. V. (Germany), 263
Deutscher Bibliotheks- und Informationsverband e. V. (Germany), 264
Deutscher Bibliotheksverband e. V. (Germany), 265
Deutscher Verband Medizinischer Dokumentare e. V. (Germany), 266
Developing Library Network (India), 291
DIK (Sweden), 468
DIK Association – Documentation, Information & Culture (Sweden), 468
Documentation Sciences Foundation (Spain), 010
Drustvo Bibliotekara Bosne i Hercegovine (Bosnia and Herzegovina), 138
Dutch Association of School Librarians (Netherlands), 385
Early Years Library Network (United Kingdom), 508
East Asian Library Resources Group of Australia (Australia), 114
East-Kazakhstan Librarians Association (Kazakhstan), 345

Ecclesiastical Archivists Association (Italy), 308
Eesti Raamatukoguhoidjate Ühing (Estonia), 219
Estonian Librarians Association (Estonia), 219
European Association for Health Information and Libraries (Netherlands), 040
European Association for Library and Information Education and Research (Norway), 041
European Association of Aquatic Sciences Libraries and Information Centres (Bulgaria), 042
European Association of Information Services (Netherlands), 043
European Association of Libraries and Information Services on Alcohol and Other Drugs (Ireland), 044
European Bureau of Library, Information and Documentation Associations (Netherlands), 045
European Information Association (United Kingdom), 046
European Theological Libraries (Belgium), 029
Evangelical Church Library Association (United States of America), 572
Evangelisches Literaturportal e. V. (Germany), 267
Ex Libris Association (Canada), 181
Federaçao Brasileira de Associaçoes de Bibliotecários (Brazil), 143
Federação Brasileira de Associações de Bibliotecários, Cientistas da Informação e Instituições (Brazil), 144
Federaçao Brasileira de Associaçoes de Bibliotecários – Comissao Brasileira de Bibliotecas Centrais Universitárias (Brazil), 145
Federación Española de Sociedades de Archivística, Biblioteconomía, Documentación y Museística (Spain), 462
Federal Council of Librarianship (Brazil), 142
Federal Libraries Coordination Secretariat (Canada), 182
Federal Library and Information Center Committee (United States of America), 573
Federal Union of German Library and Information Associations (Germany), 261
Federatie van Organisaties op het gebied van het Bibliotheek-, Informatie-en Documentatiewezen (Netherlands), 381
Fédération des enseignants documentalistes de l'Éducation nationale (France), 242
Fédération Internationale des Archives du Film (Belgium), 047
Federation of Associations of Documentalists-Librarians of National Education (France), 242
Federation of Organizations in the Fields of Library, Information, and Documentation Services (Netherlands), 381
Federation of Spanish Archival, Library, Documentation, and Museum Associations (Spain), 462
Félag skólasafnskennara (Iceland), 289
Fiji Library Association (Fiji), 220
Finlands Svenska Biblioteksförening r. f. (Finland), 223
Finnish Association of Information Studies (Finland), 224
Finnish Association of Medical Librarians (Finland), 222
Finnish Research Library Association (Finland), 227
Flemish Association of Librarians, Archivists and Documentalists (Belgium), 135
FOBID Netherlands Library Forum (Netherlands), 382

Forskerforbundets Bibliotekforening (Norway), 409
Forum of Asian Theological Libraries (Indonesia), 048
French Association for the Information Sciences and Technologies (France), 239
French Association of Information Scientists and Special Librarians (France), 238
Friends of African Village Libraries (United States of America), 049
Friends of Libraries Australia Incorporated (Australia), 115
Fundashon Biblioteka Publiko Kòrsou (Curaçao), 203
General Association of the Romanian Archivists (Romania), 439
Georgian Library Association (Georgia), 246
German Association for Information Science and Practice (Germany), 262
German Classification Society (Germany), 269
German Law Libraries Association (Germany), 255
German Library and Information Association (Germany), 264
German Library Association (Germany), 265
Gesellschaft für Bibliothekswesen und Dokumentation des Landbaues – Fachliche Arbeitsgemeinschaft der ASpB (Germany), 268
Gesellschaft für Klassifikation e. V. (Germany), 269
Ghana Library Association (Ghana), 276
Ghana Library Board (Ghana), 277
Göteborgs University Library (Sweden), 469
Gruppo Italiano Documentalisti dell'industria Farmaceutica e degli Istituti di Ricerca Biomedica (Italy), 314
Guyana Library Association (Guyana), 283
Hanguk Tosogwan Hyophoe (Korea, Republic), 349
Haykakan Gradaranayin Asotsiatsia (Armenia), 104
Health Information Association of New Zealand (New Zealand), 397
Health Information Management Association of Australia Ltd. (Australia), 116
HK/KOMMUNAL Library Committee (Denmark), 214
Hong Kong Library Association (China), 189
Hong Kong Teacher Librarians' Association (China), 190
Hrvatsko Arhivisticko Drustvo (Croatia), 199
Hrvatsko knjiznicarsko drustvo (Croatia), 200
Hungarian Medical Library Association (Hungary), 288
IAML Nihon Shibu (Kokusai Ongaku Bunken-Kyokai Nihon Shibu) (Japan), 319
Igud Ha'arkhiyy Yona Yim Be-Israel (Israel), 303
Igud Menahalei Archyyionim Ba-Rashuiot Ha-Mekomyiot (Israel), 304
Ikatan Pustakawan Indonesia (Indonesia), 296
Independent Research Libraries Association (United States of America), 574
Indexing and Abstracting Society of Canada / Société Canadienne d'indexation (Canada), 183
Indian Association of Special Libraries and Information Centres (India), 292
Indian Association of Teachers of Library and Information Science (India), 050
Indonesian Library Association (Indonesia), 296
Information Processing Association of Israel (Israel), 305
Information Processing Society of Japan (Japan), 321
Information Science and Technology Association (Japan), 322

Index of Associations

Information Society in Brazil (Brazil), 147
Information – the Icelandic Library and Information Science Association (Iceland), 290
Instituto Nacional de Estudos e Pesquisa (Guinea-Bissau), 282
Inter-American Association of Agricultural Librarians, Documentalists and Information Specialists (Peru), 011
International Association for Social Sciences Information Services and Technology (Denmark), 051
International Association of Agricultural Information Specialities (United Kingdom), 052
International Association of Aquatic and Marine Science Libraries and Information Centers (United States of America), 053
International Association of Law Librarians (United Kingdom), 054
International Association of Law Libraries (Ireland), 055
International Association of Music Information Centres (Belgium), 056
International Association of Music Libraries, Archives, and Documentation Centres – United States Branch (United States of America), 575
International Association of Music Libraries, Archives and Documentation Centers – Japanese Branch (Japan), 319
International Association of Music Libraries, Archives and Documentation Centres (New Zealand), 021
International Association of Music Libraries, Archives and Documentation Centres, Australian Branch (Netherlands), 383
International Association of Music Libraries, Archives and Documentation Centres, New Zealand Branch, Incorporated (New Zealand), 398
International Association of Music Libraries, Archives and Documentation Centres – German Branch/FRG (Germany), 270
International Association of Music Libraries, Archives and Documentation Centres – Italian Branch (Italy), 315
International Association of Music Libraries, Archives and Documentation Centres – United Kingdom and Ireland Branch (United Kingdom), 509
International Association of Orientalist Librarians (Russia), 057
International Association of School Librarianship (Australia), 058
International Association of Schools of Information Science (Romania), 022
International Association of Scientific and Technological University Libraries (Ireland), 059
International Association of Sound and Audiovisual Archives (Denmark), 060
International Association of Users and Developers of Electronic Libraries and New Information Technologies (Russia), 061
International Council for Scientific and Technical Information (France), 062
International Council on Archives / Conseil International des Archives (France), 063
International Federation for Information Processing (Austria), 064
International Federation of Film Archives (Belgium), 047
International Federation of Library Associations and Institutions (Netherlands), 065
International Group of Publishing Libraries (United Kingdom), 066
International Information Centre for Terminology (Austria), 067
International Network for the Availability of Scientific Publications (United Kingdom), 068

International Society for Knowledge Organization e. V. (Germany), 069
International Society of Libraries and Museums of the Performing Arts (Canada), 089
International Working Group of Archival, Library and Graphic Restorers (Switzerland), 070
Internationale Arbeitsgemeinschaft der Archiv-, Bibliotheks-, und Graphikrestauratoren (Switzerland), 070
Internationale Vereinigung der Musikbibliotheken, Musikarchive und Musikdokumentationszentren – Gruppe Bundesrepublik Deutschland (Germany), 270
Internet Chinese Librarians Club (United States of America), 071
Iranian Library and Information Science Association (Iran), 297
Irish Association of School Librarians (Ireland), 302
Irish Society for Archives (Ireland), 300
Israel Archives Association (Israel), 303
Israeli Center for Libraries (Israel), 306
Israeli Society of Libraries and Information Centers (Israel), 307
Italian Association for Advanced Documentation (Italy), 312
Italian Libraries Association (Italy), 311
Japan Art Documentation Society (Japan), 317
Japan Association of Agricultural Librarians and Documentalists (Japan), 332
Japan Association of Private University Libraries (Japan), 338
Japan Library Association (Japan), 335
Japan Library Group (United Kingdom), 510
Japan Medical Library Association (Japan), 331
Japan Nursing Library Association (Japan), 323
Japan Pharmaceutical Library Association (Japan), 336
Japan School Library Association (Japan), 342
Japan Society for Archival Science (Japan), 330
Japan Society for Information and Media Studies (Japan), 320
Japan Society of Archives Institutions (Japan), 343
Japan Society of Library and Information Science (Japan), 333
Japan Special Libraries Association (Japan), 337
Joho Shori Gakkai (Japan), 321
Jordan Library and Information Association (Jordan), 344
Jouhou Kagaku Gijutsu Kyokai (Japan), 322
Junior College Library Association (Japan), 339
Kango Toshokan Kyogikai (Japan), 323
Keizai Shiryo Kyogikai (Japan), 324
Kenya Library Association (Kenya), 347
Knowledge Management Society of Japan (Japan), 325
Kokkoshiritsu Daigaku Toshokan Kyoryoku Iinkai (Japan), 326
Kokuritsu Daigaku Toshokan Kyogikai (Japan), 327
Koninklijke Vereniging van Archivarissen in Nederland (Netherlands), 384
Korean Library and Information Science Society (Korea, Republic), 350
Korean Library Association (Korea, Republic), 349
Korean Medical Library Association (Korea, Republic), 351
Korean Society for Information Management (Korea, Republic), 352

Index of Associations

Kouritsu Daigaku Kyokai Toshokan Kyogikai (Japan), 328
Landelijke Werkgroep Schoolmediathecarissen Voortgezet Onderwijs (Netherlands), 385
Latin American Association of Archives (Colombia), 012
Latvian School Librarian Association (Latvia), 355
Latvijas Bibliotekāru bierdrība (Latvia), 354
Latvijas Skolu bibliotekāru asociācija (Latvia), 355
League of European Research Libraries (Netherlands), 074
Legal Information Preservation Alliance (United States of America), 072
Lesotho Library Association (Lesotho), 357
LIASA Interest Group for Bibliographic Standards (South Africa), 456
Librarians' Christian Fellowship (United Kingdom), 511
Librarians association of France (France), 231
Library and Information Association of Eritrea (Eritrea), 218
Library and Information Association of Jamaica (Jamaica), 316
Library and Information Association of New Zealand Aotearoa (New Zealand), 399
Library and Information Association of South Africa (South Africa), 457
Library and Information Technology Association (United States of America), 576
Library Association of Antigua and Barbuda (Antigua and Barbuda), 098
Library Association of Barbados (Barbados), 128
Library Association of China (Taiwan), 480
Library Association of Costa Rica (Costa Rica), 198
Library Association of Cuba (Cuba), 201
Library Association of Guatemala (Guatemala), 280
Library Association of Latvia (Latvia), 354
Library Association of Malaysia (Malaysia), 362
Library Association of Samoa (Samoa), 446
Library Association of Singapore (Singapore), 451
Library Association of Slovenia (Slovenia), 454
Library Association of the Democratic People's Republic of Korea (Korea, Democratic People's Republic), 348
Library Association of the Republic of Kazakhstan (Kazakhstan), 346
Library Association of the Republic of Moldova (Moldova), 373
Library Association of Trinidad and Tobago (Trinidad and Tobago), 485
Library Leadership and Management Association (United States of America), 577
Library Promotion Bureau (Pakistan), 415
Library Public Relations Council (United States of America), 578
Library Society of China (China), 191
Lietuvos bibliotekininkų draugija (Lithuania), 358
Ligue des Bibliothèques Européennes de Recherche (Netherlands), 074
Lithuanian Librarians' Association (Lithuania), 358
Luxembourgish Librarians', Archivists' and Documentalists' Association (Luxembourg), 359
Macau Library and Information Management Association (China), 193
Macedonian Library Association (Macedonia), 360
Magyar Könyvtárosok Egyesülete (Hungary), 286
Magyar Levéltárosok Egyesülete (Hungary), 287

Magyar Orvosi Könyvtárak Szövetsége (Hungary), 288
Major Orchestra Librarians' Association (United States of America), 075
Maldives Library Association (Maldives), 363
Malta Library and Information Association (Malta), 365
Marshall Islands Library Association (Marshall Islands), 366
Mauritius Library Association (Mauritius), 368
Media Archives Austria (Austria), 122
Medical and Health Librarians Association of the Philippines (Philippines), 424
Medical Librarians Group of Malaysia (Malaysia), 361
Medical Library Association Inc. (United States of America), 580
Medical Library Association of India (India), 293
Metropolitan Libraries Section (Singapore), 076
Metropolitan Library of Bucharest (Romania), 440
Mexican Association of Librarians (Mexico), 013
Middle East Librarians Association (Egypt), 077
Mita Society for Library and Information Science (Japan), 329
Mita Toshokan Joho Gakkai (Japan), 329
Mountain Plains Library Association (United States of America), 581
Museum Librarians and Archivists Group (United Kingdom), 513
Museums, Libraries and Archives Council (United Kingdom), 514
Music Library Association, Inc (United States of America), 582
Myanmar Library Association (Myanmar), 377
National Archives of Malaysia (Malaysia), 005
National Association of Government Archives and Records Administrators (United States of America), 583
National Association of Information Specialists (Morocco), 376
National Association of Italian Archivists (Italy), 313
National Association of Public Libraries and Librarians in Romania (Romania), 441
National Association of State Information Resource Executives (United States of America), 584
National Association of Toy and Leisure Libraries (United Kingdom), 515
National Church Library Association (United States of America), 585
National Committee of Archivists (India), 294
National Federation of Abstracting and Information Services (United States of America), 586
National Institute for Studies and Research (Guinea-Bissau), 282
National Iranian Oil Company, NIOC Central Library (Iran), 298
National Library Association of Brunei (Brunei), 148
Nederlandse Bibliotheek Dienst (Netherlands), 386
Nederlandse Vereniging van Beroepsbeoefenaren in de Bibliotheek-, Informatie- en Kennissector (Netherlands), 387
Nederlandse Vereniging van Gebruikers van Online Informatiesystemen (Netherlands), 388
Nepal Community Library Association (Nepal), 378
Nepal Library Association (Nepal), 379

Netherlands Association for Library, Information and Knowledge Professionals (Netherlands), 387
Netherlands Association of Users of Online Information Systems (Netherlands), 388
Netherlands Institute for Public Libraries (Netherlands), 390
Netherlands Library Supply Service (Netherlands), 386
Network of Government Library and Information Specialists (United Kingdom), 516
New Zealand Law Librarians Inc. (New Zealand), 400
New Zealand Society of Archivists (New Zealand), 401
Nicaraguan Association of Librarians and Related Professionals (Nicaragua), 403
Nigerian Library Association (Nigeria), 405
Nihon Akaibuzu Gakkai (Japan), 330
Nihon Igaku Toshokan Kyokai (Japan), 331
Nihon Nougaku Toshokan Kyogikai (Japan), 332
Nihon Toshokan Joho Gakkai (Japan), 333
Nihon Toshokan Kenkyukai (Japan), 334
Nihon Toshokan Kyokai (Japan), 335
Nihon Yakugaku Toshokan Kyogikai (Japan), 336
Nippon Association for Librarianship (Japan), 334
NORDBOK (Norway), 078
Nordic Association for Medical and Health Information (Estonia), 079
Nordic Literature and Library Committee (Norway), 078
Norsk Arkivråd (Norway), 410
Norsk Bibliotekforening (Norway), 411
Norsk Fagbibliotekforening (Norway), 412
North American Fuzzy Information Processing Society (United States of America), 080
North American Sport Library Network (Canada), 081
NorthEast Research Libraries Association (United States of America), 587
Norwegian Archive, Library and Museum Authority (Norway), 406
Norwegian Archives Council (Norway), 410
Norwegian Association of School Librarianship (Norway), 414
Norwegian Association of Special Libraries (Norway), 412
Norwegian Library Association (Norway), 411
Norwegian Union of Municipal and General Employees (Norway), 413
NVBA, vereniging van en voor personen werkzam in het beheer van organisatie (Netherlands), 389
Österreichische Bibliothekenverbund und Service GmbH (Austria), 123
Österreichische Gesellschaft für Dokumentation und Information (Austria), 124
Organisation of South African Law Libraries (South Africa), 458
Pacific Islands Association of Libraries, Archives and Museums (Guam), 082
Pacific Regional Branch of the International Council on Archives (New Zealand), 083
Pakistan Library Association (Pakistan), 416
Pakistan Library Automation Goup (Pakistan), 417
Palestinian Library and Information Association (Palestine), 418
Panafrican Institute for Development (Burkina Faso), 152
Parent Library Community of Serbia (Serbia), 449
Persatuan Perpustakaan Kebangsaan (Brunei), 148

Persatuan Perpustakaan Malaysia (Malaysia), 362
Pharma Arbeitskreis Information und Dokumentation (Germany), 271
Pharma working group for information and documentation (Germany), 271
Philippine Association of Academic and Research Librarians (Philippines), 425
Philippine Association of School Librarians (Philippines), 426
Philippine Association of Teachers of Library Science (Philippines), 427
Philippine Group of Law Librarians, Inc. (Philippines), 428
Philippine Library Association, Inc., Headquarters (Philippines), 429
Philippine Public Librarians League, Inc. (Philippines), 430
Polish Librarians Association (Poland), 434
Polish Society of Scientific Information (Poland), 432
Polski Zwiazek Bibliotek (Poland), 084
Polskie Towarzystwo Informacji Naukowej (Poland), 432
Portuguese Association of Librarians, Archivists and Documentalists (Portugal), 014
Private Libraries Association (United Kingdom), 085
Professional Association of Librarians and Documentalists (Belgium), 133
Progressive Librarians Guild (United States of America), 588
Provincial and Territorial Library Directors Council (Canada), 184
Public Library Association (United States of America), 589
Public University Library Association (Japan), 328
Puerto Rico Librarians Society (Puerto Rico), 437
Records Management Association of Australia (Australia), 118
Records Management Society of Great Britain (United Kingdom), 517
Red de Bibliotecas Universitarias Españolas (Spain), 463
Red Latinoamericana de Información Teológica (Argentina), 086
REFORMA (National Association to Promote Library Services to the Spanish Speaking) (United States of America), 590
Regroupement des Archivistes Religieux (Canada), 185
Research Council Libraries&Information Consortium (United Kingdom), 518
Research Institute for Korean Archives and Records (Korea, Republic), 353
Research Libraries UK (United Kingdom), 519
Romanian Library Association (Romania), 438
Rossiiskaya Bibliotechnaya Assotsiatsiya (Russia), 443
Royal Dutch Society of Archivists (Netherlands), 384
Russian Library Association (Russia), 443
Russian School Libraries Association (Russia), 444
Russian Society of Historians and Archivists (Russia), 445
School Library Association (United Kingdom), 521
School Library Association in Finland (Finland), 226
School Library Association in Scotland (United Kingdom), 520
School Library Association of New Zealand Aotearoa (New Zealand), 402
Scottish Health Information Network (United Kingdom), 522
Sectorinstituut Openbare Bibliotheken (Netherlands), 390
Sefydliad Siartredig Llyfrgellwyr a Gweithwyr Gwybodaeth Cymru (United Kingdom), 523

Index of Associations

Seminar on the Acquisition of Latin American Library Materials (United States of America), 087
Senegal Association of Librarians, Archivists and Documentalists (Senegal), 447
Senmon Toshokan Kyogikai (Japan), 337
Sezione Italiana dell'International Association of Music Libraries, Archives and Documentation Centres (Italy), 315
Shiritsu Daigaku Toshokan Kyokai (Japan), 338
Shiritsu Tanki Daigaku Toshokan Kyogikai (Japan), 339
Sierra Leone Association of Archivists, Librarians and Information Scientists (Sierra Leone), 450
Sistema Integrado de Bibliotecas da Universidade de São Paulo (Brazil), 146
Skolebibliotekarforeningen i Norge (Norway), 414
Slovak Librarians Association (Slovakia), 452
Sociedad Argentina de Información (Argentina), 088
Sociedad Columbiana de Archivistas (Colombia), 196
Sociedad Cubana de Ciencias de la Información (Cuba), 202
Sociedad de Bibliotecarios de Puerto Rico (Puerto Rico), 437
Sociedad Española de Documentación e Información Científica (Spain), 464
Sociedad Para el Desarollo Científico de la Archivistica S. C. (Mexico), 372
Sociedade da Informação (Brazil), 147
Société Française des Sciences de l'Information et de la Communication (France), 243
Société Franco-Japonaise des Bibliotecaires et des Documentalistes (Japan), 340
Société Internationale des Bibliothèques et des Musées des Arts du Spectacle (Canada), 089
Society for Finnish Information Specialists (Finland), 228
Society for Information Science (India), 295
Society of American Archivists (United States of America), 591
Society of Archivists (United Kingdom), 524
Society of Chief Librarians (United Kingdom), 525
Society of College, National and University Libraries (United Kingdom), 526
Society of Filipino Archivists, Inc (Philippines), 431
Society of Finnish Archivists (Finland), 221
Society of Hellenic Archives (Greece), 279
Society of Indexers (United Kingdom), 527
Society of School Librarians International (United States of America), 592
Society of Serbian Librarians (Serbia), 448
Society of Study on Academic Library Problems (Japan), 318
South African Society of Archivists (South Africa), 459
South and West Asian Regional Branch of the International Council on Archives (Pakistan), 090
Spanish Association of Archivists, Librarians, Museologists and Documentalists (Spain), 461
Spanish Society for Scientific Information and Documentation (Spain), 464
Special Libraries Association (United States of America), 593
Spolok slovenskych knihovnikov (Slovakia), 452
Sri Lanka Library Association (Sri Lanka), 091

Standing Conference of African National and University Libraries in Eastern, Central and
   Southern Africa (Uganda), 092
Standing Conference of African University Libraries, Western Area (Senegal), 093
Standing Conference of Eastern, Central and Southern African Librarians (Uganda), 094
Standing Conference on Library Materials on Africa (United Kingdom), 528
State Library of New South Wales, Collection Services (Australia), 119
Stichting Cultureel Centrum Suriname (Suriname), 465
Stowarzyszenie Archivistów Polskich (Poland), 433
Stowarzyszenie Bibliotekarzy Polskich (Poland), 434
Study Group of Archives and Libraries in the Evangelical Church (Germany), 247
Substance Abuse Librarians&Information Specialists (United States of America), 095
Suid-Africaanse Vereniging van Archivarisse (South Africa), 459
Suomen Kirjastoseura – Finlands Biblioteksförening (Finland), 225
Suomen koulukirjastoyhdistys ry (Finland), 226
Suomen Tieteellinen Kirjastoseura r.y. – Finlands Vetenskapliga Biblioteksamfund r. f.
   (Finland), 227
Svaz knihovniku a informacních pracovniku CR (Czech Republic), 205
Svensk Biblioteksförening (Sweden), 470
Svensk förening för informationsspecialister (Sweden), 471
Svenska Arkivsamfundet (Sweden), 472
Svenska Musikbiblioteksföreningen (Sweden), 473
Swaziland Library Association (Swaziland), 466
Swedish Association for Information Specialists (Sweden), 471
Swedish Branch of the International Association of Music Libraries, Archives and
   Documentation Centres / IAML-Swedish Branch (Sweden), 473
Swedish Library Association (Sweden), 470
Tanzania Library Association (Tanzania), 481
Thai Library Association (Thailand), 483
The Association of Thai Archives (Thailand), 482
The Bibliographical Society (United Kingdom), 498
The Chartered Institute of Library and Information Professionals in Ireland (United
   Kingdom), 504
The coordinating Committee for Japanese University Libraries (Japan), 326
The Finnish Library Association (Finland), 225
The Finnish-Swedish Library Association (Finland), 223
The Lebanese Library Association (Lebanon), 356
The Libraries and Documents Association of Syria (Syria), 478
The Library Assembly of Eurasia (Russia), 073
The Library Association of Ireland (Ireland), 301
The Library Campaign (United Kingdom), 512
The Manuscript Society (United States of America), 579
The Netherlands Public Library Association (Netherlands), 392
The Swedish Archival Association (Sweden), 472
Theatre Library Association (United States of America), 594
Theological Library Association (Netherlands), 394
Tietoasiantuntijat ry (Finland), 228

Index of Associations

Tonga Library Association (Tonga), 484
Towarzystwa Nauczycieli Bibliotekarzy Szkól Polskich (Poland), 435
Türk Kütüphaneciler Dernegi (Turkey), 486
Turkish Librarians' Association (Turkey), 486
U.S. National Commission on Libraries and Information Science (United States of America), 595
Udruzenje bibliotekara Crne Gore (Montenegro), 375
Üniversite ve Arastirma Kütüphanecileri Dernegi (Turkey), 487
Uganda Library and Information Association (Uganda), 489
UKB (Samenwerkingsverband van de Universiteitsbibliotheken, de Koninklijke Bibliotheek en de Bibliotheek van de Koninklijke Nederlandse Akademie van Wetenschappen) (Netherlands), 391
UKOLN (United Kingdom), 529
Ukrainian Library Association (Ukraine), 490
Ukrainska bibliotechna asociacia (Ukraine), 490
University and Research Librarians Association (Turkey), 487
University Health and Medical Librarians Group (United Kingdom), 530
University Hospital Medical Information Network (Japan), 341
University Medical School Librarians Group (United Kingdom), 531
University of São Paulo Integrated Library System (Brazil), 146
Upplýsing – Félag bókasafns- og upplýsingafræða (Iceland), 290
Urban Libraries Council (United States of America), 596
Uruguayan Library Association (Uruguay), 600
Uzbekistan Library Association (Uzbekistan), 601
Verband der Biblioheken des Landes Nordrhein-Westfalen (Germany), 272
Verband Österreichischer Archivarinnen und Archivare (Austria), 125
Verein Deutscher Archivarinnen und Archivare e. V. (Germany), 273
Verein Deutscher Bibliothekare e. V. (Germany), 274
Vereinigung der juristischen Bibliotheken der Schweiz / Association des bibliothèques juridiques suisses (Switzerland), 476
Vereinigung deutscher Wirtschaftsarchivare e. V. (Germany), 275
Vereinigung Österreichischer Bibliothekarinnen und Bibliothekare (Austria), 126
Vereinigung Schweizerischer Archivare Associazione degli Archivisti Svizzeri / Uniun da las archivarias e dals archivaris svizzers (Switzerland), 477
Vereniging Openbare Bibliotheeken in Nederland (Netherlands), 392
Vereniging van Pers- en Omroepdocumentalisten (Netherlands), 393
Vereniging van Religieus-Wetenschappelijke Bibliothecarissen (Belgium), 134
Vereniging voor het Theologisch Bibliothecariaat (Netherlands), 394
Virgin Islands Library Association / St. Croix Library Association (United Kingdom), 532
Visual Resources Association (United States of America), 597
Vlaamse Vereniging voor Bibliotheek-, Archief- en Documentatiewezen (Belgium), 135
Welsh Library Association (United Kingdom), 507
Women's National Book Association inc. (United States of America), 598
Working Group Art and Museum Libraries (Germany), 251
Young Adult Library Services Association (United States of America), 599
Zambia Library Association (Zambia), 602

Zenkoku Gakkou Kouritsu Toshokan Kyougikai (Japan), 342
Zenkoku Rekishi Shiryo Hozon Riyo Kikan Renraku Kyogikai (Japan), 343
Zhongguo Kexue Jishu Qingbao Xuehui (China), 194
Zimbabwe Library Association (Zimbabwe), 603
Zveza Bibliotekarskih Drustev Slovenije (Slovenia), 454

List of Acronyms

AABevK (Arbeitsgemeinschaft der Archive und Bibliotheken in der Evangelischen Kirche), 247
AAE (Associazione Archivistica Ecclesiastica), 308
AAHSL (Association of Academic Health Sciences Libraries), 548
AALL (American Association of Law Libraries), 534
AAS (Arkivradet), 467
AASL (Association of Architecture School Librarians), 549
ABADCAM (Association des Bibliothécaires, Archivistes, Documentalistes et Muséographes du Cameroun), 154
ABADIN (Asociación de Bibliotecarios, Archivistas, Documentalistas e Informáticos), 100
ABBA (Asociación de Bibliotecas Biomedicas Argentinas), 103
ABCF (Association des Bibliothèques Chrétiennes de France), 232
ABD/BVD (Association Belge de Documentation / Belgische Vereniging voor Documentatie), 131
ABDC (Association des Bibliothécaires et Documentalistes Cambodgiens), 153
ABDOS (Arbeitsgemeinschaft der Bibliotheken und Dokumentationsstellen der Ost-, Ostmittel- und Südosteuropaforschung e.V.), 248
ABECIN (Associaçao Brasileira de Educação em Ciência da Informação), 140
ABEI (Associazione dei Bibliotecari Ecclesiastici Italiani), 310
ABES (Agence Bibliographique de l'Enseignement Supérieur), 229
ABF (Association des Bibliothécaires de France), 231
ABGID (Association Burkinabé des Gestionnaires de l'Information Documentaire), 150
ABGRA (Asociación de Bibliotecarios Graduados), 419
ABINIA (Asociación de Estados Iberoamericanos para el Desarrollo de la Bibliotecas de Iberoamérica), 009
ABL (Association des Bibliothèques du Liban), 356
ABR (Asociatia Bibliotecarilor din România), 438
ABTAPL (Association of British Theological and Philosophical Libraries), 493
ABU (Asociación de Bibliotecólogos del Uruguay), 600
ACA (Association of Canadian Archivists), 156
ACARM (Association of Commonwealth Archivists and Records Managers), 024
ACB (Association des Conservateurs de Bibliothèques), 233
ACL (Association of Christian Librarians), 550
ACMLA/ACACC (Association of Canadian Map Libraries and Archives/Association des Cartothèques et des Archives Canadiennes), 157
ACRL (Association of College and Research Libraries), 551
ACURIL (Association of Caribbean University, Research and Institutional Libraries), 023
ADAB (Asociación de Titulados Universitarios en Documentación y Biblioteconomía), 460
ADBGV (Association des directeurs des bibliothèques municipales et intercommunales des grandes villes de France), 235
ADBS (Association des professionnels de l'information et de la documentation), 238
ADBU (Association des Directeurs et des personnels de direction des Bibliothèques Universitaires et de la Documentation), 236

List of Acronyms

ADDNB (Association pour le Développement des Documents Numériques en Bibliothèques), 241
ADEBD (Association des Diplômés de l'École de Bibliothécaires-Documentalistes), 234
ADG (Association des documentalistes du Gabon), 244
ADMA (Igud Menahalei Archyyionim Ba-Rashuiot Ha-Mekomyiot), 304
AFFIRM (Association for Federal Information Resources Management), 541
AFIA (Association Francophone d'Informatique en Agriculture), 019
AFLI (Arab Federation for Libraries and Information), 003
AGDAB (Association Guineenne des Documentalistes, Archivistes et Bibliothecaires), 281
AGLIN (Australian Government Libraries Information Network), 108
AGMB (Arbeitsgemeinschaft für Medizinisches Bibliothekswesen), 256
AHDI (Asociación Hispana de Documentalistas en Internet), 010
AHILA (Association for Health Information and Libraries in Africa), 015
AIAF (Association Internationale des Archives Francophones), 020
AIB (Associazione Italiana Biblioteche), 311
AIBDA (Asociación Interamericana de Bibliotecarios, Documentalistas y Especialistas en Información Agrícola), 011
AIDA (Associazione Italiana per la Documentazione Avanzata), 312
AIESI (Association Internationale des Écoles des Sciences de l'Information), 022
AIFBD (Association internationale francophone des bibliothécaires documentalistes), 151
AIIM (Association for Information and Image Management), 542
AIIP (Association of Independent Information Professionals), 552
AILA (American Indian Library Association), 001
AIS (Association of Information Specialists), 245
AISP (Association of Information Systems Professionals), 554
AjBD (Arbeitsgemeinschaft für juristisches Bibliotheks- und Dokumentationswesen), 255
AJL (Association of Jewish Libraries), 555
AKMB (Arbeitsgemeinschaft der Kunst- und Museumsbibliotheken), 251
AKThB (Arbeitsgemeinschaft Katholisch-Theologischer Bibliotheken), 258
ALA (American Library Association), 536
ALAP (Agricultural Librarians Association of the Philippines), 422
ALBAD (Association Luxembourgeoise des Bibliothécaires, Archvistes et Documentalistes), 359
ALC (Africana Librarians Council), 533
ALCC (Australian Libraries Copyright Committee), 110
ALCTS (Association for Library Collections and Technical Services), 544
ALHHS (Association of Librarians in the History of the Health Sciences), 556
ALIA (Australian Library and Information Association), 111
ALISE (Association for Library and Information Science Education), 543
ALLA (Australian Law Librarians Association), 109
ALLCU (Association of Librarians in Land-Based Colleges and Universities), 495
ALSC (Association for Library Service to Children), 545
ALTAFF (Association for Library Trustees, Advocates, Friends and Foundations), 546
AMABPAC (Asociación Mexicana de Archivos y Bibliotecas Privados, A.C.), 369
AMBAC (Asociación Mexicana de Bibliotecarios, A.C.), 013
AMBAD (Association Malienne des Bibliothécaires, Archivistes et Documentalistes), 364

AMHL (Association of Mental Health Librarians), 557
AMIA (Association of Moving Image Archivists), 558
AMTEC (Association for Media and Technology in Education in Canada), 155
ANABAD (Asociación Española de Archiveros, Bibliotecarios, Museólogos y Documentalistas), 461
ANAI (Associazione Nazionale Archivistica Italiana), 313
ANAID (Asociación Nacional de Administradores de la Información Documental, A.C.), 370
ANBPR (National Association of Public Libraries and Librarians in Romania), 441
ANDEP (Association Nationale des Documentalistes de l'Enseignement Privé), 240
ANIBIPA (Asociación Nicaragüense de Bibliotecarios y Profesionales Afines), 403
ANZMapS (Australian and New Zealand Map Circle), 106
ANZSI (Australian and New Zealand Society of Indexers), 107
ANZTLA (Australian and New Zealand Theological Library Association Ltd), 026
APALA (Asian Pacific American Librarians Association), 540
APBB (Arbeitsgemeinschaft der Parlaments- und Behördenbibliotheken), 252
APBD (Association Professionnelle des Bibliothécaires et Documentalistes), 133
APDIS (Associação Portuguesa de Documentação e Informação de Saúde), 436
APLA (Association of Parliamentary Libraries of Australasia), 025
APLIC-I (Association for Population/Family Planning Libraries and Information Centers – International), 018
APLIC/ABPAC (Association of Parliamentary Librarians in Canada/Association des Bibliothécaires Parlementaires au Canada), 158
Arabcin (Arab Club for Information), 002
ARANZ (Archives and Records Association of New Zealand, Inc.), 395
ARBICA (Arab Regional Branch of the International Council on Archives), 004
ARL (Association of Research Libraries), 559
ARLIS-ANZ (Arts Libraries Society of Australia and New Zealand), 008
ARLIS/NA (Art Libraries Society of North America), 007
ARLIS/UK & Ireland (Art Libraries Society of the United Kingdom & the Republic of Ireland), 491
ARMA International (Association for Information Management Professionals), 016
ARSC (Association for Recorded Sound Collections), 547
ASA (Australian Society of Archivists (Inc.)), 113
ASAIB (Association of South African Indexers and Bibliographers), 455
ASBAD (Association Sénégalaise des Bibliothécaires, Archivistes et Documentalistes), 447
ASBL (Association des Bibliothécaires Belges d'Expression Française), 132
ASBL/VZW (Archives et Bibliothèques de Belgique / Archief- en Bibliotheekwezen in België), 130
ASCEL (Association of Senior Children's and Education Librarians), 496
ASCLA (Association of Specialized and Cooperative Library Agencies), 560
ASCOLBI (Asociación Colombiana de Bibliotecologos y Documentalistas), 195
ASCUBI (Asociación Cubana de Bibliotecarios), 201
ASI (American Society of Indexers), 538
ASIDIC (Association of Information and Dissemination Centers), 553

ASIS&T (American Society for Information Science and Technology), 537
ASLA (Australian School Library Association), 112
ASLIB (Aslib Informatuion Ltd), 492
ASLP (Association of Special Libraries of the Philippines), 423
ASNID (Association des Spécialistes Nigériens de l'Information Documentaire), 404
ASpB (Arbeitsgemeinschaft der Spezialbibliotheken e.V.), 254
ASSOCLE (Association des Amis de la Lecture), 136
ASTED (Association pour l'Avancement des Sciences et des Techniques de la Documentation), 159
ASTI (Association Française des Sciences et Technologies de l'information), 239
ATLA (American Theological Library Association), 539
ATSILIRN (Aboriginal & Torres Strait Islander Library & Information Resource Network), 105
AUKML (Association of UK Media Librarians), 497
AVSL (Association of Vision Science Librarians), 561
AY-AF (Arkistoyhdistys r.y. – Arkivföreningen r.f.), 221
BAD (Associaçâo Portuguesa de Bibliotecários, Arquivistas e Documentalistas), 014
BAILER (British Association for Information and Library Education and Research), 501
BCA (Bureau of Canadian Archivists / Bureau Canadien des Archivistes), 162
BDS (Associazione Bibliotecari Documentalisti Sanita), 309
BETH (Bibliothèques Européenne de Théologie), 029
BF (Bibliotekarforbundet: Forbundet for Informationsspecialister og kulturformidlere), 207
BIALL (British and Irish Association of Law Librarians), 500
BIASLIC (Britain and Ireland Association of Aquatic Sciences Libraries and Information Centres), 499
BIB (Berufsverband Information Bibliothek e.V.), 260
BID (Deutscher Bibliotheks- und Informationsverband e.V.), 264
BIS (Bibliothèque Information Suisse), 475
BLA (Business Librarians Association), 503
BLF (Bibliotekslederforeningen), 208
BLIA (Bulgarian Library and Information Association), 149
BMB (Biblioteca Metropolitan Bucaresti), 440
BMF (Bibliothecarii Medicinae Fenniae), 222
BPM (Beta Phi Mu (International Library Science Honor Society)), 027
BRA (British Records Association), 502
BRAIN (Branchevereniging Archiefinstellingen Nederland), 380
BS (Biblioteksstyrelsen), 209
BSA (Bibliographical Society of America), 562
BSANZ (Bibliographical Society of Australia and New Zealand), 028
BSC/SBC (Bibliographical Society of Canada/La Société Bibliographique du Canada), 160
BVÖ (Büchereiverband Österreichs / formerly Verband Österreichischer Volksbüchereien und Volksbibliothekare), 120
CACL (Canadian Association of Children's Librarians), 165

CACUL/ACBCU (Canadian Association of College and University Libraries / Association Canadienne des Bibliothèques de Collège et d'Université), 166
CAIS/ACSI (Canadian Association for Information Science / Association Canadienne des Sciences de l'Information), 163
CALA (Chinese-American Librarians Association), 566
CALL/ACBD (Canadian Association of Law Libraries / Association Canadienne des Bibliothèques de Droit), 168
CAML/ACBM (Canadian Association of Music Libraries (A Branch of the International Association of Music Libraries, Archives and Documentation Centres / Association Canadienne des Bibliothèques Musicales), 169
CAPL (Canadian Association of Public Libraries), 170
CARBICA (Caribbean Archives Association – Regional Branch of the International Council on Archives), 030
CARL/ABRC (Canadian Association of Research Libraries / Association des Bibliothèques de Recherche du Canada), 171
CASL (Canadian Association for School Libraries), 164
CASLIS (Canadian Association of Special Libraries and Information Services), 172
CAUL (Council of Australian University Librarians), 037
CBHL (Council on Botanical and Horticultural Libraries, Inc.), 038
CBP (Colegio de Bibliotecólogos del Perú), 420
CCA (Canadian Council of Archives / Conseil Canadien des Archives), 173
CCBES (Comité de Cooperación Bibliotecaria de El Salvador), 217
CCL (Central Catholic Library Association, Inc.), 299
CCS (Stichting Cultureel Centrum Suriname), 465
CDNL (Conference of Directors of National Libraries), 034
CDNLAO (Conference of Directors of Directors of National Libraries of Asia and Oceania), 033
CEAL (Council on East Asian Libraries, Inc.), 570
CENL (Conference of European National Librarians), 035
CFB (Conselho Federal de Biblioteconomia), 142
CHLA/ABSC (Canadian Health Libraries Association / Association des Bibliothèques de la Santé du Canada), 175
CILA (Chinese Information Literacy Association), 479
CILIP (Chartered Institute of Library and Information Professionals), 506
CILIP Wales (Sefydliad Siartredig Llyfrgellwyr a Gweithwyr Gwybodaeth Cymru), 523
CILIPS (Chartered Institute of Library and Information Professionals in Scotland), 505
CLA (Catholic Library Association), 563
CLIR (Council on Library and Information Resources), 571
CLS (Cumann Leabharlannaithe Scoile), 302
CLTA (Canadian Library Trustees Association), 177
CNB (Colegio Nacional de Bibliotecarios, A.C.), 371
CNI (Coalition for Networked Information), 568
COLT (Council on Library/Media Technicians), 039
COMLA (Commonwealth Library Association), 032
CONSAL (Congress of South-East Asian Libraries), 036
CONSALD (Committee on South Asian Libraries and Documentation), 569

List of Acronyms

CONZUL (Council of New Zealand University Librarians), 396
COPPUL (Council of Prairie and Pacific University Libraries), 180
COSLA (Chief Officers of State Library Agencies), 565
CRL (Center for Research Libraries), 564
CSC (Cultural Service Centre Austria), 121
CSLA (Church and Synagogue Library Association), 567
CSSTI (Zhongguo Kexue Jishu Qingbao Xuehui), 194
CUUL (Consortium of Uganda University Libraries), 488
DB (Danmarks Biblioteksforening), 210
DB BiH (Drustvo Bibliotekara Bosne i Hercegovine), 138
DBV (Deutscher Bibliotheksverband e.V.), 265
DELNET (Developing Library Network), 291
DF (Danmarks Forskningsbibliotheksforening), 211
DGI (Deutsche Gesellschaft für Informationswissenschaft und Informationspraxis e.V.), 262
DMBF (Dansk Musikbiblioteks Forening), 213
DVMD e. V. (Deutscher Verband Medizinischer Dokumentare e.V.), 266
EAHIL (European Association for Health Information and Libraries), 040
EALRGA (East Asian Library Resources Group of Australia), 114
EBLIDA (European Bureau of Library, Information and Documentation Associations), 045
ECLA (Evangelical Church Library Association), 572
EIA (European Information Association), 046
ELA (Eesti Raamatukoguhoidjate Ühing), 219
eliport (Evangelisches Literaturportal e.V.), 267
ELISAD (European Association of Libraries and Information Services on Alcohol and Other Drugs), 044
ELNIT Association (International Association of Users and Developers of Electronic Libraries and New Information Technologies), 061
EUCLID (European Association for Library and Information Education and Research), 041
EURASLIC (European Association of Aquatic Sciences Libraries and Information Centres), 042
EUSIDIC (European Association of Information Services), 043
EYLN (Early Years Library Network), 508
FADBEN (Fédération des enseignants documentalistes de l'Éducation nationale), 242
FAVL (Friends of African Village Libraries), 049
FBF (Forskerforbundets Bibliotekforening), 409
FEBAB (Federação Brasileira de Associações de Bibliotecários, Cientistas da Informação e Instituições), 144
FEBAB/CBBCU (Federaçao Brasileira de Associaçoes de Bibliotecários – Comissao Brasileira de Bibliotecas Centrais Universitárias), 145
FESABID (Federación Española de Sociedades de Archivística, Biblioteconomía, Documentación y Museística), 462
FIAF (Fédération Internationale des Archives du Film), 047
FLA (Suomen Kirjastoseura – Finlands Biblioteksförening), 225
FLCS (Federal Libraries Coordination Secretariat), 182

FLICC (Federal Library and Information Center Committee), 573
FOBID (FOBID Netherlands Library Forum), 382
FOLA (Friends of Libraries Australia Incorporated), 115
For ATL (Forum of Asian Theological Libraries), 048
FRP Canada (Canadian Association of Family Resource Programs), 167
GBDL (Gesellschaft für Bibliothekswesen und Dokumentation des Landbaues – Fachliche Arbeitsgemeinschaft der ASpB), 268
GfKl (Gesellschaft für Klassifikation e.V.), 269
GIDIF-RBM (Gruppo Italiano Documentalisti dell'industria Farmaceutica e degli Istituti di Ricerca Biomedica), 314
GLA (Guyana Library Association), 283
GMDS (Deutsche Gesellschaft für Medizinische Informatik, Biometrie und Epidemiologie e.V.), 263
HAD (Hrvatsko Arhivisticko Drustvo), 199
HIANZ (Health Information Association of New Zealand), 397
HIMAA (Health Information Management Association of Australia Ltd.), 116
HKLA (Hong Kong Library Association), 189
HKTLA (Hong Kong Teacher Librarians' Association), 190
IAA (Igud Ha'arkhiyy Yona Yim Be-Israel), 303
IAALD (International Association of Agricultural Infornation Specialities), 052
IADA (Internationale Arbeitsgemeinschaft der Archiv-, Bibliotheks-, und Graphikrestauratoren), 070
IALL (International Association of Law Libraries), 055
IAMIC (International Association of Music Information Centres), 056
IAML (UK&Irl) (International Association of Music Libraries, Archives and Documentation Centres – United Kingdom and Ireland Branch), 509
IAML-Australian Branch (International Association of Music Libraries, Archives and Documentation Centres, Australian Branch), 383
IAML Italia (Sezione Italiana dell'International Association of Music Libraries, Archives and Documentation Centres), 315
IAML-NZ (International Association of Music Libraries, Archives and Documentation Centres, New Zealand Branch, Incorporated), 398
IAML-US (International Association of Music Libraries, Archives, and Documentation Centres – United States Branch), 575
IAML; AIBM; IVMB (Association Internationale des Bibliothèques, Archives et Centres de Documentation Musicaux/Internationale Vereinigung der Musikbibliotheken, Musikarchive und Musikdokumentationszentren), 021
IAMSLIC (International Association of Aquatic and Marine Science Libraries and Information Centers), 053
IAOL (International Association of Orientalist Librarians), 057
IASA (International Association of Sound and Audiovisual Archives), 060
IASL (International Association of School Librarianship), 058
IASLIC (Indian Association of Special Libraries and Information Centres), 292
IASSIST (International Association for Social Sciences Information Services and Technology), 051
IATLIS (Indian Association of Teachers of Library and Information Science), 050

List of Acronyms 424

IATUL (International Association of Scientific and Technological University Libraries), 059
ICA; CIA (International Council on Archives / Conseil International des Archives), 063
ICLC (Internet Chinese Librarians Club), 071
ICSTI (International Council for Scientific and Technical Information), 062
IFIP (International Federation for Information Processing), 064
IFLA (International Federation of Library Associations and Institutions), 065
IGBIS (LIASA Interest Group for Bibliographic Standards), 456
IGPL (International Group of Publishing Libraries), 066
ILISA (Iranian Library and Information Science Association), 297
INASP (International Network for the Availability of Scientific Publications), 068
INEP (Instituto Nacional de Estudos e Pesquisa), 282
INFOSTA (Jouhou Kagaku Gijutsu Kyokai), 322
Infoterm (International Information Centre for Terminology), 067
Interdoc (Association des Documentalistes de Collectivités Territoriales), 237
IPA (Information Processing Association of Israel), 305
IPI (Ikatan Pustakawan Indonesia), 296
IRLA (Independent Research Libraries Association), 574
ISA (Cumann Cartlannaíochta Éireann), 300
ISC/SCI (Indexing and Abstracting Society of Canada / Société Canadienne d'indexation), 183
ISKO (International Society for Knowledge Organization e.V.), 069
IVMB – Deutsche Gruppe/BRD; IAML-FRG (Internationale Vereinigung der Musikbibliotheken, Musikarchive und Musikdokumentationszentren – Gruppe Bundesrepublik Deutschland), 270
JADS (Ato Dokyumenteshon Kenkyukai), 317
JASPUL (Shiritsu Daigaku Toshokan Kyokai), 338
JBS (Vereinigung der juristischen Bibliotheken der Schweiz / Association des bibliothèques juridiques suisses), 476
JLG (Japan Library Group), 510
JLIA (Jordan Library and Information Association), 344
JMLA (Nihon Igaku Toshokan Kyokai), 331
JSAS (Nihon Akaibuzu Gakkai), 330
JSIMS (Japan Society for Information and Media Studies), 320
JSLIS (Nihon Toshokan Joho Gakkai), 333
KLSS (Korean Library and Information Science Society), 350
KODAIKYO (Kouritsu Daigaku Kyokai Toshokan Kyogikai), 328
KOSIM (Korean Society for Information Management), 352
KVAN (Koninklijke Vereniging van Archivarissen in Nederland), 384
LAB (Library Association of Barbados), 128
LAC (Chung-kuo t'u-shu-kuan hsüeh-hui), 480
LAE (The Library Assembly of Eurasia), 073
LAI (Cumann Leabharlann na h-Éireann), 301
LAS (Library Association of Singapore), 451
LATT (Library Association of Trinidad and Tobago), 485
LBB, LAL (Latvijas Bibliotekāru bierdrība), 354

LCF (Librarians' Christian Fellowship), 511
LIAJA (Library and Information Association of Jamaica), 316
LIANZA (Library and Information Association of New Zealand Aotearoa), 399
LIASA (Library and Information Association of South Africa), 457
LIBER (Ligue des Bibliothèques Européennes de Recherche), 074
LIPA (Legal Information Preservation Alliance), 072
LITA (Library and Information Technology Association), 576
LLA (Lesotho Library Association), 357
LLAMA (Library Leadership and Management Association), 577
LPB (Library Promotion Bureau), 415
LPRC (Library Public Relations Council), 578
LSBA (Latvijas Skolu bibliotekāru asociācija), 355
LWSVO (Landelijke Werkgroep Schoolmediathecarissen Voortgezet Onderwijs), 385
MAA (Media Archives Austria), 122
MAHLAP (Medical and Health Librarians Association of the Philippines), 424
MaLIA (Malta Library and Information Association), 365
MELA (Middle East Librarians Association), 077
MILA (Marshall Islands Library Association), 366
MKE/AHL (Magyar Könyvtárosok Egyesülete), 286
MLA (Music Library Association, Inc), 582
MLAI (Medical Library Association of India), 293
MLE (Magyar Levéltárosok Egyesülete), 287
MLG (Medical Librarians Group of Malaysia), 361
MLIMA (Macau Library and Information Management Association), 192
MOKSZ (Magyar Orvosi Könyvtárak Szövetsége), 288
MOLA (Major Orchestra Librarians' Association), 075
MPLA (Mountain Plains Library Association), 581
NA (Norsk Arkivråd), 410
NAFIPS (North American Fuzzy Information Processing Society), 080
NAGARA (National Association of Government Archives and Records Administrators), 583
NAMHI (Nordic Association for Medical and Health Information), 079
NASCIO (National Association of State Information Resource Executives), 584
NASLIN (North American Sport Library Network), 081
NATLL (National Association of Toy and Leisure Libraries), 515
NBF (Norsk Bibliotekforening), 411
NBLC (Nederlandse Bibliotheek Dienst), 386
NCA (National Committee of Archivists), 294
NCLIS (U.S. National Commission on Libraries and Information Science), 595
NERL (NorthEast Research Libraries Association), 587
NFAIS (National Federation of Abstracting and Information Services), 586
NFF (Norsk Fagbibliotekforening), 412
NGLIS (Network of Government Library and Information Specialists), 516
NITOKYO; JLA (Nihon Toshokan Kyokai), 335
NITTOKEN; NAL (Nihon Toshokan Kenkyukai), 334
NLA (Nigerian Library Association), 405

NOTOKYO; JAALD (Nihon Nougaku Toshokan Kyogikai), 332
NVB (Nederlandse Vereniging van Beroepsbeoefenaren in de Bibliotheek-, Informatie- en Kennissector), 387
NZLLA (New Zealand Law Librarians Inc.), 400
NZSA (New Zealand Society of Archivists), 401
ÖGDI (Österreichische Gesellschaft für Dokumentation und Information), 124
OSALL (Organisation of South African Law Libraries), 458
P.A.I.D. (Pharma Arbeitskreis Information und Dokumentation), 271
PAARL (Philippine Association of Academic and Research Librarians), 425
PakLAG (Pakistan Library Automation Goup), 417
PARBICA (Pacific Regional Branch of the International Council on Archives), 083
PASL (Philippine Association of School Librarians), 426
PATLS (Philippine Association of Teachers of Library Science), 427
PGLL (Philippine Group of Law Librarians, Inc.), 428
PIALA (Pacific Islands Association of Libraries, Archives and Museums), 082
PLA (Public Library Association), 589
PLAI (Philippine Library Association, Inc., Headquarters), 429
PLG (Progressive Librarians Guild), 588
PLIA (Palestinian Library and Information Association), 418
PPLL (Philippine Public Librarians League, Inc.), 430
PPM (Persatuan Perpustakaan Malaysia), 362
PTLDC (Provincial and Territorial Library Directors Council), 184
PZB (Polski Zwiazek Bibliotek), 084
RBA, RLA (Rossiiskaya Bibliotechnaya Assotsiatsiya), 443
RESCOLINC (Research Council Libraries&Information Consortium), 518
RIKAR (Research Institute for Korean Archives and Records), 353
RLIT (Red Latinoamericana de Información Teológica), 086
RLUK (Research Libraries UK), 519
RMAA (Records Management Association of Australia), 118
RMS (Records Management Society of Great Britain), 517
SAA (Society of American Archivists), 591
SAI (Sociedad Argentina de Información), 088
SALALM (Seminar on the Acquisition of Latin American Library Materials), 087
SALIS (Substance Abuse Librarians&Information Specialists), 095
SAP (Stowarzyszenie Archivistów Polskich), 433
SASA (Suid-Africaanse Vereniging van Archivarisse), 459
SBP; PLA (Stowarzyszenie Bibliotekarzy Polskich), 434
SBPR (Sociedad de Bibliotecarios de Puerto Rico), 437
SCA (Sociedad Columbiana de Archivistas), 196
SCANUL-ECS (Standing Conference of African National and University Libraries in Eastern, Central and Southern Africa), 092
SCAULWA (Standing Conference of African University Libraries, Western Area), 093
SCECSAL (Standing Conference of Eastern, Central and Southern African Librarians), 094
SCL (Society of Chief Librarians), 525
SCLA (Virgin Islands Library Association / St. Croix Library Association), 532

SCOLMA (Standing Conference on Library Materials on Africa), 528
SCONUL (Society of College, National and University Libraries), 526
SEDIC (Sociedad Española de Documentación e Información Científica), 464
SEK (Spolok slovenskych knihovnikov), 452
SEMEL ASMI (Israeli Society of Libraries and Information Centers), 307
SENTOKYO; JSLA (Senmon Toshokan Kyogikai), 337
SFSIC (Société Française des Sciences de l'Information et de la Communication), 243
SHINE (Scottish Health Information Network), 522
SHITANTOKYO (Shiritsu Tanki Daigaku Toshokan Kyogikai), 339
SI (Society of Indexers), 527
SIBMAS (Société Internationale des Bibliothèques et des Musées des Arts du Spectacle), 089
SIS (Society for Information Science), 295
SKIP (Svaz knihovniku a informacních pracovniku CR), 205
SLA (Special Libraries Association), 593
SLAALIS (Sierra Leone Association of Archivists, Librarians and Information Scientists), 450
SLANZA (School Library Association of New Zealand Aotearoa), 402
SLLA (Sri Lanka Library Association), 091
SMBF (Svenska Musikbiblioteksföreningen), 473
SOCICT (Sociedad Cubana de Ciencias de la Información), 202
SSLI (Society of School Librarians International), 592
SWALA (Swaziland Library Association), 466
SWARBICA (South and West Asian Regional Branch of the International Council on Archives), 090
TiAs (Tietoasiantuntijat ry), 228
TKD (Türk Kütüphaneciler Dernegi), 486
TLA (Theatre Library Association), 594
TLS (Svensk förening för informationsspecialister), 471
TOHYOP; KLA (Hanguk Tosogwan Hyophoe), 349
ÜNAK (Üniversite ve Arastirma Kütüphanecileri Dernegi), 487
UHMLG (University Health and Medical Librarians Group), 530
ULA (Uzbekistan Library Association), 601
ULC (Urban Libraries Council), 596
ULIA (Uganda Library and Information Association), 489
UMIN (University Hospital Medical Information Network), 341
UMSLG (University Medical School Librarians Group), 531
USP/SIBi (Sistema Integrado de Bibliotecas da Universidade de São Paulo), 146
V.R.B (Vereniging van Religieus-Wetenschappelijke Bibliothecarissen), 134
VdA (Verein Deutscher Archivarinnen und Archivare e.V.), 273
VDB (Verein Deutscher Bibliothekare e.V.), 274
VdW (Vereinigung deutscher Wirtschaftsarchivare e.V.), 275
VÖA (Verband Österreichischer Archivarinnen und Archivare), 125
VÖB (Vereinigung Österreichischer Bibliothekarinnen und Bibliothekare), 126
VOGIN (Nederlandse Vereniging van Gebruikers van Online Informatiesystemen), 388
VPOD (Vereniging van Pers- en Omroepdocumentalisten), 393

VRA (Visual Resources Association), 597
VSA/AAS/AAS/UAS (Vereinigung Schweizerischer Archivare Associazione degli Archivisti Svizzeri / Uniun da las archivarias e dals archivaris svizzers), 477
VTB (Vereniging voor het Theologisch Bibliothecariaat), 394
VVBAD (Vlaamse Vereniging voor Bibliotheek-, Archief- en Documentatiewezen), 135
WLA (Cymdeithas Llyfrgelloedd Cymru), 507
WNBA (Women's National Book Association inc.), 598
YAKUTOKYO; JPLA (Nihon Yakugaku Toshokan Kyogikai), 336
YALSA (Young Adult Library Services Association), 599
ZBDS (Zveza Bibliotekarskih Drustev Slovenije), 454
ZENKOKU SLA; JSLA (Zenkoku Gakkou Kouritsu Toshokan Kyougikai), 342
ZLA (Zimbabwe Library Association), 603

Index of Official Journal

A

AASL Hotlinks (American Association of School Librarians), 535
ABD-BVD INFO (Association Belge de Documentation / Belgische Vereniging voor Documentatie), 131
ABDOS-Mitteilungen (Arbeitsgemeinschaft der Bibliotheken und Dokumentationsstellen der Ost-, Ostmittel- und Südosteuropaforschung e.V.), 248
ABM-Skrift; Scandinavian Public Library Quarterly (ABM-utvikling – Statens senter for arkiv, bibliotek og museum), 406
ACARM Newsletter (Association of Commonwealth Archivists and Records Managers), 024
Acceso (Sociedad de Bibliotecarios de Puerto Rico), 437
ACCESS (Australian School Library Association), 112
Actualidades Bibliotecológicas (Asociación de Bibliotecólogos del Uruguay), 600
ACURIL Newsletter/Carta Informativa (Association of Caribbean University, Research and Institutional Libraries), 023
African Research & Documentation (Standing Conference on Library Materials on Africa), 528
Africana Libraries Newsletter (Africana Librarians Council), 533
Agenda del bibliotecario (Associazione Italiana Biblioteche), 311
AIB Notizie (Associazione Italiana Biblioteche), 311
AIDA Informazioni (Associazione Italiana per la Documentazione Avanzata), 312
AIS newsletter (Association of Information Specialists), 245
Akaibuzu Kenkyu (Nihon Akaibuzu Gakkai), 330
ALLCU Bulletin (Association of Librarians in Land-Based Colleges and Universities), 495
Allgemeine Mitteilungen (Arbeitsgemeinschaft der Archive und Bibliotheken in der Evangelischen Kirche), 247
American Archivist (Society of American Archivists), 591
American Indian Libraries Newsletter (American Indian Library Association), 001
American Libraries (American Library Association), 536
AMIA Newsletter (Association of Moving Image Archivists), 558
An Leabharlann. The Irish Library (Cumann Leabharlann na h-Éireann), 301
Anai Notizie (Associazione Nazionale Archivistica Italiana), 313
ANZTLA Newsletter (Australian and New Zealand Theological Library Association Ltd), 026
APALA Newsletter (Asian Pacific American Librarians Association), 540
AppliCommunicator (Association for Population/Family Planning Libraries and Information Centers – International), 018
ARBIDO (Vereinigung Schweizerischer Archivare Associazione degli Archivisti Svizzeri / Uniun da las archivarias e dals archivaris svizzers), 477
ARC Magazine (Society of Archivists), 524
Archiv und Wirtschaft (Vereinigung deutscher Wirtschaftsarchivare e.V.), 275
Archiva Ecclesiae (Associazione Archivistica Ecclesiastica), 308
Archivar. Zeitschrift für Archivwesen (Verein Deutscher Archivarinnen und Archivare e.V.), 273

Archivaria (Association of Canadian Archivists), 156
Archives (British Records Association), 502
Archives and Manuscripts (Australian Society of Archivists (Inc.)), 113
Archives et Bibliothèques de Belgique/Archief- en Bibliotheekwezen in België (Archives et Bibliothèques de Belgique / Archief- en Bibliotheekwezen in België), 130
Archivi per la Storia (Associazione Nazionale Archivistica Italiana), 313
Archivum (International Council on Archives / Conseil International des Archives), 063
Archiwista (Stowarzyszenie Archiwistów Polskich), 433
ARHIVI (Arhivsko Drustvo Slovenije), 453
ARKHIYYON (Igud Ha'arkhiyy Yona Yim Be-Israel), 303
Arkiv, samhälle och Forskning (Svenska Arkivsamfundet), 472
ARL: A Bimonthly Report on Research Library Issues and Actions from ARL, CNI, and SPARC (Association of Research Libraries), 559
ARLIS-ANZ Journal (Arts Libraries Society of Australia and New Zealand), 008
ARLIS-Nytt (ARLIS/Norden – Norge. Forening for Kunstbibliotekarbeid), 408
ARLIS/Norden Info (ARLIS/Norden), 006
Arquivo e administraçao (Associaçao dos Arquivistas Brasileiros), 141
ARSC Journal (Association for Recorded Sound Collections), 547
Art Documentation (Art Libraries Society of North America), 007
Art Libraries Journal (Art Libraries Society of the United Kingdom & the Republic of Ireland), 491
ASCUBI Informa (Asociación Cubana de Bibliotecarios), 201
ASIDIC Newsletter (Association of Information and Dissemination Centers), 553
Aslib Managing Information (Aslib Informatuion Ltd), 492
ASLP Bulletin (Association of Special Libraries of the Philippines), 423
Association of Architecture School Librarians Newsletter (Association of Architecture School Librarians), 549
ASTI-Hebdo (Association Française des Sciences et Technologies de l'information), 239
ATLA Newsletter (American Theological Library Association), 539
ATSILIRN Newsletter (Aboriginal & Torres Strait Islander Library & Information Resource Network), 105
Australian Law Librarian (Australian Law Librarians Association), 109
Australian Library Journal (Australian Library and Information Association), 111

B

Bericht über die Tagung (Conference report) (Arbeitsgemeinschaft der Spezialbibliotheken e.V.), 254
BIBLIO (Library Association of Trinidad and Tobago), 485
BiblioMAGAZIN (National Association of Public Libraries and Librarians in Romania), 441
Biblioteca Bucurestilor (Biblioteca Metropolitan Bucaresti), 440
Bibliotekarstvo Godisnjak Drustva Bibliotekara Bosne i Hercegovine (Drustvo Bibliotekara Bosne i Hercegovine), 138
Bibliotekforum (Norsk Bibliotekforening), 411
Biblioteksbladet (BBL) (Svensk Biblioteksförening), 470

Bibliotekspressen (Bibliotekarforbundet: Forbundet for Informationsspecialister og kulturformidlere), 207
Biblioteksvejviser (Danmarks Biblioteksforening), 210
Bibliotheek- en Archiefgids. 1983-. (formerly Bibliotheekgids. 1922–83) (Vlaamse Vereniging voor Bibliotheek-, Archief- en Documentatiewezen), 135
Bibliotheek en Samenleving (Nederlandse Bibliotheek Dienst), 386
Bibliotheksdienst (Deutscher Bibliotheksverband e.V.), 265
Bibliotheksdienst: Organ der Bundesvereinigung Deutscher Bibliotheksverbände (Bibliothek&Information Deutschland), 261
Bibliothèque(s) (Association des Bibliothécaires de France), 231
Biblos: Österreichische Zeitschrift für Buch- und Bibliothekswesen. Dokumentation. Bibliographie und Bibliophilie (Vereinigung Österreichischer Bibliothekarinnen und Bibliothekare), 126
Bilten Drustva Bibliotekara Bosne i Hercegovine (Drustvo Bibliotekara Bosne i Hercegovine), 138
Bladen voor Documentatie (Association Belge de Documentation / Belgische Vereniging voor Documentatie), 131
BLATT (Library Association of Trinidad and Tobago), 485
BLOC-Notes (Association Professionnelle des Bibliothécaires et Documentalistes), 133
Boletim (Associaçao dos Arquivistas Brasileiros), 141
Boletim Annual do Departamento do SIBi/USP (Sistema Integrado de Bibliotecas da Universidade de São Paulo), 146
Boletín (Asociación de Bibliotecólogos del Uruguay), 600
Boletín ANABAD (Asociación Española de Archiveros, Bibliotecarios, Museólogos y Documentalistas), 461
Boletín CLIP (Sociedad Española de Documentación e Información Científica), 464
Boletín de la Asociación Bibliotecoiógica de Guatemala (Asociación Bibliotecológica de Guatemala), 280
Boletin de Novedades (Sociedad Española de Documentación e Información Científica), 464
Boletin del Bibliotecario Teológico Latinoamericano (Red Latinoamericana de Información Teológica), 086
Boletín Informativo del CBP (Colegio de Bibliotecólogos del Perú), 420
Boletín Interamericano de Archivos (Asociación Latinoamericana de Archivos), 012
Boletín Online (Asociación Hispana de Documentalistas en Internet), 010
Boletín: Asociación de Bibliotecarios Profesionales (Asociación de Bibliotecarios Profesionales de Rosario), 102
Bolletino AIB (Associazione Italiana Biblioteche), 311
Bolletino di Informacione (Associazione dei Bibliotecari Ecclesiastici Italiani), 310
Botswana Library Association Journal (Botswana Library Association), 139
Briefe zur Klassifikation (Gesellschaft für Klassifikation e.V.), 269
BRIO (International Association of Music Libraries, Archives and Documentation Centres – United Kingdom and Ireland Branch), 509
Broadside (Theatre Library Association), 594
BSANZ Bulletin (Bibliographical Society of Australia and New Zealand), 028

BuB – Forum für Bibliothek und Information (Berufsverband Information Bibliothek e.V.), 260

Bücherei Perspektiven (Büchereiverband Österreichs / formerly Verband Österreichischer Volksbüchereien und Volksbibliothekare), 120

Bulletin d' information de l'ABDC; CLDA Newsletter (Association des Bibliothécaires et Documentalistes Cambodgiens), 153

Bulletin d'Information de l'Association des Diplômés de l'École de Bibliothécaires-Documentalistes (Association des Diplômés de l'École de Bibliothécaires-Documentalistes), 234

Bulletin de l'Informatiste (Association Nationale des Informatistes), 376

Bulletin de la société franco-japonaise des bibliothécaires et des ducumentalistes (Société Franco-Japonaise des Bibliotecaires et des Documentalistes), 340

Bulletin de Liaison de l'ABEF (Association des Bibliothèques Chrétiennes de France), 232

Bulletin de Liaison de l'Association des Documentalistes du Gabon (Association des documentalistes du Gabon), 244

Bulletin of the Association of British Theological & Philosophical Libraries (Association of British Theological and Philosophical Libraries), 493

Bulletin of the Library Assembly of Eurasia (The Library Assembly of Eurasia), 073

Bulletin of the Library Association of Barbados (Library Association of Barbados), 128

Bulletin of the Library Association of China/Chung-kuo t'u-shu-kuan hsüeh-hui hui-pao (Chung-kuo t'u-shu-kuan hsüeh-hui), 480

Bulletin of the Philippine Library Association. Inc. (Philippine Library Association, Inc., Headquarters), 429

Bulletin SKIP (Svaz knihovniku a informacních pracovniku CR), 205

C

C.L.S. Bulletin (Cumann Leabharlannaithe Scoile), 302

Cadernos (Associaçâo Portuguesa de Bibliotecários, Arquivistas e Documentalistas), 014

Cahiers de la Documentation (Association Belge de Documentation / Belgische Vereniging voor Documentatie), 131

CAML review (Canadian Association of Music Libraries (A Branch of the International Association of Music Libraries, Archives and Documentation Centres / Association Canadienne des Bibliothèques Musicales), 169

Canadian Journal of Information Science/Revue Canadienne des Sciences de l'Information (Canadian Association for Information Science / Association Canadienne des Sciences de l'Information), 163

Canadian Journal of Learning and Technology (Association for Media and Technology in Education in Canada), 155

Canadian Law Library Review (Canadian Association of Law Libraries / Association Canadienne des Bibliothèques de Droit), 168

Canadian Library Journal (Canadian Library Association), 176

CAPL newsletter (Canadian Association of Public Libraries), 170

Caribbean Archives (Caribbean Archives Association – Regional Branch of the International Council on Archives), 030

Carta al Bibliotecario (supersedes Boletín de la Asociación Colombiana de Bibliotecarios. 1957–79) (Asociación Colombiana de Bibliotecologos y Documentalistas), 195

Catholic Library World (Catholic Library Association), 563
CBHL Newsletter (Council on Botanical and Horticultural Libraries, Inc.), 038
CDNLAO Newsletter (Conference of Directors of Directors of National Libraries of Asia and Oceania), 033
Children and Libraries (Association for Library Service to Children), 545
Christian Librarian (Librarians' Christian Fellowship), 511
Church & Synagogue Libraries (Church and Synagogue Library Association), 567
Church Libraries (Evangelical Church Library Association), 572
CILIP News (The Chartered Institute of Library and Information Professionals in Ireland), 504
Clearinghouse (National Association of Government Archives and Records Administrators), 583
CLIR Reports (Council on Library and Information Resources), 571
College and Research Libraries (Association of College and Research Libraries), 551
COMLA Newsletter (Commonwealth Library Association), 032
Continuo (International Association of Music Libraries, Archives and Documentation Centres, Australian Branch), 117
Cosas de la ADAB (Asociación de Titulados Universitarios en Documentación y Biblioteconomía), 460
Coyright Bulletin (Australian Libraries Copyright Committee), 110
Crescendo (International Association of Music Libraries, Archives and Documentation Centres, New Zealand Branch, Incorporated), 398
Crossroads (National Association of Government Archives and Records Administrators), 583

D

Daigaku Toshokan Kenkyu (Kouritsu Daigaku Kyokai Toshokan Kyogikai), 328
Danmarks Biblioteker (Danmarks Biblioteksforening), 210
Das audiovisuelle Archiv 1988-. (formerly Das Schallarchiv. 1976–1987) (Media Archives Austria), 122
Deadline (Association of UK Media Librarians), 497
Dec Info (Association Nationale des Documentalistes de l'Enseignement Privé), 240
Der Evangelische Buchberater (Evangelisches Literaturportal e.V.), 267
DF-Revy (Danmarks Forskningsbiblioteksforening), 211
DIK-forum (DIK), 468
Documentaliste-Sciences de l'Information (Association des professionnels de l'information et de la documentation), 238
Documentation et Bibliothèques (Association pour l'Avancement des Sciences et des Techniques de la Documentation), 159
Dokumenteshon Kenkvu (Nihon Nougaku Toshokan Kyogikai), 332
Dokumenteshon Kenkvu (Nihon Yakugaku Toshokan Kyogikai), 336

E

EALRGA Newsletter (East Asian Library Resources Group of Australia), 114
EBLIDA Hot News (European Bureau of Library, Information and Documentation Associations), 045

ELA Yearbook (Eesti Raamatukoguhoidjate Ühing), 219
ELAN Ex Libris Association Newsletter (Ex Libris Association), 181
Elisad journal (European Association of Libraries and Information Services on Alcohol and Other Drugs), 044
EURASLIC Newsletter (European Association of Aquatic Sciences Libraries and Information Centres), 042

F
Feuille de liaison (Association Luxembourgeoise des Bibliothécaires, Archvistes et Documentalistes), 359
Fiji Library Association Journal (formerly Newsletter) (Fiji Library Association), 220
FLICC Newsletter (Federal Library and Information Center Committee), 573
Focus (European Information Association), 046
Focus on The Center for Research Libraries (Center for Research Libraries), 564
Fontes artis musicae (Association Internationale des Bibliothèques, Archives et Centres de Documentation Musicaux/Internationale Vereinigung der Musikbibliotheken, Musikarchive und Musikdokumentationszentren), 021
Forum (International Council for Scientific and Technical Information), 062
Forum Musikbibliothek (Internationale Vereinigung der Musikbibliotheken, Musikarchive und Musikdokumentationszentren – Gruppe Bundesrepublik Deutschland), 270
Fregnir; Bókasafnid (Upplýsing – Félag bókasafns- og upplýsingafræða), 290

G
Gakkou Toshokan (Zenkoku Gakkou Kouritsu Toshokan Kyougikai), 342
Gakkou Toshokan Sokuhou-ban (Zenkoku Gakkou Kouritsu Toshokan Kyougikai), 342
Ghana Library Journal (Ghana Library Association), 276
Greek Library Association Bulletin (Association of Greek Librarians and Information Scientists), 278
Guyana Library Association Bulletin (Guyana Library Association), 283

H
Handbuch der Öffentlichen Büchereien (Deutscher Bibliotheksverband e.V.), 265
Hong Kong Library Association Journal (Hong Kong Library Association), 189
Hong Kong Library Association Newsletter (Hong Kong Library Association), 189
Horse-Texte (Association genevoise des bibliothécaires et professionnels diplômés en information documentaire), 474

I
IAMSLIC Newsletter (International Association of Aquatic and Marine Science Libraries and Information Centers), 053
IAOL Bulletin (International Association of Orientalist Librarians), 057
IASA Journal (International Association of Sound and Audiovisual Archives), 060
IASLIC Bulletin (Indian Association of Special Libraries and Information Centres), 292
IASSIST Quarterly (International Association for Social Sciences Information Services and Technology), 051

IATLIS Communication (Indian Association of Teachers of Library and Information Science), 050
IFLA Journal (International Federation of Library Associations and Institutions), 065
Igaku Toshokan (Nihon Igaku Toshokan Kyokai), 331
IGPL Newsletter (International Group of Publishing Libraries), 066
Il Mondo degli Archivi (Associazione Nazionale Archivistica Italiana), 313
ILA Bulletin (Iranian Library and Information Science Association), 297
ILSA (Indian Library Science Abstracts) (Indian Association of Special Libraries and Information Centres), 292
INASP Newsletter (International Network for the Availability of Scientific Publications), 068
Indonesian Learned Periodicals Index (Ikatan Pustakawan Indonesia), 296
INFORM: The Magazine of Information and Image Management (Association for Information and Image Management), 542
Informa: Boletín Mensual (Asociación de Bibliotecarios de El Salvador), 216
Informaatiotutkimus (Finnish Association of Information Studies), 224
Information – Wissenschaft und Praxis (Deutsche Gesellschaft für Informationswissenschaft und Informationspraxis e.V.), 262
Information and Librarianship (Israeli Society of Libraries and Information Centers), 307
Information Bulletin (International Federation for Information Processing), 064
Information Outlook (Special Libraries Association), 593
Information Scotland (Chartered Institute of Library and Information Professionals in Scotland), 505
Information Technology and Libraries (Library and Information Technology Association), 576
Infoterm Newsletter (International Information Centre for Terminology), 067
Interface (Association of Specialized and Cooperative Library Agencies), 560
Interim (Scottish Health Information Network), 522
Intermezzo (International Association of Music Libraries, Archives and Documentation Centres, Australian Branch), 117
International Journal of Approximate Reasoning (North American Fuzzy Information Processing Society), 080
International Journal of Legal Information (International Association of Law Libraries), 055
ISC/SCI Bulletin (Indexing and Abstracting Society of Canada / Société Canadienne d'indexation), 183

J

Japanese Agricultural Sciences Index (JASI). (Nihon Nougaku Toshokan Kyogikai), 332
JLA Bulletin (Library and Information Association of Jamaica), 316
Journal of East Asian Libraries (Council on East Asian Libraries, Inc.), 570
Journal of Education for Library and Information Science (Association for Library and Information Science Education), 543
Journal of Film Preservation (Fédération Internationale des Archives du Film), 047
Journal of Information and Media Studies; JSIMS Newsletter (Japan Society for Information and Media Studies), 320

Journal of Library and Information Science (Chinese-American Librarians Association), 566

Journal of Macau Library and Information Management Association (Macau Library and Information Management Association), 192

Journal of Paper Conservation (Internationale Arbeitsgemeinschaft der Archiv-, Bibliotheks-, und Graphikrestauratoren), 070

Journal of the American Society for Information Science and Technology (American Society for Information Science and Technology), 537

Journal of the Canadian Health Libraries Association (Canadian Health Libraries Association / Association des Bibliothèques de la Santé du Canada), 175

Journal of the China Society of Scientific and Technical Information (Zhongguo Kexue Jishu Qingbao Xuehui), 194

Journal of the French Libraries (Romanian version (Biblioteca Metropolitan Bucaresti), 440

Journal of the Medical Library Association (Medical Library Association Inc.), 580

Judaica Librarianship (Association of Jewish Libraries), 555

K

Kelias News (Kenya Library Association), 347

Key Words (American Society of Indexers), 538

Kirjastolehti (Suomen Kirjastoseura – Finlands Biblioteksförening), 225

Knjiznica (Zveza Bibliotekarskih Drustev Slovenije), 454

Knowledge Organization (International Society for Knowledge Organization e.V.), 069

Koudaikyo Toshokan Kyogikai Kenshu Houkokusho (Kouritsu Daigaku Kyokai Toshokan Kyogikai), 328

Kouritsu Daigaku Jittai Chosa. Fuzoku Toshokanhen (Kouritsu Daigaku Kyokai Toshokan Kyogikai), 328

Kouritsu Daigaku Kyokai Toshokan Kyogikai Kaihou (Kouritsu Daigaku Kyokai Toshokan Kyogikai), 328

Kouritsu Daigaku Toshokan Gaiyou (Kouritsu Daigaku Kyokai Toshokan Kyogikai), 328

L

La Gazette des Archives (Association des Archivistes Français), 230

La lettre d'Inforcom (Société Française des Sciences de l'Information et de la Communication), 243

Law Library Journal (American Association of Law Libraries), 534

LCF Newsletter (Librarians' Christian Fellowship), 511

Le Bibliothécaire: Revue d'Information Culturelle et Bibliographique (Association des Bibliothécaires Belges d'Expression Française), 132

Le Courrier Bibliographique (Udruzenje bibliotekara Crne Gore), 375

Legal Information Management (British and Irish Association of Law Librarians), 500

Lesotho Books and libraries (Lesotho Library Association), 357

Lettre de L'ADBU (Association des Directeurs et des personnels de direction des Bibliothèques Universitaires et de la Documentation), 236

Levéltári Szemle (Magyar Levéltárosok Egyesülete), 287

LIBER Quarterly: The Journal of European Research Libraries (Ligue des Bibliothèques Européennes de Recherche), 074
Library and Information Science (Mita Toshokan Joho Gakkai), 329
Library and Information Science Journal for Uganda (Uganda Library and Information Association), 489
Library Association of Samoa Newsletter (Library Association of Samoa), 446
Library Campaigner (The Library Campaign), 512
Library Media & PR (Library Public Relations Council), 578
Library Resources and Technical Services (Association for Library Collections and Technical Services), 544
Literatorul-Review (Biblioteca Metropolitan Bucaresti), 440
Lutheran Libraries (National Church Library Association), 585

M

Maase Hoshev (Information Processing Association of Israel), 305
MAHLAP Newsletter (Medical and Health Librarians Association of the Philippines), 424
Majalah Ikatan Pustakawan Indonesia (Ikatan Pustakawan Indonesia), 296
Majallah Perpustakaan Malaysia (Persatuan Perpustakaan Malaysia), 362
Maktaba (Kenya Library Association), 347
MaLIA Newsletter (Malta Library and Information Association), 365
Manuscripts (The Manuscript Society), 579
Marcato (Major Orchestra Librarians' Association), 075
Mauritius Library Association Newsletter (Mauritius Library Association), 368
mdi – Forum der Medizin-Dokumentation und Medizin-Informatik (Deutscher Verband Medizinischer Dokumentare e.V.), 266
Medelingen van de VTB (Vereniging voor het Theologisch Bibliothecariaat), 394
medizin-bibliothek-information (Arbeitsgemeinschaft für Medizinisches Bibliothekswesen), 256
MEIDA (Igud Ha'arkhiyy Yona Yim Be-Israel), 303
MELA Notes (Middle East Librarians Association), 077
Mitteilungen (Arbeitsgemeinschaft der Parlaments- und Behördenbibliotheken), 252
Mitteilungen der Gesellschaft für Bibliothekswesen und Dokumentation des Landbaues (Gesellschaft für Bibliothekswesen und Dokumentation des Landbaues – Fachliche Arbeitsgemeinschaft der ASpB), 268
Mitteilungen der IADA (Internationale Arbeitsgemeinschaft der Archiv-, Bibliotheks-, und Graphikrestauratoren), 070
Mitteilungen der Vereinigung Österreichischer Bibliothekare (Vereinigung Österreichischer Bibliothekarinnen und Bibliothekare), 126
Mitteilungsblatt der AKThB (Arbeitsgemeinschaft Katholisch-Theologischer Bibliotheken), 258
MKE-Hírlevél Archívum (Magyar Könyvtárosok Egyesülete), 286
MLG newsletter (Medical Librarians Group of Malaysia), 361
MPLA Newsletter (Mountain Plains Library Association), 581
MusikBIB. Journal for Music Libraries (Dansk Musikbiblioteks Forening), 213

Index of Official Journal 438

N

NASLINE (North American Sport Library Network), 081
Nederlands Archievenblad (Koninklijke Vereniging van Archivarissen in Nederland), 384
New Zealand Archivist (New Zealand Society of Archivists), 401
New Zealand Library & Information Management Journal (Library and Information Association of New Zealand Aotearoa), 399
Newsidic (European Association of Information Services), 043
Newsletter (REFORMA (National Association to Promote Library Services to the Spanish Speaking)), 590
Newsletter of the Lebanese Library Association (Association des Bibliothèques du Liban), 356
Newsupdate (Friends of Libraries Australia Incorporated), 115
NFAIS electronic newsletter (National Federation of Abstracting and Information Services), 586
NFF-Informasjon (Norsk Fagbibliotekforening), 412
Nieuwsbrief (Landelijke Werkgroep Schoolmediathecarissen Voortgezet Onderwijs), 385
Nigerian Libraries (Nigerian Library Association), 405
Nihon Nougaku Toshokan Kyogikai Kaiho (Nihon Nougaku Toshokan Kyogikai), 332
Nihon Toshokan Joho Gakkaishi (Nihon Toshokan Joho Gakkai), 333
Norsk Arkivforum (Arkivarforeningen), 407
Notes (Music Library Association, Inc), 582
Noticiero de la AMBAC (Asociación Mexicana de Bibliotecarios, A.C.), 013
Notizie (Gruppo Italiano Documentalisti dell'industria Farmaceutica e degli Istituti di Ricerca Biomedica), 314
NVB Nieuwsbrief (Nederlandse Vereniging van Beroepsbeoefenaren in de Bibliotheek-, Informatie- en Kennissector), 387
NZLLG News (New Zealand Law Librarians Inc.), 400

O

OSALL newsletter (Organisation of South African Law Libraries), 458

P

PAARL Newsletter (Philippine Association of Academic and Research Librarians), 425
Pakistan Library & Information Science Journal (Library Promotion Bureau), 415
Papers of the Bibliographical Society of America (Bibliographical Society of America), 562
Papers/Cahiers (Bibliographical Society of Canada/La Société Bibliographique du Canada), 160
PATLS Newsletter (Philippine Association of Teachers of Library Science), 427
PLA Newsletter (Pakistan Library Association), 416
Play and Parenting Connections (Canadian Association of Family Resource Programs), 167
Proceedings of SCECSAL (Lesotho Library Association), 357
Progressive Librarian (Progressive Librarians Guild), 588
Przeglad Biblioteczny (Library Review) (Stowarzyszenie Bibliotekarzy Polskich), 434
Public Libraries (Public Library Association), 589

Q

Quarterly Bulletin of IAALD (International Association of Agricultural Infornation Specialities), 052

R

Raamatukogu (Eesti Raamatukoguhoidjate Ühing), 219
Recht, Bibliothek, Dokumentation (RBD): Mitteilungen der AjBD (Arbeitsgemeinschaft für juristisches Bibliotheks- und Dokumentationswesen), 255
Records Management Bulletin (Records Management Society of Great Britain), 517
REFERENCIAS (Asociación de Bibliotecarios Graduados de la República Argentina), 101
Repeat (NVBA, vereniging van en voor personen werkzam in het beheer van organisatie), 389
Revista AIBDA (Asociación Interamericana de Bibliotecarios, Documentalistas y Especialistas en Información Agrícola), 011
Revista ALA (Asociación Latinoamericana de Archivos), 012
Revista Argentina de Documentación Biomedica (Asociación de Bibliotecas Biomedicas Argentinas), 103
Revista Brasileira de Biblioteconomía e Documentaçao (Federaçao Brasileira de Associaçoes de Bibliotecários), 143
Revista de Bibliotecología y Ciencias de la Información. 1986–2/yr. Free for members. Address: Alvaro Perez. email: perquir@racsa.co.cr. Boletín 3/yr. Address: Laura Guevara. email: laugue@yahoo.com (Colegio de Bibliotecarios de Costa Rica), 198
Revista española de documentación (Sociedad Española de Documentación e Información Científica), 464
Revista Romana de Biblioteconomie si Stiinta Informarii/Romanian Review of Library and Information Science (Asociatia Bibliotecarilor din România), 438
Revue de l'Association des Bibliothécaires du Monténégro et de la Bibliothèque nationale de la R. S. de Monténégro à Cetinje (Udruzenje bibliotekara Crne Gore), 375
RIKAR Newsletter (Research Institute for Korean Archives and Records), 353
Rissalat at-Maktaba (Jordan Library and Information Association), 344
RLA Information Bulletin (Rossiiskaya Bibliotechnaya Assotsiatsiya), 443

S

Sakartvelos Biblioteka (Georgian Library Association), 246
SALALM Newsletter (Seminar on the Acquisition of Latin American Library Materials), 087
SALIS News (Substance Abuse Librarians&Information Specialists), 095
SARBICA Journal (Arkib Negara Malaysia), 005
SASA Journal (Suid-Africaanse Vereniging van Archivarisse), 459
SCANUL-ECS Newsletter (Standing Conference of African National and University Libraries in Eastern, Central and Southern Africa), 092
SCAULWA Newsletter (Standing Conference of African University Libraries, Western Area), 093
School Librarian (School Library Association), 521
School Libraries in Canada (SLIC) (Canadian Association for School Libraries), 164
School Libraries Worldwide (International Association of School Librarianship), 058

Schrifttum zur Informationswissenschaft und -praxis (Gesellschaft für Bibliothekswesen und Dokumentation des Landbaues – Fachliche Arbeitsgemeinschaft der AspB), 268
Scrinium (Verband Österreichischer Archivarinnen und Archivare), 125
Senmon Toshokan (Senmon Toshokan Kyogikai), 337
Shiritsu Daigaku Toshokan Kyokai Kaihou (Shiritsu Daigaku Toshokan Kyokai), 338
Shiritsu Tanki Daigaku Toshokan Kyogikai Kaihou (Shiritsu Tanki Daigaku Toshokan Kyogikai), 339
Sierra Leone library Journal (Sierra Leone Association of Archivists, Librarians and Information Scientists), 450
Signum (Suomen Tieteellinen Kirjastoseura r.y. – Finlands Vetenskapliga Biblioteksamfund r.f.), 227
Singapore Journal of Library and Information Management (Library Association of Singapore), 451
Singapore Libraries Bulletin (Library Association of Singapore), 451
SISCOM (Society for Information Science), 295
Skole Biblioteket (Danmarks Skolebibliotekarer), 212
Skolebiblioteket (Skolebibliotekarforeningen i Norge), 414
Someni (Tanzania Library Association), 481
Soronda (Instituto Nacional de Estudos e Pesquisa), 282
South African Journal of Libraries & Information Science; LIASA-IN-TOUCH (Library and Information Association of South Africa), 457
Special Issues (Canadian Association of Special Libraries and Information Services), 172
Sri Lanka Library Review (Sri Lanka Library Association), 091
State Librarian (Network of Government Library and Information Specialists), 516
SWALA Journal (Swaziland Library Association), 466
SWALA Newsletter (Swaziland Library Association), 466
SWARBICA Journal (South and West Asian Regional Branch of the International Council on Archives), 090

T

Tanki Daigaku Toshokan Kenkvu (Shiritsu Tanki Daigaku Toshokan Kyogikai), 339
Tarp knygų (Lietuvos bibliotekininkų draugija), 358
Tema arkiv (Arkivradet), 467
The AFFIRMation (Association for Federal Information Resources Management), 541
The Arab Archives (al-Watha'ig al Arabiyah) (Arab Regional Branch of the International Council on Archives), 004
The Bookwoman (Women's National Book Association inc.), 598
The Bulletin (Association of Canadian Map Libraries and Archives/Association des Cartothèques et des Archives Canadiennes), 157
The Christian Librarian (Association of Christian Librarians), 550
The Globe (Australian and New Zealand Map Circle), 106
The Indexer (Society of Indexers), 527
The Information Management Journal (Association for Information Management Professionals), 016
The Library (The Bibliographical Society), 498
The Manuscript Society News (The Manuscript Society), 579

The Moving Image (Association of Moving Image Archivists), 558
The Pipeline Beta Phi Mu Newsletter (Beta Phi Mu (International Library Science Honor Society)), 027
The Private Library (Private Libraries Association), 085
The Thai Library Association Bulletin (Thai Library Association), 483
The ULC Exchange (Urban Libraries Council), 596
The Watermark (Association of Librarians in the History of the Health Sciences), 556
Tidskrift för Dokumentation (TD) (Svensk förening för informationsspecialister), 471
Tietoasiantuntija magazine (Tietoasiantuntijat ry), 228
Tohyop Wolbo (KLA Bulletin). (Hanguk Tosogwan Hyophoe), 349
Tonga Library Association Newsletter (Tonga Library Association), 484
Toshokan-Kai (Nihon Toshokan Kenkyukai), 334
Toshokan Zasshi (Nihon Toshokan Kyokai), 335
Tosogwan Hak (Korean Library and Information Science Society), 350
Türk Kütüphaneciligi (Türk Kütüphaneciler Dernegi), 486

U
Uganda Information Bulletin (Uganda Library and Information Association), 489
UKOLN Newsletter; Ariadne (UKOLN), 529
UMIN Brochure (University Hospital Medical Information Network), 341

V
VDB-Mitteilungen (Verein Deutscher Bibliothekare e.V.), 274
Visual Resources Association Bulletin (Visual Resources Association), 597
Vjesnik Bibliotekara Hrvatske (Hrvatsko knjiznicarsko drustvo), 200
VR.B.-Informatie (Vereniging van Religieus-Wetenschappelijke Bibliothecarissen), 134

W
Wadah Pustaka (Persatuan Perpustakaan Kebangsaan), 148

Y
Y Ddolen: Cylchgrawn Cymdeithas Llvfrgelloedd Cymru/Journal of The Welsh Library Association (Cymdeithas Llyfrgelloedd Cymru), 507
Yakugaku Toshokan (Nihon Yakugaku Toshokan Kyogikai), 336
Young Adult Library Services (Young Adult Library Services Association), 599

Z
Zambia Library Association Journal (ZLAJ) (Zambia Library Association), 602
Zimbabwe Librarian (Zimbabwe Library Association), 603

Index of Officers

A

Abate, Helen; PA to Chief Exec (Museums, Libraries and Archives Council), 514
Abbas Khan, Prince; Gen Secr (South and West Asian Regional Branch of the International Council on Archives), 090
Abbott-Stout, Sandra; Treas (International Association of Aquatic and Marine Science Libraries and Information Centers), 053
Abdallah, Fawz; Pres (Association des Bibliothèques du Liban), 356
Abrantes, Paul Maria; Pres (Federaçao Brasileira de Associaçoes de Bibliotecários – Comissao Brasileira de Bibliotecas Centrais Universitárias), 145
Absalom, Umarov; Chair (Uzbekistan Library Association), 601
Abu Harb, Qasem; 2nd VP (Arab Regional Branch of the International Council on Archives), 004
Accart, Jean-Philippe; VP (Association genevoise des bibliothécaires et professionnels diplômés en information documentaire), 474
Acosta-Rodrígue, Fernando; Pres (Seminar on the Acquisition of Latin American Library Materials), 087
Adair, Helen; 1st VP (Société Internationale des Bibliothèques et des Musées des Arts du Spectacle), 089
Adamides, Nicole; Training Manager (Aslib Informatuion Ltd), 492
Adams, Cecily; Secr (Australian Law Librarians Association), 109
Adamson, Kathy; Treas (Association Internationale des Bibliothèques, Archives et Centres de Documentation Musicaux/Internationale Vereinigung der Musikbibliotheken, Musikarchive und Musikdokumentationszentren), 021
Aguilar, Laura; Secr (Asociación de Bibliotecarios de El Salvador), 216
Ahmed, Sharif Uddin; VP (South and West Asian Regional Branch of the International Council on Archives), 090
Ahoranta, Laura; Secr (Arkistoyhdistys r.y. – Arkivföreningen r.f.), 221
Ajmal Khan, Muhammad; Secr Gen (Pakistan Library Automation Goup), 417
Ajuwon, Grace; Treas (Association for Health Information and Libraries in Africa), 015
Akzhigitova, Khabiba; Pres (East-Kazakhstan Librarians Association), 345
Al Ibrahim, Baho; Treas (Arab Regional Branch of the International Council on Archives), 004
Alberts, Marietta; Alternate VP (International Information Centre for Terminology), 067
Ali Kamal, Asif; IT Manager (Pakistan Library Automation Goup), 417
Ali, Mohsin; IT Consultant (Pakistan Library Automation Goup), 417
Ali, Salizah; Secr (Medical Librarians Group of Malaysia), 361
Allick, Susan K.; Pres (Virgin Islands Library Association / St. Croix Library Association), 532
Amadou, Diop; Manager (Panafrican Institute for Development), 152
Amarasiri, P.B.; Immediate Past Pres (Sri Lanka Library Association), 091
Amarasiri, Upali; Pres (Sri Lanka Library Association), 091
Ambrozic, Melita; Pres (Zveza Bibliotekarskih Drustev Slovenije), 454
Anagnostelis, Betsy; Chair (University Health and Medical Librarians Group), 530
Andersen, Tore K.; Pres (Norsk Bibliotekforening), 411

Index of Officers 444

Anderson, Bill; Treas (Church and Synagogue Library Association), 567
Anderson, J. THeodore; Past Pres (Church and Synagogue Library Association), 567
Ando, Masahito; VP (Nihon Akaibuzu Gakkai), 330
Andradi, D.I.D.; Treas (Sri Lanka Library Association), 091
Andreev, Igor; Deputy PR-officer (Council of PCLI Programme Coordinators), 442
Angelov, Kiril; Secr (Bibliothkarsko Drustvo na Makedonija), 360
Anley, Cath; Secr (Society of Chief Librarians), 525
Ansari, Abdul Samad; Secr Gen (Library Promotion Bureau), 415
Apostoleanu, Corina; Secr Gen (Asociatia Bibliotecarilor din România), 438
Arb, Jacqueline von; VP (International Association of Sound and Audiovisual Archives), 060
Arèvalo, Angela; Treas (Asociación de Bibliotecarios de El Salvador), 216
Arlindo Rodrigues, Nêmora; Pres (Conselho Federal de Biblioteconomia), 142
Armstrong, Eileen; VChair (School Library Association), 521
Arpad, Tyekvicska; Pres (Magyar Levéltárosok Egyesülete), 287
Arsenault, Clément; Dir/Membership (Canadian Association for Information Science / Association Canadienne des Sciences de l'Information), 163
Arthur, Rhona; Asst Dir (Chartered Institute of Library and Information Professionals in Scotland), 505
Aryal, Rem Raj; VP (Nepal Community Library Association), 378
Arzumanyan, Nazeni; Secr (Haykakan Gradaranayin Asotsiatsia), 104
Ashari, Ali Akbar; Pres (South and West Asian Regional Branch of the International Council on Archives), 090
Assmann, Ilase; Secr Gen (International Association of Sound and Audiovisual Archives), 060
Aston, Jennefer; Secr (International Association of Law Libraries), 055
Aubin, Paul; 1st VP (Bibliographical Society of Canada/La Société Bibliographique du Canada), 160
Auer, Margaret E.; Treas (Women's National Book Association inc.), 598
Auksoriútè, Albina; Pres (International Information Centre for Terminology), 067
Avram, Chris; Treas (International Federation for Information Processing), 064
Aydin, Ahmet Emre; Controller (Türk Kütüphaneciler Dernegi), 486

B

Babic, Silvija; Member of the Exec Board (Hrvatsko Arhivisticko Drustvo), 199
Bagûés, Jon; VP (Association Internationale des Bibliothèques, Archives et Centres de Documentation Musicaux/Internationale Vereinigung der Musikbibliotheken, Musikarchive und Musikdokumentationszentren), 021
Baier, Prof. Dr. D.; Treas (Gesellschaft für Klassifikation e.V.), 269
Baildon, Michelle; Immediate Past Pres (Asian Pacific American Librarians Association), 540
Baillargeon, Diane; Dir (Canadian Council of Archives / Conseil Canadien des Archives), 173
Baird, Iain; Vive Chair (University Health and Medical Librarians Group), 530
Bakos, Klára; Pres (Magyar Könyvtárosok Egyesülete), 286

Ballantyne, Peter; Pres (International Association of Agricultural Infornation Specialities), 052
Ballhausen, Thomas; Vice Chair (Media Archives Austria), 122
Baltar Carneiro de Albuquerque, Maria Elizabeth; Treas (Conselho Federal de Biblioteconomia), 142
Banfield, Paul; Pres (Association of Canadian Archivists), 156
Bannerman, Valentina J.A.; Pres (Ghana Library Association), 276
Baqar, Shri S.M.R.; Dir (National Committee of Archivists), 294
Barber, Jeff; Chair (Canadian Urban Libraries Council), 178
Barbini, Palmira Maria; Treas (Associazione Italiana Biblioteche), 311
Barnard, John; Pres (The Bibliographical Society), 498
Barnett, Kristina; VP (Friends of Libraries Australia Incorporated), 115
Barone, Joseph M.; Pres (North American Fuzzy Information Processing Society), 080
Barrenechea, Idoia; Pres (Red de Bibliotecas Universitarias Españolas), 463
Barreto Pereira Silva, Rosa Maria; Lis Training (Associaçâo Portuguesa de Bibliotecários, Arquivistas e Documentalistas), 014
Barrie, Lita; Pres (Canadian Association of Children's Librarians), 165
Barringer, Terry; Edi (Standing Conference on Library Materials on Africa), 528
Barrionuevo, Gerardo; Secr (Sociedad Argentina de Información), 088
Bartlett, Joan; Past Pres (Canadian Association for Information Science / Association Canadienne des Sciences de l'Information), 163
Bartos, Éva; VP (Magyar Könyvtárosok Egyesülete), 286
Batazzi, Claudine; Treas (Société Française des Sciences de l'Information et de la Communication), 243
Bazile, Bea; Pres (Association of Caribbean University, Research and Institutional Libraries), 023
Beard, Colleen; Past Pres (Association of Canadian Map Libraries and Archives/Association des Cartothèques et des Archives Canadiennes), 157
Beaudry, Guylaine; Pres (Corporation des bibliothécaires professionnels du Québec), 179
Beaudry, Rcihard; Past Pres (Canadian Association for School Libraries), 164
Beaumont, Nancy; Exec Dir (Society of American Archivists), 591
Becker, Dr. Irmgard Christa; Treas (Verein Deutscher Archivarinnen und Archivare e.V.), 273
BeDell, Suzanne; Treas (National Federation of Abstracting and Information Services), 586
Behr, Michèle; Pres (Association des Bibliothèques Chrétiennes de France), 232
Bellas Vilariño, Margarita; Pres (Asociación Cubana de Bibliotecarios), 201
Belluzo, Regina Célia; VP (Federação Brasileira de Associações de Bibliotecários, Cientistas da Informação e Instituições), 144
Bendo, Mark; VP (Medical and Health Librarians Association of the Philippines), 424
Benzner, Sonja; Chair (Arbeitsgemeinschaft der Kunst- und Museumsbibliotheken), 251
Bepler, Jochen; Pres (Arbeitsgemeinschaft Katholisch-Theologischer Bibliotheken), 258
Bérard, Raymond; Treas (Ligue des Bibliothèques Européennes de Recherche), 074
Berdigaliyeva, Rosa A.; Pres (Library Association of the Republic of Kazakhstan), 346
Berezansky, Tracey; Pres (National Association of Government Archives and Records Administrators), 583

Index of Officers

Berg, Marc Van den; VP (Association Belge de Documentation / Belgische Vereniging voor Documentatie), 131
Berger, Gabriele; Vice Pres (Deutscher Bibliotheks- und Informationsverband e.V.), 264
Bergeron, Paul R.; VP (National Association of Government Archives and Records Administrators), 583
Bethel, Alison; Treas (Britain and Ireland Association of Aquatic Sciences Libraries and Information Centres), 499
Bettington, Jackie; Pres (Australian Society of Archivists (Inc.)), 113
Beute, Idelette; VChair (Suid-Africaanse Vereniging van Archivarisse), 459
Bickeböller, Prof. Dr. H.; 1st VP (Deutsche Gesellschaft für Medizinische Informatik, Biometrie und Epidemiologie e.V.), 263
Bier, Marilyn; Exec Dir (Association for Information Management Professionals), 016
Bihl, Elisabeth; VP (International Association of Music Information Centres), 056
Bird, Blaine; Hon Secr (British and Irish Association of Law Librarians), 500
Bispinck, Julia; Treas (Internationale Arbeitsgemeinschaft der Archiv-, Bibliotheks-, und Graphikrestauratoren), 070
Bitsch, Britta; Manager (Bibliotekslederforeningen), 208
Blank, Claudia; Ex-Pres (Société Internationale des Bibliothèques et des Musées des Arts du Spectacle), 089
Blanks, Robert; Past Pres (Mountain Plains Library Association), 581
Bleicher, Martin; Dir (International Network for the Availability of Scientific Publications), 068
Boelt, Kirsten; 2nd VP (Danmarks Biblioteksforening), 210
Boillat, Pierre; Pres (Association genevoise des bibliothécaires et professionnels diplômés en information documentaire), 474
Bolton, Larysa; Hon Treas (Society of Archivists), 524
Bomsey, Edward N.; Pres (The Manuscript Society), 579
Bonanno, Karen; Exec Secr (International Association of School Librarianship), 058
Boon, Christopher; Secr (Association Belge de Documentation / Belgische Vereniging voor Documentatie), 131
Borilovic, Branislav; Pres (Associations of Montenegrin Librarians), 374
Bostley, Jean R.; Exec Dir (Catholic Library Association), 563
Boulanger, Laurence; Pres (Association Professionnelle des Bibliothécaires et Documentalistes), 133
Bouthiellier, France; Pres (Canadian Council of Information Studies/ Le Conseil Canadien des écoles de sciences de l'information), 174
Bouvard, Franciane; Secr (Association des Documentalistes de Collectivités Territoriales), 237
Bowers, Alden; Treas (British and Irish Association of Law Librarians), 500
Boyd, Angela; Treas (Asian Pacific American Librarians Association), 540
Bracke, Wouter; Gen Secr (Archives et Bibliothèques de Belgique / Archief- en Bibliotheekwezen in België), 130
Bradbeer, Gayle; Secr (Council on Botanical and Horticultural Libraries, Inc.), 038
Bradley, Kevin; Pres (International Association of Sound and Audiovisual Archives), 060
Brady, Susan; VP (Theatre Library Association), 594

Bragard, Marianne; VP (Association Professionnelle des Bibliothécaires et Documentalistes), 133
Brandão Toutain, Lídia Maria; Pres (Associaçao Brasileira de Educação em Ciência da Informação), 140
Brandsen, Nicola; Treas (Health Information Association of New Zealand), 397
Braun, Linda W.; Pres (Young Adult Library Services Association), 599
Brellochs, Andreas; Pres (Bibliothèque Information Suisse), 475
Brennan, Karen; Edi (Pacific Regional Branch of the International Council on Archives), 083
Bridge, David; Vice Chair (Records Management Society of Great Britain), 517
Briggs, Ronald; Treas (Aboriginal & Torres Strait Islander Library & Information Resource Network), 105
Brink, Dr. Brian; Treas (Library and Information Association of South Africa), 457
Brlic, Sanja; Treasurer (Hrvatsko Arhivisticko Drustvo), 199
Brodie, Lynn; Secr (Association of Parliamentary Librarians in Canada/Association des Bibliothécaires Parlementaires au Canada), 158
Brooks Clark, Robin; Recording Secr (Mountain Plains Library Association), 581
Brown, Mark; Chair (Research Libraries UK), 519
Browne, Junior; Pres (Library Association of Barbados), 128
Brunner, Meg; Chair-elect (Substance Abuse Librarians&Information Specialists), 095
Bryson, Tim; Chair (Committee on South Asian Libraries and Documentation), 569
Buelow, Anna; Secr (Internationale Arbeitsgemeinschaft der Archiv-, Bibliotheks-, und Graphikrestauratoren), 070
Bundy, Dr. Alan; Pres (Friends of Libraries Australia Incorporated), 115
Buntrock, Logan; Treas (Association of Information Systems Professionals), 554
Burger, Marlene; Pres (Association of South African Indexers and Bibliographers), 455
Burillo, Jeanette Z.; P. R. O. (Medical and Health Librarians Association of the Philippines), 424
Burlacu, Sorin; Deputy-Pres (National Association of Public Libraries and Librarians in Romania), 441
Burns, Maureen; Pres (Visual Resources Association), 597
Butler, James; Treas (Australian Law Librarians Association), 109
Butros, Amy; Pres-Elect (International Association of Aquatic and Marine Science Libraries and Information Centers), 053
Byrne, Gillian; Dir-Memebership (Canadian Association of College and University Libraries / Association Canadienne des Bibliothèques de Collège et d'Université), 166

C

Cabrales, Aida; Treas (Comité de Cooperación Bibliotecaria de El Salvador), 217
Caidi, Nadia; VP (Canadian Association for Information Science / Association Canadienne des Sciences de l'Information), 163
Calimano, Ivan; Pres (Sociedad de Bibliotecarios de Puerto Rico), 437
Calvo, Hortensia; Exec Secr (Seminar on the Acquisition of Latin American Library Materials), 087
Cannell, Sheila; Treas (Research Libraries UK), 519
Caplan, Audra; Pres-elect (Public Library Association), 589

Carlblom, Sheila O.; Treas (Association of Christian Librarians), 550
Carr, Ben; Pres (Association of Information Systems Professionals), 554
Carter, Sarah; Secr (Britain and Ireland Association of Aquatic Sciences Libraries and Information Centres), 499
Case, Mary; Pres (Association for Library Collections and Technical Services), 544
Cassaro, Jim; VP (Association Internationale des Bibliothèques, Archives et Centres de Documentation Musicaux/Internationale Vereinigung der Musikbibliotheken, Musikarchive und Musikdokumentationszentren), 021
Cavalcanti de Miranda, Marcos Luiz; 2nd Secr (Associaçao Brasileira de Educação em Ciência da Informação), 140
Céli de Sousa, Regina; VP (Conselho Federal de Biblioteconomia), 142
Celik, Güler; Secr (HK/KOMMUNAL Library Committee), 214
Centeno, Dalia; VP (Asociación Nicaragüense de Bibliotecarios y Profesionales Afines), 403
Ceylan, Humeyra; Hon Edi (Association of British Theological and Philosophical Libraries), 493
Chakraborty, Arun K.; Gen Secr (Indian Association of Special Libraries and Information Centres), 292
Champ-Blackwell, Siobhan; Secr/Recorder (REFORMA (National Association to Promote Library Services to the Spanish Speaking)), 590
Chan, Shik-Tong; Chair (Fundashon Biblioteka Publiko Kòrsou), 203
Chandnary, Rajendra; VP (Nepal Community Library Association), 378
Chandra, Dr. Hanish; Treas (Developing Library Network), 291
Chang, Durk Hyuan; Exec Secr (Korean Library and Information Science Society), 350
Chang, Jim; Pres (Hong Kong Library Association), 189
Chanturishvili, Irina; VP (Association of Information Specialists), 245
Chaparro, Luis; Immediate Past Pres (REFORMA (National Association to Promote Library Services to the Spanish Speaking)), 590
Chapman, Natalie; VP (Canadian Association of Family Resource Programs), 167
Charles, Henry; Pres (Council on Library and Information Resources), 571
Chase, Donald; Pres (American Society for Information Science and Technology), 537
Chesser, Richard; Pres (International Association of Music Libraries, Archives and Documentation Centres – United Kingdom and Ireland Branch), 509
Chikhi, M. Abdelmadjid; Pres (Arab Regional Branch of the International Council on Archives), 004
Choi, Key-Sun; VP (International Information Centre for Terminology), 067
Chou, Min; Incoming VP/Pres Elect (Chinese-American Librarians Association), 566
Christie, Pat; Chair (Art Libraries Society of the United Kingdom & the Republic of Ireland), 491
Cid, Victor; Secr (Asociación Mexicana de Bibliotecarios, A.C.), 013
Cieplinski, Stan; Treas (Council on Library/Media Technicians), 039
Clapp, Mary; Recording Secr (Evangelical Church Library Association), 572
Clare, David; Hon Treas (Business Librarians Association), 503
Clare, Roy; Chief Exec (Museums, Libraries and Archives Council), 514
Clarke, Marie; VP (Australian School Library Association), 112
Clarke, Paul; Chair (European Information Association), 046

Index of Officers

Clemens, G. Scott; Treas (Bibliographical Society of America), 562
Cochrane, Tom; Chair (Australian Libraries Copyright Committee), 110
Cognetti, Gaetana; Pres (Associazione Bibliotecari Documentalisti Sanita), 309
Cohen, Nancy; Past Pres (Canadian Association of Children's Librarians), 165
Colby, Michael; Treas (International Association of Music Libraries, Archives, and Documentation Centres – United States Branch), 575
Cole-Phoenix, Odean; Secr (Library and Information Association of Jamaica), 316
Coleman, Casey; Pres (Association for Federal Information Resources Management), 541
Colindres, Carlos R.; Pres (Comité de Cooperación Bibliotecaria de El Salvador), 217
Combs, Kathleen; Exec Dir (Association for Library and Information Science Education), 543
Coninx, Stef; Gen Secr (International Association of Music Information Centres), 056
Connor, Sheila; Pres (Council on Botanical and Horticultural Libraries, Inc.), 038
Cooke, Ian; Treas (Standing Conference on Library Materials on Africa), 528
Copioso, Lina C.; Treas (Agricultural Librarians Association of the Philippines), 422
Coravu, Robert; Secr Gen (Asociatia Bibliotecarilor din România), 438
Core, Jane; Chair (Society of College, National and University Libraries), 526
Cornish Debraski, Sarah; Past Pres (Young Adult Library Services Association), 599
Corrall, Sheila; Chair (British Association for Information and Library Education and Research), 501
Crnogorac, Vesna; Secr (Bibliotekarsko društvo Srbijé), 448
Crookston, Mark; Secr Gen (Pacific Regional Branch of the International Council on Archives), 083
Croy-Vanwely, Marcia; Pres-Elect (International Association of Aquatic and Marine Science Libraries and Information Centers), 053
Crwaford, Ellen; Secr (American Theological Library Association), 539
Cummings, Leanne; Pres (Australian Law Librarians Association), 109
Cunningham, Adrian; Treas (Pacific Regional Branch of the International Council on Archives), 083
Currie, Debbie; Edi (International Association of Agricultural Infornation Specialities), 052

D

da Silva de Oliveira, João Carlos Salvador; Editorial (Associaçâo Portuguesa de Bibliotecários, Arquivistas e Documentalistas), 014
Daelemans, Frank; Pres (Archives et Bibliothèques de Belgique / Archief- en Bibliotheekwezen in België), 130
Dahl, Hanne; Secr (Danmarks Forskningsbiblioteksforening), 211
Dale, Michele; Secr/Treas (Association of Canadian Archivists), 156
Danner, Richard A.; 1st VP (International Association of Law Libraries), 055
Dato Paduka Haji Sunny, Puan Nellie; Pres (Persatuan Perpustakaan Kebangsaan), 148
Dato Pakuda Haji Sunny, Nellie; Pres (Congress of South-East Asian Libraries), 036
Davidsen, Jan; Pres (Norwegian Union of Municipal and General Employees), 413
De Klerk, Karlien; Secr (Library and Information Association of South Africa), 457
De Landtsheer, Simone; Treas (Vlaamse Vereniging voor Bibliotheek-, Archief- en Documentatiewezen), 135

Index of Officers

Deane, Christopher; Secr (Health Information Association of New Zealand), 397
Decker, Prof. Dr. R.; 1st VP (Gesellschaft für Klassifikation e.V.), 269
Dediu, Liviu Iulian; Deputy-Pres (National Association of Public Libraries and Librarians in Romania), 441
Delgado, Edgar Allan; Pres (Asociación Colombiana de Bibliotecologos y Documentalistas), 195
Delrue, Laure; Secr (Association des Directeurs et des personnels de direction des Bibliothèques Universitaires et de la Documentation), 236
Demidov, Alexei; Chair (Council of PCLI Programme Coordinators), 442
Dennis, Nicole; Secr (Business Librarians Association), 503
Devine, Heather; Secr (American Indian Library Association), 001
Dewe, Ainslie; Dep Pres (Council of Australian University Librarians), 037
Dhawan, SC; VP (Society for Information Science), 295
Dhungana, Basudev; Chair (Nepal Community Library Association), 378
Diaz Ruiz, Silvia; Pres (Colegio de Bibliotecarios de Costa Rica), 198
Didier Tengeneza, Desire; Pres (Association des Bibliothecaires, Archivistes, Documentalistes et Museologues), 197
Diefenbacher, Dr. Michael; Chair (Verein Deutscher Archivarinnen und Archivare e.V.), 273
Dilomama, Kone; Secr Gen (Association Burkinabé des Gestionnaires de l'Information Documentaire), 150
Dingwall, Orvie; VP (Canadian Health Libraries Association / Association des Bibliothèques de la Santé du Canada), 175
Dione, Bernard; Secr Gen (Association Sénégalaise des Bibliothécaires, Archivistes et Documentalistes), 447
Djalo, Iaguba; Pres (Association Guineenne des Documentalistes, Archivistes et Bibliothecaires), 281
Djekovic-Sachs, Dr. Liliana; Vice-Chair (Arbeitsgemeinschaft der Bibliotheken und Dokumentationsstellen der Ost-, Ostmittel- und Südosteuropaforschung e.V.), 248
Dlamini, Jabulile; Secr (Swaziland Library Association), 466
Dobbs Mackenzie, Barbara; Secr (National Federation of Abstracting and Information Services), 586
Dobrica, Ladislav; Member of the Exec Board (Hrvatsko Arhivisticko Drustvo), 199
Doina, Popa; Pres (National Association of Public Libraries and Librarians in Romania), 441
Dondertman, Anne; Pres (Bibliographical Society of Canada/La Société Bibliographique du Canada), 160
Donven, Dr. Michel; Secr Gen (Association Luxembourgeoise des Bibliothécaires, Archvistes et Documentalistes), 359
Dorado, Ma. Lutgarda M.; Pres (Medical and Health Librarians Association of the Philippines), 424
Doran, Antoinette; Hon Membership Secr (Cumann Cartlannaíochta Éireann), 300
Dorgan, Marlene; Pres (Canadian Health Libraries Association / Association des Bibliothèques de la Santé du Canada), 175
Doucette, Wendy; Councillor (Canadian Association for School Libraries), 164
Dougherty, Robin; Webmaster (Middle East Librarians Association), 077

Douselle-Melish, Caroline; Secr (Bibliographical Society of America), 562
Drost, Pernille; Pres (Bibliotekarforbundet: Forbundet for Informationsspecialister og kulturformidlere), 207
Dubin, Susan; Pres (Association of Jewish Libraries), 555
Duda, Dan; 1st VP (Association of Canadian Map Libraries and Archives/Association des Cartothèques et des Archives Canadiennes), 157
Duffin, Therese; Treas (New Zealand Law Librarians Inc.), 400
Duller, Paul; Exec Secr (Records Management Society of Great Britain), 517
Dumitrescu, Gabriela; VP (Asociatia Bibliotecarilor din România), 438
Dunham, Joanne; Treas (University Health and Medical Librarians Group), 530
Dupont, Odile; VP (Association des Bibliothèques Chrétiennes de France), 232
Duval, Anne-Sophie; VP (Association Nationale des Documentalistes de l'Enseignement Privé), 240
Dzuma, Irgashev; Prov Exec Dir (Uzbekistan Library Association), 601

E
Echiverri, Lilia F.; Pres (Philippine Library Association, Inc., Headquarters), 429
Edminster, Matt; VP (Association of Information Systems Professionals), 554
Edwards, Adelle; VP (Australian and New Zealand Map Circle), 106
Egan, Chris; VP/Pres Elect (Council on Library/Media Technicians), 039
Egloff, Gregor; VP (Vereinigung Schweizerischer Archivare / Association des Archivistes Suisses / Associazione degli Archivisti Svizzeri / Uniun da las archivarias e dals archivaris svizzers), 477
Eichhorn, Rachel; Conference Secr (Association of British Theological and Philosophical Libraries), 493
Elliott, Crystal; Pres (Canadian Association of Family Resource Programs), 167
Ellis-King, Deirdre; Pres (Cumann Leabharlann na h-Éireann), 301
Emmet, Joan; Program Librarian (NorthEast Research Libraries Association), 587
Engel, Gerald; VP (International Federation for Information Processing), 064
Engstom, Carlene; Interim Treas (American Indian Library Association), 001
Erbach, Gertrud; Treas (Association of UK Media Librarians), 497
Erichsen Nassif, Mõnica; 1st Secr (Associaçao Brasileira de Educação em Ciência da Informação), 140
Erviti, Manuel; Secr (International Association of Music Libraries, Archives, and Documentation Centres – United States Branch), 575
Escandar, Raúl; Dir (Sociedad Argentina de Información), 088
Essinger, Catherine; VP/Pres-elect (Association of Architecture School Librarians), 549
Etten, Ryan; Secr (Association of Information Systems Professionals), 554
Evans, Jon; VP/Pres-elect (Art Libraries Society of North America), 007
Everly, Robin; 2nd VP (Council on Botanical and Horticultural Libraries, Inc.), 038
Eyre, Gaynor; Secr (British Association for Information and Library Education and Research), 501
Ezzat, Mohamed; Pres (Central Bank of Egypt (Library Economic Research Sector)), 215

F
Faezi, A.; Pres (National Iranian Oil Company, NIOC Central Library), 298

Index of Officers

Fakudze, Queeneth; Vice Chair (Swaziland Library Association), 466
Falãdo, António José de Pina; Pres (Associaçâo Portuguesa de Bibliotecários, Arquivistas e Documentalistas), 014
Farley-Chevrier, Francis; Exec Dir (Association pour l'Avancement des Sciences et des Techniques de la Documentation), 159
Farrugia, Charles; Chair (Association of Commonwealth Archivists and Records Managers), 024
Fátima Portela Cysne, Maria do Rosário de; VP (Associaçao Brasileira de Educação em Ciência da Informação), 140
Febo, Loida Garcia; Pres (REFORMA (National Association to Promote Library Services to the Spanish Speaking)), 590
Fedorov, Viktor; Pres (The Library Assembly of Eurasia), 073
Feldman, Sari; Pres (Public Library Association), 589
Fennell, Catherine; Past Pres (Catholic Library Association), 563
Ferguson, Daniel; Exec Dir (Friends of Libraries Australia Incorporated), 115
Ferrero, Jean-Marc; Treas (Association Francophone d'Informatique en Agriculture), 019
Fiels, Keith Michael; Exec Dir (American Library Association), 536
Filev, Dimitar; Past Pres (North American Fuzzy Information Processing Society), 080
Findlay, Margaret; Treas (Australian and New Zealand Society of Indexers), 107
Fisher, Biddy; Pres (Chartered Institute of Library and Information Professionals), 506
Fisher, Melanie; Chair (Association of Librarians in Land-Based Colleges and Universities), 494
Fletcher, Stephen; Pres (National Association of State Information Resource Executives), 584
Flury, Roger; Secr Gen (Association Internationale des Bibliothèques, Archives et Centres de Documentation Musicaux/Internationale Vereinigung der Musikbibliotheken, Musikarchive und Musikdokumentationszentren), 021
Focht, Marcia; Secr (Visual Resources Association), 597
Ford, Meg; Hon Secr (The Bibliographical Society), 498
Ford, Terence; Past Pres (National Federation of Abstracting and Information Services), 586
Forsyth, Ian; Chair (Canadian Council of Archives / Conseil Canadien des Archives), 173
Fortelius, Robin; Chair (Finlands Svenska Biblioteksförening r.f.), 223
Fortna, Nancy; Treas (National Association of Government Archives and Records Administrators), 583
Foster, Ann; Secr/Treas (Canadian Association of Children's Librarians), 165
Fox, Peter K.; Secr (Ligue des Bibliothèques Européennes de Recherche), 074
François, Sylvie; Secr Gen (Société Internationale des Bibliothèques et des Musées des Arts du Spectacle), 089
Frankenberger, Henning; 1st Vice Chair (Arbeitsgemeinschaft der Spezialbibliotheken e.V.), 254
Frankland, Kathy; VP (Aboriginal & Torres Strait Islander Library & Information Resource Network), 105
Franks, Debbie; Chair (Research Council Libraries&Information Consortium), 518
Fras-Popovic, Sabina; VP (Zveza Bibliotekarskih Drustev Slovenije), 454
Fraser, Linda; VP (Bureau of Canadian Archivists / Bureau Canadien des Archivistes), 162

Fredriksson, Berndt; VP (Svenska Arkivsamfundet), 472
Frey, Sue; Dir (Friends of African Village Libraries), 049
Frigimelica, Giovanna; Gen Secr (Associazione Italiana Biblioteche), 311
Friskney, Janet; 2nd VP (Bibliographical Society of Canada/La Société Bibliographique du Canada), 160
Fructus, Isabelle; Pres (Fédération des enseignants documentalistes de l'Éducation nationale), 242
Funk, Carla J.; Pres (Medical Library Association Inc.), 580
Funke, Claudia; VP (Bibliographical Society of America), 562
Furui, Zhan; Dir (Library Society of China), 191

G
Galibert, Olivier; Gen Secr (Société Française des Sciences de l'Information et de la Communication), 243
Gallego Cuadrado, Maria Pilar; Pres (Asociación Española de Archiveros, Bibliotecarios, Museólogos y Documentalistas), 461
Galvin, Brian; Treas (European Association of Libraries and Information Services on Alcohol and Other Drugs), 044
Garner, Imogen; Exec Committee Members (Council of Australian University Librarians), 037
Garner, Jane; Treas (Seminar on the Acquisition of Latin American Library Materials), 087
Garriock, Barbara; Pres (Library and Information Association of New Zealand Aotearoa), 399
Garvey, Deborah; Dir (Friends of African Village Libraries), 049
Gaunt, Marianne; Pres (Association of Research Libraries), 559
Gauthier, Diana; Secr/Treas (Canadian Association for School Libraries), 164
Gauvin, Rodrigue; Pres-elect (Association for Library Trustees, Advocates, Friends and Foundations), 546
Gayon, Elisabeth; Pres (Association des professionnels de l'information et de la documentation), 238
Geifand, Joan; Pres (Women's National Book Association inc.), 598
Geleijnse, Hans; Pres (Ligue des Bibliothèques Européennes de Recherche), 074
Gélinas, Nathalie; Pres (Bureau of Canadian Archivists / Bureau Canadien des Archivistes), 162
Gensler, Elena; Recording Secr (Association of Jewish Libraries), 555
Gentili-Tedeschi, Massimo; Past Pres (Association Internationale des Bibliothèques, Archives et Centres de Documentation Musicaux/Internationale Vereinigung der Musikbibliotheken, Musikarchive und Musikdokumentationszentren), 021
Gerard, Fabienne; Secr (Association Professionnelle des Bibliothécaires et Documentalistes), 133
Gey James, Mary; VP/Pres-elect (Women's National Book Association inc.), 598
Ghazaryan, Rafik; VP (Haykakan Gradaranayin Asotsiatsia), 104
Giambi, M. Dina; Past Pres (Association for Library Collections and Technical Services), 544
Gibbons, Frances; Exec Officer (School Library Association of New Zealand Aotearoa), 402

Index of Officers 454

Gieser, Christa; Treas (Arbeitsgemeinschaft für Medizinisches Bibliothekswesen), 256
Gilbert, Jefferson; Exec Dir (Canadian Urban Libraries Council), 178
Gitachu, Rosemary; Pres (Kenya Library Association), 347
Giuliani, Luca; VP (Fédération Internationale des Archives du Film), 047
Glanfield, Marilyn; Programme Secr (Standing Conference on Library Materials on Africa), 528
Glass, Bligh; Treas (International Association of Music Libraries, Archives and Documentation Centres, Australian Branch), 117
Glynn, Lindsay; Dir/CE-Coord (Canadian Health Libraries Association / Association des Bibliothèques de la Santé du Canada), 175
Gnoli, Claudio; 2nd VP (International Society for Knowledge Organization e.V.), 069
Göcking, Dominikus OFM; VP (Arbeitsgemeinschaft Katholisch-Theologischer Bibliotheken), 258
Goetsch, Lori; Pres (Association of College and Research Libraries), 551
Golick, Great; Secr (Bibliographical Society of Canada/La Société Bibliographique du Canada), 160
Gomez, Olinda; VP (Asociación de Bibliotecarios de El Salvador), 216
González, Lucia; VP/Pres elect (REFORMA (National Association to Promote Library Services to the Spanish Speaking)), 590
Goodair, Christine; Chair (European Association of Libraries and Information Services on Alcohol and Other Drugs), 044
Goodey, Lorna; Chair (Network of Government Library and Information Specialists), 516
Goodine, Scott; Pres (Bureau of Canadian Archivists / Bureau Canadien des Archivistes), 162
Goodrum, Katy; Chair (Society of Archivists), 524
Gordon, Heather; Exec Committee Members (Council of Australian University Librarians), 037
Goulay, Véronique; Secr (Association des Diplômés de l'École de Bibliothécaires-Documentalistes), 234
Graham, Pamela; Past Pres (Seminar on the Acquisition of Latin American Library Materials), 087
Grashkina, Vanja; Pres (Bulgarian Library and Information Association), 149
Gray, Jody; VP/Pres-elect (American Indian Library Association), 001
Gray, Leslie; VP (Friends of African Village Libraries), 049
Green, Richard; Past Pres (International Association of Sound and Audiovisual Archives), 060
Greenberg, Stephen J.; Pres-elect (Association of Librarians in the History of the Health Sciences), 556
Greenidge, Ernesta; Pres (Library Association of Trinidad and Tobago), 485
Greeves, Susan; Treas (Association of Canadian Map Libraries and Archives/Association des Cartothèques et des Archives Canadiennes), 157
Gref, Karin; Treas (Arkistoyhdistys r.y. – Arkivföreningen r.f.), 221
Gregory, Vicky; Treas (American Society for Information Science and Technology), 537
Greider, Toni; Secr/Treas (International Association of Agricultural Information Specialities), 052
Greve, Eli; VP (Danmarks Forskningsbiblioteksforening), 211

Griffiths, Peter; Immediate Past Pres (Chartered Institute of Library and Information Professionals), 506
Grillo, Gaetano; Secr (Associazione Bibliotecari Documentalisti Sanita), 309
Grima, Eman; Co-Edi (Malta Library and Information Association), 365
Großer, Andrea; VP (Deutscher Verband Medizinischer Dokumentare e.V.), 266
Gruttemeier, Herbert; Pres (International Council for Scientific and Technical Information), 062
Gudin de Vallerin, Gilles; Pres (Association des directeurs des bibliothèques municipales et intercommunales des grandes villes de France), 235
Guerrini, Mauro; Pres (Associazione Italiana Biblioteche), 311
Guèye, Oumar; Treas (Association Sénégalaise des Bibliothécaires, Archivistes et Documentalistes), 447
Guinery, Annick; Dep Secr Gen (Association des Bibliothécaires de France), 231
Gustafson, Ruth; Pres (International Association of Aquatic and Marine Science Libraries and Information Centers), 053
Gwynn, Sara; Dir (International Network for the Availability of Scientific Publications), 068

H

Haas, Didier; Treas (Association Belge de Documentation / Belgische Vereniging voor Documentatie), 131
Haas, Laurie; VP/membership (Association of Jewish Libraries), 555
Habeeb, Habeeba Husein; Advisor (Maldives Library Association), 363
Haerting, Prof. Dr. J.; Pres (Deutsche Gesellschaft für Medizinische Informatik, Biometrie und Epidemiologie e.V.), 263
Hagafny, Shahaf; Chair (Israeli Society of Libraries and Information Centers), 307
Hajdu Barát, Agnes; VP (Magyar Könyvtárosok Egyesülete), 286
Haji Mohd Shahminan bin Pg Haji Sulaiman, Pg; VP (Persatuan Perpustakaan Kebangsaan), 148
Haji Tahir, Haji Abdullah; VP (Congress of South-East Asian Libraries), 036
Hall, Brian; Vice-Pres (Chartered Institute of Library and Information Professionals), 506
Halle, Dr. Axel; 1st Vice Chair (Arbeitsgemeinschaft der Regionalbibliotheken im Deutschen Bibliotheksverband), 253
Hamedinger, Wolfgang; Manag Dir (Österreichische Bibliothekenverbund und Service GmbH), 123
Hannesdottir, Sigrun Klara; Pres (Upplýsing – Félag bókasafns- og upplýsingafræða), 290
Hansen, Per Steen; Pres (Danmarks Forskningsbiblioteksforening), 211
Harboe-Ree, Cathrine; Pres (Council of Australian University Librarians), 037
Harris, Gordon A.; Pres (Librarians' Christian Fellowship), 511
Hart, Liz; Immediate Past Pres (International Association of Music Libraries, Archives and Documentation Centres – United Kingdom and Ireland Branch), 509
Hasrah bin Haji Kamis, Abu; Hon Treas (Persatuan Perpustakaan Kebangsaan), 148
Hass, V. Heidi; Secr (Art Libraries Society of North America), 007
Hayn, Brigitta; Chair (Arbeitsgemeinschaft Patientenbibliotheken im Deutschen Bibliotheksverband), 259
Heath, Fred; Chair (Center for Research Libraries), 564

Index of Officers 456

Hedges, Graham; Secr+Publ Off (Librarians' Christian Fellowship), 511
Heijne, M.A.M.; Pres (UKB (Samenwerkingsverband van de Universiteitsbibliotheken, de Koninklijke Bibliotheek en de Bibliotheek van de Koninklijke Nederlandse Akademie van Wetenschappen)), 391
Heijne, Maria; Pres (FOBID Netherlands Library Forum), 382
Heil, Kathleen; Secr (International Association of Aquatic and Marine Science Libraries and Information Centers), 053
Heim, Ortwin; Secr (Vereinigung Österreichischer Bibliothekarinnen und Bibliothekare), 126
Hellemans, Jacques; Treas (Association internationale francophone des bibliothécaires documentalistes), 151
Henderson, Bob; Treas (Ex Libris Association), 181
Henri, Janine; Past Pres (Association of Architecture School Librarians), 549
Hentze, Sybille; Secr (Arbeitsgemeinschaft der Kunst- und Museumsbibliotheken), 251
Herkert, Mary Beth; Immediate Past Pres (National Association of Government Archives and Records Administrators), 583
Hernandez, Marta; Trustee (Comité de Cooperación Bibliotecaria de El Salvador), 217
Hertogs, Daan; Treas (Branchevereniging Archiefinstellingen Nederland), 380
Hicks, Shauna; Managing Êdi (Australian Society of Archivists (Inc.)), 113
Hilal, Riffat; 1st VP (Arab Regional Branch of the International Council on Archives), 004
Hill, Ruth S.; Sevr (American Association of Law Libraries), 534
Hirmasto, Johanna; Pres (Suomen koulukirjastoyhdistys ry), 226
Hirsch, David; VP/Pres-elect (Association of Jewish Libraries), 555
Hite, Jackie; Pres (Council on Library/Media Technicians), 039
Hnetschel, Dr. Eike; 1st Vice Chair (Arbeitsgemeinschaft für Medizinisches Bibliothekswesen), 256
Hoh, Anchi; Pres (Middle East Librarians Association), 077
Hohoff, Ulrich; Vice Pres (Deutscher Bibliotheks- und Informationsverband e.V.), 264
Hoklotubbe, Robin; Secr / Treas (Association for Library Trustees, Advocates, Friends and Foundations), 546
Holmes, Robyn; Pres (International Association of Music Libraries, Archives and Documentation Centres, Australian Branch), 117
Hoover, John Neal; Pres (Bibliographical Society of America), 562
Hopper, Michael; VP/Program Chair (Middle East Librarians Association), 077
Horinstein, Régine; Exec Dir (Corporation des bibliothécaires professionnels du Québec), 179
Horley, Nick; Treas (Librarians' Christian Fellowship), 511
Horta, Cristina; 1st VP (Association for Health Information and Libraries in Africa), 015
Houšková, Zlata; Secr (Svaz knihovniku a informacních pracovniku CR), 205
Houston, Kerry; Hon Treas (Cumann Cartlannaíochta Éireann), 300
Hubert, Dr. Rainer; Chair (Media Archives Austria), 122
Hudson, Claire; Pres (Société Internationale des Bibliothèques et des Musées des Arts du Spectacle), 089
Huemer, Dr. Hermann; Treas (Österreichische Gesellschaft für Dokumentation und Information), 124
Hungwe, Vimbai; Pres (Association for Health Information and Libraries in Africa), 015

Hurtado, Norma Málan de; Pres (Colegio de Bibliotecologos del Peru), 421
Husbands, Jillian; VP (Library Association of Barbados), 128
Hutley, Sue; Ecec Dir (Australian Library and Information Association), 111
Hwa, Kang Mi; Secr (Library Association of the Democratic People's Republic of Korea), 348

I
Ibanez, Florante Peter; VP/Pres-elect (Asian Pacific American Librarians Association), 540
Ibánez Marmolejo, Martha; Treas (Colegio Nacional de Bibliotecarios, A.C.), 371
Ibrahim, Zoungo; Pres (Association Burkinabé des Gestionnaires de l'Information Documentaire), 150
Igarashi, Tetsuya; Chair (University Hospital Medical Information Network), 341
Ignatova, Ekaterina; Exec Off of Dep of Educ Technologie (Council of PCLI Programme Coordinators), 442
Ikeuchi, Atushi; Exec Committee (Nihon Toshokan Joho Gakkai), 333
Ingoldsby, Tim; Pres (Association of Information and Dissemination Centers), 553
Ishihara, Kazunori; VP (Nihon Akaibuzu Gakkai), 330
Issem, Renate van; VP (Internationale Arbeitsgemeinschaft der Archiv-, Bibliotheks-, und Graphikrestauratoren), 070
Itier-Coeur, Martine; Treas (Association des Bibliothécaires de France), 231

J
Jaber, Hani; Pres (Palestinian Library and Information Association), 418
Jackson, Ian; Hon Treas (Association of British Theological and Philosophical Libraries), 493
Jackson, Melissa; Pres (Aboriginal & Torres Strait Islander Library & Information Resource Network), 105
Jackson, Pat; VP (Australian Society of Archivists (Inc.)), 113
Jacobson, Janet; Past Pres (Ex Libris Association), 181
Jallab, Hedi; GenSecr (Arab Regional Branch of the International Council on Archives), 004
Jansson, Gunilla; Pres (Bibliothecarii Medicinae Fenniae), 222
Jason Muscadin, Jean-Yves; Pres (Association des Archivistes Haitiens), 284
Jenkin, Alistair; Pres (New Zealand Law Librarians Inc.), 400
Jenkins, Alun; Treas (Society of College, National and University Libraries), 526
Jiang, Shuyong; Treas (Chinese-American Librarians Association), 566
Jin, Xudong; Pres (Chinese-American Librarians Association), 566
Jobst, Dr. Herwig; Secr (Österreichische Gesellschaft für Dokumentation und Information), 124
Jodor, Daniel; Secr (Sociedad Argentina de Información), 088
Johnsen, Tove Haavi; Secr (Norsk Fagbibliotekforening), 412
Johnson, Carherine; Pres (Canadian Association for Information Science / Association Canadienne des Sciences de l'Information), 163
Johnson, Roger; Hon Secr (International Federation for Information Processing), 064
Johnston, Janis; Board member (Legal Information Preservation Alliance), 072

Johnston, Stanley; 1st VP (Council on Botanical and Horticultural Libraries, Inc.), 038
Jones Morris, Donna; Secr (Chief Officers of State Library Agencies), 565
Jorgensen, Lis; Secr (Australian School Library Association), 112
Joshi, Elaine E.; VP (Agricultural Librarians Association of the Philippines), 422
Joslin, Ann; Treas (Chief Officers of State Library Agencies), 565
Joye, Volker; Chair (Arts Libraries Society of Australia and New Zealand), 008
Jürgens, Prof. E.C.M.; Chair (Vereniging Openbare Bibliotheeken in Nederland), 392
Juliano, Liana; Pres (American Indian Library Association), 001
Julien, Heidi; Ex-Officio Member (Canadian Association for Information Science / Association Canadienne des Sciences de l'Information), 163
Jurk, Michael; Chair (Vereinigung deutscher Wirtschaftsarchivare e.V.), 275

K

Kaddu, Sarah; Secr Gen (Uganda Library and Information Association), 489
Kadir, Maimunah; Chair (Medical Librarians Group of Malaysia), 361
Kaestner, Jürgen; Chair (Arbeitsgemeinschaft der Parlaments- und Behördenbibliotheken), 252
Kahl, Chris; Treas (Australian School Library Association), 112
Kalibjian, Cliff; Treas (Association of Independent Information Professionals), 552
Kallenborn, Reiner; Treas (International Association of Scientific and Technological University Libraries), 059
Kalra, Dr. H.P.S.; Joint Secr (Indian Association of Teachers of Library and Information Science), 050
Kanazawa, Masakata; Pres (IAML Nihon Shibu (Kokusai Ongaku Bunken-Kyokai Nihon Shibu)), 319
Karatas, Ahmet; Deputy (Türk Kütüphaneciler Dernegi), 486
Kartal, Ali Fuat; Chair (Türk Kütüphaneciler Dernegi), 486
Kassenbrock, Gabriele; Manag Dir (Evangelisches Literaturportal e.V.), 267
Kato, Kiyofumi; Secr (Nihon Akaibuzu Gakkai), 330
Kaul, H. K.; Dir (Developing Library Network), 291
Kaur, Dr. Trishanit; Gen Secr (Indian Association of Teachers of Library and Information Science), 050
Kaya, Ebru; Deputy (Türk Kütüphaneciler Dernegi), 486
Kearney, Cathy; Asst Dir (Chartered Institute of Library and Information Professionals in Scotland), 505
Keightley, Jane; Secr (Association of Librarians in Land-Based Colleges and Universities), 494
Keirstead, Robin; Dir (Canadian Council of Archives / Conseil Canadien des Archives), 173
Kevane, Michael; Pres (Friends of African Village Libraries), 049
Khalidi, Omar; Past Pres (Middle East Librarians Association), 077
Khan, Prof. Liaquat Ali; Finance Secr (Library Promotion Bureau), 415
Khanna, Gopal; Past Pres (National Association of State Information Resource Executives), 584
Kharouba, Dianne; Past Pres (Canadian Health Libraries Association / Association des Bibliothèques de la Santé du Canada), 175

Khaskeli, Riaz Ali; Secr (Pakistan Library Association), 416
Khatoon, Aman; Asst Secr (Library Promotion Bureau), 415
Khlot, Vibolla; Pres (Association des Bibliothécaires et Documentalistes Cambodgiens), 153
Kidwell, Claire; Treas (International Association of Music Libraries, Archives and Documentation Centres – United Kingdom and Ireland Branch), 509
Kim, Hak-Joon; Pres (Research Institute for Korean Archives and Records), 353
Kim, Joy; Pres (Council on East Asian Libraries, Inc.), 570
Kim, Tae-Seung; Pres (Hanguk Tosogwan Hyophoe), 349
Kimura, Sherise; Pres (Asian Pacific American Librarians Association), 540
King, Daniella; President (British and Irish Association of Law Librarians), 500
King, Mragaret; Pres-elect (Association of Independent Information Professionals), 552
Kingdom, Ann; Chair (Society of Indexers), 527
Kirk, Darey; VP (American Association of Law Libraries), 534
Kiss, Anita; Secr (Magyar Levéltárosok Egyesülete), 287
Kiss, Gábor; VP (Magyar Könyvtárosok Egyesülete), 286
Kiyindou, Alain; Pres (Société Française des Sciences de l'Information et de la Communication), 243
Klayb, Fadil; Head (Jordan Library and Information Association), 344
Klein, Dr. Diana; Chair (Arbeitsgemeinschaft für Medizinisches Bibliothekswesen), 256
Knösel, Jens; VP (Deutscher Verband Medizinischer Dokumentare e.V.), 266
Kobayashi, Fujiko; Secr (Japan Library Group), 510
Köglmeier, Werner; VP (Gesellschaft für Bibliothekswesen und Dokumentation des Landbaues – Fachliche Arbeitsgemeinschaft der ASpB), 268
Kohl, Allan T.; Past Pres (Visual Resources Association), 597
Kokko, Narjut; Pres (Tietoasiantuntijat ry), 228
Komarova, Irina; Secr (Council of PCLI Programme Coordinators), 442
Konrad, Shauna-Lee; Secr (Canadian Health Libraries Association / Association des Bibliothèques de la Santé du Canada), 175
Koontz, Christie, Ph.D.; Exec Dir (Beta Phi Mu (International Library Science Honor Society)), 027
Kopycki, William J.; Secr/Treas (Middle East Librarians Association), 077
Koren, Dr. Marian; Exec Secr (FOBID Netherlands Library Forum), 382
Kotovchevskai, Suzana; Pres (Bibliothkarsko Drustvo na Makedonija), 360
Kovacec, Deana; Pres (Hrvatsko Arhivisticko Drustvo), 199
Kraeuchi, Barbara; Secr Gen (Bibliothèque Information Suisse), 475
Krag Dalsgaard, Susanne; Treas (Danmarks Forskningsbiblioteksforening), 211
Krajewski, Jan; Pres (Polski Zwiazek Bibliotek), 084
Krause, Dr. Detlef; Vice Chair (Vereinigung deutscher Wirtschaftsarchivare e.V.), 275
Krizanic, Arlene; Treas (Association of Mental Health Librarians), 557
Krogh Jensen, Susanne; Treas (Arkivforeningen), 206
Kuhn, K.; 2nd VP (Deutsche Gesellschaft für Medizinische Informatik, Biometrie und Epidemiologie e.V.), 263
Kulikovski, Lidia; Pres (Library Association of the Republic of Moldova), 373
Kumar, Dr. Naresh; Pres (Society for Information Science), 295

Index of Officers 460

Kumber, Dr. B.D.; VP (Indian Association of Teachers of Library and Information Science), 050
Kundra, Dr. Ramesh; VP (Society for Information Science), 295
Kusanic, Nela; Member of the Exec Board (Hrvatsko Arhivisticko Drustvo), 199
Kusen, Drazen; Member of the Exec Board (Hrvatsko Arhivisticko Drustvo), 199
Kuula, Meri; Secr (Suomen Tieteellinen Kirjastoseura r.y. – Finlands Vetenskapliga Biblioteksamfund r.f.), 227
Kwan, Billy; Treas (Visual Resources Association), 597
Kyriakopoulou, Christina; Pres-elect (Association of Greek Librarians and Information Scientists), 278

L

Labrum, Meg; Secr Gen (Fédération Internationale des Archives du Film), 047
Lachance, Janice R.; Exec Dir (Special Libraries Association), 593
Lachs, Daniela; Vice Chair (Media Archives Austria), 122
Laferla, Claudio; Secr (Malta Library and Information Association), 365
Lahary, Dominique; VP (Association des Bibliothécaires de France), 231
Lakatos, Jackie; Immediate Past Pres (Council on Library/Media Technicians), 039
Lam, Yamaka; Secr (Macau Library and Information Management Association), 193
Lambrecht, Jutta; VP (Association Internationale des Bibliothèques, Archives et Centres de Documentation Musicaux/Internationale Vereinigung der Musikbibliotheken, Musikarchive und Musikdokumentationszentren), 021
Landau, Elvita; VP/Pres-elect (Mountain Plains Library Association), 581
Langhammer, Ingrid; Treas (Canadian Association of Public Libraries), 170
Lansangan, Emeralda L.; PRO (Agricultural Librarians Association of the Philippines), 422
Larsen, Christian; Pres (Arkivforeningen), 206
Larsen, Vagn Ytte; Pres (Danmarks Biblioteksforening), 210
Latta-Guthrie, Leslie; VChair (Canadian Council of Archives / Conseil Canadien des Archives), 173
Lau, Jesus; Pres (Asociación Mexicana de Bibliotecarios, A.C.), 013
Laukkamen, Markku; Pres (Suomen Kirjastoseura – Finlands Biblioteksförening), 225
Lausen, PD Dr. B.; 2nd VP (Gesellschaft für Klassifikation e.V.), 269
Laux, Wolfrudolf; Pres (Gesellschaft für Bibliothekswesen und Dokumentation des Landbaues – Fachliche Arbeitsgemeinschaft der ASpB), 268
Lavoue, Martine; VP (Association des Documentalistes de Collectivités Territoriales), 237
Lawson, Dawn; Secr (Council on East Asian Libraries, Inc.), 570
Lazia, Liliane; VP (Asociatia Bibliotecarilor din România), 438
Leclercq, Nicole; 2nd VP (Société Internationale des Bibliothèques et des Musées des Arts du Spectacle), 089
Leconte, Mathilde; VP (Association Nationale des Documentalistes de l'Enseignement Privé), 240
Lee, Eun Joo; Treas (Korean Library and Information Science Society), 350
Lee, Jae-Wohan; Pres (Korean Library and Information Science Society), 350
Lee, Kyung-Ku; Secr (Hanguk Tosogwan Hyophoe), 349
Leenings, Anke; Treas (International Association of Sound and Audiovisual Archives), 060

Legrand, Carole; Secr Gen (Association des professionnels de l'information et de la documentation), 238
Leitch, David; Secr Gen (International Council on Archives / Conseil International des Archives), 063
Leitner, Gerald; Pres (European Bureau of Library, Information and Documentation Associations), 045
Lemann, Catherine; Past Pres (American Association of Law Libraries), 534
Lemmens, Myriam; Secr (Vlaamse Vereniging voor Bibliotheek-, Archief- en Documentatiewezen), 135
Leombroni, Claudio; VP (Associazione Italiana Biblioteche), 311
Leong-Fortier, Dianne; Councillor (Canadian Association for School Libraries), 164
LeRoy, èric; VP (Fédération Internationale des Archives du Film), 047
Lewis, Jessica; Asst Secr (Library Association of Barbados), 128
Lewis-Somers, Susan; Treas (American Association of Law Libraries), 534
Li, Haipeng; Exec Dir (Chinese-American Librarians Association), 566
Libert, Marc; Edi-in-chief (Archives et Bibliothèques de Belgique / Archief- en Bibliotheekwezen in België), 130
Lieberknecht, Sabine; Vice Chair (Arbeitsgemeinschaft für juristisches Bibliotheks- und Dokumentationswesen), 255
Light, Ruth; Secr (Women's National Book Association inc.), 598
Lindberg, Niclas; Secr Gen (Svensk Biblioteksförening), 470
Lindström, Åke; Pres (DIK), 468
Linfield, Alan; Chair (Association of British Theological and Philosophical Libraries), 493
Linger, Joyce P.; Secr (Stichting Cultureel Centrum Suriname), 465
Lippincott, Joan K.; Assoc Exec Dir (Coalition for Networked Information), 568
Lison, Barbara; Pres (Deutscher Bibliotheks- und Informationsverband e.V.), 264
LLamas, Nerea; VP/Pres-elect (Seminar on the Acquisition of Latin American Library Materials), 087
Lloyd, Ivor; VP (Chartered Institute of Library and Information Professionals in Scotland), 505
Lon, Y. Chan Kam; Pres (Association of Professional Librarians), 367
Long, Shannon; Treas (Canadian Health Libraries Association / Association des Bibliothèques de la Santé du Canada), 175
Lopérfido, Pablo; Secr (Sociedad Argentina de Información), 088
Lopes Freitas, Georgete; 1st Secr (Conselho Federal de Biblioteconomia), 142
López-Huertas, María J.; Past Pres/1st VP (International Society for Knowledge Organization e.V.), 069
López Ruelas, Sergio; Pres (Colegio Nacional de Bibliotecarios, A.C.), 371
Loscalzo, Anthony; Treas (The Manuscript Society), 579
Lougee, Wendy Pradt; VChair (Council on Library and Information Resources), 571
Loughney, Patrick; Treas (Fédération Internationale des Archives du Film), 047
Lowe, Carrie Beth; Secr (Association of Christian Librarians), 550
Lowry, Charles; Exec Dir (Association of Research Libraries), 559
Lucker, Amy; Past Pres (Art Libraries Society of North America), 007
Lunau, Carroll; Pres (Ex Libris Association), 181
Lundén, Inga; Pres (Svensk Biblioteksförening), 470

Lupu, Valentina; VP (Asociatia Bibliotecarilor din România), 438
Luther, Judy; Secr (Association of Information and Dissemination Centers), 553
Lynch, Clifford A.; Exec Dir (Coalition for Networked Information), 568

M
Macaskill, Dianne; VP (Pacific Regional Branch of the International Council on Archives), 083
Macias, Edward S.; Vice-Chair (Center for Research Libraries), 564
Mackenzie, Maggie; VP (Health Information Association of New Zealand), 397
Maes, Vincent; Pres (Association Belge de Documentation / Belgische Vereniging voor Documentatie), 131
Magan de Hurtado, Norma; Pres (Colegio de Bibliotecólogos del Perú), 420
Magnusson, Chris; Secr (National Church Library Association), 585
Maier, Robert; Dir (Chief Officers of State Library Agencies), 565
Maissen, Anna Pia; Pres (Vereinigung Schweizerischer Archivare / Association des Archivistes Suisses / Associazione degli Archivisti Svizzeri / Uniun da las archivarias e dals archivaris svizzers), 477
Maitre-Allain, Elisabeth; Exec Secr (International Council for Scientific and Technical Information), 062
Majid Al Rifai Syria, Dr. Abdel; Head (Arab Club for Information), 002
Makhafola, Tshidi; Deputy (Library and Information Association of South Africa), 457
Malhan, Dr. Inder Vir; VP (Indian Association of Teachers of Library and Information Science), 050
Mamo, Oliver; Assist Hon Secr (Malta Library and Information Association), 365
Mancini, John; Pres (Association for Information and Image Management), 542
Mann, Chuck; Pres (National Church Library Association), 585
Manna Janto, Joyce; Pres (American Association of Law Libraries), 534
Manners, Louise; Chair (Librarians' Christian Fellowship), 511
Marsh, Vicki; Treas (Arts Libraries Society of Australia and New Zealand), 008
Marshak, Boris; Managing Dir (International Association of Users and Developers of Electronic Libraries and New Information Technologies), 061
Marshall, Brian; Secr (Australian and New Zealand Map Circle), 106
Martin, Jill; VP (European Bureau of Library, Information and Documentation Associations), 045
Martindill, Robin; Secr (Council on Library/Media Technicians), 039
Martinez, Christine; Pres (Association des Archivistes Français), 230
Masalinto, Ma. Lindie D.; Auditor (Medical and Health Librarians Association of the Philippines), 424
Maslen, Jim; Hon Memebership Secr (Private Libraries Association), 085
Massa, Jeff; Treas (Association of Information and Dissemination Centers), 553
Masse, Claudine; Pres (Association des Diplômés de l'École de Bibliothécaires-Documentalistes), 234
Matabuena, Teresa; Secr (Asociación Mexicana de Archivos y Bibliotecas Privados, A.C.), 369
Matos Paula, Elaine Baptista de; Secr (Federaçao Brasileira de Associaçoes de Bibliotecários – Comissao Brasileira de Bibliotecas Centrais Universitárias), 145

Matsuoka, Kaname; Secr Gen (Nihon Toshokan Kyokai), 335
Matsushita, Hitoshi; Secr (IAML Nihon Shibu (Kokusai Ongaku Bunken-Kyokai Nihon Shibu)), 319
Matthee, Tommy; Pres (Library and Information Association of South Africa), 457
Matthews, Cindy; Councillor (Canadian Association for School Libraries), 164
Matthews, D. J.; Secr/Chair-elect (Association of Vision Science Librarians), 561
Matthews, Paul; Treas (British Association for Information and Library Education and Research), 501
May, Simon; Hon Treas (Society of Chief Librarians), 525
Mayfield, Ian; Treas (European Information Association), 046
Mazelin, Janelle; Exec Dir (Association of Christian Librarians), 550
McCann, Lucy; Secr (Standing Conference on Library Materials on Africa), 528
McCarthy, Malachy; VP (Catholic Library Association), 563
McCulloch, Ian; Chair (Britain and Ireland Association of Aquatic Sciences Libraries and Information Centres), 499
McDonald, Vickie; Information Coordinator (Metropolitan Libraries Section), 076
McEntegart, Tag; Exec Dir (International Network for the Availability of Scientific Publications), 068
Mcharazo, Dr. Alli; Chair (Tanzania Library Association), 481
McKearney, Miranda; Pres (School Library Association), 521
McKee, Susan; Secr (Association of Canadian Map Libraries and Archives/Association des Cartothèques et des Archives Canadiennes), 157
McKnight, David; Past Pres (Bibliographical Society of Canada/La Société Bibliographique du Canada), 160
McLuckie, Angela; VP (New Zealand Law Librarians Inc.), 400
McMilian, Gary; Past Pres (Association of Mental Health Librarians), 557
Mc Tyre, Ruthann B.; Pres (Music Library Association, Inc), 582
McVey, Susan; Pres (Chief Officers of State Library Agencies), 565
Mead, William; Treas (Network of Government Library and Information Specialists), 516
Meadows, Judith; Secr/Treas (Legal Information Preservation Alliance), 072
Meer, Jan van der; Exec Officer (Branchevereniging Archiefinstellingen Nederland), 380
Mehmood, Khalid; Pres (Pakistan Library Automation Goup), 417
Memon, Mumtaz; VP (Pakistan Library Association), 416
Mertens, M.M.B.; Secr/Treas (Vereniging Openbare Bibliotheeken in Nederland), 392
Mertens, Dr. Mike; Exec Dir (Research Libraries UK), 519
Mertes, Kate; Pres (American Society of Indexers), 538
Methven, Moira; Pres (Chartered Institute of Library and Information Professionals in Scotland), 505
Mikoletzky, Dr. Lorent; 3rd Chair (Österreichische Gesellschaft für Dokumentation und Information), 124
Mills, Chris; Chair (Museum Librarians and Archivists Group), 513
Millsap, Gina; Pres (Library Leadership and Management Association), 577
Miranda, Giovanna; Pres (Gruppo Italiano Documentalisti dell'industria Farmaceutica e degli Istituti di Ricerca Biomedica), 314
Miski, Abdelhamid; Pres (Association Nationale des Informatistes), 376
Mittler, Elmar; Past Pres (Ligue des Bibliothèques Européennes de Recherche), 074

Miwa, Makiko; Exec Committee (Nihon Toshokan Joho Gakkai), 333
Mix, Lisa A.; Pres (Association of Librarians in the History of the Health Sciences), 556
Mkhonta, Faith; Chair (Swaziland Library Association), 466
Moen, Jorunn; Past Chair (European Association of Libraries and Information Services on Alcohol and Other Drugs), 044
Mohamed, Guleyfa; PR Off (Maldives Library Association), 363
Mohamed, Khadheeja; Treas (Maldives Library Association), 363
Molinari, Silvia; Treas (Gruppo Italiano Documentalisti dell'industria Farmaceutica e degli Istituti di Ricerca Biomedica), 314
Moore, Kelly; Exec Dir (Canadian Library Association), 176
Moore, Robert; Pres (Australian School Library Association), 112
Moran, Jenny; Hon Secr (Society of Archivists), 524
Mori, Yoshiko; Treas (IAML Nihon Shibu (Kokusai Ongaku Bunken-Kyokai Nihon Shibu)), 319
Morita, M.; Exec Dir (Zenkoku Gakkou Kouritsu Toshokan Kyougikai), 342
Morita, Matsutaro; Pres (Knowledge Management Society of Japan), 325
Morrison, Ann; Treas (International Association of Law Libraries), 055
Moser, Dr. Eva; Treas (Vereinigung deutscher Wirtschaftsarchivare e.V.), 275
Mosley, Rose; Pres (Association for Library Trustees, Advocates, Friends and Foundations), 546
Moss, Stuart; Pres (Association of Mental Health Librarians), 557
Mucignat, Emmanuelle; Pres (Association Nationale des Documentalistes de l'Enseignement Privé), 240
Murgatroyd, Diana; VChair (Network of Government Library and Information Specialists), 516
Murphy, Julie; Chair (Substance Abuse Librarians&Information Specialists), 095
Murthy, Dr. S.S.; VP (Developing Library Network), 291
Muscat, Ruth; Hon Secr (Malta Library and Information Association), 365
Myers, Robin; Hon Librarian (The Bibliographical Society), 498

N
Naeskind, Sara; Pres (Svenska Arkivsamfundet), 472
Nagy, Anikó; Gen Secr (Magyar Könyvtárosok Egyesülete), 286
Ndiaye, Djibril; Pres (Association Sénégalaise des Bibliothécaires, Archivistes et Documentalistes), 447
Ndjock, Jerome; Pres (Association des Bibliothécaires, Archivistes, Documentalistes et Muséographes du Cameroun), 154
Neagu, Dragos Adrian; Senior Deputy-Pres (National Association of Public Libraries and Librarians in Romania), 441
Nebiker, Regula; Treas (Vereinigung Schweizerischer Archivare / Association des Archivistes Suisses / Associazione degli Archivisti Svizzeri / Uniun da las archivarias e dals archivaris svizzers), 477
Nelsson, Richard; Chair (Association of UK Media Librarians), 497
Nemoto, Akira; Pres (Nihon Toshokan Joho Gakkai), 333
Nestorescu, Silvia; Gen Secr (National Association of Public Libraries and Librarians in Romania), 441

Netiv, Ariela; Exec Officer (Branchevereniging Archiefinstellingen Nederland), 380
Neupaney, Ganesh Prasad; Gen Secr (Nepal Community Library Association), 378
Neves Tembe, Joel das; Vice-Chair (Association of Commonwealth Archivists and Records Managers), 024
Newberry, Mary; Pres (Indexing and Abstracting Society of Canada / Société Canadienne d'indexation), 183
Nicholas, Pualine; 1st VP (Library and Information Association of Jamaica), 316
Nichols, Stephen; Chair (Council on Library and Information Resources), 571
Nicholson, Andrew; Pres (Association of Canadian Map Libraries and Archives/Association des Cartothèques et des Archives Canadiennes), 157
Nicholson, Jennefer; Secr Gen (International Federation of Library Associations and Institutions), 065
Niggemann, Dr. Elisabeth; Chair (Conference of European National Librarians), 035
Nikonorova, Ekaterina; Dir Gen (The Library Assembly of Eurasia), 073
Ninkow, Jasmina; VP (Bibliotekarsko društvo Srbijé), 448
Nivakoski, Outi; Secr (Finnish Association of Information Studies), 224
Nochimson, David; Exec Secr (Theatre Library Association), 594
Nogales Herrera, Jose Maria; Secr (Federación Española de Sociedades de Archivística, Biblioteconomía, Documentación y Museística), 462
Nogoshi, Masanobu; Secr Gen (Senmon Toshokan Kyogikai), 337
Noguier, Michel; Pres (Association des Documentalistes de Collectivités Territoriales), 237
Nordström, Gunika; Secr (Svenska Arkivsamfundet), 472
Normann, Michael; 2nd Vice Chair (Arbeitsgemeinschaft der Spezialbibliotheken e.V.), 254
North, Alison; Treas (Records Management Society of Great Britain), 517
Nussbaumer, Alison; Past Pres (Canadian Association of College and University Libraries / Association Canadienne des Bibliothèques de Collège et d'Université), 166
Nxumalo, Esther; Treas (Swaziland Library Association), 466
Nyberg, Marjukka; VP (Tietoasiantuntijat ry), 228

O

O'Brian, Heather L.; Secr (Canadian Association for Information Science / Association Canadienne des Sciences de l'Information), 163
O'Kelly, Eve; Treas (International Association of Music Information Centres), 056
Obachi, Esther K.; Secr (Kenya Library Association), 347
Ocaso, Alicia; Pres (Asociación de Bibliotecólogos del Uruguay), 600
Oetting, Edward; Exec Dir (The Manuscript Society), 579
Okerson, Ann; Coordinator (NorthEast Research Libraries Association), 587
Okojie, Victoria; Pres (Nigerian Library Association), 405
Oliveira, Eneida de; Dir Planning/Marketing (Federaçao Brasileira de Associaçoes de Bibliotecários – Comissao Brasileira de Bibliotecas Centrais Universitárias), 145
Oliveira, Lucia Maria Velloso de; Pres (Associaçao dos Arquivistas Brasileiros), 141
Oliver, Patricia; Treas (Virgin Islands Library Association / St. Croix Library Association), 532
Olivier, Fanus; Chair (Organisation of South African Law Libraries), 458

Olsson, Agneta; Library Dir (Göteborgs University Library), 469
Opela, Vladimir; VP (Fédération Internationale des Archives du Film), 047
Orefice, Isabella; Pres (Associazione Nazionale Archivistica Italiana), 313
Oren, Gale; Chair (Association of Vision Science Librarians), 561
Osborne, Renata; Pres (East Asian Library Resources Group of Australia), 114
Ostinelli, Paolo; Secr (Vereinigung Schweizerischer Archivare / Association des Archivistes Suisses / Associazione degli Archivisti Svizzeri / Uniun da las archivarias e dals archivaris svizzers), 477

P

Pabbruwe, Herman; Treas (Council on Library and Information Resources), 571
Page, Andra; Pres (Internationale Arbeitsgemeinschaft der Archiv-, Bibliotheks-, und Graphikrestauratoren), 070
Papazova, Krasimira; Secr (Bulgarian Library and Information Association), 149
Parent, Ingrid; Pres-elect (International Federation of Library Associations and Institutions), 065
Paris, Martes; PRO/Int'national Secr (Malta Library and Information Association), 365
Parsons, Fiona; VChair (Society of College, National and University Libraries), 526
Patterson, Margaret; Treas (Association of Librarians in Land-Based Colleges and Universities), 494
Patton, Kim; VP/Pres-elect (Young Adult Library Services Association), 599
Payette, Suzanne; Pres (Bibliothèques publiques du Québec), 161
Pearson, David; Vice-Pres (The Bibliographical Society), 498
Pellizzari, Pio; VP (International Association of Sound and Audiovisual Archives), 060
Pendse, Liladhar R.; Secr (Asian Pacific American Librarians Association), 540
Perera, Pushpamala; Gen Secr (Sri Lanka Library Association), 091
Perez Moya, Felicia; VP (Asociación Cubana de Bibliotecarios), 201
Perez Salmeron, Gloria; Pres (Federación Española de Sociedades de Archivística, Biblioteconomía, Documentación y Museística), 462
Perrot, Christian; Treas (Association des Archivistes Français), 230
Peschers, Gerhard; Speaker (Arbeitsgemeinschaft Gefangenenbüchereien / Deutscher Bibliotheksverband (Sektion 8)), 257
Peters, Sonja; Chair (Arbeitsgemeinschaft der Fachhochschulbibliotheken), 249
Peterson, Naish; VP (Australian Law Librarians Association), 109
Phelps, Marcy; Pres (Association of Independent Information Professionals), 552
Piacquadio, Ann; Accounts Clerk (Aslib Informatuion Ltd), 492
Picchi, Isabelle; Treas (Association des Documentalistes de Collectivités Territoriales), 237
Pigonska, Hanne; 1st VP (Danmarks Biblioteksforening), 210
Pilzer, Harald; Chair (Arbeitsgemeinschaft der Großstadtbibliotheken), 250
Pimentel, D.; Treas (Fundashon Biblioteka Publiko Kòrsou), 203
Pipon, Brigitte; VP (Association des Archivistes Français), 230
Pirola, Cecilia; Secr national (Associazione Nazionale Archivistica Italiana), 313
Plaice, Michael; Secr (Cumann Leabharlann na h-Éireann), 301
Plant, Trish; Secr (Canadian Association of Family Resource Programs), 167

Plumat, Emmanuelle; VP (Association Professionnelle des Bibliothécaires et Documentalistes), 133
Poirot, Albert; Pres (Association des Directeurs et des personnels de direction des Bibliothèques Universitaires et de la Documentation), 236
Pollard, William; VP (Virgin Islands Library Association / St. Croix Library Association), 532
Poole, Connie; Pres (Association of Academic Health Sciences Libraries), 548
Poupart, Agnès; Treas (Association Luxembourgeoise des Bibliothécaires, Archvistes et Documentalistes), 359
Powell, Mandy; Chair (Sefydliad Siartredig Llyfrgellwyr a Gweithwyr Gwybodaeth Cymru), 523
Preez, Madely du; Chair (LIASA Interest Group for Bibliographic Standards), 456
Preez, Madely du; Secr (Association of South African Indexers and Bibliographers), 455
Prentice, Susan; VP & Secr (East Asian Library Resources Group of Australia), 114
Prgin, Ivana; Sectretary (Hrvatsko Arhivisticko Drustvo), 199
Priestner, Andy; Chair (Business Librarians Association), 503
Pritchard, Dafydd; VP (International Association of Sound and Audiovisual Archives), 060
Pritchard, Kate; Secr (Network of Government Library and Information Specialists), 516
Prout, Debbie; Vice Chair (Records Management Association of Australia), 118
Pryde, David; Chair (Records Management Association of Australia), 118
Ptolomey, Joanna; Chair (Scottish Health Information Network), 522
Puigjaner, Ramon; VP (International Federation for Information Processing), 064

Q
Qutab, Saima; Joint Secr (Pakistan Library Automation Goup), 417

R
Rademeyer, Gill; Treas (Organisation of South African Law Libraries), 458
Radijeng, Madzigigwa; Pres (Botswana Library Association), 139
Ragonesi, Anita; Edi (Malta Library and Information Association), 365
Railiene, Dr. Birute; VP (Lietuvos bibliotekininkų draugija), 358
Ralla, D.; Secr (Latvijas Bibliotekāru bierdrība), 354
Ramirez, Anibal; Treas (Asociación Mexicana de Bibliotecarios, A.C.), 013
Ramirez, Raul; Pro-Treas (Asociación Mexicana de Bibliotecarios, A.C.), 013
Ramos, Manuel; Pres (Asociación Mexicana de Archivos y Bibliotecas Privados, A.C.), 369
Ramos, Maria José Faria; Dir (Biblioteca Nacional de Angola), 097
Ramsden, Michael; Secr (Australian and New Zealand Society of Indexers), 107
Ranasingha, P.; Immediate Past Pres (Sri Lanka Library Association), 091
Randall, Michèle E.; Exec Secr (Bibliographical Society of America), 562
Rasul, Aamir; Treas (Pakistan Library Automation Goup), 417
Rathnayake, J.; VP (Sri Lanka Library Association), 091
Rati, Dinesh; Dir/Communications (Canadian Association for Information Science / Association Canadienne des Sciences de l'Information), 163
Raworth, Rebecca; Dir/PR (Canadian Health Libraries Association / Association des Bibliothèques de la Santé du Canada), 175

Razpotnik, Spela; VP (Zveza Bibliotekarskih Drustev Slovenije), 454
Realinho Ribeiro, Cristina Maria; VP (Associaçâo Portuguesa de Bibliotecários, Arquivistas e Documentalistas), 014
Rebetez, Jean-Paul; Pres (Vereinigung der juristischen Bibliotheken der Schweiz / Association des bibliothèques juridiques suisses), 476
Recana, Edna; Secr (Virgin Islands Library Association / St. Croix Library Association), 532
Reding, Jean-Marie; Pres (Association Luxembourgeoise des Bibliothécaires, Archvistes et Documentalistes), 359
Reekie, Carol; Hon Secr (Association of British Theological and Philosophical Libraries), 493
Refaussé, Raymond; Chair (Cumann Cartlannaíochta Éireann), 300
Reformat, Marek; Pres-Elect (North American Fuzzy Information Processing Society), 080
Regneala, Mircea; Pres (Asociatia Bibliotecarilor din România), 438
Rehm, Dr. Clemens; 1st Vice Chair (Verein Deutscher Archivarinnen und Archivare e.V.), 273
Reiher, Kerstin; Pres (Vereinigung der juristischen Bibliotheken der Schweiz / Association des bibliothèques juridiques suisses), 476
Reijnders, Wim; Exec Officer (Branchevereniging Archiefinstellingen Nederland), 380
Reilly, Bernard; Pres (Center for Research Libraries), 564
Reilly, Colleen; Treas (Theatre Library Association), 594
Reinard, Romain; VP (Association Luxembourgeoise des Bibliothécaires, Archvistes et Documentalistes), 359
Reisser, Michael; Secr (Berufsverband Information Bibliothek e.V.), 260
Reissland, Birgit; Edi (Internationale Arbeitsgemeinschaft der Archiv-, Bibliotheks-, und Graphikrestauratoren), 070
Repta, Vada; Secr (Association of Independent Information Professionals), 552
Residbegovic, Amra; Pres (Association of Information Professionals – Librarians, Archivists and Museologists), 137
Rettig, Jim; Pres (American Library Association), 536
Reusch, Rita; Board member (Legal Information Preservation Alliance), 072
Reuters, Thomson; Pres-elect (National Federation of Abstracting and Information Services), 586
Rich, Marie Josée; VP (Association des Bibliothécaires de France), 231
Richards, Jan; Pres (Australian Library and Information Association), 111
Richter, Vít; Pres (Svaz knihovniku a informacních pracovniku CR), 205
Riedel, Susanne; Pres (Berufsverband Information Bibliothek e.V.), 260
Riedel, Tom; Treas (Art Libraries Society of North America), 007
Rivest, Stephanie; Treas (Canadian Association of Family Resource Programs), 167
Riyaz, Aminath; Edi (Maldives Library Association), 363
Roberts, Ken; Past-Pres (Canadian Association of Public Libraries), 170
Robertson, Carolyn; Pres Elect (Library and Information Association of New Zealand Aotearoa), 399
Robine, Martine; Treas (Association Nationale des Documentalistes de l'Enseignement Privé), 240
Robinson, Paula; Secr (New Zealand Law Librarians Inc.), 400

Robinson, Ruth; Secr (Scottish Health Information Network), 522
Rochelle, Matthieu; Dep Secr Gen (Association des Bibliothécaires de France), 231
Rodgers, Wendy; Dir-Awards (Canadian Association of College and University Libraries / Association Canadienne des Bibliothèques de Collège et d'Université), 166
Rodrigues Galhanas, Leonarda de Jesus; Finance (Associaçâo Portuguesa de Bibliotecários, Arquivistas e Documentalistas), 014
Roe, Brent; Exec Dir (Canadian Association of Research Libraries / Association des Bibliothèques de Recherche du Canada), 171
Roeder, Corinna; Chair (Arbeitsgemeinschaft der Regionalbibliotheken im Deutschen Bibliotheksverband), 253
Røijen, Kristin; Pres (Norsk Fagbibliotekforening), 412
Rogers, Annette; Exec Dir (American Society of Indexers), 538
Rojer, M.; Secr (Fundashon Biblioteka Publiko Kòrsou), 203
Roots, Sally; Treas (Society of Indexers), 527
Roque, Yadira; Pres (Asociación Nicaragüense de Bibliotecarios y Profesionales Afines), 403
Rotaru, Florin; Gen Dir (Biblioteca Metropolitan Bucaresti), 440
Rovis, Mirjana Kontestabile; Pres (Arhivsko Drustvo Slovenije), 453
Rudgard, Stephen; VP (International Association of Agricultural Infornation Specialities), 052
Rugambwa, Innocent; Pres (Uganda Library and Information Association), 489
Ruleman, Alice; VP (Association of Christian Librarians), 550
Russell, Judith; Pres (National Federation of Abstracting and Information Services), 586
Russell, Marilyn; Pres (Art Libraries Society of North America), 007
Russell, Mary; Pres (Australian and New Zealand Society of Indexers), 107
Ryan, Pam; Pres (Canadian Association of College and University Libraries / Association Canadienne des Bibliothèques de Collège et d'Université), 166

S

Saavedra, Oscar; VP (Asociación Mexicana de Bibliotecarios, A.C.), 013
Saeteren, Liv; Chair (Metropolitan Libraries Section), 076
Saint-Amand, Sr. Emmanuel; Secr/Treas (Association des Bibliothèques Chrétiennes de France), 232
Saleh, Marlis; MELA Notes Edi (Middle East Librarians Association), 077
Salliss, Nicola; Hon Secr (Art Libraries Society of the United Kingdom & the Republic of Ireland), 491
Salminen, Seija; VP (Suomen koulukirjastoyhdistys ry), 226
Samdani, Dr. Rais Ahmed; VP (Library Promotion Bureau), 415
Sammon, Christine E.; Secr/Treas (Canadian Association of College and University Libraries / Association Canadienne des Bibliothèques de Collège et d'Université), 166
Santana, Gilda; Secr/Treas (Association of Architecture School Librarians), 549
Sanz, Pascal; Pres (Comité français IFLA), 031
Sargsyan, Davit; Pres (Haykakan Gradaranayin Asotsiatsia), 104
Satpathi, Jatindra Nath; Pres (Indian Association of Special Libraries and Information Centres), 292

Sauberer, Dr. Gabriele; 1st Chair (Österreichische Gesellschaft für Dokumentation und Information), 124
Saul, Conception DL.; Pres (Agricultural Librarians Association of the Philippines), 422
Sauvageau, Philippe; Pres (Association pour l'Avancement des Sciences et des Techniques de la Documentation), 159
Sawhney, Lalit; VP (International Federation for Information Processing), 064
Schaafsma, Roberta A.; VP (American Theological Library Association), 539
Schaeffer Young, Judith; Treas (Association of Vision Science Librarians), 561
Schafer, Kyle; VP (National Association of State Information Resource Executives), 584
Schallier, Wouter; Exec Dir (Ligue des Bibliothèques Européennes de Recherche), 074
Schenk, Marteen; Secr (Branchevereniging Archiefinstellingen Nederland), 380
Schlacher, Werner; 2nd VP (Vereinigung Österreichischer Bibliothekarinnen und Bibliothekare), 126
Schleihagen, Barbara; Exec Dir (Deutscher Bibliotheksverband e.V.), 265
Schlesinger, Kenneth; Pres (Theatre Library Association), 594
Schlindwein, Dr. Birgit; Secr/Treas (Gesellschaft für Bibliothekswesen und Dokumentation des Landbaues – Fachliche Arbeitsgemeinschaft der ASpB), 268
Schlögel, Prof. Dr. Christian; Treas (Österreichische Gesellschaft für Dokumentation und Information), 124
Schlosser, Anna; 2nd Vice Chair (Arbeitsgemeinschaft für Medizinisches Bibliothekswesen), 256
Schmalor, Dr. Hermann-Josef; Treas (Arbeitsgemeinschaft Katholisch-Theologischer Bibliotheken), 258
Schmeikal, Dr. Bettina; 2nd Chair (Österreichische Gesellschaft für Dokumentation und Information), 124
Schmidtmann, Nancy; Pres (Catholic Library Association), 563
Schoening, Paul; Secr/Treas (Association of Academic Health Sciences Libraries), 548
Schoombee, Rene; PR Off (Library and Information Association of South Africa), 457
Schuemmer, Volker; Vice Chair (Arbeitsgemeinschaft der Kunst- und Museumsbibliotheken), 251
Schweim, Prof. Dr. H.G.; Treas (Deutsche Gesellschaft für Medizinische Informatik, Biometrie und Epidemiologie e.V.), 263
Seissl, Maria; 1st VP (Vereinigung Österreichischer Bibliothekarinnen und Bibliothekare), 126
Selle, Xavier de la; VP (Association des Archivistes Français), 230
Sepp, Anneli; Pres (Eesti Raamatukoguhoidjate Ühing), 219
Sevara, Zaynutdinova; Asst (Uzbekistan Library Association), 601
Severt, Martie; Pres (Association Internationale des Bibliothèques, Archives et Centres de Documentation Musicaux/Internationale Vereinigung der Musikbibliotheken, Musikarchive und Musikdokumentationszentren), 021
Sevila, Francis; Secr (Association Francophone d'Informatique en Agriculture), 019
Shabana, Aishath; Pres (Maldives Library Association), 363
Shagufta, Nasreen; Asst Secr (Library Promotion Bureau), 415
Shakeel, Athiyya; Training Off (Maldives Library Association), 363
Shaner, Arlene; Treas/Secr (Association of Librarians in the History of the Health Sciences), 556

Shantz-Keresztes, Linda; Pres (Canadian Association for School Libraries), 164
Shaparneva, Dr. Maya; Exec Secr (Rossiiskaya Bibliotechnaya Assotsiatsiya), 443
Shatirishvili, George; Exec Dir (Association of Information Specialists), 245
Sheehan, Paul; Secr (International Association of Scientific and Technological University Libraries), 059
Sheffer, Carol; Past Pres (Public Library Association), 589
Shellburne, Brian; VP (Visual Resources Association), 597
Shen, Zhijia; VP/Pres-elect (Chinese-American Librarians Association), 566
Shepstone, Carol; Dir-Grants (Canadian Association of College and University Libraries / Association Canadienne des Bibliothèques de Collège et d'Université), 166
Sherwani, Malahat Kaleem; Pres (Pakistan Library Association), 416
Shevchenko, Iryna; Pres (Ukrainska bibliotechna asociacia), 490
Shiham, Fathimath; VP (Maldives Library Association), 363
Shin, Ali; Treas (Canadian Association for Information Science / Association Canadienne des Sciences de l'Information), 163
Shiomi, Noboru; Chair (Nihon Toshokan Kyokai), 335
Shipp, Jogn; Exec Committee Members (Council of Australian University Librarians), 037
Shiuna, Aminath; Secr (Maldives Library Association), 363
Shoujah, Rudaynah; Secr (Association des Bibliothèques du Liban), 356
Shraiberg, Yakow; Pres (International Association of Users and Developers of Electronic Libraries and New Information Technologies), 061
Shrestha, Bhola Kumar; Pres (Nepal Library Association), 379
Shwe, U Thein; Secr (Myanmar Library Association), 377
Siddique, Nadeem; VP (Pakistan Library Automation Goup), 417
Siebert, Dr. Irmgard; 2nd Vice Chair (Arbeitsgemeinschaft der Regionalbibliotheken im Deutschen Bibliotheksverband), 253
Siegel, Leora; Past Pres (Council on Botanical and Horticultural Libraries, Inc.), 038
Silva Brita Costa, Marcia Valeria da; VP (Federaçao Brasileira de Associaçoes de Bibliotecários – Comissao Brasileira de Bibliotecas Centrais Universitárias), 145
Silva, Maria Celina Soares de Mello e; Treas (Associaçao dos Arquivistas Brasileiros), 141
Silva Wendling Apparicio, Rosane da; Financial Dir (Federaçao Brasileira de Associaçoes de Bibliotecários – Comissao Brasileira de Bibliotecas Centrais Universitárias), 145
Silvester, John; Secr (Society of Indexers), 527
Silvester, Stephanie; Hon Treas (Art Libraries Society of the United Kingdom & the Republic of Ireland), 491
Simkin, John; VP (Australian and New Zealand Society of Indexers), 107
Simonetti Barbalho, Celia Regina; 2nd Secr (Conselho Federal de Biblioteconomia), 142
Singer, Andrea; Secr/Treas (Committee on South Asian Libraries and Documentation), 569
Singh, Dr. Jagtar; Pres (Indian Association of Teachers of Library and Information Science), 050
Singirankabo, Marcel; 2nd VP (Association for Health Information and Libraries in Africa), 015
Sipilä, Sinikka; Gen Secr (Suomen Kirjastoseura – Finlands Biblioteksförening), 225
Sjöblom, Kenth; Chair (Arkistoyhdistys r.y. – Arkivföreningen r.f.), 221
Sjōman, Birje; Treas (Svenska Arkivsamfundet), 472
Skjekkeland, Atle; VP (Association for Information and Image Management), 542

Index of Officers   **472**

Slöber, Thomas; Secr (Verein Deutscher Bibliothekare e.V.), 274
Slyngstad, Stein; Dir Gen (ABM-utvikling – Statens senter for arkiv, bibliotek og museum), 406
Smeeton, Don; Pres (Association of Christian Librarians), 550
Smetanova, Olga; Pres (International Association of Music Information Centres), 056
Smink, Marjorie; 1st VP/Pres-elect (Church and Synagogue Library Association), 567
Smith, Barton L.; VP (The Manuscript Society), 579
Smith, Clive; Secr/Treas (Australian Society of Archivists (Inc.)), 113
Smith, Linda; Pres-elect (American Society for Information Science and Technology), 537
Snyder Anderson, Janice; Vice Chair (Legal Information Preservation Alliance), 072
Sollenberger, Julia; Immediate Past Pres (Association of Academic Health Sciences Libraries), 548
Solms, Basie von; Pres (International Federation for Information Processing), 064
Soluk, Mehmet; Deputy (Türk Kütüphaneciler Derneği), 486
Sorensen, Chris; Pres (Health Information Association of New Zealand), 397
Speller, Randall; 2nd VP (Bibliographical Society of Canada/La Société Bibliographique du Canada), 160
Spina, Barbara; Chair (Standing Conference on Library Materials on Africa), 528
Spiteri, Josephine; Treas (Malta Library and Information Association), 365
Stahl, Sheryl; Treas (Association of Jewish Libraries), 555
Stanhope, Charles V.; Exec Dir (Federal Library and Information Center Committee), 573
Stasselová, Silvia; Pres (Spolok slovenskych knihovnikov), 452
Steen-Hansen, Michel; Exec Dir (Danmarks Biblioteksforening), 210
Steenhuis, Jantje; Pres (Branchevereniging Archiefinstellingen Nederland), 380
Stefanczyk, Elzbieta; Pres (Stowarzyszenie Bibliotekarzy Polskich), 434
Steffe, Jerôme; VP (Association Francophone d'Informatique en Agriculture), 019
Stein, Nadja; Chair (Deutsche Gesellschaft für Informationswissenschaft und Informationspraxis e.V.), 262
Steinlechner, Siegfried; Vice Chair (Media Archives Austria), 122
Stephenson, Mattew; Chair (Records Management Society of Great Britain), 517
Sterchan, Monan Kunari; VP (Nepal Community Library Association), 378
Stern, Deborah; VP/publications (Association of Jewish Libraries), 555
Stevens, Cheryl; Secr (Arts Libraries Society of Australia and New Zealand), 008
Stewart, David R.; Pres (American Theological Library Association), 539
Stewart, Paulette; Pres (Library and Information Association of Jamaica), 316
Stiverson, Keith Ann; Chair (Legal Information Preservation Alliance), 072
Stogia, Angela; Secr (European Information Association), 046
Stowers, Marianne; 2nd VP/Membership Chair (Church and Synagogue Library Association), 567
Strettmatter, Aimee; Exec Dir (Association for Library Service to Children), 545
Strous, Leon; Pres elect (International Federation for Information Processing), 064
Stvilia, Besiki; Pres (Association of Information Specialists), 245
Suhaimi bin Haji Abd. Karim, Haji; Hon Secr (Persatuan Perpustakaan Kebangsaan), 148
Sun, Shin O.; Pres (Library Association of the Democratic People's Republic of Korea), 348
Sutherland, John; Hon Pres (Society of Indexers), 527

Index of Officers

Sutton, Regina; Dir (State Library of New South Wales, Collection Services), 119
Suzuki, I.; Pres (Zenkoku Gakkou Kouritsu Toshokan Kyougikai), 342
Svitraite, Zivile; Secr (Lietuvos bibliotekininkų draugija), 358
Sweeney, Shelley; Secr Gen (Bureau of Canadian Archivists / Bureau Canadien des Archivistes), 162
Szekely, Adriana; VP (Asociatia Bibliotecarilor din România), 438
Szogi, László; VP (Magyar Levéltárosok Egyesülete), 287

T

Takahashi, Minoru; Pres (Nihon Akaibuzu Gakkai), 330
Takanashi, Tom; Manag Dir (Knowledge Management Society of Japan), 325
Takaro, Tom; Pres (Major Orchestra Librarians' Association), 075
Take, Setareki; Pres (Pacific Regional Branch of the International Council on Archives), 083
Takeuchi, Hiroya; Exec Committee (Nihon Toshokan Joho Gakkai), 333
Tally, Joseph; Program Chair / Pres-elect (Association of Mental Health Librarians), 557
Tamura, Shunsaku; Exec Committee (Nihon Toshokan Joho Gakkai), 333
Tay, Ai Cheng; Secr+Treas (Metropolitan Libraries Section), 076
Taylor, Martin; VChair (Society of Archivists), 524
Taylor, Mary; Exec Dir (Library and Information Technology Association), 576
Tchafack, Rosemary; VP (Association des Bibliothécaires, Archivistes, Documentalistes et Muséographes du Cameroun), 154
Teague, Edward H.; Pres (Association of Architecture School Librarians), 549
Teskey, John; Pres (Canadian Association of Public Libraries), 170
Thapa, Prakash; Secr (Nepal Library Association), 379
Theaker, Margaret; Treas (Scottish Health Information Network), 522
Theis, Kenneth; Secr/Treas (National Association of State Information Resource Executives), 584
Theissen, Guy; VP (Association Luxembourgeoise des Bibliothécaires, Archvistes et Documentalistes), 359
Thibodeau, Pat; Pres-elect (Association of Academic Health Sciences Libraries), 548
Thomas, Claudette; 2nd VP (Library and Information Association of Jamaica), 316
Thomason, Geoff; Gen Secr (International Association of Music Libraries, Archives and Documentation Centres – United Kingdom and Ireland Branch), 509
Thompson, Brian R.; Treas (Council on Botanical and Horticultural Libraries, Inc.), 038
Thorn, Katharina; Chair (Deutscher Verband Medizinischer Dokumentare e.V.), 266
Tiemann, Katharina; 2nd Vice Chair (Verein Deutscher Archivarinnen und Archivare e.V.), 273
Tilcsik, Gyorgy; VP (Magyar Levéltárosok Egyesülete), 287
Timsley, Pete; Exec Dir (Association for Information Systems), 017
Tin, U Khin Maung; Pres (Myanmar Library Association), 377
Tise, Ellen; Pres (International Federation of Library Associations and Institutions), 065
Tjoa, A Min; VP (International Information Centre for Terminology), 067
Todd, Hamish; Chair (Japan Library Group), 510
Todo, Yasuko; VP (IAML Nihon Shibu (Kokusai Ongaku Bunken-Kyokai Nihon Shibu)), 319

Index of Officers

Togbé Deguenon, Denis; Pres (Association des Amis de la Lecture), 136
Tondreau, Guy; Treas (Association Professionnelle des Bibliothécaires et Documentalistes), 133
Topp Fargion, Dr. Janet; Edi (International Association of Sound and Audiovisual Archives), 060
Touré, Khady Kane; VP (Association Sénégalaise des Bibliothécaires, Archivistes et Documentalistes), 447
Trautwein, Paul; Treas (Evangelical Church Library Association), 572
Tretjakova, Silvija; Pres (Latvijas Bibliotekāru bierdrība), 354
Trevvett, Melissa; VP (Center for Research Libraries), 564
Tryon, Rusty; Pres (Church and Synagogue Library Association), 567
Tseronis, Peter; VP (Association for Federal Information Resources Management), 541
Tsou, Judy; Pres (International Association of Music Libraries, Archives, and Documentation Centres – United States Branch), 575
Turek, Judi; Secr (Evangelical Church Library Association), 572

U

Üerry, Laurence; VP (Association des Archivistes Français), 230
Ugricic, Sreten; Pres (Parent Library Community of Serbia), 449

V

Vaglini, Maurizio; VP (Associazione Bibliotecari Documentalisti Sanita), 309
Valdez, Andriette S.; Secr (Agricultural Librarians Association of the Philippines), 422
Van Goethem, Jan; Treas (Société Internationale des Bibliothèques et des Musées des Arts du Spectacle), 089
Van Heyst, Wenonah; 2nd VP (Association of Canadian Map Libraries and Archives/Association des Cartothèques et des Archives Canadiennes), 157
Vanmarque, Maïté; Secr Gen (Association des Bibliothécaires de France), 231
Vannieuwenhuyse, Johan; Pres (Vlaamse Vereniging voor Bibliotheek-, Archief- en Documentatiewezen), 135
Vanouplines, Patrick; VP (Vlaamse Vereniging voor Bibliotheek-, Archief- en Documentatiewezen), 135
Vanrie, André; Treas (Archives et Bibliothèques de Belgique / Archief- en Bibliotheekwezen in België), 130
Varadarajan, S.; Pres (Developing Library Network), 291
Varniene, Regina; VP (Lietuvos bibliotekininkų draugija), 358
Vasas, Dr. Lívia; Pres (Magyar Orvosi Könyvtárak Szövetsége), 288
Vatanen, Pirjo; Library Dir (Suomen Tieteellinen Kirjastoseura r.y. – Finlands Vetenskapliga Biblioteksamfund r.f.), 227
Vawter, Edward; Past Pres (Association of Independent Information Professionals), 552
Veatch, Lamar; VP/Pres-elect (Chief Officers of State Library Agencies), 565
Veluz, Imelda B.; Auditor (Agricultural Librarians Association of the Philippines), 422
Verhagen, Nol; Treas (FOBID Netherlands Library Forum), 382
Viciedo Valdes, Miguel; VP (Asociación Cubana de Bibliotecarios), 201
Vida, Garunkstyte; VP (Lietuvos bibliotekininkų draugija), 358
Vides, Yensi; Pres (Asociación de Bibliotecarios de El Salvador), 216

Vigneron, Claire-Hélène; VP (Association Nationale des Documentalistes de l'Enseignement Privé), 240
Vigo-Cepeda, Luisa; Exec Secr (Association of Caribbean University, Research and Institutional Libraries), 023
Vilanculos, Flatiel; Secr Gen (Association for Health Information and Libraries in Africa), 015
Vincent, Tom; Treas (Bibliographical Society of Canada/La Société Bibliographique du Canada), 160
Vitarino Gonçalves, Maria José; Secr (Associaçâo Portuguesa de Bibliotecários, Arquivistas e Documentalistas), 014
Vreugd, Ilse; Chair (Stichting Cultureel Centrum Suriname), 465
Vuckovic, Zeljko; Pres (Bibliotekarsko društvo Srbijé), 448

W

Wadhwa, NR; Secr (Society for Information Science), 295
Wagner, Pascal; Pres (Association des Bibliothécaires de France), 231
Wala, Dr. Carola; Secr (Österreichische Gesellschaft für Dokumentation und Information), 124
Walk, Paul; Dep Dir (UKOLN), 529
Walker, Glen; Immediate Past Pres (Library and Information Association of New Zealand Aotearoa), 399
Walker, Julie; Exec Dir (American Association of School Librarians), 535
Walker, keith; VP (Canadian Association of Public Libraries), 170
Walker, Mike; Immediate Past Pres (Association of Information and Dissemination Centers), 553
Walksman, Guy; Pres (Association Francophone d'Informatique en Agriculture), 019
Wall, June; VP (Australian School Library Association), 112
Wallace Davidson, Mary; Past Pres (International Association of Music Libraries, Archives, and Documentation Centres – United States Branch), 575
Wallenborn, Michéle; Secr (Association Luxembourgeoise des Bibliothécaires, Archvistes et Documentalistes), 359
Waln, Donna; Pres (Evangelical Church Library Association), 572
Walsh, Jan; Dir (Chief Officers of State Library Agencies), 565
Walsh, KIrstin; Pres (Canadian Association of Music Libraries (A Branch of the International Association of Music Libraries, Archives and Documentation Centres / Association Canadienne des Bibliothèques Musicales), 169
Walters, John Paul; Program Dir (Beta Phi Mu (International Library Science Honor Society)), 027
Warmbrunn, Dr. Jürgen; Chair (Arbeitsgemeinschaft der Spezialbibliotheken e.V.), 254
Warriach, Nosheen Fatima; Joint Secr (Pakistan Library Automation Goup), 417
Washington, Sheryl; Secr (Library Association of Trinidad and Tobago), 485
Way, David; Secr (International Group of Publishing Libraries), 066
Wegenast, Christoph; Treas (Vereinigung der juristischen Bibliotheken der Schweiz / Association des bibliothèques juridiques suisses), 476
Weigel, Harald; Pres (Vereinigung Österreichischer Bibliothekarinnen und Bibliothekare), 126

Weihs, Prof. Dr. Claus; Pres (Gesellschaft für Klassifikation e.V.), 269
Weihs, Jean; Secr+Memeber Secr (Ex Libris Association), 181
Weiner, Barbara S.; Treas (Substance Abuse Librarians&Information Specialists), 095
Weir, Leslie; Pres (Canadian Association of Research Libraries / Association des Bibliothèques de Recherche du Canada), 171
Weiss Dutra, Sigrid Karin; Pres (Federação Brasileira de Associações de Bibliotecários, Cientistas da Informação e Instituições), 144
Westh, Kirsten; Pres (HK/KOMMUNAL Library Committee), 214
Westhuizen, Anri van der; Secr (Suid-Africaanse Vereniging van Archivarisse), 459
Wettasinghe, Saroja; Treas (South and West Asian Regional Branch of the International Council on Archives), 090
Whitacre, Cynthia; Pres-elect (Association for Library Collections and Technical Services), 544
White, Andrew; Hon Secr (Cumann Cartlannaíochta Éireann), 300
White, Annemarie; Treas (Library Association of Barbados), 128
White, Caroline; Meeting Secr (Association of UK Media Librarians), 497
White, Senga; Pres (School Library Association of New Zealand Aotearoa), 402
Wight, Jill; Dir (The Library Campaign), 512
Will, David; Pres-Elect (British and Irish Association of Law Librarians), 500
Williams, Alec; Chair (School Library Association), 521
Williams, Fiona; Pres (Society of Chief Librarians), 525
Williams, James; Secr (Council on Library and Information Resources), 571
Williams, Mavis; Immediate Past Pres (Library and Information Association of Jamaica), 316
Williams, Pat; Treas (School Library Association), 521
Wilson, Clive; Webmaster (Standing Conference on Library Materials on Africa), 528
Wilson, Ian E.; Pres (International Council on Archives / Conseil International des Archives), 063
Wilson, Kristen; MELANET-L List Manager (Middle East Librarians Association), 077
Winiarz, Elizabeth; Past-Pres (International Association of Aquatic and Marine Science Libraries and Information Centers), 053
Winter, Sabine; Treas (Arbeitsgemeinschaft der Kunst- und Museumsbibliotheken), 251
Winterton, Jules; Pres (International Association of Law Librarians), 054
Winton, Peggy; VP (Association for Information and Image Management), 542
Witter-Thomas, Koren; Treas (Library and Information Association of Jamaica), 316
Wojcik, Caryn; Secr (National Association of Government Archives and Records Administrators), 583
Woldering, Dr. Britta; Secr (Conference of European National Librarians), 035
Wolfson, Laurel; Past Pres (Association of Jewish Libraries), 555
Wong Cubelo, Marta; VP (Asociación Cubana de Bibliotecarios), 201
Wong, Raymond; Pres (Macau Library and Information Management Association), 193
Wong, Wan; Treas (East Asian Library Resources Group of Australia), 114
Woodroffe-Holder, Caroline; Secr (Library Association of Barbados), 128
Woods, Dr. Martin; Pres (Australian and New Zealand Map Circle), 106
Wright, Eileen; Pres (Mountain Plains Library Association), 581

Y

Yablonskaya, Marina N.; Exec Secr (Library Association of the Republic of Kazakhstan), 346
Yamaguchi, Nobuo; Pres (Senmon Toshokan Kyogikai), 337
Yang, Ai-lin; Treas (Council on East Asian Libraries, Inc.), 570
Yanning, Zheng; Secr Gen (Zhongguo Kexue Jishu Qingbao Xuehui), 194
Yasmeen, Nuzhat; VP (Pakistan Library Association), 416
Yegon, Elizabeth J.; Treas (Kenya Library Association), 347
Yeomans, Yoanne; Dir (European Bureau of Library, Information and Documentation Associations), 045
Yeow, Puspa; Pres (Library Association of Singapore), 451
Yeung, Blick-har; Edi (East Asian Library Resources Group of Australia), 114
Yoshida, Yuko; Exec Committee (Nihon Toshokan Joho Gakkai), 333
You, Young-Koo; Chair (Research Institute for Korean Archives and Records), 353
Young, William R.; Parliamentary Librarian (Association of Parliamentary Librarians in Canada/Association des Bibliothécaires Parlementaires au Canada), 158
Yue, Wu; Pres (Library Society of China), 191
Yuen, Iris; Secr (Hong Kong Library Association), 189
Yusi, Rita P.; Treas (Medical and Health Librarians Association of the Philippines), 424

Z

Zadeh, Loffi; Hon Pres (North American Fuzzy Information Processing Society), 080
Zain, Faizah; Treas (Medical Librarians Group of Malaysia), 361
Zaitsev, Vladimir N.; Pres (Rossiiskaya Bibliotechnaya Assotsiatsiya), 443
Zardo, Daniela; Secr (European Association of Libraries and Information Services on Alcohol and Other Drugs), 044
Zecheru, Mihaela; VP (Asociatia Bibliotecarilor din România), 438
Zechner, Gerhard; Treas (Vereinigung Österreichischer Bibliothekarinnen und Bibliothekare), 126
Zerafa, Laurence; Chair (Malta Library and Information Association), 365
Zetter, Julio; Pro-Secr (Asociación Mexicana de Bibliotecarios, A.C.), 013
Zhou, Peter; VP/Pres-elect (Council on East Asian Libraries, Inc.), 570
Ziegler, Hans-Peter; Chair (Arbeitsgemeinschaft für juristisches Bibliotheks- und Dokumentationswesen), 255
Zink, Lori; Dir (Friends of African Village Libraries), 049
Zoodsma, Lieuwe; Exec Officer (Branchevereniging Archiefinstellingen Nederland), 380
Zurlys, Petras; Pres (Lietuvos bibliotekininkų draugija), 358

Subject Index

Abstracting and Indexing, 107, 183, 187, 455, 527, 538, 586
Administration and Management, 005, 092, 111, 173, 230, 236, 275, 294, 524, 526, 577
Africa and Africana, 049, 092, 093, 094, 528, 533, 602
Agriculture, 011, 019, 052, 268, 332, 422, 494
Arab Countries, 003, 004, 478
Architecture, 549
Archives, 004, 005, 012, 014, 020, 023, 024, 030, 063, 082, 083, 090, 113, 125, 130, 135, 141, 150, 154, 156, 162, 173, 188, 196, 199, 204, 206, 215, 221, 230, 273, 275, 279, 281, 282, 284, 287, 294, 300, 303, 304, 313, 343, 344, 353, 364, 369, 372, 380, 384, 389, 395, 401, 406, 407, 410, 431, 433, 439, 445, 447, 450, 453, 459, 461, 462, 464, 467, 472, 477, 482, 513, 514, 524, 591
Art (Fine Arts), 006, 007, 008, 251, 317, 408, 491
Asia, 540
Associations, Organizations of, 045, 144, 381
Audiovisual Archives, 060, 122
Automation, 123, 389, 412, 417
Bibliography, 028, 160, 229, 251, 255, 455, 456, 493, 498, 562, 582
Bibliophiles, 511
Biomedical Documentation and Information, 103, 233, 314, 548
Botany and Horticulture, 038
Caribbean, 023, 030
Catholic Libraries and Collections, 258, 299, 308, 563
Children, 165, 167, 496, 508, 515, 545
Christian Churches, 550
Church-affiliated Libraries, 029, 247, 310, 550, 567
Church Archives, 247, 308
Classification and Knowledge Organization, 269

College and University Libraries, 166, 326, 339, 405, 494, 495, 503
Commonwealth, The, 032
Continuing Education, 164, 210, 273, 341
Cooperation, 003, 004, 030, 065, 074, 217, 233, 241, 246, 251, 254, 261, 273, 290, 326, 340, 359, 391, 412, 505, 564, 565
Copyright, 037, 110, 587
Documentation and Information Science, 010, 011, 014, 016, 046, 100, 124, 131, 143, 149, 150, 159, 195, 237, 243, 244, 262, 269, 271, 281, 292, 312, 322, 324, 344, 370, 393, 404, 418, 447, 460, 461, 462, 468, 471, 478, 569
East Asia, 570
Economics, 142, 275, 324
Education, 155, 167, 448, 496, 508, 551
Ethnic Groups, 001
Film and Video, 558, 594
Film Archives, 047, 558
Fuzzy Sets Theory, 080
Government Archives, 583
Government Libraries and Information Services, 108, 182, 252, 304, 516, 541
Health Sciences, 015, 040, 044, 095, 116, 175, 309, 397, 522, 530, 556
Honor Society, 027
Hospital Libraries, 259
Humanities, 146, 574
Image Managemant and Technology, 597
Independent Information Professionals, 552
Information Centers, 042, 192, 442, 450, 499, 573
Information Management, 016, 088, 116, 124, 228, 352, 464, 492, 529, 542, 584
Information Processing, 064, 305, 321
Information Science, 013, 022, 027, 088, 135, 137, 147, 163, 172, 194, 202, 224, 239, 242, 262, 295, 297, 303, 304, 320, 322, 329, 331, 333, 376, 399, 415, 437, 464, 474, 479, 481, 492, 504, 507, 523, 537, 595
Information Services, 002, 023, 043, 051, 062, 065, 068, 098, 137, 227, 228, 271,

Subject Index

283, 292, 301, 312, 327, 350, 364, 376, 381, 422, 429, 432, 434, 442, 448, 475, 489, 512, 518, 536, 552, 571, 586
Information Systems, 017, 238, 388, 541, 554
Information Technology, 111, 124, 144, 202, 239, 241, 322, 452, 537, 553, 568, 576
International (General), 065
International Libraries, 382
Jewish Libraries and Collections, 555, 567
Knowledge Management, 069, 124, 144, 264, 325, 464
Language or Ethnic Groups, 590
Latin America and Latin Americana, 009, 012, 087
Law, 054, 055, 072, 109, 168, 255, 382, 400, 428, 458, 476, 500, 534
Librarianship; Library Science, 009, 013, 014, 023, 032, 036, 041, 057, 065, 071, 073, 078, 082, 091, 092, 094, 100, 101, 104, 111, 114, 126, 128, 130, 135, 139, 143, 149, 150, 153, 154, 186, 192, 195, 198, 200, 201, 207, 215, 219, 223, 224, 231, 240, 242, 245, 246, 247, 260, 261, 271, 272, 274, 278, 280, 281, 286, 290, 296, 297, 306, 311, 316, 329, 330, 331, 333, 334, 335, 344, 346, 347, 348, 350, 354, 356, 357, 358, 360, 362, 363, 364, 365, 368, 369, 375, 376, 377, 390, 399, 403, 406, 411, 415, 416, 418, 420, 435, 437, 438, 443, 447, 450, 451, 452, 454, 457, 460, 461, 462, 464, 466, 470, 478, 480, 481, 485, 486, 488, 490, 492, 501, 504, 505, 506, 507, 513, 514, 523, 566, 569, 595, 600, 601, 602, 603
Library and Information Science Education (Professional Training), 003, 011, 016, 022, 041, 050, 092, 101, 102, 104, 111, 138, 140, 153, 154, 174, 189, 192, 198, 200, 201, 205, 207, 216, 219, 220, 234, 240, 242, 245, 259, 260, 274, 275, 283, 296, 311, 363, 365, 366, 369, 387, 395, 416, 420, 427, 431, 451, 454, 480, 501, 505, 506, 509, 524, 543, 566
Library and Information Technology, 061,

073, 121, 602
Library Collections, 544
Library Directors, 033, 034, 059, 184, 235, 236
Library History, 181
Library Promotion, 133, 189, 192, 200, 217, 276, 290, 306, 355, 375, 378, 573, 578, 581, 603
Library Services, 009, 032, 042, 049, 082, 084, 087, 115, 127, 129, 138, 148, 176, 189, 200, 201, 210, 216, 220, 225, 231, 265, 274, 276, 283, 296, 301, 346, 348, 349, 360, 366, 377, 379, 381, 409, 429, 434, 446, 483, 484, 488, 489, 490, 499, 512, 518, 536, 571, 599, 601
Library Staff/Personnel (General) (including Archives, Documentation Centers), 039, 105, 205, 207, 231, 307, 401, 407, 453, 495, 504, 506, 523
Literature, 078
Lutheran Church, 267, 572, 585
Management, 208
Manuscripts, 579
Maps, 106, 157
Marine Science, 053
Media, 320, 542
Media Centers, 497
Medicine, medical librarianship and documentation, 015, 040, 044, 079, 095, 222, 256, 263, 266, 288, 293, 331, 341, 351, 361, 424, 436, 531, 548, 556, 580
Mental Health, 557
Metropolitan City Libraries, 076, 235, 250
Middle East and Middle Eastern Collections, 077
Museums, 082, 154, 251, 406, 461, 462, 513, 514
Music, 021, 056, 075, 117, 169, 213, 270, 315, 319, 383, 398, 473, 509, 575, 582
Music Archives, 021, 117, 315, 319, 473, 509, 575
Muslims and Islam, 057
National Associations (General), 096, 098
National Libraries, 033, 035, 209, 264, 277, 526

Networks, 002, 264, 266, 291, 475, 496, 568
Orientalia, 057
Pacific, 540
Parliament and Government Libraries, 025, 158, 252
Personnel, 313, 588
Pharmacology, 271, 336
Philosophy, 493
Population Planning (1) 15, 018
Preservation, 072, 156, 230, 300, 353, 395, 502, 547, 558
Private Libraries, 085, 369
Private Universities, 338
Professional (Graduate Level), 101, 102, 234, 419
Professional Development, 132, 133, 142, 144, 147, 162, 212, 221, 223, 225, 233, 240, 260, 273, 274, 280, 286, 358, 371, 403, 438, 459, 468, 505, 599, 600
Public Libraries, 120, 132, 170, 186, 203, 208, 210, 214, 265, 277, 302, 386, 387, 392, 405, 430, 440, 441, 486, 525, 589
Public Relations, 578
Publishing, 066, 393
Recorded Sound, 393, 547
Records Management, 005, 016, 024, 063, 083, 090, 113, 118, 156, 303, 304, 353, 384, 389, 395, 431, 433, 477, 502, 517, 524, 583
Regional Libraries, 105, 184, 253, 581
Religion, 099, 185, 511, 550
Research and Research Materials, 037, 587
Research Libraries, 074, 171, 211, 227, 265, 327, 387, 425, 487, 519, 551, 559, 564, 574

Restoration and Conservation, 070
Retired Librarians and Archivists, 181
School Libraries/Media Centers, 058, 112, 164, 186, 212, 226, 342, 355, 385, 402, 414, 426, 444, 520, 521, 532, 535, 592
Science and Technology, 042, 062, 146, 194, 282, 432, 499, 574
Social Sciences/Social Studies, 051, 146, 282
Sound Archives and Sound Collections, 060
South Asia, 090, 569
Southeast Asia, 005, 036
Special Libraries (General), 172, 238, 248, 254, 257, 292, 307, 337, 387, 405, 412, 423, 593
Specialized and Cooperative Library Agencies, 254, 560
Sport libraries, 081
State Librarians, 516
State Libraries, 516
State Library Agencies, 565
Teacher librarians, 190, 427
Technology, 039, 155, 544
Terminology, 067
Theatre (Performing Arts), 089, 594
Theology, 026, 029, 048, 086, 134, 232, 394, 493, 539
Toy Libraries, 515
Trustees, 177, 546
University Libraries, 059, 092, 093, 145, 180, 236, 249, 318, 328, 391, 396, 487, 510, 526
Urban Libraries, 235, 596
Visual Science, 561
Women, 598

Countries with international Associations

Algeria, 004
Argentina, 086, 088
Australia, 008, 026, 028, 033, 034, 037, 058
Austria, 064, 067
Belgium, 029, 047, 056
Bulgaria, 042
Canada, 007, 020, 081, 089
Colombia, 012
Denmark, 051, 060
Egypt, 077
Estonia, 079
Finland, 006
France, 019, 031, 062, 063
Germany, 069
Guam, 082
India, 050
Indonesia, 048
Ireland, 044, 055, 059
Jamaica, 032
Malaysia, 005
Mali, 015
Martinique, 030
Mexico, 013
Netherlands, 040, 043, 045, 065, 074
New Zealand, 021, 025, 083
Norway, 041, 078
Pakistan, 090
Peru, 011
Poland, 084
Portugal, 014
Puerto Rico, 023
Romania, 022
Russia, 057, 061, 073
Senegal, 093
Singapore, 076
Spain, 010
Sri Lanka, 091
Switzerland, 035, 070
Syria, 002
Tunisia, 003
Uganda, 092, 094
United Kingdom, 024, 046, 052, 054, 066, 068, 085
United States of America, 001, 016, 017, 018, 027, 038, 039, 049, 053, 071, 072, 075, 080, 087, 095
Venezuela, 009
Vietnam, 036

Countries with national Associations

Albania, 096
Angola, 097
Antigua and Barbuda, 098
Argentina, 099, 100, 101, 102, 103
Armenia, 104
Australia, 105, 106, 107, 108, 109, 110, 111, 112, 113, 114, 115, 116, 117, 118, 119
Austria, 120, 121, 122, 123, 124, 125, 126
Azerbaijan, 127
Barbados, 128
Belarus, 129
Belgium, 130, 131, 132, 133, 134, 135
Benin, 136
Bosnia and Herzegovina, 137, 138
Botswana, 139
Brazil, 140, 141, 142, 143, 144, 145, 146, 147
Brunei, 148
Bulgaria, 149
Burkina Faso, 150, 151, 152
Cambodia, 153
Cameroon, 154
Canada, 155, 156, 157, 158, 159, 160, 161, 162, 163, 164, 165, 166, 167, 168, 169, 170, 171, 172, 173, 174, 175, 176, 177, 178, 179, 180, 181, 182, 183, 184, 185
Chile, 186
China, 187, 188, 189, 190, 191, 192, 193, 194
Colombia, 195, 196
Congo, Democratic Republic, 197
Costa Rica, 198
Croatia, 199, 200
Cuba, 201, 202
Curaçao, 203
Czech Republic, 204, 205
Denmark, 206, 207, 208, 209, 210, 211, 212, 213, 214
Egypt, 215
El Salvador, 216, 217
Eritrea, 218
Estonia, 219
Fiji, 220

Finland, 221, 222, 223, 224, 225, 226, 227, 228
France, 229, 230, 231, 232, 233, 234, 235, 236, 237, 238, 239, 240, 241, 242, 243
Gabon, 244
Georgia, 245, 246
Germany, 247, 248, 249, 250, 251, 252, 253, 254, 255, 256, 257, 258, 259, 260, 261, 262, 263, 264, 265, 266, 267, 268, 269, 270, 271, 272, 273, 274, 275
Ghana, 276, 277
Greece, 278, 279
Guatemala, 280
Guinea-Bissau, 281, 282
Guyana, 283
Haiti, 284
Hungary, 285, 286, 287, 288
Iceland, 289, 290
India, 291, 292, 293, 294, 295
Indonesia, 296
Iran, 297, 298
Ireland, 299, 300, 301, 302
Israel, 303, 304, 305, 306, 307
Italy, 308, 309, 310, 311, 312, 313, 314, 315
Jamaica, 316
Japan, 317, 318, 319, 320, 321, 322, 323, 324, 325, 326, 327, 328, 329, 330, 331, 332, 333, 334, 335, 336, 337, 338, 339, 340, 341, 342, 343
Jordan, 344
Kazakhstan, 345, 346
Kenya, 347
Korea, Democratic People's Republic, 348
Korea, Republic, 349, 350, 351, 352, 353
Latvia, 354, 355
Lebanon, 356
Lesotho, 357
Lithuania, 358
Luxembourg, 359
Macedonia, 360
Malaysia, 361, 362
Maldives, 363
Mali, 364
Malta, 365

Countries with national Associations

Marshall Islands, 366
Mauritius, 367, 368
Mexico, 369, 370, 371, 372
Moldova, 373
Montenegro, 374, 375
Morocco, 376
Myanmar, 377
Nepal, 378, 379
Netherlands, 380, 381, 382, 383, 384, 385, 386, 387, 388, 389, 390, 391, 392, 393, 394
New Zealand, 395, 396, 397, 398, 399, 400, 401, 402
Nicaragua, 403
Niger, 404
Nigeria, 405
Norway, 406, 407, 408, 409, 410, 411, 412, 413, 414
Pakistan, 415, 416, 417
Palestine, 418
Paraguay, 419
Peru, 420, 421
Philippines, 422, 423, 424, 425, 426, 427, 428, 429, 430, 431
Poland, 432, 433, 434, 435
Portugal, 436
Puerto Rico, 437
Romania, 438, 439, 440, 441
Russia, 442, 443, 444, 445
Samoa, 446
Senegal, 447
Serbia, 448, 449
Sierra Leone, 450
Singapore, 451
Slovakia, 452

Slovenia, 453, 454
South Africa, 455, 456, 457, 458, 459
Spain, 460, 461, 462, 463, 464
Suriname, 465
Swaziland, 466
Sweden, 467, 468, 469, 470, 471, 472, 473
Switzerland, 474, 475, 476, 477
Syria, 478
Taiwan, 479, 480
Tanzania, 481
Thailand, 482, 483
Tonga, 484
Trinidad and Tobago, 485
Turkey, 486, 487
Uganda, 488, 489
Ukraine, 490
United Kingdom, 491, 492, 493, 494, 495, 496, 497, 498, 499, 500, 501, 502, 503, 504, 505, 506, 507, 508, 509, 510, 511, 512, 513, 514, 515, 516, 517, 518, 519, 520, 521, 522, 523, 524, 525, 526, 527, 528, 529, 530, 531, 532
United States of America, 533, 534, 535, 536, 537, 538, 539, 540, 541, 542, 543, 544, 545, 546, 547, 548, 549, 550, 551, 552, 553, 554, 555, 556, 557, 558, 559, 560, 561, 562, 563, 564, 565, 566, 567, 568, 569, 570, 571, 572, 573, 574, 575, 576, 577, 578, 579, 580, 581, 582, 583, 584, 585, 586, 587, 588, 589, 590, 591, 592, 593, 594, 595, 596, 597, 598, 599
Uruguay, 600
Uzbekistan, 601
Zambia, 602
Zimbabwe, 603